The Evidence Act 2006:
Act and Analysis

The Evidence Act 2006: Act and Analysis

Richard Mahoney

Elisabeth McDonald

Scott Optican

Yvette Tinsley

PUBLISHED BY:
Brookers Ltd
Level 1, Guardian Trust House
15 Willeston St
Wellington

ISBN 978-0-86472-606-3

Production Editor: Matthew Heaphy

Cover: Base Two, Wellington, New Zealand

Typeset by Brookers XBook Processor

Printed by Printlink, Wellington, New Zealand

Foreword

I am delighted to offer a foreword to this work on the reform and codification of the law of evidence. The Evidence Act 2006 comes as close to a codification of evidence law in New Zealand as is ever likely to be achieved. The journey of this measure to the statute books was long and tortuous.

The evidence law project began with a reference given to the Law Commission when I was Minister of Justice in 1989. The reference stated its purpose as follows:[1]

> "To make the law of evidence as clear, simple and accessible as is practicable, and to facilitate the fair, just and speedy resolution of disputes. With this purpose in mind the Law Commission is asked to examine the statutory and common law governing evidence in proceedings before courts and tribunals and make recommendations for its reform with a view to codification."

The task took the Law Commission 10 years. The final report of the Law Commission was tabled in Parliament in 1999. In the course of the decade the Law Commission produced no fewer than seven discussion papers covering in total 624 pages. The final report was in two volumes and came to 291 pages. A Bill based on the report was introduced into Parliament on 3 May 2005. The Bill received the royal assent on 4 December 2006. The new law came into force on 1 August 2007.

Essentially, the Act was designed to bring the rules of evidence into one place and state them authoritatively in statute form. However, in many instances, the changes made by the Act mark a significant departure from previous law. The reform was based on the policies and principles now contained in ss 6 and 7 of the Act.

The Act was designed by the Law Commission as a code, although this is a term that suffers from ambiguity in New Zealand's legal system. The purpose was to provide a set of statutory rules to replace the common law. But section 10(1)(c) of the Act makes it clear that the Act

> "(c) may be interpreted having regard to the common law, but only to the extent that the common law is consistent with—
>
> "(i) its provisions; and

---

1   New Zealand Law Commission, *Evidence Law: Principles for Reform: A Discussion Paper*, NZLC PP13, Wellington, 1991, v.

"(ii)   the promotion of its purpose and its principles; and

"(iii) the application of the rule in section 12 [which deals with evidential matters not provided for in the Act]."

Despite these qualifications the Parliamentary Select Committee that scrutinised the Bill stated in a report considering an amendment in 2007 that the Act "should be regarded as a codification of the law of evidence in New Zealand".[2]

The Law Commission has been given a statutory responsibility to keep the new law under review. Section 202 of the Act states that, as soon as practicable after 1 December 2011, the Minister of Justice must ask the Law Commission to report on the operations of the Act and whether changes are required. Another review must take place no later than 1 December 2014.

This novel provision is welcome. Too much legislation is passed and never reviewed. We need to see whether the Act has achieved its objectives. This book will be of substantial assistance to the Commission in carrying out its review.

It is never easy to bring to fruition a law reform project of such size and complexity. It is an occasion for celebration that is has been completed. It is also to be hoped that the effect of the Act will be to make evidence law more accessible, make it clear, and cut down the range of argument over how the rules of evidence should be applied.

I should perhaps record that the reason the Law Commission was given a reference on the law of evidence resulted from the writer taking a course on that subject at the University of Chicago Law School in 1966. The course met for one hour, five days a week, and was taught by the late Professor Bernard D Meltzer — a master of the "Socratic method". The course convinced me that the common law was in need of radical reform. It was an experience that led to one of my first law review articles, "The Admissibility of Judgments in Subsequent Proceedings", which concluded with the observation:[3]

"Perhaps the increasing reluctance of Judges to change judge-made rules can be compensated for by bold legislative activity."

Having started the project to reform the law of evidence in New Zealand in 1989, I found it a fascinating and serendipitous experience to appear, as Chair of the Legislation Advisory Committee and President of the Law Commission, in front of the Select Committee that considered the Evidence Bill in 2006. My task was to say why the Bill should be enacted.

There was concern raised at the Select Committee that the law was not sufficiently flexible, and that it did not give Judges the necessary room to manoeuvre in difficult trials. In my view, this will not be the case. I look forward to this Act settling in and contributing to the better functioning of the New Zealand legal system.

---

2   Justice and Electoral Committee, *Select Committee Report: Evidence Amendment Bill 2007*, 2

3   Palmer, "The Admissibility of Judgments in Subsequent Proceedings" (1968) 3 NZULR 142.

Writing a text of this character is an incredibly difficult burden to bear. But these authors are particularly well qualified to do so. All of them had a close association with the project when it was at the Law Commission. For 2 years at its concluding stages, Elisabeth McDonald was seconded to the Commission as Research and Policy Manager for the evidence law project. Likewise, Richard Mahoney was a consultant to the Commission virtually throughout the project. Yvette Tinsley and Scott Optican both provided commentary on various aspects of the proposed Evidence Code during the Commission's work.

The authors should be congratulated on their industry and the publishers on their initiative. This is a comprehensive and timely book.

Sir Geoffrey Palmer
President
New Zealand Law Commission

Acknowledgements

As Sir Geoffrey Palmer notes in his kind foreword, the Evidence Act 2006 had its origins as reference to the New Zealand Law Commission in 1989. Over the next 10 years, the Commission published numerous preliminary and consultation papers in carrying out the reference. It also consulted widely with members of the profession, the judiciary, government departments, the police, interest groups and other professionals — as well as taking advice from the Commission's Maori Advisory Committee. Consultation with the legal profession on a full draft of a proposed "Evidence Code" was undertaken during a travelling seminar in March 1998.

A large number of people were involved in the evidence reference. However, the careful stewardship of Justice John Wallace, Judge Margaret Lee and Justice David Baragwanath was most significant in developing and finalising the Law Commission's Evidence Code — which was presented to Parliament in August 1999. Grant Thornton undertook the drafting of the Code, a large part of which forms the basis of the Evidence Act 2006. His work, although little recognised during the legislative process, was painstakingly accurate while also challenging conventional drafting practices.

Almost 20 years after the Law Commission began its work and following extensive Select Committee modifications, this book offers analysis, explanations and questions concerning the scope and meaning of the Act's present provisions (over 200 in all including amendments and regulations). During the course of writing, with respect to both content and production, the authors have been fortunate to receive support in many forms. Assistance has been given by the supplying of helpful cases and documents, through valuable conversations concerning particular sections and issues, and by comments from colleagues on various drafts. In particular, we have been aided in our endeavours by Judge Murray Abbott, Justice Simon France, Peter Sankoff and Chelly Walton. We also thank Valmai Bilsborough-York, Bernice Ng, Blair Keown and John Lloyd, together with the hardworking staff at Thomson Brookers — especially Matthew Heaphy, Sarah Hunt and Amanda Reid. Much before the Act came into force, Brookers saw the need for this project and patiently worked with us through its completion.

The support and understanding of our families — from whom we have been absent more than we wished in order to complete this work — is gratefully acknowledged and deeply appreciated.

Finally, Scott Optican would like to dedicate his work on this book to his mother, Barbara Warren.

The law is stated as of 15 November 2007.

Richard Mahoney

Elisabeth McDonald

Scott Optican

Yvette Tinsley

Authors

Richard Mahoney

BA, LLB (British Columbia), BCL (Oxford)

Professor of the Faculty of Law, University of Otago

Elisabeth McDonald

ATCL, ASB, BA, LLB (Victoria), LLM (Michigan)

Associate Professor of the Faculty of Law, Victoria University of Wellington

Scott Optican

BA (Berkeley), MPhil (Cambridge), JD (Harvard)

Associate Professor of the Faculty of Law, University of Auckland

Yvette Tinsley

LLB (Hons), PhD (Birmingham)

Senior Lecturer of the Faculty of Law, Victoria University of Wellington

Abbreviations

The texts listed below have been referred to in *The Evidence Act 2006: Act and Analysis* in an abbreviated form, the full citation for each text is provided in the right-hand column.

Adams on Criminal Law	Robertson (ed), *Adams on Criminal Law* (looseleaf), Wellington, Brookers Ltd, 1992
Adams on Criminal Law — Evidence	Robertson (ed), *Adams on Criminal Law — Evidence* (looseleaf), Wellington, Brookers Ltd, 2007
Cabinet Paper 1	Office of the Associate Minister of Justice, *Evidence Bill: Paper 1: General Principles, Documentary Evidence and Overseas Evidence*, Cabinet Paper (CAB100/2002/1), December 2002
Cabinet Paper 2	Office of the Associate Minister of Justice, *Evidence Bill: Paper 2: Admissibility of Evidence*, Cabinet Paper (CAB100/2002/1), December 2002
Cabinet Paper 4	Office of the Associate Minister of Justice, *Evidence Bill: Paper 4: The Trial Process*, Cabinet Paper (CAB100/2002/1), December 2002
Cross on Evidence (8th NZ ed)	Mathieson (ed), *Cross on Evidence* (8th NZ ed), Wellington, LexisNexis, 2005
Cross on Evidence (online)	*Cross on Evidence* (online), Wellington, LexisNexis
Departmental Report (EV/MOJ/2)	Crime Prevention and Criminal Justice Group, *Departmental Report for the Justice and Electoral Committee: Evidence Bill — Part 3 — Trial Process*, Wellington, Ministry of Justice, May 2006
Departmental Report (EV/MOJ/3)	Crime Prevention and Criminal Justice Group, *Departmental Report for the Justice and Electoral Committee: Evidence Bill — Part 4 — Evidence from Overseas or to be Used Overseas*, Wellington, Ministry of Justice, May 2006

Departmental Report (EV/MOJ/4)	Crime Prevention and Criminal Justice Group, *Departmental Report for the Justice and Electoral Committee: Evidence Bill — Part 5 — Miscellaneous*, Wellington, Ministry of Justice, May 2006
Departmental Report (EV/MOJ/5)	Crime Prevention and Criminal Justice Group, *Departmental Report for the Justice and Electoral Committee: Evidence Bill — Part 1 — Preliminary Provisions*, Wellington, Ministry of Justice, June 2006
Departmental Report (EV/MOJ/6)	Crime Prevention and Criminal Justice Group, *Departmental Report for the Justice and Electoral Committee: Evidence Bill — Part 2 — Admissibility Rules, Privilege, and Confidentiality*, Wellington, Ministry of Justice, June 2006
Departmental Report (EV/MOJ/7)	Crime Prevention and Criminal Justice Group, *Departmental Report for the Justice and Electoral Committee: Evidence Bill — General Comments and Miscellaneous Issues*, Wellington, Ministry of Justice, June 2006
LC *Evidence Code*	New Zealand Law Commission, *Evidence: Volume 2 — Evidence Code and Commentary*, NZLC R55, Wellington, 1999
LC *Evidence Reform*	New Zealand Law Commission, *Evidence: Volume 1 — Reform of the Law*, NZLC R55, Wellington, 1999
McGechan on Procedure	*McGechan on Procedure* (looseleaf), Wellington, Brookers Ltd, 1989
NZLS *Intensive: Evidence Act 2006*	New Zealand Law Society, *Intensive: Evidence Act 2006*, Wellington, June 2007
NZLS *Submission on the Evidence Bill*	New Zealand Law Society, *Submission on the Evidence Bill*, 2005
Select Committee Report on the Evidence Bill	Justice and Electoral Select Committee, *Select Committee Report on Evidence Bill*, 24 October 2006
Select Committee Report on the Evidence Amendment Bill	Justice and Electoral Select Committee, *Select Committee Report on Evidence Amendment Bill*, 22 June 2007

Contents

Contents

Chapter 1

Evidence Act 2006

Evidence Act 2006

2006 No 69

AMENDMENT

2007 No 24

Contents

[4 December 2006

The Parliament of New Zealand enacts as follows:

1   Title

This Act is the Evidence Act 2006.

2   Commencement

This Act comes into force on a date to be appointed by the Governor-General by Order in Council; and 1 or more Orders in Council may be made appointing different dates for different provisions.

Editorial Note

Sections 203 to 214 of this Act came into force, as from 18 July 2007, pursuant to cl 2(1) Evidence Act 2006 Commencement Order 2007 (2007/190).

The rest of this Act came into force, as from 1 August 2007, pursuant to cl 2(2) Evidence Act 2006 Commencement Order 2007 (2007/190).

Part 1
Preliminary provisions
(s 3 to s 15)

General

3   Act to bind the Crown

This Act binds the Crown.

4   Interpretation

(1)   In this Act, unless the context otherwise requires,—

EV4.00.01   Introduction

The introductory words to s 4, as used at the start of most interpretation sections, may well have particular significance for the application of this Act. One of the consequences of the amendments to the Law Commission's draft Code, which provided the basis for the Act, is that changes in drafting (in particular the use of certain words) have not been employed consistently throughout the Act. This means that the same word or phrase may have to be interpreted differently depending on the section in which it is used. This commentary will discuss which sections may be affected by drafting irregularities (see, for example, the discussion of the definition of "witness").[1]

Section 4 does not contain all the definitions used in the Act (for example those found in ss 16, 40, or 51). Nor does the Act indicate at the end of each section (as the Code did) which words are defined in s 4.

admission, in relation to a civil proceeding, means a statement that is—

(a)   made by a person who is or becomes a party to the proceeding; and

(b)   adverse to the person's interest in the outcome of the proceeding

EV4.01.01   Admission

The definition of admission only applies in civil proceedings.[2] Statements by defendants in criminal cases offered by the prosecution are not referred to in the Act as either admissions or confessions (see ss 27-30).

child means a person under the age of 18 years

EV4.02.01   Child

This is a change from the definition in s 23C(b) of the Evidence Act 1908. The increase from 17 to 18 years was made so the Act is consistent with the definition of child in the United Nations Convention on the Rights of the Child.[3]

child complainant, in relation to any proceeding, means a complainant who is a child when the proceeding commences

EV4.03.01   Child complainant

For the purposes of the Act (see, for example, s 107) a child complainant must be under the age of 18 years at the commencement of the proceeding rather than the beginning of the trial. (Section 12 of the Summary Proceedings Act 1957 provides that a proceeding commences when an information is laid.)

---

1   See EV4.46.01-03.
2   See EV34.01 and accompanying discussion.
3   *Departmental Report* (EV/MOJ/5), 2.

(1)   No definition of child witness

Some of the provisions in the Act (see s 95) however also apply to witnesses who are children in proceedings other than those that are criminal in nature. There is no guidance given as to when the Act should treat a witness as being a child for the purposes of its provisions (except for s 77), although given that the relevant discretions also apply to adult witnesses, this may not be of much importance in practice.

common bundle means a compilation of documents that the parties to a civil proceeding wish to offer in evidence at the hearing of the proceeding, being a compilation that—

(a)   is prepared in accordance with rules of court or the practice of a court; and

(b)   is filed in court

EV4.04.01   Common bundle

This definition was included as a result of the addition of s 132 by the Select Committee, justified on the basis that the section "parallels" the appropriate High Court Rules (in this case rr 441N, 441O, and 441P).[4] The Act does not define "hearing" (although see s 4(2) for guidance on when a hearing commences) but in this context at least it must mean the substantive hearing of the issues that are the subject of the proceedings.

communication assistance means oral or written interpretation of a language, written assistance, technological assistance, and any other assistance that enables or facilitates communication with a person who—

(a)   does not have sufficient proficiency in the English language to—

(i)   understand court proceedings conducted in English; or

(ii)   give evidence in English; or

(b)   has a communication disability

EV4.05.01   Communication assistance

This definition was intended by the Law Commission to be sufficiently general so as to encompass current and future forms of assistance appropriate to all communication needs. Communication "disability" is not defined in the Act but its ordinary meaning must be sufficient so that people who are hearing-impaired as well as those who have difficulty speaking will be included.

Although the Law Commission did consider proposing the use of "intermediaries" for the purpose of enhancing communication with some witnesses, by rephrasing questions and answers,[5] this was not ultimately

---

4   *Select Committee Report on the Evidence Bill*, 2.

recommended and consequently this kind of help is not intended to be "communication assistance".

The definition also does not make any reference to te reo Maori, as the relevant provisions (see ss 80 and 81) are intended to be subject to the Maori Language Act 1987 (the draft Code's version expressly provided for this — see s 81(8)).[6] Where a person wishes to speak Maori in court, the provisions of the Maori Language Act 1987 will apply (allowing for the provision of interpreters) even if the te reo speaker can also communicate in English. If a witness cannot speak English, the broader range of options that allow for communication assistance under the Evidence Act 2006 will be available.[7]

conviction means,—

(a)   in sections 47 to 49, a subsisting conviction entered before or after the commencement of this Act by—

(i)   a New Zealand court or a court-martial conducted under New Zealand law in New Zealand or elsewhere; or

(ii)   a court established by, or a court-martial conducted under, the law of Australia, United Kingdom, Canada, or any other foreign country in respect of which an Order in Council has been made under section 140(5); and

(b)   in sections 139 and 140, a subsisting conviction entered before or after the commencement of this Act by a New Zealand or foreign court or a court-martial conducted under New Zealand or foreign law

EV4.06.01   Conviction

This definition is in essence the same as the one in the draft Code, which in turn incorporated parts of s 12A of the Evidence Act 1908 and s 22 of the Evidence Amendment Act (No 2) 1980. No Order in Council was ever made under s 12A of the 1908 Act. The definition excludes a conviction that a court has overturned or one that is the subject of a free pardon.[8]

---

5   New Zealand Law Commission, *The Evidence of Children and Other Vulnerable Witnesses*, NZLC PP26, Wellington, 1996, para 167ff.
6   LC *Evidence Code*, para C312.
7   See further LC *Evidence Code*, para C312.
8   LC *Evidence Code*, para C10.

copy, in relation to a document, includes a copy of a copy and a copy that is not an exact copy of the document but is identical to the document in all relevant respects

EV4.07.01   Copy

This definition is the same as that proposed by the Law Commission in the draft Code. It is relevant to a number of sections: see ss 22(3), 138, 149. When discussing this definition, the Law Commission stated:[9]

> "Whether something is a copy in terms of the definition depends on the purpose for which it is proffered. Thus, a black and white photocopy of a document printed in colour or a typed copy of a hand-written original would both be within this definition, if the purpose is to convey the contents of the document, because the copy would be identical in content to the original. If the purpose is to convey the colour or form of the original, however, neither would be a copy within the definition."

While it is likely that this approach will be adopted, it is not guaranteed by the actual wording of the definition. Despite the Law Commission's explanation, the Act's definition does not depend on identity *in content*. It is conceivable that a court may not agree that a hand-written version of a typed original is "identical in all relevant respects".

The Law Commission's first version of this definition included the words in italics: "includes a copy of a copy, *a hand-written copy* and a copy that is not an exact copy ...".[10] The original commentary to this definition also stated:[11]

> "When the missing feature (eg colour) is relevant to an issue, the document cannot be treated as a copy. Such a document may still be admissible under s 5(2)(b), which allows all relevant evidence of the contents of a document to be received if the original is shown to be unavailable."

Section 5 from the Law Commission's preliminary paper (which provided for the admission of secondary evidence) is not in the Act. The use of the word "copy" therefore has much less significance in the Act than in the earlier versions of the documentary evidence rules (drafted in 1994) given the development of technology and the liberalisation of the hearsay rule.

---

9   LC *Evidence Code*, para C11.
10   New Zealand Law Commission, *Evidence Law: Documentary Evidence and Judicial Notice: A Discussion Paper*, NZLC PP22, Wellington 1994, 98.
11   New Zealand Law Commission, *Evidence Law: Documentary Evidence and Judicial Notice: A Discussion Paper*, NZLC PP22, Wellington 1994, 99.

country includes a State, territory, province, or other part of a country

EV4.08.01   Country

This definition makes it clear that a country includes Australian states and Canadian provinces. Its main relevance is as part of the definition of "foreign country", as "country" is used infrequently in the Act and is limited to a reference to those parts of a country that enact laws or enter into treaties (see ss 140 and 141).

court includes the Supreme Court, the Court of Appeal, the High Court, and any District Court

EV4.09.01   Court

A definition of "court" was not included in the Law Commission's draft Code. This version is from the Evidence Act 1908, but without the reference to "any Court of summary jurisdiction", on the basis that apart from the District Court there are no courts of summary jurisdiction.[12] This addition was recommended by the New Zealand Law Society in their submission to the Select Committee.

The definition is not exhaustive and may cause some difficulties given the use of "court" in the Act. Although the Disputes Tribunal and the Environment Court are not bound by the rules of evidence that apply to judicial proceedings (see, for example, s 276(2) of the Resource Management Act 1991), the Disputes Tribunal is constituted as a division of the District Court by s 4B of the District Courts Act 1947. A number of uses of "court" in the Act must, at times, be widened to include tribunals (or the Environment or Employment Courts) — see, for example, "judgment of a court" (s 139(1)(c)).

(1)   Application of the Evidence Act rules in tribunals

The combination of the definition of "proceedings" and "court" in the Act seems to prevent tribunals or the Environment Court, for example, from electing to use the provisions of the Act, unless the definition of court can include any court (but presumably not a tribunal). This is because many sections of the Act apply "in any proceedings" — that is, proceedings conducted in a court. This makes it difficult for tribunals to "opt in" to the Act when the language of the Act seems to preclude them from doing so. This cannot have been the intention. This position is further complicated by s 5(1), which renders the Act subject to other "enactments" in the case of inconsistencies.

However, the Act also recognises a difference in admissibility rules for tribunals by the wording of s 53(5), which operates to preserve claims of "legal professional privilege" at common law outside of "proceedings". This may mean that legal professional privilege survives for the purposes of hearings by

---

12   *Departmental Report* (EV/MOJ/5), 3.

tribunals (see the discussion of s 53(5)),[13] indicating the Act is not intended to apply to tribunals.

Other sections that deal with the application of the Act to the work of tribunals include s 150 that defines a New Zealand court as including "a tribunal declared by the Minister of Justice under s 152 to be a New Zealand court".[14]

The definition of "Judge" in s 4 also includes a tribunal.[15]

District Court includes—

(a)   a Family Court; and

(b)   a Youth Court

EV4.10.01   District Court

See also the discussion of "court".[16]

document means—

(a)   any material, whether or not it is signed or otherwise authenticated, that bears symbols (including words and figures), images, or sounds or from which symbols, images, or sounds can be derived, and includes—

(i)   a label, marking, or other writing which identifies or describes a thing of which it forms part, or to which it is attached:

(ii)   a book, map, plan, graph, or drawing:

(iii)   a photograph, film, or negative; and

(b)   information electronically recorded or stored, and information derived from that information

EV4.11.01   Removal of the reference to "record"

This definition of document is different to that in the version of the Bill reported back from the Select Committee and was contained in Supplementary Order Paper No 79. The explanatory note to the Supplementary Order Paper states that the definition of document was replaced "to avoid the possibly limiting word 'record' and to ensure that the definition is so comprehensive so as to avoid a technical and limiting interpretation". The previous version read:[17]

"**document** means any *record* of information, and includes—

"(a)   anything on which there is writing or any image; and

---

13   See EV53.06.
14   See EVPt4Sub1.02.
15   See further discussion at EV4.26.01.
16   See EV4.09.01.
17   LC *Evidence Code*, para C13 (emphasis added).

"(b)   anything on which there are marks, figures, symbols, or perforations that have a meaning for persons qualified to interpret them; and

"(c)   anything from which sounds, images, or writing can be reproduced, with or without the aid of anything else"

The Select Committee's concern with the use of the word "record" was not noted with regard to the definition of "business record" in s 16.

The Act's definition is now exceptionally wide — especially given the potential scope of para (b) and the use of the word "material" instead of "record". The list contained in para (a)(i)-(iii) appear in contrast quite limited — especially when compared to the "technologically non-specific version"[18] that the Law Commission recommended.

domestic violence has the same meaning as in section 3(1) of the Domestic Violence Act 1995

EV4.12.01   Domestic violence

This definition has relevance to s 95.

enforcement agency means the New Zealand Police or any body or organisation that has a statutory responsibility for the enforcement of an enactment

EV4.13.01   Enforcement agency

This definition is taken from the draft Code, the Law Commission noting that it is intended to include not just the Police "but also organisations like the New Zealand Customs Service, the Ministry of Fisheries and the Inland Revenue Department which have a statutory responsibility for enforcing an enactment: for example, the Customs and Excise Act 1996."[19]

The inclusion of the wide range of bodies charged with "the enforcement of an enactment" was clearly intended for the purposes of s 64 (relating to informers' privilege).[20] Inclusion of this definition now in s 4 of the Act now means the term presumably also applies for the purposes of s 45 (the process of obtaining visual identification evidence), which may not have been intended.[21]

---

18   *Departmental Report* (EV/MOJ/5), 3.
19   LC *Evidence Code*, para C14.
20   See EV64.02. See also New Zealand Law Commission, *Evidence Law: Privilege: A Discussion Paper*, NZLC PP23, Wellington, 1994, 216 — in which the definition of "enforcement agency" was included in draft s 10.
21   See EV45.04.

expert means a person who has specialised knowledge or skill based on training, study, or experience

EV4.14.01   Expert

The Law Commission noted that this definition "codifies the common law rule" — and is intended to be wide and flexible. "Thus a formal qualification is not the only way of proving that a person possesses the requisite knowledge and skill."[22]

expert evidence means the evidence of an expert based on the specialised knowledge or skill of that expert and includes evidence given in the form of an opinion

EV4.15.01   Expert evidence

Expert evidence is that offered by a properly qualified expert and is within that expert's area of expertise.[23] The definition makes it clear that expert opinion evidence is just one type of expert evidence (see further the definition of "opinion evidence").[24] It is not uncommon for an expert to give a combination of expert evidence (which may or may not be opinion evidence) as well as other non-expert evidence. Section 25 of the Act controls the admission of the expert's evidence that is a statement of opinion.[25]

foreign country means a country other than New Zealand

EV4.16.01   Foreign country

See the definition of country.

give evidence means to give evidence in a proceeding—

(a)   in the ordinary way, as described in section 83; or

(b)   in an alternative way, as provided for by section 105; or

(c)   in any other way provided for under this Act or any other enactment

EV4.17.01   Give evidence

This definition came from the draft Code — a definition needed because of the particular use of the phrase in the Code (especially the provisions concerning directions as to how as witness may "give evidence" in an "alternative way"). However, given the modifications made to the Code during the legislative process, the definition of "giving evidence" (which is what traditionally may be thought of as "offering evidence") which is found in

---

22   LC *Evidence Code*, para C15.
23   "The court is required to consider both whether the expert has the requisite knowledge and skill, and whether the proposed testimony is within the witness's competence.": LC *Evidence Code*, para C16.
24   See EV23.02.
25   See EV25.01.

ss 186(5) and 195(3) may have been helpfully included in s 4 so as to apply to the whole Act.

The Law Commission's draft intentionally included all forms of giving evidence provided for in the Code and in other enactments — with para (c) aimed at "evidence taken on commission, or under an order for examination of a witness under Rule 369 of the High Court Rules".[26]

harassment has the same meaning as in section 3 of the Harassment Act 1997

EV4.18.01   Harassment

This definition was added as a result of the addition of "harassment" to s 95(1), the Select Committee stating: "We consider it appropriate to treat harassment cases in a similar way to domestic violence and sexual cases."[27]

hearsay rule means the rule described in section 17

hearsay statement means a statement that—

(a)   was made by a person other than a witness; and

(b)   is offered in evidence at the proceeding to prove the truth of its contents

EV4.20.01   Statements of witnesses are not excluded by the hearsay rule

This definition of "hearsay statements" means that out-of-court statements made by a "witness" (that is, someone who gives evidence and is able to be cross-examined in a proceeding) are not excluded by the hearsay rule (but may be excluded by the rule against previous consistent statements, for example), on the basis that the maker is available to be cross-examined (see also the discussion of the definition of "witness" and s 14 on the issue of "past" and "future" testifiers).[28]

The ability to cross-examine the maker of the statement means that the primary rationale for the rule against hearsay (the inability to test the credibility and accuracy of the maker) is not applicable.[29] This means, for example, that a complaint of sexual assault made close in time to the alleged event (prior to the Act referred to as evidence of "recent complaint") would not be excluded by the rule against hearsay if, as would usually be the case, the complainant testifies at the trial (is a "witness"), but will be excluded under s 35, unless an exception applies.[30]

---

26   LC *Evidence Code*, para C17. See also the statutory authority to accept evidence by video link in civil proceedings (s 26IB of the Judicature Act 1908 and rr 72B-72E of the High Court Rules).

27   *Select Committee Report on the Evidence Bill*, 11.

28   See EV4.46.01 and EV14.01.

29   LC *Evidence Reform*, para 50.

30   See EV35.04.

EV4.20.02   Statements not intended to be assertions are not excluded by the hearsay rule

The definition of "hearsay statement" requires reference to the definition of "statement", which has broad application throughout the Act.[31] The definition of "statement" does not include a statement or non-verbal conduct which is not intended to be an assertion.[32] This means that for the purpose of the hearsay rule (s 17), arguments may well be more focussed than prior to the Act on the extent to which a particular statement contains an intentional assertion, or whether the relevance of the statement is dependent on the various inferences or implications.[33] The Act's definition of "statement" clarifies the position with regard to whether "implied" or "unintended" assertions fall outside the rule against hearsay,[34] but will require good understanding of the distinction, as the implications of falling outside the definition will mean the evidence will not be subject to ss 18 or 19 or, in criminal proceedings, the notice requirement in s 22.

EV4.20.03   Offered to prove the truth of its contents

The second part of the definition of hearsay statement confirms that, as at common law, the focus of the rule is on hearsay "use" or "purpose" rather than just the fact that the statement was made out-of-court. A statement offered for some other purpose, for example merely to show that the statement was made or uttered, is not a hearsay statement and need not meet s 18's admissibility test. Its admissibility will depend on ss 7 and 8 if no other specific admissibility rules apply.

EV4.20.04   Removal of "limited use" rules and the definition of hearsay

The Act does not preserve most of the common law's "limited use" rules. For example, at common law a prior inconsistent statement that was not adopted by the witness could only be used to assess credibility, not to prove the "truth" of that prior statement.[35] Evidence of "recent complaint" could also only be used to show consistency (credibility), not to prove the truth of the prior complaint.[36]

Under the Act, however, most admissible evidence will be admissible for all purposes (that is, to prove the truth of the statement, the guilt of the accused, the veracity of the maker),[37] except in some instances.[38]

---

31   See EV27.01.
32   LC *Evidence Code*, para C37.
33   *Cross on Evidence* (online), EVA17.6; *R v Fung* 6/7/07, Wild J, HC Palmerston North CRI-2006-054-5024, para 57.
34   Illingworth QC and Mathias, "The Admisibility of Hearsay Statements and Opinion Evidence" in NZLS *Intensive: Evidence Act 2006*, 18-22.
35   *Adams on Criminal Law — Evidence*, EC11.09(1).
36   *Adams on Criminal Law — Evidence*, EC12.03(1).
37   LC *Evidence Code*, paras C168 and C352.
38   See, for example, the discussion at EV37.09 and EV38.08.

The removal of most "limited use" rules means that the distinction drawn in the definition of hearsay statement has a different significance than at common law. Statements that are not offered to prove their truth, so fall outside the hearsay rule, may actually be used for any purpose once they are admitted. For example, evidence of out-of-court statements, that have traditionally been admitted when only offered to prove that they were made, includes some "state of mind" evidence. Such statements, if not offered to prove their truth, may nevertheless be used to prove their truth once admitted. This may mean that under the Act there will continue to be argument concerning the purpose of offering the evidence in order to fall outside the scope of the definition of hearsay. This is because under the Act once evidence is admitted, it is admitted for all purposes, so the evidence can be *used* to prove its truth notwithstanding that it has not been *offered* to prove its truth and therefore is not subject to the reliability filter under s 18, nor the subject of notice under s 22.

To the extent that such a result is considered undesirable, it will be a matter for the judge to consider whether to give a suitable limited use direction (see the possibility of this under s 12)[39] in indictable proceedings.

EV4.20.05   Treatment of multiple hearsay

As noted by the Law Commission, the definition of hearsay statement makes no distinction between firsthand and multiple hearsay, "but this will be one factor to take into account when examining the circumstances relating to the statement in order to assess reliability".[40]

hostile, in relation to a witness, means that the witness—

(a)   exhibits, or appears to exhibit, a lack of veracity when giving evidence unfavourable to the party who called the witness on a matter about which the witness may reasonably be supposed to have knowledge; or

(b)   gives evidence that is inconsistent with a statement made by that witness in a manner that exhibits, or appears to exhibit, an intention to be unhelpful to the party who called the witness; or

(c)   refuses to answer questions or deliberately withholds evidence

EV4.21.01   Introduction

This definition is the prerequisite to a party's ability to cross-examine a witness called by that party (s 94). It does not necessarily reflect the common law definition. Paragraphs (a) and (b) of the definition include the (mere) *appearance* of a lack of veracity or an intention to be unhelpful. In contrast, before a finding of hostility can be made under para (c) of the definition, the judge must conclude that the witness was *deliberately* withholding evidence. By including "appearances", paras (a) and (b) avoid the necessity to prejudge

---

39   See EV12.02.
40   LC *Evidence Code*, para C21.

whether the witness actually lacks veracity or does in fact have an intention to be unhelpful to the party who called the witness.

EV4.21.02   "Supposed to have knowledge"

An actual or apparent lack of veracity amounts to hostility under para (a) of the definition only when displayed "on a matter about which the witness may reasonably be supposed to have knowledge". It is difficult to conceive of circumstances where a witness can properly be questioned about some matter upon which he or she *cannot* reasonably be supposed to have knowledge. In any event, whenever such circumstances exist it is also difficult to understand why the witness's lack of veracity should not amount to hostility.

EV4.21.03   Inconsistent statement

Paragraph (b) of the definition settles a controversy that had existed before the Act. It can no longer be said that hostility is demonstrated by the mere fact that the witness has given evidence that is inconsistent with another *statement* he or she has made. An actual or apparent intention to be unhelpful to the party calling the witness must also be present.

Italics were used to highlight the fact that in para (b) of the definition of hostile, "statement" is unqualified by any modifier such as *previous* statement. Although it is natural to think of the "statement" referred to in para (b) as a statement made by the witness prior to testifying at the current proceeding, such a restriction is not warranted. The result is that the inconsistent statement referred to in para (b) of the definition could be a statement made by the witness while testifying in the current proceeding.

EV4.21.04   Withholding evidence

Para (c) of the definition (deliberately withholding evidence) is justified in terms of a witness's oath or affirmation to tell the *whole* truth. However, this is not of assistance in determining the extent to which a witness is under an obligation to volunteer information that is not specifically elicited by a question asked in the witness's examination. Only that uncertain boundary line will determine when a witness has deliberately withheld evidence so as to demonstrate hostility.

In sum, the Act's definition of a hostile witness indicates that the mere fact that a witness gives evidence adverse to a party, suffers a loss of memory, or provides evidence inconsistent with another statement does not, by itself, justify a finding that the witness is hostile. Under the various prongs of s 4, there must some additional indications — whether stemming from the witness's demeanour, behaviour, statements, course of conduct, or any other relevant facts and circumstances — to demonstrate that the witness is not desirous of telling the truth at the instance of the calling party, or is deliberately withholding evidence that would assist the party, the jury or the judge.

The definition of "hostile" in s 4(1) speaks of the term "in relation to a witness" — a clear indication that, if someone does not "give evidence" at all in a civil or criminal trial, they cannot be a "witness" to whom the designation "hostile" may be applied (see further the discussion of "witness").[41] The definition of "hostile" pursuant to s 4(1) will thus be reserved for a witness who, after being sworn, gives some evidence for a calling party in a case but, at some point, falls within the definition of "hostile" under s 4(1).

incriminate means to provide information that is reasonably likely to lead to, or increase the likelihood of, the prosecution of a person for a criminal offence

EV4.22.01   Incriminate

The definition of this crucial term does not expressly cover the provision of information that would increase the likelihood that an *existing* prosecution will result in a conviction. If an existing prosecution is not included, the effect would be to deny the privilege against self-incrimination for information about an offence once a charge has been laid.

To avoid that result, perhaps the definition will be interpreted to include the phrase "… increase the likelihood of, the [*successful*] prosecution of a person for a criminal offence". This would be in keeping with the policy and history of the common law privilege against self-incrimination.[42]

international organisation means an organisation of States or governments of States or an organ or agency of an organisation of that kind, and includes the Commonwealth Secretariat

EV4.23.01   International organisation

This definition relates to ss 141 and 142 of the Act. The term "international organisation" was not used in the Evidence Act 1908 (or its various amendments), sections from which are replaced by ss 141 and 142. The definition is based on that used in the Official Information Act 1982 and the Privacy Act 1993.[43]

interpreter includes a person who provides communication assistance to a defendant or a witness

EV4.24.01   Interpreter

The Law Commission noted that the wide definition of "communication assistance" means that "interpreter" has an extended meaning and includes anyone who "enables or facilitates communication in any way."[44] This

---

41   See EV4.46.01.
42   *Adams on Criminal Law — Evidence*, EC20.07. The definition does not include providing information likely to expose a person to liability for a civil penalty, which was an addition was initially proposed by the Law Commission: LC *Evidence Reform*, para 278.
43   LC *Evidence Code*, para C26.

definition of interpreter means that a person who provides communication assistance of any kind (s 80) must take an oath or make an affirmation (s 78).

investigative questioning means questioning in connection with the investigation of an offence or a possible offence by, or in the presence of,—

(a)   a member of the police; or

(b)   a person whose functions include the investigation of offences

EV4.25.01   Investigative questioning

This definition is relevant to s 32 which, in some circumstances, prohibits the fact-finder drawing the inference of guilt from a defendant's silence in response to "investigative questioning" before trial.[45]

The Select Committee recommended that the definition be widened to include questioning by regulatory enforcement officers such as fisheries officers and also persons such as store detectives,[46] however the broad scope of the definition was initially intended by the Law Commission — note their commentary on the phrase "official questioning":[47]

> "The term **official questioning** is limited to questioning by or in the presence of a police officer or person whose functions include investigating offences. The latter category will include officials conducting investigations in order to enforce an enactment, such as customs or fisheries officers, and persons such as insurance investigators or store security staff. The width of this category means greater protection for a defendant's right of silence before trial".

The Ministry of Justice recommended a return to the Law Commission's definition (renaming it "investigative questioning") after concern that the definition in the Evidence Bill was too narrow.[48]

Judge includes a Justice of the Peace, a community magistrate, and any tribunal

EV4.26.01   Judge

The broad definition of "Judge" includes any *tribunal*. This raises an issue about the Act's scope of operation. The great majority of sections are limited to apply (only) *in a proceeding*. Because of s 4's definition of "proceeding", all of such sections are limited to proceedings conducted by a "court". The references to "Judge" in such sections must be limited accordingly, to exclude "mere" tribunals. This conclusion appears to follow despite the Act's reference to a "*court* proceeding" in s 62(1). Such a term should be seen as tautological.

---

44   LC *Evidence Code*, para C27.
45   See EV32.01(3).
46   *Select Committee Report on the Evidence Bill*, 2.
47   LC *Evidence Code*, para C30.
48   *Departmental Report* (EV/MOJ/5), 4ff.

Despite this general approach, there are some provisions, not governing admissibility of evidence, which are not expressly limited to proceedings and which refer to a judge. Section 13 is an early example. On the face of it, s 13 applies to all *tribunals* whether or not they are conducting a "proceeding".[49] See similarly ss 52(4) and 61(2).

This appears to be in line with the approach occasionally taken in legislation governing proceedings conducted by tribunals. For example, s 106(1)(d) of the Human Rights Act 1993 permits the Human Rights Review Tribunal to receive material as evidence "whether or not it would be admissible in a court of law".[50] This provision is given priority over the Act because of s 5(1) of the Act. However, in matters other than admissibility, s 106(4) of the Human Rights Act states "the Evidence Act 2006 shall apply to … the Tribunal in the same manner as if the Tribunal were a court within the meaning of that Act."

The New Zealand Law Society's submission on the Evidence Bill recommended the removal of the reference to "any tribunal" as the words may limit the powers of tribunals to regulate their own procedure — and the flexibility tribunals have should be retained.[51] The Ministry of Justice was of the view that the inclusion of tribunals (as recommended by the Law Commission) within the definition of "Judge" would not preclude tribunals from regulating their own procedures — and s 5 makes it clear that in the case of an inconsistency the legislation that the tribunals operate under will prevail. The Ministry was also of the view that including tribunals within the definition of judge would have the advantage of requiring tribunals to have regard to the legislation when it is enacted.[52] This view was expressed before the Select Committee added the definition of "court", however.[53]

lawyer means a barrister or solicitor, as those terms are defined in section 2 of the Law Practitioners Act 1982

EV4.27.01   Lawyer

Section 51(1) has a separate definition of "legal adviser", which is applicable for the purposes of Subpart 8 of Part 2 (privilege), as well as a definition of "lawyer" which refers to the Lawyers and Conveyancers Act 2006 under which a lawyer is defined as a person who holds a current practising certificate as a barrister or as a barrister and solicitor. The definition of "lawyer" is also needed for later provisions, such as s 95(5)(a) (personal cross-examination).

Although the definition of "lawyer" in s 4 refers to the soon to be repealed Law Practitioners Act 1982, the effect of s 207 is that s 51(1) must be read as

---

49   See EV13.01.
50   See also s 276(2) of the Resource Management Act 1991: "The Environment Court is not bound by the rules about evidence than apply to judicial proceedings".
51   NZLS *Submission on the Evidence Bill*, 4.
52   *Departmental Report* (EV/MOJ/5), 4.
53   See the discussion of that definition and its impact on tribunal hearings at EV4.09.01(1).

though the s 4 (1982) definition applies until the "commencement of s 6 of the Lawyers and Conveyancers Act 2006".[54]

leading question means a question that directly or indirectly suggests a particular answer to the question

EV4.28.01 Leading question

One guide for when a question is leading is whether or not it seeks a "yes or no" answer. However, there are no comprehensive tests and much will depend on what fact is in issue and what questions have already been asked. A classic leading question would be "was the car red?" in a case where the colour of the car was the crucial fact in dispute.

The Law Commission stated that this definition codifies the current meaning and does not include "questions that assume the existence of a fact about which the witness has given no evidence", which is part of the definition used in the Evidence Act 1995 (Aust),[55] and often included in textbook discussions of what is a leading question.[56] The Law Commission was of the view that this latter type of question could be dealt with under s 85.[57]

offer evidence includes eliciting evidence by cross-examining a witness called by another party

EV4.29.01 Offer evidence

A party "offers" evidence and one method of doing so is by calling a witness who "gives evidence". The party who testifies is both offering and giving evidence. This definition makes it clear that the mere process of cross-examination does not itself amount to offering evidence. This is confirmed by s 96(1).[58] Some evidence must be "elicited" by the questioning before evidence has been offered. This means that the Act is consistent with the common law that to merely "put" a proposition to a witness in cross-examination does not amount to evidence of the proposition.[59] The witness must accept the proposition before it can be said that there is some evidence of its truth.

---

54 The Lawyers and Conveyancers Act 2006 is likely to come into force on 1 July 2008: New Zealand Law Society, *Law Talk*, Issue 697, 15 October 2007, 16.

55 See the Dictionary of the Act in Odgers, *Uniform Evidence Law* (5th ed), Sydney, Thomson Lawbook Co, 2002, 576.

56 *Cross on Evidence* (8th NZ ed), para 9.13.

57 LC *Evidence Code*, para C28. See further the discussion of "hypothetical questions" at EV85.04.

58 See EV96.03.

59 *R v McKenzie* [2004] 1 NZLR 181. See also EV90.03(1).

opinion, in relation to a statement offered in evidence, means a statement of opinion that tends to prove or disprove a fact

EV4.30.01   Opinion

See the discussion at EV23.02.

opinion rule means the rule described in section 23

party means a party to a proceeding

EV4.32.01   Party

Although this definition requires no further elucidation for anyone with legal training, some uncertainty may yet exist for lay persons. Parties are the litigants who are actually named in a proceeding, most commonly the plaintiff and defendant in a civil proceeding and the defendant and the prosecutor (usually the police or the Crown) in a criminal proceeding. Again, given the definition of "proceeding" (which relies on the definition of "court"), this definition of party may be too narrow in some instances — see, for example, ss 34, 47, 57, 131, 132, and 134 — if it excludes those whose disputes are not heard by a "court".

previous consistent statements rule means the rule described in section 35

previous statement means a statement made by a witness at any time other than at the hearing at which the witness is giving evidence

EV4.34.01   Previous statement

The definition makes it clear that it includes a statement made by a witness at an earlier hearing in the same proceeding. As pointed out by the Law Commission,[60] the previous statement of a *witness* is not hearsay and is admissible unless excluded by the previous consistent statements rule in s 35. It is not hearsay because, per the definition of a "hearsay statement", it is not a statement made by a person *other than a witness*.[61]

proceeding means—

(a)   a proceeding conducted by a court; and

(b)   any interlocutory or other application to a court connected with that proceeding

EV4.35.01   Arbitration is not a "proceeding"

The Law Commission stated that because a proceeding is conducted by a court, a hearing before an arbitration is not a proceeding:[62]

---

60   LC *Evidence Code*, para C32.
61   See EV4.20.01.

"An arbitral tribunal has much greater flexibility than a court in determining the admissibility, relevance and weight of evidence — article 19(1) and (2) of the First Schedule of the Arbitration Act 1996. However, by virtue of article 19(3), witnesses appearing before an arbitral tribunal have the same privileges and immunities as witnesses in proceedings before a court, and will therefore have the privileges and other protection conferred by Part 4 of this Code [Subpart 8 of Part 2 of the Act]."

The Law Commission's commentary does not make it clear whether witnesses before an arbitral tribunal can also rely on the procedural sections of the Act — those dealing with the use of alternative ways of giving evidence, for example.

EV4.35.02   Criminal proceedings not defined

The New Zealand Law Society recommended a separate definition of "criminal proceedings" which should include "any proceeding commenced by an enforcement agency where the defendant is liable to a sanction of some form".[63] The principal advantage of separately defining a criminal proceeding, according to the Ministry of Justice, was that "the definition might provide greater certainty as to who was entitled to the procedural and substantive protections in Parts 2 [admissibility rules] and 3 [trial process] of the Bill."[64] The Ministry preferred that "the Bill [leave] it to the courts to make that determination [what is a criminal proceeding] on a case-by-case basis ... a similar approach should be taken to these provisions as a way of maintaining flexibility and to ensure that the rights and protections ... would apply in appropriate cases."[65]

EV4.35.03   "Proceeding" is wide enough to include the discovery process

The Act uses the phrases "civil and criminal proceeding" and "any" or "a proceeding" alternatively and presumably without intending any difference (see, for example, ss 37 and 71 as compared to ss 53 and 75). This commentary proceeds on the basis that the definition of proceeding is wide enough to cover any relevant process or procedure once proceedings are filed — for example, discovery.[66]

propensity rule means the rule described in section 40

---

62   LC *Evidence Code*, para C33. In the consultation version of the Code (*The New Zealand Law Commission Consultative Workshop on the Proposed Evidence Code*, Wellington, New Zealand Law Society, 1998, 9) "proceeding" was defined as "a proceeding conducted by a court, tribunal, or arbitrator having authority by law to hear, receive and examine evidence in New Zealand."

63   NZLS *Submission on the Evidence Bill*, 4.

64   *Departmental Report* (EV/MOJ/5), 5.

65   *Departmental Report* (EV/MOJ/5), 6.

66   Contra to the more narrow view taken by Panckhurst J in *R v S* 17/9/07, Panckhurst J, HC Christchurch CRI-2006-009-1151.

public document —

(a)   means a document that—

    (i)   forms part of the official records of the legislative, executive, or judicial branch of the Government of New Zealand or of a foreign country or of a person or body holding a public office or exercising a function of a public nature under the law of New Zealand or a foreign country; or

    (ii)   forms part of the official records of an international organisation; or

    (iii)   is being kept by, or on behalf of, a branch of any government, person, body, or organisation referred to in subparagraph (i) or (ii), for the purpose of carrying out the official functions of that government, person, body, or organisation; but

(b)   in sections 145 to 147, has the meaning set out in section 145

EV4.37.01   Public document

This exceptionally broad definition is relevant to ss 138, 148 and 149. Paragraph (b) of the definition refers to the separate definition in s 145.[67] See too ss 141 and 142 which deal with "official documents".

The definition was drawn from the Evidence Act 1995 (Aust).[68]

seal includes a stamp

self-incrimination means the provision by a person of information that could reasonably lead to, or increase the likelihood of, the prosecution of that person for a criminal offence

EV4.39.01   Self-incrimination

See the discussion of "incriminate".

sexual case means a criminal proceeding in which a person is charged with, or is waiting to be sentenced or otherwise dealt with for,—

(a)   an offence against any of the provisions of sections 128 to 142A or section 144A of the Crimes Act 1961; or

---

67   New Zealand Law Commission, *Evidence Law: Documentary Evidence and Judicial Notice: A Discussion Paper*, NZLC PP22, Wellington 1994, paras C18-C21:

    "The definition of public document also includes the records of a person or body holding a public office or exercising a function of a public nature under the law of New Zealand or of a foreign county. It covers, therefore, the full range of public agencies, including local authorities in New Zealand and overseas. The definition is, however, intended to exclude both the records of the companies or associations of a private nature incorporated under the law of New Zealand or a foreign country and the records of persons holding offices of a private nature."

68   Odgers, *Uniform Evidence Law* (5th ed), Sydney, Thomson Lawbook Co, 2002, 577-578.

(b)   any other offence against the person of a sexual nature

EV4.40.01   Sexual case

This definition is relevant to ss 44, 88, 95(1), and 127 of the Act. It is similar drafting to s 23A(1) of the Evidence Act 1908, but makes no specific reference to party liability or conspiracy (compare s 23A(1)(c) and (d)).

statement means—

(a)   a spoken or written assertion by a person of any matter; or

(b)   non-verbal conduct of a person that is intended by that person as an assertion of any matter

EV4.41.01   Statement

This definition was viewed by the Law Commission as the "natural meaning" of statement[69] and does not include a statement or non-verbal conduct which is not intended to be an assertion.[70]

veracity rules means the rules described in section 37

video record means a recording on any medium from which a moving image may be produced by any means; and includes an accompanying sound track

EV4.43.01   Video record

This definition is taken from the Law Commission's draft Code and is "widely defined to include what is currently meant by videotapes and also any means of recording available in the future that preserves both visual and sound images."[71] It is of relevance to s 46 (visual identification), and ss 105-106, which deal with evidence given in "alternative ways". The comparable sections in the Evidence Act 1908 used the term "videotape", which was not defined in that Act. See also the Evidence Regulations 2007,[72] which deal with video record evidence.

visual identification evidence means evidence that is—

(a)   an assertion by a person, based wholly or partly on what that person saw, to the effect that a defendant was present at or near a place where an act constituting direct or circumstantial evidence of the commission of an offence was done at, or about, the time the act was done; or

---

69   LC *Evidence Code*, para C37.
70   See further the discussion at EV4.20.02, EV17.01, and EV27.01.
71   LC *Evidence Code*, para C38.
72   The Evidence Regulations 2007 (SR 2007/204) are reproduced in Chapter 2 of this text.

(b)   an account (whether oral or in writing) of an assertion of the kind described in paragraph (a)

EV4.44.01   Visual identification evidence

The revolutionary provisions of s 45 of the Act apply only to visual identification evidence.[73] In contrast, the judicial warning required by s 126 of the Act is triggered by a different class of identification evidence.[74]

As with the definition of "voice identification evidence", the definition of visual identification evidence includes any assertion, as long as it is "*to the effect* that a defendant was present ...". This flexibility may have been intended to include cases where the person making the assertion admits to some uncertainty about the identification.

Visual identification evidence includes an assertion that the defendant was present at or near a place where an act constituting *circumstantial evidence* of the offence was done. This would include an assertion that the defendant was the person seen fleeing the scene of the crime. It would also include an assertion that the defendant was the person involved in an act that the prosecution offers as propensity evidence (a form of circumstantial evidence) against the defendant. Although such evidence amounts to visual identification evidence, it does not trigger the warning required by s 126 of the Act.

(1)   Pre-trial assertions

The Law Commission explained the difference between paras (a) and (b) of the definition of visual identification evidence on the basis that para (a) refers to the actual assertion by a witness *in court* that the defendant is the offender. Paragraph (b) is meant to cover "the ... usual case" where an alleged offender is identified out of court (for example, in an identification parade or photographic montage) and the identifier or another witness gives an account of that identification in court.[75] No such distinction is made in the case of "voice identification evidence", discussed below. Despite the Law Commission's view, there is nothing in para (a) of the definition of visual identification evidence that restricts it to an assertion made by a person while giving evidence. A witness could give evidence of a pre-trial assertion of identification made by himself or herself or by another person and such evidence would fit para (a) of the definition.[76]

voice identification evidence means evidence that is an assertion by a person to the effect that a voice, whether heard first-hand or through mechanical or electronic transmission or recording, is the voice of a defendant or any other

---

73   See EV45.01.
74   See EV126.01.
75   LC *Evidence Code*, para C39.
76   See further the discussion at EV45.01(2) and EV46.01(1).

person who was connected with an act constituting direct or circumstantial evidence of the commission of an offence

EV4.45.01 Voice identification evidence

See also the discussion of "visual identification evidence". An important distinction between visual identification evidence and voice identification evidence is that the latter includes evidence identifying the voice of *any person* having the "connection" required by the definition. Therefore, it is not merely voice identification evidence that identifies the defendant that must satisfy the test for admissibility set by s 46.[77] As with visual identification evidence, voice identification includes evidence that the voice of the defendant (or another person) was "connected with" an act constituting *circumstantial* evidence of the commission of the offence. An example would be an assertion that it was the defendant's voice that called out near the time of a robbery "time to go; the police are here". The definition of voice identification does not contain a provision similar to para (b) of the definition of visual identification evidence. The result must be that evidence which can be described as *an account* of evidence coming within the definition of voice identification evidence need not meet the test for admissibility set by s 46. However, such an "account" may well be a hearsay statement and have to meet the prerequisites for admissibility of hearsay evidence.

witness means a person who gives evidence and is able to be cross-examined in a proceeding.

EV4.46.01 Witness: introduction

This is the most troublesome of all the definitions in the Act. It is clear that "witness" at least involves a person who is actually engaged in the process of giving evidence and is able to be then cross-examined. The difficulties are caused by the person who is scheduled to be, or is likely to give evidence in the future (the "future testifier") and the person who has already given evidence and left the courtroom (the "past testifier").

EV4.46.02 The future testifier

Difficulties arise in determining the meaning of a "witness" when applying the "core admissibility" provisions governing hearsay (s 18), admissions in civil proceedings (s 34), and previous consistent statements (s 35). These provisions would be almost unworkable if "witness" includes a future testifier.

Consider the hearsay provisions. Paragraph (a) of the definition of a "hearsay statement" makes it clear that a hearsay statement is a statement made by a person *other than a witness*. If a future testifier is a "witness", this means that an out-of-court statement by such a person is *not* a hearsay statement. The pre-trial statements by such a person would be admissible regardless of the controls

---

77   See EV46.01.

on hearsay evidence of reliability, unavailability, and (in criminal proceedings) notice.

Insofar as *admissions* in civil proceedings are concerned, s 34(2) would be rendered largely meaningless. Section 34(2) focuses on "an admission that is a hearsay statement".[78] But if "witness" includes a future testifier, an admission that is a hearsay statement will almost never exist. This is because the parties in civil proceedings almost always give evidence. If the mere fact that the party is scheduled to give evidence at some future point in the proceeding is enough to make the party a "witness", his or her out-of-court statement will not be a hearsay statement (because it does not qualify as a statement by someone *other than a witness*).

The *previous consistent statements* rule applies only to previous statements by "witnesses". If the rule is applied to statements by future testifiers, intractable difficulties will be caused by the attempt to determine if the statement offered in evidence is "consistent" with the evidence that it is anticipated that the future testifier will eventually give.

Section 14, which deals with provisional admissibility, may need to be employed in such situations — the court will have to assess the admissibility of the evidence based on what the parties indicate about who will be called as a witness in the future and what their evidence will consist of.[79]

There are other provisions in the Act that undoubtedly treat future testifiers as "witnesses". The most obvious examples are the provisions dealing with privacy as to a witness's address (s 87), directions about alternative ways of giving evidence (s 103), witness anonymity orders (s 113), and New Zealand subpoenas served on Australian witnesses (s 154).

The result is that this commentary relies on the introductory words in s 4(1) that the definitions in that section apply "unless the context otherwise requires".[80] The context of provisions such as alternative ways of giving evidence, witness anonymity orders, and subpoenas for Australian witnesses requires that "witness" includes a person who will give evidence at a future point in the proceeding.

EV4.46.03   The past testifier

For reasons similar to those just discussed relating to the future testifier, it could be argued that a past testifier should likewise be excluded from the definition of "witness", at least for the purposes of the Act's core admissibility provisions. However, it does not appear that such arguments troubled either the Law Commission or the author of the explanatory notes to the Evidence Bill.

---

78   See EV34.03(4).
79   See EV14.01.
80   See EV4.00.01.

Both the explanatory notes to the Bill's definition of a "hearsay statement" and the Law Commission[81] agreed that when one witness *repeats an out-of-court statement by another "witness"*, this is not a hearsay statement. The inability of two people to testify at one time means that when the explanatory notes and the Law Commission speak of one witness repeating a statement made by another witness they are referring to the statement of a past testifier. Accordingly, the explanatory notes and the Law Commission are saying that a past testifier comes within the Act's definition of a "witness", presumably because at some stage of the proceeding he or she gave evidence and was able to be cross-examined.

In summary, the Law Commission and the explanatory notes to the Evidence Bill agree that for the core admissibility provisions such as hearsay, admission in civil proceedings, and previous consistent statements, a "witness" is a person who is actually engaged in the process of giving evidence *or* who has previously given evidence in the proceeding. As stated above, there can be no doubt that, for the purpose of provisions such as those governing alternative ways of giving evidence and anonymous witness, the definition of "witness" must also include a future testifier.[82]

EV4.46.04   Refusal to answer questions

A person who refuses to take an oath or make an affirmation is not a witness because such a person does not "give evidence".

(2)   A hearing commences for the purposes of this Act when at the substantive hearing of the issues that are the subject of proceedings the party having the right to begin commences to state that party's case or, having waived the right to make an opening address, calls that party's first witness.

EV4.47.01   Subsection (2)

Although the Act never explicitly defines its scope of application, individual provisions such as s 4(2) reflect that, in general, the Act does not regulate matters of procedure. Accordingly, although s 4(2) defines the commencement of a hearing as the moment that "the party having the right to begin" starts to present their case, the Act gives no guidance on which party to a dispute has that right. The Law Commission explained the purpose of s 4(2) as having particular relevance to s 5(3).[83]

---

81   LC *Evidence Code*, para C19.

82   However, these difficulties may have been avoided had the initial wording of the Law Commission been retained. In New Zealand Law Commission, *Evidence Law: Hearsay: A Discussion Paper*, NZLC PP15, Wellington, 1991, 32, the following draft was proposed: "'Hearsay' means a statement that … was made by a person other than a person *who is giving evidence* of the statement at a proceeding." (Emphasis added.)

83   LC *Evidence Code*, para C43.

5   Application

(1) If there is an inconsistency between the provisions of this Act and any other enactment, the provisions of that other enactment prevail, unless this Act provides otherwise.

(2) Despite subsection (1), if there is any inconsistency between rules of court made under any enactment with the concurrence of 2 or more members of the Rules Committee and this Act, the provisions of this Act prevail.

(3) This Act applies to all proceedings commenced before, on, or after the commencement of this [section] except—

    (a) the continuation of a hearing that commenced before the commencement of this [section]; and

    (b) any appeal from, or review of, a determination made at a hearing of that kind.

History

Subsection (3) was amended, as from 4 July 2007, by s 4 Evidence Amendment Act 2007 (2007 No 24) by substituting "section" for "Act" in the second and third places it appears.

EV5.01   Priority of other enactments in the case of inconsistency

Section 5(1) is likely to be one of the more commonly cited provisions in the Act. It was extended during the legislative process to include reference to "enactments" (which includes regulations — see s 29 of the Interpretation Act 1999)[84] and the phrase "inconsistency" was added. There is likely to be much discussion of whether an inconsistency exists.[85] Many other enactments contain provisions dealing with the admissibility of evidence and other matters also dealt with by the Act.[86] Section 5(1) gives precedence to those other enactments when there is an inconsistency between the provisions unless the Evidence Act "provides otherwise". The Act does "provide otherwise" in a number of places — see, for example, ss 95(7), 114(3), and 120(3). The Act also effectively repeats s 5(1), perhaps for the avoidance of doubt, in the case of a number of specific provisions (for example, ss 55(2), 60(3), 84(1), and 116(3)).

If the Act is silent on a matter dealt with in another enactment, this may well amount to an inconsistency as s 12 (the "gap-filling" section) only takes effect if there is no

---

84   Section 5(1) is a change from that proposed by the Law Commission, which provided that the Code "applies subject to the express provisions of any other Act". This drafting was contained in the relevant Cabinet Paper (*Cabinet Paper 1*, para 10), but was altered to include a reference to enactments in the Bill. This is a significant policy shift accompanied by no easily accessible rationale. It seems contrary to the Law Commission's prioritising of the principles of the Act to guide future development of the law to have the Act subject to secondary legislation, or Acts that do not expressly take priority.

85   *Adams on Criminal Law — Evidence*, EA5.01(1).

86   During the Law Commission's work, for example, a large number of Acts were identified that dealt with the admissibility of hearsay: LC *Evidence Reform*, para 9.

provision "in the [Evidence] Act or any other enactment".[87] The fact that an enactment, which has not been subject to scrutiny for consistency with the purposes and principles of the Act, should take priority may potentially undermine the significance of the Act, and the value of having most of the rules of evidence in one statute.[88] The lessened significance of the Evidence Act, which is made possible by the redrafting of ss 5, 10 and 12, may not have been clear to the members of the Select Committee. When speaking of the meaning of s 5(1), Russell Fairbrother MP stated: "The statute prevails over other legislation unless it is stated otherwise."[89]

Note that ss 7 and 17 only refer to the provisions of other Acts, not other enactments.[90]

EV5.02   The priority of the Act over some rules of court

Section 5(2) contains the one general exception to s 5(1). In the case of an inconsistency, the Act takes priority over "rules of court made under any enactment with the concurrence of 2 or more members of the Rules Committee" — effectively for the present, the rules of court for the High Court and District Court. It is not entirely clear why those words were favoured over the wording of the Bill, which just referred to the Act taking priority over the High Court Rules and the District Courts Rules 1992.[91] Due to the addition of "enactment" to s 5(1), the Act takes *priority over* the High Court and District Courts Rules, but is *subject to* the rules of the Family Court, Environment Court, Employment Court and indeed to the practices of any tribunals which are the subject of regulations.

Reference to the Family Courts Rules 2002 in s 5(2) was viewed by the Ministry of Justice as undesirable given the less formal approach taken by the Family Court (with regard to applying the law of evidence) — and the fact that there is no formal rules committee — which "may lead to difficulties where there is an unanticipated consequence of an inconsistency between the Evidence Act and the Family Courts Rules."[92] However, the consequence of this decision is that the Family Courts Rules will prevail over the Act when there is an inconsistency.[93]

Issues will arise regarding the identification of an inconsistency between the Act and the High Court Rules. Some provisions of the Act are intended to ensure consistency between the Act and the High Court Rules by essentially incorporating the relevant rule into a section of the Act — see, for example ss 20, 26, 57(3)(c), 83(1)(c), 131 and 132, or providing that the section is subject to the relevant rules of court — see s 154(6).

---

87   See EV12.01.

88   Hansard, *Nandor Tanczos: Evidence Bill: Second Reading*, 15 November 2006 ((2006) 635 NZPD 6563).

89   Hansard, *Russell Fairbrother: Evidence Bill: Second Reading*, 15 November 2006 ((2006) 635 NZPD 6561).

90   See EV7.01.

91   There is no explanation for the change in the Select Committee's report.

92   *Departmental Report* (EV/MOJ/5), 7.

93   See, eg, r 179 of the Family Courts Rules 2002.

For an example where it may not be clear if an inconsistency exists, see r 273 of the District Courts Rules 1992 which states that an admission made for the purpose of an interlocutory application is not otherwise binding on a party. Section 34 of the Act, which governs the admissibility of admissions, contains no such limitation. Would the Act take priority?

Section 5(3) is the general transitional provision in the Act. The specific transitional provisions, which came into force on 18 July 2007, are found in ss 203-214.

With regard to s 5(3) the Law Commission stated:[94]

> "A proceeding may be made up of a number of hearings: for example, a bail application, application under s 344A of the Crimes Act 1961 or other pretrial application, and the substantive hearing itself. The effect of s 5(3) is that the Code applies to any hearing commenced on or after the Code's date of commencement, even if the proceeding commences before that date. Hearings commenced before the Code comes into operation must be completed under the former law, as must appeals or reviews arising from such hearings."

Purpose, principles, and matters of general application

6   Purpose

The purpose of this Act is to help secure the just determination of proceedings by—

(a)   providing for facts to be established by the application of logical rules; and

(b)   providing rules of evidence that recognise the importance of the rights affirmed by the New Zealand Bill of Rights Act 1990; and

(c)   promoting fairness to parties and witnesses; and

(d)   protecting rights of confidentiality and other important public interests; and

(e)   avoiding unjustifiable expense and delay; and

(f)   enhancing access to the law of evidence.

EV6.01   Introduction

Section 6 sets out the purpose of the Act, a section which also has significance when the court is interpreting the Act (s 10), exercising inherent powers (s 11) and making admissibility decisions when the Act (or any other enactment) does not fully cover the matter (s 12). The overarching purpose of the Act is to "help secure the just determination of proceedings". The Act's primary purpose[95] is therefore to be achieved through the six objectives in s 6.

---

94   LC *Evidence Code*, para C47.
95   Compared to the four purposes originally drafted in New Zealand Law Commission, *Evidence Law: Codification: A Discussion Paper*, NZLC PP14, Wellington, 1991, 19.

EV6.02   Paragraph (a): "providing for facts to be established by the application of logical rules"

The draft Code's s 6(a) read as "promoting the rational ascertainment of facts". The wording was changed at the Cabinet stage to "providing for facts to be established by the application of logical rules", on the basis that "the proposed wording captures the same concept and expresses it in plain English".[96] Although the current wording captures some of the same sense, it is not an objective as easily applied as an interpretative tool. It is more useful to ask whether the admissibility decision promotes the rational ascertainment of facts, than whether it provides for the facts to be established by the application of logical rules. If both phrases require consideration of the same matters of policy, the original wording may be easier for judges to take into consideration.

EV6.03   Paragraph (b): "providing rules of evidence that recognise the importance of the rights affirmed by the New Zealand Bill of Rights Act 1990"

The addition by the Select Committee of s 6(b) may be more significant than the Select Committee thought.[97] Arguments over the proper interpretation of provisions of the Evidence Act will no doubt often include references to the New Zealand Bill of Rights Act 1990, with one or more of the parties suggesting that a particular interpretation should be preferred because it is consistent with the Bill of Rights Act. The rights in the Bill of Rights Act are also wider and include substantive rights (for example, freedom from discrimination and freedom of religion) as well as the procedural rights, which are arguably covered by s 6(c).[98] The inclusion of the reference to all of the rights in the Bill of Rights Act may have an impact on the sections in which judges are instructed to take account of "religious beliefs", for example ss 95 and 103. Section 5(1) will apply, if required, with regard to inconsistencies between the Bill of Rights Act and the Evidence Act, as opposed to matters of interpretation.

In commenting on what is now s 6(d), the Law Commission considered that privacy issues and human rights would be included as "important public interests".[99]

---

96   *Cabinet Paper 1*, fn 1.

97   The New Zealand Law Society was of the view that the application of the Bill of Rights Act to proceedings is "axiomatic" and argued there should be an express reference (NZLS *Submission on the Evidence Bill*, 5) . The Select Committee agreed: "We consider it important to recognise the fundamental importance of that Act in the purpose section of the bill." (*Select Committee Report on the Evidence Bill*, 2). The Hon Rick Barker MP said: "The reference to the New Zealand Bill of Rights Act requires legal practitioners to have regard to the rights in that Act." (Hansard, *Hon Rick Barker: Evidence Bill: Second Reading*, 14 November 2006 ((2006) 635 NZPD 6483)).

98   LC *Evidence Code*, para C50.

99   LC *Evidence Code*, para C51.

EV6.04   Paragraph (e): "avoiding unjustifiable expense and delay"

This objective is also reflected in the general exclusion provision: s 8(1)(b).[100] The Law Commission considered the importance of efficiency and finality early in their work:[101]

> "We do not see efficiency and finality as subsidiary policies for the trial. They are important trial policies and therefore must play an appropriate role in evidence law. In particular, efficiency provides a good justification for minimising complications in the exclusionary rules of evidence (simply to avoid the time-wasting and confusion caused by arguing about them). Considerations of efficiency and finality also provide a justification for excluding evidence in cases where its probative value cannot justify the time, cost and general complexity involved in considering it."

EV6.05   Paragraph (f): "enhancing access to the law of evidence"

Section 6(f) was added by the Select Committee. There is no doubt that enhancing access to the law of evidence is an important purpose of the legislation — in fact the express purpose of the Law Commission's law reform reference was "[t]o make the law of evidence as ... accessible as possible" — but it is difficult for this to be applied as an interpretative aid in the sense of "access" that the Select Committee contemplated:

> "Th[is] is an important consideration, because one of the difficulties in the past has been that the laws of evidence have been scattered in case law as well as in legislation. The attempt here is to bring it all together. ... [It] basically provides a central place where the law of evidence can be found. I think for the public that is enormously helpful."[102]

Interpreting a section of the Act, or deciding on an admissibility point not covered by the Act in a way that "enhances access to the law of evidence" is not necessarily a straightforward undertaking, unless it means that such decisions should themselves be "accessible" or easy to understand. Read this way, however, s 6(f) does not add anything of significance to the purpose provision that was intended primarily as an interpretative tool. That s 6(f) was added for a different reason is clear from advice given on the point from the specialist adviser to the Select Committee, the Hon Robert Fisher QC:[103]

> "It has been brought home to me in my dealings with the judiciary that not everyone appreciates the role of the Act in enhancing access to the law of evidence. This impacts indirectly upon the perceived need to promulgate other

---

100   See EV8.03.

101   New Zealand Law Commission, *Evidence Law: Principles for Reform: A Discussion Paper*, NZLC PP13, Wellington, 1991, para 54.

102   Hansard, *Nandor Tanczos: Evidence Bill: Second Reading*, 15 November 2006 ((2006) 635 NZPD 6563).

103   Fisher QC, *Fifth Memo for Justice and Electoral Select Committee re Evidence Bill* (EV/ADV/5), 27 September 2006, paras 3-4.

aspects of the law of evidence which are not contained in the Act e.g. Regulations and the Judges' Rules.

"I recommend that the Committee consider adding to the purposes in cl 6 of the Bill something along these lines:

"(e)   enhancing access to the law of evidence."

7   Fundamental principle that relevant evidence admissible

(1)   All relevant evidence is admissible in a proceeding except evidence that is—

(a)   inadmissible under this Act or any other Act; or

(b)   excluded under this Act or any other Act.

(2)   Evidence that is not relevant is not admissible in a proceeding.

(3)   Evidence is relevant in a proceeding if it has a tendency to prove or disprove anything that is of consequence to the determination of the proceeding.

EV7.01   Relevance

Rather than admitting any and all evidence offered by a party, a judge will only admit evidence that bears such a sufficient relationship to the matters in dispute that it may be deemed "relevant" to the case. Section 7 sets out the fundamental principal of relevance governing the admissibility of any type of evidence in civil and criminal proceedings.

Subject to certain exceptions, s 7(1) makes it clear that all relevant evidence will be admissible and that evidence can be admitted on any basis for which it is relevant.[104] Under s 7(1)(a), relevant evidence will not be admitted if another provision of the Act, or any other Act, renders such evidence inadmissible (such as the s 8 requirement of general exclusion). Similarly, s 7(1)(b) indicates that otherwise relevant evidence will not be considered in a proceeding if the Act, or any other Act, excludes the evidence for some particular use (such as the s 31 prohibition against the prosecution relying on improperly obtained evidence (s 30), even if offered by another party in a criminal trial).[105] Section 7(2) states that all irrelevant evidence is inadmissible.[106]

The combined effect of these provisions is that relevance is a *necessary* but not *sufficient* condition of admissibility under the Act. Relevant evidence will be entitled to admissibility at first instance, but may still be kept out of civil or criminal proceedings by a separate provision of the Act or some other specific statutory rule. The reference to "any other *Act*" rather than "any other *enactment*" in s 7 appears to be a legislative oversight. Indeed, subject to the exception contained in s 5(2), s 5(1) makes it clear that, unless the Evidence Act provides otherwise, its provisions

---

104   See, eg, *R v Wyatt* 10/10/07, CA311/07; [2007] NZCA 436, para 14; *Cash for Scrap Ltd v Auckland Regional Council* 9/10/07, Cooper J, HC Auckland CIV-2006-404-4270, para 87; *Wardle v Attorney-General* 24/4/07, Miller J, HC Wellington CIV-1999-485-85, para 36.
105   See EV31.01.
106   See, eg, *R v Cooper* 2/11/07, CA361/07; [2007] NZCA 481, para 25.

are subordinate to any other inconsistent "enactment" (which, under s 29 of the Interpretation Act 1999, would include both Acts and regulations).[107]

The s 7 requirement of relevance should be read in conjunction with two other rules of admissibility contained in the Act. Section 13 codifies a specific judicial approach to establishing the relevance of a document. Section 14 deals with the provisional admission of evidence "subject to evidence being offered later which establishes its admissibility" (such as evidence offered at a subsequent point in a civil or criminal proceeding that establishes the relevance of the previously offered evidence).[108]

EV7.02   Materiality and probativeness

The test of relevance under s 7(3) contains two prongs: materiality and probativeness.

Materiality asks whether the evidence is offered on a matter or fact at issue in the case ("of consequence to the determination of the proceeding"). Probativeness asks whether the evidence has a logical "tendency to prove or disprove" the material proposition on which it is offered.

Both prongs of relevance must be satisfied to pass the s 7(3) relevance test. Evidence will be irrelevant if it is not offered on a material issue in the proceeding, or has no tendency to prove or disprove anything about a material point.

Relevance is a relational concept. It requires the proponent of the evidence to explain what the offered proof is relevant to and why. Questions of materiality and probativeness can therefore be assessed only within the concrete circumstances of a particular proceeding.[109]

For example, in a homicide case, the fact that the defendant's fingerprints were found on the murder weapon is material to the issue of the murderer's identity and hence to the accused's guilt or innocence. Identifying the killer is clearly a matter of consequence to the determination of a homicide trial. However, the probativeness of the fingerprint evidence depends on a chain of reasoning linking fingerprints to the question of identity based on the facts of the case. Such a chain of reasoning can be derived from commonsense, logic, science or experience. With respect to the hypothetical above, the probativeness of the proof depends on the judge accepting the science of fingerprint investigation, as well as a chain of reasoning suggesting that a person in possession of a murder weapon was likely to be a murderer.

In *R v Herewini*,[110] a murder case involving a claim of self-defence, Stevens J rejected evidence offered by the defendant on the deceased's general propensity for violent behaviour. While accepting the materiality of the victim's actual aggression to

---

107   See EV5.01. As discussed further at EV17.02, s 17(a) contains a similar drafting mistake.

108   See, respectively, EV13.01 and EV14.01.

109   See, eg, *R v Tye* 3/8/07, CA86/07; [2007] NZCA 330, para 37; *R v Russell* 2/11/07, Stevens J, HC Auckland CRI-2006-092-11084, paras 27-32 (ruling that the historic criminal convictions of a prosecution witness could not be the subject of defence cross-examination since the convictions were irrelevant both to the facts at issue in the proceeding and the veracity of the witness. See EV37.07); and *R v Cooper* 2/11/07, CA361/07; [2007] NZCA 481, para 13.

110   *R v Herewini* 15/8/07, Stevens J, HC Rotorua CRI-2006-063-3151.

Herwini's argument of self-defence, the Court ruled that none of the offered proof would be "probative of violence or the type of violence" alleged to have been exhibited by the deceased during the particular encounter leading to the homicide.[111] Accordingly, the evidence failed the test for admissibility under s 7(3).

EV7.03 Multiple uses of admissible evidence

The Act does not specify whether evidence may be relied upon for multiple purposes. However, in line with s 6(a) and s 7, the general rule should be that, once admitted, evidence will be available to prove "*anything* that is of consequence to the determination of the proceeding" (s 7(3)).[112] Admissible evidence may thus be used in different ways and for diverse purposes in a particular proceeding. While not completely free from doubt, an example is provided by the prior consistent statement of a witness offered under s 35. As discussed at EV35.04(1), such a statement should be admissible both to prove the truth of its contents *and* to respond to certain challenges to a witness's veracity or accuracy pursuant to s 35(2).

The general rule outlined must itself be subject to various provisions of the Act specifically limiting the use to which some admissible evidence can be put; examples include: s 27 (controlling the use of the pre-trial statements of defendants and co-defendants); s 31 (forbidding the prosecution from relying on certain evidence offered by defendants in a criminal case); s 32 (forbidding the fact-finder from using a criminal defendant's pre-trial silence as evidence of guilt); and s 34(2) (limiting the use of hearsay admissions in respect of the case of a third party[113]). In a few cases, the Act also tasks judges with warning juries against relying on certain types of evidence or trial procedures for an unauthorised purpose; examples include: s 123 (judicial directions about alternative modes of witness testimony in a criminal proceeding); and s 124 (judicial warnings in a criminal proceeding about evidence that the defendant has lied). Additionally, as suggested at EV38.08, it may be that evidence attacking a defendant's veracity which is admitted under s 38(2) can only be used for the purpose of assessing the defendant's veracity and not as evidence of guilt.

EV7.04 Relevance (admissibility) versus weight

To satisfy the test of relevance, s 7 requires only that the evidence have a "tendency" to prove or disprove a material proposition in the proceeding, not prove or disprove it absolutely. This is a low threshold.[114] As a result, the links in the chain of reasoning need not be ironclad. A defendant might argue, for example, that his fingerprints were found on a murder weapon because he merely stumbled across the weapon on a street and picked it up. While such evidence would itself satisfy the s 7 test of relevance — because it tends to disprove the defendant's identity as the murderer — it does not

---

111   *R v Herewini* 15/8/07, Stevens J, HC Rotorua CRI-2006-063-3151, para 31.
112   Emphasis added.
113   See EV34.03(2).
114   See *R v Smith* 10/9/07, CA267/07; CA343/07; [2007] NZCA 400, para 16 (noting that the "substantially helpful test" for the admissibility of veracity evidence under s 37(1) of the Act "creates a higher threshold than mere relevance" under s 7(3)).

diminish the legal admissibility of the fingerprint evidence as relevant to proving that the defendant committed the crime. In other words, the determination that evidence is relevant — a legal question for the judge — merely settles the preliminary question as to whether a party's proffered chain of reasoning on a particular issue is sufficient to satisfy the s 7 requirements of materiality and probativeness. If so, and subject to any other legal rules of inadmissibility or exclusion (s 7(1)(a) and (b)), the party will be entitled to present such evidence in the proceeding. However, once received, the degree of probative force, or "weight", to be given to the evidence is exclusively a question for the trier of fact.

8   General exclusion

(1)   In any proceeding, the Judge must exclude evidence if its probative value is outweighed by the risk that the evidence will—

      (a)   have an unfairly prejudicial effect on the proceeding; or

      (b)   needlessly prolong the proceeding.

(2)   In determining whether the probative value of evidence is outweighed by the risk that the evidence will have an unfairly prejudicial effect on a criminal proceeding, the Judge must take into account the right of the defendant to offer an effective defence.

EV8.01   Exclusion of relevant evidence

Section 8 sets out a general and overriding requirement for exclusion of evidence that is otherwise relevant (s 7) and not excluded, or rendered inadmissible, by some specific provision of the Act or any other Act (s 7(1)(a) and (b)).[115] The requirement of general exclusion is made mandatory in all civil and criminal proceedings — whether judge-alone or a judge sitting with a jury.[116] The judge "must" exclude evidence that runs afoul of s 8. The s 8 test involves balancing the probative value of an item of evidence against the risk that the evidence will have an "unfairly prejudicial effect on the proceeding" (s 8(1)(a)), or "needlessly prolong the proceeding" (s 8(1)(b)). Evidence should not be kept out under s 8 if its probative value: (a) outweighs the risk of any unfairly prejudicial effect on the proceeding; or (b) is strong enough to support a prolonging of the proceeding in order to receive the offered proof. Conversely, s 8 should render inadmissible evidence posing a risk of unfair prejudice disproportionate to its probative value, or where reception of the evidence would unnecessarily extend a civil or criminal trial.[117]

The s 8 requirement of general exclusion is intended to help a judge manage the length of a trial and/or advance a fair course for the proceeding itself. Accordingly, any party in a civil or criminal trial can invoke the protections of the rule.[118]

---

115   See EV7.01. See, eg, *R v Wyatt* 10/10/07, CA311/07; [2007] NZCA 436, para 15; *R v Smith* 10/9/07, CA267/07; CA343/07; [2007] NZCA 400, para 18.
116   See *Wardle v Attorney-General* 24/4/07, Miller J, HC Wellington CIV-1999-485-85, para 36.
117   See *Wardle v Attorney-General* 24/4/07, Miller J, HC Wellington CIV-1999-485-85, para 39.

EV8.02   Unfair prejudice

The s 8(1)(a) test will not be met merely because evidence is adverse to a party's case. Inadmissibility under s 8(1)(a) requires that the evidence present some credible risk of *unfair* prejudice to the proceeding *and* that such risk outweighs the probative value of the evidence. Such balancing is a quintessentially idiosyncratic exercise and must be made by a judge on the concrete facts and circumstances of a particular situation.[119] The same is true with evidence whose probative value may or may not be worth the expenditure of additional court time pursuant to the s 8(1)(b) test.[120]

In the context of s 8, the term "probative value" will be incapable of bearing an exact meaning. As the Law Commission has observed: "[t]he positive side of the s 8 balancing test ... will depend on such matters as how strongly the evidence points to the inference it is said to support, and how important the evidence is to the ultimate issues in the trial".[121] Similarly, in s 8(1)(a), the phrase "unfairly prejudicial" is not a term capable of precise or exclusive definition. One writer has noted the following useful definition:[122]

> "Prejudice, in the evidentiary context, means the drawing of an inference ... along an impermissible chain of reasoning — not one of logic, commonsense and experience, but one of hunch, gut-reaction and lack of logic. It is the reaching of a conclusion for the wrong reason and whether that conclusion is 'right' or 'wrong' is quite immaterial.".

Like the balancing exercise itself mandated under s 8, allegations of unfair prejudice may encompass myriad arguments and be conceptualised in numerous ways. However, as contemplated by s 8, the risk of "unfair prejudice" will typically refer to the danger that a trier of fact — most likely a jury — will:

(a)   Give some piece of evidence more effect than it deserves (as opposed to appreciating its logical, rational weight);

(b)   Be misled by evidence; or

(c)   Use evidence for an illegitimate purpose.[123]

Examples will include material that appeals to a jury's sympathies, arouses its sense of contempt or horror,[124] provokes its instinct to punish, or appears more persuasive

---

118   Compare s 43(1), discussed at EV43.05. See, eg, *R v Wyatt* 10/10/07, CA311/07; [2007] NZCA 436.

119   See, eg, *R v Waaka* 12/10/07, Potter J, HC Auckland CRI-2006-092-15178.

120   See *Wardle v Attorney-General* 24/4/07, Miller J, HC Wellington CIV-1999-485-85, para 39 (noting that a court will find it "sometimes difficult to reach firm conclusions about relevance before trial, and no doubt ... be slow to exclude evidence that may possess significant probative value").

121   LC *Evidence Code*, para C58. See, eg, *R v T* 6/11/07, Venning J, HC Auckland CRI-2006-092-11737 (excluding some gruesome photographic evidence in a prosecution for murder where the photos were not relevant to any contested issue at trial).

122   Mahoney, "Evidence" [1993] NZ Recent Law 57, 59 (quoting "Editorial" (1992) 34 Crim LQ 385).

123   See *R v During* [1973] 1 NZLR 366, 375.

than it actually is (a situation encountered with "some types of expert and statistical" evidence).[125] In such cases, s 8(1)(a) essentially requires the judge to decide whether the trial will be better and more fairly conducted without the presence of the offered evidence. Should a judge decide that the probative value of a piece of evidence outweighs the risk of unfair prejudice, the judge will usually attempt to ameliorate such prejudice by instructing the jury as to the item's appropriate role in the proceeding and its proper or improper evidential use.[126]

In *R v Herewini*, Stevens J noted that, by referring broadly to any "unfairly prejudicial effect on the proceeding", s 8(1)(a) is "consistent with the concept of promoting fairness to the parties and witnesses mentioned in s 6(c)" of the Act.[127] In a criminal proceeding, such orientation will allow the exclusion of evidence that operates unfairly on the prosecution case, or that will "invite improper speculation and divert the attention of the jury away from the key issues" in a criminal trial.[128] While ultimately finding the evidence irrelevant under s 7(3), Stevens J would have applied this principal to exclude proof concerning the victim's general propensity for violence in a prosecution for murder involving a claim of self-defence.[129]

EV8.03 Needlessly prolonging the proceeding

The second prong of s 8 makes it clear that the general exclusion of otherwise probative evidence may occur in situations other than that of unfair prejudice to a court proceeding. Under s 8(1)(b), probative evidence that poses an unacceptable risk of "needlessly" prolonging a case will be material that unnecessarily delays the end of trial, or mires the court in the presentation of repetitive, trivial or superfluous proof.

An example would be a defendant in a criminal hearing who, pursuant to ss 38(1) or 41(1) of the Act, respectively, wishes to call a dozen witnesses to give evidence regarding his veracity (s 38(1)) or propensity to behave in an upright manner (s 41(1)). Assuming it otherwise passed muster under ss 7 and 8(1)(a), most judges would rely on s 8(1)(b) to limit this type of veracity or propensity evidence to one or two witnesses. Indeed, the evidence of all 12 would likely be cumulative, repetitive and generally unnecessary to establish the defendant's contention of truth telling or law-abiding character.[130] Section 6(e) would likewise support such a result. That provision makes it clear that one purpose of the Evidence Act is "to help secure the just determination of proceedings by … avoiding unjustifiable expense and delay".

---

124   See, eg, *R v Marson* 25/5/01, Nicholson J, HC Whangarei T002936 (ruling admissible in the accused's murder trial photographs of the victim's body as found by the police); *R v T* 6/11/07, Venning J, HC Auckland CRI-2006-092-11737 (excluding and admitting gruesome photographic evidence in a prosecution for murder); *R v Phillips* 15/9/94, CA208/94 (ruling inadmissible at his trial for sexual assault pornographic videotapes found in the accused's possession).

125   LC *Evidence Code*, para C59.

126   See, eg, *Selvey v DPP* [1970] AC 304; [1968] 2 All ER 497.

127   *R v Herewini* 15/8/07, Stevens J, HC Rotorua CRI-2006-063-3151, para 16.

128   *R v Herewini* 15/8/07, Stevens J, HC Rotorua CRI-2006-063-3151, paras 32-33.

129   See EV7.02.

EV8.04   Right to an effective defence

In criminal proceedings, the judicial balancing act between probative value and the risk of unfair prejudice under s 8(1)(a) "must take into account the right of the defendant to offer an effective defence" (s 8(2)). This mandatory direction reflects ss 25(e) (the right of criminal defendants to present a defence) and 25(a) (the right to a fair trial) of the New Zealand Bill of Rights Act 1990. Its potential impact involves judicial determinations under s 8(1)(a) that might otherwise be finely balanced between admitting and excluding a particular piece of proof. In a close decision where the evidence is helpful to the defence, s 8(2) might cause a judge to err on the side of admissibility under s 8(1)(a). Conversely, s 8(2) might result in a finding of inadmissibility where prosecution evidence risks an "illegitimate prejudicial impact on [the accused's] defence".[131] On the other hand, nothing in s 8(2) requires the admission of evidence where its unfairly prejudicial effect on a proceeding is held by a court to outweigh its probative value in the case.[132]

9   Admission by agreement

(1)   In any proceeding, the Judge may,—

    (a)   with the written or oral agreement of all parties, admit evidence that is not otherwise admissible; and

    (b)   admit evidence offered in any form or way agreed by all parties.

(2)   In a criminal proceeding, a defendant may admit any fact alleged against that defendant so as to dispense with proof of that fact.

(3)   In a criminal proceeding, the prosecution may admit any fact so as to dispense with proof of that fact.

EV9.01   Judge retains ultimate control

Although the power given by s 9 is unfettered, it is possible to imagine cases where, despite agreement by the parties, the judge would refuse to admit the evidence or not allow it to be offered in an agreed form or way. The most obvious example would be where, in the judge's view, the evidence or the mode of offering it would amount to a breach of s 8. It is also important that the judge retains control in cases that involve unrepresented parties.

---

130   In *R v Smith* 10/9/07, CA267/07; CA343/07; [2007] NZCA 400, paras 18-19, the Cour Appeal noted that "the party who called a witness whose veracity is being attacked [under of the Act] could still mount an objection to the contradictory evidence under s 8(1)(h) objection, which mirrors the justification for the former collateral fact rule, would b . un .e tangential inquiry into the validity of the proposition that was denied by the witness would 'needlessly prolong the proceeding'". See EV37.03(7).

131   *R v Taea* 31/10/07, CA442/07; [2007] NZCA 472, para 25 (commenting on the connection between the prejudice/probative balancing tests of ss 8 and 43 ("Propensity evidence offered by prosecution against defendants") of the Act. For further discussion, see EV43.05).

132   *R v Herewini* 15/8/07, Stevens J, HC Rotorua CRI-2006-063-3151, para 23.

EV9.02   Subsection (1)(a): what amounts to "written or oral agreement"

The Bill used the phrase "with the consent of all parties". The New Zealand Law Society in their submission suggested the addition of the word "*express* consent" — arguing that "[g]iven the importance of the provision there should be no suggestion that the consent of the parties may be implied from their conduct or from the surrounding circumstances".[133] The Ministry of Justice agreed,[134] recommending that the clause be amended to read "with the express consent of all parties." The Select Committee however added the phrase "with the written or oral agreement of all parties." The current drafting does not therefore necessarily reflect the concern noted by the New Zealand Law Society that informed consent should be given (of particular importance in the case of unrepresented defendants in criminal cases).

(1)   Extension to s 369 of the Crimes Act 1961

Section 9(2) and (3) replace and extend the provisions of s 369 of the Crimes Act 1961 to enable both the prosecution and the defence to admit facts so they need not be proved.[135] However, existing authorities under s 369 illustrate that the mere fact that the defendant offers to admit particular *facts* does not always mean that the prosecution will willingly forego the chance to offer *evidence* giving "colour and context" to the admitted facts.[136] In the face of an offer to admit facts, argument over admissibility of evidence proving these and "associated" facts will often focus on any unfairly prejudicial effect of such evidence.[137]

10   Interpretation of Act

(1)   This Act—

    (a)   must be interpreted in a way that promotes its purpose and principles; and

    (b)   is not subject to any rule that statutes in derogation of the common law should be strictly construed; but

    (c)   may be interpreted having regard to the common law, but only to the extent that the common law is consistent with—

        (i)   its provisions; and

        (ii)   the promotion of its purpose and its principles; and

        (iii)   the application of the rule in section 12.

---

133   NZLS *Submission on the Evidence Bill*, 6.

134   "The issue of whether the consent should be express or could be implied was not addressed by the Law Commission. However, there is potential for the quality and nature of that consent to be challenged. We agree that the significance of the clause means that there should be no room for doubt as to whether the parties consented or not and understood what they were being asked to consent to and why.": *Departmental Report* (EV/MOJ/5), 12.

135   LC *Evidence Code*, para C64.

136   *R v Marshall* 30/10/01, Rodney Hansen J, HC New Plymouth T5/01, para 9.

137   Under the Act this will be by reference to s 8(1)(a); see *R v Marshall* 30/10/01, Rodney Hansen J, HC New Plymouth T5/01 and *R v Pender* 15/7/05, CA143/05.

(2) Subsection (1) does not affect the application of the Interpretation Act 1999 to this Act.

EV10.01 The Act is not a code

Section 10 is a much changed provision from that proposed by the Law Commission which merely provided: "This Code is to be liberally construed in such a way as to promote the purpose and principles and is not subject to any rule that statutes in derogation of the common law should be strictly construed." The commentary to the Code simply stated that the section "is a reminder that it is to the purpose and principles of the Code, rather than to the common law, that judges and lawyers should look for answers to evidential issues."[138] The section therefore reflected the Law Commission's reform project: to codify the law of evidence. This was seen as desirable as the Law Commission saw the "need to break out of the complexity and incoherence which over the years the sheer number of cases and a technical approach to the rules of evidence have created."[139]

The Law Commission's codification exercise was fully supported at that general level, even though not all agreed with the substance of the particular rules proposed. The amendments to ss 5, 10, and 12 have the effect of ensuring that the Act is no longer a code. Such a significant policy change was only accompanied by the following justification in a briefing to the Minister of Justice: "The Bill adds reference to the status of common law with respect to the Bill that that did not appear in the Code. This was thought to be a helpful addition to aid interpretation."[140] There were no submissions on this section and it was passed unamended by the Select Committee. Despite this clear message that the common law is still relevant, the Select Committee stated as recently as July 2007 that "the Evidence Act should be regarded as codification of the law of evidence in New Zealand."[141]

EV10.02 Subsection (1)(a): promoting the Act's purpose and principles

Aside from the policy implications of this section, the drafting of the provision is not without difficulties. The *requirement* imposed by s 10(1)(a) to interpret the Act in a way that promotes its purpose and principles may not always be easy to follow, particularly if the wording of one of the Act's provisions appears to lead to a result that conflicts with the Act's stated purpose or principles. Beyond this, there are substantial difficulties in coming to grips with what, in practical terms, is required by s 10(1)(a). How does s 10(1)(a) actually apply to the interpretation of a provision of the Act dealing with, for example, hearsay, communication assistance, or the conduct of a cross-examination? Somehow, such a provision *must* be interpreted in such a way as to *promote* the overall purpose set out in s 6 of helping to secure the just

---

138 LC *Evidence Code*, para C64.

139 New Zealand Law Commission, *Evidence Law: Principles for Reform: A Discussion Paper*, NZLC PP13, Wellington, 1991, para 77.

140 Ministry of Justice, *Letter of Advice to the Minister of Justice*, 8 February 2005.

141 *Select Committee Report on Evidence Amendment Bill*, 2. See also, Hansard, *Hon Rick Barker: Evidence Bill: Second Reading*, 14 November 2006 ((2006) 635 NZPD 6483): "Consolidating the laws of evidence so they are in one location is consistent with the objectives of the bill."

determination of proceedings, and to do so by the means particularised in s 6(a)-(f). This means that the interpretation should, for example, promote "fairness for parties and witnesses" (s 6(c)) and promote "enhancing access to the law of evidence" (s 6(f)). None of this presents an easy task for a judge.

EV10.03   Subsection (1)(c): reference to "the common law"

Section 10(1)(c) permits, and s 12(b) requires, the judge to "have regard to" the common law in particular circumstances. Insofar as ss 10(1)(c) and 12(b) are concerned, it is suggested that when a judge "has regard to" the common law, the result will usually be a direct application of the common law. Although ss 10 and 12 give priority to the Act's purpose and principles, in most cases these will not provide a barrier to applications of the common law. The purpose and principles in ss 6-8 are sufficiently flexible to accommodate much of the common law.

More difficulty may occur when deciding whether the common law referred to is consistent with the provisions of the Act. For example, the Court of Appeal has decided a number of cases by applying the common law residual exception to the rule against hearsay.[142] One inquiry under this exception that the Act codifies is the reliability of the hearsay statement. The Act defines, at least in part, what is the appropriate scope of that reliability inquiry. A couple of matters were deliberately excluded from the Act's definition — for example, the relevance of the credibility (now "veracity") of the witness who is offering evidence of the hearsay statement.[143] The question to be asked is whether the common law's acceptance of those matters as being relevant is consistent or inconsistent with the Act's definition of reliability. If it is inconsistent, then the common law should not be applied — but if the matter is instead regarded as a gap, as per s 12, then the common law must be applied. This example also raises the significance of the difference in scope and wording of ss 10 and 12. What is considered a "gap" and what amounts to an "inconsistency" will be a line-drawing exercise by the courts, which may be of some significance in some cases.

It is also likely that, in applying ss 10 and 12 of the Act, "the common law" will be taken to refer to the law of evidence as it existed prior to the Act. This may well permit (or indeed require under s 12) reference to judicial interpretations of earlier statutes in instances where those statutes have been modified and incorporated into the Evidence Act 2006. Such references to statute law are to be expected and must be taken to be authorised if they abide by the constraints set out in ss 10(1)(c) and 12(b). Such an approach is contrary to the intention of the reform and care will need to be taken to ensure wholesale reversion to the pre-2006 Act law does not occur.

11   Inherent and implied powers not affected

(1)   The inherent and implied powers of a court are not affected by this Act, except to the extent that this Act provides otherwise.

---

142   *R v Shortland* 2/3/07, CA314/06; CA315/06; [2007] NZCA 37; *R v Collier* 20/9/06, CA13/06; *R v Hamer* [2003] 3 NZLR 757; (2003) 20 CRNZ 731 (CA).

143   See EV16.03.02.

(2) Despite subsection (1), a court must have regard to the purpose and the principles set out in sections 6, 7, and 8 when exercising its inherent or implied powers.

EV11.01   A change to the existing law?

The Bill's version of this provision stated that "the powers inherent in a court to regulate and prevent abuse of its procedure". The Rules Committee submitted that the words "to regulate and prevent abuse of its procedure" should be omitted, as it would limit the operation of the court's inherent jurisdiction to just those matters. The Select Committee accepted this argument, adding the word "implied" as well as specifying in s 11(2) the particular sections that contain the purposes and principles (which are not specifically mentioned in s 10). This was done on the basis that it "would ensure that the inherent powers of the courts were retained and continued to co-exist with their statutory jurisdiction wherever possible."[144] However, as stated by the Law Commission, in reliance on the common law principles:[145]

> "a superior court may exercise its inherent jurisdiction 'even in respect of matters which are regulated by statute or by rule[s] of court, so long as it can do so without contravening any statutory provisions' … . Thus, the effect of the Code on the court's inherent powers and jurisdiction is limited to requiring that they should not be exercised contrary to the express provisions of the Code."

The Law Commission's draft, according to the Ministry of Justice, simply codified the existing law.[146] It is not clear, then, what the amendment has achieved.

EV11.02   The current extent of inherent and implied powers

One reason why s 11(1) may require further elucidation by appellate courts is because the extent of a court's inherent and implied powers is uncertain.[147] One area of controversy that existed before the Act was whether a court's inherent power to regulate its procedure could justify the use of an alternative means for a witness to give evidence in a case where no statutory justification for such a procedure exists.[148] Because ss 102-104 now expressly provide for an order to be made that permits any witness to give evidence in an alternative way, that particular controversy should not resurface — although this has been the primary use of inherent powers in recent times, along with controlling the personal cross-examination of complainants in cases of a sexual nature[149] (a matter dealt with in s 95 of the Act). However, if ss 102-104 are interpreted to not permit pre-trial recorded cross-examination,[150] then such a process may require resort to s 11.

---

144   *Select Committe Report on the Evidence Bill*, 3.

145   LC *Evidence Code*, para C65.

146   *Departmental Report* (EV/MOJ/5), 13.

147   Joseph, "Inherent Jurisdiction and Inherent Powers in New Zealand" (2005) 11 Canta LR 220.

148   See, eg, the argument made in *R v Lewis* 28/11/06, CA311/06, para 9.

149   *R v Cumming* [2006] 2 NZLR 597; (2005) 22 CRNZ 171 (CA).

150   See EV103.03.

EV11.03   Subsection (2): "having regard to"

Although s 11(2) requires a court to "have regard to" the purpose and principles of the Act when exercising its inherent or implied powers, it is unlikely that this instruction will have much practical effect, as compared to the importance of the purposes and principles with regard to ss 10 and 12.

12   Evidential matters not provided for

If there is no provision in this Act or any other enactment regulating the admission of any particular evidence or the relevant provisions deal with that question only in part, decisions about the admission of that evidence—

(a)   must be made having regard to the purpose and the principles set out in sections 6, 7, and 8; and

(b)   to the extent that the common law is consistent with the promotion of that purpose and those principles and is relevant to the decisions to be taken, must be made having regard to the common law.

EV12.01   Introduction

This section has already been considered in the discussion of s 10.[151] Of particular importance is s 12's requirement that the judge "have regard to" the common law when the Act (or another enactment) deals only in part with the question of admissibility of evidence. There are a substantial number of occasions when the Act does not deal completely with all admissibility issues raised by a particular class of evidence (for example, the admissibility of "reputation" evidence under ss 37 or 40).[152] Section 12 requires that the judge who is determining such an issue must turn to the common law as long as that can be done by concurrently "having regard to" the purpose and principles of the Act.

EV12.02   "Admission of evidence"

Many provisions of the Act deal with issues other than "the admission of evidence", which is the focus of s 12. Part 3 of the Act (trial process) contains numerous examples of such provisions. When there is a gap in one of these provisions, s 12 has no direct relevance. It is suggested that in such a case, s 10 would apply, permitting (but not requiring) the judge to have regard to the common law in dealing with such a gap. That process could only be adopted if the result was consistent with promoting the purpose and principles in ss 6-8 (s 10(1)(c)(ii)). However, some procedural matters may be considered matters of admission — for example, *Cross on Evidence* suggests

---

151   See EV10.03. This is a change from the draft Code's "gap-filling" provision which merely stated that "matters of evidence that are not provided for by this Code are to be determined consistently with the purposes and principles of this Code." Given the changes made to ss 5 and 10 during the legislative process, s 12 was also amended to give greater importance to other enactments and the common law, with little justification given. If the Act's purposes and principles are sound, it is suggested that there should be no need to refer to the common law.

152   See EV37.03(4) and EV40.02(3).

that "admissibility" (as the term is used in s 344A of the Crimes Act 1961) "extends to the mode in which the evidence will be admitted".[153]

Other matters, other than trial process, which may fall to be dealt with under s 10 rather than s 12, include rules relating to the burden and standard of proof and those relating to the limited use of admissible evidence.[154] With regard to the last matter, although a number of limited use rules exist at common law, the argument that they should survive the "codification" process will not necessarily be easy to resolve simply by the terms of s 10, even though the legislative history on the point is relatively clear.[155] The most useful aspect of s 6 for this purpose would be s 6(a), although it would be more easily applicable in its original form — does the limited use rule "promot[e] the rational ascertainment of facts?"[156]

EV12.03   "Having regard to the common law"

As was discussed in relation to s 10, the extent to which the common law is had "regard to" (ie, applied) under s 12 may either support or undermine the goals of the reform. Section 12 could also have very limited effect. As ss 7 and 8 are provisions that regulate all "particular evidence", it may be that the gaps to be filled by s 12 will only be those filled by the exercise of inherent powers. The Ministry of Justice's comments seem to support such an interpretation:[157]

> "The purpose of the clause is to provide the Act with some flexibility in cases where courts are faced with new developments in technology (say) which were not contemplated at the time the Act was drafted. The courts could give effect to these changes but only to the extent whereby use of the technology was consistent with the purposes and principles of the Act."[158]

[12A   Rules of common law relating to statements of co-conspirators, persons involved in joint criminal enterprises, and certain co-defendants preserved

Nothing in this Act affects the rules of the common law relating to—

(a)   the admissibility of statements of co-conspirators or persons involved in joint criminal enterprises; or

---

153   *Cross on Evidence* (8th NZ ed), para 9.11A.
154   See also EV43.07(9).
155   See EV35.04(1) and EV7.03.
156   Further on this matter, the portion of s 8 (the general exclusion) which was originally proposed also gives some guidance as to the Law Commission's thinking: that evidence should be excluded if there is a danger it will confuse the issues (necessitating, for example, complicated jury instructions). (See New Zealand Law Commission, *Evidence Law: Codification: A Discussion Paper*, NZLC PP14, Wellington, 1991, 24.)
157   *Departmental Report* (EV/MOJ/5), 13.
158   If this is the section's purpose, it remains unclear why any reference to the common law was thought to be "helpful": Ministry of Justice, *Letter of Advice to the Minister of Justice*, 8 February 2005, 2.

(b)   the admissibility of a defendant's statement against a co-defendant in circumstances where the defendant's statement is accepted by the co-defendant.]

History

Section 12A was inserted, as from 4 July 2007, by s 5 Evidence Amendment Act 2007 (2007 No 24).

EV12A.01   Two common law exceptions to the co-accused rule preserved

Section 12A was added after debate as to whether the common law exceptions to the "co-accused" rule (that evidence offered by the prosecution of an out-of-court statement made by one defendant cannot be used as evidence against their co-defendant) could continue to operate notwithstanding s 27(1) of the Act, which seemed to read prior to the amendment as an absolute prohibition.[159] Whether or not the common law as to the use of co-defendant's out-of-court statements could have been preserved by ss 10 and 12 of the Act also exercised Members of Parliament during the second reading of the Amendment Bill: "[T]here is a very respectable argument that the legislation we are dealing with today is not, in fact, necessary."[160] The enactment of s 12A ends that debate but may well introduce others.

The intent of the amendment (see also s 27(4) and the consequential amendments to ss 28(1), 29(1), and 30(1)) was to preserve two common law exceptions to the co-accused rule: s 12A(a) concerns the "co-conspirators' rule" and s 12A(b) relates to the use of a defendant's out-of-court statement which has been accepted or adopted by the co-defendant.

EV12A.02   The co-conspirators' rule

The scope of the co-conspirators' rule at common law was considered prior to the passing of the amendment by the Supreme Court in *Qui v R*.[161] The Court confirmed that:[162]

> "in some circumstances involving an alleged criminal combination, including but not limited to criminal conspiracies, statements made by one or more alleged offenders in the absence of another [in furtherance of the common design], implicating that other, are admissible as evidence of their truth, notwithstanding their hearsay nature."

There must also be some independent evidence to show the existence of the conspiracy and that the other conspirator was a party to it.[163]

---

159   See Jones QC and Verrall, "Admissibility and Identification" in NZLS *Intensive: Evidence Act 2006*, 133 and *R v Pearce* 2/3/07, CA453/06; [2007] NZCA 40, para 50. As the Code did not contain the wording of s 27(1), the co-conspirators' rule was not needed as an exception to the co-accused rule: LC *Evidence Reform*, para 61.

160   Hansard, *Christopher Finlayson: Evidence Amendment Bill: Second Reading*, 28 June 2007 ((2007) 640 NZPD 10336).

161   *Qui v R* 5/7/07, SC41/06; [2007] NZSC 51. See also, generally, Kinsler, "The Co-Conspirators' Exception to the Hearsay Rule in New Zealand: *R v Qui*" (2007) 13 Auckland U L Rev 200.

162   *Qui v R* 5/7/07, SC41/06; [2007] NZSC 51, para 15.

In *Qui* the Court was concerned with the quality of the evidence offered to prove the existence of the joint enterprise or conspiracy and the complicity of the person whose statement "in furtherance of the common intention" is sought to be admitted.[164] Of the two options considered, the Court favoured a test assessing the "reasonableness" of the evidence offered to establish these two preliminary matters,[165] also expressing the view that such a test "appears to be in harmony with the general test of admissibility of hearsay evidence provided by the Evidence Act 2006, which is concerned with an assurance of reliability."[166]

(1)   Impact on hearsay provisions

The addition of s 12A may, however, have complicated the position with regard to the admissibility of hearsay evidence generally under the Act and its admissibility when offered in the context of the co-conspirators' rule.

The wording of s 12A(a) states that nothing in the Act (including the Act's rules relating to the admissibility of hearsay — see s 17) affects the rules of the common law relating to "the admissibility of statements of co-conspirators ...". This presumably means that both in relation to the evidence offered to prove the existence of the conspiracy *and* the statements of the co-conspirator in the furtherance of the common intention are not subject to the hearsay provisions of the Act, including any reliability inquiry or notice requirement.

(2)   "Use" of a co-defendant's statement

Section 12A(a) says nothing about the second purpose of the co-conspirators' exception. It is a significant exception for the prosecution not just because it allows the admission of hearsay evidence (and, as such, less important for this reason under the Act), but because it allows those hearsay statements (by a defendant) to be offered as part of the prosecution's case *against* another defendant. Section 12A(a) is silent about the *use* of such a co-defendant's statement, as contrasted with s 12A(b) — yet this was clearly the intended effect of the amendment.[167]

EV12A.03   Acceptance of a co-defendant's statement

Section 12A(b) preserves the common law exception to the co-accused rule in situations where the co-defendant, by his or her words or conduct, accepts the truth of the out-of-court statement made by the defendant.[168] By adopting the truth of the defendant's statement, the co-defendant has in effect made the statement their own.

---

163   See *Adams on Criminal Law — Evidence*, EC10.06(4)(c); Keane, *The Modern Law of Evidence* (6th ed), Oxford, Oxford University Press, 2006, 422-423.

164   *Qui v R* 5/7/07, SC41/06; [2007] NZSC 51, para 24.

165   *Qui v R* 5/7/07, SC41/06; [2007] NZSC 51, para 28.

166   *Qui v R* 5/7/07, SC41/06; [2007] NZSC 51, para 29; see also Mathias, "Hearsay: the Pre-concert Exception" [1996] NZLJ 391.

167   Hansard, *Mark Burton: Evidence Amendment Bill: Second Reading*, 28 June 2007 ((2007) 640 NZPD 10335).

168   Keane, *The Modern Law of Evidence* (6th ed), Oxford, Oxford University Press, 2006, 425, *Adams on Criminal Law — Evidence*, EC6.03(2).

What may amount to accepting or adopting a defendant's statement (or part of the statement — in which case only that part can be admissible against the co-defendant) will vary according to the circumstances, and such acceptance may take place pre-trial, in the course of police questioning,[169] or when the co-defendant testifies,[170] and directions as to use of the out-of-court statement will follow accordingly. Mere silence will not usually amount to acceptance.[171]

EV12A.04   The preservation of other common law exceptions

Section 12A preserves two common law exceptions to the co-accused rule. It does not include reference to the development of a third exception at common law — which was identified in the context of the very specific facts of *R v Hayter*.[172] Although the application of this exception by Ronald Young J in *R v Clayton*[173] was overturned on appeal,[174] the Court noted: "On the facts of [*Hayter*] we do not see anything surprising about the outcome."[175] In that case, which concerned a contract killing, it was alleged that Ms Bristow, the wife of the deceased, had arranged through Hayter that a man called Ryan should kill her husband. The evidence against Ryan was based solely on a confession he had allegedly made to his girlfriend. The House of Lords agreed that if the jury found Ryan guilty of murder on the basis of the confession, they could use that finding of guilt to conclude that Hayter was guilty as a party to the murder, but when deciding the case against Hayter the jury "must disregard entirely everything said out of court by [Ryan] which might otherwise be thought to incriminate [Hayter]."[176]

If a case with facts more similar to *Hayter* does come before the courts, the ability of ss 10 and 12 to preserve such an exception will be tested. Given the enactment of s 12A it may well be harder to successfully mount such an argument.

Another possible exception to the co-accused rule was discussed as the result of the Court of Appeal's comments in *R v Fenton*.[177] The Court of Appeal noted that "it is the hearsay rule which makes an out of Court statement by accused A inadmissible against accused B unless made in B's presence."[178] On this basis, the Court of Appeal noted that the liberalisation of the hearsay rule proposed by the Law Commission, and subsequently adopted in *R v Manase*,[179] would allow reliable hearsay statements of a defendant to be offered in evidence against a co-defendant. Although s 27(1) of

---

169   *Adams on Criminal Law — Evidence*, EA12A.03.
170   *Adams on Criminal Law — Evidence*, EA12A.03.
171   See EV32.01.
172   *R v Hayter* [2005] 2 All ER 209 (HL); Keane, *The Modern Law of Evidence* (6th ed), Oxford, Oxford University Press, 2006, 422; *Adams on Criminal Law — Evidence*, EC10.6(4)(a).
173   *R v Clayton* 23/11/06, Ronald Young J, HC Wellington CRI-2005-078-1785, para 29.
174   *R v Pearce* 2/3/07, CA453/06; [2007] NZCA 40, paras 46-47.
175   *R v Pearce* 2/3/07, CA453/06; [2007] NZCA 40, para 46.
176   *R v Hayter* [2005] 2 All ER 209 (HL), para 86.
177   *R v Fenton* 14/9/00, CA223/00; CA299/00: see *Adams on Criminal Law — Evidence*, EC10.05(1) and *R v Pearce* 2/3/07, CA453/06; [2007] NZCA 40, para 28.
178   *R v Fenton* 14/9/00, CA223/00; CA299/00, para 31.
179   *R v Manase* [2001] 2 NZLR 197; (2000) 18 CRNZ 378 (CA).

the Act rejects the Law Commission's approach to this issue, if the rationale of the co-accused rule does turn on reliability, can the development of this common law exception to the rule against hearsay survive the Act? The answer is probably "no" — given that both the wording of s 27(1) and the two specifically preserved exceptions are not subject to any independent reliability inquiry. Given the Act's overall approach to the admissibility of hearsay, this may be viewed as an odd result.

EV12A.05   Unintended effects of s 12A

It must be hoped that the enactment of s 12A, which codifies the common law exception by reference to the common law, rather than to the substance of the exception, will not have the effect of encouraging the survival of numerous other common law admissibility exceptions. In any event, this amendment is primarily about the *use* that can be made of an admissible statement (presuming for the moment that it is reliable), not one primarily about admissibility per se.

13   Establishment of relevance of document

If a question arises concerning the relevance of a document, the Judge may examine it and draw any reasonable inference from it, including an inference as to its authenticity and identity.

EV13.01   Self-authentication

This provision was first proposed, essentially in this form, in the Law Commission's discussion paper dealing with documentary evidence. The initial commentary to the draft section stated:[180]

> "[T]he discussion paper points out that the authenticity of a document is an aspect of relevance. It is, therefore, unnecessary to have code rules concerning authenticity. [Section 13] is, however, inserted to clarify one aspect of the relevance rule [s 7]. [Section 13] empowers the court to examine and draw inferences from any document or thing, the relevance of which is in question. Thus a document which contains the necessary information can be self-authenticating. This makes it clear that the common law rule that extrinsic evidence is required to authenticate a document is abrogated".

The earlier version allowed examination of any "thing" — it is now clear that s 13 only relates to "documents", as defined in s 4.[181]

Note that the Law Commission referred to a *court* examining a document, whereas s 13 refers to "the Judge", which includes a tribunal, according to the s 4 definition.[182]

Section 13 complements s 130 under which a party may offer a document as evidence without calling a witness to produce the document.[183]

---

180   New Zealand Law Commission, *Evidence Law: Documentary Evidence and Judicial Notice: A Discussion Paper*, NZLC PP22, Wellington 1994, 143.
181   See EV4.11.01.
182   See EV4.26.01.

Although the New Zealand Law Society objected to "the unwarranted expansion of the judicial role" under s 13,[184] the Ministry of Justice expressed the view that the change from the common law was consistent "with the objectives of the Bill to avoid unnecessary delay without undue unfairness as the weight and significance of the document is something that can be tested during the proceeding."[185]

By leaving the issue of authentication as a matter of inferences, which may or may not be drawn, s 13 does however leave room for uncertainty. There are numerous occasions where the Act avoids such uncertainty by providing specific presumptions of the authenticity of documents (see most of the sections in Subpart 8 of Part 3).

EV13.02   Relevance at issue

Although s 13 appears to have been intended to have a wide scope of operation, the section states it only applies if there is a question concerning the relevance of a document. This may not have much significance as a matter of practice. The important inferences authorised by s 13, as to authenticity and identity, may be sufficient to determine the document's relevance in the proceeding. In most cases an inauthentic or forged document will not be relevant.[186]

14   Provisional admission of evidence

If a question arises concerning the admissibility of any evidence, the Judge may admit that evidence subject to evidence being later offered which establishes its admissibility.

EV14.01   Analysis

Section 14 reflects the practice before the Act. Sometimes referred to as the "de benne esse" rule, it appears to be most used in summary proceedings.[187] Some argue that it leads to unnecessary prolonging of proceedings as the opposing party needs to respond to provisionally admitted evidence which may be ultimately disregarded. A common complaint has also been that judges unfamiliar with the law of evidence have tended to use the de bene esse rule as a means of escaping the need to give contested evidence rulings. In the words of the authors of the New Zealand Law Society seminar on the Evidence Act 2006, "this would be a misuse of section 14. Section 14 is limited to cases in which the admissibility of evidence will turn on an evidentiary platform yet to be established."[188] It is therefore essential that the admissibility issue is

---

183   See EV130.01.

184   The New Zealand Law Society argued that: "[w]hile a judge should properly be permitted to examine a document for the purpose of deciding its relevance, it is undesirable to confer powers on the judge to draw further inferences, such as inferences as to the authenticity and identity of the document, in the course of this process. This is especially the case in circumstances where evidence on these matters may not have been given in the course of a proceeding." (NZLS *Submission on the Evidence Bill*, 7). The Law Society recommended that a judge could only examine a document for the purpose of determining its relevance — although such a section would be of limited additional use, given the scope of s 14. (See s 58 of the Evidence Act 1995 (Aust).)

185   *Departmental Report* (EV/MOJ/5), 14.

186   See further the discussion at EV7.01.

ultimately determined. If the required other evidence to establish admissibility is not forthcoming "the provisionally admitted evidence must be excluded from consideration."[189]

In the context of the 2006 Act, whether a person will be called as a witness later in the proceeding will impact on the admissibility of the evidence, in particular, whether the evidence being offered should be treated as hearsay or as a previous consistent statement. In summary proceedings at least, s 14 could be used to admit the (hearsay) evidence on the basis that the maker of the statement will later be called as a witness.[190]

A court will normally accept counsel's representations that the relevance of the offered evidence will be demonstrated when further witnesses have been called or after later argument.[191] However, if counsel subsequently defaults on that promise, the provisionally admitted evidence should be excluded as irrelevant under s 7. A mistrial might also be declared, depending on the degree and remediable nature of any prejudice or unfairness caused by the party's failure to demonstrate finally the relevance of the previously offered proof.

The presence of a jury may be influential in determining whether evidence should be admitted on a provisional basis. The courts in exercising their discretion should have regard to whether the jury would be able to disregard the evidence should the party offering the evidence be unable to establish its admissibility. The Ministry of Justice, in responding to the New Zealand Law Society's submission that the wording be tightened to ensure that the judge is satisfied later evidence will establish its admissibility, noted that the warnings provision (s 122), dealing with the treatment of unreliable evidence as a matter of weight, could also be used to prevent unfairness in indictable proceedings.[192]

In the first draft of this provision, "relevance" was used instead of "admissibility",[193] which probably makes little difference in practice, although later evidence will need to demonstrate not just its relevance but also its admissibility. In the context of the hearsay rules, for example, whether the maker of the statement is

---

187   In New Zealand Law Commission, *Evidence Law: Documentary Evidence and Judicial Notice: A Discussion Paper*, NZLC PP22, Wellington 1994, paras 53-54, the Law Commission stated the reason for including this rule in the Code: "At present provisional relevance problems are often dealt with by the court accepting the party's assurance that later evidence will be adduced which links the disputed item of evidence to the issues in the case. The judge may accept such an assurance over the objection of the other party, though in criminal cases where the disputed evidence is important the judge may require the connecting evidence to be given first." (To use the hearsay example again, this may mean confirmation that the maker will indeed be a witness.) "This pragmatic approach to the problem ought to continue under a codified law of evidence … [A] provisional relevance rule us useful in a code to indicate that a pragmatic approach to relevance is to be taken."

188   Cull QC, Fisher QC, and Robertson, "Overview" in NZLS *Intensive: Evidence Act 2006*, 9.

189   LC *Evidence Code*, para C71.

190   See EV4.46.02.

191   See *Shaw Savill & Albion Co Ltd v Skilton* [1950] NZLR 588.

192   *Departmental Report* (EV/MOJ/5), 15.

to testify will take the evidence outside of the rules and therefore impacts on the statement's admissibility — indeed on the rules it will be subject to (see further the discussion of "witness" in s 4).[194]

15   Evidence given to establish admissibility

Evidence given by a witness to prove the facts necessary for deciding whether some other evidence should be admitted in a proceeding—

(a)   is admissible in the proceeding if the evidence given by the witness is inconsistent with the witness's subsequent testimony in the proceeding (whether or not the other evidence is admitted):

(b)   is not otherwise admissible in the proceeding.

EV15.01   Admissibility of voir dire testimony

There will be numerous occasions when a judge who is determining the admissibility of an item of evidence is called upon to determine issues of fact. Such a hearing is commonly referred to as a "voir dire", particularly in a case where the jury is excluded from the courtroom for the duration of the admissibility hearing.[195] Facts determined at a voir dire are sometimes referred to as "preliminary facts".[196] Section 15 settles an issue that had given rise to substantial controversy at common law, namely the admissibility at other stages of the proceeding, of the evidence offered on the voir dire in proof or disproof of the preliminary facts. Before the Act, the controversy settled by s 15 arose most commonly in disputes over the admissibility of a defendant's confession, where the defendant testified at the voir dire.[197]

(1)   The general rule and the exception

The general rule stated in s 15(b) is that the evidence is inadmissible in the other stages of the proceeding. The one exception is set out in s 15(a). If a witness at the voir dire testifies at another stage of the same proceeding (especially the substantive hearing or trial) in a way that is inconsistent with his or her testimony at the voir dire (that is, the "preliminary facts"), the witness's voir dire testimony will be admissible to demonstrate the inconsistency. (Section 15 makes no attempt to control admissibility in other proceedings.)

---

193   See New Zealand Law Commission, *Evidence Law: Documentary Evidence and Judicial Notice: A Discussion Paper*, NZLC PP22, Wellington 1994, 142 and s 57 of the Evidence Act 1995 (Aust).

194   See EV4.46.02.

195   For the form in which applications for pre-trial admissibility orders should be made from 1 December 2007, see *Practice Note — Pre-Trial Applications in Criminal Jury Cases* (5 November 2007) regarding the process of making such applications in criminal jury cases. The practice note is available at: www.courtsofnz.govt.nz/business/practice-directions.html.

196   Mahoney, "Proving Preliminary Facts" (1993) 15 NZULR 225.

197   Mahoney, "Using Improperly Obtained Evidence to Impeach the Accused's Testimony: Should We Let the Phoenix Fly?" (1994) 16 NZULR 46. See also EV28.04(1).

The Act therefore departs from the rule in *Wong Kam-Ming v R*,[198] in which the Privy Council held that if a statement is ruled inadmissible, the defendant may not be cross-examined on his or her voir dire evidence,[199]. The Ministry of Justice, however, noted that the court "retains the discretion to disallow such cross-examination if such questioning is unfair or the probative value is outweighed by the risk that the evidence will have an unfairly prejudicial effect on the outcome of the proceeding"[200] — that is, s 15 is subject to s 8. Although this view is consistent with the structure of the Act, its effect might be to require consideration of why the voir dire testimony was ruled inadmissible — essentially reconsideration of the fairness or reliability inquiry under ss 28 or 30. To subject s 15 to s 8 might have the consequence, at least in some cases, of rendering the reform ineffective.

The effect of s 15 has been noted by the Court of Appeal in *R v Ram*,[201] in which the Court of Appeal allowing the appeal on the basis that the trial judge erred in ruling that the Crown could cross-examine the accused on an inconsistency between his testimony and what he had said in the (inadmissible) video interview. Although the issue before the Court was the use in cross-examination of a statement excluded on the grounds of unfairness (a matter clarified by s 90 of the Act), the Court also commented on the effect of s 15:[202]

> "Whatever the arguments are for and against the policy matters behind these issues, the net result appears to us to be that for the future in New Zealand, an accused who gives evidence at a voir dire is at risk of being cross-examined on any prior inconsistencies, should he or she give evidence at their trial. But the accused cannot be cross-examined on a statement which is excluded under ss 29 or 30. This has the benefit that the law is at least certain. Counsel will have to be very careful to advise their clients accordingly. The change to the rule relating to evidence on a voir dire has real implications for criminal law practitioners."

The Law Commission noted that s 15 applies to all witnesses (not only defendants), "to evidence given in any type of hearing held to determine the admissibility of evidence — whether pre-trial or in a voir dire", and whether the admissibility hearing is pursuant to the Evidence Act, s 344A of the Crimes Act 1961, or under any other enactment.[203] The rule therefore also applies to civil proceedings, which concerned the New Zealand Law Society.[204]

198　*Wong Kam-Ming v R* [1980] AC 247 (PC).

199　LC *Evidence Code*, para C73.

200　*Departmental Report* (EV/MOJ/5), 16.

201　*R v Ram* [2007] 3 NZLR 322 (CA).

202　*R v Ram* [2007] 3 NZLR 322 (CA), para 70.

203　LC *Evidence Code*, para C72.

204　"There are no adequate reasons advanced by the Law Commission to justify a common law ruling in criminal trials applying in a civil proceeding." NZLS *Submission on the Evidence Bill*, 7.

Part 2
Admissibility rules, privilege, and confidentiality
(s 16 to s 70)

Subpart 1—Hearsay evidence
(s 16 to s 22)

16   Interpretation

(1)   In this subpart,—

business—

(a)   means any business, profession, trade, manufacture, occupation, or calling of any kind; and

(b)   includes the activities of any department of State, local authority, public body, body corporate, organisation, or society

EV16.01.01   "Business"

This definition, required as part of the definition of "business record", repeats that found in s 2 of the Evidence Amendment Act (No 2) 1980 and as such the earlier cases applying this definition may be referred to.[205]

business record means a document—

(a)   that is made—

     (i)   to comply with a duty; or

     (ii)   in the course of a business, and as a record or part of a record of that business; and

(b)   that is made from information supplied directly or indirectly by a person who had, or may reasonably be supposed by the court to have had, personal knowledge of the matters dealt with in the information he or she supplied

EV16.02.01   "Business record"

This comprehensive definition is also taken from s 2 of the Evidence Amendment Act (No 2) 1980 with a drafting change with the use of the phrase "comply with" as compared to "pursuant to". The definition is required due to the admissibility rule in s 19 of the Act. The Law Commission noted problems with the phrase "record ... relating to any business" — specifically whether a business record included correspondence or invoices or consignment notices.[206] This phrase has been changed in the Act version to "record ... of that business". This definition is wide enough to capture a statement made to

---

205   See EV10.03.
206   New Zealand Law Commission, *Hearsay Evidence: An Options Paper*, NZLC PP10, Wellington, 1989, para 32.

a police officer and then written down in his or her notebook.[207] The scope of the definition therefore has significant implications for the operation of s 19 in the context of criminal proceedings.[208]

circumstances, in relation to a statement by a person who is not a witness, include—

(a)   the nature of the statement; and

(b)   the contents of the statement; and

(c)   the circumstances that relate to the making of the statement; and

(d)   any circumstances that relate to the veracity of the person; and

(e)   any circumstances that relate to the accuracy of the observation of the person

EV16.03.01   Indicia of reliability

This non-exhaustive definition provides the list of matters the court should consider when determining whether the "circumstances relating to the statement provide reasonable assurance that the statement is reliable" for the purposes of the admissibility rule in s 18.[209]

In determining whether "the circumstances relating to the statement provide reasonable assurance of reliability" a judge should, therefore, consider (at least):

•   The nature of the statement (whether it is written or oral, signed, witnessed, first-hand etc);[210]

•   The contents of the statement;

•   The circumstances relating to the making of the statement (the physical environment, when it was made — ie how long after the event the statement refers to, what was the relationship between the maker and the witness etc);[211] and

•   Any circumstances that relate to the "veracity"[212] of the person who is not a witness (the "maker") or the accuracy of the observation of the "maker" of the statement.[213]

---

207   *R v Hovell* [1986] 1 NZLR 500; (1986) 2 CRNZ 145 (CA).
208   See EV19.01.
209   See EV18.02.
210   See LC *Evidence Code*, para C76.
211   See LC *Evidence Code*, para C27 and *Adams on Criminal Law — Evidence*, EA18.06.
212   See s 37(5) and EV37.15.
213   The maker being "a person who is not a witness". Although the term "maker" is not defined in the Act, it is used in ss 18 and 22 but not in ss 16 and 19, perhaps a legislative oversight. The Law Commission stated: "Whether a person is the maker of the statement is a question of fact. The question is likely to only arise in cases where more than one person was involved in preparing a statement" (LC *Evidence Code*, para C79). See also *R v Hovell* [1986] 1 NZLR 500; (1986) 2 CRNZ 145 (CA).

EV16.03.02   The veracity or accuracy of the witness offering evidence of a hearsay statement

The list of factors to be considered (or "indicia" of reliability) does not include any reference to the veracity or accuracy of the witness (who is giving evidence of the statement) because according to the Law Commission the veracity and accuracy "of the witness who relates the hearsay can be tested before, and assessed by, the fact-finder."[214] This approach was recently questioned by the Court of Appeal in *R v Shortland*, in which the Court stated:[215]

> "We have reservations as to whether, in practice, it will prove practicable to segment reliability assessments so as to exclude from consideration the accuracy and truthfulness of the witness who gives evidence of the statement".

The reference to the "contents" of the hearsay statement in s 16(1) may also invite consideration of the veracity of the maker — an investigation the courts have been willing to undertake in the context of discussing the impact of a lack of cross-examination.[216]

EV16.03.03   The existence of supporting or conflicting evidence

The Law Commission also noted that the factors do not include reference to "the consistency of the statement with other evidence not directly related to the statement."[217] In the Law Commission's view:[218]

> "It is important to distinguish between the circumstances relating to the statement and other evidence in the case: hearsay that the circumstances relating to the statement indicate to be reliable should not be held inadmissible because it contradicts other evidence."

Whether there is other corroborating or conflicting evidence can be assessed by the fact-finder rather than considered as an admissibility question because "[l]ogically, the general strength of the case does not affect the reliability of individual items of evidence."[219] The Law Commission also considered that limiting the admissibility inquiry in this way would allow an admissibility decision to be made at the time the statement is offered in evidence (when the existence and weight of other evidence will not be known).[220]

---

214   LC *Evidence Code*, para C75.
215   *R v Shortland* 2/3/07, CA314/06; CA315/06; [2007] NZCA 37, para 44.
216   See, eg, *R v L* [1994] 2 NZLR 54; (1993) 11 CRNZ 8 (CA) and *R v Hamer* [2003] 3 NZLR 757; (2003) 20 CRNZ 731 (CA).
217   LC *Evidence Code*, para C75.
218   LC *Evidence Code*, para C75.
219   New Zealand Law Commission, *Evidence Law: Hearsay: A Discussion Paper*, NZLC PP15, Wellington, 1991, para 35.
220   New Zealand Law Commission, *Evidence Law: Hearsay: A Discussion Paper*, NZLC PP15, Wellington, 1991, para 35.

Under the common law, judges have been willing to consider other items of evidence when making the admissibility decision, whether as part of the residual discretion "reliability" inquiry,[221] or as part of the discretion to exclude hearsay under s 18 of the Evidence Amendment Act (No 2) 1980.[222]

The definition of "circumstances" in s 16 may also require some consideration of other evidence. First, the reference to the "contents" of the statement in s 16(1) only has meaning (as being different from the "nature" of the statement) if the contents can be compared to other evidence. Also, the fact that the court can consider the "veracity" of the maker of the statement must mean that other conflicting statements or conflicting evidence can be taken into account as part of that inquiry.[223]

The wording of s 8(2)[224] also indicates that in criminal proceedings, if the hearsay statement is the only evidence supporting the defence's theory of the case, it should be admitted if sufficiently reliable, without having regard to the existence or not of other corroborating evidence.[225]

EV16.03.04   Impact of inability to cross-examine the maker

Another factor not mentioned expressly in the Act, but one that underlies the rationale and consequently the scope of the rule,[226] is the extent to which the inability to cross-examine the maker of the statement should be taken into account as part of the admissibility decision. At common law, the courts have clearly weighed reliability against the loss of ability to cross-examine — to use the words of Cooke P in *R v Baker*: "it is reasonably safe and of sufficient relevance to admit the evidence notwithstanding the dangers against which the hearsay rule guards".[227] This has been applied at common law to mean that, especially in criminal cases, unless cross-examination of the maker would have made no, or no appreciable, difference, the hearsay will not be admitted.[228]

The Law Commission referred to considering the significance of an inability to cross-examine in criminal cases the following way:[229]

> "A judge may be expected to take different factors into account, depending on whether the prosecution or the defence is offering the hearsay. If a hearsay statement forms part of the prosecution case and

---

221   *R v Manase* [2001] 2 NZLR 197; (2000) 18 CRNZ 378 (CA); *Adams on Criminal Law — Evidence*, EC10.05(3).

222   *R v L* [1994] 2 NZLR 54; (1993) 11 CRNZ 8 (CA); *R v Hamer* [2003] 3 NZLR 757; (2003) 20 CRNZ 731 (CA); *Adams on Criminal Law — Evidence*, EC10.06(1).

223   See, eg, *R v Hamer* [2003] 3 NZLR 757; (2003) 20 CRNZ 731 (CA).

224   See EV8.04.

225   *R v Bain* [1996] 1 NZLR 129; (1995) 13 CRNZ 684 (CA) provides an example of a hearsay statement the defence sought to introduce that was seemingly uncorroborated.

226   And provides the reason for definition of "witness" — one who can be cross-examined. See LC *Evidence Reform*, para 50.

227   *R v Baker* [1989] 1 NZLR 738; (1989) 4 CRNZ 282 (CA), 741; 285.

228   See *R v L* [1994] 2 NZLR 54; (1993) 11 CRNZ 8 (CA) and s 25(f) of the Bill of Rights.

229   LC *Evidence Code*, para C88.

is crucial to proving a defendant's guilt, a judge will want to ensure that the circumstances relating to the statement give such assurance of reliability that the defendant's right to a fair trial will not be jeopardised by his or her inability to cross-examine the making of the statement."

The fact that the maker of the statement is not available to be cross-examined may be treated as a matter to take into account when determining whether the circumstances relating to the statement "provide reasonable assurance that the statement is reliable" (s 18). Alternatively, once the judge considers that the statement is sufficiently reliable, the extent to which lack of cross-examination is significant in the particular circumstances of the case could form part of the inquiry under s 8(1)(a) and (2). The Law Commission's comment and the structure of the Act seem consistent with either approach. The result should be the same, although only the second approach preserves a clear and separate role for the exercise of the s 8 discretion.

duty includes any duty imposed by law or arising under any contract, and any duty recognised in carrying on any business practice.

EV16.04.01   Duty

The definition of "duty" is necessary to clarify the scope of the definition of "business record".[230]

(2)   For the purposes of this subpart, a person is **unavailable as a witness** in a proceeding if the person—

(a)   is dead; or

(b)   is outside New Zealand and it is not reasonably practicable for him or her to be a witness; or

(c)   is unfit to be a witness because of age or physical or mental condition; or

(d)   cannot with reasonable diligence be identified or found; or

(e)   is not compellable to give evidence.

EV16.05.01   "Unavailable as a witness"

This definition of unavailability is different from that contained in s 2 of the Evidence Amendment Act (No 2) 1980 in a number of ways, although some of the existing case law on s 2 will remain relevant.[231] The emphasis in para (b) is on whether the person cannot be a "witness" (that is, give evidence and be cross-examined — see s 4)[232] rather than whether the evidence can be obtained. Note that other provisions in the Act (see s 168 for example) reflect an increased use of technology (video-link in particular) to enable witnesses from outside the jurisdiction to give evidence in a proceeding.

---

230   See EV16.02.01.
231   *Adams on Criminal Law — Evidence*, EC10.06(1)(d); *R v Harmer* [2002] 3 NZLR 560.
232   See EV4.46.01.

Paragraph (c) removes the reference to "old" age, so that the inquiry into unavailability can relate to the effect of youth on the ability to be a witness, as well as age.[233] When discussing this ground, the Law Commission stated that:[234]

> "Trauma, or the severe impairment of a statement maker's emotional state will make it necessary for the judge to consider under *para (c)* whether the maker is unfit to attend because of his or her mental condition …"

The Law Commission ultimately rejected earlier suggestions that the definition should include reference to witnesses who refuse to give evidence even though physically present in court, or those who cannot reasonably be expected to recollect matters dealt with in the statement.[235] However, s 19(1)(b) of the Act effectively re-introduces the second of these inquiries in the context of business records only.[236]

Paragraph (d) makes it clear that an inability to either *identify or find* a person renders them unavailable, in comparison to the former provision that referred only to an inability to be found.

EV16.05.02   Subsection (2)(e): non-compellability

The most important change is the addition of the factor now contained in para (e), namely unavailability by reason of non-compellability. Those who cannot be compelled to testify (for example, the Sovereign (s 74) and the defendant in a criminal case) are considered "unavailable as a witness" for the purposes of the hearsay rule. The consequences of classifying a non-compellable defendant, or co-defendant, as "unavailable", are discussed in the context of s 21.[237]

The addition of the ground of non-compellability may also result in the courts treating witnesses who are excused from testifying (for example, under s 352(1) of the Crimes Act 1961 for "just excuse", or s 20 of the Summary Proceedings Act 1957 for "sufficient cause") as "unavailable". Given that the effect of such sections is to set aside a subpoena, this may well have the effect of rendering such a person non-compellable.

---

233   The Australian Law Reform Commission have recently recommended a similar reform of the Uniform Evidence Act's definition of "unavailability of persons" so that the focus is on mental and physical inability regardless of age (Australian Law Reform Commission, *Uniform Evidence Law*, ALRC 102, Canberra, 2005, Recommendation 8.2).

234   LC *Evidence Code*, para C80.

235   See s 12(2), (3), and (f) of the draft Code in *The New Zealand Law Commission Consultative Workshop on the Proposed Evidence Code*, Wellington, New Zealand Law Society, 1998 and s 2(f) of the draft sections in New Zealand Law Commission, *Evidence Law: Hearsay: A Discussion Paper*, NZLC PP15, Wellington, 1991.

236   See EV19.01.

237   See EV21.01.

Under the common law, Simon France J considered himself bound by the Court of Appeal's decision in *R v M-T*[238] so that he did not treat a non-compellable spouse as "unable" to testify for the purposes of the common law exception to the rule against hearsay.[239] The requirement of an "inability" to testify does not survive the Act,[240] so it will be open to the courts to decide the status of an excused witness for the purposes of the definition of unavailability. If excused witnesses are considered to be non-compellable, this could have implications for the prosecution of domestic violence offences in situations where the complainant is not required to testify.

In *R v Lologa*,[241] Lang J considered, in a different context, the application of the woman partner of a defendant charged with murder that, pursuant to s 352(1), she possessed a "just excuse" not to testify for the prosecution. According to Lang J, the determination of a "just excuse" in the case involved weighing "the adverse consequences to the witness if she is compelled to give evidence against the adverse consequences for the administration of justice if she is not required to do so".[242]

In rejecting the application, Lang J noted that spousal non-compellability had been abolished under the Evidence Act 2006. According to Lang J, this demonstrated Parliament's view that "persons who are in a close personal relationship with an accused person must nevertheless in the ordinary course of events fulfil their duty to the community to give evidence against such persons should that be required".[243] Such reasoning suggests that, with respect to spouses and partners of criminal defendants, successful appeals to the "just cause" provision of s 352(1) will be rare, if based on claimed detriment to the relationship. If an application to be excused is made on the basis that the applicant will suffer serious physical or psychological harm if he or she testifies, it is suggested the result may well be different.

(3)   Subsection (2) does not apply to a person whose statement is sought to be offered in evidence by a party who has caused the person to be unavailable in order to prevent the person from attending or giving evidence.

EV16.06.01   Subsection (3): causing unavailability

This subsection (which had no equivalent in the Evidence Amendment Act (No 2) 1980) has been rendered less comprehensible due to the change from the Code version which provided:[244]

---

238   *R v M-T (CA269/02)* [2003] 1 NZLR 63; (2002) 19 CRNZ 659 (CA); McDonald, "Hearsay in Domestic Violence Cases" [2003] NZLJ 174.
239   *R v G D A* 1/8/06, Simon France J, HC Auckland CRI-2005-004-17305.
240   See EV17.03.
241   *R v Lologa* 19/7/07, Lang J, HC Auckland CRI-2005-092-7703.
242   *R v Lologa* 19/7/07, Lang J, HC Auckland CRI-2005-092-7703, para 15.
243   *R v Lologa* 19/7/07, Lang J, HC Auckland CRI-2005-092-7703, para 17. Compare *R v M-T (CA269/02)* [2003] 1 NZLR 63; (2002) 19 CRNZ 659 (CA).

"Notwithstanding subsection (2), the maker of a statement is not to be regarded as unavailable as a witness if the unavailability was brought about by the party offering the statement for the purpose of preventing the maker of the statement from attending or giving evidence."

The Code version made it clear that s 16(3) is aimed at preventing a party from potentially benefiting from rendering someone unavailable to testify (for example, the party kidnaps or kills the maker of the statement, or pays him or her to go into hiding).[245] The subsection would apply when a party anticipates that the maker may not testify consistently with the out-of-court statement, and so causes them to be unavailable in an attempt to offer the preferred hearsay evidence.

EV16.06.02 Difficulties with the section as enacted

When a party has caused the unavailability of a statement maker, the result under s 16(3) is that the s 16(2) definition of unavailability no longer applies. But s 16(3) does not expressly prevent a party from offering the statement in evidence.

Section 16(3) applies only to "a person whose statement is sought to be offered in evidence …". However the concept of unavailability is also relevant to suppliers of information (s 19(1)(a)). When the supplier of the information is not the statement maker in a business record, s 16(3) will not apply.

Section 16(3) requires that the party intentionally cause the unavailability of the statement maker. If a party negligently causes the death of a witness, that party will still be able to apply s 16(2)'s definition of unavailability.

17 Hearsay rule

A hearsay statement is not admissible except—

(a) as provided by this subpart or by the provisions of any other Act; or

(b) in cases where—

(i) this Act provides that this subpart does not apply; and

(ii) the hearsay statement is relevant and not otherwise inadmissible under this Act.

---

244 The subsection was taken from s 29(3) of the Canadian draft Code (see New Zealand Law Commission, *Evidence Law: Hearsay: A Discussion Paper*, NZLC PP15, Wellington, 1991, 33), but there is no discussion of the rationale for the provision in Law Reform Commission of Canada, *Hearsay*, Study Paper 9, Ottawa, 1974. The proposed formulation in that paper was "provided that the person's [maker's] inability … to testify is not due to any wrongdoing of the proponent of his statement committed for the purpose of preventing the person from attending or testifying." This was part of a section which provided that the hearsay rule did not apply to statements of an unavailable witness — therefore if the maker was rendered unavailable by the proponent, the hearsay rule would apply, thereby amounting to a disadvantage.

245 LC *Evidence Code*, para C82.

EV17.01   The exclusionary rule

This section (which relies on the definitions of "hearsay statement", "statement" and "witness" discussed in s 4) contains the general exclusionary rule. The combination of those definitions means that the exclusionary rule only applies to statements intended to be assertions made by a person who is not a witness in the proceeding and which are offered to prove their truth.[246]

The combination of paras (a) and (b) means that hearsay made admissible by other provisions in the Act (for example, visual identification evidence as defined in s 4)[247] must nevertheless also comply with the hearsay rules, unless the operation of the hearsay rule is expressly excluded (as it is in ss 27(3) and 138(3) for example). Further, even though the Act permits a party to ignore the hearsay provisions in a particular context, the veracity and propensity provisions, for example, may still render inadmissible an otherwise admissible hearsay statement.

EV17.02   Preservation of admissibility rules in other Acts (and enactments)

The Law Commission was also of the view that the many provisions found in other Acts which govern the admissibility of hearsay evidence should continue to operate, at least in the short term.[248] Section 17 therefore provides that hearsay can be admissible under other Acts, and the effect of s 5(1) of the Act means that "if a hearsay statement fails to comply with the statutory regime governing the admissibility of the particular class of hearsay to which the statement belongs, the statement will not be admissible under the [Act's] hearsay rules."[249]

The Law Commission considered that the provisions found in other Acts that deal with the admissibility of hearsay evidence could be reviewed by the relevant departments administering those Acts in order to determine whether the provisions could be replaced by the Evidence Act 2006 rules. For example, the new definition of hearsay in the Act may render such provisions otiose. Further, it would be consistent with the general acceptance of the reliability and necessity test that all hearsay should be subject to the same test. At present, hearsay evidence admissible under the Act's regime may not be admissible under the Land Transport Act 1998, for example, because of some procedural requirements that may or may not still be considered helpful.

EV17.03   Limited preservation of the common law

What s 17 does make clear is that any common law exceptions to the rule against hearsay can no longer be relied on. Section 17 only permits a hearsay statement to be admitted pursuant to the Evidence Act or some other Act. However, s 17 must also be read as being subject to s 12A, which specifically preserves a common law exception to the rule against hearsay.[250]

---

246   See further NZLS *Intensive: Evidence Act 2006*, 24-25 and EV4.20.01-04.
247   See EV4.44.01.
248   LC *Evidence Reform*, para 9.
249   LC *Evidence Code*, para C83.

Apart from s 12A, the wording of s 17 means that for the most part there will be no need to refer to the numerous common law exceptions to the hearsay rule — including the general residual common law exception which was being developed in the years immediately preceding the Act.[251] However, as discussed with regard to the definition of "circumstances",[252] the common law may still have a role to play with regard to the assessment of reliability under the Act.[253]

There can no longer be direct reliance on the res gestae exception to the rule.[254] Such evidence will be subject to the admissibility test in s 18 (unavailability and reliability). Spontaneous utterances were often admitted as part of the res gestae — such statements will usually have sufficient assurance of reliability to be admitted under the Act.

18   General admissibility of hearsay

(1)   A hearsay statement is admissible in any proceeding if—

   (a)   the circumstances relating to the statement provide reasonable assurance that the statement is reliable; and

   (b)   either—

      (i)   the maker of the statement is unavailable as a witness; or

      (ii)   the Judge considers that undue expense or delay would be caused if the maker of the statement were required to be a witness.

(2)   This section is subject to sections 20 and 22.

EV18.01   The admissibility provision

Section 18 contains the main exception to the exclusionary rule and thus the major reform of the common law rule. The criteria for admissibility are reliability and unavailability, or, the alternative to unavailability, that "undue expense or delay would be caused". Section 22 contains a notice provision for criminal proceedings.

EV18.02   Reliability of the statement

The focus of s 18(1)(a) is the reliability of the *hearsay statement*, not the reliability of the *evidence* through which that hearsay statement is offered in evidence. Hence the assessment of reliability should not be concerned with potential problems with the testimony of a witness who offers evidence that some person (other than a witness)

---

250   This amendment (see the discussion at EV12A.01) was not primarily needed because of the rigors of the hearsay rule, as s 27(3) provides that the rule does not apply when the prosecution is offering statements of a defendant, but because of the *use* that can be made of such statements under the common law.

251   McDonald, "Going 'straight to basics': the role of Lord Cooke in reforming the rule against hearsay — from *Baker* to the Evidence Act 2006" (2008) VUWLR (forthcoming), *Adams on Criminal Law — Evidence*, EC10.05, and *Cross on Evidence* (8th NZ ed), para 16.28A.

252   See EV16.03.02-03.

253   See also EV18.02.

254   *Adams on Criminal Law — Evidence*, EC9.04.

made a hearsay statement. The reliability of a witness's testimony is not part of the inquiry under s 18 (however, see the discussion of "circumstances" in s 16).[255]

The reference to "reasonable assurance" of reliability means presumably that the evidence is considered reliable enough for the fact-finder to consider it, and draw its own conclusions as to weight (sometimes referred to as "threshold reliability", as opposed to "ultimate reliability").[256] However, s 122(2)(a) empowers a judge in a criminal proceeding to warn the jury of the need for caution when the judge concludes that admissible hearsay evidence may be unreliable. This provision is difficult to reconcile with the requirement that a hearsay statement can only be admitted into evidence when there is a reasonable assurance of its reliability.[257]

EV18.03   Undue expense and delay

Section 18(1)(b) provides two alternative prerequisites to admissibility of a hearsay statement. "Unavailability" was discussed under s 16(2).[258] The alternative prerequisite (s 18(1)(b)(ii)) is satisfied when the judge considers that undue expense or delay would be caused if the statement maker were required to be a witness (that is, to give evidence and be cross-examined on it). Under the Evidence Amendment Act (No 2) 1980 this alternative was only applicable in relation to documentary hearsay in civil proceedings. Section 18 however applies in both civil and criminal proceedings and whatever the nature of the hearsay statement (oral *or* documentary).

The ability for witnesses to give evidence in a range of ways under the Act (see ss 102-106) means that mere distance will not necessarily mean that a witness is deemed unavailable or that it would be too expensive to require them to be a witness. What needs to be considered is whether there would be "undue" expense involved or it would not be "reasonably practicable" — for example, if the evidence is only relevant "to prove a minor issue about which there is unlikely to be any real doubt."[259] In this way, the seriousness of the issue and the importance of the hearsay statement may be considered (matters which are more contentious with regard to the assessment of reliability).[260]

EV18.04   Notice requirement

Section 18(1) is subject to s 22, which means that in criminal proceedings the notice requirement in s 22 must be met before the hearsay statement can be admitted, even if the prerequisites to admissibility in s 18(1) are met.

19   Admissibility of hearsay statements contained in business records

(1)   A hearsay statement contained in a business record is admissible if—

---

255   See EV16.03.02.
256   *R v Khelawon* [2006] SCJ No 57 (SCC).
257   See EV122.04(1).
258   See EV16.05.01.
259   LC *Evidence Code*, para C85.
260   LC *Evidence Reform*, para 54.

(a)   the person who supplied the information used for the composition of the record is unavailable as a witness; or

(b)   the Judge considers no useful purpose would be served by requiring that person to be a witness as that person cannot reasonably be expected (having regard to the time that has elapsed since he or she supplied the information and to all the other circumstances of the case) to recollect the matters dealt with in the information he or she supplied; or

(c)   the Judge considers that undue expense or delay would be caused if that person were required to be a witness.

(2)   This section is subject to sections 20 and 22.

EV19.01   Business record exception applies in both civil and criminal proceedings

This section is essentially a re-enactment of s 3(1) of the Evidence Amendment Act (No 2) 1980. However, in that Act the equivalent of s 19(1)(c) only applied in civil proceedings. This version is consistent with s 18 of the 2006 Act, which allows hearsay evidence to be offered even when the maker is available, in criminal or civil proceedings. Section 19 however provides a different test of admissibility for hearsay statements contained in business records as there is no requirement of "reasonable assurance that the statement is reliable", and the "necessity" part of the admissibility inquiry is extended due to the operation of s 19(1)(b). The definitions of "business record", "business", and "duty" in s 16 are relevant to this provision.

The Law Commission considered that re-enactment of the "business record" exception was not required given the generality of the hearsay admissibility rule they proposed.[261] The Select Committee was however of the view that "business records as a class of documents are accepted as reliable",[262] hence time and cost would be saved by not subjecting such material to the reliability test.

The fact that notice of offering hearsay statements contained in business records in criminal proceedings must be given may not mean a time and cost saving in practice. The wide definition of "business record" also means it is unlikely that all material of this kind will be inherently reliable. As noted in the discussion of s 16,[263] statements recorded in police notebooks and in job sheets were held to be "business records" at common law.[264] Presumably if the records are challenged as not being sufficiently reliable that can be dealt with as a matter of weight, or may even lead to exclusion under s 8(1)(a) of the Act.

---

261   New Zealand Law Commission, *Evidence Law: Hearsay: A Discussion Paper*, NZLC PP15, Wellington, 1991, para 37.
262   *Select Committee Report on the Evidence Bill*, 3.
263   See EV16.02.01.
264   *R v Hovell* [1986] 1 NZLR 500; (1986) 2 CRNZ 145 (CA).

20   Admissibility in civil proceedings of hearsay statements in documents related to applications, discovery, or interrogatories

(1)   In a civil proceeding, a hearsay statement in an affidavit made to support or oppose an application is admissible for the purposes of that application if, and to the extent that, the applicable rules of court require or permit a statement of that kind to be made in the affidavit.

(2)   In a civil proceeding, a hearsay statement in a document by which documents are discovered or interrogatories are answered is admissible in that proceeding if, and to the extent that, the applicable rules of court require or permit the making of a statement of that kind.

Compare: HCR 138(5), 248, 249, 283(2)(a)

EV20.01   Analysis

This section was added in Select Committee. The rationale given for its addition was given by Christopher Finlayson MP who stated:[265]

> "The second change, which is contained in clause 18B [s 20], picks up a couple of the High Court Rules that deal with hearsay, or statements of belief, in certain circumstances. In civil proceedings, hearsay statements and documents related to interlocutory applications, interrogatories, or discovery will be admissible, provided that grounds are given. It is appropriate that those sorts of rules are contained in the Evidence Act and are not simply contained in the High Court Rules or their equivalent."

As s 5(2) gives the Act priority over various rules of court, this section permits parties to offer hearsay evidence in particular circumstances. These rules do not impose prerequisites for admissibility that are found in ss 18 or 19. Section 20 makes it clear that evidence falling within s 20 does not need to satisfy ss 18 or 19. However, s 20 operates to admit hearsay only to the extent permitted by the rules of court — beyond this the Act's controls on admissibility will take priority.

21   Defendant who does not give evidence in criminal proceeding may not offer own statement

(1)   If a defendant in a criminal proceeding does not give evidence, the defendant may not offer his or her own hearsay statement in evidence in the proceeding.

(2)   To avoid any doubt, this section does not limit the previous consistent statement rule.

---

265   Hansard, *Christopher Finlayson: Evidence Amendment Bill: Second Reading*, 21 November 2006 ((2006) 635 NZPD 6642).

EV21.01 Admissibility of a defendant's hearsay statements when offered by the defendant

As a defendant in a criminal proceeding is not compellable,[266] they are deemed to be unavailable for the purposes of the hearsay rule. Provided that their out-of-court statement was sufficiently reliable it could be admitted under s 18. This was the intention of the Law Commission, which was of the view that repetitive, or fabricated, self-serving statements made by a defendant leading up to their trial could be controlled by the reliability filter in s 18 as well as by s 8(1)(b). The Evidence Bill 2005 contained the substance of s 21, so the policy decision to reject the Law Commission's approach was made by Cabinet:[267]

> "[A] defendant who elects not to give evidence will not be permitted to offer his or her own hearsay statement as evidence in a criminal proceeding ... as a defendant is not, in reality, 'unavailable' to him or herself. This departs from the Law Commission's recommendation."

In this form, s 21 is also a major change from the common law.[268]

EV21.02 Defendants' statements offered by the prosecution

Pre-trial statements of a defendant in a criminal case may be offered by the prosecution in accordance with ss 27-30, to which the hearsay rule does not apply. Current case law supports the practice that even exculpatory portions of such "mixed" statements are admissible as an exception to the rule against hearsay (even though not strictly statements against interest which is the basis for the traditional exception).[269]

The purpose of this section is seemingly to prevent a defendant offering their pre-trial statement in evidence as they cannot be cross-examined on it, although the addition of the section during the legislative process was probably intended only to control the introduction of fabricated self-serving statements. The section now also prevents a defendant's statements being elicited through cross-examination of prosecution witnesses unless the defendant will later give evidence.[270] It also excludes evidence of statements made by the defendant when confronted by the police, which will now only be admissible if the prosecution offers them under s 27.[271]

---

266   See EV16.05.02.

267   *Cabinet Paper 2*, 3-4. Contrary to the statement in Illingworth QC and Mathias, "The Admisibility of Hearsay Statements and Opinion Evidence" in NZLS *Intensive: Evidence Act 2006*, 48, the Law Commission did not revise the Code and prepare the Bill, nor did the Law Commission add s 21.

268   For further discussion of the possible (unintended) effects of s 21, see Illingworth QC and Mathias, "The Admisibility of Hearsay Statements and Opinion Evidence" in NZLS *Intensive: Evidence Act 2006*, 47-51.

269   *Adams on Criminal Law — Evidence*, EC4.02(3); *R v Pearce* 2/3/07, CA453/06; [2007] NZCA 40, para 7. See also EV27.01(3).

270   Illingworth QC and Mathias, "The Admisibility of Hearsay Statements and Opinion Evidence" in NZLS *Intensive: Evidence Act 2006*, 51.

271   See EV27.06.

EV21.03   "Give evidence"

The section uses the phrase if a defendant "does not give evidence", but the preferable reading is probably if the defendant "is not a witness". The definition of "witness" is someone who gives evidence *and* is able to be cross-examined. The use of the phrase "gives evidence" may have the effect that if a defendant testifies at a pre-trial hearing, they will have "given evidence" as required by the section so at trial may offer their hearsay statements without having to testify (subject only to s 8). "Does not give evidence" must mean "is not a witness" for the section to give effect to the policy behind it.

EV21.04   Offering hearsay statements of a co-defendant

Section 21(1) does not prevent a co-defendant offering the hearsay statement of another co-defendant, so this may mean cooperative co-defendants can circumvent the rule (by offering evidence through cross-examination of each others' hearsay statements), while uncooperative ones will effectively be forced to testify in order to offer in evidence exculpatory statements made to a co-defendant. The other prerequisites for admissibility in ss 18 and 22 would need to be met as well. There is however no bar on a defendant offering inculpatory pre-trial statements of a co-defendant.[272]

The definition of a hearsay statement (which excludes from its scope statements made by a witness) also means that if a co-defendant testifies, a defendant can offer evidence of the co-defendant's out-of-court statements without any need to satisfy s 18.[273]

EV21.05   Res gestae

This section will also exclude evidence which was admitted prior to the Act as an exception to the hearsay rule, but will now only be admitted if admissible under s 18 of the Act — those statements referred to as res gestae under the common law.[274] This means s 21 will prevent a defendant who does not testify from also being able to question a prosecution witness about what the defendant allegedly said at the time of the crime ("offer evidence" being defined in s 4 as including "eliciting evidence by cross-examining a witness called by another party").[275]

EV21.06   Business record

Section 21(1) also applies to prevent a defendant offering evidence of a business record if the record contains a hearsay statement by a defendant.

EV21.07   Subsection (2): previous consistent statement

Section 21(2) clarifies the position once a defendant becomes a witness and is not prevented by s 21(1) from offering evidence of his or her pre-trial statement. Usually s 35 will prevent such evidence being given. This is because usually the defendant will want to offer a pre-trial self-serving statement that is consistent with the

---

272   See EV31.01(3).
273   See further the discussion of "witness" at EV4.46.01.
274   *Adams on Criminal Law — Evidence*, EC9.04.
275   See EV4.29.01.

defendant's testimony. Section 35(1) excludes such evidence unless an exception in s 35(2) applies.[276]

22   Notice of hearsay in criminal proceedings

(1)   In a criminal proceeding, no hearsay statement may be offered in evidence unless—

    (a)   the party proposing to offer the statement has complied with the requirements of subsections (2), (3), and (4); or

    (b)   every other party has waived those requirements; or

    (c)   the Judge dispenses with those requirements.

(2)   A party who proposes to offer a hearsay statement in a criminal proceeding, must provide every other party with a written notice stating—

    (a)   the party's intention to offer the hearsay statement in evidence; and

    (b)   the name of the maker of the statement, if known (subject to the terms of any witness anonymity order); and

    (c)   if the hearsay statement was made orally, the contents of the hearsay statement; and

    (d)   if section 18(1)(a) is relied on, the circumstances relating to the statement that provide reasonable assurance that the statement is reliable; and

    (e)   if section 19 is relied on, why the document is a business record; and

    (f)   if section 18(1)(b)(i) or 19(1)(a) is relied on, why the person is unavailable as a witness; and

    (g)   if section 18(1)(b)(ii) or 19(1)(c) is relied on, why undue expense or delay would be caused if the person were required to be a witness.

(3)   If the hearsay statement was made in writing, the notice must be accompanied by a copy of the document in which the statement is contained.

(4)   The requirements of subsections (2) and (3) must be complied with in sufficient time before the hearing to provide all other parties to the proceeding with a fair opportunity to respond to the statement.

(5)   The Judge may dispense with the requirements of subsections (2), (3), and (4) if,—

    (a)   having regard to the nature and contents of the statement, no party is substantially prejudiced by the failure to comply with the requirements; or

    (b)   compliance was not reasonably practicable in the circumstances; or

    (c)   the interests of justice so require.

---

276   See EV35.04.

EV22.01   Required pre-trial disclosure by defendants in criminal proceedings

Prior to the Act, a defendant had few pre-trial disclosure obligations (sometimes viewed as part of the right to silence before trial). The effect of s 22 may be to force the defendant to disclose his or her defence pre-trial to the extent that it becomes apparent by the notice requirement.

Some members of the criminal bar opposed the introduction of a notice requirement on the basis that there is no obligation on an accused to disclose his or her defence and giving notice of an intention to offer hearsay evidence should not therefore have adverse effects on an accused.[277] The Law Commission made it clear that a defendant in a criminal case who gives notice "of an intention to offer hearsay evidence should not be treated as having elected to call evidence, and there should be no adverse comment about any later decision not to offer the evidence."[278] With regard to the power to excuse a party from giving notice, the Law Commission noted that unexpected or un-notified hearsay could be met by allowing any other party to call or recall a witness to rebut that hearsay. One example of a situation where a judge may dispense with the notice requirement in s 22(5)(c) is where "the hearsay evidence was not known to counsel and is unexpectedly disclosed while a witness gives evidence at trial."[279]

EV22.02   Rationale for notice requirement

The rationale for the notice provision was to encourage admissibility decisions concerning hearsay to be made pre-trial where possible, given the move from a category-based approach to one relying on the exercise of judicial discretion. Specific reference to a requirement for notice was not considered necessary for civil proceedings — it being presumed that this would occur as part of the usual discovery process.[280]

EV22.03   Content of the notice and waiver

Consistent with the Law Commission's view that admissibility decisions should be made pre-trial, s 20(2) of the draft Code provided that a party in a criminal proceeding who objects to the admission of the statement should give notice of that objection as soon as practicable.[281] The Act's notice provision however does not include reference to such a process. The Act is also more prescriptive about the content of the notice — the Code only specified reference to the contents of the statement and the name of the maker. Other than the requirement that the notice be in writing, the Act does not state how notice is to be communicated.

---

277   LC *Evidence Reform*, para 65.
278   LC *Evidence Code*, para C92.
279   LC *Evidence Code*, para C94.
280   LC *Evidence Code*, para C86.
281   LC *Evidence Code*, para C93. For the form in which applications for pre-trial admissibility orders should be made from 1 December 2007, see *Practice Note — Pre-Trial Applications in Criminal Jury Cases* (5 November 2007) regarding the process of making such applications in criminal jury cases. The practice note is available at: www.courtsofnz.govt.nz/business/practice-directions.html.

The Act gives no guidance, however, as to when a party has waived the requirement of s 22 (see s 22(1)(b)). Controversies may develop over the extent to which there may have been an implied waiver.

Missing from s 22(2) is any requirement for reference to the grounds for a reliance on s 19(1)(b), presumably a legislative oversight. Nor is there any requirement that there is disclosure of the name of the person who supplied the information used for the compilation of a business record.

Section 22(2)(d) will require pre-trial work. The process will be more difficult until there is a body of case law dealing with matters that are considered to be relevant to the reliability inquiry.[282]

Subpart 2—Statements of opinion and expert evidence

(s 23 to s 26)

23   Opinion rule

A statement of an opinion is not admissible in a proceeding, except as provided by section 24 or 25.

EV23.01   Overview

Section 23 states the general exclusionary rule that opinions are not admissible to prove the truth of what is believed or inferred. A witness in a case is called to give evidence of what he or she has experienced, and the testimony must comprise direct evidence of his or her own perceptions of the facts. The general premise is that a witness's opinions, beliefs or inferences are not their perceptions but are conclusions drawn from those perceptions.

EV23.02   Distinction between fact and opinion

The Act defines "opinion" as "a statement of opinion that tends to prove or disprove a fact".[283] The distinction between what is fact and what is opinion is sometimes unclear. The traditional definition of opinion evidence as "an inference from observed and communicable data" belies both theoretical and practical difficulties in distinguishing between fact and opinion. Clearly conjecture without personal knowledge or observation would hold little relevance and would be unreliable, and in everyday life (and indeed in the courtroom) we do group statements into opinion or fact.

The difficulty comes when trying to closely define what is fact or opinion, necessary for the exclusionary rule in s 23. In the commentary to the draft Code, Law Commission, in defining opinion evidence as "an opinion offered in evide[nce] tending to prove or disprove any fact", sought to exclude from the definition ev[idence] offered to prove that a person held a particular opinion,[284] and it is likely that [th]e definition in the Act seeks to do likewise. Hence, where A's preference in [m]usic is

---

282   See EV16.03.01.

283   See EV4.30.01.

284   LC *Evidence Code*, 19.

an issue in the proceeding, the opinion rule should not operate to exclude a statement by A as to her favourite recording artist. Although the fine distinction between fact and opinion could make this intention difficult to achieve, it is clear that s 23 should only be applied where a statement of opinion is offered in evidence in order to prove a fact other than that the person who made the statement held a particular opinion.

EV23.03   Rationale of the opinion evidence rule

The rationale of the exclusionary rule is essentially to prevent the admission of unreliable, superfluous or misleading evidence. To admit such evidence would lead to a waste of court time and the admission of evidence with doubtful relevance. The justifications for the rule can be brought under the umbrella of this rationale, and can essentially be broken down into three main strands: first, where a witness offers a bare opinion it holds little probative weight, but there is a danger that such uninformed speculation would sway the tribunal of fact (particularly in jury trials) disproportionately. This leads to the second strand, which is the danger that a witness offering opinion evidence will "usurp" the function of the tribunal of fact, whose job it is to draw the necessary inferences from the facts presented in evidence. It may be that the evidence would confuse the tribunal of fact and prolong proceedings, and in the case of an expert witness may result in unquestioning acceptance of the opinion because of impressive qualifications and confident manner. Although the exclusionary rule may exclude potentially useful evidence, the policy behind it acts to try and prevent juries in particular from being drawn into a mere acceptance of a witness's opinion without considering it further. Thirdly, a witness's evidence of opinion may be based on other evidence which, if stated expressly, would be inadmissible — for example where an opinion is based largely on propensity evidence.

EV23.04   Relationship of s 23 to the other rules of admissibility in the Act

Section 23 could be interpreted to mean that other rules of admissibility are not relevant once a statement of opinion is admissible under ss 24 or 25. For example, a statement of opinion could breach the rule against hearsay — if the statement satisfies ss 24 or 25, there is nothing in the section directing that other rules should still be satisfied before the evidence is admissible. However, it can be assumed that the intention is that a statement of opinion that is admissible under ss 24 or 25 should also satisfy any other rules under the Act that apply. The Act generally states when particular rules or Subparts do not apply (including where the opinion rule does not apply),[285] and therefore an absence of such a statement in s 23 leads to the conclusion that other rules of admissibility still apply, even where ss 24 or 25 are satisfied. For example, s 17 provides that any hearsay statement is not admissible unless it either satisfies the provisions of that Subpart, or where the "Act provides that this subpart does not apply; and the hearsay statement is … not otherwise inadmissible under this

---

285   See, eg, s 27 at EV27.05(2).

Act".[286] We can therefore assume that other admissibility rules *do* apply, because there is nothing in s 23 to suggest that they do not.

The justifications for the exclusionary rule highlight concerns that could be addressed under the general exclusion provision in s 8 of the Act. For example, concerns that opinion evidence could be accepted without question, that the evidence holds little probative weight and that the opinion may be based on inadmissible evidence could result in exclusion of such opinion evidence because its probative value is outweighed by the risk that the evidence will have an unfairly prejudicial effect on the outcome of the proceeding (s 8(1)(a)). Similarly, the concern about unreliable and superfluous evidence could be covered by s 8 where the probative value of the evidence is outweighed by the risk that the evidence will needlessly prolong the proceeding (s 8(1)(b)). For example, cross-examination or calling other witnesses could test potentially unreliable opinion evidence, but this could be time consuming and, where the opinion is that of an expert, could lead to the problem of a "battle of the experts". However, some opinion evidence is valuable and helpful, and as such reliance on the general exclusion in s 8 alone would offer less clarity and specific guidance than can be offered by ss 23-25.

24   General admissibility of opinions

A witness may state an opinion in evidence in a proceeding if that opinion is necessary to enable the witness to communicate, or the fact-finder to understand, what the witness saw, heard, or otherwise perceived.

EV24.01   Overview

Section 24 summarises the common law approach to admissibility of non-expert opinion evidence, which has presented few problems in practice. There is no closed list of areas in which non-expert opinion is admissible, there being "an apparently anomalous miscellany"[287] of exceptions to the general exclusionary rule, including opinion evidence from a witness about topics such as identity, speed, emotional state, weather, age and so on.

In order to be admissible under s 24, the statement of opinion must fulfil two basic criteria. First, opinion must be the only way in which to effectively communicate the information to the finder of fact (and therefore the information must be something that the finder of fact cannot infer without the statement of opinion).[288] Secondly, the

---

286   See EV17.01.
287   Australian Law Reform Commission, *Evidence (Interim)*, Vol 1, ALRC 26, Canberra, 1985, para 739.
288   See *R v Toka* (1994) 11 CRNZ 601; *R v Konia* 28/3/06, Goddard J, HC Palmerston North CRI-2005-054-2095; *R v Williams* (1993) 11 CRNZ 34; and *Smith v R* (2001) 206 CLR 650 (HCA), for examples where the court excluded non-expert opinion evidence (confining the witnesses to evidence of perceived facts) on the basis that the jury could draw the inference or conclusions itself. Where there may be additional assistance or value because the witness has a particular skill (such as in *R v Tipene* (2001) 19 CRNZ 93 (CA)), the evidence should be assessed under s 25.

witness must be stating an opinion (be it conclusion, inference etc) from something personally perceived. This is often termed the "compendious mode" of giving evidence.[289]

EV24.02   Mixture of fact and inference

In general, non-expert opinion evidence will be accepted where the perceptions and statements of fact of the witness are conclusions in themselves, or where there is a mixture of inference and fact that cannot be separated. The justification for this is that, given the difficulties in separating fact and opinion, and the artificiality in some circumstances of demanding that evidence be presented as statements of fact only, clear and useful evidence will be sacrificed where the rule is strictly adhered to:[290]

> "It is important that witnesses be able to present their testimony in such a way that they are able to articulate their thoughts clearly and rationally, but at the same time be of maximal assistance to the court. The natural flow of speech and of thought processes however, can be detrimentally interrupted by the demand that testimony be expressed in the form of facts, not opinions."

Whether the non-expert opinion should be admitted is determined on the particular facts of each case. Courts in New Zealand have never had any particular problem in admitting statements by witnesses that consist of inferences based on perceived facts.

The more difficult it is to disentangle fact and inference in a witness's testimony, the more likely it is that it will be admitted. For example, where a witness offers evidence that she identified the accused as the offender in an identification parade, she is giving evidence of the fact that she chose the accused from a parade of other people, but the belief that the defendant and the offender are one and the same is a mixture of fact and inference. The two are almost impossible to separate. Similarly, where a witness gives evidence about a car accident, he or she may be asked whether the car was speeding. The witness may use the sound of the car or other perceptions to give an opinion on whether the car was travelling at a fast speed: the perception and the opinion are closely bound together.

25   Admissibility of expert opinion evidence

(1)   An opinion by an expert that is part of expert evidence offered in a proceeding is admissible if the fact-finder is likely to obtain substantial help from the opinion in understanding other evidence in the proceeding or in ascertaining any fact that is of consequence to the determination of the proceeding.

(2)   An opinion by an expert is not inadmissible simply because it is about—

(a)   an ultimate issue to be determined in a proceeding; or

(b)   a matter of common knowledge.

---

289   See New Zealand Law Commission, *Evidence Law: Expert Evidence and Opinion Evidence*, NZLC PP18, Wellington, 1991, para 31.

290   Australian Law Reform Commission, *Evidence (Interim)*, Vol 1, ALRC 26, Canberra, 1985, para 734.

(3)   If an opinion by an expert is based on a fact that is outside the general body of knowledge that makes up the expertise of the expert, the opinion may be relied on by the fact-finder only if that fact is or will be proved or judicially noticed in the proceeding.

(4)   If expert evidence about the sanity of a person is based in whole or in part on a statement that the person made to the expert about the person's state of mind, then—

(a)   the statement of the person is admissible to establish the facts on which the expert's opinion is based; and

(b)   neither the hearsay rule nor the previous consistent statements rule applies to evidence of the statement made by the person.

(5)   Subsection (3) is subject to subsection (4).

EV25.01   Overview

Section 25 outlines the new rules for admissibility of expert opinion evidence. In order to comply with s 25, the opinion must be that of an "expert", it must comprise "expert evidence" and it must offer substantial help to the fact-finder in understanding other evidence or ascertaining any fact in the proceeding. "Expert" and "expert evidence" are defined in s 4,[291] and form a rule of qualification before the opinion evidence can be assessed under s 25.

The Law Commission originally recommended that a notice provision was included for expert opinion evidence in criminal proceedings (civil proceedings were provided for by virtue of the High Court Rules and District Courts Rules 1992).[292] However, this provision did not appear in the Evidence Bill, but is part of the new criminal disclosure regime proposed in the Criminal Procedure Bill 2004.[293]

(1)   History of expert opinion evidence

Expert opinion evidence has long been allowed in matters which the jury would either have difficulty in resolving alone or which involve counter-intuitive issues upon which an expert can offer enlightenment. Experts were allowed to testify as long ago as 1555, when the English court in the case of *Buckley v Rice Thomas* stated that:[294]

> "[I]f matters arise in our Law which concern other Sciences or Faculties, we commonly apply for the aid of that Science or Faculty which it concerns. Which is an honourable and commendable thing in our Law. For thereby it appears that we do not despise all other Sciences but our own, but we approve of them and encourage them as things worthy of commendation."

---

291   See EV4.14.01 and EV4.15.01.
292   LC *Evidence Code*, 71.
293   Criminal Procedure Bill 2004, Part 2.
294   *Buckley v Rice Thomas* (1555) 1 Plowd 118, 124.

(2)   Qualification as an expert

Section 4 of the Act defines an "expert" as "a person who has specialised knowledge or skill based on training, study or experience".[295] This codifies the common law rule as to qualification as an expert. The judge must determine whether the expert witness is properly qualified to testify: opinions given by non-experts on matters calling for expertise are inadmissible. The expert is therefore required to demonstrate to the court that he or she has the requisite qualification to be deemed "expert" in the field in question. Evidence offered by an expert should be within his or her area of expertise — in other words, it replicates the common law rule that experts should testify only within their own competence.

The expert may be qualified through formal study and training, through experience, or both.[296]

(3)   Ambit of s 25

Section 25 is concerned only with the admissibility of expert *opinion* evidence. Expert evidence may consist of fact, opinion, or a mixture of the two.[297] Factual evidence from an expert will therefore be governed only by the general rules in ss 7 and 8, and any other admissibility rules applicable in the individual case.

(4)   Demonstrations and reconstructions

Although there was some authority that evidence of reconstructions was inadmissible prior to the Act,[298] this was becoming less certain[299] where the evidence of reconstruction was relevant, reliable and not unduly prejudicial. Experiments and demonstrations were also admissible on the same footing (with demonstrations needing to be fair representations of what actually occurred in the circumstances in question).[300] Where the reconstruction, experiment or demonstration involves technical knowledge in its performance, s 25 will apply.[301]

EV25.02   Subsection (1): "likely to obtain substantial help"

The requirement of substantial help to the fact-finder is intended to replace the common knowledge and ultimate issue rules. The common knowledge rule stated that an expert could not give an opinion on matters that were within the common knowledge of the jury. The ultimate issue rule provided that an expert could not give an opinion on the ultimate issue in the case. These were the two defining common

---

295   See EV4.14.01.

296   *R v Silverlock* [1894] 2 QB 766 offers the classic description of what will make a witness an "expert" in the eyes of the court. What was important to the court was the extent to which the skill had been developed, not how it was acquired: "[T]he expert must be peritus; he must be skilled in doing so; but we cannot say that he must have become peritus in the way of his business or in any definite way. The question is, is he peritus? Is he skilled?"

297   See EV23.02.

298   *R v Baker* (1989) 4 CRNZ 687, 689.

299   For discussion of reliability, relevance, and lack of undue prejudice, see *R v Kingi* 17/2/06, Wild J, HC Palmerston North CRI-2005-054-305, para 9.

300   *R v Allison* 28/2/03, Williams J, HC Auckland T002481.

301   See also *Adams on Criminal Law — Evidence*, EC14.06(5).

law rules relating to expert opinion evidence that are effectively abolished in s 25(2).

(1) Rationale of the substantial helpfulness test

The requirement of substantial helpfulness seeks to offer a "more rational test which assesses the reliability and value of the expert opinion on its merits"[302]. It essentially confirms the position arrived at in the common law in New Zealand prior to the Act's enactment.[303]

The effect of the substantial helpfulness test is to conflate separate assessments under the old common law rules (including that relating to evidence from novel scientific disciplines),[304] into one holistic assessment of reliability and value.

(2) "Substantial" helpfulness

There is a danger that all relevant evidence can be helpful to some degree — it is assumed that the term "substantial" is to prevent this danger. Guidance will be needed as to the interpretation of the substantial helpfulness test.

EV25.03   Novel disciplines

The traditional approach used by the courts in New Zealand to new and possibly unreliable evidence has been that a discipline need not be generally accepted before expert evidence is admissible, but it must be sufficiently established to pass the ordinary threshold of reliability.[305] This offered a simple and straightforward test of admissibility, but led to dangers of over-inclusiveness and hasty acceptance of novel procedures, which were left to be ameliorated by the restrictions placed upon the scope of expert evidence by the operation of the ultimate issue and common knowledge rules. From now on they will be addressed by operation of the "substantial helpfulness" test under s 25(1), which is also designed to assess reliability, leaving the judge to draw the fine and difficult balance between helpful information and uncertain or untested theories (so-called "junk science").

(1) Judge as gatekeeper

The Law Commission drew inspiration not only from New Zealand judgments, but also from the leading United States case of *Daubert v Merrell Dow*,[306] which looked to reliability indicators such as empirical testing, peer review, error rates, and

---

302   New Zealand Law Commission, *Evidence Law: Expert Evidence and Opinion Evidence*, NZLC PP18, Wellington, 1991, para C10. This is similar to the motivation of the court in *Daubert v Merrell Dow* (1993) 509 US 579 (see discussion below at EV25.03(1)).

303   *R v Decha-Iamsakun* [1993] 1 NZLR 141; *Diagnostic Medlab Ltd v Auckland District Health Board* 5/12/06, Asher J, HC Auckland CIV-2006-404-4724, para 21.

304   Sometimes referred to as the "field of expertise" inquiry.

305   This is the approach in many common law jurisdictions: see *R v Robb* (1991) 93 Cr App R 161, *R v Mohan* [1994] 2 SCR 9. Although the usual approach is one of relevance and reliability, the New Zealand courts have sometimes proposed a higher threshold: see *R v B* [1987] 1 NZLR 362.

306   *Daubert v Merrell Dow* (1993) 509 US 579. Rule 702 of the Federal Rules of Evidence (US) acts as the basis of this approach.

acceptance of the scientific community. The *Daubert* approach places the judge in a gatekeeper role, giving him or her the burden of determining whether the reasoning and methodology underlying the expert testimony is scientifically valid. This can require the trial judge to distinguish not only between respectable and "junk" science, but more specifically between good and bad science, something which he or she may not be qualified to do. The Law Commission may have been referring to these drawbacks when it stated that evidence based on specialised knowledge and skills "is not amenable to verification by empirical testing".[307] In other words, the reliability inquiry may differ according to the measure used and the purpose of introducing the evidence. For example, reliability of evidence may not need to meet the threshold of empirical error rating in some circumstances. If this was strictly required, the substantial helpfulness test would operate to exclude many novel forms of scientific evidence.

(2) Understanding other evidence and ascertaining facts

Under s 25(1), evidence will be substantially helpful where it helps the fact-finder to understand other evidence in the proceeding or ascertain any fact that is of consequence to the determination of the proceeding.

(a) *Understanding other evidence*

The Law Commission described as an example of "understanding other evidence" situations where wrong inferences could easily be drawn from the evidence of other witnesses, such as the way an intellectual disability affects a witness's behaviour, understanding and communication.[308] It is unclear from this description whether the substantial helpfulness test is designed to not only dispel myths or prevent the drawing of wrong inferences,[309] but also to admit expert psychological evidence pertaining to a witness's veracity. Although the courts were historically reluctant to admit evidence relating to veracity prior to the Act,[310] it is a possible interpretation of s 25(1) that such evidence could be admissible in order to aid the fact-finder in "understanding other evidence", particularly where a witness has reduced capacity or an "abnormality".

Another example of "substantial help in understanding other evidence" is expert opinion evidence about the level of intellectual and emotional development of a child witness.[311] As no equivalent of s 23G of the Evidence Act 1908, which governed the admissibility of expert opinion evidence in child sexual abuse cases,[312] features in the new Act, evidence previously admitted under the section (for example, as to the

---

307   LC *Evidence Code*, para C101.
308   LC *Evidence Code*, para C102. A similar view was articulated by the court in *R v Decha-Iamsakun* [1993] 1 NZLR 141 as a reason for departing from a strict application of the common knowledge rule.
309   As per *R v Decha-Iamsakun* [1993] 1 NZLR 141.
310   There was arguably a changing mood to allow expert evidence as to the veracity of those considered "abnormal": *R v Pinfold* [2004] 2 Cr App R 5 (CA); *R v Hurihanganui* [2004] 2 NZLR 1 (CA).
311   LC *Evidence Code*, para C102.

child's intellectual attainment, emotional maturity, or mental capability) will now be treated as any other expert opinion evidence under s 25. Such evidence may well aid the fact-finder in understanding the evidence of a child complainant of sexual abuse, but there may be difficulties in asserting the reliability of such evidence under the substantial helpfulness test.

EV25.04   Subsection (2): ultimate issue and common knowledge rules no longer determinative

Section 25(2) abolishes the common knowledge and ultimate issue rules. Expert opinion evidence will not be inadmissible simply because it is about the ultimate issue or a matter of common knowledge. In other words, common knowledge and ultimate issue are no longer determinative of admissibility; substantial helpfulness is.

(1)   Ultimate issue rule

The ultimate issue rule traditionally prevented witnesses from giving their opinion on the point that the jury had to decide.[313]

The rule aimed to prevent some of the dangers of opinion evidence, namely usurpation of the fact-finding role or undue weight placed on expert evidence.[314] In practice, the ultimate issue rule was often ignored, or was circumvented by a play on words. It was claimed that "the fact that an opinion may be given as to the ultimate issue is no longer a reason for excluding it".[315] The courts were inclined to exclude questions where the words used were exactly the same as those used in the formulation of an offence or defence. However, where the question was being asked by way of a different form of words, or where hypothetical questions were used, the expert was usually allowed to express an opinion. The result was that the rule was largely symbolic, and its abolition as a determinative factor in the admissibility of expert opinion evidence is likely to make little practical difference.

---

312   Section 23G allowed for limited expert opinion on the general development level of children the same age as the complainant, and limited comment on whether the behaviour of the complainant (as evidenced in court) was consistent with sexually abused children of the same age group. The section proved to be problematic to apply: see, eg, *R v J* 4/8/03, CA51/03. The Act does not replicate the enhanced qualification requirements found in s 23G of the Evidence Act 1908 (see EV25.01(2)).

313   As stated in *Joseph Crosfield and Sons Ltd v Techno-Chemical Laboratories Ltd* (1913) 29 TLR 378, 379: "It is not competent in any action for witnesses to express their opinions upon any of the issues, whether of law or fact, which the court or jury has to determine."

314   *Wigmore*'s view was that the language of usurpation of the jury's function was "so misleading, as well as unsound, that it should be entirely repudiated. It is a mere bit of empty rhetoric", and this was reflected in the more recent treatment of the rule by the courts (Chadbourn (ed), *Wigmore on Evidence*, Boston, Little, Brown & Co, 1978). See also the amusing visualisation in Murphy, "An evaluation of the arguments against the use of expert testimony on eyewitness identification" (1987) 8 *University of Bridgeport Law Review* 21, 27.

315   *R v Kaukasi* 9/8/02, Fisher J, HC Auckland T014047, para 16; see also *R v Eade* (2002) 19 CRNZ 470 (CA), para 19.

---

(2)   Substantial help versus common knowledge

(a)   *Common knowledge*

If matters do not call for expertise, "expert" evidence can offer no help to the court and may serve to cause confusion.[316] For example, experts have been prevented from giving evidence to explain the ordinary meaning of words such as "obscene and indecent"; and have not been allowed to give evidence on whether behaviour is within the "bounds of normality". *R v Turner* offers the classic exposition of such concerns:[317]

> "An expert's opinion is admissible to furnish the court with scientific information which is likely to be outside the experience and knowledge of a judge or jury. If on the proven facts a judge or jury can form their own conclusions without help, then the opinion of an expert is unnecessary ... The fact that an expert witness has impressive scientific qualifications does not by that fact alone make his opinion on matters of human nature and behaviour within the limits of normality any more helpful than that of the jurors themselves; but there is a danger that they may think it does."

Although the common knowledge rule was logical in theory, in practice it could be too rigid. The rule, for example, could exclude testimony as to the capacity of an accused where he or she had an IQ just within the normal range, because jurors would be expected to know the abilities of "normal" people. When interpreted rigidly, it could result in valuable evidence being excluded.[318]

(b)   *Dissatisfaction with the common knowledge rule*

Well before the finalisation of the Law Commission's draft Code, the courts in New Zealand had begun to question the strict interpretation of the common knowledge rule and in *R v Decha-Iamsakun*[319] the Court made it clear that in some circumstances expert evidence falling within common knowledge may still be helpful to the jury, and should be admitted. For example, some research findings may be counter-intuitive, there may be a need to dispel commonly held myths, or it may be helpful to explain and supplement the ordinary knowledge in a given area:[320]

> "Matters which to a considerable extent are within the experience of a judge trying the facts or jury can arise, yet expert evidence may help materially in coming to a conclusion. The information provided may well be outside

---

316   As discussed at EV23.03.

317   *R v Turner* [1975] QB 834, 841.

318   See Mackay and Colman, "Excluding expert evidence; A tale of ordinary folk and common experience" [1991] Crim LR 800; Mackay and Colman, "Equivocal Rulings on Expert Psychological and Psychiatric Evidence: Turning a Muddle into a Nonsense" [1996] Crim LR 88; and Sheldon and MacLeod, "From Normative to Positive Data: Expert Psychological Evidence Re-examined" [1991] Crim LR 811.

319   *R v Decha-Iamsakun* [1993] 1 NZLR 141.

320   *R v Decha-Iamsakun* [1993] 1 NZLR 141, 146. See also *R v Kaukasi* 9/8/02, Fisher J, HC Auckland T014047; and Pattenden, "Conflicting approaches to psychiatric evidence in criminal trials: England, Canada and Australia" [1986] Crim LR 92, 100.

ordinary experience and cause the judge or jury to review impressions or instinctive judgments based on ordinary experience, and to do so in the direction of either confirmation or doubt of what ordinary experience suggests."

The Law Commission's view was also that the common knowledge rule worked too restrictively, acting to limit useful evidence "because the rule excludes evidence by its subject matter without regard to its reliability and value in the trial".[321]

(c)   *Likely effect of abolition of the common knowledge rule*

As was intended by the Law Commission, the use of a substantial helpfulness test is unlikely to result in a change in the admissibility inquiry from the use of the common knowledge rule in the majority of cases,[322] but will do so in borderline cases, especially ones involving evidence from psychologists. The Law Commission argued that if the evidence is within the common knowledge of jury members then it is likely to be of little help to them. On this analysis, it may appear that a requirement that the evidence be of help to the jury is little more than a reformulation of the old common knowledge rule.

However, a "helpfulness" test may make a difference in those cases where the condition is within the common knowledge of the jury, but where that common knowledge is based, in part at least, on fallacy; or where the jury will not be able to fully comprehend the intricacies of the condition. Expert witnesses could then be of help in dispelling common myths about the condition in question, or in explaining the finer details. As such, it is likely that the operation of the substantial helpfulness test will result in some increase in expert opinion evidence in the courts.[323] However, this depends on its application in relation to novel scientific disciplines.[324]

EV25.05   Subsection (3): evidence based on proven facts

Section 25(3) largely reflects the common law position prior to the Act, so that expert opinion based on the general body of knowledge in the expert's field carries no requirement to prove the facts upon which it is based.[325] Opinion based on facts outside the general body of information will need to be proved or judicially noticed.[326] In *R v Turner* the Court said that:

"Before a court can assess the value of an opinion it must know the facts upon which it is based. If the expert has been misinformed about the facts or has taken irrelevant ones into consideration or has omitted to consider relevant ones, the opinion is likely to be valueless. In our judgment, counsel calling an

---

321   New Zealand Law Commission, *Evidence Law: Expert Evidence and Opinion Evidence*, NZLC PP18, Wellington, 1991, para 40.

322   LC *Evidence Reform*, para 76.

323   The introduction of a similar provision in Australia was designed to have this effect: see Australian Law Reform Commission, *Uniform Evidence Law*, ALRC 102, Canberra, 2005, para 9.134.

324   See EV25.03.

325   *Holt v Auckland CC* [1980] 2 NZLR 124 (CA).

326   See EV128.01.

expert should in examination in chief ask his witness to state the facts upon which his opinion is based. It is wrong to leave the other side to elicit the facts by cross-examination."

The factual basis of an expert opinion needs to be proven because without it the opinion can be given little weight. Indeed, where there is no factual basis proven, the evidence may carry so little weight that it will not be relevant.[327]

(1) Body of knowledge

Where material is part of the general body of information on any given topic, such as books and journal articles, an expert witness is allowed to base his or her opinion partly on the research of others working in the area.[328] To do otherwise would involve a costly and time-consuming parade of experts in court: for example, research on memory processes has been conducted by a large number of scientists, the results of which make up a body of knowledge, but no one scientist has personally conducted a high enough number of experiments to be able to give sufficient breadth of comment on the basis of personal experience alone.

(2) Assumed facts

An expert opinion may also be based on facts that are supplied by others, such as analyses of body tissues carried out by colleagues or the research findings of other scientists. In this way, the facts upon which an expert witness bases his or her opinion may be assumed facts or facts of which they have no first hand knowledge. For example, where there are marks on a body, a surgeon who has not seen the body may be asked whether, given the nature of the wounds, they could be self-inflicted. When giving evidence, an expert should state the assumed facts upon which the opinion is based, so that admissible evidence is offered of the facts themselves.[329] If research findings were relayed directly to the court, rather than being used to support and explain the conclusions reached by the expert witness, they would be hearsay evidence and may be excluded under s 18.

(3) Proven facts and provisional admissibility

Section 25(3) requires that the fact "is or will be proved". This means that the expert witness may either state the facts upon which the opinion is based during evidence in chief, or give the evidence on the basis that it "will be" proven, ie that it is provisionally admissible. As it is a conditional process, admissibility in such cases will depend on whether the factual basis of the opinion is indeed proven. If the evidence proving the factual basis does not eventuate, or if it is insufficient to establish the admissibility of the expert opinion (in a jury trial there will be a direction to rely

---

327   New Zealand Law Commission, *Evidence Law: Expert Evidence and Opinion Evidence*, NZLC PP18, Wellington, 1991, para 71; Australian Law Reform Commission, *Uniform Evidence Law*, ALRC 102, Canberra, 2005, 289-295.

328   *H v Schering Chemicals Ltd* [1983] 1 All ER 849, 853 (per Bingham J); *Holt v Auckland CC* [1980] 2 NZLR 124 (CA). See EV129.01.

329   See EV25.05(3).

on the expert opinion only if it finds the factual basis proved), then the opinion will be disregarded (see EV14.01 for further discussion on provisional admissibility).

Expert opinion evidence led later in the case will be based on matters already led, and admissibility of the evidence able to be determined straight away. Provisional admissibility for expert opinion evidence will be necessary in those cases where expert opinion evidence is led early in the party's case, because the evidence on which the expert bases his or her opinion may not yet itself have been led.

(4)   Theory and hypotheses without factual basis

Section 25(3) will not apply to opinions on theory or hypotheses that do not depend on a factual basis.[330] In the past, although expert witnesses were not allowed to speculate as to possibilities for which there was no supporting evidence, in some circumstances experts have been allowed to give evidence based on or about unproven theories. This applies even where the majority of those working within the discipline do not support the theory, but was only allowed where the expert was well-qualified and where the reliability of the evidence could be tested in cross-examination.[331] The operation of the substantial helpfulness test will take into account the level of acceptance of the theory in the scientific community, but as this will be tempered by a more liberal view of helpfulness than the common knowledge rule allowed, it is likely that similar types of evidence will be admissible under s 25 as under the previous law.

EV25.06   Subsection (4): expert evidence about sanity

Section 25(4) provides for the admissibility of a person's statement about his or her state of mind in order to establish the factual basis for the expert's opinion on the sanity of that person. Although s 25(5) states that s 25(3) is subject to s 25(4), there is nothing incompatible about the two subsections.

Section 25(4) represents an (arguably restricted) form of the common law treatment of expert opinions about mental state based on hearsay statements. The precise boundaries of the common law approach are difficult to assess, but in general where the statements were of general background or verified by medical records, the opinion was admissible without requiring the statement-maker to testify.[332] However, where the statements were simply self-serving, on a controversial matter,[333] or where the evidence was the sole evidence upon which a defence was mounted, it was less likely that the opinion would be admitted, because there was no admissible basis for the opinion.

Unlike under the common law, s 25(4) limits its ambit to opinions based on statements made by the person whose sanity is in issue, thereby excluding from coverage statements by others, or statements pertaining to mental disorders falling short of legal insanity. Furthermore, the statements must be about the person's state of mind, and

---

330   LC *Evidence Reform*, 24.
331   A common law example can be seen in *R v Robb* (1991) 93 Cr App R 161 (CA).
332   *R v Rongonui* [2000] 2 NZLR 385 (CA); *R v Smith* [1989] 3 NZLR 405 (CA).
333   *R v Rapira* [2003] 3 NZLR 794 (CA).

so any statements informing the expert's opinion made about other issues will not be covered by s 25(4).[334]

Where the expert's opinion is based on a statement satisfying s 25(4)(a), s 25(4)(b) provides that neither the hearsay rule nor the previous consistent statements rule applies to evidence of the statement made by the person whose sanity is in issue. This means that, if the person whose sanity is in issue does not testify, the hearsay rule will not prevent evidence being given of the statements made to the expert; and if the person does testify, then the previous consistent statements rule cannot operate to make statements within s 25(4) inadmissible by virtue of the fact that they are consistent with his or her testimony. If the statements are used for any purpose other than an expert opinion about the sanity of the person, the hearsay and previous consistent statements rules will apply, because the statements will not be being used "to establish the facts on which the expert's opinion is based" under s 25(4)(a).

26   Conduct of experts in civil proceedings

(1)   In a civil proceeding, experts are to conduct themselves in preparing and giving expert evidence in accordance with the applicable rules of court relating to the conduct of experts.

(2)   The expert evidence of an expert who has not complied with rules of court of the kind specified in subsection (1) may be given only with the permission of the Judge.

Compare: HCR 330A

EV26.01   Analysis

Section 26 was one of a number of sections added to the Evidence Bill by the Select Committee which "parallel the appropriate High Court Rules". Section 26 was added because it refers to the Code of Conduct for expert witnesses in civil proceedings, as recognised in r 330A of the High Court Rules and found in Schedule 4 to the High Court Rules. The section applies to civil proceedings only.

Although s 26 was introduced with reference to the Code of Conduct, it is not limited to that Code, covering as it does "the applicable rules of the court relating to the conduct of experts", and therefore being wide enough to apply to any future rules relating to expert's conduct regarding the preparation and giving of expert evidence in civil proceedings.

The current Code of Conduct includes a reminder that experts should remain impartial,[335] and specifically provides that the expert witness must state his or her

---

334   Although such statements may be admissible under the hearsay rule: see EV18.01-02.
335   The Code of Conduct (Schedule 4 to the High Court Rules) requires both "impartiality" and that experts do not act as advocates for the party calling him or her. This line between advocacy and support was characterised in *Maritime Union of New Zealand Inc v TLNZ Ltd* 7/9/07, Judge Colgan, EMC Auckland AC51/07; ARC34/07, para 39, as being "between persuasive/party supportive opinion evidence (admissible) and opinion evidence that is partial and/or amounts to advocacy for the party calling it (inadmissible)".

qualifications, state the issues that the expert evidence addresses and that it is within his or her area of expertise, state the facts and assumptions upon which the opinion is based, and give details regarding material relied upon in forming the opinion given. Aside from the duty to confer, many of the issues within the Code of Conduct will be covered by the operation of s 25 and the substantial helpfulness test. For example, qualification is a prerequisite to admissibility; and a statement as to the facts upon which the opinion is based is required under s 25(3). There is therefore only limited value in the inclusion of s 26 as a separate general provision given the substantial overlap between the current Code and the ambit of s 25.

Section 26(2) states that evidence may be inadmissible where the rules covered by s 26(1) are not complied with. The subsection unfortunately gives no guidance as to when, or on what grounds, expert evidence should be admitted where the rules of the court have not been complied with. The absence of guidance as to the exercise of judicial discretion is disappointing when the provision is part of a codification exercise that seeks to give such guidance where possible. However, as discussed above, unless different rules as to the conduct of expert witnesses in civil proceedings are generated, non-compliance with the Code of Conduct will usually mean that s 25 has not been satisfied, and the evidence will be excluded on that basis.

Subpart 3—Defendants' statements, improperly obtained evidence, silence of parties in proceedings, and admissions in civil proceedings

EVPt2Sub3.01   Overview

Sections 27-31 substantially alter the common law governing the admissibility of pre-trial statements of defendants in criminal proceedings. Although the Act does not refer to *confessions*, these sections will be the focus for disputes over the admissibility of that much litigated issue in criminal proceedings.

Section 30, governing the admissibility of *improperly obtained evidence* in criminal proceedings, is of obvious importance. Section 30 will often be referred to in arguments over the admissibility of a defendant's statements but the scope of the section is much wider. It covers all forms of improperly obtained evidence in criminal proceedings. Any form of evidence obtained by a wide range of possible improprieties, including *breaches of the Bill of Rights*, will require the application of s 30.

Section 31 attempts to prevent the prosecution obtaining any advantage when another party offers evidence that would be inadmissible under ss 28, 29, or 30 if offered by the prosecution.

Section 32 is one of the few provisions in the Act which purports to restrict the way in which admissible evidence may be used by the fact-finder. It is also an important affirmation of one aspect of the *right of silence*. Section 32 governs a defendant's right of silence before trial. It is supplemented by s 33, which limits "comment" on what could be viewed as an item of evidence, namely the fact that a defendant did not give evidence.

Section 34 governs aspects of admissibility and use of *admissions in civil proceedings*.

(s 27 to s 34)

27   Defendants' statements offered by prosecution

(1)   Evidence offered by the prosecution in a criminal proceeding of a statement made by a defendant is admissible against that defendant, but not against a co-defendant in the proceeding.

(2)   However, evidence offered under subsection (1) is not admissible against that defendant if it is excluded under section 28, 29, or 30.

(3)   Subpart 1 (hearsay evidence), subpart 2 (opinion evidence and expert evidence), and section 35 (previous consistent statements rule) do not apply to evidence offered under subsection (1).

[(4)   To avoid doubt, this section is subject to section 12A.]

History

Subsection (4) was inserted, as from 4 July 2007, by s 6 Evidence Amendment Act 2007 (2007 No 24).

EV27.01   Statements

Section 27(1) applies to all *statements made by a defendant* which are offered by the prosecution in a criminal proceeding.

(1)   Implied assertions

The Act's definition of a "statement" in s 4 does not include what were known at common law as "implied assertions". Thus ss 27-31 are not relevant to the admissibility of, for example, evidence that the defendant acted in a way which demonstrated that he or she had a consciousness of guilt or was aware of a fact which only the offender could know.

(2)   Not limited to proof of contents

Section 4 defines a "hearsay statement" as a "statement that … (b) is offered in evidence … to prove the truth of its contents". However, s 27 applies to all statements by a defendant and not merely to hearsay statements. Accordingly, the Act's controls on the admissibility of evidence offered by the prosecution of statements made by a defendant apply even to statements offered for a purpose other than to prove the truth of their contents. See the discussion of "lies" below.[336]

(3)   Admissible against defendant: mixed statements

Section 27(1) speaks only of admissibility *against* a defendant. This raises an issue concerning "mixed" statements, a term used by earlier authorities to describe a defendant's statement which contains both inculpatory and exculpatory material. The common law accepted that when the prosecution offered evidence of a mixed statement, all of the statement was admissible as evidence of the truth of its contents.[337] The defendant could rely on the exculpatory portions of the mixed statement.

It could be argued that s 27(1) changes the earlier law because it does no more than set out a rule of admissibility *against* the defendant. However, it is inconceivable that the legislature could have intended such a dramatic change in the law. It is suggested that the issue of the admissibility in favour of the defendant of the exculpatory portions of a "mixed" statement will be analysed as a gap in the Act. Section 12 would then require that regard be had to the common law position, outlined above.

(4)   Lies

Because the common law focused on confessions, substantial case law had grown up over the issue whether the common law confessions rule (also referred to as the "voluntariness" rule) applied to *exculpatory* statements made by a defendant. It is not difficult to imagine occasions when the prosecution will want to offer evidence of a defendant's statement that appears to be exculpatory. The prosecution might want to show that the statement was a lie or that it demonstrated the defendant's cavalier attitude upon being confronted with an allegation of wrongdoing. Regardless of the

---

336   See EV27.01(4).
337   See *Adams on Criminal Law — Evidence*, EC4.02.

earlier controversies, it is clear that ss 27-31 apply to statements by the defendant which the prosecution offers for such purposes.

The effect of this new approach may be surprising. See further discussions under ss 28(2) and (3) for the suggestion of difficulties caused by an application of the reliability rule to evidence of a defendant's lie.

EV27.02   Not admissible against a co-defendant

Section 27(1) imposes an important limitation on the use which can be made of evidence offered by the prosecution of a statement made by a defendant. Such evidence is not admissible against a co-defendant. However, see EV27.07.

EV27.03   Co-defendant's testimony

Section 27(1) does not merely prohibit the use against one defendant of prosecution evidence of a hearsay statement made by another defendant. The section prohibits such use of *any* "statement" made by a defendant.

Because of the broad definition of "statement" in s 4, it could be argued that s 27(1) applies to in-court *testimony* by a defendant. However, the legislature could not have intended s 27(1) to mean that the prosecution is prohibited from relying on one defendant's testimony as evidence against a co-defendant. Therefore, s 27(1) must be an example where the opening words of s 4(1) apply and "the context otherwise requires" that, in s 27(1), "statement" refers only to a pre-trial, out-of-court statement by a defendant.

EV27.04   Subsection (2): hurdles for the prosecution

Section 27(2) confirms that despite the general rule of admissibility set out in s 27(1), there are still three substantial hurdles to be overcome when the prosecution offers evidence of a statement made by a defendant. These are what will be referred to as the reliability rule (s 28), the oppression rule (s 29), and the improperly obtained evidence rule (s 30).

EV27.05   Subsection (3): assistance for prosecution

The task set for the prosecution by s 27(2) is counterbalanced by the assistance provided by s 27(3).

Section 27(3) emphasises the central "admissibility" message of s 27(1) by rendering irrelevant three rules which might otherwise have led to the exclusion of prosecution evidence of a defendant's statement, namely the rules governing hearsay, opinion and previous consistent statements.

(1)   Hearsay

Because s 27(3) renders the hearsay provisions irrelevant, s 22 does not apply to prosecution evidence of a defendant's statement. Therefore, there is no requirement that the prosecution give notice of their intention to offer this class of evidence. This result is not likely to be the source of many problems. The lack of a notice requirement rarely caused practical difficulties before the Act came into effect. In view of the extensive pre-trial disclosure obligation already resting on the prosecution, the defence will usually be well aware of the prosecution's intention to offer evidence of the defendant's statement.

Similarly, although the reliability prerequisite to the admissibility of hearsay evidence (s 18(1)(a)) is rendered irrelevant by s 27(3), the "reliability rule" in s 28(2) imposes a more stringent standard for the admissibility of prosecution evidence of a defendant's statement.

(2)   Opinion

By rendering irrelevant the opinion rule, s 27(3) has the effect that no objection can be made to a defendant's statement on the ground that it contains a statement of opinion, whether an expert opinion or not.

(3)   Previous consistent statements

It is difficult to imagine cases in which the prosecution would offer evidence of a defendant's (pre-trial) statement which is consistent with the defendant's testimony (as a witness). In any event, the effect of s 27(3) is that, whenever this rare phenomenon occurs, the prosecution need not be concerned with the potential bar to admissibility provided by s 35(1).

EV27.06   No similar assistance for defendants or co-defendants

Section 27(3) only benefits the prosecution. Therefore, if a defendant offers evidence of his or her own statement or if one defendant offers evidence of a statement made by another defendant, such evidence is subject to the three rules referred to in s 27(3). See too s 21.

Whether or not a statement made by a defendant is a hearsay statement or a previous consistent statement will largely depend on whether, in the circumstances of the particular case, the defendant whose statement is being offered in evidence is a "witness".[338]

EV27.07   Subsection (4): co-defendant's statements

Section 27(4) confirms that s 12A preserves certain common law exceptions to the general rule of inadmissibility set forth in the concluding portion of s 27(1).

EV27.08   Does s 27 preclude the applicability of other provisions?

Section 27(1) provides for the admissibility of prosecution evidence of a defendant's statement. The only qualifications on admissibility that are acknowledged by s 27(1) are those set forth in s 27(1) itself and in s 27(2).

It is unclear whether *other* admissibility rules, not referred to in s 27(1) or (2), can be relied on to qualify s 27(1)'s statement of admissibility. For example, what of the controls in Subpart 5 of Part 2 on veracity evidence and propensity evidence? On the one hand, s 27(1)'s universal statement of admissibility appears to leave no room for the application of such provisions. On the other hand, the drafting of the rules in Subpart 5 appear to assume their own universal application.

---

338   See EV4.20.01, EV4.46.01-03, and EV35.03.

Because the Act offers no express solution to this conflict, little more can be done than offer a prediction which is based on the approach taken by the common law (s 10). It is suggested that, despite s 27(1), a defendant's statement will be inadmissible if it contains evidence which is inadmissible under Subpart 5 of Part 2 of the Act (veracity and propensity). An example would be a defendant's statement to the police in which the defendant admitted numerous offences which were broadly similar to the offence being tried, but the circumstances of the case are such that, under s 43, the prosecution would not otherwise be permitted to offer this form of propensity evidence.

28   Exclusion of unreliable statements

(1)   This section applies to a criminal proceeding in which the prosecution offers or proposes to offer a statement of a defendant if—

   (a)   the defendant [or, if applicable, a co-defendant] against whom the statement is offered raises, on the basis of an evidential foundation, the issue of the reliability of the statement and informs the Judge and the prosecution of the grounds for raising the issue; or

   (b)   the Judge raises the issue of the reliability of the statement and informs the prosecution of the grounds for raising the issue.

(2)   The Judge must exclude the statement unless satisfied on the balance of probabilities that the circumstances in which the statement was made were not likely to have adversely affected its reliability.

(3)   However, subsection (2) does not have effect to exclude a statement made by a defendant if the statement is offered only as evidence of the physical, mental, or psychological condition of the defendant at the time the statement was made or as evidence of whether the statement was made.

(4)   Without limiting the matters that a Judge may take into account for the purpose of applying subsection (2), the Judge must, in each case, take into account any of the following matters that are relevant to the case:

   (a)   any pertinent physical, mental, or psychological condition of the defendant when the statement was made (whether apparent or not):

   (b)   any pertinent characteristics of the defendant including any mental, intellectual, or physical disability to which the defendant is subject (whether apparent or not):

   (c)   the nature of any questions put to the defendant and the manner and circumstances in which they were put:

   (d)   the nature of any threat, promise, or representation made to the defendant or any other person.

History

Subsection (1)(a) was amended, as from 4 July 2007, by s 7 Evidence Amendment Act 2007 (2007 No 24) by inserting "or, if applicable, a co-defendant" after "the defendant".

EV28.01   Reliability rule

Section 28 sets out what will be referred to as the reliability rule. Although the section incorporates much of the ground previously covered by s 20 of the Evidence Act 1908, the law under that earlier section has been substantially altered.

In *R v McCallum*, Asher J said:[339]

> "Reliability is not defined in the Act, but I interpret the word as relating to the accuracy and soundness of the statement, rather than to the fairness of the circumstances that led to it being made."

EV28.02   Subsection (1): raising the issue of reliability

As with the oppression rule (s 29) and the improperly obtained evidence rule (s 30), the prosecution will not be called upon to argue for the admissibility of a defendant's statement under s 28 unless the issue is raised by the defendant or a co-defendant against whom the evidence is offered or by the judge (s 28(1)(a) and (b)).

The words "or, if applicable, a co-defendant" were added to s 28(1)(a) by the same amendment which added s 12A to the Act. A co-defendant will only be able to raise the issue of reliability of another defendant's statement under s 28(1) when the prosecution is offering the statement as evidence against the co-defendant in one of the classes of cases envisioned by s 12A. In all other cases, s 27(1) renders one defendant's statement inadmissible against the co-defendant. See too ss 29(1)(a) and 30(1)(a).

By permitting the judge to raise the issue of the reliability of a defendant's statement, s 28(1)(b) anticipates the case where the defendant has not put reliability in issue but the judge is concerned about the issue. It is possible to imagine circumstances where a defendant (or a co-defendant) decides for tactical reasons not to raise the issue of reliability of his or her statement, but the judge nonetheless does so.

(1)   Evidential foundation

Section 28(1)(a) sets a minimum standard to be met by the defendant (or co-defendant) who seeks to have a statement excluded because of a breach of the reliability rule. He or she must be able to point to an "evidential foundation". Undoubtedly, this must amount to some evidence suggesting that the defendant's statement may be unreliable.

The effect of successfully "raising the issue" of reliability is pivotal. By virtue of s 28(2), the onus of proof then shifts to the prosecution to prove that the Act's test for reliability has been met. A failure to satisfy that onus results in the inadmissibility of the defendant's statement.

EV28.03   Subsection (2): the test of reliability

It is suggested that the test set by s 28(2) should be more difficult for the prosecution to meet than the test that existed under the broadly similar s 20 of the Evidence Act

---

339   *R v McCallum* 29/8/07, Asher J, HC Auckland CRI-2006-004-17181, para 64.

1908. A long line of cases demonstrated the ease with which the prosecution could show, per the earlier provision, that the means by which a confession was obtained "were not in fact likely to cause an untrue admission of guilt to be made". It will be a more onerous task for the prosecution to satisfy the judge that, per s 28(2) of the Act, "the circumstances ... were not likely to have adversely affected" the reliability of the statement. The range of factors set forth in s 28(4) acknowledges the many ways in which reliability may be adversely affected.

However, in *R v Cameron*,[340] Venning J referred to the earlier law governing the reliability of confessions and said:

> "The issue will generally properly be one for the jury. I do not consider that the test under s 28 has made a marked difference to the approach to be taken to reliability. Underlying the exclusion is that the statement is too unreliable to go to a jury. It follows that even though a statement may have certain features of unreliability, it may still be admissible and be a matter for the jury to consider."

EV28.04   Truth of the statement

Although the Select Committee recommended that s 28(2) "be amended to provide that the truth of a statement is not a relevant consideration when determining whether to admit a statement where the issue of its reliability has been raised", no such provision was enacted.[341] All that occurred was the deletion of a controversial clause in the Evidence Bill which would have rendered the defendant's statement admissible if the judge determined that the statement was true.

(1)   Defendant testifies at the voir dire

The final version of s 28 leaves it uncertain whether a judge determining admissibility under the reliability rule can consider evidence about the truth or falsity of the statement. This question is likely to be of particular relevance when the defendant gives evidence at a voir dire which is held to determine the admissibility of the defendant's statement. A much litigated issue before the Act was whether at such a hearing the defendant could be *cross-examined about the truth or falsity of his or her statement*.

The earlier law leaned against any enquiry into the truth or falsity of the defendant's statement.[342] Under the Act, however, a different approach may be possible. The lack of any express prohibition in s 28 on considering the truth or falsity of the statement is contrasted with s 29(3) of the oppression rule, which does contain such a prohibition. The result may be that the truth or falsity of a defendant's statement is treated as a relevant issue in enquiries into reliability under s 28. We may soon see voir dires at which the first question put to the defendant by the prosecution will be whether his or her statement is true. If this development occurs, it will dramatically

---

340   *R v Cameron* 10/8/07, Venning J, HC Gisborne CRI-2006-016-3325, para 33.
341   Cf s 29(3) in the oppression rule. This issue may have suprising effects. See EV30.09(2).
342   *Adams on Criminal Law — Evidence*, EC4.06(4); EC4.07(4).

affect the defendant's decision whether or not to testify on a voir dire which is enquiring into the questions posed by the reliability rule.

(2) The reliability of lies

The discussion of s 27(1) emphasised that this Subpart's controls on the admissibility of a defendant's statement apply to *all* such statements offered by the prosecution. Accordingly, s 28 applies to those statements which are offered by the prosecution for a reason other than proving the truth of their contents.

The classic example of such a reason is a statement offered by the prosecution to show that the defendant had *lied* to the police about some circumstance relating to the offence (see, generally, s 124). Needless to say, there is no possibility in such a case that the prosecution would attempt to satisfy the s 28(2) test for reliability. The whole point of offering the statement in evidence is to show that it is *not* reliable. As it stands, the defendant who wishes to prevent the prosecution offering evidence of a lie told to the police by the defendant should simply raise the issue of reliability and rely upon the inability of the prosecution to satisfy s 28(2).

As discussed below, it may be that s 28(3) will be seized upon as a means of avoiding this anomaly.

(3) Definition of improperly obtained evidence

The reliability rule may have an effect on the definition of "Improperly Obtained Evidence".[343]

EV28.05 Voluntariness

The Act does not refer to the common law concept of voluntariness. The vast body of previous law on that issue is no longer directly relevant.

EV28.06 Subsection (2): burden of proof

Although the common law required the prosecution to prove the voluntariness of a defendant's confession beyond reasonable doubt, s 28(2) requires only that the prosecution satisfy the test for reliability on the balance of probabilities. Compare s 29(2) of the oppression rule.

EV28.07 Person in authority

The common law voluntariness rule was framed in terms of an inducement held out to the defendant by a *person in authority*. Even in cases where the involvement of a person in authority was not required, the common law insisted that any factor alleged to have adversely affected voluntariness must have emanated from someone other than the defendant himself or herself.[344] In this way, circumstances such as tiredness or self induced drunkenness were irrelevant to the determination of voluntariness.

No such qualification exists in Subpart 3 of Part 2 of the Act.[345] It is no longer an express requirement that a person in authority was in some way involved in obtaining

---

343   See EV30.09(2).
344   *Adams on Criminal Law — Evidence*, EC4.03(6); EC4.05(1).
345   Cf s 30(5)(a).

the statement. Further, s 28(4) confirms that it is not necessary that any person other than the defendant himself or herself was responsible for creating the circumstances which may have affected reliability. Tiredness or self-induced drunkenness are now relevant to the enquiry into reliability under s 28(2).

However, in *R v Cameron*, Venning J said:[346]

> "By s 28(4)(d) the Court is directed to consider the nature of any threat, promise or representation made to the accused. In my judgment the threat, promise or representation must be by a person in authority, as is the position at common law."

In *Cameron* the police suspected that the defendant had committed a murder. The police posed as a criminal gang and the defendant told them of the murder in order to impress the supposed gang. On the basis of the earlier cases,[347] Venning J concluded that the defendant did not view the police as persons in authority.

EV28.08   Subsection (3): exception to reliability rule

Section 28(3) creates a two pronged exception to the reliability rule.

(1)   Evidence of defendant's condition

The first limb of the exception covers the case where the prosecution wishes to use the defendant's statement as evidence of his or her "physical, mental, or psychological condition … at the time the statement was made."[348] It is understandable that in such a case there is likely to be no concern over the literal truth of the statement. An example would be where the prosecution was attempting to prove that the defendant was under the influence of an hallucinogenic drug and the defendant's statement purports to describe to the police the appearance of an elephant said by the defendant to be present in the police station interview room.

Nonetheless, there may be difficulties in determining the scope of operation of this limb of s 28(3). What of the case where the prosecution are attempting to prove that the defendant was in a dangerously aggressive rage and the prosecution offers evidence that the defendant told the police "I am so mad that I want to kill anyone I see". The prosecution may assert that they are only offering the evidence to demonstrate the defendant's psychological condition. Yet it is hard to accept that the reliability of this statement is irrelevant.

(2)   Lies

It was suggested in the discussion of s 28(2) that the prosecution could never satisfy the subsection's test for admissibility of a defendant's statement when the prosecution alleges that the statement is a *lie* told by the defendant to the police.

Section 28(3) provides the only potential means of avoiding this difficulty. However, the first limb of s 28(3) is unlikely to assist. The prosecution could perhaps argue that

---

346   *R v Cameron* 10/8/07, Venning J, HC Gisborne CRI-2006-016-3325, para 30.
347   Discussed in *Adams on Criminal Law — Evidence*, EC4.03(6)(e).
348   Section 28(3).

the accused's lie demonstrated his or her consciousness of guilt and that this amounted to the pertinent "mental or psychological condition" referred to in s 28(3). Such an argument appears unduly strained.

The second limb of s 28(3) excludes the operation of the reliability rule if the prosecution offers the defendant's statement "only ... as evidence of whether the statement was made". This may be the means by which the prosecution could successfully offer evidence of the defendant's lie. The prosecution could argue that they are not offering the defendant's statement for the purpose of proving the truth of its contents. They wish only to show that the defendant made the statement, which other evidence demonstrates to be a lie.

The defendant's counter argument would be that the prosecution has a purpose for offering the evidence that goes beyond merely showing that the statement was made. They also wish to show that the statement was untrue. Section 28(3) is expressly limited to those cases where the *only* reason that the prosecution offers evidence of the defendant's statement is for the purpose of showing that the statement was made.

(3) Other rules may exclude lies

Neither s 29, the oppression rule, nor s 30, the improperly obtained evidence rule, contains any provision similar to s 28(3). Accordingly, the defendant will still be able to rely on these two rules to oppose the prosecution's offer of evidence of a statement by the defendant that is said to be a lie. Such evidence will be inadmissible if it was influenced by oppression (s 29(2)) or improperly obtained (s 30) (and excluded by application of s 30's balancing test).

EV28.09   Subsection (4): Assessing reliability

Section 28(4) sets out a list of factors which must be taken into account by a judge in making the determination required by s 28(2), namely whether the prosecution has shown on the balance of probabilities "that the circumstances in which the [defendant's] statement was made were not likely to have adversely affected its reliability". Other factors may be considered, but the listed factors must be taken into account insofar as they are "relevant to the case".

Although it is possible to discover subtle distinctions between s 28(4)(a) and (b), the more important message is that the Act is emphasising the broad range of factors which may "affect" reliability.

(1)   Police fault

The bracketed portions of s 28(4)(a) and (b) mean that in the typical case of a statement obtained by police questioning, it is irrelevant to the assessment of reliability under s 28(2) whether or not the police were aware of the pertinent condition or characteristic of the defendant. The assessment focuses on reliability rather than any fault on the part of the police.

(2)   Range of factors

Although s 28(4)(b) singles out "any mental, intellectual, or physical disability" of the defendant, the Law Commission believed that the additional factors of age, sex, ethnic or national origin, sexual orientation, or health status carried the potential to adversely affect reliability.[349] This merely emphasises the vast potential for argument under the reliability rule.

(3)   Inducements

In referring to promises and threats, s 28(4)(d) hearkens back to the common law voluntariness rule and to s 20 of the Evidence Act 1908. However, in speaking of "representations", s 28(4)(d) casts a wide net and avoids the complications which had developed under the earlier law in determining what amounts to an "inducement", which was the other term employed by s 20 of the 1980 Act.[350]

(4)   Other than the defendant

Another way in which s 28(4)(d) requires the judge to consider a wide range of circumstances is by referring to threats, promises, or representations made to *someone other than the defendant*.

A line of earlier authorities generally accepted that the prosecution had met the test for admitting a defendant's confession set by s 20 of the Evidence Act 1908 even though the defendant admitted guilt in response to a police threat that a spouse or other associate of the defendant would suffer some detrimental consequence.[351] Such consequences could include, for example, being charged with an offence or not being granted bail.

The combination of the specific reference in s 28(4)(d) to persons other than the defendant and the high standard regarding reliability set by s 28(2) may see a change in the way such cases are decided under the Act.

29   Exclusion of statements influenced by oppression

(1)   This section applies to a criminal proceeding in which the prosecution offers or proposes to offer a statement of a defendant if—

    (a)   the defendant [or, if applicable, a co-defendant] against whom the statement is offered raises, on the basis of an evidential foundation, the issue of whether the statement was influenced by oppression and informs the Judge and the prosecution of the grounds for raising the issue; or

    (b)   the Judge raises the issue of whether the statement was influenced by oppression and informs the prosecution of the grounds for raising the issue.

(2)   The Judge must exclude the statement unless satisfied beyond reasonable doubt that the statement was not influenced by oppression.

(3)   For the purpose of applying this section, it is irrelevant whether or not the statement is true.

---

349   LC *Evidence Code*, para C135.
350   Cf *R v Potae* [2000] 3 NZLR 375 (CA).
351   *Adams on Criminal Law — Evidence*, EC2.4.05(6).

(4)   Without limiting the matters that a Judge may take into account for the purpose of applying subsection (2), the Judge must, in each case, take into account any of the following matters that are relevant to the case:

(a)   any pertinent physical, mental, or psychological condition of the defendant when the statement was made (whether apparent or not):

(b)   any pertinent characteristics of the defendant including any mental, intellectual, or physical disability to which the defendant is subject (whether apparent or not):

(c)   the nature of any questions put to the defendant and the manner and circumstances in which they were put:

(d)   the nature of any threat, promise, or representation made to the defendant or any other person.

(5)   In this section, **oppression** means—

(a)   oppressive, violent, inhuman, or degrading conduct towards, or treatment of, the defendant or another person; or

(b)   a threat of conduct or treatment of that kind.

History

Subsection (1)(a) was amended, as from 4 July 2007, by s 8 Evidence Amendment Act 2007 (2007 No 24) by inserting "or, if applicable, a co-defendant" after "the defendant".

EV29.01   The oppression rule

Section 29 draws on the common law in rendering a defendant's statements inadmissible if they were offered by the prosecution and were "influenced by oppression." (s 29(2)).

The section is structurally similar to s 28 and much of the previous discussion of that section will be relevant to s 29.

EV29.02   Subsection (1): raising the issue

As with the reliability rule (s 28) and the improperly obtained evidence rule (s 30), the Crown will not be called upon to argue for the admissibility of a defendant's statement under s 29 unless the issue is raised by the defendant or a co-defendant against whom the evidence is offered or by the judge (s 29(1)(a) and (b)).

The words "or, if applicable, a co-defendant" were added to s 28(1)(a) by the same amendment which added s 12A to the Act. A co-defendant will only be able to raise the issue under s 29(1) and suggest that another defendant's statement was influenced by oppression where the prosecution is offering the statement as evidence against the co-defendant in one of the classes of cases envisioned by s 12A. In all other cases, s 27(1) renders a defendant's statement inadmissible against the co-defendant.

EV29.03   Subsection (2): a high threshold for the prosecution

In the discussion of the test for reliability in s 28(2), the point was made that it imposed a high threshold on the prosecution. The prosecution faces an even higher hurdle under s 29(2) of the oppression rule. In contrast to the lower "balance of probabilities" standard of proof to be met by the prosecution in satisfying the test imposed by the reliability rule, s 29(2) requires the prosecution to satisfy the judge *beyond reasonable doubt* that the defendant's statement was not influenced by oppression.

In attempting to achieve that result, it may often be a difficult task for the prosecution to counter the suggestion that the defendant's statement was *influenced by* oppression. Presumably, this test requires the prosecution to prove that there was no possibility of any causal link between any oppression and the defendant's decision to make a statement. Proving a negative is always difficult and this is particularly so in an area such as causation. It is predicted that, once a judge determines that oppression was present, it will be rare that a finding of a breach of the oppression rule does not quickly follow.

EV29.04   Oppression

The likely approach of prosecution arguments in disputes under s 29(2) will be to deny the presence of any oppression, as defined in s 29(5). However, there are no certain boundaries at to what conduct towards the defendant (or another person) will amount to oppression, particularly in view of s 29(4), discussed below. Added to this is the fact that the beyond reasonable doubt standard imposed by s 29(2) will mean that any doubt as to the existence of oppression must be resolved in the defendant's favour.

EV29.05   Subsection (3): Irrelevance of the truth of the statement

The problems facing prosecution attempts to satisfy the test imposed by s 29(2) are compounded by s 29(3). This provision makes it clear that in an enquiry under s 29(2), it is irrelevant whether the defendant's statement is true. The result is that a judge will have to exclude a defendant's statement under s 29(2) even though the judge is certain that the statement is true.

In contrast to the uncertainty expressed in the discussion of the reliability rule, a defendant who invokes the oppression rule need not be concerned that the Act may have opened the door to a new focus for cross-examination by the prosecution on a voir dire held to determine the admissibility of the defendant's statement. Section 29(3) means that the defendant cannot be asked in cross-examination whether or not the statement in question was true.

EV29.06   Lack of exceptions

Section 29 contains no provision corresponding to s 28(3), discussed above. Accordingly, a defendant can rely on the oppression rule to oppose prosecution evidence of a statement by the defendant even when the prosecution relies on the statement for the limited purposes set forth in s 28(3). The message from Parliament is that the prosecution can obtain no benefit at all from a defendant's statement that may have been influenced by oppression.

EV29.07   Assessing the influence of oppression

Both s 29(5), which contains a definition of oppression, and s 29(4), which sets out factors to consider in the enquiry, must be considered in tandem when making the determination required by s 29(2).

EV29.08   Need for an oppressor

Section 29(5) defines oppression in terms of "conduct towards" or "treatment of" the defendant or another person (or a threat of such conduct or treatment). This must mean that oppression requires the involvement of someone other than the defendant. This contrasts with the position under the reliability rule.[352]

EV29.09   Subsection (4): no fault required

Section 29 contains no suggestion that a finding of oppression is only possible when the person who engages in the oppressive conduct or treatment is a "person in authority" as defined by the common law. More important is the message which is implicit in the bracketed portions of s 29(4)(a) and (b). The "oppressor" need not be acting with any particular state of mind. He or she may be completely unaware that his or her interaction with the defendant could be characterised as oppressive.

(1)   Defendant's perspective

The effect of s 29(4)(a) and (b) is that oppression is to be judged solely from the perspective of the defendant. Conduct or treatment by the oppressor which could in no way be characterised as "oppressive, violent, inhuman, or degrading" (s 29(5)) if directed at a normal, reasonable person, may yet be so due to some unperceivable, idiosyncratic quality of the defendant. This emphasises the difficult task facing the prosecution in satisfying the test set by s 29(2).

EV29.10   Subsection (5): conduct or treatment of some person other than the defendant

As with s 28(4)(d) of the reliability rule, the judge considering the oppression rule must, under s 29(4)(d), take into account *representations* etc, made to any person. However, the oppression rule takes matters further. This is because s 29(5) makes it clear that oppression may result from a broad range of *conduct or treatment* (or a threat of such) of persons other than the defendant. Once again, this emphasises the breadth of the enquiry under s 29(2). Some remarkable, irrational sensitivity of the defendant may lead him or her to view as oppressive some representation, conduct or treatment directed at a third party and this belief may influence the defendant's decision to make a statement. Section 29(2) requires that any doubt on this issue must result in the statement being ruled inadmissible.

---

352   See EV28.07 (above).

30   Improperly obtained evidence

(1)   This section applies to a criminal proceeding in which the prosecution offers or proposes to offer evidence if—

   (a)   the defendant [or, if applicable, a co-defendant] against whom the evidence is offered raises, on the basis of an evidential foundation, the issue of whether the evidence was improperly obtained and informs the prosecution of the grounds for raising the issue; or

   (b)   the Judge raises the issue of whether the evidence was improperly obtained and informs the prosecution of the grounds for raising the issue.

(2)   The Judge must—

   (a)   find, on the balance of probabilities, whether or not the evidence was improperly obtained; and

   (b)   if the Judge finds that the evidence has been improperly obtained, determine whether or not the exclusion of the evidence is proportionate to the impropriety by means of a balancing process that gives appropriate weight to the impropriety but also takes proper account of the need for an effective and credible system of justice.

(3)   For the purposes of subsection (2), the court may, among any other matters, have regard to the following:

   (a)   the importance of any right breached by the impropriety and the seriousness of the intrusion on it:

   (b)   the nature of the impropriety, in particular, whether it was deliberate, reckless, or done in bad faith:

   (c)   the nature and quality of the improperly obtained evidence:

   (d)   the seriousness of the offence with which the defendant is charged:

   (e)   whether there were any other investigatory techniques not involving any breach of the rights that were known to be available but were not used:

   (f)   whether there are alternative remedies to exclusion of the evidence which can adequately provide redress to the defendant:

   (g)   whether the impropriety was necessary to avoid apprehended physical danger to the police or others:

   (h)   whether there was any urgency in obtaining the improperly obtained evidence.

(4)   The Judge must exclude any improperly obtained evidence if, in accordance with subsection (2), the Judge determines that its exclusion is proportionate to the impropriety.

(5)   For the purposes of this section, evidence is **improperly obtained** if it is obtained—

(a)   in consequence of a breach of any enactment or rule of law by a person to whom section 3 of the New Zealand Bill of Rights Act 1990 applies; or

(b)   in consequence of a statement made by a defendant that is or would be inadmissible if it were offered in evidence by the prosecution; or

(c)   unfairly.

(6)   Without limiting subsection (5)(c), in deciding whether a statement obtained by a member of the police has been obtained unfairly for the purposes of that provision, the Judge must take into account guidelines set out in practice notes on that subject issued by the Chief Justice.

History

Subsection (1)(a) was amended, as from 4 July 2007, by s 9 Evidence Amendment Act 2007 (2007 No 24) by inserting "or, if applicable, a co-defendant" after "the defendant".

EV30.01   Improperly obtained evidence

Section 30 brings into a single section a vast area of earlier law governing the admissibility of improperly obtained evidence in criminal cases. Previously, separate lines of authority dealt with unfairly obtained confessions, evidence obtained through a breach of the Bill of Rights, and evidence obtained through a breach of some other statutory provision or common law doctrine. Now, argument in all such cases will focus on s 30.

EV30.02   Civil proceedings

Section 30 applies only to criminal proceedings. The Act does not specifically control the admissibility of improperly obtained evidence in civil proceedings other than to the limited extent provided for by s 53(4) and potentially s 90.[353]

EV30.03   Offered by the prosecution

Another important limitation on the scope of s 30 is that it only applies to evidence offered by the prosecution. Other than the potential application of ss 53(4) and 90(1), the Act contains no obvious controls on admissibility of improperly obtained evidence that is offered by a defendant or a co-defendant. Such evidence is potentially admissible, as is recognised by s 31. Arguments that improperly obtained evidence offered by a defendant or co-defendant should be inadmissible would likely concentrate on ss 10 and 12 of the Act and common law precedents.[354]

EV30.04   Subsection (1): raising the issue

As with ss 28(1)(a) and 29(1)(a), the words "or, if applicable, a co-defendant" were added to s 30(1)(a) by the same amendment which added s 12A to the Act. However, s 30 deals with all types of evidence and is not restricted to statements by a defendant.

---

353   See EV53.05 and EV90.04(4).
354   See *Adams on Criminal Law — Evidence*, EC10.04(12); EC3.13(3).

When the evidence in question is a statement by a defendant, s 30(1)(a) operates in the same way as ss 28(1)(a) and 29(1)(a). A co-defendant will only be able to raise the issue under s 30(1) of whether the statement was improperly obtained when the prosecution is offering the statement as evidence against the co-defendant in one of the classes of cases envisioned by s 12A. In all other cases, s 27(1) renders a defendant's statement inadmissible against the co-defendant.

The same position does not apply when the enquiry under s 30 involves evidence that is not a defendant's *statement*. Insofar as all classes of evidence other than a defendant's statement, s 30(1)(a) means that any defendant can raise the issue that the evidence was improperly obtained in any case when the prosecution offers the evidence against that defendant. This has brought about an important change to the earlier law of standing, as now discussed.

EV30.05   Standing

Section 30 appears to bring about a change in the law relating to the standing of a defendant to apply for exclusion of evidence that was obtained through a breach of someone else's rights. There are many circumstances which give rise to this issue but it is typically raised in cases involving an unreasonable search, which is in breach of s 21 of the New Zealand Bill of Rights Act 1990.

(1)   Examples: unreasonable search

Before *R v Williams*,[355] the prosecution would have been able to successfully argue that the defendant had no *standing* to apply for exclusion of evidence in a case where the defendant was charged with drug offending and the prosecution offered evidence of drugs found in an unreasonable search of premises where the defendant was a mere visitor or in an unreasonable search of an automobile in which the defendant was a gratuitous passenger. The usual judicial response before *Williams* was that the defendant's lack of a reasonable expectation of privacy in those circumstances meant that he or she had no standing to argue for exclusion of the evidence found in the unreasonable search. The defendant's lack of standing meant that the evidence remained admissible to prove the defendants guilt, despite the improper way in which the evidence was obtained.

(2)   Not restricted to breach of own right

The law was reviewed in *R v Williams*.[356] The Court confirmed the general proposition that breaches of other peoples' rights under the New Zealand Bill of Rights Act 1990 cannot be relied upon by third parties to claim the personal remedy of exclusion of evidence.[357] However, the Court also held that in search and seizure cases, a broad range of people could raise the issue of a breach of s 21 of the Bill of Rights (protection against unreasonable search and seizure) on the basis that they had a reasonable expectation of privacy in the area searched. Such people would include everyone actually present at a search of private property, with the likely exception of pure

---

355   *R v Williams* (2007) 23 CRNZ 1 (CA).
356   *R v Williams* (2007) 23 CRNZ 1 (CA), paras 47-78 and 235-240.
357   *R v Williams* (2007) 23 CRNZ 1 (CA), para 235.

trespassers on a property for unlawful purposes, such as burglars. For those not present during a search, any type of licence to occupy the premises searched and any type of proprietary or possessory interest in the property searched or seized would give a sufficient expectation of privacy to satisfy the requirement of standing.

(3) Position under s 30

Although *Williams* liberalised the law governing standing, at least in search and seizure cases, s 30 has gone even further. Section 30(1) contains no requirement that the defendant can only apply for an exclusion on the basis of a breach of his or her *own* right. The section applies whenever improperly obtained evidence is offered against the defendant who asks for its exclusion.

(a) *Parliament's intention*

It is conceivable that the drafters of s 30 never actually had any of this in their collective mind. Such indications as there are in s 30 suggest that the legislature only anticipated a defendant applying for exclusion of evidence obtained through a breach of his or her rights, or at least the rights of another defendant in the proceeding. Thus, in s 30(3) (the non-exhaustive list of factors to be considered by the judge in the balancing process which determines admissibility) para (f) asks whether there are remedies other than that of exclusion which will adequately "provide redress to the defendant". It is difficult to imagine that the legislature was contemplating the possibility of any form of "redress" for a defendant, alternative to exclusion of evidence or not, that could be based on a breach of someone else's rights. A similar indication occurs in the definition of improperly obtained evidence in s 30(5). Section 30(5)(b) refers only to an inadmissible statement made by "a defendant", as opposed a statement made by anyone at all.

Despite these indications, it appears that we must accept the bold proposition set out in s 30(1) that a defendant has standing to apply for exclusion regardless of whose rights were breached in obtaining the evidence now offered against the defendant. The change to the previous law brought about by this aspect of s 30 will be substantial because it will apply to all forms of improperly obtained evidence that are governed by s 30 (see s 30(5)). It will also apply to all ways in which the prosecution may "offer evidence", including eliciting evidence through examination of a witness whose rights have been breached (in this way the Act should change the result reached in *R v King*).[358]

(b) *Standing does not determine admissibility*

The s 30 abolition of the former requirement of standing does no more than give the defendant the right to make the application for exclusion of the tainted evidence. It by no means settles the dispute over admissibility. A defendant will argue for exclusion from a far stronger foundation if he or she is asking for vindication of his or her own rights rather than those of someone else. In this way, standing can be viewed as a matter of degree and itself become a factor in the balancing process that

---

358   *R v King* 15/12/03, CA227/03 (discussed in *Adams on Criminal Law — Evidence*, EC3.10(1)).

s 30 sets out as the means of determining the admissibility of improperly obtained evidence. This is confirmed in *R v Williams*.[359]

EV30.06   Subsection (2): Burden of proof

Once the issue is raised under s 30(1), the judge must then determine whether or not the evidence was improperly obtained.[360]

Section 30(2)(a) does not specify the party who bears the burden of proof on the issue of whether the evidence in question was improperly obtained. However, the *standard* of proof is the "balance of probabilities".[361]

(1)   Probabilities in equilibrium

The balance of probabilities standard is well known in civil litigation. One of the most important functions of the burden of proof in that context is determining which of the parties wins if, at the end of the case, the judge determines that the probabilities are in equilibrium. In such a case, the party who bore the burden of proof will lose because that party has not tipped the *balance* of probabilities in his or her favour.

Section 30(2)(a) does not permit the judge to let matters rest at a point of equilibrium. The judge *must* determine that the balance of probabilities does or does not weigh in favour of a finding that the evidence was improperly obtained.

EV30.07   Definition of improperly obtained evidence

Section 30(5) contains an exhaustive definition of improperly obtained evidence.

(1)   Causation

Section 30(5)(a) and (b) defines improperly obtained evidence as evidence obtained "in consequence" of stated forms of impropriety. The effect of this is to require a causative link between the impropriety and the obtaining of the evidence. The same message must likewise apply to s 30(5)(c). Even though that provision does not state "in consequence of unfairness", the terminology used of "unfairly obtained" evidence must necessarily involve a causative link between the unfairness and the obtaining of the evidence.

Before the Act, controversy over the difficult topic of a causative link between an impropriety and the obtaining of evidence arose most commonly in Bill of Rights litigation, although there are numerous authorities on causation in confession cases that involved improprieties other than breaches of the Bill of Rights. The Act makes no attempt to alter that earlier law and it should be referred to when issues of causation are raised under s 30(5).[362] See in particular the discussion in *R v Williams*.[363] In that case, the Court of Appeal held that the relative strength of the causative link may itself be a factor to be weighed in the balancing process which determines admissibility.

---

359   *R v Williams* (2007) 23 CRNZ 1 (CA), para 74.

360   Section 30(2)(a).

361   See, generally, *Adams on Criminal Law — Evidence*, EC2.03(5).

362   See *Adams on Criminal Law — Evidence*, EC4.03(3); *Adams on Criminal Law*, Ch10.24.03(5).

363   *R v Williams* (2007) 23 CRNZ 1 (CA), paras 79-103 and 241-244.

EV30.08   Subsection (5)(a): breaches of law

Section 30(5)(a) defines improperly obtained evidence in terms of a "breach of any enactment or rule of law …". By s 29 of the Interpretation Act 1999, "enactment" includes "regulation". However, there may still be some uncertainty as to what is encompassed in a breach of a "rule of law". It appears safe to assume that the legislative intent was that the phrase referred to breaches of *common law doctrines*. An obvious example is a search of property conducted by trespassing police officers. Incriminating evidence discovered in the course of that search appears to fit the definition in s 30(5)(a) of evidence obtained in consequence of a breach of a rule of law.

(1)   Which common law breaches?

But which common law "rules of law" are still relevant after the Act has come into force? It can hardly be argued that the common law "voluntariness" rule, which governed the earlier law of confessions, has survived the enactment of ss 28-30 of the Act. Accordingly, it would be impossible to argue that a confession obtained in breach of the voluntariness rule amounts to improperly obtained evidence for the purposes of s 30(5)(a). Other examples may not be as clear. The way in which courts answer the question of which common law doctrines are within the scope of s 30(5)(a) will also provide guidance on ss 10 and 12 of the Act.[364]

(2)   Unreasonable search

It is possible that s 30(5)(a) may render irrelevant much of the earlier law interpreting s 21 of the Bill of Rights Act. This section protects against unreasonable search and seizure.

Before the Act, s 21 of the Bill of Rights Act was the focus for most arguments over the admissibility of evidence discovered in a search by police. The Court of Appeal had made it clear that the mere fact that a search was conducted in breach of an enactment or in breach of a rule of law (such as the law of trespass, alluded to in the example discussed above) did not necessarily mean that the search was unreasonable and in breach of s 21 of the Bill of Rights. A variety of circumstances could lead a court to conclude that the search was still reasonable. When a court determined that a search, although illegal, was not unreasonable, this usually ended any argument that evidence obtained through such a search should be ruled inadmissible.

Such an approach should no longer be viable under s 30(5)(a). Once it is determined that a search by the police was conducted in breach of an enactment or a rule of law, s 30(5) dictates the conclusion that the evidence obtained in consequence of the search was improperly obtained. Pursuant to s 30(2)(b), a finding that the evidence was improperly obtained triggers the balancing process which determines admissibility. Unlike the position before the Act, s 30(2)(b) does not expressly impose a requirement to pass on to the further question whether the illegality rendered the search unreasonable and in breach of s 21 of the Bill of Rights.

---

364   See also EV30.10.

However, see the discussion below of *R v Williams*.[365]

(3)   Section 198(1) of the Summary Proceedings Act 1957: search warrants

The most important application of the above analysis occurs in relation to s 198(1) of the Summary Proceedings Act 1957. This section governs the issuance of search warrants. It requires that the evidence in support of an application for a search warrant must disclose reasonable grounds for believing that evidence of an offence exists on the property to be searched.

Prior to the Act, a controversy had developed about the admissibility of evidence discovered in a search conducted pursuant to a warrant that is subsequently determined to have been "illegally" issued because the standard set by s 198(1) of the Summary Proceedings Act had not actually been met. Some Court of Appeal judgments concluded that such a search could still be reasonable in terms of s 21 of the Bill of Rights Act.[366]

Section 30(5)(a) of the Act should require the conclusion that evidence has been improperly obtained if it was discovered in a search conducted pursuant to a warrant that was issued in breach of the standard set by s 198(1) of the Summary Proceedings Act. In such a case, the balancing process to determine admissibility pursuant to s 30(2)(b) of the Act should be mandatory. There can be no justification for cases decided under s 30 of the Act to adopt the approach taken by the Court of Appeal in the earlier authorities to which reference was just made. The breach of s 198(1) of the Summary Proceedings Act means that the evidence was improperly obtained, with the effect that s 30(2)(b)'s admissibility enquiry is triggered. There is no need to also determine if the search was unreasonable under s 21 of the Bill of Rights.

However, the effect of *R v Williams*,[367] now discussed, may yet make such an enquiry desirable in most cases.

(4)   Effect of *R v Williams*

In *Williams* the Court reviewed the law as summarised above and concluded that "an unlawful search will normally be an unreasonable search".[368] The effect will be to minimise the dichotomy discussed above. The Court in *Williams* also discussed the Evidence Act 2006 and pointed out that when considering s 30(3)(a) (the importance of the right that has been breached) exclusion of evidence will be the more likely result when a breach of the New Zealand Bill of Rights Act 1990 has occurred, as opposed to a breach of some other right.[369] Thus, even in search and seizure cases, it will continue to be important to determine if an illegal search amounts to an unreasonable search, in breach of s 21 of the Bill of Rights.

---

365   *R v Williams* (2007) 23 CRNZ 1 (CA), discussed at EV30.08(4).
366   See *Adams on Criminal Law*, Ch10.8.13(3).
367   *R v Williams* (2007) 23 CRNZ 1 (CA).
368   *R v Williams* (2007) 23 CRNZ 1 (CA), para 16.
369   *R v Williams* (2007) 23 CRNZ 1 (CA), para 150.

(5) Limited class of persons whose improprieties are relevant

Not all evidence obtained in consequence of a breach of law will be "improperly obtained" so as to trigger the balancing process under s 30(2)(b). Section 30(5)(a) limits the relevant breaches of law to those committed by "a person to whom s 3 of the New Zealand Bill of Rights Act 1990 applies". Because of the "evidence gathering" focus of s 30 of the Act, s 3(b) of the Bill of Rights will be the subsection most commonly turned to in this context ("acts done … by any person … in the performance of any public function, power, or duty conferred … by … law.").

Police officers are the most obvious class of persons whose breaches of law will give rise to improperly obtained evidence. Consideration of the existing law on s 3(b) of the Bill of Rights will provide guidance on the additional classes of persons who come within s 30(5)(a). A person performing a "citizen's arrest" is not likely to be included.[370]

In a case where a person who does not come within the class of persons referred to in s 30(5)(a) obtains evidence in consequence of a breach of the law, the evidence is not "improperly obtained" unless the circumstances are such as to bring into play s 30(5)(b) or (c). Consider a case where a person not coming within s 3 of the Bill of Rights, such as a neighbour of the defendant, unlawfully detains the defendant and searches the defendant's jacket. When checking the jacket's pockets, the neighbour discovers illicit drugs, which he or she turns over to the police. Although s 30(5)(a) does not apply, the amorphous concept of unfairness, enshrined in s 30(5)(c), may result in this evidence being classified as improperly obtained.

EV30.09 Subsection (5)(b): in consequence of a statement

Section 30(5)(b) focuses on the common circumstance where a suspected offender makes a statement to the police and that statement refers to other incriminating evidence such as a weapon ("real evidence"). The subsection ensures that if the pivotal statement is inadmissible, the real evidence comes within the definition of improperly obtained evidence. This is because the real evidence has been obtained "in consequence" of the statement. Guidance on the causative link required by s 30(5)(b) may be assisted by the general discussion in *R v Williams*.[371]

Section 30(5)(b) anticipates the case where, for one reason or another, the prosecution decides not to offer in evidence the statement by the defendant which refers to an item of real evidence. Where the prosecution attempts to offer the real evidence which was obtained in consequence of the statement, the issue whether that real evidence is improperly obtained will turn on the judge's decision whether the initial statement was inadmissible. If it was, then the real evidence comes within the definition of improperly obtained evidence and its admissibility is determined by the balancing process set by s 30(2)(b). It is inconsequential that the prosecution made no actual attempt to offer the statement in evidence.

---

370   Discussed in *Adams on Criminal Law*, Ch10.3.07. Contrast the s 4 definition of "investigative questioning", which is applicable to s 28.

371   *R v Williams* (2007) 23 CRNZ 1 (CA).

(1)   Multiple reasons why a statement may be inadmissible

The most common reason why a defendant's statement would be inadmissible is because of the operation of ss 28-30. However, s 30(5)(b) contains no restriction on the reasons for the inadmissibility of the statement.

Section 27(3) has the result that three of the most obvious reasons why a defendant's statement might have been inadmissible (hearsay, opinion, previous consistent statement) will not be permitted to stand in the way of the statement's admissibility. However, the earlier discussion of s 27(3) also suggested that there may well be *other* reasons why a defendant's statement could be inadmissible, such as a breach of the provisions governing propensity evidence.[372] The surprising result is that, in such a case, s 30(5)(b) would classify as "improperly obtained evidence", real evidence that had been obtained in consequence of a defendant's statement that was inadmissible because of a breach of the controls on propensity evidence. This hardly seems an appropriate label when there was no impropriety involved in the *obtaining* of the evidence.

This anomaly could be reflected in the balancing process conducted under s 30(2)(b) to determine the admissibility of real evidence. The fact that there was *no* impropriety committed would inevitably lead to the conclusion of admissibility.

(2)   Circularity: the reliability rule

At common law there were divergent lines of authority governing an issue which occasionally arose when a confession was initially held to be inadmissible because it had been obtained through an inducement offered by the police. If that confession referred to real evidence which was then located by the police, this process *confirmed the accuracy of the confession*. The question that was litigated was, could this proof of the confession's reliability render the confession suddenly admissible, despite the impropriety which had occurred? The Privy Council answered "no" to this question, relying on the fact that the common law rule governing the admissibility of confessions was aimed at promoting additional policies beyond that of reliability (eg control of police practices).[373]

An awareness of that earlier controversy raises an issue regarding the effect of the reliability rule (s 28) in the context of s 30(5)(b).

Consider a case in which, per s 28(2), the judge concludes that the circumstances in which the defendant's statement was made were likely to have adversely affected its reliability. This conclusion would appear to render the statement inadmissible. However, what if the statement refers to real evidence, such as the location of hidden drugs and, in reliance on the statement, the police find the drugs and thereby confirm the statement's reliability?

---

372   See EV27.08.
373   *Lam Chi-ming v R* [1991] 2 AC 212; [1991] 2 All ER 172 (PC). See *Adams on Criminal Law —
       Evidence*, EC4.09(2).

How does this affect the issue of the statement's admissibility under s 28(2)? Wrapped up in that question is a second question regarding the drugs. Were they "improperly obtained" pursuant to s 30(5)(b)? The drugs will only be improperly obtained if the statement is inadmissible. However, the question of the statement's admissibility may be affected by the evidence of the finding of the drugs.

The solution to this problem may be determined by the extent to which a judge who is applying the reliability rule is permitted to consider the actual truth or falsity of the defendant's statement. The earlier discussion of s 28(2) suggested that the Act gives no clear guidance on this issue.[374] However, it is suggested that the proper approach to be taken in the example under discussion is for the judge to focus solely on the test for admissibility established by s 28(2). In a case where the prosecution cannot satisfy the judge that the circumstances in which the statement was made were not likely to have adversely affected its reliability, the statement should remain inadmissible. This decision should not be altered by the finding of the drugs, because the enquiry under s 28(2) is not an enquiry into actual truth or falsity. The result is that the evidence of the finding of the drugs was improperly obtained, pursuant to s 30(5)(b).

EV30.10   Subsection (5)(c): unfairly obtained

It is difficult to overestimate the importance of s 30(5)(c), which makes evidence improperly obtained if it was obtained *unfairly*. By this means, the Act has incorporated a vast area of the common law governing all classes of evidence in criminal proceedings.

Before the Act, New Zealand judges refused to be limited in the scope of circumstances which could be characterised as unfair. Likewise, they jealously guarded their discretion to exclude prosecution evidence on the ground of unfairness. Although that discretion has now been altered and codified in s 30, there is no reason to believe that the Act will result in a narrowing of circumstances which hold the potential of unfairness.[375] The former law interpreting "unfairly obtained" was applied to s 30(5)(c) in *R v Petricevich*.[376]

Section 30(5)(c) will likely be interpreted in a way that will fill in gaps which appear to exist in the other provisions of this Subpart of the Act. As stated by the Law Commission, a judge could decide that a defendant's statement had been obtained unfairly even though the prosecution could satisfy the tests for admissibility under s 28 (the reliability rule) or s 29 (the oppression rule).[377] Likewise, as discussed under s 30(5)(a), evidence (whether a statement or not) could be characterised as having been unfairly obtained if it was obtained by a breach of law committed by someone *other than* a member of the class of persons referred to in s 30(5)(a).[378]

---

374   See EV28.04.
375   See *Adams on Criminal Law — Evidence*, EC4.06. See also *R v Williams* (2007) 23 CRNZ 1 (CA), paras 77 and 150.
376   *R v Petricevich* 6/8/07, CA236/07; [2007] NZCA 325. See, similarly, *R v Hall* 11/9/07, CA242/07; [2007] NZCA 405.
377   LC *Evidence Code*, para C144.
378   See EV30.08(5).

(1)   Police questioning practices

Before the Act, the Judges' Rules provided a prime focus for arguments that a defendant's statement had been obtained unfairly.

A new version of the Judges' Rules has now been incorporated into the Practice Note on Police Questioning, issued by the Chief Justice under s 30(6) of the Act. Section 30(6) requires judges to take into account the guidelines set out in the Practice Note when deciding whether a statement obtained by a member of the police has been unfairly obtained.

The Practice Note purports to govern only the police. However, when a judge is considering the fairness of "investigative questioning" (defined in s 4) by someone other than a police officer, the Practice Note may serve as a source of general guidance.

(a)   *Practice Note*

The following Practice Note was issued by the Chief Justice on 16 July 2007:

"Practice Note on Police Questioning

"(s 30(6) Evidence Act 2006)

"The courts will continue to apply judicially-developed guidelines for police questioning. The former Judges' Rules are (with some developments) restated here for the purposes of s 30(6) of the Evidence Act 2006. The obligation to advise that legal advice may be available without charge under the Police Detention Legal Assistance Scheme is new. As well the advice requirements under s 23 of the New Zealand Bill of Rights Act 1990 are brought into the required caution. Giving such advice prior to a suspect being arrested or detained does not obviate the necessity to repeat the advice upon arrest or detention. The practice note also favours the use of video recording of statements. In other aspects, the practice note is not intended to change existing case law on application of the Judges' Rules in New Zealand and does not preclude further judicial development. The guidelines in this practice note supplement enactments relevant to police questioning and must be read consistently with those enactments. In particular they do not affect the rights and obligations under the New Zealand Bill of Rights Act 1990. The practice note takes effect on the commencement of section 30 of the Evidence Act 2006.

"1.   A member of the police investigating an offence may ask questions of any person from whom it is thought that useful information may be obtained, whether or not that person is a suspect, but must not suggest that it is compulsory for the person questioned to answer.

"2.   Whenever a member of the police has sufficient evidence to charge a person with an offence or whenever a member of the police seeks to question a person in custody, the person must be cautioned before being invited to make a statement or answer questions. The caution to be given is:

"(a)   that the person has the right to refrain from making any statement and to remain silent

"(b)   that the person has the right to consult and instruct a lawyer without delay and in private before deciding whether to answer questions and that such right may be exercised without charge under the Police Detention Legal Assistance Scheme.

"(c)   that anything said by the person will be recorded and may be given in evidence.

"3.   Questions of a person in custody or in respect of whom there is sufficient evidence to lay a charge must not amount to cross-examination.

"4.   Whenever a person is questioned about statements made by others or about other evidence, the substance of the statements or the nature of the evidence must be fairly explained.

"5.   Any statement made by a person in custody or in respect of whom there is sufficient evidence to charge should preferably be recorded by video recording unless that is impractical or unless the person declines to be recorded by video. Where the statement is not recorded by video, it must be recorded permanently on audio tape or in writing. The person making the statement must be given an opportunity to review the tape or written statement or to have the written statement read over, and must be given an opportunity to correct any errors or add anything further. Where the statement is recorded in writing, the person must be asked if he or she wishes to confirm the written record as correct by signing it."

(b)   *Judges' Rules*

It appears clear from the introductory passage to the Practice Note that much of the extensive jurisprudence under the old Judges' Rules will be of continued relevance under the Act.[379]

There are many ways in which the Practice Note *increases* the protections which are granted by the Judges' Rules. In particular:

- As stated in the Introduction to the Practice Note, the advice requirements under s 23 of the New Zealand Bill of Rights Act 1990 have been incorporated into the caution required by the Judges' Rules;

- Practice Note No 1 adds to Judges' Rule No 1 the express prohibition on any suggestion by the police that the person questioned must answer questions;

- Practice Note No 2 clarifies Judges' Rule No 2 by requiring the new, extended caution "whenever a member of the police has sufficient evidence to charge a person with an offence …".[380]

---

379   For a full discussion of the Judges' Rules, see *Adams on Criminal Law — Evidence*, EC5.
380   See *Adams on Criminal Law — Evidence*, EC5.03(1).

- Practice Note No 3 is more strict than the judicial interpretations of Judges' Rules Nos 3 or 7. The earlier law was that questioning of persons in custody would only be classified as unfair if the cross-examination was excessive or oppressive.[381] Practice Note No 3 prohibits *any* cross-examination. Additionally, it applies to questioning of persons in custody or "in respect of whom there is sufficient evidence to lay a charge".

- Practice Note No 5 avoids many of the controversies which had arisen with respect to Judges' Rule No 9.[382] The preference for video recording enshrines a long held judicial view.[383]

(c)   *New Zealand Bill of Rights Act 1990*

The Practice Note supplements the protections granted by the Bill of Rights in two ways:

- By requiring the advice requirements under s 23 of the Bill of Rights Act to be given before a suspect is arrested or detained; and

- By requiring the police to include a reference to the Police Detention Legal Assistance Scheme when initially giving suspects s 23 advice. There is no doubt that the Practice Note has changed the earlier law, effectively reversing *R v Alo*.[384]

(d)   *Additional protection*

Practice Note No 4 sets down a positive obligation that was not clear under the earlier law. Some cases had held that it was unfair for the police to intentionally mislead a suspect as to the strength of the evidence against him or her.[385] However, Practice Note No 4 imposes a positive obligation on the police to fairly explain the substance of statements or the nature of the evidence when these matters are the subject of questions posed by the police.

(e)   *Guide for fairness*

A breach of the Practice Note will not inevitably result in the inadmissibility of a statement obtained by the police. Section 30(6) makes it clear that the breach must be taken into account by the judge, but a finding of unfairness is not mandatory. This is similar to the approach previously taken to a breach of the Judges' Rules.[386]

Additionally, even when it is determined that a statement has been obtained unfairly, this only means that the statement has been "improperly obtained" (s 30(5)(c)). The balancing process required by s 30(2)(b) must still be undertaken to determine admissibility.

---

381   See *Adams on Criminal Law — Evidence*, EC5.04 and EC5.08.
382   See *Adams on Criminal Law — Evidence*, EC5.10.
383   See *Adams on Criminal Law — Evidence*, EC5.15.
384   *R v Alo* 3/5/07, CA155/06; [2007] NZCA 172. See *R v Tye* 3/8/07, CA86/07; [2007] NZCA 330.
385   See *Adams on Criminal Law — Evidence*, EC4.06(8).
386   See *Adams on Criminal Law — Evidence*, EC5.12.

EV30.11 The balancing process

Section 30(2)(b) requires the judge to engage in a balancing process to determine the admissibility of evidence offered by the prosecution which the judge has determined to have been improperly obtained. Section 30(3) provides further guidance on the factors which may be considered in the balancing process.

There is no doubt that the balancing process is closely modelled on *R v Shaheed*.[387] A useful summary of *Shaheed*'s balancing process can be found in *R v Williams*.[388] *Williams* involved a breach of s 21 of the Bill of Rights (unreasonable search and seizure) and this must be kept in mind when reading the following summary, which often refers to privacy interests — a factor not necessarily relevant in cases involving, for example, improperly obtained confessions. In *Williams* the Court said:[389]

> "The first step in the *Shaheed* balancing test is to assess the magnitude of the breach ...

> "Having assessed the seriousness of the breach, the next stage is to balance the breach against the public interest factors pointing away from the exclusion of the evidence. These factors are considered in combination and not in isolation ...

> "They are:

> "(a)   The seriousness of the crime. A crime is considered serious if the starting point of any sentence is likely to be in the vicinity of 4 years or more or where there are elements of a threat to public safety involved, such as the carrying of a loaded weapon in public. The more serious the crime the more weight this factor is accorded. Crimes involving a serious incursion into the personal bodily integrity of the victim, particularly where there is a significant risk of there being further victims, are regarded as particularly serious ...

> "(b)   The nature and quality of the evidence. The more probative, reliable and crucial the evidence is, the more likely it is that the public interest in the conviction of criminals might outweigh the breach of rights. Conversely, where there is a significant issue of unreliability because of the breach, the balancing test would come down in favour of exclusion ...

> "The aim of the balancing exercise is to assess whether the remedy of exclusion of evidence is proportionate to the breach. The fact that there has been a breach of a quasi-constitutional right and the seriousness of the particular breach in question must be given due weight. Strict rules cannot be laid down. The exclusion of evidence under the *Shaheed* balancing test must be tailored to the

387   *R v Shaheed* [2002] 2 NZLR 377; (2002) 19 CRNZ 165 (CA).
388   *R v Williams* (2007) 23 CRNZ 1 (CA).
389   *R v Williams* (2007) 23 CRNZ 1 (CA), paras 245-252. For a detailed discussion, see *Adams on Criminal Law*, Ch10.24.04.

circumstances of each case and it remains an evaluative decision for the individual Judge ...

"Generalisations can be made, however. The reliability and probative value of the evidence will often outweigh a minor breach where the crime is of a serious nature ... When the illegality or unreasonableness is serious, however, and supported by a strong privacy interest, then, in the absence of any mitigating factors such as an attenuation of causation or a weak personal connection to the property searched or seized, any balancing exercise would normally lead to the exclusion of the evidence, even where the crime was serious. This result would be almost inevitable where the breach was deliberate, reckless or grossly careless on the part of the police."

The above remarks in *Williams* must be read with the caveat that they reflect the law before the Evidence Act 2006. In *R v McGaughey*,[390] the Court emphasised that although the proportionality test set by s 30(2)(b) is "similar" to that laid down by *Shaheed*, the actual wording of the subsection must take priority.

(1) Burden of proof: proportionality

The Act avoids assigning any burden of proof for the "proportionality" test which determines the admissibility of improperly obtained evidence under s 30(2)(b). In practice, the prosecution will attempt to persuade the judge that, despite the impropriety that has occurred, the "need for an effective and credible system of justice", referred to in s 30(2)(b), means that exclusion of the evidence is not proportionate. The defence will argue the contrary and both parties will rely heavily on the factors set forth in s 30(3) as well as the existing jurisprudence under *R v Shaheed*.[391]

(2) Policies in equilibrium

As was suggested in the discussion of s 30(2)(a), problems may arise in the rare case where the judge's mind is left in equilibrium, namely when he or she concludes that the policies referred to in s 30(2)(b) are equally balanced. In such a case, it appears that the evidence will be admissible. Although s 30(4) does not *require* the judge to admit improperly obtained evidence when exclusion is not proportionate to the impropriety, the scheme of s 30 implies that exclusion of improperly obtained evidence is only permissible when the standard set by s 30(4) has been met. That standard has not been met in a case where the judge's mind is left in equilibrium.

EV30.12   Subsection (3): balancing factors

Section 30(3) sets out a non-exhaustive list of factors which the judge *may* take into account in conducting the balancing process mandated by s 30(2)(b). With one important exception, discussed immediately below, the list of factors has been taken

---

390   *R v McGaughey* 17/9/07, CA269/07; [2007] NZCA 411, para 20.
391   *R v Shaheed* [2002] 2 NZLR 377; (2002) 19 CRNZ 165 (CA). See *Adams on Criminal Law*, Ch10.24.04.

almost verbatim from *Shaheed*.[392] Accordingly, existing case law on that important judgment can be relied upon until a new appellate jurisprudence is created.[393]

(1)   Importance of evidence for prosecution

The one major change from *Shaheed* is the absence of any reference in the balancing factors listed in s 30(3) to how important the evidence is for the case for the prosecution. This factor from *Shaheed* was in the original Evidence Bill, but was removed by the Select Committee. Not suprisingly, this legislative history has not stood in the way of reliance on the factor of the importance to the Crown case of the improperly obtained evidence. In *R v Boon*,[394] Asher J relied on *R v Williams*[395] and took this factor into account in the balancing process, albeit "with appropriate caution".

(2)   Known alternative investigative technique

When the factor stated in s 30(3)(e) was set out by Blanchard J in *R v Shaheed*,[396] his Honour referred to "other investigatory techniques ... *known to the police*." This italicised qualification may perhaps be implied into s 30(3)(e). If so, the enquiry under this subsection will continue to be whether the police (or other person who committed the impropriety) knew of the alternative, benign investigative technique.

EV30.13   Remedies other than exclusion

Section 30(3)(f) refers to the balancing factor of "whether there are alternative remedies to exclusion of the evidence which can adequately provide redress to the defendant". In *R v Shaheed*,[397] the Court largely dismissed the relevance of this factor. This was because of the Court's view that exclusion of evidence provides the only practical means of vindicating the rights of the defendant. However, in *R v Williams*,[398] the Court noted that the express inclusion of this factor in s 30 may require "modification" of the view taken in *R v Shaheed*.

31   Prosecution may not rely on certain evidence offered by other parties

Evidence that is liable to be excluded if offered by the prosecution in a criminal proceeding because of section 28 or 29 or 30 may not be relied on by the prosecution if that evidence is offered by any other party.

EV31.01   Evidence offered by parties other than the prosecution

Section 31 recognises that evidence which is inadmissible for the prosecution under s 28 (the reliability rule), s 29 (the oppression rule), or s 30 (the improperly obtained evidence rule) may yet be admissible when *offered by another party* to a criminal proceeding.

---

392   *R v Shaheed* [2002] 2 NZLR 377; (2002) 19 CRNZ 165 (CA).
393   *Adams on Criminal Law*, Ch10.24.04.
394   *R v Boon* 13/8/07, Asher J, HC Auckland CRI-2006-004-21763, paras 75-76.
395   *R v Williams* (1990) 7 CRNZ 378 (CA), para 141.
396   *R v Shaheed* [2002] 2 NZLR 377; (2002) 19 CRNZ 165 (CA), para 150.
397   *R v Shaheed* [2002] 2 NZLR 377; (2002) 19 CRNZ 165 (CA).
398   *R v Williams* (1990) 7 CRNZ 378 (CA), para 152.

(1) Conflict with s 90(1)

There appears to be an insoluble conflict between s 31 and s 90(1).[399]

(2) Any other party

Although s 31 refers to evidence offered by "any other party" (than the prosecution), in all but the most exceptional cases (eg where the court joins an intervenor when a Bill of Rights issue is raised) the "other parties" to a criminal prosecution will be *defendants*.

(3) Offered by a co-defendant

The purpose of s 31 is to attempt to deprive the prosecution of any advantage which might otherwise flow from evidence which could incriminate a particular defendant (D1) in a case where the only reason the evidence is admitted is because a co-defendant (D2) offered the evidence to assist his or her defence.

(4) No reliance of any sort

Although it is likely that s 31 is primarily aimed at protecting D1 in the above example, the wording of s 31 goes further. The prosecution is deprived of any advantage which the evidence might have given them against even the co-defendant (D2) who offered the evidence. The prosecution cannot rely on the evidence *at all*.

(5) Liable to be excluded

Section 31 will apply whether or not the prosecution has actually attempted to offer the evidence and been met with a ruling that the evidence is inadmissible because of ss 28, 29 or 30. In many cases the prosecution will not have bothered to offer the classes of evidence referred to in s 31. The most obvious reason for the prosecution to adopt that stance is because they conclude that the judge would inevitably rule the evidence inadmissible. In such a case, if a co-defendant offers the same evidence, s 31 will still come into play. The judge will be required to decide if the evidence would have been inadmissible under ss 28, 29, or 30 if the prosecution had offered it. If so, s 31 applies because the evidence "is liable to be excluded."

(6) Relevance of reliability rule

The discussion of s 31 has to this point followed the approach taken by the section in not drawing any distinctions among ss 28, 29 and 30. However, there is some difficulty imagining occasions when s 28, the reliability rule, will have practical relevance in this context.

Consider the most common application of s 31, where one defendant (D2) offers evidence of a statement by another defendant (D1) because the statement advances the defence of D2. There will be no difficulty envisioning the operation of s 31 when D1's statement was influenced by oppression (a breach of s 29) or was improperly obtained (a breach of s 30) and which states "I robbed the bank and my co-defendant (D2) is innocent". However, examples involving s 28 (the reliability rule) are more problematic.

---

399   See the discussion of s 90(1) at EV90.04(3).

If the statement just hypothesised was inadmissible for the prosecution because of a breach of s 28, this means that the prosecution was unable to prove that the statement was reliable (s 28(2)). This does not prevent D2 offering the evidence. However, in doing so, D2 will have to deal with the fact that D1's statement is hearsay. Accordingly, D2 will have to satisfy the prerequisites for admissible hearsay, which (except in the case of a business record, s 19) include a reasonable assurance of the statement's reliability (s 18(1)(a)). It is difficult to see how that prerequisite could be met in the face of the prosecution's inability to satisfy s 28(2).

32   Fact-finder not to be invited to infer guilt from defendant's silence before trial

(1)   This section applies to a criminal proceeding in which it appears that the defendant failed—

     (a)   to answer a question put, or respond to a statement made, to the defendant in the course of investigative questioning before the trial; or

     (b)   to disclose a defence before trial.

(2)   If subsection (1) applies,—

     (a)   no person may invite the fact-finder to draw an inference that the defendant is guilty from a failure of the kind described in subsection (1); and

     (b)   if the proceeding is with a jury, the Judge must direct the jury that it may not draw that inference from a failure of that kind.

(3)   This section does not apply if the fact that the defendant did not answer a question put, or respond to a statement made, before the trial is a fact required to be proved in the proceeding.

EV32.01   Silence before trial

Section 32 preserves an important aspect of the right of silence as it applies to a defendant's silence before trial in a criminal proceeding. With a possible qualification,[400] the section attempts to prevent the fact-finder from using the defendant's silence as evidence of guilt.

(1)   Subsection (1): silence

The classes of silence within the scope of the section are broad. Section 32(1)(a) includes the common circumstance of a failure to answer a question put in the course of investigative questioning before trial. Also included is a failure to *respond to a statement* made in the course of investigative questioning. This means that there is no room for the prosecution to argue that (in accordance with some common law authorities) the defendant's failure to respond to an allegation of wrongdoing amounts to an acceptance of the allegation.[401]

---

400   See EV32.02(2).
401   *Adams on Criminal Law — Evidence*, EC6.03.

Very few people actually remain silent in response to questions posed or allegations made as a part of investigative questioning. The most common response is to give some form of apparently exculpatory response. When this occurs, s 32 has no application.

It may be that courts will show some flexibility in interpreting the scope of protection offered by s 32(1)(a). Perhaps a response of "no comment" will be seen as tantamount to a failure to answer a question or respond to a statement.

(2)   Failure to disclose a defence

Section 32(1)(b) completes the picture by including within the classes of protected "silence" a defendant's failure to *disclose a defence* before trial. There may be other controls on certain "ambush" defences raised for the first time at trial.[402] However, s 32(2) ensures that even when such a defence has not been disclosed before trial, the defendant is entitled to be protected from any argument by the prosecution that such a tactic demonstrates the defendant's guilt.

In view of the express protection granted by s 32(1)(b), it is likely that many defendants will make the tactical decision not to disclose a defence before trial.

(3)   Investigative questioning

Section 32(1)(a) only applies to "investigative questioning". The Act's definition of the phrase is discussed under s 4.

Section 32(1)(a) provides no protection for the defendant who remains silent in response to questions put or allegations made to the defendant in circumstances that do not amount to investigative questioning. The result is reminiscent of the common law, where an inference of guilt could be drawn from a defendant's silence in the face of an allegation put by someone with whom the defendant was "on even terms". Practically speaking, a defendant is on even terms with a lay person who does not wield any of the power that is associated with an enforcement body such as the police. At common law, if it would have been reasonable for an innocent person to have denied an allegation put by someone with whom the defendant was on even terms, an inference of guilt could be drawn from the defendant's silence.[403]

EV32.02   Subsection (2): extent of protection

Although s 32(2) provides broad protections for a defendant whose exercise of the right of silence comes within the scope of s 32(1), there are some gaps and uncertainties.

(1)   No inference of guilt by jury

Section 32(2) is a comprehensive attempt to prohibit the jury from drawing any inference of the defendant's guilt from the classes of evidence outlined in s 32(1). Section 32(2)(a) prevents any person "inviting" the jury (as the "fact-finder") to draw

---

402   *Adams on Criminal Law*, CA367A.01.
403   *Adams on Criminal Law — Evidence*, EC6.03(2)(b).

such an inference. Section 32(2)(b) imposes an obligation on the judge to direct the jury that they may not draw any such inference.

It is likely that courts will give a broad interpretation to "invites". It is suggested that a court will construe as a prohibited "invitation", any *suggestion* that the defendant's pre-trial silence is a factor which the jury can consider in determining guilt.

(2)   No inference of guilt: judge alone

Section 32(2) does not specifically prevent the judge in a judge alone trial from relying on the defendant's pre-trial silence as the basis for an inference of guilt. Although s 32(2)(a) prevents any person inviting the judge to draw such an inference, the Act makes no attempt to mirror s 32(2)(b) by specifically preventing the judge from drawing the inference. The Law Commission's draft Code (s 32(1)) had taken this step and its omission from the Act suggests that the legislature has left the door open for a judge, as opposed to the jury, to draw an inference of guilt from a defendant's pre-trial silence. Perhaps it was felt that a judge would not put undue weight on a defendant's exercise of the right of silence.[404] The contrary argument is that it is incongruous to make the ability to use the same fact — a pre-trial exercise of the right of silence — dependent on whether the fact-finder at trial is a jury or a judge.

EV32.03   Admissibility of evidence of silence

It might have been thought that because s 32(2) renders a defendant's pre-trial silence *irrelevant* to the determination of guilt (at least in a jury trial: see above discussion), evidence of that silence should be inadmissible. Because of the lack of relevance of such evidence, a rule of inadmissibility would be in accordance with s 7(2). However there are strong indications that the Act permits the prosecution to offer evidence of the defendant's exercise of his or her right to remain silent before trial.

If such evidence was inadmissible, there would be no need for s 32(2). Further, the Law Commission's draft Evidence Code prohibited *cross-examination* by the prosecution of a defendant about the defendant's pre-trial exercise of the right of silence. The omission from the Act of this prohibition of cross-examination suggests that there is nothing standing in the way of the prosecution employing this method of "offering evidence" of the defendant's pre-trial silence (see s 4's definition of "offer evidence").

Even though evidence of a defendant's pre-trial silence remains admissible, the question remains, what use can be made of such evidence? The following two possibilities appear arguable:

(1)   Judge may draw an inference of guilt

As discussed above, s 32(2) does not specifically prohibit a judge (as opposed to a jury) drawing an inference of guilt from evidence that the defendant exercised his or her right of silence before trial.

---

404   See, generally, *Adams on Criminal Law*, Ch10.12.

(2)   Truthfulness/guilt

Particularly in cases involving a defendant's failure to disclose a defence before trial (s 32(1)(b)), the common law had drawn a distinction which may well have carried over to s 32. At common law, when a defendant had not taken the opportunity to disclose a defence before trial, this fact could be relied upon to detract from the defendant's veracity at trial, when he or she testified in support of that defence. Court of Appeal authorities stressed that such a negative impact on veracity was not mandatory and there could be many explanations as to why the defendant exercised his or her right of silence.[405]

The Law Commission's draft Evidence Code specifically prohibited the fact-finder from using a defendant's pre-trial silence as the basis for an inference about the defendant's veracity.[406] The omission of this clause from s 32 is telling. Given that the very existence of s 32(2) means that *some* use can be made of evidence of the defendant's exercise of the right of silence, a weakening of the defendant's veracity is the most likely use to which such evidence can be put that is in keeping with the rest of s 32.

Of course, as was the case at common law, it is questionable whether there is any meaningful distinction between an inference of guilt, which is prohibited (at least in jury trials) by s 32(2) and "mere" damage to the defendant's veracity when he or she asserts a defence.

EV32.04   Subsection (3): when silence is an element of an offence

The Law Commission's explanation of s 32(3) consisted in giving the example of the trial of an offence of failing to answer questions under s 185 of the Customs and Excise Act 1996.[407] Clearly, in such a proceeding, the intention of s 32(3) is to permit a finding of guilt from evidence that the accused failed to answer a question in circumstances which concurrently fit within the boundaries of s 32(1)(a).

33   Restrictions on comment on defendant's right of silence at trial

In a criminal proceeding, no person other than the defendant or the defendant's counsel or the Judge may comment on the fact that the defendant did not give evidence at his or her trial.

EV33.01   Overview

Section 33 is to the same effect as s 366(1) of the Crimes Act, which s 33 replaces. See s 215 and Schedule 1 to the Act.[408] The extensive law applicable to s 366(1) will provide the necessary guidance for the interpretation of s 33.[409]

---

405   *Adams on Criminal Law — Evidence*, EC6.03(8).
406   LC *Evidence Code*, 90 (s 32(2)).
407   LC *Evidence Reform*, para C160.
408   See EV215.01.
409   See *Adams on Criminal Law — Evidence*, EC15.

Section 366(2) of the Crimes Act continues in force. It prevents adverse comment on a defendant's failure to call his or her spouse as a witness. The Act makes no attempt to deal with this topic.

34   Admissions in civil proceedings

(1)   Subpart 1 (hearsay evidence), subpart 2 (opinion evidence and expert evidence), and section 35 (the previous consistent statements rule) do not apply to evidence of an admission offered in a civil proceeding that is—

    (a)   given orally by a person who saw, heard, or otherwise perceived the admission being made; or

    (b)   contained in a document.

(2)   Evidence of an admission that is a hearsay statement may not be used in respect of the case of a third party unless—

    (a)   the circumstances relating to the making of the admission provide reasonable assurance that the admission is reliable; or

    (b)   the third party consents.

(3)   In this section, **third party** means a party to the proceeding concerned, other than the party who—

    (a)   made the admission; or

    (b)   offered the evidence.

EV34.01   Introduction

Section 34 applies only in civil proceedings. Admissions in criminal proceedings are, in effect, dealt with in ss 27-30.

"Admission" is defined in s 4.

EV34.02   Purpose of s 34

Section 34 has remained unchanged since the Law Commission first released its draft Evidence Code. It is therefore safe to assume that the following statement by the Law Commission accurately reflects the legislative intent behind s 34:[410]

"Under the common law, a statement against interest (defined as an 'admission' in the Code) is admissible against the party who made it. Under the Code, an admission is admissible because it is relevant and generally reliable, since a party is unlikely to make an admission that is untrue. The restrictions of the hearsay rule are therefore unnecessary if a witness offers evidence of a party's admission made in writing or an admission the witness personally heard or saw the party making. The witness who offers the evidence can be cross-examined on any motive he or she may have to lie, or on the accuracy of his or her observation. However, a reasonable assurance of

---

410   LC *Evidence Code*, para C165.

reliability is expressly required before an admission may be used to implicate a third party, unless there is consent."

(1)   Subsection (1): inapplicability of other rules

Although in the passage just quoted the Law Commission referred only to the hearsay rule, s 34(1) renders irrelevant two additional admissibility rules when a party offers evidence of an admission. These are the opinion and expert evidence rule, and the previous consistent statement rule. In this way, s 34 is designed to more readily admit evidence of an admission than may have been the case if the party offering the evidence had to surmount the hurdles presented by these potential bars to admissibility.

Brief comments can be made about each of the three admissibility rules referred to in s 34(1).

(a)   *Opinion and expert evidence*

The effect of s 34(1) is to permit oral or documentary evidence of an admission even though the admission contains a statement of opinion which would otherwise not have met the tests for admissibility set by Subpart 2. Thus, in a lawsuit alleging faulty building construction, a plaintiff could offer evidence that the defendant builder said "I did a negligent job". The plaintiff could offer this evidence without the need to consider the tests for lay opinion evidence set by s 24. The plaintiff could also ignore the question whether the defendant was an expert or whether other aspects of s 25 might have presented difficulties with the admissibility of this evidence of opinion.

Because s 34(1) renders inapplicable the whole of Subpart 2, the plaintiff in this example would not need to be concerned with s 26, which normally imposes controls on expert witnesses.

(b)   *Previous consistent statements*

Section 34(1) also renders the previous consistent statement rule irrelevant to evidence of an admission. This aspect of s 34(1) appears to have been included out of an abundance of caution. It is difficult to imagine realistic examples where the previous consistent statements rule would ever have applied to evidence of an admission. This is because, as reflected in the definition in s 4, an admission involves a statement by a party that is adverse to his or her interest. The previous consistent statement rule would only be relevant in a case where a party testifies in a way which is adverse to his or her interests and that party or an opposing litigant offers evidence of the party's previous statement which contains a similar (consistent) adverse statement. Such circumstances are unlikely to occur.

(c)   *Hearsay*

Section 34(1) aims to admit evidence of an admission without the necessity to consider s 18(1)'s prerequisites for admissibility of reliability (or s 19's qualification as a business record) and of the unavailability of the statement maker. As confirmed by the Law Commission, quoted above, the Act assumes that admissions are inherently reliable. However, the distinctions drawn by s 34(1)(a) and (b) demonstrate that the Act is concerned with the issue of evidence of an admission in the form of *multiple hearsay*. That issue is now discussed

Section 34(1)(a) limits the occasions when the hearsay rule is irrelevant. There need be no consideration of the hearsay rule in a case where oral evidence is given by a person who actually "perceived the admission being made". This means that if a witness (W) testifies, "X told me that the defendant admitted his liability", the hearsay rule would still apply. W did not perceive the actual making of the admission by the defendant. The statement by X is a hearsay statement and it would only be admissible if the tests set forth in s 18 were satisfied.

It is strange that s 34(1)(a) speaks of oral evidence given by a *person* who perceived the making of an admission. Such a "person" must almost always be a "witness". By virtue of the definition of "witness" in s 4, the only person who could *give oral evidence* yet not be a "witness" is someone who testifies but who is not able to be cross-examined — a difficult circumstance to imagine.

It is possible that s 34(1)(b) meant to apply only to a case where a party uses a document as the means of making an admission. For example, party D writes in her diary, "I am liable in the lawsuit". Section 34(1)(b) would certainly have the effect of rendering the hearsay rule irrelevant in such a case. The documentary evidence of the admission would be admissible despite the fact that D was available to give evidence. Additionally, there would be no need to enquire into the reliability of the admission. These tests for admissibility of hearsay would be inapplicable.

D's diary is a simple example of "first hand" documentary hearsay. The document itself was written by the party who made the admission. Yet in stark contrast to s 34(1)(a), s 34(1)(b) is not expressly restricted to first hand hearsay. The inescapable conclusion is that s 34(1)(b) was intended to permit "multiple hearsay" of an admission in the case of documentary evidence.

Consider a case where X is a person who does not give evidence. It is possible to interpret the broad wording of s 34(1)(b) as covering the case where a document written by X records that a party (D) made a admission to X. This is "second hand" hearsay (because X does not give evidence). It is not difficult to imagine circumstances where the reliability of X's statement is questionable. Nonetheless, if it is correct to characterise this example as one of evidence of an admission "contained in a document", s 34(1)(b) negates the Act's normal controls over hearsay evidence of reliability and unavailability (s 18). The document can be admitted without further ado under s 34(1)(b).

EV34.03 The limited effect of s 34(2) and (3)

A first reading of s 34(2) and (3) might suggest that these subsections attempt to deal with the much litigated common law issue of when a damaging pre-trial statement by X becomes admissible as an admission made by one of the parties to a proceeding ("vicarious admissions"). The issue is usually raised when X is an agent of the party in question. However, the effect of s 34(2) and (3) is much narrower.

(1)   Third party

Analysis can start with s 34(3)'s definition of a "third party". This makes it clear that s 34(2) is only dealing with statements (admissions) made by one *party* in a proceeding that are sought to be used as evidence by another *party* in that proceeding. Section 34(2) has little to do with the general issue of "vicarious admissions" described above. The modest aim of the section is to limit the occasions when one party's admission can be "used in respect of the case" of another party.

(2)   Restricted use of admissible evidence

Section 34(2) limits the occasions when "an admission that is a hearsay statement" can be used against a "third party". Section 34(2) is, then, one of the rare occasions when the Act restricts the *use* to which admissible evidence may be put. As discussed more fully under s 7,[411] the normal position under the Act is that once evidence is admitted, it can be used for any purpose.

The class of evidence that is the focus of s 34(2) (an admission that is a hearsay statement) remains available to damage the position of *the party who made the admission* or to help the case of *the party who offered evidence* of the admission. This is the effect of s 34(3). However, this same class of evidence (an admission that is a hearsay statement) is not available to damage the case of the third party *unless* the third party consents (s 34(2)(b)) or "the circumstances relating to the making of the admission provide reasonable assurance that the admission is reliable" s 34(2)(a).

(3)   Circumstances

With respect to the latter prerequisite, it was probably intended that s 16(1)'s definition of "the circumstances in relation to a statement" would apply to s 34(2)(a), but that definition may actually have no application. The opening phrase of s 16(1) limits its operation to "this Subpart" and s 34 is not contained in the same Subpart as s 16.

(4)   An admission that is a hearsay statement

Subsections (2) and (3) apply only to "an admission that is a hearsay statement". This means that these provisions do not purport to affect an admission made by a party when he or she is *giving evidence*. That class of evidence, once admitted, will be available for all purposes, including its use for or against all other parties in the proceeding.

EV34.04   Rationale for s 34(2) and (3)

The thinking behind s 34(2) and (3) is likely to be as follows: Because admissions are inherently reliable, s 34(1) renders them admissible *against the party who made them* without the need to engage in the assessment of reliability which is normally applicable to hearsay under s 18(1).

Under the common law, except in the case of "vicarious admissions", a pre-trial admission made by one party is not admissible against another party. The Act

---

411   See EV7.03.

continues that rule in criminal proceedings (s 27(1)). Insofar as civil proceedings are concerned, without special controls the Act would permit one party's pre-trial admission to be used against another party to the proceeding.[412] Section 34 attempts to be that special control. A party (D1) should not have his or her position in a civil proceeding damaged by another party's (D2's) admission unless D1 consents (s 34(2)(b)) or unless there is an assessment and an assurance of the reliability of D2's admission (s 34(2)(a)).

Thus it appears that s 34(2) focuses on "an admission that is a hearsay statement" in order to negate the effect of s 34(1) (which generally gets rid of s 18(1)'s assessment of reliability in the case of admissions) and to thereby restore the normal hearsay reliability assessment in the particular case of admissions by one party that are sought to be used against another party.

EV34.05   Vicarious admission

The above discussion pointed out that s 34 makes no attempt to deal with the general issue of vicarious admissions. Under s 12, we are therefore left to turn to the common law (and statute law such as s 18 of the Partnership Act 1908) for guidance.

The ultimate solution will depend on an analysis of the various circumstances in which the common law admitted, as evidence against a party, the damaging pre-trial statements of his or her agent, referee, or predecessor in title etc. The pivotal question is whether this result was dictated by a body of substantive law other than the law of evidence. The issue is best illustrated by the most commonly litigated example of a vicarious admission, namely where one party seeks to offer evidence of a damaging statement made by the *agent* of an opposing party. To determine the position under the Act it is first necessary to determine the basis upon which the common law justified the vicarious admission against the principal. On the one hand, admissibility of the agent's statement could be seen as "a corollary of the whole idea of the vicarious liability of the principal in substantive law".[413] Under this rationale, an admission made by a suitably authorised agent[414] is "admissible as if said by the principal himself".[415] In this way, the agent's statement *becomes the party's own admission*. As such, s 34(1) applies without further ado to admit the statement which the law of agency has transformed into the principal's admission.[416]

The same result will not follow if the common law cases are characterised as simply demonstrating an expedient invention of evidence law to render admissible the agent's hearsay statement. If the agent's statement is treated as having a separate existence from any statement made by the principal, there is nothing in the Act to

---

412   This is because of the general rule that, once admitted, evidence becomes available for use for all purposes. See EV7.03.

413   Fridman, *Law of Agency* (7th ed), London, Butterworths, 1996, 347.

414   A much litigated issue at common law was whether the agent was authorised to make admissions. See, generally, *Maxwell v Inland Revenue Commissioner* [1959] NZLR 708 (CA).

415   *Kirkstall Brewery Co v The Furness Railway Co* (1874) LR 9 QB 468, 469.

416   See EV34.02(1).

serve as a basis for reinventing the doctrine of vicarious admissions. Litigants will search in vain for any express provision in the Act permitting the agent's statement to "become" the principal's admission. Under this analysis, s 34(1) is inapplicable. The agent's statement remains a hearsay statement, subject to the tests for admissibility set by s 18. In the typical case where the agent is not "unavailable as a witness", s 18(1)(b)(i) will mean that the statement will be inadmissible.[417]

Subpart 4—Previous consistent statements made by witness

(s 35)

35   Previous consistent statements rule

(1)   A previous statement of a witness that is consistent with the witness's evidence is not admissible unless subsection (2) or subsection (3) applies to the statement.

(2)   A previous statement of a witness that is consistent with the witness's evidence is admissible to the extent that the statement is necessary to respond to a challenge to the witness's veracity or accuracy, based on a previous inconsistent statement of the witness or on a claim of recent invention on the part of the witness.

(3)   A previous statement of a witness that is consistent with the witness's evidence is admissible if—

(a)   the circumstances relating to the statement provide reasonable assurance that the statement is reliable; and

(b)   the statement provides the court with information that the witness is unable to recall.

EV35.01   Significant changes to the common law admissibility rules

Section 35 substantially alters the common law with regard to both the admissibility and use of a witness's previous consistent statements.

Section 35(1) sets out the general rule that the previous consistent statements of a witness are inadmissible unless the exceptions contained in s 35(2) or (3) apply. This means that the common law exceptions no longer apply — except to the extent they are preserved by s 35(2).

The Ministry of Justice stated that "the common law rules governing previous consistent statements will continue to apply where those rules are consistent with the aims of the Bill."[418] However, this would require a wide interpretation of s 12 — such that that s 35 only deals with the admissibility of previous consistent statements "in part". If such an interpretation was followed (notwithstanding the wording of

---

417   Section 18(1)(b)(ii) (undue expense or delay) may permit the agent's statement to be admissible if s 18(1)(a) (reliability) was also satisfied. If the agent testifies, his or her pre-trial statement is no longer hearsay (see EV4.20.01). Numerous circumstances may be imagined which would result in the agent's statement becoming admissible if he or she testifies.

418   *Departmental Report* (EV/MOJ/6), 22.

s 35(1)), it would have the potential to undermine much of the reform project if applied more generally.

EV35.02   Rationale for excluding previous consistent statements

The Law Commission stated that the intention of the section is "to prevent the parties from inundating the courts with voluminous amounts of repetitive material in order to shore up a witness's consistency. So if the witness's testimony is silent on a matter that is the subject of a previous statement, or if the witness's testimony is different from the content of a previous statement, [s 35] will not exclude evidence of the previous statement."[419] Therefore if an out-of-court statement of the witness (which is not hearsay under the Act because the definition of "hearsay statement" excludes statements made by a "witness"[420]) contains evidence not covered by the witness when testifying, it is not excluded by s 35. The Law Commission also said that "consistent" does "not simply mean the lack of inconsistency: there must be something in the witness's testimony with which the previous statement is consistent".[421]

EV35.03   Difficulty of assessing admissibility if witness is yet to testify

In the context of discussing the definition of witness, it was noted that it is difficult to treat a person who has yet to testify as a "witness" for the purpose of s 35.[422] No assessment about consistency can sensibly be made before the witness has testified. This person's statement may have to be treated as a hearsay statement if offered in evidence before he or she testifies. To be admissible, the hearsay statement of this person (offered by another witness) will have to meet the requirements of ss 18 or 19 of the Act, even though the maker is not "unavailable" (recourse presumably will have to be to s 18(1)(b)(ii) or s 19(1)(b) or (c), as well as to s 22(5) in the criminal context). Alternatively, s 14 could be used[423] to allow the statement to be admitted on the basis that the maker will be a witness, but then the eventual testimony will need to be limited to evidence not already heard, unless s 35(2) is satisfied.

EV35.04   Subsection (2): the two exceptions to the rule

Section 35(2) sets out two exceptions to the general prohibition on previous consistent statements. A previous consistent statement will only be admissible to the extent that the statement is necessary to respond to a challenge to the witness's veracity or accuracy. These challenges must also be based on either a previous inconsistent statement or a claim of recent invention (which is not defined by the Act and may require reference to the common law).[424] This second requirement was added by the Select Committee, who adopted the suggested re-drafting from the New Zealand Law Society's submission. This addition will affect most significantly the admissibility of "recent complaint" evidence,[425] as the second aspect to the New Zealand Law

---

419   LC *Evidence Code*, para C167.
420   See EV4.20.01.
421   LC *Evidence Code*, para C167.
422   See EV4.46.02.
423   See EV14.01.
424   *Adams on Criminal Law — Evidence*, EC12.05; *R v W* 11/9/07, CA164/07; [2007] NZCA 408.

Society's recommendation — that "the law relating to recent complaint in sexual offences should be codified"[426] — was not adopted.

(1)   Use which can be made of a previous consistent statement

The New Zealand Law Society also submitted that "it is unclear whether the previous consistent statement is admissible as evidence of its truth or the fact that it was made", and that the "admission of a previous consistent statement should never be admitted as the truth". It was the Law Commission's view that under the Act, a witness's previous consistent statement would be admissible to prove the truth of its contents.[427] (The Act provides only a few examples of limited use provisions,[428] these can be viewed as exceptions to the general rule which is that, consistent with the Law Commission's policy position, that once evidence is admitted, it is admitted to prove "anything that is of consequence" (s 7).) Despite the Law Society's concern to clarify the use of admissible previous consistent statements, no change was made to the section. This must mean that no change to the Law Commission's position was intended.

In discussing the submissions on the Bill with regard to "recent complaint" evidence the Ministry of Justice stated: "The Bill treats recent complaints in the same way as the previous statements of any witness. In addition, the statement, once admitted can go to support the truthfulness and accuracy of the witness and to prove the truth of the contents of the statement."[429] However the wording of s 35(2) "to the extent necessary to respond to a challenge to veracity …" may mean it will be argued that statements admitted under this subsection should only be used to prove consistency, not to prove their truth.[430]

Nonetheless, s 35 is best interpreted as simply creating a bar to the admission of a previous consistent statement and then providing exceptions. It does not purport to limit the use that can be made of the previous statement once it is admitted as evidence.

(2)   Control on the number of prior consistent statement admitted under s 35(2)

Judicial control on the number of previous consistent statements that can be admitted will be exercised through an interpretation of the extent to which the evidence is "necessary" to respond to the challenge and use of s 8(1)(b) — the extent to which the admission of the evidence will "needlessly prolong the proceeding." Section 8 may also be used to control the extent to which other aspects of a statement, not necessary to respond to the challenge, should be admitted. The authors of the New Zealand Law Society seminar stated: "Section 35(2) makes a previous statement admissible evidence in the proceeding, so it can be produced as an exhibit."[431]

---

425   See EV35.05(2).

426   NZLS *Submission on the Evidence Bill*, 15-16.

427   LC *Evidence Code*, para C168.

428   See ss 27(1) and 34(2), and further at EV7.03.

429   *Departmental Report* (EV/MOJ/6), 24.

430   See EV37.09 and EV38.08. See also *Cross on Evidence* (online), EVA35.5.

431   Burston and Verrall, "Questioning of Witnesses" in NZLS *Intensive: Evidence Act 2006*, 117.

However, whether the whole of a previous statement is admissible will depend on whether all of the statement is "necessary" to respond to the relevant challenge.

EV35.05   Challenging veracity

The first of the two classes of challenges described by s 35(2) is a challenge to the witness's veracity. Section 37(5) defines veracity (changed from "truthfulness" by the Select Committee). Is s 35 also subject to s 37? The Law Commission was of the view that "if a previous consistent statement is solely or mainly about [veracity] and is admitted to meet a challenge to [veracity], it will almost always be substantially helpful ... and therefore admissible".[432] Further, although more contentiously, the Law Commission stated that most previous statements will not be solely or mainly about the veracity of the witness — but about the truthfulness of the content of the statement (which can also be used to prove its truth). The Ministry of Justice, however, stated that under s 35(2) "statements can be ruled admissible to support the fact that the *witness's testimony* is truthful or accurate, not the truthfulness of the witness."[433]

Section 35(2) appears to require that a challenge has been made before there is any possibility of admitting the previous consistent statement. However, it is conceivable that a judge could adopt the approach taken in *R v Manuchhima*[434] and permit evidence to be given of a previous consistent statement in advance of an anticipated challenge.[435]

It is likely that courts will be easily persuaded that s 35(2)'s trigger of a "challenge" has occurred. Any suggestion in cross-examination that the witness is lying or mistaken should be sufficient.

Nothing in s 35(2) requires that a challenge must be by evidence. However, it is reasonable to assume that a challenge could take the form of an offer of evidence. This raises the question whether a "challenge" occurs through the mere act of offering evidence that contradicts the evidence of the witness whose previous statement is in issue. There is no specific provisions which states that an offer of contradictory evidence cannot amount to a challenge under s 35(2). Such a specific provision does exist in another context. Section 37(4)(a) prohibits a party challenging the veracity of a witness called by that party (except in the case of a hostile witness). However, s 37(4)(b) goes on to make it clear that a mere offer of evidence which contradicts the evidence given by the witness does not amount to the sort of "challenge" prohibited by s 37(4)(a).[436]

The lack of any comparable provision for the purpose of s 35(2) could support the argument that a challenge to a witness's veracity or accuracy occurs under s 35(2) whenever an opposing party offers evidence which contradicts that given by the witness. Such contradictory evidence could be offered before the witness gives

---

432   LC *Evidence Code*, para C172. See also EV37.03(2).
433   *Departmental Report* (EV/MOJ/6), 22 (emphasis in original).
434   *R v Manuchhima* 13/10/05, CA272/05.
435   *Adams on Criminal Law — Evidence*, EC12.05(9).
436   See EV37.13(1).

evidence, as would be the case if the contradictory evidence was offered by a witness for the plaintiff or the prosecution and the witness whose previous statement is in issue is a witness for the defence. The contradictory evidence could also be offered during the time that the witness is giving evidence. This is possible because s 4 defines "offer evidence" as including eliciting evidence by cross-examining a witness.[437] Finally, the contradictory evidence could be offered after the witness has finished giving evidence.

(1) Previous exceptions: evidence of a prior identification

This previous exception to the general rule prohibiting previous consistent statements allowed evidence to be given that not only has the witness identified the defendant in court as the offender, the witness has also done so on an occasion before the trial (see s 22A of the Evidence Act 1908). This exception applied even though in some cases the earlier identification was not consistent with the witness's evidence in court.[438]

The Law Commission was of the view that s 22A was replaced by s 35.[439] There may be some difficulties with the overlap with s 45, however. If there is no identification of the defendant at trial then s 45 permits the evidence to be given of the witness's pre-trial identification of the defendant (s 35 does not bar this).[440] However, where the witness identifies the defendant at trial and this is consistent with a pre-trial identification by the witness, s 35(1) appears to prohibit evidence of the pre-trial identification but s 45 appears to permit it. If s 45 is subject to s 35 then evidence of a prior identification will only be admissible if s 35(2) or (3) is satisfied — a change to the current law.

(2) The previous "recent complaint" exception

This common law exception operated to admit the previous consistent statement of the victim of a sexual offence if that statement was made at the "first reasonable opportunity" (and to the person the complainant would be expected to complain to) following the offence.[441] Under the Act such complaints will only be admissible under s 35(2), which will limit the amount of "recent complaint" evidence that can be admitted. The Law Commission's aim was to treat all previous complaints in the same way (regardless of type of offence) and to do away with the requirement of being recent — on the basis that evidence of earlier complaints could bolster any complainant's (or witness's) credibility, if challenged. This means that what is now considered "recent complaint evidence" will not be led as a matter of course and can only be led in re-examination or in rebuttal. However, the common law limitations on what amounts to a recent complaint will not apply — for example, there is no longer any requirement for the complaint to be made at the first reasonable

---

437   See EV4.29.01.
438   *Adams on Criminal Law — Evidence*, EC12.07.
439   LC *Evidence Code*, para C168.
440   See EV45.01.
441   *Adams on Criminal Law — Evidence*, EC12.04(2).

opportunity. There is also no requirement to call the person to whom the complaint was made, although this may be prudent as a matter that may go to weight.[442]

EV35.06   Section 127

Given the changes to the admissibility of what is currently "recent complaint" evidence under the Act, s 127 (a retention of s 23AC) seems oddly worded.[443] The Ministry of Justice supported its retention in this form, stating that it "provides a mechanism that enables a Judge to inform the jury that good reasons may exist for the victim of a sexual offence where there has been a delay in making a complaint. If a defence counsel improperly challenges the complainant's credibility for the first time in closing, [s 98(3)] allows further may be offered with the leave of the Judge."[444]

EV35.07   Subsection (3): statements the witness is "unable to recall"

Although s 35(3) reads as an exception to s 35(1), the Law Commission recognised that such evidence cannot really be described as a previous consistent statement. The Law Commission stated that the provision was:[445]

> "intended to cover the situation where a witness may wish to consult a previous statement containing details the witness cannot recall. Such a statement is not, strictly speaking, a previous consistent statement because the witness's evidence will not contain the details recorded in the statement. Paragraph (b) has been inserted to avoid unnecessary argument that such a statement is inadmissible and therefore cannot be used for the purpose of questioning a witness or cannot be consulted by a witness while giving evidence."

However, this argument was based on the Code's version of s 90 which provided that any inadmissible statement could not be used when questioning a witness[446] — hence this part of the rule was added to render statements used to refresh memory admissible.

Section 35(3)(a) imposes the prerequisite that the "circumstances relating to the statement" provide reasonable assurance that the statement is reliable. This is the concept defined by s 16(1) to be used when assessing the reliability of a hearsay statement[447] — however it is not clear that s 16(1)'s definition of such "circumstances" applies to s 35(3)(a) because s 16(1) states that its definitions apply "in this subpart". This requirement did not form part of the Law Commission's draft and was added prior to the Bill being introduced as "[c]oncerns were expressed about the broadness of the provision",[448] but no cross-reference to the s 16 was discussed, nor was the issue raised in submissions. This amendment was also accompanied by a leave requirement

---

442   See also *Cross on Evidence* (online), EA35.6.
443   See EV127.02.
444   *Departmental Report* (EV/MOJ/6), 24.
445   LC *Evidence Code*, para C169.
446   See EV90.02.
447   See EV16.03.01.
448   Ministry of Justice, *Letter of Advice to the Minister of Justice*, 8 February 2005, 5.

in the Bill (cl 31(4)) which was deleted by the Select Committee as it was viewed as "superfluous" given the consequential amendment to s 90(5).

EV35.08   Refreshing memory

As discussed at EV90.06, s 90(5) governs the process of refreshing memory and s 35(3) governs the issue of the admissibility of the document used to refresh the witness's memory. A document may, however, be "consulted" under s 90(5) even though not admissible under s 35(3) — as the dual requirements of reliability and the witness being unable to recall may not necessarily be satisfied, even if s 90(5) is. According to the specialist adviser to the Select Committee: "The existing common law requirement for refreshing memory turns on freshness of memory when the note is made or adopted, not reliability. There are sound reasons for this."[449] Others may consider that the common law requirement of contemporaneity[450] is in fact an "indicia" of reliability.

Section 35(3) will also apply to a case where the witness makes no attempt to refresh their memory (and it may be that the document is reliable but does not meet the contemporaneity requirement in s 90(5)), but simply testifies that they cannot recall (a common law inquiry)[451] the information contained in the statement. There may be examples in which the witness has some imperfect recollection as opposed to an inability to recall the information — only the latter leads to admissibility under s 35(3).

(1)   Recalling only imperfectly

The Evidence Bill contained the additional phrase "or able to recall only imperfectly" which was removed by the Select Committee following the New Zealand Law Society's submission that if there is an imperfect recollection it might suggest the statement is not reliable and may then be admitted to prove the statement's truth and perhaps contradict the witness's "imperfect recollection".[452] This removal was not supported by Hon Robert Fisher QC:[453]

> "I do not recall the reason for the deletion but suggest it would be unwise. At present it is routine to have witnesses produce business records and other documents they made at an earlier time in circumstances where they have some recollection of the matter but consider that the document is more comprehensive and accurate. By allowing production of the document in addition to the oral evidence in those circumstances one gets the best of both worlds."

---

449   Fisher QC, *Third Memo for Justice and Electoral Select Committee re Evidence Bill* (EV/ADV/ 3), 29 June 2006, para 3.
450   *Adams on Criminal Law — Evidence*, EC13.03.
451   *Adams on Criminal Law — Evidence*, EC13.03(4).
452   NZLS *Submission on the Evidence Bill*, 15.
453   Fisher QC, *Fifth Memo for Justice and Electoral Select Committee re Evidence Bill* (EV/ADV/ 5), 27 September 2006, para 6.

Whether the whole statement, or just the part "unable to be recalled" is admitted, will be a matter for the judge.[454]

It is clear that statements admitted under s 35(3) can be used to prove their truth. The New Zealand Law Society's concern seems to be about a matter better viewed as going to weight rather than admissibility. More often than not, the witness will remember most of a previous statement but not all of the statement.

Section 35(3) will also apply when the witness is making no attempt to refresh their memory (or indeed, is still unable to "recall", even when having consulted the relevant document), but simply testifies that although the statement is their own, they cannot recall the information in the statement. Although this is not then a previous consistent statement, this must be the result of the subsection for it to have any purpose at all.[455]

Subpart 5—Veracity and propensity

(s 36 to s 44)

EVPt2Sub5.01   Overview

Subpart 5 governs the admissibility of a wide range of evidence that has given rise to a difficult body of common law.

Subpart 5 departs from the common law by dividing what used to be referred to as "character" evidence into the two classes of evidence of "veracity" and "propensity". This may well have resulted in some improvements over the common law but it has undoubtedly created some difficulties of interpretation, including difficulties sorting out the relationship between the two classes of evidence dealt with in Subpart 5.[456]

The definition of "veracity" is set out in s 37(5) and is of obvious importance in interpreting this Subpart of the Act. See the discussion of s 37(5) for possible uncertainties caused by the precise terms of that definition.[457]

Application

36   Application of subpart to evidence of veracity and propensity

(1) This subpart does not apply to evidence about a person's veracity if that veracity is an ingredient of the claim in a civil proceeding or one of the elements of the offence for which a person is being tried in a criminal proceeding.

(2) This subpart does not apply so far as a proceeding relates to bail or sentencing.

(3) Subsection (2) is subject to section 44.

---

454   See also the discussion of "editing" at EV91.01.

455   For the contrary view, see Burston and Verrall, "Questioning of Witnesses" in NZLS *Intensive: Evidence Act 2006*, 118.

456   For further discussion of that relationship, see EV40.05.

457   For the definition of "propensity evidence" see EV40.02.

EV36.01   Subsection (1): when veracity determines liability

Section 36(1) assures that Subpart 5 of Part 2 does not apply to evidence of a person's veracity when that is one of the crucial factors being litigated.

(1)   Civil proceedings

Section 36(1) excludes the application of Subpart 5 when a person's veracity "is an ingredient of the claim in a civil proceeding". A straightforward example of this would be an action for deceit. Evidence demonstrating the defendant's lack of veracity in the particular transaction upon which the claim in deceit is based is not subject to the controls otherwise applicable to veracity or propensity evidence.

(2)   Criminal proceedings

In so far as criminal proceedings are concerned, a prosecution for perjury would be an obvious example where s 36(1) renders the remainder of Subpart 5 irrelevant. The defendant's veracity (on the specific occasion alleged) is one of the elements of the offence of perjury for which he or she is being tried.

(3)   Whole of Subpart inapplicable

It is noteworthy that in the cases to which it is directed, s 36(1) excludes not only the veracity rules but also the rules governing propensity evidence. The whole of Subpart 5 is rendered inapplicable. This could give rise to an argument that is best illustrated by a perjury trial in which the prosecution offers evidence of a multitude of occasions where the defendant has lied. The prosecution could argue that s 43's controls on propensity evidence are not applicable because of s 36(1).

Such an argument leads to a result that appears to be contrary to the intention of the Act's controls on propensity evidence. The counter argument would be that the example does not come within s 36(1). In speaking of "that veracity", the subsection is exempting from the Subpart's controls only the class of veracity evidence which is *one of the elements of the offence*. The defendant's veracity on occasions other than the one that has been charged is outside that class of veracity evidence.[458]

(4)   Subsection (2): bail or sentencing

Section 36(2) excludes the operation of Subpart 5 in proceedings relating to bail or sentencing. Accordingly, at a bail or sentencing hearing, the prosecution can offer evidence about the defendant's veracity without reference to the veracity rules contained in ss 37 or 38.

It is likely that s 36(2) is largely directed at propensity evidence, the other main component of Subpart 5. Accordingly, at bail or sentencing hearings the prosecution will be able to offer evidence about the defendant's propensity (commonly, his or her record of convictions) without regard to s 43 of the Act. Other sections of the Act outside Subpart 5 will remain applicable. Thus, although s 36(2) means that at bail or sentencing hearings the prosecution can offer evidence about the defendant's lack

---

458   See also the discussion at EV40.05(3).

of veracity without reference to the veracity rules, such evidence may often be excluded as irrelevant, in accordance with s 7(2).

(5)   Subsection (3): sexual experience of complainant

Section 36(3) provides an exception to s 36(2). The veracity and propensity rules *will* apply to proceedings relating to bail or sentencing when the veracity or propensity evidence in question "relates directly or indirectly to the sexual experience of the complainant with any person other than the defendant" (s 44(1)). The same is true of evidence offered in a proceeding relating to bail or sentencing when such evidence "relates directly or indirectly to the reputation of the complainant in sexual matters" (s 44(2)).

This means that when a defendant in a sexual case is applying for bail or being sentenced after conviction, he or she will be subject to the limitations or prohibitions on evidence concerning the complainant that are set forth in s 44. For example, a defendant would be subject to the restrictions set by s 44 in any attempt to argue for a lesser sentence because the complainant was a prostitute.

Evidence of veracity

37   Veracity rules

(1)   A party may not offer evidence in a civil or criminal proceeding about a person's veracity unless the evidence is substantially helpful in assessing that person's veracity.

(2)   In a criminal proceeding, evidence about a defendant's veracity must also comply with section 38 or, as the case requires, section 39.

(3)   In deciding, for the purposes of subsection (1), whether or not evidence proposed to be offered about the veracity of a person is substantially helpful, the Judge may consider, among any other matters, whether the proposed evidence tends to show 1 or more of the following matters:

(a)   lack of veracity on the part of the person when under a legal obligation to tell the truth (for example, in an earlier proceeding or in a signed declaration):

(b)   that the person has been convicted of 1 or more offences that indicate a propensity for dishonesty or lack of veracity:

(c)   any previous inconsistent statements made by the person:

(d)   bias on the part of the person:

(e)   a motive on the part of the person to be untruthful.

(4)   A party who calls a witness—

(a)   may not offer evidence to challenge that witness's veracity unless the Judge determines the witness to be hostile; but

(b)   may offer evidence as to the facts in issue contrary to the evidence of that witness.

(5)   For the purposes of this Act, **veracity** means the disposition of a person to refrain from lying, whether generally or in the proceeding.

EV37.01   Veracity rules

Section 37 sets out the veracity rules. Certain specific applications of these rules are governed by ss 38 and 39.

(1)   Accuracy

Section 37(5) defines "veracity" as a person's disposition to refrain from lying. The result is that ss 37-39 make no attempt to control evidence about the *accuracy* of a statement by a person who is attempting to tell the truth.[459]

EV37.02   Substantial helpfulness

Section 37(1) sets out the basic veracity rule. Veracity evidence must be *substantially helpful* in assessing the veracity of the person in question. This is reminiscent of the test for admissibility of expert opinion evidence in s 25(1).

The substantial helpfulness test marks a higher threshold than mere relevance, as that term is defined by s 7(3). Evidence is not admissible simply because it "has a tendency to prove or disprove" a person's veracity. To be admissible under s 37(1), the evidence must be "substantially helpful" in assessing veracity.

EV37.03   Wide application of s 37(1)

Section 37(1)'s substantial helpfulness test will apply in a number of surprising contexts that are concurrently governed by other provisions in the Act. Some of these are now discussed.

(1)   Hearsay

There is no qualification on the scope of s 37(1) which would render it inapplicable in determining the admissibility of hearsay evidence. An important prerequisite for the admissibility of a hearsay statement is that "the circumstances relating to the statement provide reasonable assurance that the statement is reliable" (s 18(1)(a)). Paragraph (d) of s 16(1)'s definition of "circumstances" includes "any circumstances that relate to the veracity of the person" making the hearsay statement in question. Although this provision envisions a wide range of evidence concerning veracity ("*any* circumstances that relate to veracity"), s 37(1) is still paramount. Evidence directed at this aspect of "circumstances" must meet the "substantial helpfulness" test set by s 37(1).

(2)   Previous consistent statements

The discussion of s 35(2)[460] suggested that it could be argued that when evidence of a witness's previous consistent statement is offered under s 35(2) on the basis that it is necessary to respond to a challenge to the witness's veracity, the statement must

---

459   See EV40.05(5).
460   See EV35.05.

also meet s 37(1)'s substantial helpfulness test. However, in the majority of such cases, that test will be automatically satisfied.

(3)   Previous inconsistent statements

In so far as previous inconsistent statements are concerned, the same conclusion does not necessarily follow. This is because, unlike s 35's general prohibition of previous consistent statements, the Act contains no similar prohibition of previous inconsistent statements. Accordingly, previous inconsistent statements can be admitted without any necessary focus on the topic of veracity. In the discussion of s 37(3)(c) it will be argued that the freedom to offer evidence of previous inconsistent statements *for a variety of purposes*, means that in a majority of cases such evidence will *not* be evidence "about" a person's veracity. Whenever it is not, a party's ability to offer evidence of a person's previous inconsistent statements will, therefore, not be subject to s 37(1)'s substantial helpfulness test.

(4)   Reputation

Section 37(1)'s test for evidence about veracity contains no limit on the *type* of evidence that may be offered. However, although the Act contains no prohibition on evidence of a person's reputation for veracity (or a lack of veracity), the Evidence Bill had a specific provision permitting the judge to consider a person's reputation for being untruthful. This provision was deleted by the Select Committee. Therefore, it will be difficult to convince a court to allow reputation evidence in this context — at least when it is evidence of a *lack* of veracity. However, an argument in support of an offer of reputation evidence of a person's veracity would emphasise the absence of any specific prohibition on such evidence, as *is* provided for in s 44(2) with respect to complainants in sexual cases.

In *R v Bensitel*,[461] the Court referred to the Evidence Bill in the form it stood before the Select Committee had removed the provisions which specifically authorised evidence of reputation for being untruthful. The Court also referred to a line of common law authority which permitted one witness to testify that he or she would not believe the evidence given by another witness. The Court said:

> "If the Evidence Bill is passed, the cases [concerning one witness's opinion of another's veracity] may have to be reconsidered in light of the new test. It does not seem to us that evidence of one person's view of whether a witness is truthful or not (with no indication as to the grounds for belief) is, in most cases, likely to be substantially helpful in assessing a witness's truthfulness. Evidence of general reputation among the relevant community for telling lies may, however, be of more assistance."

Following the Act, the topic was touched on by the Court of Appeal in *R v C (CA391/07)*.[462] As discussed at EV40.05(5), the central issue in *R v C* was whether, in a sexual case, s 37 or s 44 determined the admissibility of evidence that the

---

461   *R v Bensitel* 5/10/06, CA133/06, para 18.
462   *R v C (CA391/07)* 12/10/07, CA391/07; [2007] NZCA 439.

complainant had made (allegedly false) complaints that persons other than the defendant had also abused her. In the course of the judgment the Court apparently concluded that, in view of the legislative history outlined above, evidence of a person's reputation for a lack of veracity was *never* admissible under s 37.[463] The Court said:

> "The 2006 Act prohibits the admission of evidence of reputation in sexual matters (s 44(2)) and does not allow for the admission of evidence of reputation for untruthfulness (s 37). If the evidence which the appellant seeks to adduce at trial is evidence of reputation, it will be inadmissible whether the case falls under s 37 or s 44."

(5)   Cross-examination

Because s 4 defines "offer evidence" as including eliciting evidence by cross-examination, s 37(1)'s substantial helpfulness test governs cross-examination as well as examination in chief. Previously, a lawyer's explanation to the judge that the lawyer's cross-examination was "directed at credibility" was a sufficient justification for wide latitude in questioning. That former explanation may no longer be sufficient. Cross-examination directed at attacking veracity must now meet the standard of substantial helpfulness.

Section 37(1) will force cross-examiners to look to the substantial helpfulness test instead of earlier statutory provisions that no longer exist. For example, the ability to ask any witness whether they have been convicted of an indictable offence (and prove the conviction if denied), enshrined in s 12 of the Evidence Act 1908, is not preserved in the new Act. See the discussion below of s 37(3)(b). Whether such a question is permissible in any particular case will now be determined by the substantial helpfulness test. Similarly, the new test replaces the more detailed guidance for permissible cross-examination as to credibility that was set forth in s 13 of the Evidence Act 1908. See the discussion of s 92 at EV92.02 for a possible limitation on all cross-examination designed to attack a witness's veracity.

(6)   Oath helping

Previously, the law had a general aversion to "oath helping", namely evidence called by a party that is designed to show that one of the party's witnesses is a truthful person. This aversion was most pronounced in a case where the attempt at oath helping was made before any attack had been launched by an opposing party (*Sungsuwan v R*[464]). Under the Act, there is no obvious bar to oath helping evidence. Section 37(1) will allow such evidence as long as it meets the substantial helpfulness test.[465]

The law's traditional aversion to oath helping evidence may lead a court to turn to ss 7 or 8 as a means of limiting evidence supporting a witness's veracity. Section 7 appears to be a weaker source for argument, because oath helping evidence is surely

---

463   *R v C (CA391/07)* 12/10/07, CA391/07; [2007] NZCA 439, para 21. See also EV38.01(1) and EV40.02(3).

464   *Sungsuwan v R* [2006] 1 NZLR 730; (2005) 21 CRNZ 977 (SC), para 84.

465   See also EV37.05(3).

---

relevant. It tends to prove a witness's veracity, which is nearly always "of consequence to the determination of the proceeding" (s 7(3)). Section 8(1)(b) provides a stronger base for exclusion because, at least until a witness's veracity has been attacked, oath helping evidence may be judged to "needlessly prolong the proceeding".

(7) Collateral issues rule

One of the most substantial changes brought about by s 37 is the end to the rule known as "the collateral issues" rule, or "the rule in *Hitchcock*'s case".[466] This rule prevented a cross-examining party from offering evidence to contradict the denial of a proposition put to a witness when the focus of the cross-examination was the "collateral" issue of the witness's veracity. "Collateral" here is meant to distinguish such cross-examination from questioning on the issues in dispute in the litigation (in which case, evidence contradicting the witness's answer was always permitted).

The collateral issues rule was justified on the basis that it was necessary to avoid extended controversies over facts that were not central to the determination of liability. Such tangential enquiries into collateral issues would unjustifiably extend the time and resources expended in litigation.

Under s 37, there is no explicit bar on evidence about veracity that contradicts a witness's denial of a proposition put to the witness during cross-examination. Of course, the "substantial helpfulness" test in s 37(1) must be met before such contradictory evidence can be offered by the cross-examiner. Additionally, the party who called the witness whose veracity is being attacked could still mount an objection to the contradictory evidence on the basis of s 8(1)(b). This objection, mirroring the justification for the former collateral issues rule, would be that the tangential enquiry into the validity of the proposition that was denied by the witness would "needlessly prolong the proceedings".[467]

(8) Exceptions to the collateral issues rule

The collateral issues rule was subject to various exceptions. When the proposition that was denied by the witness during cross-examination involved a topic coming within one of the exceptions, the cross-examining party *was* able to call evidence contradicting the witness's denial. As a general proposition, the major exceptions to the collateral issues rule appear, in somewhat modified form, in s 37(3)(a)-(e). However, as the discussion of s 37(3) makes clear, the listed factors are now merely possible indicators of whether or not the "substantial helpfulness" test has been met.

(9) Priority of veracity rules over propensity rule

See EV40.05.

---

466 *A-G v Hitchcock* (1847) 1 Exch 91; 154 ER 38.
467 In *R v Smith* 10/9/07, CA267/07; CA343/07; [2007] NZCA 400, paras 14-20, the Court discussed the collateral issues rule and concluded that the combined operation of s 37(1)'s "substantial helpfulness" test and s 8(1)(b) would mean that "often in practice there will be little, if any, difference between the Act and the common law". However, see the discussion in *Adams on Criminal Law — Evidence*, EC11.04.

EV37.04   Subsection (2): criminal proceedings

Section 37(2) makes the point that, in the case of the two classes of veracity evidence referred to in the subsection, satisfaction of s 37(1)'s substantial helpfulness test alone will not be enough to ensure admissibility. These two classes of veracity evidence both involve a criminal proceeding where the evidence is about a *defendant's veracity*. Section 38 imposes additional requirements for admissibility of such evidence when it is offered by the prosecution. Section 39 does so when such evidence is offered by a co-defendant.

EV37.05   Subsection (2): factors for assessing substantial helpfulness

Section 37(3) provides guidance for a judge who is called upon to determine whether proposed veracity evidence has met s 37(1)'s substantial helpfulness test. Section 37(3) merely says that the judge "may consider" whether the proposed evidence tends to show one or more of the matters set out in paras (a)-(e). However, in a case where the evidence does raise an issue under one or more of these subsections, a judge would be opening himself or herself to criticism if he or she did not take the relevant factor into consideration.

(1)   Physical or mental condition

One factor relevant to a witness's veracity that earlier authorities often grouped with those listed in s 37(3)(a)-(e) was evidence of a witness's *physical or mental condition that detrimentally affects the witness's veracity*. Presumably, in a case where a party proposed to offer evidence that a witness suffered from such a condition, the judge could, without considering any of the matters set forth in s 37(3)(a)-(e), conclude that such evidence was admissible because it satisfied the substantial helpfulness test.

(2)   One or more

In encouraging judges to consider whether "1 or more" of the factors listed in paras (a)-(e) are shown by the evidence, the opening portion of s 37(3) is indicating that the likelihood that the substantial helpfulness test has been met increases when the proposed evidence tends to show more than one of the factors. However, it is not difficult to imagine cases where, although the evidence tends to show only one of the matters listed, the substantial helpfulness test is satisfied because of the high relevance to veracity exhibited by the evidence in the particular case.

(3)   Negative factors

All of the factors set forth in s 37(3)(a)-(e) are "negative" in the sense that they tend to indicate a *lack of veracity*. Despite this focus, it is not possible to argue that s 37(1) is concerned only with a person's lack of veracity. Other than s 37(3), the remainder of ss 36-39 refer only to "veracity". There is ample justification for applying s 37(1)'s substantial helpfulness test to evidence *supporting* a person's veracity.

EV37.06   Lies

By highlighting evidence showing lack of veracity when under a *legal* obligation to tell the truth, s 37(3)(a) may tend to *restrict* a party's ability to offer evidence about veracity when compared to the position before the Act. The subsection suggests that evidence of lying when there is no legal obligation to tell the truth will not usually be substantially helpful in assessing the veracity of the person who lied.

(1)   Earlier proceeding

Some difficulty may be caused by the bracketed portion of s 37(3)(a), which gives the example of a lack of veracity at an *earlier* proceeding. Perhaps this example can be explained on the basis that the legislative drafter wished to avoid the accusation of begging the question of the person's veracity in the *current* proceeding. Nonetheless, the suggestion appears to be that evidence will not meet the substantial helpfulness test if it tends to show a lack of veracity at the *current* hearing.

Such a suggestion is difficult to justify, given that s 37(5) defines veracity as the disposition to refrain from lying, whether generally *or in the proceeding*. It cannot be the case that a judge engaged in the process of determining the veracity of a witness should somehow feel constrained in placing reliance on evidence that the witness has been shown to have lied in the current proceeding.

(2)   Lies by complainant in sexual case

See EV40.05(5).

EV37.07   Convictions

Four points are raised by s 37(3)(b)'s emphasis on convictions of 1 or more offences that indicate a propensity for dishonesty or lack of veracity:[468]

(i)   By singling out convictions for offences that indicate a propensity for dishonesty or lack of veracity, s 37(3)(b) implies that, in the usual case, convictions for offences which do *not* carry that connotation do not meet the substantial helpfulness test.

(ii)   There is no easy explanation for the distinction drawn by s 37(3)(b) between *dishonesty* and *lack of veracity*. Section 37(5) makes it clear that veracity is solely concerned with a person's disposition to refrain from lying. It might therefore have been thought that lack of veracity has already been defined as "dishonesty", rendering s 37(3)(b)'s distinction meaningless.

(iii)   The wording of s 37(3)(b) makes it clear that a single conviction for an offence that indicates a *propensity* for dishonesty or lack of veracity may be enough to satisfy the substantial helpfulness test in assessing the veracity of the convicted person. This speaks volumes about the legislature's understanding of what qualifies as "propensity evidence" as defined by s 40(1) and as governed by the second half of Subpart 5. Section 37(3)(b)'s reference to a *propensity* for dishonesty or lack of veracity demonstrates the legislature's view that there are certain offences (and, presumably, other acts or omissions)

---

468   It is likely that s 49(3) will be interpreted to require counsel (in a criminal case) to obtain permission from the judge before offering evidence (including cross-examination) about a person's convictions: *R v Russell* 2/11/07, Stevens J, HC Auckland CRI-2006-092-11084, para 10.

which are capable of indicating a person's propensity from a *single occurrence*.

(iv)   The point just made highlights that s 37(3)(b) does not focus on convictions for offences of dishonesty or lack of veracity simpliciter. The substantial helpfulness test will (in most cases) only be met by convictions for offences that indicate a *propensity* for dishonesty or lack of veracity.

Matters would have been simpler if the enquiry was merely whether the convictions were of the sort that are commonly referred to as "an offence of dishonesty" (or "an offence of lack of veracity"). This would have permitted the conclusion that, for example, convictions for theft or perjury were aimed at by s 37(3)(b). Matters are much less clear when the focus is that of a propensity. Remembering that a single conviction is enough to satisfy s 37(3)(b), it is legitimate to ask whether every conviction for an offence of, for example, perjury, indicates a propensity for dishonesty or lack of veracity? If it does not, what additional factors are required before a conviction does carry such an indication?

This enquiry is not assisted by the fact that "propensity" is not defined in the Act other than by the definition of "propensity evidence" in s 40(1). By its terms, that definition only applies to ss 41-43. Even greater problems are caused by s 37(5)'s definition of "veracity". Those problems are discussed at EV37.15.

The perjury example was used because, even in the case of an offence so readily characterised as an offence of dishonesty (or lack of veracity), the focus of propensity adds uncertainty. This uncertainty is only increased in the case of most other offences which are not as easily characterised as offences of dishonesty or lack of veracity. For example, although theft is routinely referred to as an offence of dishonesty, theft offences are usually performed with no lie being told. Sexual abuse of young children is not normally considered an offence of dishonesty, yet the modus operandi of many sexual offenders does involve extensive lying.

This issue is not a new one. See the differing judicial viewpoints expressed in *R v Lumsden*[469] (drug convictions); see too *Bugg v Day*[470] (traffic convictions). More recently, in *R v Wood*,[471] the Court said, "credibility can be affected by conviction other than for dishonesty. A lack of trustworthiness may be demonstrated by repeated instances of contempt for the law".[472]

---

469   *R v Lumsden* [2003] NSWCCA 83.
470   *Bugg v Day* (1949) 79 CLR 442 (HCA).
471   *R v Wood* [2006] 3 NZLR 743 (CA), paras 39-41.
472   In *R v Russell* 2/11/07, Stevens J, HC Auckland CRI-2006-092-11084, para 25, Stevens J concluded that two convictions for indecency, nearly 30 years old, would not meet s 37(1)'s substantial helpfulness test in assessing a witness's veracity.

EV37.08   Previous inconsistent statements

Section 37(3)(c) suggests that the substantial helpfulness test will likely be satisfied whenever the proposed evidence "tends to show" that the person whose veracity is in question made a *previous inconsistent statement.*

The opportunity is taken here to begin a consideration of previous inconsistent statements under the Act. The central focus will be s 37(3)(c), but broader issues will be touched on. This discussion is supplemented by the later discussion of s 96, which provides controls on the method of questioning a witness about his or her previous inconsistent statements.[473]

(1)   Inconsistent

The Act does not give any assistance in determining when a previous statement is inconsistent. Guidance on this issue is found in *R v Speers.*[474] That case involved testimony which added a detail not found in the witness's previous statement. Fisher J held that this would amount to an inconsistency if it would have been expected that a truthful witness would have referred to the detail in the previous statement.[475]

(2)   Witnesses and Others

There is some uncertainty over the class of evidence caught by s 37(3)(c). Section 4 of the Act defines "previous statement" as a statement made by a *witness* at any time other than at the hearing at which the witness is giving evidence. Presumably, the core of this definition will still apply to a "previous inconsistent statement". A statement *by a witness* is surely the framework that is most readily brought to mind by s 37(3)(c). The subsection's main purpose is to confirm that an inconsistency between a witness's testimony and a statement made by the witness prior to coming to court is a substantially helpful method of showing that the witness lacks veracity.

However, s 37 controls evidence about *any* person's veracity, not only witnesses. It is easy to imagine situations where a party may wish to offer evidence about the veracity of a person who is not a witness in a proceeding. The most obvious example will be evidence about the veracity of a person whose hearsay statement has been offered by another party to the proceeding. The party wishing to weaken the effect of that hearsay statement may want to offer evidence that the statement maker contradicted himself or herself in some statement made on a different occasion (whether earlier or later). Because of the definition of a "previous statement" (applying only to *witnesses*), it does not seem that the inconsistent statement by the hearsay statement maker will amount to a "previous inconsistent statement" as that phrase appears in s 37(3)(c). It is even less likely to do so if the contradictory statement was made some time *after* the making of the hearsay statement that has been admitted into evidence (it would not be a *previous* statement).

---

473   See, generally, *Adams on Criminal Law — Evidence,* EC11.
474   *R v Speers* 18/2/91, Fisher J, HC Hamilton T60/90.
475   See, generally, *Adams on Criminal Law — Evidence,* EC11.02.

These points should hardly prevent the offer of such evidence. Section 37(3) is expressly stated to be a non-exhaustive list of factors relevant to an application of the substantial helpfulness test. Accordingly, even if the inconsistent statement does not fit within s 37(3)(c), it should still have the potential to be a substantially helpful indicator of the statement maker's lack of veracity. Whether or not it is actually substantially helpful will depend on the predictably variable circumstances surrounding the two statements in any particular case.

EV37.09　Admissibility of previous inconsistent statements

Section 37(1)'s substantial helpfulness test only applies to evidence offered about a person's veracity. It is suggested that the factor determining whether evidence is offered "about" a person's veracity is the *purpose* for which the evidence is offered. If the party offering the evidence does so to bolster or attack a person's veracity, then the evidence is about veracity. If the evidence is offered for some other purpose, it is not evidence about veracity.

(1)　Multiple purposes for offering evidence

There is little doubt that the Act accepts a party's ability to offer evidence for one of two (or more) possible purposes. This is made clear, for example, in s 4's definition of a hearsay statement as a statement "offered in evidence to prove the truth of its contents." As was the case before the Act, if a party offers a statement in evidence for some other purpose, such as simply to show that the statement was made, it is not a hearsay statement.[476]

This proposition is important when considering previous inconsistent statements. Undoubtedly, one common purpose for offering evidence of a previous inconsistent statement is to attack the veracity of the person who made the statement. When this occurs, the evidence is offered about veracity and it must meet s 37(1)'s test of substantial helpfulness. This is so regardless of what may have been the actual topic of the previous statement. (The Law Commission did not agree with this analysis.)[477]

On the other hand, when a party offers evidence of a person's previous inconsistent statement for a purpose other than attacking veracity, it is no longer evidence *about* veracity. Section 37(1)'s substantial helpfulness test is not relevant in such a case. Unlike previous consistent statements (see s 35(2)), the Act contains no general prohibition on a party's ability to offer evidence of a person's previous inconsistent statements. Admissibility is not tied to a challenge to veracity.

The most obvious purpose for which a party will want to offer evidence of a person's previous inconsistent statement is to *prove the truth* of the contents of the statement. Before the Act, it was clear that (in most cases) this purpose was not available.[478] The most that the previous inconsistent statement could accomplish was to weaken the

---

476　See further discussion at EV4.20.03; EV7.03.
477　LC *Evidence Code*, para C171. The Law Commission's view was that evidence of a previous statement is "about" whatever topic is dealt with in the statement.
478　*Adams on Criminal Law — Evidence*, EC11.09.

witness's credibility. Under the Act, however, this limitation has been removed. A previous inconsistent statement can now be used to help prove the truth of its contents.

(2)   Few controls on admissibility

Where a party offers evidence that a witness made a previous inconsistent statement and the party offers that evidence to prove the truth of the contents of the statement, there appears to be little control on the admissibility of the statement. Because the statement was made by a *witness*, it does not meet the definition of a hearsay statement under s 4(1) (which defines hearsay as a statement by a person "other than a witness"). Thus it need not pass the reliability threshold for hearsay statements set by s 18(1)(a). Because it is not evidence "about a person's veracity", it need not comply with s 37(1)'s substantial helpfulness test. Section 37(3)(c) is only relevant when the purpose for offering the evidence of the previous inconsistent statement is to demonstrate the statement maker's lack of veracity, as opposed to proving the truth of what was stated.

(3)   Need to confront the witness

Section 37(3)(c) has no requirement that a witness whose veracity is being attacked must first be given a chance to comment on his or her alleged previous inconsistent statement. However, such a requirement may arise from s 96(2).[479]

EV37.10   Bias

Section 37(3)(d) suggests that s 37(1)'s substantial helpfulness test will be met by evidence that the person whose veracity is in issue is *biased*. There is little doubt that this will most commonly apply to bias in favour of or against any party to the proceeding, although it is possible to imagine a witness who was biased against courts or authority to such an extent that his or her veracity was affected.

Some common law authorities lumped together with bias, the factors of corruption and interest in the outcome of the litigation (as well as a motive to be untruthful, covered separately by s 37(3)(e)). Although these additional factors may not be identical to bias, it is probably safe to assume that their presence is equally likely to satisfy s 37(1)'s substantial helpfulness test.[480]

EV37.11   Motive to be untruthful

Section 37(3)(e) adds to the list of factors likely to be substantially helpful in assessing veracity, evidence tending to show that the person whose veracity is in question had a motive to be untruthful. As referred to above, this factor has traditionally been linked with bias, s 37(3)(d). See too s 122(2)(c), which is applicable in criminal proceedings.

EV37.12   Three separate concepts in s 37(3)

In referring to "untruthfulness", s 37(3)(e) has not added clarity to s 37. The concept of truthfulness was the focus of cls 36-39 in the Evidence Bill, but the Select

---

479   See also EV92.02(1).

480   See, generally, *Adams on Criminal Law — Evidence*, EC11.13(1)(b).

Committee changed the rules from "truthfulness" rules to the current "veracity" rules on the ground that:

> "we consider the word 'veracity' is more appropriate as it places the emphasis upon the intention to tell the truth, whereas 'truthfulness' is more readily confused with factual correctness".

The unhelpful result is that we now have the three concepts in s 37(3) of veracity, dishonesty (s 37(3)(b)), and untruthfulness (s 37(3)(e)). Given the view stated by the Select Committee, lawyers will be understandably tempted to make arguments which draw esoteric distinctions among these three concepts.

EV37.13   Subsection (4): party challenges veracity of his or her own witness

Section 37(4)(a) states the general rule that a party who calls a witness may not offer evidence to challenge that witness's veracity.

In considering s 37(4) it will be helpful to compare s 9 of the Evidence Act 1908. That section prohibited a party "impeaching the credit" (a phrase broadly equivalent to s 37(4)'s "challenging the veracity") of the party's own witness *by general evidence of bad character*. Section 37(4) prohibits a challenge to veracity by *any* means (not merely by "general evidence of bad character").

(1)   Challenge

Section 37(4) may be contrasted with s 35(2) (part of the previous consistent statement rule). Section 35(2) does not limit the type of challenge dealt with by that subsection.[481] For example, a witness could be challenged by a suggestion made by the cross-examiner that the witness was lying. In contrast, s 37(4) focuses on a challenge in the form of an *offer of evidence*.

The similarity between s 37(4) and s 9 of the Evidence Act 1908 makes it likely that *R v Eagles*[482] will still apply. In *Eagles* the Court agreed that s 9 did not prohibit a party from *inviting the fact-finder* not to accept the evidence of a witness called by that party. It appears that such an invitation will not breach s 37(4)(a).

Section 37(4)(b) makes it clear that a prohibited "challenge" does not occur simply because the party who called the witness offers "evidence as to the facts in issue contrary to the evidence of that witness". Presumably, this wording is meant to imply that *other* classes of evidence, such as evidence of the matters set out in s 37(3), *can* amount to the sort of challenge that is prohibited by s 37(4).

EV37.14   Hostile witness

Section 37(4)(a) contains one exception to its general prohibition. A party can offer evidence to challenge the veracity of a witness called by the party if the judge determines that the witness is hostile.

(1)   Hostile

See the discussion of the definition of "hostile" at EV4.21.01-04.

---

481   See EV35.05.
482   *R v Eagles* [2004] 2 NZLR 468 (CA).

(2)   Other controls

Section 37(4)(a) gives a *right* to offer evidence challenging the veracity of a hostile witness. However, it is suggested that such evidence must still meet s 37(1)'s substantial helpfulness test.

When the particular offer of evidence takes the form of an attack on the witness in *cross-examination*, s 94 will apply to give the judge a more direct source for controlling the process. Such controls may go well beyond s 37(1)'s substantial helpfulness test for admissibility.

The most common focus for a party's cross-examination of the party's own hostile witness is a *previous statement* by the witness. Section 96 provides controls on the way such a cross-examination should be conducted.

EV37.15   Subsection (5): definition of veracity

The negative definition of veracity in s 37(5) creates some potential for confusion in the enquiries required by s 37(3), in particular s 37(3)(b). That this is so is demonstrated when the precise definition set forth in s 37(5) is substituted for "veracity" in s 37(3)(b). A judge considering s 37(1)'s substantial helpfulness test will be required to determine whether the proposed evidence about veracity tends to show that the person whose veracity is in question has been convicted of one or more offences that "indicate a propensity for … lack of … a disposition to refrain from lying".

(1)   Disposition

Section 37(5) introduces the concept of "disposition", not found elsewhere in the Act. It might have been thought that "propensity" would have served the same purpose and brought about some consistency.

An enquiry into a person's disposition to refrain from lying is different than an enquiry whether the person refrained from lying on a *particular occasion*. This distinction may provide a solution to one of the difficulties presented by s 38(2).[483]

38	**Evidence of defendant's veracity**
(1)	A defendant in a criminal proceeding may offer evidence about his or her veracity.
(2)	The prosecution in a criminal proceeding may offer evidence about a defendant's veracity only if—
	(a) the defendant has offered evidence about his or her veracity or has challenged the veracity of a prosecution witness by reference to matters other than the facts in issue; and
	(b) the Judge permits the prosecution to do so.
(3)	In determining whether to give permission under subsection (2)(b), the Judge may take into account any of the following matters:

---

483   See EV38.02(2).

(a)   the extent to which the defendant's veracity or the veracity of a prosecution witness has been put in issue in the defendant's evidence:

(b)   the time that has elapsed since any conviction about which the prosecution seeks to give evidence:

(c)   whether any evidence given by the defendant about veracity was elicited by the prosecution.

EV38.01   Subsection (1): evidence supporting defendant's veracity

Section 38(1) confirms the ability of a defendant in criminal proceedings to offer evidence about his or her veracity. See, similarly, s 41(1), which permits a defendant to offer propensity evidence about himself or herself.

As discussed at EV4.29.01, a party may offer evidence although he or she never testifies. A defendant could offer evidence about the defendant's veracity by questioning a defence witness or by cross-examining a prosecution witness.

Although a defendant may wish to offer evidence supporting his or her veracity, such a tactic can have the undesirable result set out in s 38(2). As discussed below, with the permission of the judge, the prosecution can respond by offering evidence showing the defendant's lack of veracity.

Section 37(1)'s substantial helpfulness test will apply to evidence offered by a defendant under s 38(1). This is made clear by s 37(2).

(1)   General reputation

At common law there was a rule that evidence of the defendant's "good character" could only take the form of evidence of the defendant's *general reputation* rather than evidence of specific instances of demonstrating good character. Not only is there no suggestion that this rule applies under the Act, the Select Committee's specific removal from the Evidence Bill of references to evidence of reputation is likely to be relied upon to preclude the sort of evidence that the common law required.

However, nothing in the Act specifically prohibits evidence of a defendant's reputation (cf s 44(2)). The Select Committee's concern appeared to be directed at evidence of a person's reputation for a lack of veracity. This is not the focus of s 38(1) because, under that subsection, a defendant will be offering evidence *supporting* his or her veracity. Evidence of a reputation for veracity may still be permissible.[484]

EV38.02   Subsection (2): attack on defendant's veracity

Section 38(2) prevents the prosecution in a criminal proceeding from offering evidence about a defendant's veracity except in the limited circumstances described in s 38(2)(a) and (b). When the prosecution is permitted to offer such evidence it will inevitably be evidence *attacking* the defendant's veracity.

---

484   See *Adams on Criminal Law — Evidence*, EC8.15(2). However, see the discussion of *R v C (CA391/07)* 12/10/07, CA391/07; [2007] NZCA 439 at EV37.03(4). See also EV40.02(3).

(1)   Broader prohibition than before the Act

In the Select Committee's Report on the Evidence Bill, the Committee explained s 38(2) as "reinstat[ing] the existing law that limits the opportunity for the prosecution to call evidence as to the defendant's bad character".[485] However, the result of the Select Committee's tinkering with the Evidence Bill is that s 38(2) prevents *all classes* of prosecution evidence about a defendant's veracity, not merely evidence of "bad character". On the face of it, this means that unless the defendant "opens the door" to such evidence in the ways set out in s 38(2)(a), the prosecution is absolutely prohibited from suggesting that the defendant is lying when the defendant gives evidence of his or her innocence. In view of s 4's definition of "offer evidence", this prohibition on the prosecution offering evidence of the defendant's veracity will cover the process of *cross-examination of the defendant* as well.

All of this means that in a case where the defendant gets into the witness box and gives evidence of his or her innocence, but not about his or her veracity, the prosecution is prevented from cross-examining the defendant by such traditional means as were described by the Court of Appeal in the pre-Act case of *R v Leef*, as follows:[486]

> "It is, … a perfectly proper approach, for prosecuting counsel to suggest an accused has a motive to lie and has lied because of previous convictions, the improbability of his evidence, its conflict with proved facts or other circumstances of the case."

In other words, s 38(2) prevents the prosecution from offering evidence challenging the defendant's veracity when the defendant has not offered evidence of the sort referred to in s 38(2)(a) but has merely denied his or her guilt and offered evidence of innocence.

This problem could perhaps have been avoided if the general prohibition on prosecution evidence of the defendant's veracity, set out in the opening clause of s 38(2), had recognised the same exception concerning "the facts in issue", as appears in the separate, concluding clause of s 38(2)(a). However, this did not occur.

(2)   Possible contrary arguments

There are some arguments against this remarkable proposition. One is based on s 37(5)'s definition of "veracity". It could be argued that prosecution evidence that the defendant's testimony of innocence is a lie does not meet s 37(5)'s definition of evidence about the defendant's *disposition* to refrain from lying. As such, it does not come within s 37(5)'s definition of evidence about "veracity" and therefore is not caught by the prohibition in s 38(2).

Beyond this general argument, there is a further argument which will only apply to support specific classes of prosecution evidence that are designed to show that the defendant's testimony of innocence is a lie. This second argument is best exemplified

---

485   *Select Committee Report on the Evidence Bill*, 6.
486   *R v Leef* 24/8/06, CA14/06, para 29.

by prosecution evidence that the defendant made a previous statement that is inconsistent with his or her testimony.

Although the fact that the defendant has made a previous inconsistent statement will almost always suggest a lack of veracity, the prosecution could argue that this result is not the *purpose* for which they offered the evidence. Rather, the evidence was offered to prove the truth of what was stated in the previous inconsistent statement and thus is relevant evidence on one of the disputed issues in the case. This being the purpose for which the evidence was offered, it was *not* offered "about" the defendant's veracity. Therefore, it does not come within the terms of the opening clause of s 38(2).

Without the acceptance of one of these or some other argument, s 38(2) must stand among the worst of the errors of the Select Committee's last minute changes to the Evidence Bill.

EV38.03   Substantial helpfulness

As with all evidence about a person's veracity, s 37(1) requires that prosecution evidence about a defendant's veracity, offered under s 38(2), must meet the substantial helpfulness test. Any doubt about this is laid to rest by s 37(2).

EV38.04   Defendant opens the door

Section 38(2)(a) sets out the two ways in which the defendant will "open the door" to otherwise prohibited prosecution evidence about the defendant's veracity.

(1)   Defendant must be responsible

An implied prerequisite to the operation of s 38(2)(a) must be that the defendant is responsible for the circumstances which have opened the door to the damning veracity evidence offered by the prosecution. The defendant can hardly be said to have offered evidence of his or her own veracity or to have challenged the veracity of a prosecution witness if all that has happened is that some defence witness has blurted out a gratuitous comment and there is no suggestion that the defendant has orchestrated this.

EV38.05   Defendant's own veracity

The first of the two ways envisioned by s 38(2)(a) occurs when the defendant offers evidence about his or her own veracity.

The common law did not draw such a clear distinction between veracity evidence and propensity evidence as the Act does. The common law treated both these topics as aspects of "character" evidence. The defendant exposed himself or herself to cross-examination about his or her disreputable veracity or propensity when the defendant "put character in issue" by offering evidence supporting his or her veracity or propensity. Despite these differences, it is likely that guidance as to when the defendant has opened the door under s 38 can still be obtained from the earlier law on when a defendant has "put character in issue" by offering evidence of his or her good character.[487]

(1)   Veracity

As with s 38(1), s 38(2)(a) is only concerned with evidence about the defendant's veracity, as defined by s 37(5). It is likely that occasions will arise where, to avoid the effects of s 38(2)(a), a defendant will argue that although he or she has offered evidence to back up the truth of his or her evidence, that evidence has not been offered about his or her *disposition* to refrain from lying. See the discussion of s 37(5).

EV38.06   Challenge the veracity of prosecution witness

The second way in which the defendant opens the door to prosecution evidence about the defendant's veracity is by challenging the veracity of a prosecution witness.

(1)   Challenge

The triggering challenge by the defendant need not consist in an offer of evidence.[488] Presumably, a challenge could occur through an accusation by defence counsel. See similarly s 35(2).[489]

(2)   By reference to the facts in issue

Section 38(2)(a) adds the sudden qualification set forth in the concluding phrase of the subsection. When the challenge by the defendant can be characterised as a challenge "by reference to … the facts in issue", such a challenge will *not* open the door to the prosecution's counter-attack. This unclear phrase will become a constant source of controversy, with the defence arguing that their challenge to the veracity of a prosecution witness has only been in reference to the facts in issue.

Consider a case in which the defence evidence, offered to challenge the veracity of a prosecution witness, is of the sort referred to in s 37(3)(a). If the occasion demonstrating the lack of veracity when under a legal obligation to tell the truth occurred long before the events currently being litigated, it would be difficult for the defendant to argue that, nonetheless, the challenge "referred to the facts in issue" (s 38(2)(a)).

However the situation is not as clear when the focus shifts to s 37(3)(c) and a previous inconsistent statement made by the prosecution witness about the events being litigated. This example has a higher likelihood of being classified as a challenge "by reference to the facts in issue". If it is, s 38(2)(a) means that the prosecution is unable to respond with evidence about the defendant's veracity.

Similar arguments could arise when the defence challenge to the veracity of a prosecution witness is based on evidence coming within s 37(3)(d) or (e) and the challenge suggests that the witness is lying because they actually committed the crime for which the defendant is being tried or the witness stood to profit from that crime or from their testimony. Such challenges may be argued to be made "by reference to the facts in issue" under s 38(2)(a).[490]

---

487   See *Adams on Criminal Law — Evidence*, EC3.04(1).
488   Cf s 37(4)(a).
489   See, however, EV38.07(2).
490   See, generally, *Adams on Criminal Law — Evidence*, EC3.04(2).

(3)   Only challenges to witnesses are relevant

Section 38(2)(a) refers only to a challenge to the veracity of a prosecution *witness*. Because of the definition of "witness" in s 4, s 38(2)'s consequences do not arise if the defendant challenges the veracity of some other class of person, for example a person who made a hearsay statement that is offered by the prosecution. Because the maker of a hearsay statement is not a "witness", such a challenge does not come within the terms of s 38(2)(a). The defendant can launch such a challenge with impunity.

EV38.07   Permission by the judge

Section 38(2)(b) imposes a further prerequisite to the admissibility of prosecution evidence about the veracity of a defendant. Even when the prosecution overcomes the hurdles set by s 38(2)(a), they must obtain permission from the judge to offer such evidence. This is in keeping with the common law.[491]

(1)   Procedure

It is likely that the procedural controls in place before the Act will continue to apply to jury trials. These controls are designed to avoid any prejudice to a defendant if the judge refuses the application by the prosecution to offer evidence about the defendant's veracity.[492]

(2)   Guidance for the judge

Section 38(3) provides guidelines which the judge *may* take into account in deciding whether or not to grant permission under s 38(2). Despite this terminology, it is suggested that in view of the protective attitudes taken by judges under the earlier law, the factors set out in s 38(3) will be treated as essentially mandatory. It is also likely that earlier authorities will continue to be consulted for guidance on factors beyond those listed in s 38(3).[493]

The "question of degree" raised by s 38(3)(a) appears to assume that s 38(2)(a) only involves a challenge to the veracity of a prosecution witness that is based on an offer of evidence. The earlier discussion of s 38(2)(a) suggested that such a challenge could be made by other means, such as an accusation by defence counsel.

(3)   Trap by prosecution

Section 38(3)(c) marks a potential change from the earlier law. Before the Act, courts considered it improper for the prosecution to lure a defendant into offering evidence of his or her "good character" or into an attack on the character of a prosecution witness: ("Are you an honest person? Are you saying that the police officer is lying?"). In such circumstances, the judge would not grant permission to offer evidence about the defendant's bad character.[494]

---

491   *Adams on Criminal Law — Evidence*, EC3.04(3).
492   *Adams on Criminal Law — Evidence*, EC3.07.
493   See, generally, *Adams on Criminal Law — Evidence*, EC3.04(2)-(3).
494   *Adams on Criminal Law — Evidence*, EC3.04(2)(c).

In contrast, s 38(3)(c) makes this prosecution tactic merely a factor for the judge to consider in the decision whether to grant permission under s 38(2)(b).

(4)   Defendant's veracity must be in issue

In accordance with the basic requirement of relevance in s 7, a judge could not grant permission under s 38(2) if the defendant's veracity was not in issue. Prosecution evidence attacking the defendant's veracity would not be relevant in a case where the defendant did not testify and there is no evidence of a pre-trial exonerating statement made by the defendant.

EV38.08   What uses may be made of evidence attacking defendant's veracity?

When the prosecution offers evidence under s 38(2), is it open to the fact-finder to use the evidence for a purpose beyond that of assessing the defendant's veracity? This question is posed because evidence offered on the basis that it is substantially helpful in assessing veracity may have additional relevance. For example, s 39(1) expressly recognises that evidence challenging the veracity of one defendant may be relevant to the defence of a co-defendant. In the particular context of s 38(2), the important question is whether the fact-finder can use the "veracity" evidence as direct evidence of the defendant's guilt of the crime charged.

This is but one example of the wider question that arises with respect to all classes of evidence about veracity and indeed all classes of evidence admitted under the Act. Once evidence has been admitted, are there any restrictions on how it may be used by the fact-finder? The discussion of this issue at EV4.20.03 and EV7.03 suggested the general rule that, once admitted, evidence can be used for multiple purposes. However, it is here suggested that evidence attacking a defendant's veracity which is admitted under s 38(2) should stand as an exception to that general rule.

The specific question raising this issue in the context of s 38(2) could be rephrased to ask whether prosecution evidence about the defendant's veracity can be relied upon by the jury for what is essentially a propensity use, namely circumstantial evidence of the defendant's guilt. Take the example of a theft trial in which prosecution evidence is offered under s 38(2) that the defendant had numerous previous convictions for obtaining by deception. Is it open to the jury to rely on this evidence not simply to disbelieve a statement made by the defendant (a "veracity" purpose) but also as evidence of the defendant's guilt of the theft charge being tried?

Despite the general rule proposed in the discussion of s 7, it is suggested that, in keeping with the former law,[495] it will be the duty of the judge to direct the jury that veracity evidence offered by the prosecution under s 38(2) can only be used for the purpose of assessing the defendant's veracity and not as evidence of guilt.[496]

---

495   *R v M* (2002) 19 CRNZ 300 (CA).
496   See, generally, *R v Highton* [2005] EWCA Crim 1985; [2005] 1 WLR 3472 (CA).

39   Evidence of co-defendant's veracity

(1)   A defendant in a criminal proceeding may offer evidence that challenges the veracity of a co-defendant only if—

(a)   the evidence is relevant to a defence raised or proposed to be raised by the defendant; and

(b)   the Judge permits the defendant to do so.

(2)   A defendant in a criminal proceeding who proposes to offer evidence that challenges the veracity of a co-defendant must give notice in writing to that co-defendant and every other co-defendant of the proposal to offer that evidence unless the requirement to give notice is waived by—

(a)   all the co-defendants; or

(b)   the Judge in the interests of justice.

(3)   A notice must—

(a)   include the contents of the proposed evidence; and

(b)   be given in sufficient time to provide all the co-defendants with a fair opportunity to respond to that evidence.

EV39.01   Challenging a co-defendant's veracity

Section 39 limits the occasions when one defendant in a criminal proceeding may offer evidence that challenges the veracity of a co-defendant. Such evidence may only be offered if the conditions set forth in s 39(1)(a) and (b) are met. Subsections (2) and (3) impose what is essentially a third prerequisite, that of written notice.

(1)   Challenge

Jointly charged defendants do not always turn on each other at their trial. In a case where both defendants are asserting their common innocence, s 39 is irrelevant. The section only applies when one defendant offers evidence that *challenges the veracity* of a co-defendant. Where one defendant wants the fact-finder to accept what the co-defendant says, that defendant may wish to offer evidence *in support* of the co-defendant's veracity. In such a case, s 37(1)'s substantial helpfulness standard is the only prerequisite to admissibility. Contrast s 42(1) of the propensity rules, which does not require a challenge.

(2)   Substantial helpfulness

Section 37(2) makes it clear that the prerequisites to admissibility set by s 39 are in addition to s 37(1)'s substantial helpfulness test.

EV39.02   Relevance

Section 39(1)(a) requires that the evidence challenging the veracity of the co-defendant must be relevant to a defence raised or proposed to be raised by the defendant who wishes to offer the evidence. Section 42(1) imposes the same requirement for propensity evidence.

There will inevitably be arguments raised as to whether, in a particular case, a challenge to the co-defendant's (D2's) veracity is actually relevant to the defence of the defendant (D1) who is offering the evidence. In the common situation where, while testifying, D2 alleges that it was D1 who committed the crime being tried, a challenge to D2's veracity must surely be relevant to the defence raised by D1. The defence is that D2 is lying. The same conclusion will likely follow in any case where what D2 says would, if true, weaken the chance of success of the defence raised by D1.

(1)   Pre-trial statement

Section 39(1)(a)'s test of relevance to D1's defence will not usually be satisfied when D2 makes his or her allegation against D1 in a pre-trial statement. The general rule in s 27(1) is that when the prosecution offers evidence of D2's pre-trial statement, it cannot be used against D1. Without more, D2's veracity will not be relevant to D1's defence. However, s 12A sets out specific exceptions to this general proposition in s 27(1). When D2's pre-trial statement fits within one of these exceptions, the statement can be relied upon by the prosecution as evidence against D1. In such a case, D2's veracity has become relevant to D1's defence.

EV39.03   Permission by the judge

Section 39(1)(b) provides the second prerequisite to admissibility of evidence offered by one defendant that challenges the veracity of a co-defendant. The judge must grant permission.

It is surprising that when the Select Committee added this prerequisite to s 39, they did not see fit to add a provision similar to s 38(3). The latter subsection was also added by the Select Committee, who did so in order to provide guidance to a judge who is called upon to decide whether or not to allow prosecution evidence about a defendant's veracity.

The resulting lack of guidance means that the earlier law may still be referred to in determinations whether a defendant should be permitted to offer evidence challenging the veracity of a co-defendant.[497] All that the Select Committee said was that they added s 39(1)(b) to "ensure a proper balance between the interests of the defendant and the interests of the co-defendant".[498]

EV39.04   Notice

There were indications before the Act that a rule of practice existed which required a defendant to give notice to a co-defendant of any proposed attack on the co-defendant.[499] Section 39(2) confirms and expands that rule in the context of veracity evidence offered by one defendant that challenges the veracity of a co-defendant. See s 42(2), which imposes a similar obligation when one defendant proposes to offer propensity evidence about a co-defendant.

---

497   *Adams on Criminal Law — Evidence*, EC3.05.
498   *Select Committee Report on the Evidence Bill*, 6.
499   *R v Rhodes & Nikara* (1991) 7 CRNZ 641.

The notice that s 39(2) requires from the defendant who proposes to challenge the veracity of a co-defendant must be *in writing* and given to *every other co-defendant* (but not to the prosecution). Section 39(2)(a) permits the notice requirement to be waived, but only by *all* the co-defendants. Failing unanimity, the judge can waive the notice requirement, but this is only possible "in the interests of justice". This phrase would probably cover the case where the evidence challenging the co-defendant's veracity was exceptionally strong. It would also cover a case where the notice that was given did not quite meet the requirements set by s 39(3). Although s 65 demonstrates that in the case of waiver of *privilege* it was felt necessary to provide some guidance in interpreting the concept of waiver, no such provision exists to define what amounts to waiver in the context of s 39(2).

(1)   Notice requirements

Section 39(3)(a) requires that the notice must include the *contents* of the proposed evidence challenging the co-defendant's veracity. A substantial summary of the proposed evidence will likely suffice. However, the approach taken by the courts to a notice of hearsay pursuant to s 22(2)(b) may spill over to influence the degree of detail required under s 39(3)(a).

Section 39(3)(b) follows the pattern of similar provisions in the Act which require that the notice be given in sufficient time to provide a fair opportunity to "respond".[500] The required time will probably differ among the various co-defendants. All must be given notice, but in many cases the challenge will only be to the veracity of one co-defendant. The latter must surely be entitled to the earliest notice.

Evidence of propensity

40   Propensity rule

(1)   In this section and sections 41 to 43, **propensity evidence**—

   (a)   means evidence that tends to show a person's propensity to act in a particular way or to have a particular state of mind, being evidence of acts, omissions, events, or circumstances with which a person is alleged to have been involved; but

   (b)   does not include evidence of an act or omission that is—

      (i)   1 of the elements of the offence for which the person is being tried; or

      (ii)   the cause of action in the proceeding in question.

(2)   A party may offer propensity evidence in a civil or criminal proceeding about any person.

(3)   However, propensity evidence about—

   (a)   a defendant in a criminal proceeding may be offered only in accordance with section 41 or 42 or 43, whichever section is applicable; and

---

500   See ss 22(4) and 42(3)(b).

(b)   a complainant in a sexual case in relation to the complainant's sexual experience may be offered only in accordance with section 44.

(4)   Evidence that is solely or mainly relevant to veracity is governed by the veracity rules set out in section 37 and, accordingly, this section does not apply to evidence of that kind.

EV40.01   Similar fact evidence

The Act's definition of propensity evidence is discussed further under s 40(1). However, one common law term not found in the Act is "similar fact" evidence. At its broadest, this term referred to any evidence in a criminal proceeding disclosing disreputable aspects of a defendant's character, other than evidence of the actual commission of the offence being tried. Sections 40-43 govern this class of evidence.

A glimpse at any evidence law text published before the Act will reveal the vast extent of the law governing evidence of propensity, particularly in the field referred to above as similar fact evidence. In its treatment of similar fact evidence, the common law sought to reach a compromise between two extremes. On the one hand, evidence that the defendant has a propensity to commit criminal acts is relevant to the determination of guilt or innocence, particularly when those acts are similar to the circumstances giving rise to the charge that the defendant is currently facing. On the other hand, there is an understandable concern that the fact-finder may give undue emphasis to the revelation that the defendant has formerly offended a similar way to that alleged in the current proceeding.

The Act has made no attempt to dramatically alter the earlier law governing similar fact evidence. As discussed in leading authorities such as *R v Holtz*,[501] in the years immediately preceding the Act the common law had reached the stage where the admissibility of similar fact evidence was determined by weighing up the probative value of the evidence against its prejudicial effect. This is very close to the test adopted by s 43(1). Beyond this central test for admissibility, the majority of the issues that previously made similar fact evidence one of the most difficult areas of evidence law are still with us.

The early indicators are that the jurisprudence existing before the Act will continue to be applied in this much litigated area of evidence law.[502]

EV40.02   Subsection (1): definition of propensity evidence

Section 40(1) provides a broad definition of propensity evidence.[503]

(1)   Single incident

Before turning to the specific terms of this definition, it is worth recalling the earlier discussion of s 37(3)(b), part of the veracity rules.[504] That subsection provides express acknowledgement that a person's propensity for dishonesty or lack of veracity can be shown by a *single* conviction for an offence. There appears to be no reason why

---

501   *R v Holtz* [2003] 1 NZLR 667; (2002) 20 CRNZ 14 (CA).

other propensities cannot also be shown by a single event. Regarding broadly similar, recently introduced, legislation, the UK Court of Appeal said in *R v Hanson*:[505]

> "The fewer the number of convictions the weaker is likely to be the evidence of propensity. A single previous conviction for an offence of the same description or category will often not show propensity. But it may do so where, for example, it shows a tendency to unusual behaviour or where its circumstances demonstrate probative force in relation to the offence charged (compare *DPP v P* [1991] 2 AC 447 at 460E to 461A). Child sexual abuse or fire setting are comparatively clear examples of such unusual behaviour but we attempt no exhaustive list."

(2) State of mind

Section 40(1) casts a wide net. Not only is a person's propensity to act in a particular way included in the definition of propensity evidence, but also a person's propensity to have a particular *state of mind* (eg a love of violence; a lack of inhibition; a hatred of women; an unrealistic optimism).

(3) Reputation

The Evidence Bill made specific reference to propensity evidence in the form of evidence of a person's reputation. However, the Select Committee deleted those references on the basis that "a person's reputation should not affect current proceedings." In view of that legislative history, it will be difficult to argue that evidence of a person's reputation can ever be admitted as propensity evidence.

---

502   *Healy v R* 1/8/07, Asher J, HC Auckland CRI-2006-044-6242. See also *R v Herewini* 15/8/07, Stevens J, HC Rotorua CRI-2006-063-3151, where the earlier law (see *Adams on Criminal Law — Evidence*, EC8.15(3)) was applied to the issue of propensity evidence about the deceased in a murder trial. However, in *R v Taea* 31/10/07, CA442/07; [2007] NZCA 472, para 20, the Court said, "We do not consider it necessary to refer back to the law in force before the advent of the Evidence Act for guidance in dealing with the issue raised in the present case. In our view, s 43 gives adequate guidance on the approach to be taken and we approach the present task by following the requirements of the section itself."
In *R v Te Pania* 4/10/07, CA317/07; [2007] NZCA 429, para 11, the Court characterised as "part of the narrative", evidence that in a single evening the defendant had committed numerous offences involving weapons, intentional damage, and violence. The Court relied on this characterisation to conclude that the whole of the evidence of offending was admissible to assist proving each individual offence. The Court concluded that there was therefore no need to consider the test for admissibility of propensity evidence under s 43. This approach is questionable because the evidence appears to be caught by the definition of propensity evidence in s 40(1). However, this method of avoiding an application of the test for admissibility of propensity evidence was well known in the earlier law: *Adams on Criminal Law — Evidence*, EC8.09(2); EC8.14.

503   See *R v Te Pania* 4/10/07, CA317/07; [2007] NZCA 429, discussed immediately above.
504   See EV37.07(iii).
505   *R v Hanson* [2005] 1 WLR 3169; [2005] 2 Cr App R 21 (CA), para 9. This passage from *Hanson* was quoted with apparent approval in *R v Taea* 31/10/07, CA442/07; [2007] NZCA 472, para 38. See also EV37.07(iii).

Nonetheless, other than the particular case dealt with by s 44(2), the Act does not contain any specific prohibition on propensity evidence in the form of evidence of reputation. Such evidence comes within s 40(1)'s definition of propensity evidence, because it "tends to show a person's propensity to act in a particular way". To be admissible, propensity evidence in the form of a reputation would have to overcome the hurdles presented by the hearsay rules and the rules governing opinion evidence and expert evidence. The Evidence Bill had exempted propensity evidence in the form of reputation evidence from these controls. However, that provision was also deleted by the Select Committee.[506]

(4)   Alleged propensity

The concluding phrase of s 40(1)(a) assumes the potential admissibility of evidence of "… circumstances with which a person is alleged to have been involved". It may appear surprising that, for the purposes of admissibility, it is sufficient that someone has merely *alleged* that the person in respect of whom the evidence is being offered has been, on other occasions, connected with circumstances showing a certain propensity. This is largely a reflection of the common law, at least in criminal cases involving "similar fact" evidence. Nonetheless, the more extended discussion of s 43(3)(d) and (e) below suggests that the Act's specific controls on admissibility of prosecution evidence about a defendant's propensity have actually brought about a subtle change to the common law approach in this context.

(5)   When propensity is the ultimate issue in dispute

Paragraph (b) of s 40(1)'s definition of "propensity evidence" confirms that ss 40-43 have no application when the charge against a criminal defendant or the claim against a civil defendant requires proof that the defendant exhibited a particular propensity. Section 36(1) produces the same result for evidence about veracity.

An example where para (b) of the definition of propensity evidence would apply in a criminal case is s 98A(1) of the Crimes Act (participating in an organised criminal group). An example from civil proceedings is evidence that the defendant created the continuing nuisance that is the subject of the plaintiff's cause of action. In such cases, any controls on the admissibility of evidence offered on the issue of liability will be found in other parts of the Act, such as s 7.

EV40.03   Subsection (2): propensity evidence is generally admissible

Subject to the restrictions set out in subsequent provisions, s 40(2) grants a general permission to offer propensity evidence about any person in civil and criminal proceedings.

(1)   Civil proceedings

The subsequent controls on propensity evidence are mainly directed at criminal proceedings. In *civil proceedings*, the result of s 40(2) is that the law remains largely as it was before the Act.[507] Relevance is the main determinant of admissibility.[508]

---

506   See also EV37.03(4) and EV38.01(1).

(2)   Propensity of a witness or victim

Section s 7's control of relevance (and s 8(1)) will provide the main check on the admissibility of propensity evidence in all circumstances that are not specifically provided for in ss 40-43. For instance, the wide scope of s 40(2) may lead parties to consider offering propensity evidence about *witnesses*, whether in criminal or civil proceedings. Section 7 will prevent this in many circumstances because, other than a witness's propensity to exhibit veracity or a lack of veracity, such evidence is likely to be irrelevant to anything of consequence to the determination of the proceeding. Where the propensity evidence is "solely or mainly relevant to veracity" (of a witness), s 40(4) gives the veracity rules priority over the propensity rules, as further discussed below.

Section 40(2) provides the necessary authority for defence evidence about the propensity of the victim of the crime with which the defendant is charged. The ultimate decision about the admissibility of such evidence will be determined by "the principles of general application set out in ss 6, 7 and 8".[509]

(3)   Acknowledged relevance of propensity

Section 40(2)'s open acknowledgement of the admissibility of propensity evidence is a symbolic development. Before the Act, there had been a continuing debate among New Zealand judges whether, in criminal cases at least, "propensity evidence" was *ever* admissible. This debate was largely semantic, depending on what meaning was ascribed to "propensity" evidence. If the term was used to describe evidence that the defendant had general criminal leanings, then the evidence would undoubtedly be ruled inadmissible. However, if the evidence showed that the defendant had a tendency to act in a manner that was strikingly similar to the circumstances currently alleged against him or her, the evidence was likely to be admissible. The Act has done away with this controversy of semantics by acknowledging that this class of "character" evidence is indeed about propensity and that label does not, by itself, determine admissibility.

(4)   Subsection (3): criminal proceedings

Section 40(3)(a) ensures that, despite the broad terms of s 40(2), admissibility of propensity evidence about a *defendant in a criminal proceeding* is subject to the specific limitations set out in ss 41, 42 and 43.

---

507   See, generally, *O'Brien v Chief Constable of South Wales* [2005] UKHL 265; [2005] 2 WLR 1038 (HL).

508   See also s 8(1).

509   *R v Herewini* 15/8/07, Stevens J, HC Rotorua CRI-2006-063-3151, para 9. In the pre-Act case of *R v Farquhar* 20/3/06, CA4/06, para 16, the Court discussed defence evidence about a complainant's propensity (for violence) and said: "The key question to be answered is how is evidence of the complainant's previous convictions relevant to the case in question. Unlike in the case of an accused, there is no consideration of prejudicial effect, as the only potential prejudice is to the complainant."

EV40.04   Complainant's sexual history

Section 40(3)(b) is a reminder of s 44's special restrictions on admissibility of propensity evidence in a sexual case in relation to the complainant's sexual experience.

EV40.05   Subsection (4): priority of veracity rules

Section 40(4) deals with the relationship between the veracity rules and the propensity rule. The need to do so arises because parties may wish to offer evidence showing that they, opposing parties, witnesses, or other persons (eg the makers of hearsay statements) have a *propensity for veracity* (or lack of veracity). The solution adopted by s 40(4) is to give priority to the veracity rules when the propensity evidence in question "is solely or mainly relevant to veracity".

(1)   Defendant's veracity

Consider the high profile example of a criminal case in which the prosecutor offers evidence about the defendant's propensity for a lack of veracity. As long as it is determined that the evidence is "solely or mainly relevant to veracity", s 40(4) dictates that s 37(1)'s "substantial helpfulness" test governs admissibility, rather than s 43(1)'s assessment of probative value and prejudicial effect.

(2)   Mainly relevant to veracity

Whether propensity evidence is "mainly" relevant to veracity is necessarily a question of degree. It is suggested that the declared purpose of the party offering the evidence should not be determinative of this issue.

This can be illustrated by a criminal trial for theft in which the prosecution offers evidence about a propensity of the defendant to commit what are commonly referred to as "offences of dishonesty", such as theft or obtaining by deception. Although there is as yet no judicial guidance, it is predicted that s 37(1)'s "substantial helpfulness" test for admitting evidence about veracity will be easier to satisfy than s 43's test for prosecution evidence of a defendant's propensity, namely whether probative value outweighs the risk of an unfairly prejudicial effect. Accordingly, in this example the prosecution would likely declare that the purpose for offering the evidence about the defendant's history of committing dishonesty offences is "solely or mainly" directed at an assessment of the defendant's veracity, rather than being offered to show the defendant's propensity to commit offences of dishonesty. If this declaration of purpose by the prosecution was enough to trigger s 40(4), the prosecution would avoid s 43(1)'s more stringent test for admitting propensity evidence about a defendant. Section 40(4) cannot have been intended to authorise such a result. The judge should remain the ultimate arbiter whether or not s 40(4) applies.[510]

(3)   Perjury trial

The discussion of s 36(1) considered the example of a perjury trial where the prosecution offers evidence of the defendant's propensity to lie.[511] The prosecution

---

510   See also EV41.01(2); EV42.02(4).

will be offering this evidence as circumstantial evidence that the defendant lied on the occasion which forms the subject of the charge.

Is the prosecution's evidence solely or mainly relevant to veracity within the meaning of s 40(4)? It is suggested that the purpose for which this evidence has been offered properly characterises it as propensity evidence. This will ensure the application of s 43.

(4)   False accusations by complainant in sexual case

Section 40(4) was not referred to by the Court of Appeal in *R v C*.[512] In that case the defendant was charged with sexual offences against his sister, the complainant. The defendant wished to offer evidence of numerous allegations made by the complainant that other men had sexually abused her. The defence would then attempt to show that these other allegations were false.

As discussed at EV44.02(2), the Court held that s 44 (which governs propensity evidence in the form of a complainant's previous sexual experience) was engaged by this evidence of allegations by the complainant against others.[513] The defence had argued that although the evidence may have tangentially related to the subject dealt with by s 44, the evidence was primarily about the complainant's veracity. Therefore, the question of admissibility should be governed by s 37.[514] The defence argument appears to have been a restatement of the proposition embodied in s 40(4).

The Court rejected the defence argument and stated, "section 37 does not trump s 44".[515] The Court concluded that s 44 governed the admissibility of the evidence of the complainant's allegations against other persons.

It is submitted that the judgment in *R v C* is open to attack because of its lack of any reference to or discussion of s 40(4).

(5)   Propensity to be accurate

In considering s 40(4) it must be remembered that s 37(5) defines veracity as the disposition to refrain from lying. There can be no suggestion that a person's veracity has anything to do with his or her disposition to be *accurate*, or his or her accuracy on any particular occasion. Thus, in giving priority to the veracity rules, s 40(4) is not purporting to affect evidence relating to a person's ability to give an accurate account when honestly attempting to do so. This means that evidence about person's propensity to be accurate or inaccurate would continue to be governed by the rules controlling propensity evidence. Section 40(4) would not give priority to the veracity rules in such a case.[516]

511   See EV36.01(2)-(3).
512   *R v C (CA391/07)* 12/10/07, CA391/07; [2007] NZCA 439.
513   *R v C (CA391/07)* 12/10/07, CA391/07; [2007] NZCA 439, para 23.
514   *R v C (CA391/07)* 12/10/07, CA391/07; [2007] NZCA 439, para 4.
515   *R v C (CA391/07)* 12/10/07, CA391/07; [2007] NZCA 439, para 22.
516   See EV35.05.

41   Propensity evidence about defendants

(1)   A defendant in a criminal proceeding may offer propensity evidence about himself or herself.

(2)   If a defendant offers propensity evidence about himself or herself, the prosecution or another party may, with the permission of the Judge, offer propensity evidence about that defendant.

(3)   Section 43 does not apply to propensity evidence offered by the prosecution under subsection (2).

EV41.01   Defendants in criminal trials

Section 41(1) permits a defendant in a criminal proceeding to offer propensity evidence about himself or herself. Usually, such evidence will be of a laudable propensity — what the common law referred to as "good character" evidence.

(1)   Not necessarily evidence of good propensity

However, it is conceivable that, for tactical reasons, a defendant may want to offer evidence that he or she has a disreputable propensity or at least a propensity that is neither laudable or disreputable. Section 41(1) permits this.

An example of the former situation would be where the defendant denies making the verbal confession testified to by the police and supports this denial by saying that his years of dealings with the police have taught him to invariably exercise the right of silence.

An example of a "neutral" propensity is evidence offered to support an alibi. If the defendant wants to show that at the time of the offence he or she was dining with friends, s 41(1) permits the defendant to offer evidence that he or she has dined with those same friends at the same locale on that particular night of the week for the past three years.

(2)   Jury direction

In separating evidence of veracity and propensity, Subpart 5 brought about a major change from the common law. "Good character" evidence offered by a defendant at common law would generally incorporate aspects of the defendant's character that were relevant to both veracity and propensity. As confirmed by authorities such as *R v Falealili*,[517] the common law required the judge to direct the jury that evidence that the defendant was a person of good character was evidence that could be used both (i) to support the credibility of the defendant and also (ii) to support his or her innocence of the offence charged.[518]

It is difficult to predict if the law established by *Falealili* will continue under the Act. On the one hand, the defence may be forced to clarify whether "good character" evidence about the defendant is being offered pursuant to s 38(1) (veracity) or s 41(1) (propensity) and the jury directed accordingly. If the evidence is solely about

---

517   *R v Falealili* [1996] 3 NZLR 664; (1996) 14 CRNZ 157 (CA).
518   See *Adams on Criminal Law — Evidence*, EC8.15(2).

the defendant's propensity, then it will likely be treated as relevant only to (ii) above, namely the issue of guilt or innocence. However, if the evidence is "solely or mainly" about veracity, per s 40(4), then the judge may restrict his or her direction to the defendant's veracity, per (i) above.

On the other hand, witnesses testifying to the defendant's good character are likely to continue to give such evidence in the same general way in which this class of testimony has been traditionally offered. The result may be that the defence will routinely submit that the evidence is being offered under both ss 38(1) and 41(1). This could lead to a continuation of the requirement for a jury direction in accordance with *Falealili*, even though there is no such express requirement under the Act.[519]

EV41.02   Subsection (2): rebuttal of defence evidence

Section 41(2) largely codifies the current law that, by offering evidence of his or her propensity to act in a laudable fashion, the defendant opens the door to evidence from the prosecution *or another party* (see below) demonstrating that the defendant actually has one or more disreputable propensities.[520] The rationale for allowing such evidence, particularly in view of the effect of s 41(3), discussed below, is that the fact-finder should not be left under the wrong impression about the defendant's character.

(1)   No restriction on method of offering evidence

Neither s 41(1) nor s 41(2) contain any restrictions on the means by which propensity evidence may be given. A defendant may offer propensity evidence about himself or herself through other witnesses, even though the defendant never testifies. Subject to the need to obtain the judge's permission, as set out in s 41(2), the rebutting evidence offered by the prosecution or another party about the defendant's propensity can come through the questioning of any witness, including *cross-examination of the defendant* if he or she decides to testify.

(2)   Another party

It is not easy to explain why s 41(2) speaks of "another party" in addition to the prosecution. There would be no difficulty if s 41(2) applied in civil cases, because in that context the phrase could refer to, for example, third parties to the proceedings. However, the indications appear overwhelmingly that s 41(2) applies only in criminal proceedings. The subsection flows on from s 41(1), which is expressly limited to criminal proceedings, and the reference to "the prosecution" in s 41(2) confirms that the subsection has a criminal focus.[521]

Except in the rarest case, such as an intervenor in a trial involving the Bill of Rights, the only parties to a criminal proceeding are the prosecution and defendants. If "another party" in s 41(2) is meant to simply refer to co-defendants, it is impossible to understand why that term was not used, as it is in a multitude of other subsections

---

519   See, however, EV38.07(4).
520   *Adams on Criminal Law — Evidence*, EC3.04(1); EC8.15(2)(f).
521   See also s 40(3)(a).

in the Act. At least the term "another party" in s 41(2) must *include* a co-defendant. But even in that context the result is an undesirable confusion. Section 42 purports to completely cover the field of propensity evidence about one defendant that is offered by another. Section 42 will be discussed below, but it can be summarised by saying that it provides a right for one defendant to offer propensity evidence about a co-defendant when the evidence is relevant to a defence of the defendant who is offering the evidence. There is no need to obtain leave from the judge, as is required under s 41(2). It is simply unclear if s 41(2) supplements s 42 and allows one defendant to offer evidence about a co-defendant, with leave of the judge, despite a lack of relevance to a defence raised by the defendant offering the evidence.

None of these problems arise in relation to evidence of the defendant's *veracity*. Section 38(2) makes no reference to "another party".

(3)   Permission from the judge

In keeping with the earlier law, s 41(2) requires the prosecution to obtain the judge's permission before offering propensity evidence about the defendant when the justification for the prosecution evidence is that the defendant has offered propensity evidence about himself or herself.

Although s 41(2)'s scope of operation is not expressly restricted in any way, the vast majority of cases will involve prosecution evidence of the defendant's unsavoury propensities, offered to rebut evidence offered by the defendant about his or her laudable propensities. Authorities such as *R v Anderson*[522] demonstrate that it is by no means inevitable that such rebutting evidence from the prosecution will be allowed. The possibility of unfair prejudice to the defendant is always high. The discussion below of s 41(3) suggests that, despite the terms of that subsection, a concern about prejudice will still be relevant when a judge is deciding whether to grant permission under s 41(2). *Anderson* was decided in the context of *prosecution cross-examination of the defendant*, a much litigated area in the pre-Act era. The judgment is likely to be treated as having continued relevance after the Act.[523]

(4)   Subsection (3): is prejudice irrelevant?

Section 41(3) makes the important point that propensity evidence offered by the prosecution under s 41(2) is admissible even though it does not meet the test for admissibility set by s 43(1) of the Act. As discussed below, when the prosecution does rely on s 43(1) in offering propensity evidence about a defendant, the probative value of such evidence must outweigh the risk of an unfairly prejudicial effect on the defendant. However, when the prosecution offers propensity evidence under s 41(2), s 41(3) renders irrelevant the need for the judge to engage in that process.

(5)   Effect of s 8(1)(a)

Although as just discussed, s 41(3) renders irrelevant the probative versus prejudicial calculation found in s 43(1), a similar calculation is nonetheless required by

---

522   *R v Anderson* [2000] 1 NZLR 667; (1999) 17 CRNZ 506 (CA).
523   See, generally, *Adams on Criminal Law — Evidence*, EC3.

s 8(1)(a). The following discussion suggests that this does not nullify the effect of s 41(3).

(6)   Subtle difference in balancing process

The most important difference between s 8(1)(a) and the specific test set forth in s 43(1) is that s 8(1)(a) is concerned with a prejudicial effect on the *outcome of the proceedings*, which is a wider focus than s 43(1)'s focus on a prejudicial effect *on the defendant*. That wider focus in s 8(1)(a) should mean that, in considering a grant of permission under s 41(2), the judge will recognise that the prosecution evidence about the defendant's propensity is being offered to *correct the misleading picture* created by the defence evidence about the defendant's propensity. This will justify admitting prosecution evidence under s 41(2) without any undue concern for the effect *on the defendant*, which would have been given more weight if the evidence had been offered under s 43(1).

The only concern in these circumstances will be the risk of an unfairly prejudicial effect on the proceeding (s 8(1)(a)). Although s 8(2) (right of the defendant to offer an effective defence) must always be considered, it will often be the case that prosecution evidence offered under s 41(2) will *promote* the fairness of the proceeding by making the fact-finder aware that the defendant's evidence of his or her laudable propensity is actually suspect or simply untrue.

(7)   Lack of guidance

Despite the above explanation, it remains regrettable that the Act gives no guidance along the lines of s 38(3) (veracity rules) to assist the judge's decision whether to grant permission under s 41(2).

Section 8(1)(a) is also referred to in the discussions of ss 42 and 43.[524]

(8)   Attack on prosecution witness

When, under s 40(2), a defendant offers damaging propensity evidence about a prosecution witness, this does not open the door to propensity evidence about the defendant under s 41(2). Contrast s 38(2)(a) of the veracity rules, discussed at EV38.06.

However, if the evidence offered by the defendant could be characterised as evidence that the prosecution witness had a propensity for a lack of veracity, the effect of s 40(4) may be to give priority to the veracity rules and s 38(2)(a) in particular.[525]

42   Propensity evidence about co-defendants

(1)   A defendant in a criminal proceeding may offer propensity evidence about a co-defendant only if—

(a)   that evidence is relevant to a defence raised or proposed to be raised by the defendant; and

---

524   See EV42.02(3) and EV43.05.
525   See, generally, EV40.05.

       (b)   the Judge permits the defendant to do so.

(2)   A defendant in a criminal proceeding who proposes to offer propensity evidence about a co-defendant must give notice in writing to that co-defendant and every other co-defendant of the proposal to offer that evidence unless the requirement to give notice is waived—

       (a)   by all the co-defendants; or

       (b)   by the Judge in the interests of justice.

(3)   A notice must—

       (a)   include the contents of the proposed evidence; and

       (b)   be given in sufficient time to provide all the co-defendants with a fair opportunity to respond to that evidence.

EV42.01   Three prerequisites

Section 42 mirrors s 39 in the veracity rules by imposing three prerequisites before one defendant can offer propensity evidence about a co-defendant. First, the evidence must be relevant to a defence raised or proposed to be raised by the defendant who offers the evidence. Second, the judge must grant permission. Finally, the defendant must give written notice to all co-defendants (unless the notice requirement is waived by all co-defendants or the judge).

EV42.02   Relevance

An example of the sort of case envisioned by s 42(1) is where it is clear that one of two defendants committed a murder and the only issue is which of the two was the offender. If the judge grants permission, s 42(1) would permit one defendant to offer expert evidence that the other defendant had a propensity for violence that was not shared by the defendant who offered the evidence. The common law had reached this position before the Act.[526]

(1)   No need for a challenge

Section 39(1) of the veracity rules is solely concerned with evidence offered by one defendant which *challenges* the veracity of a co-defendant. However, s 42(1) does not contain any similar limitation. The propensity evidence offered by one defendant about a co-defendant may be offered to show that the co-defendant has a laudable propensity. The test for admissibility remains that of relevance, set by s 42(1).

When one defendant offers evidence of a co-defendant's laudable propensity, it will not usually amount to evidence "offered by" that co-defendant, so as to bring s 41(2) into play. However, a case can be imagined where a judge determines that s 41(2) is engaged because the co-defendant about whom the laudable propensity evidence was offered had sufficiently connived with the defendant who offered the evidence.

---

526   *Adams on Criminal Law — Evidence*, EC8.16.

(2)   Prejudice

The most important aspect of s 42(1) is its omission of any reference to *prejudice*. Under s 43(1), propensity evidence about a defendant that is offered *by the prosecution* must satisfy the test of having a probative value which outweighs the risk of an unfairly prejudicial effect on the defendant. Subject to the following comments, it is the lack of any such concern for the prejudicial effect of propensity evidence offered under s 42(1) by one defendant against a co-defendant which distinguishes s 42 from s 43.

(3)   Relationship to s 8(1)(a)

It is worth giving further consideration to a point touched on in the discussion of s 41(3). Section 8(1)(a) *requires* the judge in any proceeding to exclude evidence if its probative value is outweighed by the risk that it will have an unfairly prejudicial effect on the outcome of the proceeding.

Does s 8(1)(a) operate to negate the difference between s 42(1) and s 43(1) that was suggested above? The only argument for avoiding this result is to once again emphasise that s 8(1)(a), which superimposes a concern for prejudicial effect onto s 42(1), speaks of an unfairly prejudicial effect on the *outcome of the proceedings*. Section 43(1) is directed only at the prejudicial effect *on the defendant* against whom the evidence is offered.

In considering propensity evidence offered under s 42(1), a judge who is applying s 8(1)(a) will need to consider the interests of the defendant who is offering the evidence as well as the interests of the co-defendant who is the subject of the evidence.

See too the related discussion of s 8(1)(a) under s 43.[527]

(4)   Priority of veracity rules

Section 42 should be read in tandem with s 39, which permits one defendant to offer evidence that challenges the veracity of a co-defendant. If a defendant proposes to offer propensity evidence that is properly characterised as challenging the veracity of the co-defendant (for example, evidence that the co-defendant is a habitual liar), s 39 will take priority. This is because of s 40(4). The result in such a case will be that s 37(1)'s substantial helpfulness test for admissibility will apply, as it does to all propensity evidence that is "solely or mainly relevant to veracity" (s 40(4)).

EV42.03   Permission by the judge

Section 42(1)(b) requires that the judge must give permission before a defendant may offer propensity evidence about a co-defendant.[528]

EV42.04   Notice

Subsections (2) and (3) requires that the defendant who is proposing to offer propensity evidence about a co-defendant must give *written* notice to that effect to

---

527   See EV43.05.
528   See EV39.03.

the co-defendant *and every other co-defendant*. See the discussion at EV39.04 of the similar notice requirement in respect of veracity evidence.

43   Propensity evidence offered by prosecution about defendants

(1)   The prosecution may offer propensity evidence about a defendant in a criminal proceeding only if the evidence has a probative value in relation to an issue in dispute in the proceeding which outweighs the risk that the evidence may have an unfairly prejudicial effect on the defendant.

(2)   When assessing the probative value of propensity evidence, the Judge must take into account the nature of the issue in dispute.

(3)   When assessing the probative value of propensity evidence, the Judge may consider, among other matters, the following:

     (a)   the frequency with which the acts, omissions, events, or circumstances which are the subject of the evidence have occurred:

     (b)   the connection in time between the acts, omissions, events, or circumstances which are the subject of the evidence and the acts, omissions, events, or circumstances which constitute the offence for which the defendant is being tried:

     (c)   the extent of the similarity between the acts, omissions, events, or circumstances which are the subject of the evidence and the acts, omissions, events, or circumstances which constitute the offence for which the defendant is being tried:

     (d)   the number of persons making allegations against the defendant that are the same as, or are similar to, the subject of the offence for which the defendant is being tried:

     (e)   whether the allegations described in paragraph (d) may be the result of collusion or suggestibility:

     (f)   the extent to which the acts, omissions, events, or circumstances which are the subject of the evidence and the acts, omissions, events, or circumstances which constitute the offence for which the defendant is being tried are unusual.

(4)   When assessing the prejudicial effect of evidence on the defendant, the Judge must consider, among any other matters,—

     (a)   whether the evidence is likely to unfairly predispose the fact-finder against the defendant; and

     (b)   whether the fact-finder will tend to give disproportionate weight in reaching a verdict to evidence of other acts or omissions.

EV43.01   Similar fact evidence

Section 43 encapsulates the central features of the common law governing what was traditionally known as "similar fact evidence".[529]

Although s 43(1) purports to deal with all propensity evidence about a defendant that is offered by the prosecution, the earlier discussions of ss 40(4) and 41(2) show that there are additional provisions which are relevant to that process.

EV43.02   Prosecution must be responsible for "offering" evidence

Section 43(1) only applies to an *offer* of evidence by the prosecution. The definition of "offer evidence" in s 4 does not state the extent to which a party must be "responsible for" the giving of an item of evidence before it can be said that the party has offered that evidence. The issue can arise in the context of propensity evidence because it is not uncommon for a prosecution witness, during his or her examination in chief, to blurt out negative propensity evidence about a defendant.

It is suggested that in a case where it is clear that prosecution counsel did not prompt the witness to give such evidence, s 43(1) is not engaged. This is because the prosecution has not "offered" the propensity evidence. The same conclusion is even more certain to follow where the prosecution witness volunteers some negative propensity evidence about the defendant during the witness's cross-examination by defence counsel.

In such a case, if the issue of admissibility is raised, s 8(1)(a) is likely to be the focus for the determination because no party can be said to have "offered the evidence". However, the real issue is likely to be whether the trial should be aborted. If it is not, the issue on an appeal from conviction is whether a miscarriage of justice resulted. The earlier law is likely to continue to apply.[530]

EV43.03   Cross-examination of defendant

The result of s 4's definition of "offer evidence" is that s 43(1) governs the *cross-examination* of the defendant by the prosecution as well as the admissibility of evidence offered by other means, such as the testimony of a prosecution witness. Under the former law, an 1898 UK statutory provision (s 1(f) of the Criminal Evidence Act 1898 (UK)) was used by New Zealand courts to guide the exercise their discretion to permit cross-examination of the defendant on aspects of his or her "bad character". Section 43(1) ends that rather indirect source of guidance. The sole test is that set forth in s 43(1), supplemented by s 8(1)(a), as discussed below.

EV43.04   Risk of prejudice

The actual test for admissibility set out in s 43(1) has clearly taken as its model the test that had evolved at common law prior to the Act, namely whether the probative value of the evidence outweighs its prejudicial effect. However, there may be grounds for arguing that the standard for admissibility set by s 43(1) is more difficult for the prosecution to attain than under the former test.[531]

---

529   See EV40.01.
530   *Adams on Criminal Law — Evidence*, EC8.08(2).
531   None of the cases listed at EV40.01, n 502, drew any distinction between the weighing up
        process at common law and the test set by s 43(1).

First, s 43(1) focuses solely on the risk of a prejudicial effect *on the defendant*. Some common law authorities had spoken of a wider focus, namely a prejudicial effect on the proceeding. That common law standard permitted a judge to justify admissibility of propensity evidence about the defendant by considering factors which would not be relevant in an enquiry under s 43(1).

Additionally, under s 43(1), probative value must outweigh the *risk* of an unfairly prejudicial effect. The common law authorities did not routinely draw such a distinction and spoke only of weighing probative value against (actual) prejudicial effect. This too may lead to less evidence being admitted under s 43(1) than under the common law test for admitting similar fact evidence, but this appears unlikely.

(1)   Issue in dispute

Section 43(1) speaks of probative value *in relation to an issue in dispute in the proceedings*. This seemingly innocuous phrase could have a surprising effect. Presumably, the primary purpose of this aspect of s 43(1) is to focus the judge's mind on the particular issue upon which the evidence is being offered — a point emphasised by s 43(2). However, s 43(1)'s requirement that an issue be "in dispute" may be seized upon by a defendant who wishes to keep the fact-finder from learning about a particular item of propensity evidence which the prosecution seeks to offer.

Section 9(2) of the Act permits a defendant to admit any fact alleged against the defendant "so as to dispense with proof of that fact". A defendant may choose to make such an admission rather than suffer through devastating propensity evidence offered by the prosecution to prove the same fact. This phenomenon was not unknown before the Act, but the drafting of s 43(1) is likely to crystallize the attention of more defence lawyers. Argument will inevitably focus on the precise boundaries of the "issue in dispute". A defendant may be willing to make a tactical admission that he or she has one rather vague personality defect, but not that he or she has a propensity to offend in the precise manner that is reflected in the charge being tried.

(2)   Unfairly prejudicial effect

The "weighing up" process that s 43(1) adopts as the test for admissibility pits the risk of an *unfairly* prejudicial effect against the probative value of the evidence. The "unfairly" qualification is likely designed to meet a point that had arisen under the earlier law. Some judges articulated the test for admissibility of similar fact evidence in terms of probative value outweighing (mere) prejudicial effect. This led to problems because it was open to defendants to argue that *any* prosecution evidence tending to prove the defendant's guilt was "prejudicial" in the sense that it could lead to the defendant's conviction.

Such an argument rendered the test for admissibility meaningless because the probative value of the similar fact evidence was being weighed up against its tendency to convict the defendant (ie against probative value). Hence the Court of Appeal confirmed that, as now set out in s 43(1), it is the risk of an *unfairly* prejudicial effect on the defendant that is to be taken into account.[532] Section 43(4), discussed below, provides some guidance on the assessment of "prejudicial effect".

EV43.05   Relationship with s 8(1)(a)

The earlier discussions of ss 41(3) and 42(1) considered s 8(1)(a), which requires the judge to exclude evidence if its probative value is outweighed by the risk that the evidence will have an unfairly prejudicial effect on the outcome of the proceedings.[533] What role does s 43(1) play that is independent of the function already performed by s 8(1)(a)?

The earlier discussion of ss 41(3) and 42(1) referred to the main difference between s 8(1)(a) and s 43(1), namely that the former focuses on prejudicial effect on "the outcome of the proceedings" whereas the latter is concerned *only* with the effect "on the defendant". This could support an argument that s 43(1) may lead to the exclusion of some evidence that would not necessarily be excluded under s 8(1)(a), given the wider spectrum of interests (eg convicting the guilty) accommodated by the "outcome of the proceedings" with which s 8(1)(a) is concerned.

(1)   Equal probative value and prejudicial effect

There is a further difference between the operation of ss 8(1)(a) and 43(1). This involves the case where the probative value and the risk of unfairly prejudicial effect are equal. When this occurs, the risk of an unfairly prejudicial effect would not *outweigh* probative value. In such a case, s 8(1)(a) would not require exclusion because it only does so when probative value *is* outweighed. However, because probative value does not outweigh the risk of an unfairly prejudicial effect in such a case, s 43(1) would exclude the evidence. This is because s 43(1) only permits the evidence to be admitted if probative value *does* outweigh the risk of prejudicial effect.

There is no conflict between the two sections in the hypothetical case of equal probative value and risk of unfairly prejudicial effect. Section 43(1) operates to exclude the evidence even though s 8(1)(a) does not *require* exclusion.

Apart from these peripheral issues, s 43 can be seen as an attempt to provide more specific guidance on the application of s 8(1)(a) in the much litigated context of propensity evidence offered by the prosecution about the defendant in a criminal proceeding.

EV43.06   Subsection (2): nature of the issue in dispute

Section 43(2) requires that in determining the admissibility of propensity evidence about a defendant, the judge must take into account the nature of the issue in dispute. The subsection provides explicit recognition that the probative value of propensity evidence cannot be assessed in the abstract. For example, on a charge of burglary, evidence that the defendant has committed burglaries in the past is more likely to be admitted if the defendant testifies that he entered a stranger's house by mistake than if the defendant had not been seen near the scene of the crime and the issue is who committed the burglary.

---

532   See *Adams on Criminal Law — Evidence*, EC8.03(1). See also *R v Taea* 31/10/07, CA442/07; [2007] NZCA 472, para 47.

533   See EV41.02(5)-(6) and EV42.02(3).

EV43.07   Subsection (3): factors relevant to probative value

Section 43(3) flows on from s 43(2) in giving further assistance to a judge who is determining the admissibility of propensity evidence against a defendant. Although s 43(2) is mandatory, s 43(3) says only that the judge "may" consider (among other matters) the factors that are then listed as s 43(3)(a)-(f). This may also be contrasted with s 43(4), which *requires* the judge to consider listed factors when assessing the prejudicial effect of propensity evidence. The obvious explanation for the permissive framework for s 43(3) is that the circumstances of a particular case will often mean that some of the listed factors will not be relevant. However, in a case where a factor is relevant to the determination of admissibility, it is safe to assume that a judge would be in error not to consider it.

(1)   Corroborative evidence

Probably the most important of the "other matters" which s 43(3) anticipates that a judge will take into account is the *strength of other evidence of the defendant's guilt*. Leading common law decisions such as *R v Holtz*[534] decided that propensity evidence that might not otherwise carry a sufficiently high degree of probative value may yet be admissible on the foundation of other evidence in the case that indicates the defendant's guilt.

(2)   Positive or negative operation

Although none of the provisions in s 43(3) state expressly how the listed factors affect probative value — positively or negatively — the choices made in the following discussion are probably uncontroversial.

(3)   Frequency

Section 43(3)(a) recognises that the probative value of propensity evidence increases with the number of acts, omissions etc that demonstrate the defendant's propensity. The fact that the defendant has committed 20 previous burglaries is stronger evidence of a propensity to commit burglaries than merely one prior incident. Of course, frequency alone will not ensure admissibility, except in a sufficiently clear case. The risk of an unfairly prejudicial effect may still be too high. Accordingly, it is probably safe to predict that under the Act there will be no change to the common law position that, without more, evidence of the 20 previous burglaries will still be inadmissible. By the same token, evidence of a single burglary may be admissible if, for example, it involved idiosyncratic features matching the circumstances of the offence being tried (s 43(3)(c)) and it took place within a few hours of the occurrence of the offence being tried and at a nearby location (s 43(3)(b)).[535]

(4)   Timing

Section 43(3)(b) reflects parliament's view that probative value increases as the acts, omissions, etc making up the propensity evidence occur closer in time to the occurrence of the offence being charged.

---

534   *R v Holtz* [2003] 1 NZLR 667; (2002) 20 CRNZ 14 (CA).
535   See *R v Taea* 31/10/07, CA 442/07; [2007] NZCA 472, paras 41-45. See also EV40.02(1).

(5)   Similarity

Section 43(3)(c) makes a point that is wrapped up in the common law "similar fact" label. Probative value increases with the degree to which the circumstances of the propensity evidence match those of the offence that is currently being tried. The common law has long accepted that a "striking similarity" between the propensity evidence and the offence being tried provides a near guarantee of admissibility. Nonetheless, the authorities prior to the Act were also clear that a high degree of similarity is not a prerequisite to admissibility in every case. Other factors, such as are found in the other subsections of s 43(3), can operate to admit propensity evidence despite the lack of a high degree of similarity.[536]

(6)   Number of propensity accusers

Section 43(3)(d) impliedly asserts that probative value increases with an increase in the number of persons making *allegations* against the defendant that are "the same as, or are similar to the subject of the offence being tried". Despite the uncontroversial nature of the general message of s 43(3)(d), there are the following difficulties presented by the subsection. The term "propensity accusers" will be used to refer to the persons making allegations against the defendant.

(7)   Degree of similarity

The *number* of the propensity accusers can only be considered by the judge (at least under s 43(3)(d)) when their allegations are "the same, or are similar to" the subject of the offence for which the defendant is being tried. However, we are given no guidance as to the *degree* of similarity required before the factor set out in (d) can be considered.

The prosecution is likely to argue that this factor of similarity is a flexible concept, reducing in stringency as the number of propensity accusers increases. However, such an argument is problematic because it means that, given a sufficient number of propensity accusers, the required factor of similarity of allegations would all but disappear. Yet with no similarity, s 43(3)(d) does not apply.

(8)   The subject of the offence

Unlike s 43(3)(a)-(c) and (f), s 43(3)(d) does not speak of "acts, omissions, etc". The subsection suddenly focuses on allegations that are the same as or similar to *the subject of the offence* now being tried. This peculiarity may be seized upon by the prosecution to assist the argument referred to above, that even though in a particular case the degree of similarity may be low, a judge can still take into account the number of propensity accusers when assessing probative value.

The argument would be that, in contrast to a comparison of the similarity of "acts, omissions, etc", s 43(3)(d)'s focus on similarity to the *subject of the offence* authorises a much lower threshold of similarity. If the propensity accusers allege rape and that is also the "subject of the offence" being tried, this is enough to bring s 43(3)(d) into play — even though the "acts, omissions, etc" of the allegations and the current

---

536   See *Adams on Criminal Law — Evidence*, EC8.07.

offence are not similar at all! Not a strong argument, perhaps, but it is difficult to see what else may have led to the sudden change in focus that occurs in s 43(3)(d).

(9)   Disputed allegations: directing the jury

Section 43(3)(d) makes the *number of persons making the allegations* relevant to the assessment of the probative value of the evidence offered by propensity accusers. This must mean that a single allegation has a relatively *low* probative value. This is so even when the allegation is (in the words of s 43(3)(d) itself) "the same" as the subject of the offence being tried. In a case where the propensity evidence consists in "allegations" against the defendant which he or she denies, a high probative value will only be achieved when there is a *number* of such allegations.

In referring specifically to *allegations* against the defendant, s 43(3)(d) highlights the potential for an offer of propensity evidence to give rise to a source of complexity that long bedevilled the common law. There are enough difficulties with propensity evidence in a case where the defendant does not deny (per the wording in ss 43(3)(a)-(c) and (f)) that the "acts, omissions, etc" offered as propensity evidence did indeed occur and were the defendant's own acts, omissions etc. In such a case, the exercise of comparing probative value and the risk of an unfairly prejudicial effect must still be carried out before a decision of admissibility can be reached. However, the greatest controversies over propensity evidence have always been encountered where not only must the probative value versus prejudicial effect comparison be made, but the defendant contests the truth or accuracy of the *allegations* offered as propensity evidence. The common law never reached a firm conclusion of how to proceed in such a case.

The greatest problems arose at the stage of a trial where the propensity evidence in the form of allegations denied by the defendant had been admitted by the trial judge and the time had come to *direct the jury* on how to deal with the disputed evidence. Difficult questions were raised about the applicable standard of proof (eg, need the jury be convinced beyond reasonable doubt of the truth of the allegations before relying on them?). A new level of difficulty was added if the defendant had been previously *acquitted* of a charge that had been based on the same allegation now offered as propensity evidence. The Act makes no attempt to clarify any of this and thus the earlier authorities remain relevant.[537]

(10)   Disputed allegations: admissibility

Despite this continuing uncertainty at the stage of a trial where the judge directs the jury, s 43(3)(d) may herald a change to the law applicable to the *earlier* stage of a proceeding, when a judge is asked to consider the *admissibility* of this form of propensity evidence. This suggestion requires a discussion of s 43(3)(e) which, by its terms, is referrable solely to s 43(3)(d).

---

537   *Adams on Criminal Law — Evidence*, EC8.20(2).

(11)   Collusion among propensity accusers: common law approach

Before the Act, when determining the admissibility of propensity evidence in the form of allegations disputed by the defendant, the judge was not supposed to determine whether the allegations were truthful or not. *That* question was a matter for the jury *after* the evidence had been admitted. The issue was crystallised in a case where the defendant suggested that the propensity accusers had *colluded* to fabricate their allegations. The common law held that the judge was to assume that the allegations were truthful. His or her role was merely to determine admissibility by weighing up probative value and prejudicial effect on the basis of that assumption.[538]

(12)   Where propensity accusers do not directly implicate defendant

To avoid any confusion, we should pause to emphasise that the position just outlined is restricted to a case where the propensity accusers were directly implicating the defendant. *That* is the class of case where, before the Act, the judge determining admissibility was to assume the truth of the allegation. The same approach would not apply where the propensity accusers were alleging only that *someone* had offended in a way similar to the charge currently being tried against the defendant, but the defendant denies being the person responsible. In the latter case, even on the assumption of the truth of the allegation that someone offended against the propensity accusers, the judge could only admit the evidence when he or she concluded (to some uncertain standard) that it was indeed the defendant who committed the acts alleged by the propensity accusers.[539] This position appears unchanged under the Act.

(13)   Judge must now assess truth of allegation

What though of our original focus of a case where the propensity accusers specifically allege that it was the defendant who offended against them, but the defendant denies this? Section 43(3)(e) reminds the judge to consider whether such multiple allegations can be explained away as the result of collusion or suggestibility. This enquiry dictated by ss 43(3)(e) is completely at odds with any application of the common law, discussed above, that the judge must *assume the truth* of allegations where they are denied by the defendant.

Under s 43(3)(e), it is clear that the judge must now assess whether the allegations against the defendant are untrue because they are the result of collusion or suggestibility. This factual determination now required of a judge who is determining admissibility is one of the few important changes which the Act has brought to the earlier law governing similar fact evidence.[540]

---

538   *R v H* [1995] 2 WLR 737 (HL); *R v S* 22/9/95, CA201/95; *Adams on Criminal Law —
       Evidence*, EC8.17.

539   *Sweitzer v R* [1982] 1 SCR 949; *R v Holtz* [2003] 1 NZLR 667; (2002) 20 CRNZ 14 (CA),
       para 36.

540   *Healy v R* 1/8/07, Asher J, HC Auckland CRI-2006-044-6242, para 25. In *R v Wyatt* 10/10/07,
       CA311/07; [2007] NZCA 436, para 23, the Court said "s 43(3)(e) … suggests that if there is
       evidence of collusion or suggestibility on the face of the record that is a matter that can be put
       into the mix along with other matters."

Section 43(3)(e) refers to only one topic which the judge may consider and use in assessing the truth of the allegations against the defendant. However, it is suggested that it would be unrealistic to limit a judge's enquiry to the sole topic of collusion or suggestibility. There is a strong argument that s 43(3)(e) has merely highlighted one high profile line of common law cases. When propensity evidence consists of allegations which the defendant denies, the judge determining admissibility should make an *overall assessment* of the truth of these allegations in determining their probative value.

(14) Suggestibility

Section 43(3)(e) was discussed above, because of its close relationship to s 43(3)(d). The foregoing discussion focused on possible collusion among propensity accusers. Section 43(3)(e) places *suggestibility* on an equal footing with collusion. It might have been thought that this was an obvious reference to the discussion by the House of Lords in *R v H*.[541] This was the seminal common law judgment that required the judge, in determining admissibility, to assume the truth of the allegations made by the propensity accusers. In concluding that the possibility of collusion must be ignored (and left for the jury to consider), *R v H* also concluded that the same approach should be taken to what their Lordships referred to as "unconscious influence of one witness by another"[542] or "innocent infection".[543] Such concepts appear to fit nicely within s 43(3)(e)'s label of "suggestibility".

However, in *R v Wyatt*,[544] the Court adopted the apparently more narrow approach that s 43(3)(e)'s reference to suggestibility, "appears to envision the type of situation where, for example, the way in which a question is put may have influenced the response."[545]

(15) Unusualness

Section 43(3)(f) recognises that the probative value of propensity evidence is greater when the propensity disclosed by that evidence and the circumstances of the charge being tried are both *unusual*. It is surely safe to assume that s 43(3)(f) is speaking only of a case where the propensity evidence and the circumstances of the offence display the *same* (or at least, similar) unusual features — an assumption that is supported in part by s 43(3)(c).

---

541   *R v H* [1995] 2 WLR 737 (HL).

542   *R v H* [1995] 2 WLR 737 (HL), 749 (per Lord Mackay).

543   *R v H* [1995] 2 WLR 737 (HL), 753 (per Lord Mustill).

544   *R v Wyatt* 10/10/07, CA311/07; [2007] NZCA 436, paras 23-24.

545   *R v Wyatt* 10/10/07, CA311/07; [2007] NZCA 436, para 24. The basis for the Court's conclusion may be questioned. The specific reference at para 24 of *Wyatt* was to New Zealand Law Commission, *Evidence: Total Recall? The Reliability of Witness Testimony*, NZLC MP13, Wellington, 1999, para 124ff, which dealt with techniques for interviewing young children. Surprisingly, the preceding para of *Wyatt* referred to para 278 of the arguably more relevant Law Commission Report, *Evidence Law: Character and Credibility* (NZLC PP 27, 1997), which at least obliquely refers to *R v H*, discussed in the text above.

Although the message of s 43(3)(f) is clear enough, it is not necessarily an easy task to pinpoint precisely when the factor of "unusualness" is present. The question will always be: unusual in comparison to what? Propensity evidence is commonly offered in trials of sexual offending and this can serve as an example. Non-consensual sex is, surely, "unusual" between men and women in general. However, it would appear that, to possess heightened probative value under s 43(3)(f), some additional factor must be present in both the propensity evidence and the circumstances surrounding the offence being tried. The prosecution and the defence are likely to contest whether or not the required degree of unusualness is present. A determination of that issue may hinge on research statistics or whether notice (s 128) can be taken of the frequency of occurrence of the factor relied upon as demonstrating unusualness.

EV43.08   Subsection (4): assessment of prejudicial effect

Section 43(4) deals with the other half of the admissibility equation, namely the "prejudicial effect of [the propensity] evidence on the defendant". It may appear strange that s 43(4) speaks only of the assessment of prejudicial effect when the test for admissibility set out in s 43(1) compares probative value and the risk of an *unfairly* prejudicial effect. The explanation for this omission may be that the Act assumes the prejudicial effect of *all* propensity evidence about a defendant that is offered by the prosecution. The *assessment* that is the subject of s 43(4) is an inquiry into the extent to which that inevitable prejudicial effect carries (per the test set forth in s 43(1)), a risk of unfairness. By every indication, it appears that if, as a result of this assessment, the judge concludes that the evidence will produce either of the results specified in s 43(4)(a) or (b), a risk of unfairly prejudicial effect is present.

As with the guidance for the assessment of probative value contained in s 43(3), the list of indicators of a risk of unfairly prejudicial effect in s 43(4) is expressly not exhaustive. Other factors may be considered by the judge. However, in contrast to s 43(3), the judge *must* consider the factors set out in s 43(4).

(1)   Unfairly predispose

Section 43(4)(a) reflects a concern that some commentators have restated in terms of the presumption of innocence. Once the fact-finder learns of disreputable aspects of the defendant's character, he or she may conclude that the defendant is guilty even though the prosecution evidence has not actually reached the required standard of proof beyond reasonable doubt. Although s 43(4)(a) focuses on the danger that the propensity evidence is likely to *unfairly* predispose the fact-finder against the defendant, this qualification was probably added out of an abundance of caution. *Any* predisposition "against" the defendant is likely to give rise to the sort of risk of unfair prejudice with which s 43(1) is concerned.

(2)   Disproportionate weight

Section 43(4)(b) acknowledges that there is a risk of unfair prejudice to a defendant if the nature of the propensity evidence distracts the fact-finder from a careful assessment of the other evidence in the case. There has been a longstanding school of thought that once the fact-finder learns that the defendant has disreputable propensities, particularly when such propensities have crystallised in criminal offending that has not previously been punished, the fact-finder may convict simply as a knee-jerk reaction to the accused's bad character. Section 43(4)(b) requires the judge to take this into account.

EV43.09   Section 43(4) is not the final determination

It must be stressed that even though, with the assistance of s 43(4), a determination has been made that there is a risk that the propensity evidence will have an unfairly prejudicial effect against the defendant, this does not end the enquiry into admissibility. The judge must still move on to the process of weighing up the probative value of the evidence against the established risk of an unfairly prejudicial effect, as required by s 43(1).

(1)   No guidance on weighing up process

The Act provides no guidance on how a judge is to actually perform the weighing up process required by s 43(1) or how he or she is to recognise precisely when probative value *does* outweigh the risk of an unfairly prejudicial effect. It would be safe to predict that the Act will not diminish the extent to which this question is litigated at all levels of criminal courts in New Zealand.[546]

Complainants in sexual cases

44   Evidence of sexual experience of complainants in sexual cases

(1)   In a sexual case, no evidence can be given and no question can be put to a witness relating directly or indirectly to the sexual experience of the complainant with any person other than the defendant, except with the permission of the Judge.

(2)   In a sexual case, no evidence can be given and no question can be put to a witness that relates directly or indirectly to the reputation of the complainant in sexual matters.

(3)   In an application for permission under subsection (1), the Judge must not grant permission unless satisfied that the evidence or question is of such direct relevance to facts in issue in the proceeding, or the issue of the appropriate sentence, that it would be contrary to the interests of justice to exclude it.

(4)   The permission of the Judge is not required to rebut or contradict evidence given under subsection (1).

(5)   In a sexual case in which the defendant is charged as a party and cannot be convicted unless it is shown that another person committed a sexual offence against the complainant, subsection (1) does not apply to any evidence given, or any question put, that relates directly or indirectly to the sexual experience of the complainant with that other person.

(6)   This section does not authorise evidence to be given or any question to be put that could not be given or put apart from this section.

---

546   *Adams on Criminal Law — Evidence*, EC2.8.

EV44.01   Admissibility threshold for evidence of the complainant's sexual history

Section 44 of the Evidence Act 2006, dealing with "evidence of the sexual experience of complainants in sexual cases", is, for the most part, a re-enactment of s 23A of the Evidence Act 1908.[547] This provision subjects evidence about the complainant's sexual experience with a person other than the accused to a heightened relevance test: for the evidence to be admitted or a question be asked, it must be "of such direct relevance to a fact in issue … that it would be contrary to the interests of justice to exclude it" (s 44(3)). As the test for admissibility is the same as under s 23A, the case law on the application of that section will continue to have relevance,[548] except with regard to the admission of reputation evidence.

EV44.02   Subsection (2): bar on evidence of the complainant's reputation in sexual matters

Although the admissibility test under both sections is the same, s 44(2) of the 2006 Act introduces a significant change. It appears to contain an absolute bar on evidence, or questions, relating directly or indirectly to the reputation of the complainant in sexual matters.

Section 46 of the Law Commission's draft Code recommended an amendment to the proviso in s 23A(3):

> "In a sexual case, no evidence can be given and no question can be put to a witness relating directly or indirectly to the reputation of the complainant in sexual matters
>
> "(a)   for the purpose of supporting or challenging the truthfulness of the complainant; or
>
> "(b)   for the purpose of establishing the complainant's consent; or
>
> "(c)   for any other purpose except with the permission of the judge."

This reform was intended to prohibit questions or evidence "about the complainant's reputation in sexual matters if the purpose of such questions or evidence is merely to challenge the complainant's truthfulness [credibility] or to establish the complainant's consent".[549] As such, it arguably strengthened the effect of the s 23A proviso.

The Evidence Bill 2005 did not include the Law Commission's recommended draft. Clause 40(3) of the Bill essentially re-enacted the proviso from s 23A, while the wording of admissibility inquiry was changed.

The New Zealand Law Society, and others, questioned the wisdom of the change in wording and recommended replacing cl 40 with the Law Commission's draft. This was also the advice from the Ministry of Justice,[550] although the Ministry did not

---

547   See the definition of "sexual case" at EV4.40.01.
548   *Adams on Criminal Law — Evidence*, EC19.
549   LC *Evidence Code*, para C211.

recommend extending the admissibility requirement to evidence of the complainant's sexual history with the particular defendant.[551]

The Select Committee ultimately recommended a different version from that proposed by the Law Commission. The Select Committee called for supplementary submissions on cl 40 from the Wellington Women Lawyers Association, the New Zealand Law Society, and the Criminal Bar Association.[552] In Russell Fairbrother's words, the Wellington Women Lawyers Association "challenged us as to why evidence of reputation should any longer be part of our evidence law when it came to allegations of sexual assault or sexual violation. We were interested in this challenge, because, of course, reputation has nothing to do with what is a transaction of the moment."[553] The Select Committee's Commentary on the Evidence Bill, as reported back, reads:

> "We recommend that clause 40 be amended to provide that no evidence can be given and no question be put relating to the sexual reputation of the complainant in sexual matters. We consider that any reference to a person's sexual reputation is irrelevant and should not be admitted."[554]

Section 44(2) reads, as was the Select Committee's intent, as a total bar on the offering of evidence of a complainant's reputation in sexual matters. This means that reputation evidence going to the issue of the complainant's credibility, his or her consent or the defendant's belief in consent, cannot be offered.

(1) Reputation evidence that is relevant to the assessment of the complainant's veracity

Reputation evidence which "solely or mainly" concerns the complainant's veracity[555] may fall to be considered under the veracity rules — and therefore needs be "substantially helpful" in assessing the complainant's veracity for it to be admitted. On the basis that "substantial helpfulness" is also a heightened relevance standard, the admissibility of reputation evidence that is relevant to the complainant's credibility may remain unchanged by the 2006 Act. This was the Law Commission's view of how such evidence should be treated, stating that a reputation for making false allegations of sexual assault, for example, is evidence about "reputation for truthfulness (or lack of it), not about reputation in sexual matters, and is admissible provided that it complies with the truthfulness rules".[556]

---

550 *Departmental Report* (EV/MOJ/6), 37.
551 As was proposed by the Law Commission — see s 46 of the draft Code (LC *Evidence Code*, 124).
552 Hansard, *Russell Fairbrother: Evidence Amendment Bill: Second Reading*, 15 November 2006 ((2006) 635 NZPD 6561).
553 Hansard, *Russell Fairbrother: Evidence Amendment Bill: Second Reading*, 15 November 2006 ((2006) 635 NZPD 6561).
554 *Select Committee Report on the Evidence Bill*, 7.
555 See EV40.05(2).
556 LC *Evidence Code*, para C212. See also the discussion in *R v Macdonald* 8/4/05, CA166/04, para 30ff.

The difficulty with this approach is that at the same time the Select Committee was convinced about the unhelpfulness of reputation evidence in sexual cases, the members also came to view reputation evidence as being irrelevant for other purposes. The Committee therefore also recommended that "clause 33(3)(f) [and clause 33(5)], which refers to a person's reputation for being untruthful be deleted. We consider that a person's reputation is irrelevant and should not be considered when assessing the veracity of their evidence."[557] (The Committee made a similar recommendation in relation to the propensity rule, now s 40 of the Act, saying: "We consider it important that a person's reputation should not affect current proceedings.") The removal of the reference to reputation evidence in s 37 of the Act may well render evidence of a complainant's reputation for making false complaints inadmissible.[558] Specific evidence of such false complaints may need to be offered instead by reference to s 37(3)(a), which provides that evidence may be offered which shows a "lack of veracity on the part of the person when under a legal obligation to tell the truth."[559]

(2)   Evidence of previous complaints: *R v C*

In *R v C*,[560] despite referring to the Law Commission commentary,[561] the Court of Appeal held that s 37 "does not trump s 44".[562] The Court reasoned that the removal of the reference to reputation evidence rendered the Law Commission's comment of "little or no relevance".[563] The Court went on to say that at "a more general level, we do not see the comment by the Commission as heralding a change of approach in the 2006 Act".[564] However, the wording of s 40(4) seems to confirm that the Law Commission's approach was intended in such situations — that is, to use the words of the court, s 37 *does* trump s 44.[565]

The Court's observation that reputation evidence about the complainant "will be inadmissible whether the case falls under s 37 or s 44"[566] seems to clarify the scope of s 37 (with significant implications).[567] However, the Court did not go on to find that the evidence being offered in *R v C* must actually be inadmissible. The Court must have treated the evidence as individual examples of "the sexual experience of the complainant" under s 44, even though the effect of the combined examples could also have been conceptualised as evidence of the "complainant's reputation for telling the truth".[568]

557   *Select Committee Report on the Evidence Bill*, 7.
558   See EV37.03(4).
559   See further the discussion at EV37.06.
560   *R v C (CA391/07)* 12/10/07, CA391/07; [2007] NZCA 439.
561   See EV44.02(1) and the discussion in LC *Evidence Code*, para C212.
562   *R v C (CA391/07)* 12/10/07, CA391/07; [2007] NZCA 439, para 22.
563   *R v C (CA391/07)* 12/10/07, CA391/07; [2007] NZCA 439, para 21.
564   *R v C (CA391/07)* 12/10/07, CA391/07; [2007] NZCA 439, para 22.
565   See further EV40.05(4).
566   *R v C (CA391/07)* 12/10/07, CA391/07; [2007] NZCA 439, para 21.
567   See EV37.03(4).
568   As was argued by counsel for the appellant: *R v C (CA391/07)* 12/10/07, CA391/07; [2007] NZCA 439, para 29.

The Court did preserve a limited role for s 37 in some cases — by drawing a distinction between a "clear cases" and "other cases". Where the defendant wishes to offer "clear evidence that a complainant has probably made a false complaint", the admissibility decision will be determined under s 37.[569] In "other cases" where "the truthfulness or falseness of past complaints is in issue",[570] s 44 will determine admissibility. Although the latter approach was followed in some cases under s 23A of the Evidence Act 1908, evidence solely or mainly about truthfulness was intended to be dealt with by s 37 under the 2006 Act. Although the outcome under either test (s 37 or s 44) may well be the same, the distinction between "clean" and "other" cases has the potential to encourage unnecessary argument during s 44 applications and is regrettable.

(3) Reputation evidence going to an element of the offence

Section 44(2) also impacts on the ability of a defendant to offer reputation evidence in support of a claim of honest belief in consent. This kind of evidence has been admitted in the past (see, for example, *R v Bourke*).[571] In this case the Court of Appeal confirmed that evidence of what B understood the complainant's sexual reputation to be — based on his conversation with M and others — could be admitted at trial. The evidence could be offered to explain that it did not occur to B that "the complainant might be thinking he was someone else because she was behaving in exactly the way that he had been told she behaved with men".[572] The Court therefore held that the jury should be directed that the reputation evidence was only relevant to explain why the accused went into the complainant's room and in relation to the question whether the accused honestly believed on reasonable grounds that the complainant was consenting.[573]

The purpose of the reform is clear — reputation evidence should never be treated as relevant to what an accused believes about whether a complainant is consenting. If the evidence was not admitted in *Bourke*, would this have impacted on the accused's right "to present a defence"? (See s 25(e) of the New Zealand Bill of Rights Act 1990.) If so, the Act introduces a tension between the wording of s 44(2) and s 6(b). Section 10(1)(a) of the Act states that the Act "must be interpreted in a way that promotes its purposes and principles" — a reference to "the purpose" of the Act stated in s 6 — which includes "(b) providing rules of evidence that recognise the importance of the rights affirmed by the New Zealand Bill of Rights Act 1990". Can s 44(2) be interpreted to be consistent with those rights, notwithstanding the wording of the section and the clear legislative intent?

One possible argument is that the evidence in cases like *Bourke* is not being offered as "directly or indirectly to the reputation of the complainant in sexual matters", rather to demonstrate the accused's belief in consent. This would be to interpret s 44(2) as the proviso to s 23A has been — reputation evidence only showing propensity in

---

569   *R v C (CA391/07)* 12/10/07, CA391/07; [2007] NZCA 439, para 23.
570   *R v C (CA391/07)* 12/10/07, CA391/07; [2007] NZCA 439, para 24.
571   *R v Bourke* 15/8/06, CA207/06.
572   *R v Bourke* 15/8/06, CA207/06, para 38.
573   *R v Bourke* 15/8/06, CA207/06, para 51.

sexual matters cannot be admitted, but if it goes to a fact in issue it may be. However, the proviso was not re-enacted in s 44 of the Act, despite it forming part of the Bill. It is therefore difficult to argue that interpreting s 44(2) in this way is legitimate, given the deliberate removal of the proviso.

Subpart 6—Identification evidence

(s 45 to s 46)

45   Admissibility of visual identification evidence

(1)   If a formal procedure is followed by officers of an enforcement agency in obtaining visual identification evidence of a person alleged to have committed an offence or there was a good reason for not following a formal procedure, that evidence is admissible in a criminal proceeding unless the defendant proves on the balance of probabilities that the evidence is unreliable.

(2)   If a formal procedure is not followed by officers of an enforcement agency in obtaining visual identification evidence of a person alleged to have committed an offence and there was no good reason for not following a formal procedure, that evidence is inadmissible in a criminal proceeding unless the prosecution proves beyond reasonable doubt that the circumstances in which the identification was made have produced a reliable identification.

(3)   For the purposes of this section, a **formal procedure** is a procedure for obtaining visual identification evidence—

    (a)   that is observed as soon as practicable after the alleged offence is reported to an officer of an enforcement agency; and

    (b)   in which the person to be identified is compared to no fewer than 7 other persons who are similar in appearance to the person to be identified; and

    (c)   in which no indication is given to the person making the identification as to who among the persons in the procedure is the person to be identified; and

    (d)   in which the person making the identification is informed that the person to be identified may or may not be among the persons in the procedure; and

    (e)   that is the subject of a written record of the procedure actually followed that is sworn to be true and complete by the officer who conducted the procedure and provided to the Judge and the defendant (but not the jury) at the hearing; and

    (f)   that is the subject of a pictorial record of what the witness looked at that is prepared and certified to be true and complete by the officer who conducted the procedure and provided to the Judge and the defendant (but not the jury) at the hearing; and

    (g)   that complies with any further requirements provided for in regulations made under section 201.

(4)   The circumstances referred to in the following paragraphs are **good reasons** for not following a formal procedure:

(a)   a refusal of the person to be identified to take part in the procedure (that is, by refusing to take part in a parade or other procedure, or to permit a photograph or video record to be taken, where the enforcement agency does not already have a photo or a video record that shows a true likeness of that person):

(b)   the singular appearance of the person to be identified (being of a nature that cannot be disguised so that the person is similar in appearance to those with whom the person is to be compared):

(c)   a substantial change in the appearance of the person to be identified after the alleged offence occurred and before it was practical to hold a formal procedure:

(d)   no officer involved in the investigation or the prosecution of the alleged offence could reasonably anticipate that identification would be an issue at the trial of the defendant:

(e)   if an identification of a person alleged to have committed an offence has been made to an officer of an enforcement agency soon after the offence was reported and in the course of that officer's initial investigation:

(f)   if an identification of a person alleged to have committed an offence has been made to an officer of an enforcement agency after a chance meeting between the person who made the identification and the person alleged to have committed the offence.

EV45.01   Overview

Section 45 controls the admission of visual identification evidence in criminal proceedings. Evidence of identity usually takes the form of a witness stating that a person is the same as someone he or she saw on a previous occasion. Under s 45, visual identification evidence obtained by way of a formal procedure followed by officers of an enforcement agency will be admissible in a criminal proceeding, unless the defendant proves on the balance of probabilities that it is unreliable. The requirements for a formal procedure are outlined in s 45(3), but the detail there is not comprehensive regarding the conduct of formal identification procedures. Some further detail is contained in the revised *Police Manual of Best Practice*.[574] That detail is also not comprehensive.

If no formal procedure is followed, any visual identification evidence resulting from an informal procedure will be inadmissible unless there was a good reason for not following a formal procedure (as outlined in s 45(4)) or the prosecution can prove beyond reasonable doubt that the circumstances in which the identification was made would have produced a reliable identification (s 45(2)). In essence, then, s 45 focuses

---

574   "Identification of Offenders" in *New Zealand Police Manual of Best Practice*, August 2007.

on reliability through a formal procedure, but does allow for reliable identification to be admissible even where there was no formal procedure (s 45(2)), and also allows potentially unreliable identifications to be admitted because there was a good reason for not following a formal procedure (s 45(1)). Admissibility under s 45 is tied to the idea that a formal procedure is more likely to result in reliable evidence, but not exclusively so.

(1) Focus on reliability

In drafting the Evidence Code, the Law Commission's concern was that only reliable eyewitness identification evidence be admitted as required by "the public interest in bringing wrongdoers to justice and the public interest in protecting the innocent from wrongful conviction".[575] To this end, s 126 requires that the judge in a criminal proceeding tried with a jury gives the jury a warning in cases involving identification of the defendant or other persons. The warning is required where the identification is visual or voice, and whether or not s 45 applies.[576]

The focus on reliability of eyewitness evidence in s 45 is a reflection of the inherent potential for unreliability of both visual and voice identification: our memories are prone to incompleteness, distortion, and forgetfulness. However, psychological research suggests that jurors may believe eyewitnesses too readily, especially when they are confident or have been consistent,[577] and that there is not great ability for us to distinguish accurate from inaccurate eyewitnesses. Traditional credibility cues may not work because the witness may genuinely believe that he or she is right, when in fact they are wrong.[578] As identification evidence is inherently unreliable, care must be taken to elicit the most reliable evidence possible by means of fair and transparent procedures. The Law Commission's recommendations, which are largely replicated in ss 45 and 46, were based on scientific research of ten years ago. Their "underlying presumption" regarding formal procedures and the lack of hierarchy; and the specific terms of s 45 in particular, are therefore based on psychological research on memory processes from that time.

(2) Definition of "visual identification evidence"

Under s 4, "visual identification evidence" is an assertion "based wholly or partly on what that person saw, to the effect that a defendant was present at or near a place".[579] This is a fairly broad definition, potentially encompassing evidence where the person making the assertion is uncertain; and also covering identification evidence not only of a suspect but also of other persons or things, provided that seeing those other persons or things constituted an assertion that a defendant was present at or near the place in question (for example, identification of the defendant's car). However,

---

575   LC *Evidence Code*, para 187.

576   See EV126.01 and EV126.02(3).

577   These are not necessarily indicators of accuracy — see Bradfield, Wells, and Olsen, "The damaging effect of confirming feedback on the relation between eyewitness certainty and identification accuracy" (2002) 87(1) *Journal of Applied Psychology* 112.

578   Bradfield, Wells, and Olsen (2002).

579   See EV4.44.01.

the provisions of s 45 apply only to identifications of persons alleged to have committed an offence, and so other forms of visual identification evidence will be governed by the general provisions of ss 7 and 8.

"Visual identification evidence" includes assertions that "a defendant was present at, or near a place where an act constituting direct or circumstantial evidence of an offence was done at, or about, the time the act was done", and therefore includes evidence not only of direct identification of a defendant committing an offence, but also circumstantial evidence of him or her being in the vicinity of the offence, or fleeing the scene, for example.

EV45.02   Relationship of s 45 to other admissibility rules

Where visual identification evidence includes a pre-trial assertion that the defendant is the offender (for example, by way of a formal procedure), the evidence may fulfil the requirements of s 45 and thereby be admissible under the section. However, such an assertion, when accompanied by a consistent identification of the defendant at the trial, may fall foul of the previous consistent statements rule under s 35. There is no guidance from the Act on whether visual identification evidence that meets the requirements of s 45 should also be subject to the requirements of s 35.[580]

The better view is that s 35 will apply even where the requirements of s 45 are met. In such cases, the witness will still be able to assert that the defendant is the offender in the course of giving evidence, but will only be able to support that identification by way of the previous consistent assertion identifying the defendant where there is a challenge to the witness's accuracy or veracity (s 35(2)), for example where the defence questions the ability of the witness on the basis of poor eyesight. If there is no challenge to accuracy or veracity, bringing evidence of a previous consistent assertion will prolong proceedings without doing more than boosting a witness's consistency by use of repetitive material — the very mischief that the rule in s 35 aims to prevent. Where the witness does not identify the defendant at the trial, s 35 has no application because there is no previous consistent statement apparent. In that situation s 45 would allow evidence of the pre-trial identification to be given, usually by the enforcement officer present when the witness made the pre-trial identification (although hearsay requirements under s 18 may have to be fulfilled).

EV45.03   No application to identifications by arresting officers

Section 45 is not intended to apply to identifications made by arresting officers. As stated by the Law Commission,[581] when reading s 45(1) in conjunction with the definition of visual identification evidence under s 4, the fact that s 45(1) envisages officers of an enforcement agency "obtaining an assertion to the effect that a defendant … was present at or near a place" makes it inapplicable where the arresting officer is the person who makes the identification. This view would certainly accord with the tenor of the rest of s 45. For example, s 45(3)(a) requires that a formal procedure be

---

580   The potential conflict between sections arises a number of times throughout the Act: see, eg, ss 23 and 47.

581   LC *Evidence Reform*, para 203; LC *Evidence Code*, para C218.

conducted "as soon as practicable after an offence is reported to an officer", and s 45(3)(c) and (d) assume that the witness will have no knowledge of which person is the suspect — something the arresting officer would obviously be aware of. Section 45(4) does not provide for circumstances in which the arresting officer identifies the defendant, and yet logically this would usually constitute a good reason for not following a formal procedure. It is doubtful that s 45(4)(d) or (e) would apply: under para (d) identification may still be an issue in such circumstances; and under para (e) it would stretch construction of the provision to state that an arresting officer made the identification "to an officer of an enforcement agency soon after the offence was reported and in the course of the officer's initial investigation".

The Law Commission's view was that, where the arresting officer makes an identification of the defendant, "the reliability of identification evidence … will be a question of weight rather than admissibility".[582] However, inapplicability of s 45 to identification by arresting officers does not necessarily mean that the issue becomes one of weight only. As discussed above,[583] identification may still be a disputed issue in such circumstances (such as where the defendant is pursued after the offence and arrested from amongst a crowd of people) and as such the admissibility of the identification may be disputed on the basis that its prejudicial effect outweighs its probative value even where s 45 does not apply (see s 8(1)(a)).

(1)   Application only to identification of alleged offender

Section 45 applies only to visual identification evidence of a "person alleged to have committed an offence". The Law Commission had recommended that this be broadened to include identification of persons other than defendants, where that identification is crucial to the prosecution case,[584] but this was not incorporated into the Act, and as such the requirements for a formal procedure under s 45 do not apply to identifications of anyone other than the defendant. However, as with some identifications made by arresting officers, the admissibility of identifications of persons other than the defendant will be governed by s 8, and the law before the Act will be relevant to the determination of probative value versus prejudicial effect under s 8(1)(a).

EV45.04   Subsection (1)

Section 45(1) presents a significant change from the pre-Act law, in that the pre-eminence of the live identification parade is abolished, as is any notion of hierarchy of procedures based on greater reliability of one method over another.[585] Instead, the focus under the Act is on whether or not a formal procedure was undertaken. If the requirements of s 45(3) are met, the procedure will be deemed to be a "formal procedure" under the Act. The procedure must be conducted by "officers of an

---

582   LC *Evidence Reform*, para 203.
583   See EV45.01(2).
584   As was the identification of Heidi Paakkonen, one of the victims in *R v Tamihere* [1991] 1 NZLR 195 (CA). See LC *Evidence Code*, para C219.
585   See further EV45.06 on s 45(3).

enforcement agency" which, as defined in s 4, includes agencies other than the police.[586]

Section 45(1) states that identification evidence obtained by means of a formal procedure will be presumed to be reliable and will therefore be admissible unless the defendant proves on the balance of probabilities that the evidence is unreliable. The same presumption of admissibility applies under s 45(1) to identification evidence gained by way of an informal procedure where there were good reasons for not following a formal procedure. The stated aim of the Law Commission in admitting only reliable identification evidence could be frustrated by a presumption that evidence gained from an informal procedure is admissible, good reason or no, but such a concession is rooted in practical necessity.[587]

(1)   Introduction of burden on the accused

Section 45(1) introduces a burden carried by the defendant to prove that the evidence is unreliable, on the balance of probabilities. Before the Act, judges determined the admissibility of identification evidence by assessing reliability based on whether the probative value of the evidence outweighed the prejudicial effect. So, while a reliability inquiry in and of itself is not new, determining whether the defendant has shown that it is probable that the evidence is unreliable *is* new.

(2)   Unreliability may be due to procedural methods or to witness and offence factors

The phrase "unless the defendant proves on the balance of probabilities that the evidence is unreliable" is potentially problematic, because, as illustrated by scientific research, most visual identifications could be shown to be unreliable (or "probably unreliable") in a general sense. It is to be assumed therefore that the section anticipates greater specificity than the general assertion that memory is prone to error. There is no necessary link in s 45(1) between the evidence of unreliability and the procedure undertaken by the "officers of an enforcement agency". It is likely then that the focus can be both on the procedural reasons for asserting unreliability, and on those connected with the witness or the circumstances of the offence, such as short-sightedness, bad lighting etc (factors that are also applicable to the warning given in cases where there is admissible identification evidence under s 126).

In cases that depend substantially on the identification evidence, an assessment of whether or not evidence is probably unreliable under s 45(1) will amount to an assessment of whether or not the defendant is probably guilty. Before the Act, admissibility of identification evidence was considered in light of all of the evidence in the case, and without a particular link showing that unreliability was due to the procedure used for the identification test; it is likely that this will remain the case under s 45(1), perhaps under s 45(2), and s 46.[588]

---

586   See EV4.13.01.
587   See the discussion of s 45(4) at EV45.07.
588   See EV45.05(1) and EV46.01(3) respectively.

There will often be other circumstantial evidence in the case that can affect the likely reliability of the identification evidence and therefore its admissibility. Identification evidence can itself support other identification evidence.[589] Where the quality of identification evidence is poor, the supporting evidence will need to be strong in order to allow the evidence to be admitted.[590]

EV45.05   Subsection (2)

Where a formal procedure is not followed, and there is no good reason for not doing so, s 45(2) provides that the visual identification evidence obtained as a result of the informal procedure will be inadmissible in a criminal proceeding unless the prosecution proves beyond reasonable doubt that the circumstances in which the identification was made have produced a reliable identification. It may be that expert evidence could assist in this assessment.[591] Unlike the burden on the defence under s 45(1), the requirement on the prosecution relates to the conduct of the identification procedure, and the inquiry will firmly rest on what the police (or officers of another enforcement agency) did in order to ensure that the evidence is reliable. It follows that, as envisaged by the Law Commission,[592] a procedure which adheres to most of the requirements under s 45(3) is more likely to discharge the burden than one which falls far short. Because of this requirement, the Act is likely to focus the attention of the police, and other enforcement agencies, on their procedures and practices; and the effect of s 45(2) should be to ensure that officers follow a formal procedure except where they have a good reason not to.[593]

(1)   Effect of assessment of reliability on the case against the accused under s 45(2)

Under s 45, all identification methods will need to adhere to the requirements of a formal procedure, and as such evidence gathering practices will need to change. This will be especially important in cases where the case rests "wholly or substantially"[594] on visual identification evidence, because the assessment of reliability under s 45(2) will amount to an assessment of guilt or innocence. Inadmissibility of visual identification evidence in such cases will mean collapse of the case against the defendant. The approach taken by the courts in response to s 45(2) and the requirement to use methods that produce reliable results will be of prime importance. If, as under the previous law, the judge looks to all of the evidence

---

589   *R v Holtz* [2003] 1 NZLR 667; (2002) 20 CRNZ 14 (CA); *R v Tranter* 14/6/04, CA486/03.

590   *R v Hoto* (1991) 8 CRNZ 17, where the court held that the weaker the identification evidence, the stronger the supporting evidence will need to be to justify its admission. It was noted in the case that, unlike other strands in a rope of circumstantial evidence, identification evidence holds special dangers of prejudice.

591   See EV25.02 and EV46.01(3).

592   LC *Evidence Code*, para C223.

593   Under the previous law the reasons for not conducting an identification parade were expected to be given (*R v Dixon* 25/6/97, CA77/97) but the admissibility of the evidence did not require proof of reliability beyond reasonable doubt, and the focus on procedural standards for methods other than identification parades was negligible.

594   See EV126.01.

in the case when assessing admissibility of the visual identification evidence, then in cases where there is other evidence against the defendant, the strength of that other evidence may convince the judge that (when viewed as part of all of the evidence in the case) the visual identification evidence is reliable. The possibility of such an approach is diminished by the fact that the requirement under s 45(2) is not a general assessment of reliability of the evidence as under s 45(1), but rather requires that the *circumstances of the identification* were such that reliable evidence was produced. This reference in s 45(2) only to the circumstances in which the identification was made (and not to witness or offence factors) suggests that judges may look to the identification evidence procedure (or lack of it) alone when assessing reliability.

EV45.06   Subsection (3): formal procedure requirements

Section 45(3) sets out the requirements for a formal identification procedure. All of the requirements need to be met before the presumption for admissibility under s 45(1) is triggered. If one or more of the requirements are not met, admissibility will be governed under s 45(2). The aim of s 45(3) is to ensure that visual identification evidence is as reliable as possible.

(1)   Pre-Act hierarchy of identification methods

Before the Act, there was a stated preference for the live identification parade. However, there was no rule of law prohibiting the use of photographs as an identification test medium, and photographic identification was routinely accepted with caution (usually where the reasons for a failure to conduct a live parade had been given).[595] Initially, photographic identification was used mainly for investigative purposes, to narrow down the field where there was no known suspect. At the evidential stage, there was an assumption that an identification parade would produce more reliable evidence because it showed live, moving subjects. Furthermore, evidence from photographic identification was traditionally approached with caution by the courts because of two main dangers associated with their use. First, the photographs used would not normally be admissible evidence in themselves because of their prejudicial effect on the jury — the use of police photographs may indicate that the accused has a criminal record. Secondly, there was concern about the "displacement effect", whereby a witness who identifies from photographs replaces his or her recollection of the offender with that of the photograph, which could result in a certain but mistaken identification at a later parade or in court.[596]

Despite the clear preference for identification for a live parade before the Act, the reality was that identification parades were rarely used. There were a number of good reasons for this, including the difficulty in finding suitable volunteers, the strain on police resources involved, and a lack of cooperation from both suspect and victim.[597] As such, most visual identifications in New Zealand prior to the Act resulted

---

595   *R v Porima and Wi* (1992) 9 CRNZ 368; *R v Dixon* 25/6/97, CA77/97.

596   This second concern is irrelevant where the photographic identification is the only identification test, and where the witness is not required to identify the defendant in court.

597   Tinsley, "Identification Procedures and Options for Reform" (2000) 31(1) VUWLR 117.

from a photographic identification procedure, and this is unlikely to change greatly under s 45.

(2)   No hierarchy under s 45

Section 45(3) provides no hierarchy of different identification methods, and this is a stance supported by current psychological research, which shows that there is not necessarily one method that inherently yields more accurate identifications.[598] The way the identification test method is utilised is the key, and it is this issue that s 45 attempts to address by setting out requirements for a formal procedure (what are termed the "system" variables in the psychological research). For the sake of practical guidance for law enforcement officers, a list of the methods that are considered appropriate (which is able to be amended as technology advances) would be useful, and it is hoped that this will appear in any regulations. The *Police Manual of Best Practice* endorses the use of both formal identification parades and photo montages. Some provisions on the running of each type of procedure are included in the revised *Police Manual of Best Practice*[599] (it is envisaged that other enforcement agencies will generate their own guides).

Despite a lack of indication regarding acceptable identification methods, it is likely that photographic and, in time, video identification will be the norm in New Zealand. Photographs and video are easier to use than live parades, as illustrated by the low number of live identification parades conducted before the Act. Furthermore, some methods used in other jurisdictions would not comply with the requirements of s 45(3) under any circumstances, and are therefore only likely to be used in New Zealand where there is a good reason for not conducting a formal procedure — and then only where there is little other choice if officers are to avoid the defendant proving that the identification evidence is probably unreliable under s 45(1).

For example, a confrontation (where the witness views only the suspect) would never meet the requirements of s 45(3), and if there was no good reason for departing from a formal procedure would be highly unlikely to satisfy s 45(2)'s reliability inquiry, being only marginally more satisfactory than a dock identification. Similarly, a formal group identification, where a witness is asked to identify the suspect in the crowd at a railway station or other busy place would not necessarily fulfil s 45(3) even where other requirements, such as formal recording, are met.

(3)   Dock identification

The Law Commission suggested that the combined effect of s 45(2) and (3) is to prevent dock identification[600] — where the witness identifies the defendant in the courtroom for the first time. Under s 45(2), the prosecution is unlikely to be able to prove beyond reasonable doubt that a reliable identification can be made in such

---

598   Cutler, Fisher, and Chicvara, "Eyewitness identification from live versus videotaped lineups" (1989) 2(2) *Forensic Reports* 93.

599   "Identification of Offenders" in *New Zealand Police Manual of Best Practice*, August 2007, 4-7.

600   LC *Evidence Code*, 131

circumstances; and under s 45(3) dock identification does not fulfill the requirements of a formal procedure. However, if there was a good reason why a formal procedure was not followed under s 45(4), a dock identification could be admissible unless the defendant can prove under s 45(1) that the identification is unreliable.[601]

(4) Best practice for identification procedures not adequately reflected in s 45(3)

Section 45(3) offers some detailed provisions while omitting others. Many of the following issues are well documented in the available psychological research, which has developed substantially in the 10 years since the Law Commission's initial drafting.

(a) *Multiple suspects and witnesses*

There is no indication under s 45(3) regarding what should happen where there is more than one suspect (eg, can more than one suspect be included in the same parade and if so, how many "other persons" should be used). Similarly, there is no indication regarding the appropriate procedure where there is more than one witness. The psychological research suggests that witnesses should be shown the parade one by one,[602] and should be prevented from discussing the identification once the procedure is underway. The *Police Manual of Best Practice* states that witnesses must be brought in one-by-one and prevented from communicating with other witnesses where an identification parade is conducted.[603] No similar procedure is advocated for other types of identification methods.

(b) *Legal representation*

There is no provision in s 45(3) to allow for the suspect to have a legal representative or other support person present during the procedure, again as a check and balance that the procedure is conducted fairly. Section 344B of the Crimes Act 1961 provides for legal representation when attending an identification parade. However, most identification procedures will use photographs (or video) for which there is no provision that corresponds to s 344B.

(c) *Mode of presentation*

Section 45 gives no direction on the mode of presentation for identification. Research clearly concludes that sequential (where images or live persons are presented to the witness one by one), rather than simultaneous (where witnesses see a group at the same time), presentation is preferable.[604] Section 45 does not prevent simultaneous presentation within a formal procedure. Indeed, it appears that simultaneous presentation is anticipated, as the requisite number of foils ("other persons") was changed from eight in the draft Code to seven in the Act in order to prevent the eye

---

601   Dock identification was admissible on a similar basis before before the 2006 Act: see, eg, *R v T* (1998) 16 CRNZ 10 (CA).

602   Turtle, Lindsay, and Wells, "Best practice recommendations for eyewitness evidence procedures" (2003) *Canadian Journal of Police and Security Services* 1, 5.

603   "Identification of Offenders" in *New Zealand Police Manual of Best Practice*, August 2007, 5.

604   Turtle, Lindsay, and Wells (2003).

being drawn to the centre photograph in a photo montage.[605] There are some occasions where sequential presentation has been found to reduce accuracy,[606] but in general better accuracy and a reduction of the use of guesses and relative judgement is apparent where there is sequential presentation.[607] Research on the optimum number of foils is inconclusive: the Ministry of Justice advised that the optimum number from research was five (and further advised that seven was a suitable compromise);[608] current research suggests that larger numbers do not necessarilty reduce accuracy, and so up to 12 may be acceptable.[609] Seven is therefore to be read as a minimum requirement under s 45.[610]

(d)   *Who can conduct the procedure*

The Act itself contains no specific limitation on who may conduct an identification procedure. As it stands, the Act therefore allows for an identification procedure to be conducted by the investigating officer in the case. The Law Commission originally recommended that, because of research indicating advertent or inadvertent influence on the identifying witness, investigating officers should not be allowed to conduct an identification procedure; but resiled from this view after objections, including an objection by the police, on grounds of practicality. The revised *Police Manual of Best Practice* provides that "the identification parade should, if possible, be conducted by a non-commissioned officer. The O/C Case can be present, but must not take part in the proceeding."[611] No mention is made of the input of the O/C Case into other forms of identification procedure, such as photo montages.

Allowing investigating officers to conduct procedures may result in real or perceived unfairness, especially where there is no requirement for the suspect's legal representative to approve the written and pictorial records of the procedure. Subconsciously, the officer may give verbal or non-verbal cues to witnesses.[612] The arguments of unenforceability[613] are rather unconvincing, especially where very few formal identification procedures are conducted in the live presence of the suspect, a situation which is likely to increase with the operation of s 45 and the consequent removal of the predominance of the live identification parade.

The critical issue may be that investigating officers have no contact with witnesses while the identification procedure is under way, which would be more easily satisfied than the investigating officers having no involvement with the procedure at all. This is the case with some forms of "blind" identification testing: "blind" can refer to an

---

605   *Cabinet Paper 2*, para 43.
606   For example, with children under 10 years of age: Turtle, Lindsay, and Wells (2003).
607   Turtle, Lindsay, and Wells (2003).
608   *Cabinet Paper 2*, para 43.
609   Turtle, Lindsay, and Wells (2003).
610   This is assumed to be the case in the "Identification of Offenders" in *New Zealand Police Manual of Best Practice*, August 2007, 4.
611   "Identification of Offenders" in *New Zealand Police Manual of Best Practice*, August 2007, 4.
612   Haw and Fisher, "Effects of Administrator-Witness Contact on Eyewitness Identification Accuracy" (2004) 89(6) *Journal of Applied Psychology* 1106.
613   LC *Evidence Reform*, para 206.

unawareness of who the suspect is, but can also refer to the situation in which the identification officer knows who the suspect is but is unable to see which picture or video image the witness is viewing at any given time.[614]

It may be that these omissions, along with any other strong indications from psychological research in the future, will be provided for in any regulations issued under s 201 (see s 45(3)(g)).

(5)   The "person to be identified"

Section 45(3)(b), (c), and (d) refer to the "person to be identified", a term that obviously refers to the police suspect. The phrase appears to be left over from the draft Code, when it was adopted by the Law Commission to cover not only suspects but also other people whose identity was a crucial part of the case, an extension which was not adopted in the Act. Section 45(3)(c) asserts that no indication be given to the witness as to who is "the person to be identified", which suggests that the police suspect *is* the offender and that the role of the witness is to confirm that the police are correct in suspecting "the person to be identified". Such a suggestion undermines the reason for requiring a formal procedure under the Act — that visual identification is often unreliable and so the system should do all that it can to ensure that a correct identification is made. The best outcome in cases where the suspect is not the offender is for the witness to decline to make an identification, a fact which is belied by the phrase "person to be identified".

Similarly, s 45(3)(d) states that witnesses should be informed that "the person to be identified" may or may not be among the persons in the procedure. On the face of it, s 45(3)(d) provides that there may be a "blank" procedure, where the suspect is not one of the people on the parade, photo array or video. Certainly, the Law Commission did not refute this reading of the provision when discussing the view of one commentator that "an identification procedure would rarely take place without including the person to be identified."[615] This confusion is due in part to the phrase "person to be identified", but the real function of such an instruction is surely to say to witnesses that, even though the suspect may be there, that he or she may not be the person they witnessed. The combination of this uncertainty with the implication from the phrase "person to be identified" that the suspect and the offender are one and the same leads to a reinforcement of the idea that "there is no smoke without fire". In other words, a provision aimed at increasing fairness by decreasing pressure to choose on witnesses could in fact have the opposite effect. It would be better to say to witnesses that the person he or she saw doing X at Y date may or may not be among the persons in the procedure (eg, "the person you saw may or may not be on the parade").[616]

---

614   Turtle, Lindsay, and Wells (2003).
615   LC *Evidence Reform*, para 207.
616   See Clark, "A Re-examination of the Effects of Biased Lineup Instructions in Eyewitness Identification" (2005) 29(4) *Law and Human Behavior* 395.

(6)   Written and pictorial records required

Section 45(3)(e) requires that a written record of the identification procedure be made, and that it be available to the judge and the defendant. Section 45(3)(f) contains the same requirement for a pictoral record. The content of the written record will be governed by the *Police Manual of Best Practice*[617] and amended as feedback is received from the courts, as was the case before the Act. Written reports for live and photographic procedures had to be made under the previous version of the Manual of Best Practice, including information such as the time, date and place of the procedure, the name and address of the witness, and information about the other people involved in the procedure (the "foils").

As there is no specified right for the suspect's legal representative to be present at the procedure, it is unsurprising that there is no requirement in either s 45(3)(e) or (f) for the written and pictorial records to also be certified as true and complete by the suspect's legal representative. Pictorial records of live or video parades may be entered as evidence, for example where the integrity of the identification procedure is questioned by the defendant,[618] which on its face contradicts the provision in s 45(3)(e) or (f) for records to be provided to the judge and the defendant "but not the jury". However, it is to be assumed that this provision is not meant to be prohibitive, but rather that it is a statement only that the production of the record to the jury is not *required*. That there is no requirement for production of written and pictorial records to the jury under s 45(3) reflects the wish to avoid prejudice against the accused associated with the use of mugshots in identification procedures.[619] It is likely, however, that such prejudice will be of less concern under the Act than under previous law, as s 45 will reduce the use of mugshots, or at least will mean that all of the photographs used are of a standardized form. For example, s 45(3)(c) may preclude the use of a mugshot of the suspect where the other photographs are not mugshots, as that could indicate to the witness who the person to be identified is. Similarly, s 45(3)(b) requires that there is a comparison to at least seven other persons who are "similar in appearance" to the person to be identified. Similarity of appearance may be affected by the format of the photograph used, meaning either all of the photographs used should be mugshots, or that no mugshots are used — to do otherwise may reduce the functional size of the procedure.

EV45.07   Subsection (4): good reasons for not following a formal procedure

Under a Code that assumes greater reliability via formal procedures, it is logical that admission of evidence should be more difficult where an informal identification procedure is used. Section 45(4) outlines what circumstances constitute a good reason for not following a formal procedure. The list in s 45(4) is exhaustive. This means that it is only where there is a good reason under s 45(4) that evidence gained from an informal procedure can be presumed admissible under s 45(1). The list of good reasons comprises both those situations in which it is not practical to follow a formal

---

617   "Identification of Offenders" in *New Zealand Police Manual of Best Practice*, August 2007, 6.
618   *R v Tulafono* 24/9/98, Giles J, HC Auckland T981418.
619   Discussed at EV45.06(1).

procedure, and those where it is not necessary to do so. Following the Law Commission's underlying rationale — that formality is determinative of reliability and therefore of admissibility — leads to the conclusion that informal procedures held because it is *impractical* to follow a formal procedure will be less likely to yield reliable evidence than those held because it is *unnecessary* to follow a formal procedure.

If the prosecution wants to avoid the burden imposed by s 45(2), it must try to establish a good reason for an informal procedure in any case where the requirements of s 45(3) are not fully met. How much stricter police procedures become will depend in large part on the circumstances that judges find acceptable under s 45(2).

If the prosecution can provide a good reason under s 45(4), the identification evidence will be admissible under s 45(1), and the onus will shift to the defendant to prove that the identification is unreliable. Whether or not there is a good reason under s 45(4) will therefore be a crucial issue in many cases. The list in s 45(4) is exhaustive because of the concession that a "good reason" gives in assuring admission of the evidence. Evidence gained from an informal procedure is not deemed to be as reliable as that gained from a formal procedure, and so assuring admission in any case where there has been no formal procedure makes an inroad into the philosophy underlying the section. The list of good reasons represents practical concessions to the "ideal" envisaged by the Law Commission, and so any extension should logically be made after careful consideration of the research and policy issues, rather than on a case by case basis by the courts.

(1)   Subsection (4)(a): refusal to participate

Section 45(4)(a) recognises the right (also found in s 344B of the Crimes Act 1961) of the person to be identified to refuse to participate in an identification parade, and also recognises that the person to be identified has the right to refuse to permit a photograph or video record to be taken. Where a photograph or video already exists of the person to be identified, and it represents a true likeness of that person, refusal to participate will usually not constitute a good reason under s 45(4) because the existing photograph or video can be used in a formal procedure (however, see EV45.06(1) with regard to the use of mugshots for a formal procedure).

It is possible that, in those cases where there is no existing photograph or video, the defendant may refuse participation. This is because under s 45(1) it may be easier to challenge the reliability of an informal procedure than to challenge the reliability of a formal procedure. Defendants will have a better chance of proving probable unreliability where she or he has refused to participate and the police have thereby had good reason to resort to an informal procedure, than where a formal procedure has actually taken place. The Act contains no guidance for judges in such cases, and it is fortunate that the situation is likely to arise less frequently by virtue of the fact that identification procedures will normally take place after arrest (and so a photograph will be available — but see discussion as to mugshots at EV45.06(1)). Any inclination to exploit the operation of the Act in this way could also be addressed by allowing the suspect's legal representative to be present at the procedure. This would generate an incentive to participate in a formal procedure and ensure that the best procedure was followed, as the legal representative could highlight where the procedure needs improvement, and greater confidence would be placed by suspects in the running of a procedure that would otherwise (in the case of photo and video procedures) be conducted in their absence.

(2)   Subsection (4)(b): singular in appearance

Section 45(4)(b) acknowledges that there will be cases where the person to be identified will be so singular in appearance that the requirement in s 45(3)(b) cannot be complied with. The subsection provides that singular appearance will constitute a good reason for not following a formal procedure, where the appearance is "of a nature that cannot be disguised so that the person is similar in appearance to those with whom the person is to be compared". The acceptable limits of such disguise are unclear. Judges will determine the circumstances in which a defendant is to be deemed "singular in appearance" and the kind of features that may be disguised (and how they may be disguised). Whether the other participants in the procedure will be able to be disguised in order to comply with s 45(3)(b) is also unclear. "Disguise" may simply require a hat, or a sticking plaster to cover a scar or tattoo. However, there may be cases where singularity of appearance can be "disguised", yet the effectiveness or desirability of such disguise is questionable. For example, the use of make-up artists — sometimes even to change apparent ethnicity of participants in live identification parades (such as presenting Caucasian individuals as Indian in order to gain sufficient volunteers) — was not uncommon in the UK before a national video library of volunteers was introduced. Even in cases where disguise of the singular feature is in itself straightforward there may be other factors, such as a description referring to the feature, that will complicate the decision under s 45(4)(b).

(3)   Subsection (4)(c): change of appearance

Section 45(4)(c) is open to the same exploitation as that discussed in s 45(4)(a) (refusal to participate) in that defendants may think that it is preferable to change their appearance and challenge the reliability of identification gained from the informal procedure under s 45(1), than to be subject to a formal procedure and potentially have more difficulty in proving probable unreliability. However, live procedures will not be used in the majority of cases, and therefore s 45(4)(c) will only be relevant in those cases where there has been a delay between the offending and the arrest, when a photograph will be taken.

(4)   Subsection (4)(d): no anticipation that identification would be an issue

Section 45(4)(d) provides that a formal procedure need not be held where no officer "could reasonably anticipate that identification would be an issue at the trial of the defendant". This is a rather difficult, and often subjective, assessment for officers to make, particularly at an early stage in an investigation. The Law Commission suggested that cases where the person to be identified is well known to the witness will fall under s 45(4)(d), and this reflects the fact that in some recognition cases an identification procedure will be unnecessary. However, "well-known" will need to be carefully defined. Clearly, close relatives or friends will be covered, but the scope beyond that is questionable. For example, where a witness names a person a formal identification procedure should probably still be conducted in order to ensure that the person they have in mind is indeed the person of that name.

(5)   Subsection (4)(e): identifications made shortly after the offence

Section 45(4)(e) recognises that identifications made shortly after the occurrence of the offence may make a further, formal, procedure unnecessary. For example, a witness may be able to point out the offender to a police officer arriving at the scene of the offence. "Soon after the offence was reported" is a potentially elastic term, and guidance will be needed on its limits (it may be better to confine the subsection to identifications made immediately after reporting, where reporting is itself done as soon as practicable). The identification under s 45(4)(e) must be made in the course of the officer's initial investigation, which clearly signals that identifications made after other evidence gathering or where the police have a suspect in mind will not suffice. For example, driving around the vicinity of the offence on the next day, where there is some information that the offender is a local resident, should not satisfy the requirements of the subsection.

(6)   Subsection (4)(f): chance meetings

Section 45(4)(f) deems a formal procedure to be unnecessary where the witness identifies the alleged offender after a chance meeting. The Law Commission gave the example of a witness recognizing the offender by chance in a dairy.[620] Clearly, a "chance" meeting that is in fact orchestrated — for example taking a witness to stand outside the suspect's place of work until he or she leaves the building — will not constitute a good reason under s 45(4)(f), although the line between chance and organized meetings may sometimes be difficult to discern.[621]

46   Admissibility of voice identification evidence

Voice identification evidence offered by the prosecution in a criminal proceeding is inadmissible unless the prosecution proves on the balance of probabilities that the circumstances in which the identification was made have produced a reliable identification.

EV46.01   Overview

Section 46 represents the first statutory scheme for "voice identification evidence", and like s 45 it applies only in criminal proceedings. Prior to the Act, controls on the admissibility and use of voice identification evidence were developed by the courts. It has been noted that voice identification is even more fragile than visual

---

620   LC *Evidence Code*, para C228.
621   For example, where the "chance" meeting takes place in (or outside of) a police station that both parties are attending in relation to the alleged offence. In such cases, whether the parties have been asked to attend the police station, whether precautions were taken to avoid a chance meeting etc will be relevant to the assessment as to whether or not the meeting really was one of "chance".

identification,[622] and the Court of Appeal have referred to the special dangers of relying on voice identification evidence.[623] As well as the problems of memory inherent in visual identification evidence, identification of a voice is particularly difficult unless there are distinctive features, such as a speech impediment. A voice is relatively easy to disguise and may be distorted where the speaker shouts or is under stress.

Voice identification evidence is defined in s 4 as an assertion that a voice is that "of the defendant or any person", meaning that s 46 applies to voice identification of the defendant or of any other person who was connected with an act that constituted evidence of the commission of an offence.[624] The definition in s 4, and therefore the restrictions in s 46, apply both to voice identification evidence when the voice was heard first hand, and that heard through "mechanical or electronic transmission or recording" (s 4), which while aimed at voices heard over the telephone or through a speaker,[625] may also mean that expert evidence as to voice identification may in some circumstances come under the remit of s 46.[626]

(1)   Assertion as to identification

Unlike the definition for visual identification evidence, an "account" of the assertion as to identification is not defined as voice identification evidence under the Act, meaning that an account of an out-of-court identification will not have to meet the requirements of s 46 and will fall to be governed only by the hearsay rule and ss 7 and 8. If there is a difference between an assertion and an account of that assertion, as suggested by the Law Commission, then s 46 will govern only voice identifications where the identifying witness asserts in court that the defendant (or other person) is the person they identified earlier, and not where the witness gives an account in court of an out-of-court identification. This may be because there are no set procedures for voice identification and as such no "account" will be needed or relevant. However, it appears to be illogical and impractical: without hearing the voice of the accused in court no assertion could be made. It is therefore suggested that there is no real distinction between an assertion and the account of that assertion for the purposes of the Act, and that the additional definition of visual identification as an "account of such an assertion" is superfluous.[627]

(2)   Prosecution must prove probable reliability only

Unlike s 45, s 46 does not provide guidance as to proper procedures, which are difficult to design for voice identification. Rather, it imposes a general rule that voice identification evidence will be inadmissible unless the prosecution proves that the

---

622   *R v Waipouri* [1993] 2 NZLR 410; (1994) 9 CRNZ 330 (CA). See also *R v Monika* 13/2/04, Neazor J, HC Auckland CRI057166103, where a police officer was allowed to give voice identification evidence as he was familiar with the accused.

623   *R v Wickramasinghe* (1992) 8 CRNZ 478 (CA).

624   See EV4.45.01.

625   LC *Evidence Code*, para C39.

626   See EV25.01-02.

627   See EV4.44.01(1).

circumstances in which the identification was made have produced a reliable identification. This ties the issue of reliability to the conduct of the identification procedure, as in s 45(2). However, the burden of proof imposed on the prosecution under s 46 is proof of reliability on the balance of probabilities. Therefore, the prosecution only have to prove that the voice identification evidence is *probably reliable*. This is rather strange, given that despite the concern that voice identification is less reliable than visual identification, the standard under s 45(2) is proof beyond reasonable doubt, a significantly higher standard than under s 46. To reflect the fact that voice identification was presumed to be unreliable, the Law Commission Code required the prosecution to prove the likelihood that the voice identification was reliable beyond reasonable doubt.[628] The draft Bill reduced the standards in both ss 45(2) and 46 to proof on the balance of probabilities. The Justice and Electoral Committee then raised the standard back to "beyond reasonable doubt" for s 45(2), because:

> "strengthening up that provision was important … if there is any doubt that not following a formal procedure may lead to a reliable identification, then of course we must exclude that evidence, given the intrinsic unreliability of this kind of evidence."[629]

The Select Committee raised the standard under s 45(2) in order to both ensure reliability and to ensure control of the officers conducting procedures. As voice identification carries greater inherent risk of unreliability, the lower standard of proof is curious. This is especially the case given that the accuracy of voice identification is notoriously difficult to test.[630] Whatever procedure is used, there is likely to be doubt that the procedure is reliable, and as such only the most exceptional cases (for example, where there is a distinctive voice heard over a prolonged period) are safe to admit. A balance of probabilities standard does not adequately reflect this.

(3)   Judicial assessment of reliability under ss 45 and 46

Both ss 45 and 46 require judges to assess the reliability of identification evidence. Section 45(1) asks judges to determine whether visual identification evidence is "probably unreliable"; s 45(2) whether the prosecution has proved beyond reasonable doubt that the circumstances of the identification have produced reliable evidence; and s 46 whether the prosecution have proved that the voice identification evidence is probably reliable. It is questionable whether judges are well equipped to make assessments regarding probable (un)reliability, certainly with regard to the circumstances in which the identification was made and which circumstances are likely to produce the most reliable evidence. Most of the factors affecting the reliability of identification evidence are the subject of psychological research, and expert evidence on visual and voice identification is more likely to be admitted since the introduction of the substantial helpfulness test.[631] However, as there are areas upon

---

628   LC *Evidence Code*, 134-135.

629   Hansard, *Nandor Tanczos: Evidence Bill: Second Reading*, 21 November 2006 ((2006) 635 NZPD 6563).

630   Ormerod, "Sounds Familiar" [2001] Crim LR 595.

which there is still debate among psychologists, some form of well rounded judicial education on matters of memory research may be the preferable route.

Subpart 7—Evidence of convictions and civil judgments

(s 47 to s 50)

EVPt2Sub7.01   Overview

Subpart 7 of Part 2 of the Act extends the abolition of the rule in *Hollington v Hewthorn*[632] from ss 23 and 24 of the Evidence Amendment Act (No 2) 1980. It also codifies the common law in relation to civil judgments as evidence. Broadly speaking, the rule in *Hollington v Hewthorn* excluded convictions as evidence of the defendant's guilt in later civil proceedings. Before the 2006 Act, the rule was abolished to the extent that in defamation actions convictions were "sufficient evidence",[633] and in other actions they were "admissible as evidence" that an offence has been committed.

EVPt2Sub7.02   General effect of Subpart 7

The general thrust of Subpart 7 is that evidence of convictions will now constitute proof in subsequent proceedings, both civil and criminal, that the person committed the offence. Subpart 7 does not set out the method for proving convictions — in order for ss 47-49 to apply there has to be "proof that the person has been convicted of that offence" — which is set out in ss 139 and 140.

EVPt2Sub7.03   Rationale of allowing convictions as evidence in criminal proceedings

Despite particular concern to protect defendants in criminal proceedings, the Law Commission identified a number of policy reasons why convictions should be admissible in criminal proceedings, including savings in time and expense, convictions being available evidence that is relevant and probative, and the fact that to do so adheres to the general policy that a criminal conviction is sufficient basis to impose grave penalties.[634] It identified examples of when a conviction may be relevant to an issue in the case, including where the conviction of a third party for theft is used to support a charge of being an accessory after the fact; and where a conviction for assault is offered in a later murder trial when the victim dies of the injuries.[635]

EVPt2Sub7.04   Conviction must be subsisting

For the purposes of ss 47-49, s 4(1) provides that a "conviction" means "a subsisting conviction" entered by a New Zealand court or court martial conducted under New Zealand law, or by a court or court martial conducted under the law of another country in respect of which an Order in Council has been made under s 140(5) (such Orders in Council are likely to be made extremely rarely). As the conviction must be

---

631   See EV25.02.
632   *Hollington v Hewthorn* [1943] KB 587.
633   See EV48.01.
634   LC *Evidence Reform*, 65-66.
635   LC *Evidence Code*, 141.

subsisting, those that have been overturned by a court, or are the subject of a free pardon will not constitute "convictions" for the purposes of ss 47-49.[636]

EVPt2Sub7.05 No particular status for acquittals as evidence

There are no express provisions in the Act governing the status of acquittals as evidence in subsequent proceedings.

Section 12 guides the admission of evidence that is not regulated by a specific provision in the Act, and this may operate to allow the common law to prevail. At common law, acquittals were generally inadmissible as evidence that the person did not commit the offence charged.

However, there were occasions where the earlier law allowed a party to offer evidence of an acquittal. For example, where a defendant testifies as to an unusual defence, the prosecution may question the testimony by proving that the defendant was previously acquitted on another charge by relying on the same defence. Most commonly, evidence of acquittal could become relevant and admissible where the prosecution offered propensity evidence alleging previous offending, even though the defendant had been acquitted of the offence at an earlier proceeding.[637]

Section 12 requires reference to the purpose and principles of the Act. As such, admissibility of evidence of acquittals is likely to be guided by the general principles of the Act in ss 6, 7 and 8. Acquittals may be relevant under s 7 for some purposes (for example, malicious prosecution claims[638]) and could thereby be admissible. This was the approach taken in *R v Potter*,[639] where the Court relied on the definition of relevance in s 7(3) to state that "although acquittal is distinctly less cogent evidence of innocence than conviction is of guilt, its potential relevance is obvious".[640]

Potential admissibility of acquittals is also recognised by s 139, which governs proof of the fact of an acquittal.

47 Conviction as evidence in civil proceedings

(1) When the fact that a person has committed an offence is relevant to an issue in a civil proceeding, proof that the person has been convicted of that offence is conclusive proof that the person committed the offence.

(2) Despite subsection (1), if the conviction of a person is proved under that subsection, the Judge may, in exceptional circumstances,—

---

636 See EV4.06.01.
637 See *Adams on Criminal Law — Evidence*, EC8.10.
638 LC *Evidence Code*, 137.
639 *R v Potter* 26/4/07, CA450/06; [2007] NZCA 156.
640 *R v Potter* 26/4/07, CA450/06; [2007] NZCA 156, para.16. One viewpoint is that acquittals *generally* have little probative value, because an acquittal can prove only that the prosecution failed to establish guilt to the standard of beyond reasonable doubt — in other words, an acquittal does not prove innocence to the same extent that a conviction proves guilt: LC *Evidence Reform*, para 230; and see the discussion in Australian Law Reform Commission, *Evidence (Interim)*, Vol 1, ALRC 26, Canberra, 1985, para 781. However, this does not preclude acquittals from *ever* having probative value.

     (a)   permit a party to the proceeding to offer evidence tending to prove that the person convicted did not commit the offence for which the person was convicted; and

     (b)   if satisfied that it is appropriate to do so, direct that the issue whether the person committed the offence be determined without reference to that subsection.

(3)   This section applies—

     (a)   whether or not the person convicted is a party to the proceeding; and

     (b)   whether or not the person was convicted on a guilty plea.

(4)   This section—

     (a)   is subject to section 48; and

     (b)   does not affect a provision in any other enactment to the effect that a conviction or a finding of fact in a criminal proceeding is to constitute conclusive evidence for the purposes of any other proceeding.

EV47.01   Section 47 not restricted to parties

Section 47(1) makes it clear that s 47 applies to the relevant offending of "a person". The "person" does not have to be a party to the proceeding (see s 47(3)(a)).

EV47.02   Subsection (1): the conviction has to be relevant to an issue

The fact that the person has committed the offence in question has to be "relevant to an issue in a civil proceeding", which means that the principle of relevance in s 7 must be satisfied before s 47 can apply. Furthermore, the fact that the person committed the offence will differ in value from case to case, depending on the issues being litigated and the place of the commission of the offence within those issues.

EV47.03   "Conclusive proof"

Section 47 replaces s 23 of the Evidence Amendment Act (No 2) 1980, which provided that a conviction gave rise to a rebuttable presumption that the person was guilty of the offence for which they were convicted. The Law Commission's draft Code also stated that a conviction should constitute presumptive proof that the person committed the offence in question.[641] Section 47(1) at first appears to radically change this position by providing that proof of the conviction is *conclusive* proof that the person committed the offence. However, the limitations in s 47(2) mean that the practical effect of s 47(1) will be lessened in many cases.

EV47.04   Subsection (2): qualification of "conclusive proof" in "exceptional circumstances"

Section 47(2) provides that the judge may permit evidence to prove that the person did not commit the offence "in exceptional circumstances". This clearly qualifies the notion of "conclusive proof". The definition of "exceptional circumstances" will

---

641   LC *Evidence Code*, 136.

therefore be key in ascertaining the extent to which s 47(2) allows derogation from the concept of "conclusive proof".

Although there is no intrinsic test for "exceptional circumstances" and there is no guidance as to the meaning of the phrase in the Act, it is likely that it will be given the same meaning as that ascribed to it under witness anonymity provisions,[642] which are now contained in the Act (see ss 110 and 112). This is that exceptional circumstances are something "quite out of the ordinary".

EV47.05   Subsection (2)(a)

If there are exceptional circumstances, then the judge may permit a party to offer evidence "tending to prove" that the person did not commit the offence for which he or she was convicted (s 47(2)(a)). The phrase "tending to prove" does not indicate any particular standard of proof, but requires evidence offered to meet the threshold test of relevance in s 7(3).

EV47.06   Subsection (2)(b) — determination "without reference" to subs (1)

Subsection (2)(b) provides that the judge may direct that the question of whether the person committed the offence should be determined "without reference" to subs (1).

There is no explicit link in the section between the evidence offered under s 47(2)(a) and the satisfaction (or otherwise) of the judge in s 47(2)(b). However, without such evidence, it is difficult to see why the judge would think that it were appropriate to proceed without reference to s 47(1). It is suggested therefore that the evidence that "tends to prove" that the person did not commit the offence under s 47(2)(a) must satisfy the judge that it is appropriate that the issue be determined without reference to subs (1).

There is no guidance in the Act as to the position of the parties where a direction under s 47(2)(b) means that whether the person committed the offence should be determined without reference to s 47(1). It is therefore unclear what "without reference" will mean in practice.

It is possible that s 12 would allow for the application of the common law in such circumstances, and that the rule in *Hollington v Hewthorn*[643] would make the conviction inadmissible. This is unlikely, given that s 12 is subject to the general purposes and principles of the Act, and that the conviction will usually still be relevant under s 7. The more likely result is therefore that relevant convictions may still be admissible where there is a direction under s 47(2)(b), with the weight attached to be determined in light of the other evidence tendered (including that admitted under s 47(2)(a)). In addition, any provision in other enactments that provides for

---

642   *Police v Kelly* [1999] DCR 634. The phrase has been similarly interpreted when used in other statutes: see *Awa v Independent News Auckland Ltd (No 2)* [1996] 2 NZLR 184; (1996) 9 PRNZ 289; *Zhu v Wang* [2000] DCR 503 (both Legal Services Act 1991). As the witness anonymity provisions now appear in the Act, it would appear odd to ascribe different meanings for the same phrase within sections of the same Act.

643   *Hollington v Hewthorn* [1943] KB 587.

convictions as conclusive proof is not affected by s 47 (and in particular by s 47(2)) — see s 47(4)(b).[644]

EV47.07   Section 47 applies to convictions on guilty pleas

Section 47(3)(b) provides that the section applies whether or not the person was convicted on a guilty plea. In the general run of cases, whether or not there was a guilty plea will be irrelevant to the operation of the section. However, the fact that there was a guilty plea may form the basis of exceptional circumstances under s 47(2)(a) where there is some evidence that the plea was entered not because the person committed the offence, but for some other reason (for example, as a matter of expediency).

EV47.08   Relationship to other admissibility rules

On the face of s 47, it is unclear whether or not it is subject to other admissibility rules in the Act. For example, there is no reference in s 47(1) akin to the provision in s 49(1) that evidence of the conviction may be "excluded by any other provision in this Act".[645] There is also no equivalent in s 47 of the requirement in s 49(3) that the judge must be informed of the purpose for which the evidence is offered, which was included in order to enable judges to consider whether the evidence is excluded by the operation of any other rule in the Act.[646]

The absence of such requirements in s 47 suggests that it is not subject to the other admissibility rules in the Act. It could be argued that this is a mere oversight. However, this would be incredible, given that the difference between s 47 and s 49 is maintained from the Law Commission's draft Code. Furthermore, the sections sit close together and therefore form ready comparators. Although it may seem odd if s 47 were not subject to the other rules in the Act, it may be that the provisions in s 49 are aimed at protecting the rights of defendants in criminal cases in ensuring that there is a fair trial, and it is this rationale that sets the two apart.

EV47.09   Section 47 subject to s 48

Section 47(4)(a) provides that s 47 is subject to s 48, which governs the use of convictions as evidence in defamation proceedings.

48   Conviction as evidence in defamation proceedings

In a proceeding for defamation that is based on a statement to the effect that a person has committed an offence, proof that the person has been convicted of the offence is conclusive proof that the person committed the offence if the conviction—

(a)   subsisted at the time that the statement was made; or

(b)   subsists at the time of the proceeding.

---

644   For example, see s 5(1) of the Evidence Act, and Schedule 14 to the Local Government Act 2002. However, s 47(4)(b) is probably unnecessary: s 5(1) provides that, where there is inconsistency between the Act and another enactment, the other enactment will prevail unless the Act provides otherwise.

645   See EV49.03.

646   LC *Evidence Code*, 141.

EV48.01   Conviction is "conclusive proof"

Section 48 replaces s 24 of the Evidence Amendment Act (No 2) 1980, which provided that where there was a statement by one person (A) that another person (B) committed an offence, evidence of B's conviction was "sufficient evidence in the absence of proof to the contrary" that B committed the offence. Section 48 extends the previous law by providing that evidence of B's conviction is *conclusive proof* that B committed the offence. This means that proof of B's conviction will give A a complete defence of truth under the Defamation Act 1992.

EV48.02   No qualification of "conclusive proof"

Section 48 contains none of the qualifications of "conclusive proof" found in s 47(2), and as such there can be no evidence offered to show that the conviction was wrongful.

49   Conviction as evidence in criminal proceedings

(1)   Evidence of the fact that a person has been convicted of an offence is, if not excluded by any other provision of this Act, admissible in a criminal proceeding and proof that the person has been convicted of that offence is conclusive proof that the person committed the offence.

(2)   Despite subsection (1), if the conviction of a person is proved under that subsection, the Judge may, in exceptional circumstances,—

     (a)   permit a party to the proceeding to offer evidence tending to prove that the person convicted did not commit the offence for which the person was convicted; and

     (b)   if satisfied that it is appropriate to do so, direct that the issue whether the person committed the offence be determined without reference to that subsection.

(3)   A party to a criminal proceeding who wishes to offer evidence of the fact that a person has been convicted of an offence must first inform the Judge of the purpose for which the evidence is to be offered.

EV49.01   Overview

Section 49 provides that evidence of a conviction is admissible in a criminal proceeding, and that proof of the conviction constitutes conclusive proof that the person committed the offence. Any party to criminal proceedings can offer evidence of the conviction and any party may offer evidence rebutting this under s 49(2).

EV49.02   Subsection (2): qualification of "conclusive proof"

As is the case for civil proceedings governed by s 47, s 49 differs from the Law Commission's draft Code, which provided that a conviction constituted only "presumptive proof". Like s 47(2), s 49(2) qualifies the effect of the conclusive proof standard by providing that "in exceptional circumstances" a party may be permitted to offer evidence tending to prove that the person did not commit the offence for which he or she was convicted (s 49(2)(a)) and that where the judge is "satisfied that it is appropriate to do so", whether the person committed the offence may be determined without reference to s 49(1). See the discussion above regarding the operation of the qualifying section in s 47(2), whose terms s 49(2) replicates.[647]

EV49.03   Section 49 is subject to other provisions in the Act

Section 49(1) provides that evidence of a conviction will be admissible only where it is not excluded by any other provision in the Act. Furthermore, s 49(3) requires a party who wishes to offer evidence of a conviction to first inform the judge of the purpose for offering the evidence. These are more onerous requirements than that in s 47(1), which requires only that the conviction be relevant to an issue in the proceeding. Although s 49(3) will require the party introducing the evidence to identify which issue in the case it is relevant to, the purpose of offering the evidence will also enable the judge to consider whether the evidence is excluded by any other admissibility rule. As such, subs (3) clearly underlines the provision in subs (1) that s 49 is subject to the other provisions in the Act — for example, if the conviction is offered for the purpose of attacking the person's veracity, then the evidence would have to satisfy the veracity rules (ss 37-39) before proof of the conviction could be conclusive proof that the person committed the offence for which they had been convicted.

50   Civil judgment as evidence in civil or criminal proceedings

(1)   Evidence of a judgment or a finding of fact in a civil proceeding is not admissible in a criminal proceeding or another civil proceeding to prove the existence of a fact that was in issue in the proceeding in which the judgment was given.

(2)   This section does not affect the operation of—

    (a)   a judgment "in rem"; or

    (b)   the law relating to "res judicata" or issue estoppel; or

    (c)   the law relating to an action on, or the enforcement of, a judgment

EV50.01   Overview

Section 50 codifies the existing law and sets out a rule that both civil judgments and findings of fact are inadmissible in civil and criminal proceedings to prove the existence of a fact that was in issue in the proceeding in which the judgment was given. In criminal proceedings, the differing standards of proof are a barrier to the admission of civil judgments to prove the existence of a fact in issue. It may be difficult to justify a criminal court accepting a civil finding arrived at on the balance of probabilities in a case requiring proof beyond a reasonable doubt. In civil proceedings, s 50(2) preserves the common law position as to judgments in rem, res judicata, issue estoppel and the law relating to an action on or enforcement of a judgment. Therefore, there will continue to be no re-litigation of actions and issues where both the parties and the issue are the same. Section 50(2) does not include

---

647   See EV47.04-06.

findings where the issues are the same but the parties differ.[648] These cases will be governed by s 50(1). The exceptions in s 50(2) may not have the effect of proving a fact in issue under s 50(1), but are provided as exceptions for clarity.

Findings and judgments which are not offered to prove the existence of a fact that was in issue may be admissible where relevant under s 7. For example, an earlier civil judgment entered against a defendant may be relevant and admissible in later criminal proceedings for assault, when the assault was alleged to have occurred as a result of the defendant's reaction to the loss in the civil proceeding.

Subpart 8—Privilege and confidentiality

(s 51 to s 70)

Matters relating to interpretation and procedure

51   Interpretation

(1)   In this subpart,—

lawyer has the meaning given to it by section 6 of the Lawyers and Conveyancers Act 2006

legal adviser means—

(a)   a lawyer; or

(b)   a registered patent attorney; or

(c)   an overseas practitioner

overseas practitioner means—

(a)   a person who is entitled to practise as a barrister, or a solicitor, or both in the High Court of Australia or in a Supreme Court of a State or a territory of Australia; or

(b)   a person who is entitled to practise in Australia as a registered patent attorney or as a registered trade marks attorney; or

(c)   a person who is, under the laws of a country specified by an Order in Council made under this section, entitled to undertake work that, in New Zealand, is normally undertaken by a lawyer or a patent attorney.

(2)   A reference in this subpart to a communication or to any information includes a reference to a communication or to information contained in a document.

(3)   Despite subsection (2), in sections 60 to 63, **information** means a statement of fact or opinion given, or to be given,—

(a)   orally; or

(b)   in a document that is prepared or created—

(i)   after and in response to a requirement to which any of those sections applies; but

---

648   See s 93(c) of the Evidence Act 1995 (Aust) for a similar approach.

           (ii)   not for the principal purpose of avoiding criminal prosecution under New Zealand law.

(4)   A reference in this subpart to a communication made or received by a person or an act carried out by a person includes a reference to a communication made or received or an act carried out by an authorised representative of that person on that person's behalf.

(5)   However, subsection (4) does not apply to any of the following sections:

    (a)   section 58 (privilege for communications with ministers of religion):

    (b)   section 59 (privilege in criminal proceedings for information obtained by medical practitioners and clinical psychologists):

    (c)   section 64 (informers).

(6)   The Governor-General may, by Order in Council, for the purposes of the definition of "overseas practitioner" in subsection (1), specify any country other than New Zealand or Australia.

EV51.01   Lawyers

Section 6 of the Lawyers and Conveyancers Act 2006 defines a "lawyer" as a person who holds a current practising certificate as a barrister or as a barrister and solicitor. The same section of the Lawyers and Conveyancers Act makes it clear that this reference is to a New Zealand practising certificate.

EV51.02   Legal adviser

The most important effect of the definition of a "legal adviser" is that it is only a legal adviser who is capable of offering his or her clients the protection of the privilege protecting communications with legal advisers (s 54) and the privilege for preparatory materials for proceedings (s 56).

EV51.03   Patent attorney

Paragraph (b) of s 51(1)'s definition of "legal adviser" includes a registered patent attorney. Although it might be thought that the result would be that all communications with a registered patent attorney would be protected by privilege, s 54(2) limits protected communications to those where the object of the communication is "obtaining or giving information or advice concerning intellectual property". "Intellectual property" is defined in s 54(3).

EV51.04   Overseas practitioners

The inclusion of overseas practitioners within the definition of a legal adviser was the result of an amendment by the Select Committee. Paragraph (c) of the definition of an "overseas practitioner" (and s 51(6)) will allow lawyers and patent attorneys in jurisdictions other than Australia to become legal advisers for the purposes of the Act, if the New Zealand government considers this desirable. At present, no Orders in Council have been issued under s 51(6). The result is that only New Zealand and Australian practitioners are able to offer their clients the protection of the privilege protecting communications with legal advisers and the privilege for preparatory materials for proceedings under ss 54 and 56 of the Act.[649]

EV51.05   In house counsel

Lawyers in fulltime employment in a commercial firm or a government department ("in house counsel") who have a current practising certificate can offer their employers the protection of the privileges set out in ss 54 and 56.

EV51.06   Subsection (3)(a): privilege against self-incrimination: oral disclosures

Section 51(2) contains an apparently innocuous proposition. However it is qualified for the privilege against self-incrimination by s 51(3).

Section 51(3)(a) makes it clear that the privilege against self-incrimination (which is dealt with in ss 60-63) protects oral disclosures.

EV51.07   Subsection (3)(b): privilege against self-incrimination: documents

It is important to remember that, as set out in s 60(2), the privilege against self-incrimination is *a right not to provide information*. It does not include a right to somehow cancel the effect of a disclosure once it has been made. As soon as "the cat is out of the bag", the focus shifts to ss 27-30, which provide for exclusion in criminal proceedings of defendants' statements and improperly obtained evidence.

(1)   Document created after demand

Discussions by the Law Commission make it possible to state the aim of s 51(3)(b). Under the Act, the privilege against self-incrimination is not meant to protect from disclosure those statements that have been set down in a document *before* an official requirement for information has been made. In other words, the privilege does not provide an excuse for refusing to produce a *pre-existing document*.

Despite this intention of the legislation, s 51(3)(b) still contains some uncertainties. Section 51(3)(b)(i) gives the impression that the privilege against self-incrimination can somehow be claimed for a statement that has actually *been given* in a document prepared or created after a requirement for information. This impression is misleading because, as stated above, the privilege does not apply once a disclosure has actually been made.

It is best to read s 51(3)(b)(i) as focusing on the opening phrase of s 51(3) and applying only to a statement *to be given* in a document following a requirement to provide information. Although a government official is demanding that the statement *be given* in a document, the privilege can still be claimed as a reason to refuse to comply with the demand. However, if the privilege holder capitulates and gives the statement, there is nothing left for the privilege to protect.

---

649   New Zealand Law Society, *Law Talk*, Issue 696, 1 October 2007, 1, reports that the New Zealand Law Society has written to the Secretary for Justice as follows: "The Society sees this matter as serious and urgent. We ask that you ensure that the Minister and Cabinet are advised of that urgency and that an initial Order in Council, covering countries where the level of regulation of the professions is known to be sound, is prepared and promulgated as soon as possible".

EV51.08   Purpose of avoiding prosecution

Neither the explanatory notes to the Act nor the commentary to the Law Commission's draft Evidence Code provide any guidance to the purpose of s 51(3)(b)(ii). Two interpretations are possible but both suffer from a common defect. Whichever way s 51(3)(b)(ii) is read, it appears to be based on the erroneous view that the privilege against self-incrimination has a role to play *after* a document has actually been produced. As has been pointed out above, the privilege goes no further than granting the right to refuse to create the document in the first place.

Even if this problem is ignored, there are difficulties in determining the meaning of s 51(3)(b)(ii). On one hand, the provision could be aimed at excluding from the operation of the privilege, a *fraudulent statement* in a document that is designed to lead government investigators away from the truth of the privilege holder's culpability. Although, intuitively, this appears the more likely interpretation, it requires a substantial gloss on the actual wording of the subsection. Under a more literal reading, s 51(3)(b)(ii) has a wider objective. It appears to be an attempt to remove from the scope of the privilege, any document prepared or created because of the privilege holder's hope that it would make the spectre of a prosecution go away.

Although this reading of s 51(3)(b)(ii) is simply a restatement of its very terms, its effect would be remarkable. It seems a safe assumption that most self-incriminating documents prepared or created after a requirement of the sort set out in ss 60-63 *are* motivated by the hope that this show of cooperation may lead to the end of a threatened prosecution. But in every such case, s 51(3)(b)(ii) means there is no room for the privilege.

If this suggestion is correct, the remarkable effect of s 51(3)(b)(ii) is that a person who is the subject of a requirement for information of the sort described in s 60 can only claim the privilege and refuse to write out a self-incriminating statement in a document if he or she is *not* principally motivated by the desire to end a threatened prosecution. Not only is this a far cry from the common law, it is also lacking in any discernible policy basis.[650]

EV51.09   Privilege against self-incrimination: real evidence and testimonial acts

One uncontroversial effect of s 51(3) is to emphasise that the privilege against self-incrimination is concerned only with *statements*. Accordingly, there is no room to argue that the privilege against self-incrimination permits refusals to produce "real evidence": such as a blood sample or an item of clothing. Although the effect of producing this class of evidence may well be incriminating, such circumstances stand outside the scope of the privilege against self-incrimination. The same can be said for the difficult concept of a "testimonial act", as discussed in *NZ Apple and Pear Marketing Board v Master and Son Ltd*.[651]

---

650   See EV60.01-05.

EV51.10   Subsection (4): authorised representative

Section 51(4) recognises the practical reality that communications may often pass through "authorised representatives" of the principal parties to an otherwise privileged communication. Section 51(4) extends the protection of privilege to such communications involving these authorised representatives. For example, in the case of legal adviser privilege, although s 54 refers only to communications between a legal adviser and a person who requests legal services, s 51(4) extends the privilege to protect communications between the authorised representatives of such persons. In this way, a client's communications to the secretary or student law clerk of the legal adviser (to be passed on to the legal adviser) will be privileged, assuming that the secretary or student amounts to the legal adviser's "authorised representative". The latter term is not defined in the Act.

Similarly, s 51(4) extends privilege to "acts carried out by" authorised representatives. Although legal adviser privilege (s 54) deals only with communications, the "preparatory materials" privilege in s 56 protects some acts, such as compiling information (s 56(2)(c) and (d)). Accordingly, s 51(4) operates to extend privilege to information compiled by a party's authorised representative (see similarly s 57(2)).

EV51.11   Subsection (5): exceptions for some privileges

Section 51(5) provides three exceptions to the general proposition set forth in s 51(4).

(1)   Minister of religion

Section 51(5)(a) removes the privilege for communications with ministers of religion from the operation of s 51(4). Accordingly, a communication otherwise meeting the criteria for privilege under s 58 will not be protected if it occurred between an authorised representative of either the person seeking religious advice or the minister.

(2)   Medical privilege

Section 51(5)(b) involves the privilege protecting communications with and information obtained by medical practitioners and clinical psychologists (s 59). The reason for this exception to s 51(4) is that s 59(5) itself contains a specific "authorised representative" provision. However, it relates solely to a representative of the medical practitioner or psychologist and does not extend the protection of the privilege to cover communications by a representative of the patient.

(3)   Informer privilege

The third privilege which s 51(5) removes from the operation of s 51(4) is informer privilege (s 64). Section 64(2)(a) deals specifically with the issue of a representative of the parties involved in the circumstances creating informer privilege. Only the representative of an enforcement agency is included.

---

651   *NZ Apple and Pear Marketing Board v Master and Son Ltd* [1986] 1 NZLR 191 (CA). See, generally, the discussion at EV63.02 and EV63.05 and *Adams on Criminal Law — Evidence*, EC20.07(8).

EV51.12   Privilege against self-incrimination

Section 51(5) contains no reference to the privilege against self-incrimination. It may therefore be thought that s 51(4) applies to permit the authorised representative of the holder of the privilege against self-incrimination to claim protection on behalf of the privilege holder. However, it is suggested that there are two difficulties with such a view.

First, the privilege against self-incrimination is a right to *refuse to provide* information, whether by means of a communication or otherwise. Both at common law and under s 60 of the Act, the privilege against self-incrimination is not concerned with "communications made or received or an act carried out", which is the focus of s 51(4). Section 51(4) is aimed at the other privileges in the Act, which specifically protect communication or acts. These protected activities can hardly be said to be the same as a right to refuse to provide information.

Secondly, even if s 51(4) might otherwise be argued to apply to the privilege against self-incrimination, s 60(4)(b) contains a general prohibition on one person claiming the privilege on behalf of another.[652]

| 52 | Orders for protection of privileged or confidential material, or material relating to matters of State |

(1)   A Judge may order that evidence must not be given in a proceeding of a communication, information, opinion, or document in respect of which a person has a privilege conferred by this subpart and may make an order under this subsection—

(a)   on the Judge's own initiative; or

(b)   on the application of the person who has the privilege; or

(c)   on the application of an interested person other than the person who has the privilege.

(2)   A Judge may give a direction under section 69 (confidential information) or section 70 (matters of State) on the Judge's own initiative or on the application of an interested person.

(3)   An application under subsection (1) or (2) may be made at any time either before or after any relevant proceeding is commenced.

(4)   A Judge may give any directions that are necessary to protect the confidentiality of, or limit the use which may be made of,—

(a)   any privileged communication, information, opinion, or document that is disclosed to a Judge or other body or person in compliance with a judicial or administrative order; or

(b)   any communication or information that is the subject of a direction under section 69 (confidential information) or section 70 (matters of State) but

---

652   See EV60.05.

is disclosed to a Judge or other body or person in compliance with a judicial or administrative order.

EV52.01   Overview

Section 52 gives power to a judge to make various orders prohibiting or restricting the use of evidence that is protected by privilege or which is confidential information (s 69) or a matter of State (s 70).

As set out in s 53, the effect of a privilege is to grant to the privilege holder the right to refuse to disclose privileged material in a proceeding and the right to require that no one else may disclose it. Section 52 provides the means by which the privilege holder can obtain the practical benefits of those rights.

EV52.02   When privilege holder is not a party

An order under s 52(1) will most commonly be granted in a case where the privilege holder or the "interested person" is a party. However, s 52(1) anticipates that such persons may still apply for an order under s 52(1) even when they are not parties in the proceeding. In a case where the privilege holder or interested person is, for example, a witness, it seems clear that an informal, oral "application" will suffice.

EV52.03   Order on judge's initiative

It is easy to imagine cases where the privilege holder (or "interested person") cannot be contacted or lacks the resolve or resources to make an application to claim the benefit of the privilege. Section 52(1)(a) grants power to the judge to intervene in such cases and make an order protecting the privileged material.

EV52.04   Subsection (1)(c): interested person: waiver

The reference in s 52(1)(c) to an application by an "interested person" anticipates that a judge may prohibit evidence being given of material "of which a person has a privilege conferred by this subpart", even though the privilege holder has expressed no wish for such a prohibition or the privilege holder has *waived* the privilege (s 65).

Although it is natural to assume that a waiver "destroys" privilege, there is nothing in the Act which expressly states this proposition. Waiver by the privilege holder must surely end *his or her* ability to assert the rights in s 53 (for example, the right to require that the material not be disclosed in a proceeding). However, this does not necessarily mean that privilege has been destroyed for all purposes. Section 52(1)(c) anticipates that, despite a waiver, an "interested person" could still apply for an order under s 52 that the privileged material remains inadmissible.

Such a concept is so foreign to traditional views of privilege that it is not easy to imagine who amounts to an "interested person" (the term is nowhere defined in the Act). However, it is not difficult to imagine occasions when someone other than the holder of a privilege will want to prevent privileged material being given in evidence. Such a person's motivation may bear no relationship to the policies underlying the privilege. Fortuitously for such an "interested person", s 52(1)(c) may make it possible for him or her to keep the evidence out of court. The Act provides no guidance for when such a remarkable result is appropriate.

This is not the only occasion in which the concept of an "interested person" causes difficulties in the Act.[653]

EV52.05   Subsection (2): interested person: confidentiality

Section 52(2) raises issues in respect of an "interested person" that are similar to but not identical with those arising under s 52(1). Section 52(2) focuses on s 69 (confidential information) and s 70 (matters of State). Because neither of these two concepts are framed in terms of privilege, s 52(2) does not speak of an application by a privilege holder. The subsection envisions only directions prohibiting disclosure which are made on the initiative of the judge or on the application of an interested person.

The range of interested persons is potentially huge for both ss 69 and 70. Insofar as s 69 is concerned, certain to be included would be the parties to a confidential communication (s 69(1)(a)), the supplier and receiver of confidential information (s 69(1)(b)), the person who is a confidential source of information (s 69(1)(c)), and someone who is aware of that person's identity. Likewise included would be anyone involved in or concerned with "relationships" that are of the same or similar kind as the particular confidential relationship relied upon as requiring the protection of a direction (s 69(2)(b)).

There is no necessary limit on the number of potentially interested persons for the purpose of matters of State (s 70). That this is so becomes clear when the specific provisions of the Official Information Act 1982, referred to in s 70(2), are reviewed. All New Zealanders could lay claim to being "interested" in many of the factors set out in those central provisions of the Official Information Act (eg, s 6(a): "the security or defence of New Zealand or the international relations of the Government of New Zealand").

EV52.06   Subsection (4): limiting the effects of a disclosure

Section 52(4) deals with the strange concept of a *disclosure*, pursuant to a "judicial or administrative order", of material that is privileged (s 52(4)(a)) or the subject of a non-disclosure direction pursuant to ss 69 or 70 (s 52(4)(b)). It is not immediately apparent what circumstances are envisioned whereby a court would order the disclosure of privileged material. In any event, when such a disclosure has occurred, s 52(4) provides a method of minimising its effect.

EV52.07   Possible examples

One target of s 52(4) could be disclosures ordered in another proceeding, where no one raised a claim of privilege or confidentiality. Likewise, the power granted in s 52(4) could be exercised to minimise the effect when a judge reviews material as part of the process of determining whether it meets the criteria of a privilege or whether it should be the subject of a non-disclosure order (see r 307 of the High Court

---

653   See EV52.05; EV66.01(3); and EV66.06.

Rules). The subsection would also justify orders prohibiting publication beyond the proceeding or limiting access to or use of the material by counsel or the parties.

Privilege

53   Effect and protection of privilege

(1)   A person who has a privilege conferred by any of sections 54 to 59 in respect of a communication or any information has the right to refuse to disclose in a proceeding—

    (a)   the communication; and

    (b)   the information, including any information contained in the communication; and

    (c)   any opinion formed by a person that is based on the communication or information.

(2)   A person who has a privilege conferred by section 60 or 64 in respect of information has the right to refuse to disclose in a proceeding the information.

(3)   A person who has a privilege conferred by any of sections 54 to 59 and 64 in respect of a communication, information, opinion, or document may require that the communication, information, opinion, or document not be disclosed in a proceeding—

    (a)   by the person to whom the communication is made or the information is given, or by whom the opinion is given or the information or document is prepared or compiled; or

    (b)   by any other person who has come into possession of it with the authority of the person who has the privilege, in confidence and for purposes related to the circumstances that have given rise to the privilege.

(4)   If a communication, information, opinion, or document, in respect of which a person has a privilege conferred by any of sections 54 to 59 and 64, is in the possession of a person other than a person referred to in subsection (3), a Judge may, on the Judge's own initiative or on the application of the person who has the privilege, order that the communication, information, opinion, or document not be disclosed in a proceeding.

(5)   This Act does not affect the general law governing legal professional privilege, so far as it applies to the determination of claims to that privilege that are made neither in the course of, nor for the purpose of, a proceeding.

EV53.01   Overview

Section 53 is a pivotal section because it details the protection that flows from a privilege. In doing so, the section attempts to clarify aspects of the earlier law.

EV53.02   Distinctions among privileges

The individual subsections of s 53 vary in their focus. Some aim only at particular privileges. There is also substantial discrimination among particular classes of privileged material. For example, s 53(1) covers only the privileges set forth in ss 54-59 and only insofar as a *privileged communication* or *information* is concerned. In contrast, s 53(3) adds informer privilege (s 64) as well as a privileged *opinion* or *document*. Such variations are augmented by the fact that the individual sections defining particular privileges are themselves specific in what they aim to protect. Thus s 54 (communications with legal advisers) grants a privilege only in relation to *communications*, while s 64 (informer privilege) protects *information*.

The result is that when a claim of privilege is made, it is important to enquire whether the material in question, be it a communication, information, opinion, or document, is indeed within the scope of the privilege in question.[654]

EV53.03   Subsection (1)(c): foundation for an expert's opinion

Section 53(1)(c) ends a controversy which existed at common law, notably in the case of the privilege for preparatory materials for proceedings, now set forth in s 56 (formerly known as "litigation privilege").

At common law, legal professional privilege (including litigation privilege) was said to protect communications but not facts.[655] This could be an elusive distinction. The problem was crystallised in cases where, in preparation for pending litigation, a solicitor sends material to an expert in order to obtain the expert's opinion. Authorities such as *R v King*[656] held that although the communication between the solicitor and the expert remained privileged, no protection existed for the expert's opinion. An opposing litigant could subpoena the expert and require him or her to give that opinion in evidence. Section 53(1)(c) now prohibits such testimony from the expert. In effect, the opinion itself is privileged.

Contrast the discussion of s 57(2) below.[657]

EV53.04   Subsection (2): limited protection for some privileges

Section 53(2) applies only to the privilege against self-incrimination (s 60) and informer privilege (s 64). As with s 53(1), it specifies that privilege amounts to a right to refuse to disclose "information" in a proceeding. However, neither of the privileges focused on by s 53(2) is granted the extended protection set forth in s 53(1)(a)-(c). Presumably this is because the operation of the privilege against self-incrimination and the informer privilege do not raise the sort of issues dealt with in s 53(1)(a) or (c). Neither of these two privileges protects "communications" and it is difficult to conceive of an occasion where, per s 53(1)(c), anyone would be called upon in a

---

654   See EV57.10.
655   *Adams on Criminal Law — Evidence*, EC20.10(5).
656   *R v King* [1983] 1 All ER 929.
657   See EV57.10.

proceeding to disclose their opinion that was based upon information that was protected by ss 60 or 64.

It should be noted that, despite s 53(2), s 60 enables the privilege against self-incrimination to protect against forced disclosures in contexts beyond that of a proceeding.[658]

EV53.05   Subsections (3) and (4): restraining disclosures by others

Section 53(3) is designed to avoid potential controversy over the scope of the protection granted by privileges other than the privilege against self-incrimination. The latter privilege is exempted from the operation of s 53(3) because that privilege only protects against forced disclosures. If the holder of the privilege against self-incrimination makes a disclosure, the privilege has no further role to fulfil.

An example of the operation of s 53(3)(b) in the context of the privilege for settlement negotiations (s 57) is where a party to a dispute receives a settlement proposal and sends it on to his or her accountant for advice as to the financial consequences of the proposal. Section 53(3)(b) would give the privilege holder the right to prevent the accountant from disclosing the proposal in a proceeding.

Section 53(4) confronts the situation where privileged material somehow comes into the possession of a person who has not been authorised by the holder of the privilege to possess the material. Before the 2006 Act, there was some uncertainty whether privilege was lost when a privileged communication was surreptitiously intercepted or when one of the parties to a privileged communication made an unauthorised disclosure of its contents.[659] Under s 65(4), such circumstances do not result in a waiver of privilege. Section 53(4) grants to the judge a wide discretion to prevent disclosure of the material. This is one of the few ways that the Act provides any control over the admissibility of improperly obtained evidence in a civil proceeding (see also s 90).

EV53.06   Subsection (5): continuing common law: legal professional privilege

Commonwealth jurisdictions such as New Zealand have now accepted that the privilege protecting communication with legal advisers (s 54) is more than a mere rule of evidence. It is, rather, a rule of substantive law that protects against disclosure in all circumstances, whether or not a "proceeding" is involved.[660] The law in this area is still being developed.[661] Section 53(5) was added by the Select Committee to ensure that the Act's controls of legal professional privilege (ss 54-56) would "not affect the general law governing legal professional privilege outside the context of court proceedings".[662]

---

658   See EV60.04(1).
659   *Adams on Criminal Law — Evidence*, EC20.14(4).
660   *R (on the application of Morgan Grenfell & Co Ltd) v Special Commissioner* [2002] 3 All ER 1 (HL); *Russell McVeagh v Auckland District Law Society* [2003] UKPC 38 (PC).
661   *Adams on Criminal Law — Evidence*, EC20.09(1).
662   *Select Committee Report on the Evidence Bill*, 7.

Although s 53(5) refers to legal professional privilege, this term was probably employed in an abundance of caution. It is not a term used elsewhere in the Act and at common law it incorporated the two limbs of solicitor-client privilege (now legal advice privilege (s 54)) and litigation privilege (now preparatory materials privilege (s 55)). The common law developments beyond the confines of a proceeding which were referred to above and which are protected by s 53(5) were solely concerned with solicitor-client privilege. It is difficult to see how *litigation* privilege could develop outside the context of a *proceeding*. One possibility is that s 53(5) anticipates the development of litigation privilege in hearings before *tribunals*, which do not amount to "proceedings" under s 4's definition of that term.

54   Privilege for communications with legal advisers

(1)   A person who obtains professional legal services from a legal adviser has a privilege in respect of any communication between the person and the legal adviser if the communication was—

    (a)   intended to be confidential; and

    (b)   made in the course of and for the purpose of—

        (i)   the person obtaining professional legal services from the legal adviser; or

        (ii)   the legal adviser giving such services to the person.

(2)   In this section, **professional legal services** means, in the case of a registered patent attorney or an overseas practitioner whose functions wholly or partly correspond to those of a registered patent attorney, obtaining or giving information or advice concerning intellectual property.

(3)   In subsection (2), **intellectual property** means 1 or more of the following matters:

    (a)   literary, artistic, and scientific works, and copyright:

    (b)   performances of performing artists, phonograms, and broadcasts:

    (c)   inventions in all fields of human endeavour:

    (d)   scientific discoveries:

    (e)   geographical indications:

    (f)   patents, plant varieties, registered designs, registered and unregistered trade marks, service marks, commercial names and designations, and industrial designs:

    (g)   protection against unfair competition:

    (h)   circuit layouts and semi-conductor chip products:

    (i)   confidential information:

    (j)   all other rights resulting from intellectual activity in the industrial, scientific, literary, or artistic fields.

EV54.01 Solicitor-client communication

Under the title "Privilege for communications with legal advisers", s 54 enshrines what was formerly known as solicitor-client privilege. At common law, this privilege combined with litigation privilege (s 56) to make up what was often referred to as "legal professional privilege".[663]

EV54.02 Legal adviser

This is defined by s 51(1), as there discussed.

EV54.03 Professional legal services

Section 54(1) limits privilege to communications in the course of a person obtaining "professional legal services". However, except for s 54(2) and (3) (relevant only to patent attorneys), the Act makes no attempt to define this crucial concept. Presumably, a court faced with a case on the borderline between legal and "commercial" services will have regard to leading common law authorities.[664]

EV54.04 Patent attorneys

Subsections (2) and (3) limit the professional legal services performed by a registered patent attorney which can support a claim for legal adviser privilege. The Select Committee added the definition in s 54(3) on the basis that it "reflects the definition in the Trans-Tasman Mutual Recognition Act 1997, including the relevant wording from the Convention establishing the World Intellectual Property Organisation".[665]

The definitions in s 54(2) and (3) are perhaps wider than was intended by the Select Committee. This is because they contain no limitation on the *type of advice* given on the listed topics which will attract privilege. Because of s 54(1), advice given by lawyers will have to qualify as *legal* advice before it will attract privilege. This is not required in the case of a patent attorney or an overseas practitioner fitting within the class described in s 54(2). Privilege will arise whenever the "information or advice" given by these advisers "concerns" any of the broad topics listed in s 54(3).

EV54.05 Commencement of privilege

The equivalent in the Evidence Bill to s 54(1) made a *request* for professional legal services act as the trigger for commencement of the privilege for communication with a legal adviser. The result was that privilege would protect communications at an *initial meeting* between lawyer and potential client even though no legal services were actually performed. One reason why such a situation might occur is because the

---

663   See EV53.05.

664   See *Adams on Criminal Law — Evidence*, EC20.09(4). The early indications are that, where possible, courts will turn to the common law in interpreting the scope of s 54. Thus in *R v Huang* 19/9/07, Rodney Hansen J, HC Auckland CRI-2005-004-21953, para 54, Rodney Hansen J relied on earlier case law to conclude that, per s 54(1)(b), privilege protects documents prepared by a client as an aide memoire for better communication with his or her lawyer (prior to actual communication having taken place).

665   *Select Committee Report on the Evidence Bill*, 7.

lawyer discovers that he or she is unable to act for the client because of a conflict of interests.

The Select Committee gave no explanation for their change to s 54(1). The final version of that provision grants a privilege only when the client *obtains* professional legal services. This is emphasised by s 54(1)(b)(i). The result could support an argument that no privilege arises to protect communication occurring at an initial meeting where the legal adviser declines to represent the client and, accordingly, provides no legal services. If this argument was accepted it would bring about a substantial change from the earlier law.[666] It is difficult to find any valid policy basis for denying privilege to initial communications made between lawyer and client when discussing the possibility of the lawyer acting for the client. To circumvent this result it will be necessary to conclude that legal services are "obtained" through the mere process of a lawyer considering whether or not to represent a prospective client.

EV54.06 Confidentiality

Section 54(1)(a) only grants privilege if the communication to or from the legal adviser was intended to be confidential. This is in keeping with the earlier law.[667]

EV54.07 Agents

Communications which would be privileged if carried out directly between client and legal adviser will remain privileged if carried out between the "authorised representatives" of either or both of these parties: s 51(4).

55   Privilege and solicitors' trust accounts

(1)   This section applies to documents that are books of account or accounting records kept—

    (a)   by a solicitor in relation to any trust account money that is subject to section 112 of the Lawyers and Conveyancers Act 2006; or

    (b)   by a nominee company that—

        (i)   is subject to practice rules made by the Council of the New Zealand Law Society pursuant to section 96 of the Lawyers and Conveyancers Act 2006; and

        (ii)   is operated by a barrister and solicitor or an incorporated law firm as a nominee in respect of securities and documents of title held for clients.

(2)   Section 54 does not prevent, limit, or affect—

    (a)   the issue by a District Court Judge of a search warrant under section 198 of the Summary Proceedings Act 1957 in respect of a document to which this section applies; or

---

666   *Adams on Criminal Law — Evidence*, EC20.09(3)(a).
667   *Adams on Criminal Law — Evidence*, EC20.09(6).

(b)   the execution of that warrant in respect of a document to which this section applies; or

(c)   the admissibility, in a criminal proceeding for an offence described in the warrant, of any evidence that relates to the contents of a document obtained under the warrant.

EV55.01   Overview

Section 55 is based on s 35A of the Evidence Amendment Act (No 2) 1980.

Section 55 singles out certain accounting records kept by a solicitor and makes it clear that even if such records would otherwise be protected by legal adviser privilege, this does not stand in the way of the normal operation of a search warrant issued under s 198 of the Summary Proceedings Act 1957.

There is a substantive body of law limiting the effect of a search warrant on material protected by solicitor-client privilege.[668] That law should continue to be relevant because of s 53(5). However, s 55 ensures that that law has no effect on the accounting records that are the focus of the section.

EV55.02   Change from earlier statute

Section 55(2)(c) of the Act alters the wording of its precursor (s 35A of the Evidence Amendment Act (No 2) 1980) in a way that could support an argument that the new section has made a dramatic change.

Subsection (2)(a) and (b) are unremarkable because their operation is clearly limited to the classes of documents listed in s 51(1). Both paragraphs refer expressly to "a document to which this section applies".

EV55.03   Admissibility

Section 55(2)(c) is important because it governs the *admissibility* of evidence obtained under the search warrant. The earlier version of s 55(2)(c), namely s 35A(2)(b) of the Evidence Amendment Act (No 2) 1980, limited its operation to the classes of documents specified in what is now s 55(1). This limitation was achieved by the earlier provision referring only to "any such document". Remarkably, however, s 55(2)(c) does not repeat this drafting technique.

For this reason, s 55(2)(c) could be argued to have the effect of removing legal adviser privilege as a valid argument against the admissibility of any document "obtained under the warrant". Unlike the earlier analogous provision in the 1980 Amendment Act, s 55(2)(c) is not limited to the class of documents listed in s 55(1). It is true that, "the warrant" referred to in s 55(2)(c) must, by virtue of s 55(2)(a), have been issued "in respect of" documents of the sort listed in s 55(1). However, the mere fact that such documents were the focus of a search warrant does not ensure that they will be the only documents that are seized.[669] Section 55(2)(c) purports to guarantee the

---

668   *Adams on Criminal Law — Evidence*, EC20.09(9).
669   Cf s 198(5) of the Summary Proceedings Act 1957.

admissibility of *any* document seized pursuant to such a warrant, whether or not the document is the sort described in s 55(1).[670]

EV55.04   Limitation on s 55(2)(c)

The legislated admissibility of privileged documents which is provided for by s 55(2)(c) is limited to a proceeding "for an offence described in the warrant". Inevitably, arguments will arise as to the permissible scope of variation from the general description of offending set out in the search warrant when compared to the actual charge laid against the defendant. Too great a degree of variation will mean that s 55(2)(c) cannot be relied upon to guarantee admissibility.

56   Privilege for preparatory materials for proceedings

(1)   Subsection (2) applies to a communication or information only if the communication or information is made, received, compiled, or prepared for the dominant purpose of preparing for a proceeding or an apprehended proceeding (the "proceeding").

(2)   A person (the "party") who is, or on reasonable grounds contemplates becoming, a party to the proceeding has a privilege in respect of—

    (a)   a communication between the party and any other person:

    (b)   a communication between the party's legal adviser and any other person:

    (c)   information compiled or prepared by the party or the party's legal adviser:

    (d)   information compiled or prepared at the request of the party, or the party's legal adviser, by any other person.

(3)   If the proceeding is under, or to be under, Part 2 of the Children, Young Persons, and Their Families Act 1989 or the Care of Children Act 2004 (other than a criminal proceeding under that Part or that Act), a Judge may, if satisfied that it is in the best interests of the child to do so, determine that subsection (2) does not apply in respect of any communication or information that the Judge specifies.

EV56.01   Litigation privilege

Section 56 codifies the privilege known at common law as "litigation privilege".[671]

EV56.02   Representatives

Section 51(4) makes it clear that the "communications" referred to in s 56(2)(a) and (b) will still be protected if they were actually undertaken by an "authorised representative" of the privilege holder or his or her legal adviser. Section 51(4) has a similar effect insofar as the compiling or preparing of information referred to in s 56(2)(c) and (d). This is because these activities amount to "acts" carried out by an authorised representative, as envisioned by s 51(4).

---

670   See, generally, *Adams on Criminal Law*, Ch10.8.13(13).
671   *Adams on Criminal Law — Evidence*, EC20.10. However, see EV67.06.

EV56.03   Dominant purpose

The common law of litigation privilege is reflected in the prerequisites set forth in s 56(1) and (2), namely that preparation for a proceeding must be the "dominant purpose" of activities for which privilege is sought, and the privilege holder must be a party to a current proceeding or must contemplate, on reasonable grounds, becoming a party. It is enough if a person reasonably contemplates becoming a party to an "apprehended" proceeding.[672]

EV56.04   Proceeding

Because the privilege is limited to an actual or apprehended "proceeding", the definition in s 4 of that term means that only *court* proceedings can trigger the operation of the privilege. The privilege does not exist (under the Act) when preparations are being made for a hearing before a tribunal. See further comments in the discussion of the definitions of "proceedings", "court", and "Judge".[673]

EV56.05   Compiling

By recognising that privilege exists when information is "compiled" by the party or the legal adviser, s 56(2)(c) supports the controversial argument that documents which are in themselves not privileged become cloaked with privilege when "compiled". This may be justified on the basis that the structure of the compilation may disclose tactics planned for the anticipated litigation.

EV56.06   Subsection (3): best interests of a child

Section 56(3) reflects the decision of the House of Lords in *Re L (a minor)*.[674] The proceedings referred to in s 52(3) relate to care and protection proceedings and guardianship and custody proceedings involving children.

The result of s 56(3) is that a wide range of otherwise privileged communications and information are at risk of disclosure. However, s 56(3) only goes as far as negating the application of the specific privilege described in s 56(2). It does not purport to affect other sections of the Act. In particular, legal adviser-client communications protected by s 54 will not be subject to the power granted by s 56(3).

57   Privilege for settlement negotiations or mediation

(1)   A person who is a party to, or a mediator in, a dispute of a kind for which relief may be given in a civil proceeding has a privilege in respect of any communication between that person and any other person who is a party to the dispute if the communication—

     (a)   was intended to be confidential; and

     (b)   was made in connection with an attempt to settle or mediate the dispute between the persons.

---

672   See, generally, *Adams on Criminal Law — Evidence*, EC20.10(3).
673   See, respectively, EV4.35.01-03; EV4.09.01; and EV4.26.01. See also EV53.05.
674   *Re L (a minor)* [1988] 2 All ER 78 (HL).

(2)   A person who is a party to a dispute of a kind for which relief may be given in a civil proceeding has a privilege in respect of a confidential document that the person has prepared, or caused to be prepared, in connection with an attempt to mediate the dispute or to negotiate a settlement of the dispute.

(3)   This section does not apply to—

      (a)   the terms of an agreement settling the dispute; or

      (b)   evidence necessary to prove the existence of such an agreement in a proceeding in which the conclusion of such an agreement is in issue; or

      (c)   the use in a proceeding, solely for the purposes of an award of costs, of a written offer that—

           (i)   is expressly stated to be without prejudice except as to costs; and

           (ii)   relates to an issue in the proceeding.

Compare: HCR 48G

EV57.01   Overview

Section 57 is based on the common law privilege which prohibited disclosure of communications occurring during settlement negotiations. However, the Act has made some fundamental changes.

In keeping with "a well recognised application" of the common law rule,[675] the process of mediation has been formally incorporated into the privilege.

EV57.02   Dispute

The privilege is available when there is a "dispute" and a communication is made in an attempt to settle or mediate that dispute (s 57(1)(b)).

Subsections (1) and (2) make it clear that no privilege exists unless a dispute has already arisen. There is, therefore, no privilege when parties negotiate in an attempt to avoid any future dispute arising.[676]

However, in contrast to s 56(1) (preparatory materials privilege), s 57 grants privilege even if no proceeding has been commenced or is even "apprehended". It is enough that a *dispute* has arisen.

EV57.03   Privilege holders

It is important to be able to identify who are the holders of a privilege in respect of any particular communication. Not only will this determine who can assert the rights set forth in s 53, it will determine who is able to *waive* the privilege under s 65.

When two parties have a dispute and one of them communicates with the other within the terms of s 57(1), *both* parties become privilege holders with respect to that

---

675   *Wicks v Waitakere City Council* 13/10/06, Rodney Hansen J, HC Auckland CIV-2005-404-5146, para 21.

676   Cf *City Realties (Rural) Ltd v Wilson Neil Ltd* (1996) 9 PRNZ 164.

communication. This is because the communication is, per s 57(1), "between" the two parties, even though it was sent by one and received by the other.

Similarly, when one of two parties to a dispute sends a communication to a mediator or receives a communication from the mediator, and the communication fits the criteria set by s 57(1)(a) and (b), both the mediator and that party (but not the other party to the dispute) have a privilege in the communication.

EV57.04   Without prejudice communications

The only reference to "without prejudice" communications comes in the narrow circumstance dealt with by s 57(3)(c). At common law, the privilege protecting settlement negotiations could apply to communications which were not expressly conducted on a "without prejudice" basis, as long as the purpose of the communication was to attempt to resolve a dispute. Similarly, the mere fact that a communication was labelled "without prejudice" did not necessarily invoke the privilege. The prerequisites to the privilege still had to exist.[677]

Although these general propositions were clear, the House of Lords in *Bradford and Bingley v Rashid*[678] pointed out that, even at common law, some confusion still exists as to the effect of a party expressly labelling a communication "without prejudice".[679]

It is likely that parties, most often through their legal advisers, will continue to use the express "without prejudice" label in communications attempting to settle a dispute. It is also likely that courts will continue to rely on this label as an indication that the party making the communication was seeking the protection offered by s 57. This could be justified on the basis that the express "without prejudice" reference indicates that the party sending the communication possessed the states of mind required by s 57(1)(a) and (b).

EV57.05   In connection with

Section 57(1)(b) requires that the communication be made "in connection with" an attempt to settle or mediate the dispute. This broad test may mark a change from the common law. Consider *Bradford and Bingley*,[680] where the issue was whether a letter containing an acknowledgement of a debt for the purposes of the UK equivalent to s 25(4) of the Limitation Act 1950 (NZ) was inadmissible because the letter formed part of a negotiation conducted with a view to the creditor giving the debtor time to pay. The House of Lords held that the letter was admissible and could be relied on to establish a new commencement date for the limitation period. This was because the debtor was not disputing *liability*. The only dispute being negotiated was that of time

---

677   *Adams on Criminal Law — Evidence*, EC20.15(1).
678   *Bradford and Bingley v Rashid* [2006] 1 WLR 2066; [2006] 4 All ER 705 (HL).
679   *Bradford and Bingley v Rashid* [2006] 1 WLR 2066; [2006] 4 All ER 705 (HL), see the differences of opinion among Lord Hope (para 25); Lord Brown (paras 63-64); and Lord Mance (paras 84 and 87).
680   *Bradford and Bingley v Rashid* [2006] 1 WLR 2066; [2006] 4 All ER 705 (HL).

to pay. Because the debtor's admission of liability stood outside the dispute, it was not protected by the privilege.

The same result would not follow under s 57. In terms of s 57(1), the debtor's letter *was* made "in connection with" an attempt to settle the dispute over time to pay. Accordingly, the letter would fit within all of the criteria for privilege set by s 57(1). It does not matter that the crucial admission negated one potential area of dispute between the parties. The letter would still be privileged.

EV57.06   Criminal proceeding

It is probable that the crucial prerequisite to privilege in s 57(1), namely that there is a dispute "of a kind for which relief may be given in a civil proceeding", was meant to deny the operation of the privilege in criminal proceedings. This was the intention of the Law Commission as expressed in their 1994 Preliminary Paper, *Privilege*.[681] The Law Commission stated that because "plea bargaining" was not a formally recognised process in New Zealand, it would be inappropriate to codify a settlement negotiations privilege applying in criminal proceedings.

If, as is likely, s 57 is interpreted as having no application in criminal proceedings, lawyers may have to rethink current practices. At present, it is common for defence lawyers seeking to resolve criminal charges before trial to communicate with the police or Crown counsel on a "without prejudice" basis. Such communications are conducted on the assumption that no evidence could be given of the contents of the communications. If s 57 has achieved its intended result, this assumption of inadmissibility is misguided.

EV57.07   Negotiations in criminal proceedings may be protected

Since 1994 when the Law Commission's Preliminary Paper was written, the process of plea bargaining has become more formalised through the vehicle of status hearings and "sentencing indications" in District Court. Restorative justice meetings are common. Courts may now be motivated to interpret s 57 as providing protection for negotiations in criminal proceedings. An argument could be made to support such an interpretation.

Under s 57, the privilege exists as long as the dispute is "of a kind for which relief *may* be given in a civil proceeding". Many disputes which routinely end up in a criminal court could, in theory, support a civil proceeding (eg, for battery, conversion, or deceit). Section 57(1) does not require that any civil proceeding is ever actually launched. All that is needed is that the dispute could, in theory, follow that path. In this way, negotiations in many criminal proceedings could still be protected under s 57(1).[682]

---

681   New Zealand Law Commission, *Evidence Law: Privilege*, NZLC PP23, Wellington, 1994, 81.

682   Another potential argument is that s 30 (improperly obtained evidence) could be relied on to prevent the prosecution offering evidence that was part of plea bargaining discussions. The argument depends on a finding that the evidence was improperly *obtained* because the defence were negotiating on the understanding that no part of the negotiations would be offered in evidence.

EV57.08   Mediation

Other statutes recognise a privilege for mediation proceedings that can be stronger than the privilege provided by s 57 of the Act.[683] This is because, unlike the position under the Act, the privilege provided for by these other statutes may not be subject to waiver (s 65). Because of s 5(1) of the Act, these other statutes take priority over the Act.[684]

EV57.09   Exceptions

Section 57(3) sets out the only exceptions to the privilege for settlement negotiations or mediation which are recognised by the Act. Section 57(3)(a) and (b) cater for arguments over whether or not a dispute has actually been settled and the terms of any such settlement. Section 57(3)(c) recognises a commonly used device to promote settlements, namely a threat by one party to refer to his or her attempts to settle the dispute when the judge is determining the issue of costs. The party making the threat will urge the judge to award costs against the litigant who unnecessarily refused the settlement offer and forced a continuation of the litigation.

(1)   Common law exceptions

The common law recognised other exceptions to the privilege.[685] However, the effect of codification is that there is little room to argue for the continued existence of these earlier exceptions.

See also s 67, which relates to *disallowance* of privilege in certain circumstances.

EV57.10   Subsection (2): extent of material protected by privilege

In the discussion of s 53 the point was made that there is a substantial variation among the individual privileges dealt with in this Subpart of the Act insofar as the range of material that is protected.[686] This is well illustrated by s 57(2). Consider a case where, in an attempt to settle a dispute, a party wishes to obtain an expert's opinion on facts which are relevant to the dispute and which the party summarises in a document passed on to the expert. It is important to note that, at this point, no privilege has arisen under s 57(1) because no privileged *communication* has yet taken place.

It is submitted that s 53(1)(c) does *not* grant a privilege to the expert's opinion in this example. Section 57(2) grants a privilege (only) to the *document*. Although s 53 does, on occasion, refer to specifically to documents that are protected by privilege (eg, s 53(3) and (4)), the pertinent subsection for this example, s 53(1)(c), does not do so. Section 53(1)(c) only protects opinions based on a privileged *communication* or *information*. This does not operate insofar as s 57(2) is concerned, because that section focuses solely on *documents*.[687]

---

683   For example, s 18 of the Family Proceedings Act 1980 (mediation conference); s 37 of the Children, Young Persons, and Their Families Act 1989 (family group conferences).

684   See *Adams on Criminal Law — Evidence*, EC20.15(8).

685   *Adams on Criminal Law — Evidence*, EC20.15(2). See also EV67.06.

686   See EV53.02-03.

687   See, generally, *Adams on Criminal Law — Evidence*, EC20.15(3).

EV57.11   Agents

The discussion at EV57.03 outlined the extent of communications that are protected by the privilege for settlement negotiations or mediation. Because of s 51(4), communications between the authorised representatives of the parties to the dispute (and a mediator) are also privileged.

Insofar as s 57(2) is concerned, the terms of that subsection already provide that privilege will protect a document which a party to the dispute has "*caused* to be prepared". This would cover a document prepared by an agent of the party at the party's direction.

EV57.12   Waiver

In keeping with the common law, s 65(5) ensures that the privilege protecting settlement negotiations can only be waived by "all the persons who have the privilege". This has little effect on s 57(2) because only the party who prepared the document will have the privilege protecting that document.

In the earlier discussion of who was a "privilege holder",[688] the point was made that, under s 57(1), both parties to a communication would have a privilege with respect to a communication sent by one to the other, including a communication sent by a mediator to one of the parties in the dispute. Section 65(5) requires that, to be effective, a waiver of privilege must be made by both of the privilege holders.

58   Privilege for communications with ministers of religion

(1)   A person has a privilege in respect of any communication between that person and a minister of religion if the communication was—

    (a)   made in confidence to or by the minister in the minister's capacity as a minister of religion; and

    (b)   made for the purpose of the person obtaining or receiving from the minister religious or spiritual advice, benefit, or comfort.

(2)   A person is a **minister of religion** for the purposes of this section if the person has a status within a church or other religious or spiritual community that requires or calls for that person—

    (a)   to receive confidential communications of the kind described in subsection (1); and

    (b)   to respond with religious or spiritual advice, benefit, or comfort.

EV58.01   Expanded privilege for "communications" with a "minister of religion"

Section 58 is a more expansive version of the religious adviser privilege previously contained in s 31 of the Evidence Amendment Act (No 2) 1980.

---

688   See EV57.03.

Section 31 covered only "confession[s]", a term narrowly defined by the Court of Appeal as involving some manner of acknowledgement of sin coupled with a request for a spiritual response from the clergyman involved.[689] Similarly, s 2 of the Evidence Act 1908 defined "minister" as a "minister of religion" or an analogous functionary within a "religious body" — an approach suggesting some bias towards traditional and hierarchically organised religious groups.

(1)   Privileged communications

Section 58 broadens the definition of privileged material "to include religious and spiritual communications in a more general sense, whether or not they involve atonement for sin, and regardless of whether they are made within a structured religious community".[690] Indeed, s 58(1) now extends to any communication — which, under s 51(2), includes "a communication ... contained in a document" — made for the religious or spiritual benefit of the communicator, or for the communicator's spiritual comfort or advice.

(2)   "Minister of Religion"

Section 58 extends the term "minister of religion" beyond persons recognised as such under the traditional structures of organised faith. Instead, "minister of religion" is defined functionally. The approach under s 58(2) is to determine whether any "church or other religious or spiritual community" recognises that, because of their status within that community, a person will be required or called upon to: (a) receive confidential communications seeking spiritual advice, benefit or comfort; and (b) respond to such communications with spiritual advice, benefit or comfort. This is a self-referential description of "minister of religion" — one that looks to the religious or spiritual community itself in determining who plays a pastoral role in that community attracting the protections of s 58.[691] For example, the definition would undoubtedly apply to certain "kamatua" (elders) in the New Zealand Maori community whose role is to offer spiritual guidance or advice within that group.

EV58.02   Scope of s 58

Notwithstanding its expansive scope, s 58 will not extend privilege to any and all communications between an individual and a "minister of religion".

Focussing as it does on advice, benefit or comfort of a "spiritual" nature (s 58(1)(b)), the provision will not encompass communications (including counselling) made for purely temporal purposes, or where the "spiritual aspect of the [communication] was ... outweighed by more worldly concerns".[692] Similarly, the privilege will not extend to communities bound together by "rationalist systems of

---

689   See *R v Howse* [1983] NZLR 246 (CA), 250; *R v L* [1998] 2 NZLR 141 (CA), 149-150.

690   New Zealand Law Commission, *Evidence Law: Privilege*, NZLC PP23, Wellington, 1994, para 283.

691   See New Zealand Law Commission, *Evidence Law: Privilege*, NZLC PP23, Wellington, 1994, paras 282-284.

692   New Zealand Law Commission, *Evidence Law: Privilege*, NZLC PP23, Wellington, 1994, para 284.

ethical conduct [that] do not depend on the belief in some god, divine force or other spiritual basis for life".[693]

In addition, s 58(1)(a) makes it clear that, in order to qualify for protection, communications between an individual and a minister must be made: (a) "in confidence" (that is, in a private and confidential manner and setting); and (b) within "the minister's capacity as a minister of religion". The latter requirement suggests that an individual must seek out the minister in his or her professional role and, as s 58(1)(a) reiterates, "for the purpose" of engaging in communications involving "spiritual advice, benefit or comfort". Indeed, the core rationale behind s 58 is that "a person should not suffer temporal prejudice because of what is uttered under the dictates or influence of religious belief".[694] Accordingly, the motive, intent and objective of the communicator in seeking out the minister of religion is the key to the availability of the privilege. Section 58 requires that the putative privilege holder (the communicator): (a) be "at least partly impelled" to speak to a minister of religion by his or her own religious or spiritual "belief or practice";[695] (b) seeks out the minister with the intent of engaging in such a spiritual dialogue; and (c) aims to receive spiritual advice, benefit or comfort as a result of his or her discourse with the minister concerned.

EV58.03   Authorised representatives

Section 51(5)(a) requires that, to attract privilege, the communication must occur personally between the privilege holder and the minister of religion. Communications between "authorised representatives" (s 51(4)) of one or both parties will not be protected under s 58.[696]

EV58.04   Effect and protection of the privilege

See the discussion of s 53[697] for the effect and protection of the s 58 privilege in a civil or criminal "proceeding" (defined in s 4(1) of the Act[698]).

EV58.05   Waiver

See the discussion of s 65[699] for the circumstances in which the privilege holder (the communicator) may waive the privilege for communications with a minister or religion either "expressly or impliedly" (s 65(1)).

EV58.06   Power of judge to disallow privilege

See the discussion of s 67[700] for the circumstances in which a judge must or could disallow a claim of privilege under s 58.

---

693   New Zealand Law Commission, *Evidence Law: Privilege*, NZLC PP23, Wellington, 1994, para 284.
694   *R v Howse* [1983] NZLR 246 (CA), 251.
695   *R v Howse* [1983] NZLR 246 (CA), 251. See also *R v L* [1998] 2 NZLR 141 (CA), 149.
696   See EV51.11.
697   See EV53.01.
698   See EV4.35.01-03.
699   See EV65.01.
700   See EV67.01.

EV58.07   Joint interests in privileged material

While it is difficult to imagine the circumstances in which it would occur, s 66 will impact the operation of the privilege under s 58 where it is held "jointly" (a term left undefined in the Act) between "[a] person" and "some other person or persons" (s 66(1)).[701]

EV58.08   Relationship to s 69: discretion as to confidential information

Section 69(5) of the Act provides that a confidential communication between an individual and a minister of religion not falling within the s 58 definition of "spiritual advice, benefit or comfort" may nonetheless be protected from disclosure under a court's overriding discretion to deal with confidential information codified in s 69(1).[702]

59   Privilege in criminal proceedings for information obtained by medical practitioners and clinical psychologists

(1)   This section—

    (a)   applies to a person who consults or is examined by a medical practitioner or a clinical psychologist for drug dependency or any other condition or behaviour that may manifest itself in criminal conduct; but

    (b)   does not apply in the case of a person who has been required by an order of a Judge, or by other lawful authority, to submit himself or herself to the medical practitioner or clinical psychologist for any examination, test, or for any other purpose.

(2)   A person has a privilege in a criminal proceeding in respect of any communication made by the person to a medical practitioner or clinical psychologist that the person believes is necessary to enable the medical practitioner or clinical psychologist to examine, treat, or care for the person for drug dependency or any other condition or behaviour that may manifest itself in criminal conduct.

(3)   A person has a privilege in a criminal proceeding in respect of information obtained by a medical practitioner or clinical psychologist as a result of consulting with or examining the person to enable the medical practitioner or clinical psychologist to examine, treat, or care for the person for drug dependency or any other condition or behaviour that may manifest itself in criminal conduct.

(4)   A person has a privilege in a criminal proceeding in respect of information consisting of a prescription, or notes of a prescription, for treatment prescribed by a medical practitioner or clinical psychologist as a result of consulting with or examining the person to enable the medical practitioner or clinical psychologist to treat or care for the person for drug dependency or any other condition or behaviour that may manifest itself in criminal conduct.

---

701   See EV66.01.
702   See EV69.02(2).

(5)   A reference in this section to a communication to or information obtained by a medical practitioner or a clinical psychologist is to be taken to include a reference to a communication to or information obtained by a person acting in a professional capacity on behalf of a medical practitioner or clinical psychologist in the course of the examination or treatment of, or care for, the person by that medical practitioner or clinical psychologist.

(6)   In this section,—

clinical psychologist means a health practitioner—

(a)   who is, or is deemed to be, registered with the Psychologists Board continued by section 114(1)(a) of the Health Practitioners Competence Assurance Act 2003 as a practitioner of the profession of psychology; and

(b)   who is by his or her scope of practice permitted to diagnose and treat persons suffering from mental and emotional problems

drug dependency means the state of periodic or chronic intoxication produced by the repeated consumption, smoking, or other use of a controlled drug (as defined in section 2(1) of the Misuse of Drugs Act 1975) detrimental to the user, and involving a compulsive desire to continue consuming, smoking, or otherwise using the drug or a tendency to increase the dose of the drug.

EV59.01   Scope of privilege

Section 59 is an expanded version of the privilege previously codified in s 33 of the Evidence Amendment Act (No 2) 1980. In criminal proceedings only and under various defined circumstances, it grants a privilege for certain kinds of communications made and information generated during the course of a relationship between a "person" (the privilege holder) and a "medical practitioner" or "clinical psychologist" (s 59(1)(a)). No such privilege applies in civil proceedings since the Act contains no equivalent to s 32 of the Evidence Amendment Act (No 2) 1980. See, however, the discussion of s 69 of the Act below.[703]

EV59.02   Definition of "communication" and "information"

Pursuant to s 51(2), the reference to "communication" in s 59(2) and "information" in s 59(3) and (4) includes "a communication or information ... contained in a document". See s 4(1) for a discussion of the broad definition of "document" in the Act.[704]

EV59.03   Definition of "clinical psychologist" and "medical practitioner"

"Clinical psychologist" is defined in s 59(6)(a) by reference to s 114(1)(a) of the Health Practitioners Competence Assurance Act 2003 ("HPCA"). For purposes of s 59, the HPCA also defines the term "psychologist" (s 169 of the HPCA), along with the phrase "scope of practice" as used in s 59(6)(b) (s 5 of the HPCA). "Medical

---

703   See EV59.11.
704   See EV4.11.01.

practitioner" is not defined in s 59. However, pursuant to s 159 of the HPCA, the term will bear the meaning it does under s 5 of that Act.

Despite dealing with evidence related to an individual's "drug dependency",[705] s 59 will not cover a person's interactions with drug and alcohol practitioners who — while they may be registered with the Drug and Alcohol Practitioners' Association, Aotearoa-New Zealand ("DAPAANZ") — do not also fall within the meanings of "clinical psychologist" or "medical practitioner" as defined in s 59(6) and/or the HPCA. See, however, the discussion of s 59(5).[706] See also the discussion of s 69 of the Act below.[707]

EV59.04   Judicial order

Section 59(1)(b) makes it clear that no privilege will lie under s 59 if any interaction between the individual and a health professional — whether it be for an "examination, test, or … any other purpose" — was "required by an order of a Judge, or by some other lawful authority". An identical exception existed in s 33(3)(b) of the Evidence Amendment Act (No 2) 1980. Accordingly, case law applying that provision (which typically dealt with the scope and nature of the exception) will be relevant to the interpretation of s 59(1)(b).[708]

EV59.05   Application of the privilege

The policy justification behind s 59 is to encourage drug addicts and persons with disorders resulting in criminal behaviour "to obtain assistance … and communicate candidly with those from whom they seek help".[709] This rationale informs the nature and application of the privilege as detailed below.

(1)   Privilege extends to any person

Unlike s 33 of the Evidence Amendment Act (No 2) 1980, which granted the s 59 privilege solely to a "patient" who was a "defendant" in a criminal case (s 33(1)), s 59 can be invoked by any person involved in a criminal proceeding — such as a witness called to testify by the accused or the Crown.

(2)   Drug dependency or criminal conduct

As was the case with s 33 of the Evidence Amendment Act (No 2) 1980, the s 59 privilege will apply only "to a person who consults or is examined by a medical practitioner or a clinical psychologist for *drug dependency or any other condition or behaviour that may manifest itself in criminal conduct*" (s 59(1)(a)).[710]

While, the phrase "drug dependency" is clearly defined in s 59(6), the Act contains no explanation of "condition or behaviour that may manifest itself in criminal

---

705   See EV59.05(2).

706   See EV59.06.

707   See EV59.11.

708   See *Adams on Criminal Law — Evidence*, EC20.12(5)(g)-(h).

709   LC *Evidence Code*, para C250. See *R v Campbell* 9/2/07, Mallon J, HC Wellington CRI-2005-085-3703, para 23.

710   Emphasis added.

conduct". Indeed, there can be no closed list of circumstances caught by this prong of s 59(1)(a). The definition will clearly apply, but is not limited to, classically recognised disorders resulting in criminal acts — such as paedophilia (sexual abuse of children), pyromania (arson), and kleptomania (theft).[711] However, privilege will not attach to statements made or information obtained during medical or psychological treatment for conditions that merely result from a person's unlawful conduct, or that are simply the by-product of criminal behaviour. An example would be a burglar who, while being treated for a leg wound, discloses to a doctor that he or she received the injury after jumping from the window of a house with a bag full of stolen goods. In such circumstances, the "condition or behaviour" for which the individual is seeking treatment does not "manifest itself in criminal conduct" — a requirement of s 59(1)(a) — but is simply *caused by* a criminal act.[712]

(3)   Communications or information

Where a person's dealings with a health professional fall within the scope of s 59(1)(a), s 59 will extend privilege under three related heads in a criminal proceeding.

(a)   *Subsection (2): communications made to examine, treat or care for the person*

In protecting any "communication made" by an individual to a health professional — and by pegging the privilege to the person's belief that the communication was necessary for the type of examination, care or treatment encompassed by s 59 — s 59(2) substantially restates the scope of s 33 of the Evidence Amendment Act (No 2) 1980. Accordingly, case law under that repealed provision will remain pertinent to construing the key terms of this subsection.

For example, in *Complaints Assessment Committee v Medical Practitioners Disciplinary Tribunal*, the Court of Appeal observed that, for purposes of s 33, "a 'communication' is defined subjectively so that what a patient believes is medically relevant, even mistakenly, is privileged".[713] Similarly, in *R v Campbell*, Mallon J ruled that, because the accused's violent acts were directly connected with his methamphetamine addiction, disclosure to his general practitioner of those acts were communications that the accused believed necessary "to get action from [the doctor] for his drug dependency".[714]

---

711   See, eg, *R v Campbell* 9/2/07, Mallon J, HC Wellington CRI-2005-085-3703, para 30.

712   See, eg, *R v Neilson* 4/12/87, Tompkins J, HC Gisborne T13/87.

713   *Complaints Assessment Committee v Medical Practitioners Disciplinary Tribunal* [2005] 3 NZLR 447 (CA), 466. See *Adams on Criminal Law — Evidence*, EC20.12(5)(c). See also *M v L* [1999] 1 NZLR 747 (CA), 766 (noting that a person need not give direct evidence that they held the belief required by s 33 and that such belief may be inferred from a totality of the circumstances); *Long v Attorney-General* [2001] 2 NZLR 529 (HC); *R v Campbell* 9/2/07, Mallon J, HC Wellington CRI-2005-085-3703, para 33.

714   *R v Campbell* 9/2/07, Mallon J, HC Wellington CRI-2005-085-3703, para 33.

By contrast, in *R v Gulliver*,[715] the Court of Appeal rejected the argument that s 33 applied to communications by the accused to his counselor in order to achieve more liberal supervision and release conditions under the Wellington "STOP Programme" for sexual offenders. According to Potter J:[716]

> "The words 'examine, treat or act for', in [s 33(3)] must be interpreted within the frame of diagnosis and treatment of patients. There is no justification for extending the meaning to include protection for communications made to enable the practitioner to act for the patient in an advocacy or similar support role."

Likewise, in *R v Rapana*,[717] the High Court held that, even if she had been acting on behalf of a medical practitioner or clinical psychologist,[718] a psychiatric nurse who volunteered to assess the mental state of an accused for the police was not involved in the course of treating any person as required by s 33 of the Evidence Amendment Act (No 2) 1980.

To the extent applicable, these and other decisions under s 33 of the Evidence Amendment Act (No 2) 1980 will also be germane to judicial interpretations of s 59(3) and (4), which broaden the scope of the s 59 privilege beyond that contained in s 59(2).[719]

(b)   *Subsections (3) and (4): information obtained by a medical practitioner and prescriptions or notes of a prescription*

These two prongs of s 59 substantially extend s 33 of the Evidence Amendment Act (No 2) 1980 and supplement the s 59(2) privilege for particular communications made by a person to a medical practitioner or clinical psychologist.

Section 59(3) covers all "information obtained" by the health professional resulting from and in the course of any consultation with — or examination, treatment or care for — a person whose medical or psychological condition is encompassed by s 59(1)(a). Section 59(4) extends that privilege to information "consisting of" the health professional's "prescription, or notes of a prescription for treatment" of the individual concerned.

The broad wording contained in s 59(3) and (4) will embrace any facts, observations, medical conclusions, or treatment plans arising out of the interactions between a person and a health professional with respect to either a drug dependency or behaviour that may manifest itself in criminal conduct. It would include what the health professional discovers about the patient through oral or physical examination, observations made by the health professional related to the person's medical or

---

715   *R v Gulliver* 9/6/05, CA51/05.

716   *R v Gulliver* 9/6/05, CA51/05, para 50. See *Adams on Criminal Law — Evidence*, EC20.12(5)(e).

717   *R v Rapana* [1995] 2 NZLR 381 (HC), 383. See *R v H* [2000] 2 NZLR 257 (CA), 262-264. See also *Adams on Criminal Law — Evidence*, EC20.12(5)(d).

718   See EV59.06.

719   See EV59.05(3)(b).

psychological condition, the contents of medical records related to the individual's treatment (and any proposed follow-up or plan of action), and the results of x-rays, blood tests, or other laboratory processes sought by the health professional in the course of diagnosing or treating the person seeking care.

EV59.06   Authorised representatives

The combined effect of s 51(4) and (5)(b) make it clear that, in order to be eligible for privilege under s 59, a "communication made" or an "act carried out" by an individual who consults with or is examined by a health professional must take place in person. No privilege will attach to communications made or acts done by the individual's "authorised representative … on that person's behalf" (s 51(4)).

By contrast, s 59(5) extends privilege to an individual's interactions with the authorised representatives of the relevant health professional. It broadens the definition of a "communication to or information obtained by a medical practitioner or a clinical psychologist" to include persons "acting in a professional capacity on behalf of" such professionals "in the course of" examining, treating, or caring for an individual to whom s 59 applies (s 59(5)).

Guidance on the scope and meaning of s 59(5) will be obtained from case law dealing with the parallel provision in s 33(4) of the Evidence Amendment Act (No 2) 1980.[720] For example, in *R v Rapana*, Thomas J stated that s 33(4) would encompass a psychiatric nurse acting at the direction of "a clinical psychologist or medical practitioner employed at [a] hospital".[721] However, in *R v Gulliver*,[722] the Court of Appeal refused to accept that, when a psychologist referred Gulliver to a counsellor employed by the Wellington "STOP" programme for sexual offenders, the counsellor was acting "on behalf of" the psychologist "in the course of" treating the accused.

Such precedents suggest an uncertain scope for s 59(5) and, if privilege is claimed, will relegate the provision to a case-by-case application of its terms. In particular, questions may arise whether, in any given clinical situation involving a multi-disciplinary health team, drug and alcohol practitioners registered with the Drug and Alcohol Practitioners' Association, Aotearoa-New Zealand ("DAPAANZ") are "acting in a professional capacity on behalf of" any "medical practitioners" or "clinical psychologists" encompassed within s 59.[723] See, however, the discussion of s 69 of the Act below.[724]

EV59.07   Effect and protection of the privilege

See the discussion of s 53 at EV53.01 for the effect and protection of the s 59 privilege in a criminal "proceeding" (defined in s 4(1) of the Act).[725]

---

720   See *Adams on Criminal Law — Evidence*, EC20.12(4).
721   *R v Rapana* [1995] 2 NZLR 381 (HC), 383.
722   *R v Gulliver* 9/6/05, CA51/05, para 41.
723   See EV59.03.
724   See EV59.11.

EV59.08   Waiver

See the discussion of s 65 at EV65.01 for the circumstances in which the privilege holder may waive privilege under s 59 either "expressly or impliedly" (s 65(1)).[726]

EV59.09   Power of judge to disallow privilege

See the discussion of s 67 at EV67.01 for the circumstances in which a judge must or could disallow a claim of privilege under s 59.[727]

EV59.10   Joint interests in privileged material

While it is difficult to imagine the circumstances in which it would occur, s 66 will impact the operation of the privilege under s 59 where it is held "jointly" (a term left undefined in the Act) between "[a] person" and "some other person or persons" (s 66(1)).[728]

EV59.11   Relationship to s 69: discretion as to confidential information

In situations not covered by the s 59 privilege, s 69(5) of the Act makes it clear that communications made and information generated in the course of a person's dealings with various types of health professionals may be protected from disclosure in civil or criminal proceedings under a court's overriding discretion to deal with confidences.[729]

60   Privilege against self-incrimination

(1)   This section applies if—

    (a)   a person is (apart from this section) required to provide specific information—

        (i)   in the course of a proceeding; or

        (ii)   by a person exercising a statutory power or duty; or

        (iii)   by a police officer or other person holding a public office in the course of an investigation into a criminal offence or possible criminal offence; and

---

725   See EV4.35.01-03 and, eg, *R v Matthews* 8/3/04, CA370/03, paras 13-14 (observing that, as it applied only in a "criminal proceeding", s 33 of the Evidence Amendment Act (No 2) 1980 had no relevance to incriminating disclosures made from an accused to a doctor and revealed by that doctor to the police before the accused had been charged with an offence).

726   For a discussion of a waiver of privilege with respect to protected communications between a person and a health professional under s 33 of the Evidence Amendment Act (No 2) 1980, see *Adams on Criminal Law — Evidence*, EC20.12(10)-(11). See also *C v Complaints Assessment Committee* [2006] 3 NZLR 577 (SCNZ), 593-594; *R v Campbell* 9/2/07, Mallon J, HC Wellington CRI-2005-085-3703, paras 26-27.

727   For a discussion of this issue under s 33(2) of the Evidence Amendment Act (No 2) 1980, see *Adams on Criminal Law — Evidence*, EC20.12(9).

728   See EV66.01(1).

729   See EV69.02(2) and, eg, *R v Campbell* 9/2/07, Mallon J, HC Wellington CRI-2005-085-3703, paras 44-49 (discussing the applicability of s 35 of the Evidence Amendment Act (No 2) 1980 (the forerunner of s 69) to communications between a doctor and a patient not privileged under the terms of s 33 of the Evidence Amendment Act (No 2) 1980).

(b)   the information would, if so provided, be likely to incriminate the person under New Zealand law for an offence punishable by a fine or imprisonment.

(2)   The person—

(a)   has a privilege in respect of the information and cannot be required to provide it; and

(b)   cannot be prosecuted or penalised for refusing or failing to provide the information, whether or not the person claimed the privilege when the person refused or failed to provide the information.

(3)   Subsection (2) has effect—

(a)   unless an enactment removes the privilege against self incrimination either expressly or by necessary implication; and

(b)   to the extent that an enactment does not expressly or by necessary implication remove the privilege against self incrimination.

(4)   Subsection (2) does not enable a claim of privilege to be made—

(a)   on behalf of a body corporate; or

(b)   on behalf of any person other than the person required to provide the information (except by a legal adviser on behalf of a client who is so required); or

(c)   by a defendant in a criminal proceeding when giving evidence about the matter for which the defendant is being tried.

(5)   This section is subject to section 63.

EV60.01   Meaning and effect of privilege against self-incrimination

Section 60 codifies a modified version of the common law privilege against self-incrimination recognised by New Zealand Courts.[730] If the privilege applies, s 60(2)(a) states that the privilege holder cannot be compelled to provide information that legal rules would otherwise require him or her to supply. Similarly, s 60(2)(b) adds that the privilege holder cannot "be prosecuted or penalised for failing or refusing to provide the information" — a shield that exists whether or not a person actually "claimed the privilege" when the required information was sought.[731]

(1)   Definition of "self-incrimination"

As defined in s 4(1) of the Act, "self-incrimination" means "the provision by a person of information that could reasonably lead to, or increase the likelihood of, the prosecution of that person for a criminal offence".[732] See further the discussion of "incriminate" under s 4(1) at EV60.04(3).

---

730   For discussion of the privilege against self-incrimination at common law in New Zealand, see *Adams on Criminal Law — Evidence*, EC20.07.

EV60.02   Distinctions with common law privilege in New Zealand

In those contexts where s 60 is triggered, its scope of protection will be both similar to and different from the common law version of the privilege against self-incrimination recognised by New Zealand courts. As discussed below, the key differences between s 60 and the common law privilege applied in New Zealand involve: (a) the kinds of legal detriment to which s 60 applies;[733] (b) the definition of "information" contained in s 60(1);[734] and (c) who can and cannot assert the privilege under s 60(2).[735]

EV60.03   Abrogation of the privilege

Section 60(3) makes it clear that the protections offered by s 60(2) will apply "unless" (s 60(3)(a)) and "to the extent" (s 60(3)(b)) that a parliamentary enactment "removes the privilege against self-incrimination either expressly or by necessary implication" (s 60(3)(a)). An example of a statute explicitly abrogating the privilege against self-incrimination is s 27 of the Serious Fraud Office Act 1990.[736] As for implicit abrogation of the privilege, in *NZ Apple and Pear Marketing Board v Master and Son Ltd*,[737] the Court of Appeal stated:

> "Parliament can make the rule of no application or whittle it down by imposing a duty to supply information or answer an official's questions and provide penalties for a refusal to do so. Whether in any enactment it demonstrates an intention to take away the privilege is a matter of construction. The common law favours the liberty of the subject and, if a Court is not satisfied that a statutory power of questioning was meant to exclude the privilege, it is accordance with the spirit of the ... law to allow it ... In the end, the divined statutory intent must prevail."

---

731   See *Taylor v New Zealand Poultry Board* [1984] 1 NZLR 394 (CA). By contrast with actual criminal prosecution, the word "penalise" in s 60(2)(b) undoubtedly refers to some legal, evidential or procedural disadvantage that might otherwise arise out of a person's refusal to provide information in the circumstances encompassed by s 60(1)(a). See, eg, s 32(2)(a) of the Evidence Act 2006 (stating no inference that a "defendant is guilty" may be drawn in a criminal proceeding based on the defendant's failure to respond to "investigative questioning" (s 32(1)(a)) or "disclose a defence" before trial (s 32(1)(b)). It clearly does not refer to exposure to a civil fine or penalty, a legal detriment that, while recognised as grounds for asserting the privilege against self-incrimination under New Zealand common law, is specifically excluded from the scope of s 60 by s 60(1)(b) (which limits claims to the privilege only to the risk of incrimination for *criminal* offences and punishments). See EV60.04(6).

732   See EV4.39.01.

733   See EV60.04(6).

734   See EV60.04(7).

735   See EV60.05.

736   Section 27 of the Serious Fraud Office Act 1990 ("SFO Act") states that a person required to attend an SFO interview has no right to refuse to answer questions or produce documents on the grounds that to do so "would or might incriminate or tend to incriminate that person". However, s 28 of the SFO Act limits the use that can be made in a criminal prosecution of certain kinds of self-incriminating information generated during the course of an investigative interview pursuant to s 27.

737   *NZ Apple and Pear Marketing Board v Master and Son Ltd* [1986] 1 NZLR 191 (CA), 193.

Particularly in the area of regulatory legislation, case law suggests that the privilege will be implicitly abrogated by "regulation-making power conferred upon the Executive" allowing officials to ask questions about "business or physical actions" within the scope of a regulatory regime.[738]

The possibility of *judicial* abrogation of the privilege, which was previously achievable at common law, has not been carried over into s 60(3) of the Evidence Act.[739]

EV60.04   Nature and scope of s 60

(1)   Privilege available outside court proceedings

Consistent with the combined effect of s 60(1)(a)(i) and (2)(a), s 53(2) of the Act confirms that "a person who has a privilege conferred by s 60 … in respect of information has the right to refuse to disclose *in a proceeding* the information".[740] Pursuant to s 4(1) of the Act, a "proceeding" will include any civil or criminal proceeding "conducted by a court" and "any interlocutory or other application to a court connected with that proceeding".[741] However, while the Act does not generally attempt to regulate the admission of evidence beyond the confines of court proceedings, s 60 makes it clear that the statutory privilege against self-incrimination will operate in contexts outside the processes and procedures connected with a pending civil or criminal case. Instead, the privilege will apply if a person is "required to provide specific information" (s 60(1)(a)) in any of three separate circumstances: (a) "in the course of a proceeding" (s 60(1)(a)(i)); (b) "by a person exercising a statutory power or duty" (s 60(1)(a)(ii)); or (c) "by a police officer or other person holding a public office in the course of an investigation into a criminal offence or possible criminal offence" (s 60(1)(a)(iii)).

(2)   Requirement of compulsion

The fact that an individual must be *"required to provide* specific information" in one of the situations set out in s 60(1)(a) means that some legal rule must exist obliging a person to respond to official questioning or some type of official demand for information.[742] If such an element of legal compulsion is absent, s 60 will not apply. In practical effect, this suggests that the circumstances encompassed by s 60(1)(a)(iii) will be rare. Indeed, in light of the broad, common law "right to silence", there are comparatively few situations where an individual suspected of unlawful behaviour will actually be required to provide information to the police — or some other "person holding a public office" — during "the course of an investigation into a criminal offence" (s 60(1)(a)(iii)).[743]

---

738   *NZ Apple and Pear Marketing Board v Master and Son Ltd* [1986] 1 NZLR 191 (CA), 193. See, eg, *Taylor v New Zealand Poultry Board* [1984] 1 NZLR 394 (CA).
739   See, eg, *Busby v Thorn EMI Video Programmes Ltd* [1984] 1 NZLR 461 (CA).
740   Emphasis added.
741   See EV4.35.01-03.
742   Emphasis added.

(3)　Incrimination

The s 60 privilege will shield an individual from having to provide "specific information" that "would, if so provided, be likely to incriminate the person under New Zealand law for an offence punishable by a fine or imprisonment" (s 60(1)(b)). Pursuant to s 4(1) of the Act, "incriminate" means to "provide information that *is reasonably likely to lead to, or increase the likelihood of,* the prosecution of a person for a criminal offence".[744] This is a weak test, and will apply not only to information directly admitting criminal acts, but also to matters forming mere links in the chain of proving such acts. The fact that a prosecution is "improbable or unlikely" will not exclude the operation of s 60.[745] On the other hand, the risk of prosecution must be "real and appreciable", since the privilege will not apply to "merely imaginary or fanciful peril".[746]

(4)　Specific information

The requirement of "specific information" in s 60(1)(a) is meant to preclude "blanket claims" to the exercise of the privilege under s 60(2).[747] Instead, "[t]he privilege can only be claimed for particularised items of information" sought in response to certain questions or information-seeking requests.[748] See, however, the discussion of the term "information" in EV60.04(7).

(5)　Incrimination under New Zealand law

The s 60(1)(b) reference to incrimination "under New Zealand law" excludes a claim of privilege where the information might lead to criminal prosecution in an overseas jurisdiction. However, in such circumstances, s 61 of the Act — which codifies a judicial discretion to safeguard an individual from self-incrimination under foreign law — will offer some protection to the individual concerned.[749]

743　See Rishworth, Huscroft, Optican, Mahoney, *The New Zealand Bill of Rights*, Melbourne, Oxford University Press, 2003, 647 (discussing the common law right to silence codified in s 23(4) of the New Zealand Bill of Rights Act 1990). For criminal suspects actually "arrested or detained under an enactment", s 23(4) of the Bill of Rights confirms that they have "the right to refrain from making any statement and to be informed of that right" by the investigating authorities involved. Similarly, s 25(d) of the Bill of Rights states that a person on trial for a criminal offence has the right "not to be compelled to be a witness or to confess guilt". See also *Practice Note — Police Questioning (s 30(6) Evidence Act 2006)* [2007] 3 NZLR 297 (Chief Justice's Chambers, 16 July 2007, Elias CJ) (requiring police to inform criminal suspects of their rights to silence and counsel under s 23 of the Bill of Rights when the person is in custody or the interviewing officer has sufficient evidence to charge).

744　Emphasis added. While it does not say so specifically, the risk of incrimination envisaged by ss 4(1) and 60 probably encompasses information that, if required to be disclosed, would increase a person's likelihood of conviction in an *existing* criminal prosecution as well as the chance of a *future* criminal proceeding being brought. See the discussion of "incriminate" under s 4(1) at EV4.22.01.

745　*Busby v Thorn EMI Video Programmes Ltd* [1984] 1 NZLR 461 (CA), 478 (per Sommers J).

746　*Busby v Thorn EMI Video Programmes Ltd* [1984] 1 NZLR 461 (CA), 469 (per Cooke J).

747　LC *Evidence Code*, para C255. See also New Zealand Law Commission, *The Privilege Against Self-Incrimination: A Discussion Paper*, NZLC PP25, Wellington, 1996, para C6.

748　LC *Evidence Code*, para C255.

---

(6)   Criminal acts and punishments

Section 60(2) confines application of the privilege to prosecution for "offences punishable by a fine or imprisonment". The limiting of s 60 to *criminal* acts and punishments eliminates the common law protection in New Zealand against self-incriminating exposures to a *civil* penalty.[750] According to the Law Commission, "[e]xamples of civil penalties imposed in disciplinary or civil court proceedings could include striking off, fines, revoking of a license, etc".[751]

(7)   Definition of "information"

Section 60 limits the class of material to which the privilege against self-incrimination will apply. As set out in s 51(2) and (3), the definition of "information" encompassed by s 60 is discussed at EV51.06-09.

EV60.05   Limits on the privilege against self-incrimination

Section 60(4) sets out three separate limits on who can claim the privilege against self-incrimination in the relevant circumstances encompassed by s 60(1).

(1)   No corporate claims to the privilege

In a significant change to New Zealand law,[752] s 60(4)(a) provides that the privilege against self-incrimination can only be asserted by natural persons and not "on behalf of a body corporate" — a term that would encompass various artificial entities having a separate legal personality, such as incorporated societies, charitable incorporations, companies, universities, local authorities, and some types of partnerships.[753] On the other hand, s 60(4)(a) does not preclude the employees or officers of a body corporate from "claiming the privilege on their own behalf when they are personally liable to self-incrimination".[754] However, as will typically be the case, the privilege will not be available to such persons where: (a) a statutory regime removes the privilege implicitly or explicitly;[755] or (b) the incriminating statements are contained in pre-existing documents — a class of material excluded from the operation of s 60 pursuant to the definition of "information" under s 51(3)(b)(i).[756]

(2)   Privilege can only be claimed personally

Section 60(4)(b) affirms that, because it protects against *self*-incrimination, the privilege can only be asserted by the individual who will actually be incriminated by the information sought. One person cannot claim the privilege "on behalf of" another,

---

749   See EV61.01.

750   LC *Evidence Code*, para C253.

751   New Zealand Law Commission, *The Privilege Against Self-Incrimination: A Discussion Paper*, NZLC PP25, Wellington, 1996, para C1.

752   Compare the pre-2006 Act case of *NZ Apple and Pear Marketing Board v Master and Son Ltd* [1986] 1 NZLR 191 (CA).

753   See New Zealand Law Commission, *The Privilege Against Self-Incrimination: A Discussion Paper*, NZLC PP25, Wellington, 1996, paras 207-239.

754   LC *Evidence Code*, para C258.

755   See the discussion of s 60(3) at EV60.03.

756   See EV60.04(7).

even if the information demanded would incriminate that person's friend, spouse, relative or domestic partner (s 60(4)(b)).[757]

While worded somewhat infelicitously, an exception to this rule permits a "legal adviser" (as defined in s 51(1)) to assert the privilege "on behalf of a client" (s 60(4)(b)). To that extent, s 60 will allow an authorised representative to claim the privilege against self-incrimination in the name of the privilege holder. Moreover, when dealing with a "legal adviser", information demanded from him or her may also be protected from disclosure pursuant to the privilege for communications with legal advisers codified in s 54.[758]

(3)   Testifying defendant in a criminal proceeding

Consistent with s 5(4) of the Evidence Act 1908, s 60(4)(c) states that a "defendant in a criminal proceeding" cannot assert the privilege "when giving evidence about the matter for which the defendant is being tried". The provision is directed at a defendant's right to resist answering questions put by the prosecution (or a co-accused) during cross-examination. If a person on trial for a criminal act chooses to testify in his or her defence — an option given to defendants by the non-compellability rule of s 73(1)[759] — privilege can only be asserted "when the information sought poses a risk other than of conviction in the immediate proceeding for the particular offence" (that is, for an offence separate to the one that is the subject of the accused's criminal trial).[760]

In the pre-2006 Act decision of *R v Gunthorp*,[761] the Court of Appeal ruled that, under s 5(4) of the Evidence Act 1908, a criminal defendant facing multiple charges who chooses to testify in his or her own defence cannot limit the giving of evidence (and hence cross-examination) to one charge but not the other. Such a result is unlikely to change under s 60(4)(c).

EV60.06   Waiver

See the discussion of s 65 at EV65.01 for the circumstances in which a person may waive privilege under s 60 either "expressly or impliedly" (s 65(1)). As applied to the privilege against self-incrimination, the most likely example of waiver under s 65 would be where an individual voluntarily chooses to answer incriminating questions, or provide incriminating information, in the circumstances covered by s 60(1).

EV60.07   No power of judge to disallow privilege

The power of a judge to disallow a claim of privilege under s 67 of the Act does not apply to assertions of the privilege against self-incrimination under s 60. This follows

---

757   Likewise, an individual will be unable to invoke s 60 to stop a third party from revealing information that could not be compelled from the privilege holder himself or herself. This is a result of the exclusion of s 60 from the operation of s 53(3) and (4). See EV53.05.
758   See EV54.01.
759   See EV73.04.
760   New Zealand Law Commission, *The Privilege Against Self-Incrimination: A Discussion Paper*, NZLC PP25, Wellington, 1996, para C9.
761   *R v Gunthorp* [2003] 2 NZLR 433 (CA).

from the application of s 67 only to "a claim of privilege conferred by any of sections 54 to 59 and 64" (s 67(1) and (2)).

EV60.08   Claiming the privilege in court proceedings

See EV62.01 for a discussion of the procedural mechanisms set out in s 62 that attend a person's claim to the privilege against self-incrimination in a "court proceeding" (s 62(1)).

EV60.09   Joint interests in privileged material

Note should be taken of s 66, which purports to impact the operation of the s 60 privilege against self-incrimination where it is held "jointly" — a term left undefined in the Evidence Act — between "[a] person" and "some other person or persons" (s 66(1)). However, by definition, the circumstances under which persons might *jointly* hold a privilege against *self*-incrimination are difficult to imagine.[762]

EV60.10   Disclosure requirements in civil proceedings

The concluding portion of s 60 advises that its shield against self-incrimination will be "subject to s 63" (s 60(5)). As discussed at EV63.01, s 63 deals with the abrogation and replacement of the privilege against self-incrimination with respect to certain court-ordered disclosure requirements in civil proceedings.

61   Discretion as to incrimination under foreign law

(1)   This section applies to any specific information—

    (a)   that a person is (apart from this section) required to provide—

        (i)   in the course of a proceeding; or

        (ii)   by a person exercising a statutory power or duty; or

        (iii)   by a police officer or other person holding a public office in the course of an investigation into a criminal offence or possible criminal offence; and

    (b)   that would, if so provided, be likely to incriminate the person under foreign law for an offence punishable by—

        (i)   capital punishment; or

        (ii)   corporal punishment or imprisonment, or both.

(2)   A Judge may direct that the person cannot be required to provide the information if the Judge, after having regard to the likelihood of extradition and other relevant matters, thinks that it would be unreasonable to require the person to incriminate himself or herself by providing the information.

(3)   Subsection (2) does not enable a Judge to give a direction in respect of—

    (a)   a body corporate; or

---

762   See EV66.01(2).

    (b)   any person other than the person required to provide the information (except by a legal adviser on behalf of a client who is so required); or

    (c)   a defendant in a criminal proceeding when giving evidence about the matter for which the defendant is being tried.

EV61.01   Self-incrimination under foreign law

The privilege against self-incrimination codified in s 60 applies only to incrimination "*under* New Zealand law for an offence punishable by a fine or imprisonment" (s 60(1)(b)).[763] However, reflecting the suggestion of Lord Nicholls in the Privy Council decision of *Brannigan v Davison*,[764] s 61 codifies a judicial discretion in New Zealand "to provide protection where it would be harsh to force a person to incriminate himself or herself under foreign law".[765]

EV61.02   Scope of s 61

The broad circumstances engaging the s 61 discretion — set out in s 61(1)(a) — are similar to those triggering the privilege against self-incrimination under s 60(1)(a). Accordingly, "[t]he discretion will be available in ... situations ... where the person concerned has not yet become a witness" in a civil or criminal case.[766] Pursuant to s 61(3), the discretion will be unavailable in the same situations excluding application of the privilege under s 60(4).[767] Likewise, the definition of "incriminate" in s 61(1)(b) will bear the meaning given to it by s 4(1) of the Act (that is, where provision of information would be "reasonably likely to lead to, or increase the likelihood of ... prosecution" of the individual concerned).[768] Finally, the kinds of "information" encompassed by s 61(1) will be limited by the definition of that term contained in s 51(3).[769] Consistent with s 60(1)(a), the reference to the provision of "specific" information in s 61(1) will also preclude "blanket claims" to the exercise of the discretion under s 61(2).[770]

The s 60 privilege against self-incrimination applies where the officially compelled production of information would be likely to incriminate the person under New Zealand law for a criminal offence "punishable by a fine or imprisonment" (s 60(1)(b)). By contrast, the exercise of judicial discretion under s 61 is activated where the officially compelled production of information would be likely to incriminate the person under foreign law for a criminal offence punishable by: (a) "capital punishment" (s 61(1)(b)(i)); or (b) "corporal punishment or imprisonment, or both" (s 61(1)(b)(ii)).

---

763   Emphasis added.

764   *Brannigan v Davison* [1997] 1 NZLR 140 (PC), 147.

765   LC *Evidence Code*, para C261.

766   LC *Evidence Reform*, para 289. See EV60.04(1).

767   See EV60.05.

768   See EV4.22.01.

769   See EV60.04(7) and EV51.06-09.

770   See EV60.04(4).

EV61.03   Privilege versus discretion

Where engaged by the circumstances set out in s 61(1)(a) and not excluded by those specified in s 61(3), s 61 will grant protection to an individual similar to the privilege against self-incrimination codified in s 60 of the Act. However, the most significant differences between ss 60 and 61 stem from the fact that s 61 creates a mere judicial *discretion* to shield persons in New Zealand against self-incrimination under foreign law. As it is not a *privilege*, various provisions of the Act dealing with privileges will not apply.

For example, the exercise of judicial discretion under s 61 is specifically excluded from the operation of s 65 ("Waiver") and will not be subject to s 62 ("Claiming *privilege* against self-incrimination in court proceedings").[771] Moreover, s 60 creates an exception to the privilege where another enactment removes it from New Zealand law either "expressly or by necessary implication" (s 60(3)(a)).[772] However, no such limitation exists in s 61. As a result, a judge can exercise the discretion to protect a person from self-incrimination even when, as applied to the "specific information" sought (s 61(1)), the law of the relevant foreign jurisdiction has done away with the privilege either implicitly or explicitly. This means that an individual in New Zealand may have more protection against self-incrimination under foreign law than would result from comparable claims to the privilege in the applicable overseas court.

EV61.04   Judicial discretion

As discussed at EV61.03, s 61 does not codify a *privilege* against self-incrimination under foreign law. Accordingly, persons whose compelled disclosure of information places them at risk of criminal punishment in an overseas jurisdiction will not automatically be entitled to the benefits of judicial protection in New Zealand. Indeed, s 61(2) makes it clear that a judge "*may direct* that the person cannot be required to provide the information if the Judge, after having regard to the likelihood of extradition and other relevant matters, *thinks that it would be unreasonable* to require the person to incriminate himself or herself by providing the information".[773]

While it does not say so specifically, s 61 will require an application to a judge by a person seeking protection from the officially compelled disclosure of information encompassed by the provision. Assuming its prerequisites are met — a question of fact for the New Zealand court on the circumstances of each individual case — s 61 gives no additional guidance as to how the judicial discretion should be exercised. However, relevant considerations will likely include:

(a)   The seriousness of the offence and the nature and extent of the punishment faced in the foreign jurisdiction;

(b)   The degree to which extradition to and prosecution in the foreign jurisdiction is a real or remote possibility;

---

771   Emphasis added. See, respectively, ss 65(1) and 62(1).
772   See EV60.03.
773   Emphasis added.

(c)   The reason that the potentially incriminating information is being sought in New Zealand and the interests of the government or private party seeking the information;

(d)   The extent to which the claim of privilege would be cognisable in the foreign jurisdiction;[774] and

(e)   The likely impact of disclosure on the individual beyond the potential for overseas criminal prosecution under foreign law.

62   Claiming privilege against self-incrimination in court proceedings

(1)   If in a court proceeding it appears to the Judge that a party or witness may have grounds to claim a privilege against self incrimination in respect of specific information required to be provided by that person, the Judge must satisfy himself or herself that the person is aware of the privilege and its effect.

(2)   A person who claims a privilege against self-incrimination in a court proceeding must offer sufficient evidence to enable the Judge to assess whether self-incrimination is reasonably likely if the person provides the required information.

EV62.01   Nature and scope of s 62

Section 62 sets out a pair of procedural mechanisms tied to the operation of the s 60 privilege against self-incrimination in "a court proceeding" (s 62(1) and (2)). Accordingly, and by contrast with the scope of s 60 itself, s 62 will not be triggered in the extended contexts set out in s 60(1)(a)(ii) and (iii).[775]

When the provision applies, s 62 sets out two related obligations stemming from the privilege. One is imposed on the judge where a person appears at risk of self-incrimination under the terms of s 60(1) of the Act (s 62(1)). The other is imposed on the person seeking to claim the privilege pursuant to s 60(1) (s 62(2)).

(1)   Judicial advice

As mandated by s 62(1), if "it appears to the Judge" in a court proceeding that "a party or witness may have grounds to claim a privilege against self-incrimination in respect of specific information", the judge must "satisfy himself or herself that the person is aware of the privilege and its effect".

This judicial duty — which did not exist at common law — obligates a judge to apply s 60 of the Act to determine if, under the terms of that section, a person required to

---

774   See the discussion at EV61.03.

775   See EV60.04(1). However, in line with s 62(1) of the Act and outside court proceedings, s 23(4) of the New Zealand Bill of Rights Act 1990 imposes an obligation on police to inform persons "arrested or detained under an enactment" that they have the right to refuse to answer questions put to them during custodial interrogation. See also *Practice Note — Police Questioning (s 30(6) Evidence Act 2006)* [2007] 3 NZLR 297 (Chief Justice's Chambers, 16 July 2007, Elias CJ) (requiring police to inform criminal suspects of their rights to silence and counsel under s 23 of the Bill of Rights when they are in custody or where police have enough evidence to charge the person with an offence) (see EV30.10(1)).

give "specific information" in a court proceeding would be entitled to claim the privilege in respect of the explicit fact(s) sought. In making this determination, the definition of "information" in s 62(1) will bear the limited meaning assigned to it under s 60 pursuant to s 51(3).[776] Likewise, and consistent with s 60(1)(a), the reference to the provision of "specific" information in s 62(1) will preclude the blanket exercise of judicial advice under s 62.[777]

Once a judge determines that a party has grounds to resist the production of information in a court proceeding pursuant to s 60, s 62(1) requires the judge to: (a) notify a party or witness about the nature and operation of the privilege; and (b) explain its effect.[778]

(2)   Sufficient evidence of self-incrimination

A judge who is uncertain about a person's risk of self-incrimination will be able to invoke the obligation imposed on such individual under s 62(2). It requires a party or witness seeking to claim the privilege in court proceedings to "offer sufficient evidence to enable the Judge to assess whether self-incrimination is reasonably likely if the person provides the required information" (s 62(2)).

What amounts to "sufficient evidence" can only be determined on the facts and circumstances of a particular case. However, as the Law Commission observed in its 1996 Preliminary Paper, *The Privilege Against Self-Incrimination*, "it is not sufficient for a witness or party to baldly assert his or her right to the privilege … without elaborating on the nature of the risk".[779] While no evidentiary burden is specified in s 62(2), "sufficient evidence" that self-incrimination is "reasonably likely" will probably require proof that, on the balance of probabilities, provision of the information would be "reasonably likely to lead to, or increase the likelihood of, the prosecution of a person for a criminal offence" (the definition of "incriminate" contained in s 4(1) of the Act).[780]

While application of the provision to s 62 is not completely clear, evidence offered by a person to substantiate a claim of privilege under s 62(2) could be subject to s 15 of the Act (which deals with the admissibility in a proceeding of evidence given by a witness "to prove the facts necessary for deciding whether some other evidence should be admitted" in that proceeding (s 15(a))).[781]

EV62.02   Form of advice

Apart from specifying a judge's responsibility under s 62(1) and the privilege holder's obligation under s 62(2), s 62 offers no guidance as to how a court should actually go

---

776   See EV60.04(7) and EV51.06-09.
777   See EV60.04(4).
778   As to the form of such judicial advice, see the discussion at EV62.02.
779   New Zealand Law Commission, *The Privilege Against Self-Incrimination: A Discussion Paper*, NZLC PP25, Wellington, 1996, para C15 (citing *Triplex Safety Glass Co Ltd v Lancegaye Safety Glass (1934) Ltd* [1939] 2 KB 395, 403-404).
780   See EV4.22.01. See also *Adams on Criminal Law — Evidence*, EC20.07(4).
781   See EV15.01.

about fulfilling its terms. However, in its Preliminary Paper,[782] the Law Commission suggested the following:[783]

> "[Section 62(1)] requires a court to inform a party or witness in court proceedings that he or she may have grounds to claim the privilege against self-incrimination for specific information, if there appears to be a risk of self-incrimination. It is within the court's inherent jurisdiction to regulate its own procedure in determining how it goes about assessing whether the risk is present. The judge might, for example, adjourn proceedings until the witness has consulted a lawyer, or simply inform the witness of the privilege's existence and effect.

> "[O]nce the court is satisfied that self-incrimination is 'reasonably likely' if the party or witness gives the required information, it must inform him or her that the information need not be given. ... In order to comply with [s 62(1)], and to ensure the person is given all relevant material to make a decision (with or without the assistance of counsel), the [court] should give the following standard form direction ...

>> 'You have what is called a privilege against self-incrimination in respect of the specific information that you have been required to provide, and the effect of that privilege is that you cannot be required to provide the information in this court. You cannot be prosecuted ... if you refuse to provide it.

>> 'If you do provide the information, it could possibly be used by people who become aware of it as a basis for making further inquiries and investigations. Perhaps some people might be able to use the information against you in some way not involving the High Court or District Court. You should consider those possibilities.

>> 'If you do not understand what I have just said, you should say so now and I will explain further.' "

EV62.03   Remedy for breach of s 62

Section 62 provides no remedy for a judge's failure to satisfy the notice and warning provisions of s 62(1) in a court proceeding. However, if it were proved that the terms of the section were not complied with, and a party or witness provided self-incriminating information as a result, the inculpatory statements would be eligible for exclusion in any criminal proceeding — pursuant to s 30 of the Act — as having been "improperly obtained" (s 30(5)).[784]

---

782   Discussed at EV62.01(2).
783   New Zealand Law Commission, *The Privilege Against Self-Incrimination: A Discussion Paper*, NZLC PP25, Wellington, 1996, paras C14-C16.
784   See EV30.01.

63   Replacement of privilege with respect to disclosure requirements in civil proceedings

(1)   This section applies to a person who is required by an order of the court made for the purposes of a civil proceeding—

(a)   to disclose information; or

(b)   to permit premises to be searched; or

(c)   to permit documents or things to be inspected, recorded, copied, or removed; or

(d)   to secure or produce documents or things.

(2)   The person does not have the privilege provided for by section 60 and must comply with the terms of the order.

(3)   No evidence of any information that has directly or indirectly been obtained as a result of the person's compliance with the order may be used against the person in any criminal proceeding, except in a criminal proceeding that concerns the falsity of the information.

EV63.01   Abrogation of privilege in civil proceedings

Section 63 stands as one of the Select Committee's most far reaching amendments to the Evidence Bill. Up to the stage of the Select Committee's Report, s 63 aimed only at the particular device of discovery in civil proceedings known as an *Anton Piller* order.[785] The Bill proposed to largely codify the law in this relatively narrow area, as set forth in *Busby v Thorn EMI Video Programmes Ltd*.[786] Suddenly, the Select Committee extended s 63 to abrogate the privilege against self-incrimination in the case of *all* orders by a court for the purposes of a civil proceeding which come within the broad terms of s 63(1).[787] This is the stark effect of s 63(2).

Prior to the Act, the privilege against self-incrimination was a well recognised justification for refusing to permit an opposing litigant to inspect a relevant document.[788] In confirmation, the privilege is specifically listed in form 26 of Schedule 1 of the High Court Rules as one of the privileges which may be claimed as a reason to avoid the normal disclosure obligations that are part of the discovery process.

EV63.02   Effect of related provisions

Although s 63 brings about a major change in the law, the aim of the section is in keeping with other provisions, previously discussed.[789] Most importantly, s 51(3)

---

785   An *Anton Piller* order is an ex parte, pre-trial order requiring an opposing litigant to provide information and permit inspection by the party who obtained the order. See *Adams on Criminal Law — Evidence*, EC20.07(4).

786   *Busby v Thorn EMI Video Programmes Ltd* [1984] 1 NZLR 461 (CA).

787   *Select Committee Report on the Evidence Bill*, 7-8.

788   *Taranaki Co-op Dairy Co Ltd v Rowe* [1970] NZLR 895 (CA).

789   See EV51.06-07.

removes *pre-existing documents* from the scope of the privilege against self-incrimination. Because the privilege against self-incrimination no longer protects such documents, s 63(1)(c) and (d) (which both purport to remove the privilege from documents) actually have no practical effect on pre-existing documents. Section 51(3) means that there is nothing left for s 63(1)(c) and (d) to remove. Similarly, except for the elusive "testimonial act" argument,[790] the privilege against self-incrimination has never clearly protected against the production of real evidence (tangible items other than documents).[791] Accordingly, it is arguable that there is little practical effect for s 63(1)(c) and (d) (insofar as the production of "things"). Finally, because the privilege never granted protection against the search of premises, s 63(1)(b) is actually innocuous.

In summary, the real effect of s 63 will be felt in s 63(1)(a)'s abrogation of the privilege against self-incrimination as a reason to refuse to disclose "information".

The matters just discussed add a remarkable uncertainty to s 63(3), as discussed below.[792]

EV63.03   Order of the court

In view of the suddenness of the Select Committee's alteration to this provision of the Evidence Bill, some courts may attempt to resist the intended effect of s 63. One potential argument is that s 63 abrogates the privilege only when an *order of the court* requires a person to act in the ways set forth in s 63(1)(a)-(d). The standard discovery order under r 294 of the High Court Rules will *not* order disclosure of a document that is protected by the privilege against self-incrimination (see rr 295-298 of the High Court Rules). This is because the High Court Rules continue to specifically recognised the privilege against self-incrimination. If there is no *order* for disclosure of the document or the information contained in it, s 63 does not operate to abrogate the privilege. In this way, there is no conflict between the High Court Rules and the Evidence Act 2006 (if there was, s 5(2) would give priority to the Act).

However, in view of the stated intention of the Select Committee to abrogate the privilege in civil litigation disclosure proceedings, it is doubtful if this argument will be accepted. In any event, the High Court Rules can be amended to bring them in line with s 63.

EV63.04   Subsection (3): derivative use immunity

Section 63(3) provides a form of protection for the person who has been prevented from claiming the privilege against self-incrimination through the operation of s 63(2). This form of protection is often referred to as "derivative use immunity" in

---

790   *NZ Apple and Pear Marketing Board v Master and Son Ltd* [1986] 1 NZLR 191 (CA). See the discussion of this argument in *Adams on Criminal Law — Evidence*, EC20.07(8). It is clear that the definition of "information" in s 51(3) excludes any possibility that testimonial acts come within the scope of the privilege.

791   See *C plc v P (Attorney-General intervening)* [2007] 3 WLR 437 (CA), para 34.

792   See EV63.05.

other jurisdictions. Another example can be found in s 67(3) although, as discussed under that provision, s 67(3) offers a wider protection than is provided by s 63(3).[793]

The protection granted by s 63(3) can never be as complete as would have been the result of an application of the privilege. For example, the police may become aware of the incriminating information disclosed in response to one of the orders referred to in s 63(1) when they would otherwise have remained in ignorance. Nonetheless, the effect of the derivative use immunity provided by s 63(3) is that neither the information required to be disclosed under s 63(1), nor any information obtained by following a line of investigation suggested by the forced disclosure, can be offered as evidence in any criminal proceeding brought against the person who was forced to make the disclosure. The one exception to that proposition is that, if the information originally disclosed was false, it will be admissible against the person if a prosecution is brought alleging that it was a criminal offence to provide false information.

Of course, in the civil proceeding in which the disclosure was made, the parties are free to offer the disclosed information in evidence in support of their positions in the litigation.

EV63.05   Gratuitous immunity

As discussed at EV63.02, s 63 purports to remove the privilege against self-incrimination in situations where, under the common law or by virtue of s 51(3), no privilege existed in any event or (under the "testimonial act" argument) the existence of the privilege was at best questionable. These situations are where the incriminating material is real evidence (tangible items: s 63(1)(b) and (d)) or pre-existing documents (s 63(1)(c) and (d)).

Nonetheless, in these same situations s 63(3) goes on to provide the derivative use immunity just discussed. That immunity is clearly intended to act as a rough substitute for the privilege that is removed by s 63(2). However, in the two situations of real evidence and pre-existing documents, there may actually have been nothing of substance removed by s 63(2). In these cases it is possible to view the immunity provided by s 63(3) as quite gratuitous.

The result is that civil litigants who face potential criminal liability may be eager to comply with court orders for discovery as described in s 63(1). Compliance will invoke the protection of the immunity described in s 63(3) in cases where it is arguable that the privilege against self-incrimination never existed.

64   Informers

(1)   An informer has a privilege in respect of information that would disclose, or is likely to disclose, the informer's identity.

(2)   A person is an informer for the purposes of this section if the person—

(a)   has supplied, gratuitously or for reward, information to an enforcement agency, or to a representative of an enforcement agency, concerning the

---

793   See EV67.05(1).

possible or actual commission of an offence in circumstances in which the person has a reasonable expectation that his or her identity will not be disclosed; and

(b)   is not called as a witness by the prosecution to give evidence relating to that information.

(3)   An informer may be a member of the police working undercover.

EV64.01   Overview

Section 64 grants a relatively confined privilege to informers, a term defined in s 64(2) and (3). The privilege protects the informer's identity and extends to information that is likely to disclose that identity.

EV64.02   Informers to agencies other than the police

The definition of "enforcement agency" in s 4 of the Act has the effect that the privilege provided by s 64 is not restricted to information provided by an informer to the police.

EV64.03   Informer as witness

There is some difficulty raised by the relationship between s 64(2)(b) and s 53(2). Section 53(2) purports to give an informer the right to refuse to disclose his or her identity (being privileged information) *in a proceeding*. However, the effect of s 64(2)(b) is that a person loses their status as an informer as soon as they are called as a witness by the prosecution. By virtue of being called as a witness, the "informer" loses the very benefit that the privilege was meant to provide.

Although this appears to be a contradiction between the two provisions, it will not be of great practical importance due to the unlikelihood of the prosecution calling an informer as a witness against his or her wishes.

Another effect of s 64(2)(b) is that a person who supplies the sort of information referred to in s 64(2)(a) remains an informer and can claim the privilege if he or she has been called to testify *by the defence*. However, in such a case the privilege would offer little practical protection. The whole issue would remain dormant until the witness was asked if he or she was the informer. The witness's identity as the informer would be implicitly disclosed as soon as the judge ruled that the witness could claim the privilege.

In summary, the effect of s 64(2)(b) is that the informer privilege will be primarily governed by s 53(3), which grants the right to require that *other people* not disclose privileged information in a proceeding.

EV64.04   Undercover police

Section 64(3) protects an undercover police officer's identity as an informer on an apparently equal footing with other informers. However, the position may differ if the officer is called as a witness by the prosecution. Although, as just discussed, the effect of s 64(2)(b) would be to end the privilege in such a case, ss 108-109 may still operate to protect the officer's identity.

EV64.05   Disallowing privilege

Informer privilege is subject to s 67 and indeed has long been the principal focus of the common law power to disallow privilege upon which s 67(2) is based.[794]

EV64.06   Agents

Section 51(5)(c) exempts informer privilege from the operation of s 51(4). This means that for privilege to exist, the informer must personally supply the information referred to in s 64(2)(a). No privilege will exist if the information is supplied by the informer's "authorised representative", although the latter person may himself or herself thereby become an informer.

Despite s 51(5)(c), s 64(2)(a) ensures that informer privilege exists when an informer supplies information to "a representative of an enforcement agency".

65   Waiver

(1)   A person who has a privilege conferred by any of sections 54 to 60 and 64 may waive that privilege either expressly or impliedly.

(2)   A person who has a privilege waives the privilege if that person, or anyone with the authority of that person, voluntarily produces or discloses, or consents to the production or disclosure of, any significant part of the privileged communication, information, opinion, or document in circumstances that are inconsistent with a claim of confidentiality.

(3)   A person who has a privilege waives the privilege if the person—

    (a)   acts so as to put the privileged communication, information, opinion, or document in issue in a proceeding; or

    (b)   institutes a civil proceeding against a person who is in possession of the privileged communication, information, opinion, or document the effect of which is to put the privileged matter in issue in the proceeding.

(4)   A person who has a privilege in respect of a communication, information, opinion, or document that has been disclosed to another person does not waive the privilege if the disclosure occurred involuntarily or mistakenly or otherwise without the consent of the person who has the privilege.

(5)   A privilege conferred by section 57 (which relates to settlement negotiations or mediation) may be waived only by all the persons who have that privilege.

EV65.01   Overview

Section 65 tackles the difficult issue of waiver of privilege. Section 65(1) recognises that all the privileges dealt with by the Act may be waived. See the related discussion of "common interest privilege" at EV66.02(1).

---

794   *Adams on Criminal Law — Evidence*, EC20.17(8).

EV65.02   Effect of waiver

The Act does not spell out the *effect of* a waiver of privilege. It is natural to assume that the intention of the legislature was that once a waiver has occurred, the "effects and protections of privilege", as set out in s 53, no longer apply. However, it may be that distinctions will remain.

For example, it could be that the Act will follow the common law and recognise that a waiver of privilege may be only *partial*. At common law, a waiver of privilege occurring in one proceeding did not necessarily amount to a waiver for all purposes. Depending on the circumstances, it could sometimes be possible to claim privilege in other proceedings.[795]

See also the discussion of s 52(1)(c), which suggested that a waiver by the privilege holder may not prevent an application by an "interested person" to prohibit an offer of evidence involving privileged material.[796]

EV65.03   Tests for waiver

Subsections (2) and (3) set out a variety of circumstances which amount to a waiver, while s 65(4) lists circumstances which do not amount to waiver. Section 65(5), applicable only to the privilege protecting settlement negotiation, has already been considered in the discussion of s 57.[797]

(1)   Implied waiver

Section 65(1) confirms that a privilege can be *impliedly* waived.

There is no reason why a privilege cannot be impliedly waived in ways that are not dealt with specifically in s 65(2) or (3). The privilege against self-incrimination provides a simple example. Where the privilege holder is a witness and proceeds to answer an incriminating question, the privilege has been waived even though there has been no express acknowledgement that this has occurred (see, however, s 62(1)).

(2)   Waiver under s 65(2)

Section 65(2) may produce some unprecedented results. The key to the subsection is a *voluntary* disclosure of *any significant part of* the privileged material in circumstances that are *inconsistent with a claim of confidentiality*.

(4)   Voluntary

Not surprisingly, the Act makes no attempt to define when a disclosure is voluntary. It is likely that New Zealand courts will follow the Australian lead where, in a similar legislative context, "voluntary" has been held to mean, simply, "not by mistake".[798]

---

795   *British Coal Corp v Dennis Rye Ltd (No 2)* [1988] 3 All ER 816 (CA); *Auckland District Law Society v B* [2002] 1 NZLR 721 (CA), para 157, per Tipping J; *Adams on Criminal Law — Evidence*, EC20.09(10)(d).

796   See EV52.04.

797   See EV57.12.

798   *Ampolex Ltd v Perpetual Trustee Co (Canberra) Ltd* (1996) 40 NSWLR 12, 22.

---

(5)   Any significant part

The substance, rather than the amount of material is likely to lie at the heart of an enquiry whether "any significant part" of the privileged material has been disclosed. It is also suggested that "significant" will be interpreted to mean statements of fact or opinion which the policies underlying the particular privilege in question aim to protect.

(6)   A claim of confidentiality

Section 65(2) assumes that the privilege holder (or someone else acting with the privilege holder's authority) may voluntarily disclose privileged information *without* thereby waiving the privilege. But no guidance is provided for determining which circumstances meet the pivotal test of a disclosure that is inconsistent with a claim of confidentiality, resulting in a waiver of the privilege.

The Law Commission's draft Evidence Code provided the example (based on s 59(4)) of the privilege holder obtaining a prescription for a prohibited drug from a doctor and then selling the prescription to a third person.[799] In the Law Commission's view, the sale was a voluntary disclosure in circumstances inconsistent with a claim of confidentiality. But why is this so? The "confidentiality" with which s 65(2) is concerned must in this example be the nature of the drug that has been prescribed. A chemist would have learned of this in any event. Therefore, the only relevant disclosure is the one made to the illicit purchaser of the prescription. What is it about *this* disclosure that is inconsistent with a claim of confidentiality insofar as the rest of the world is concerned? Any answer that is suggested must recognise that the mere fact that *some* disclosure has taken place merely marks the beginning of the enquiry under s 65(2).

Examples constructed involving any of the other privileges dealt with in the Act will reveal the potential for uncertainty raised by the concluding phrase of s 65(2).[800]

(7)   Exchange of witness statements

When the procedure of pre-trial exchange of witness statements in civil proceedings was introduced in the UK there was a substantial controversy as to whether this procedure amounted to a waiver, thereby destroying privilege in any material referred to in the exchanged statements. The privilege in question was invariably the limb of legal professional privilege protecting communications to and from third parties (such as potential witnesses) in preparation for litigation (now the "preparatory materials" privilege set out in s 56). The issue was initially resolved in New Zealand by r 441J(a) of the High Court Rules, which provides that nothing in the rules requiring the exchange of witness statements "deprives any party of that party's right to treat any communication as privileged."

The point is no longer clear. It could be argued that an exchange of witness statements may amount to a waiver of privilege under s 65(2) by being a voluntary disclosure of

---

799   LC *Evidence Code*, 181.
800   See, generally, *Adams on Criminal Law — Evidence*, EC20.09(10).

privileged material in circumstances which are inconsistent with a claim of confidentiality. Because s 5(2) of the Act gives the Act priority over the High Court Rules when an inconsistency between the two enactments arises, it may be that s 65(2) negates the effect of r 441J(a) of the High Court Rules. On the other hand, courts are likely to strive to give effect to r 441J(a) and conclude that a claim of confidentiality is still consistent with an exchange of witness statements.

EV65.04   Subsection (3)(a): waiver by "putting in issue"

Section 65(3)(a) confirms that a waiver of privilege occurs when the privilege holder "puts in issue" privileged material in a proceeding. In doing so, s 65(3)(a) adopts an approach rejected by the Court of Appeal in *Shannon v Shannon*.[801]

(1)   When is privileged material "put in issue"?

It is by no means clear what circumstances will result in a conclusion that privileged material has been put in issue. The most common sort of case in which the question has been raised at common law is a proceeding where a party relies upon privileged material (usually, legal adviser privilege (s 54)) as a justification for action that he or she has taken, such as filing a caveat (as in *Shannon*).

If there has been an actual, albeit partial, *disclosure* of that otherwise privileged material, s 65(2) would be the more obvious focus in determining if a waiver had occurred. But where no more is disclosed than the bare fact that the person acted "on legal advice", the effect of s 65(3)(a) may well be that privilege has been waived. However, given the antipathy with which the Court in *Shannon* viewed such an inroad on the protection offered by solicitor-client privilege, it may be that future cases will require something more before concluding that the privileged material has been "put in issue". One example of such an additional factor could be a partial disclosure of the privileged material that does not amount to a disclosure of a sufficiently "significant" part so as to trigger s 65(2).

Shannon itself may provide some guidance because in that case the Court discussed the Law Commission's proposals, which have now been enacted as s 65(3). The Court said of s 65(3)(a):[802]

> "The paragraph talks about putting privileged communication in issue. This is not the same thing as putting a matter in issue which cannot fairly be assessed without reference to the relevant legal advice".

(2)   Witness putting material in issue

Section 65(3)(a) anticipates that a "person" other than a party could act in a proceeding in a way that amounts to putting privileged material in issue.

The most likely circumstance of such an occurrence would involve a *witness* (who is not a party to the proceeding) who holds a privilege. The argument would be that the witness has waived privilege by, for example, justifying his or her actions as being

---

801   *Shannon v Shannon* [2005] 3 NZLR 757 (CA).
802   *Shannon v Shannon* [2005] 3 NZLR 757 (CA), para 47.

in accordance with legal advice or by refreshing his or her memory by means of an otherwise privileged document.[803]

(3) Subsection (3)(b): instituting proceedings

The Court in *Shannon* hinted that it had difficulty understanding why the Law Commission felt it was necessary to include s 65(3)(b), given that that subsection appears to be but one example of the broader concept of waiver by "putting in issue", spelled out by s 65(3)(a).

The only example which the Law Commission gave for the operation of the whole of s 65(3) is a client's malpractice suit against his or her lawyer.[804] The Law Commission believed that the client should not be permitted to rely on legal adviser privilege to prevent disclosure of communications with the lawyer that are relevant to the lawyer's defence of the claim.[805]

The Court in *Shannon* understandably felt that the Law Commission's example was directed at s 65(3)(b), because it involved *instituting* proceedings. However, it could just as easily have been viewed as an example of s 65(3)(a). The particular difficulty in articulating how s 65(3)(b) differs from s 65(3)(a) simply highlights the greater difficulty in offering any prediction how courts will define the concept of waiver by putting privileged information in issue.

EV65.05 Subsection (4): disclosures without consent

Section 65(4) states that disclosures of privileged material that occur "involuntarily or mistakenly or otherwise without the consent" of the privilege holder do not amount to a waiver.

Because no waiver has occurred in these circumstances, the privilege remains intact. However, it is suggested that the protection offered by the privilege has been weakened. This is because the inadvertent disclosure means that s 53(4) will apply, rather than s 53(3). Under s 53(4), a judge has a discretion to protect the privileged material, but he or she is not required to do so.

---

66   Joint and successive interests in privileged material

(1)   A person who jointly with some other person or persons has a privilege conferred by any of sections 54 to 60 and 64 in respect of a communication, information, opinion, or document—

     (a)   is entitled to assert the privilege against third parties; and

     (b)   is not restricted by any of sections 54 to 60 and 64 from having access or seeking access to the privileged matter; and

---

803   Both examples are taken from *Shannon v Shannon* [2005] 3 NZLR 757 (CA), para 48. There is no prohibition on a witness using a privileged document to refresh his or her memory. See, generally, EV90.05.

804   LC *Evidence Code*, p 181.

805   See *Lillicrap v Nalder & Son (a firm)* [1993] 1 All ER 724 (CA); in the medical context, see *Glegg v Smith & Nephew Inc* (2005) 253 DLR (4th) 193 (SCC).

    (c)   may, on the application of a person who has a legitimate interest in maintaining the privilege (including another holder of the privilege), be ordered by a Judge not to disclose the privileged matter in a proceeding.

(2)   If a person has a privilege conferred by any of sections 54 to 57 in respect of a communication, information, opinion, or document, the personal representative of the person or other successor in title to property of the person—

    (a)   is entitled to assert the privilege against third parties; and

    (b)   is not restricted by any of sections 54 to 57 from having access or seeking access to the privileged matter.

(3)   However, subsection (2) applies only to the extent that a Judge is satisfied that the personal representative or other successor in title to property has a justifiable interest in maintaining the privilege in respect of the communication, information, opinion, or document.

(4)   A personal representative of a deceased person who has a privilege conferred by any of sections 54 to 57 in respect of a communication, information, opinion, or document and any other successor in title to property of a person who has such a privilege, may, on the application of a person who has a legitimate interest in maintaining the privilege (including another holder of the privilege), be ordered by a Judge not to disclose the privileged matter in a proceeding.

EV66.01   Novel applications of the concept of joint interest

Discussions of joint interest privilege at common law concentrate solely on legal professional privilege. Nonetheless, s 66(1) applies to all the privileges dealt with in the earlier sections, while s 66(2)-(4) applies to the privileges covered in ss 54-57. The resulting wide scope of s 66 gives rise to some difficulties. To date, the law has not had to cope with the concept of a joint interest privilege for communications with, for example, ministers of religion (s 58) or a joint interest privilege for informers (s 64).

(1)   Medical privilege

Consider the privilege dealt with in s 59 (medical practitioners). What if a married couple were both drug addicts and together sought treatment from a doctor. Does this result in a joint privilege? The example highlights the difficulty determining when people actually do have a privilege jointly with others. The common law authorities offered no clear guidance.[806] The Act provides no assistance on this issue.

(2)   Privilege against self-incrimination

The privilege against self-incrimination (s 60) provides another example where it is difficult to predict if the concept of a joint privilege is relevant.[807]

---

806   See Thanki QC (ed), *The Law of Privilege*, Oxford, Oxford University Press, 2005, Ch 6.

807   It is difficult to conceive of a joint privilege against *self*-incrimination, although this is what s 66 forces us to do.

Assume that A and B are in business together. They become involved in litigation brought against them by a third party. In the course of the litigation, A is asked a question relating to the conduct of the business, the answer to which could incriminate both A and B. Although s 60(4)(b) prevents A from claiming the privilege on B's behalf, it is still important to determine whether A and B are joint holders of the privilege against self-incrimination in this example. This is because of s 66(1)(c).

Section 66(1)(c) permits one joint privilege holder to apply to a judge to order that the other privilege holder not "disclose the privileged matter" (presumably in this context, the incriminating information) in the proceeding. If the example being discussed is one of joint privilege then A can ask a judge to prevent B from answering the question. However, if each simply holds the privilege as an individual, A's right to do so is less clear.

(3) Interested person

The actual terms of s 66(1)(c) multiply the uncertainty. By a late amendment to the Evidence Bill, s 66(1)(c) now permits *any* person "who has a legitimate interest in maintaining the privilege" to apply to prevent a joint privilege holder from disclosing privileged matters in a proceeding. No indication is given as to the sort of people who could be said to have a legitimate interest in maintaining a joint privilege *held by others*.

The strange effect of this last minute addition to s 66(1)(c) can be illustrated by the above example involving A and B. It might be thought that even if it is determined that A and B do *not* jointly hold the privilege against self-incrimination, the final version of s 66(1)(c) will still allow A to apply to prevent B answering the question. This is because it could be argued that A is a person having a "legitimate interest in maintaining the privilege". However, that first impression would be wrong. Section 66(1)(c) only operates in a case where two or more people *do* have a joint privilege. Only in such a case is a person with a legitimate interest allowed to apply under s 66(1)(c). We have assumed here that A and B have been determined not to have a joint privilege. This robs A of the chance to rely on s 66(1)(c).

The result would be different if the only alteration to the facts was that B did hold the privilege against self-incrimination jointly with another person, C. The existence of a joint privilege would mean that A was able to apply under s 66(1)(c) as an interested person.

For other instances where the Act's grant of rights to an "interested person" causes uncertainty, see ss 52(1)(c) and 66(4).

(4) Prior to a proceeding

It should further be noted that, insofar as s 66(1)(c) is concerned, the example of possible joint holders of the privilege against self-incrimination is unimportant when the requirement to provide information is made by an official at a point *before* a proceeding is commenced (s 60(1)(a)(ii) or (iii)). Section 66(1)(c) only becomes relevant when an application is made to prevent disclosure *in a proceeding*.

EV66.02   Common interest privilege

Section 66 does not deal directly with the amorphous common law concept of "common interest privilege". As articulated by the Law Commission,[808] litigants who share a common interest may exchange information for limited purposes (for example, to prepare for litigation) and protection will be given for this information when disclosure is sought by third parties.

(1)   An aspect of waiver

The Law Commission's brief discussion of common interest privilege indicates that the Commission believed that s 65(2), governing *waiver* of privilege, is adequate to deal with the issues which arise in this area. This is in keeping with one school of academic thought which views "common interest privilege" as merely a label for the conclusion that no waiver of privilege occurs when a disclosure is made between parties with a sufficient "common interest" in a subject. In other words, the disclosure to another litigant who has a "common interest" with the party making the disclosure does not amount to a waiver of privilege as far as opposing litigants are concerned. This is not a universally accepted viewpoint.[809]

In any event, nothing in the Act offers any assistance with the difficulties involved in determining when a sufficient common interest exists to invoke this doctrine.[810] Neither is it clear if privilege can be waived by the person to whom the initial disclosure was made.[811]

EV66.03   Subsection (1): rights and responsibilities of joint interest privilege

Section 66(1) describes the consequences of a joint interest privilege. As can be imagined, most problems will arise when the holders of a joint interest privilege become adversaries.

Section 66(1)(b) ensures that all of the privilege holders will have access to the privileged material. The judgment of *Gemini Personnel Ltd v Morgan & Banks Ltd*[812] held that this remains so even after the parties have become opposing litigants. There seems no reason to think that this conclusion will be altered under the Act.

However, in *Gemini* the Court considered a further issue. As with all previous discussions of joint interest privilege, *Gemini* concerned legal professional privilege (ss 54 and 56). In this context, the Court recognised that one of the privilege holders may, during the continuance of the joint interest, consult for purely personal reasons, the same solicitor who was involved in the original communication that was protected by the joint interest privilege. When this occurs, the personal communication is privileged against the other joint interest privilege holder. Section 66(1) should not change that result. This is because the subsection only applies when two or more

---

808   New Zealand Law Commission, *Evidence Law: Privilege*, NZLC PP23, Wellington, 1994, 71.
809   Thanki QC (ed), *The Law of Privilege*, Oxford, Oxford University Press, 2005, paras 6.36-37.
810   See, eg, *Nicholson v Icepak Coolstores Ltd* [1999] 3 NZLR 475.
811   See *Farrow Mortgage Services Pty Ltd (in liq) v Webb* (1996) 39 NSWLR 601 (CA).
812   *Gemini Personnel Ltd v Morgan & Banks Ltd* [2001] 1 NZLR 672 (CA).

persons hold a privilege jointly. This prerequisite will not exist when a person consults the solicitor solely to promote his or her individualised interests.[813]

EV66.04   Subsection (2): personal representatives and successors in title

Section 66(2) sets out the rights of the personal representative or "other successor in title to property" of a privilege holder. These rights are the same as are provided for joint holders of privilege by s 66(1)(a) and (b). However, in contrast to joint interest privilege, the rights granted to personal representatives or successors in title apply only insofar as the privileges governed by ss 54-57. This reduces the difficulties, discussed earlier, which arise in applying the concept of a joint interest to the other privileges dealt with in ss 58-60 or 64, in particular the privilege against self-incrimination.[814]

An additional difference, discussed below, is that the rights granted to personal representatives or successors in title by s 66(2) are qualified by s 66(3) in a way that does not apply to joint holders of a privilege.

(1)   Directors and shareholders

The Law Commission provided two examples of successors in title to property of a privilege holder.[815] The first was the Official Assignee as the successor in title to a bankrupt's property. The second was a subsequent owner of property (where the privileged material is a communication relating to some matter of title to that property). These two examples are orthodox. However, in *Privilege*,[816] the Law Commission immediately went on to refer to the US authority of *Garner v Wolfinbarger*,[817] which held that in shareholder actions for alleged wrongdoing by the company or its directors, information which is privileged as between the company and its legal advisers may be made available to the shareholders. The Law Commission clearly indicated a willingness to see New Zealand law develop along these lines.

However, one difficulty with this suggestion is that s 66(2) is unlikely to be the source for such a development. Neither shareholders, directors, nor the company itself can be accurately described as a "successor in title to the property" of each other, as is a prerequisite to the operation of s 66(2)(b). Indeed, there is no obvious source in the Act for the law to develop along the lines indicated by *Garner*. That judgment relied heavily on Wigmore's fourfold test for when a privilege should be recognised[818] as well as policy reasons why shareholders should have access to communications about company affairs. It is asking too much of s 66(2) that it be interpreted to support the result reached in *Garner*.

---

813   *Gemini Personnel Ltd v Morgan & Banks Ltd* [2001] 1 NZLR 672 (CA), para 24.

814   See EV66.01(2).

815   See New Zealand Law Commission, *Evidence Law: Privilege*, NZLC PP23, Wellington, 1994, 71; LC *Evidence Code*, 183.

816   New Zealand Law Commission, *Evidence Law: Privilege*, NZLC PP23, Wellington, 1994.

817   *Garner v Wolfinbarger* 430 F (2d) 1093 (5th Cir, 1970).

818   *Garner v Wolfinbarger* 430 F (2d) 1093 (5th Cir, 1970), 1100-1101. Wigmore's fourfold test is discussed in *Adams on Criminal Law — Evidence*, EC20.16(1).

An alternate foundation for New Zealand law to mirror *Garner* would be s 66(1) and the argument that the shareholders and directors of a company possess a joint interest in communications with the company's legal advisers. Although strained, the Act's lack of guidance as to the boundaries of joint interest privilege may see such arguments being raised.

(2)   Personal representative

"Personal representative" is not defined in the Act. The usual meaning assigned to this term is the executor or trustee of a deceased person, but it appears that the Act intends a wider meaning. Despite the lack of any such qualifying term in s 66(2) or (3), s 66(4) suddenly refers only to "a personal representative *of a deceased person*." This indicates that s 66(2) and (3) were dealing with a wider class of personal representative. Yet if this is so, the result is an undesirable uncertainty. With no guidance from the Act, a vast field opens up for people who may legitimately be described as the "personal representatives" of other people.

EV66.05   Subsection (3): justifiable interest

Unlike the operation of a joint interest privilege, s 66(3) limits the rights of a personal representative or successor in title of a privilege holder. The representative or successor will only be entitled to the rights set forth in s 66(2) if a judge determines that he or she "has a justifiable interest" in the privileged material.

Earlier discussions by the Law Commission provide some assistance in understanding when a "justifiable interest" does or does not exist. *Privilege* gave one example when a personal representative of a deceased person may not be entitled to assert privilege against a third party (s 66(2)(a)), namely when the court is hearing a claim under the Family Protection Act 1955.[819] In the Law Commission's view, the personal representative should have to disclose communications between the deceased and his or her lawyer. This is because of the personal representative's duty to use the otherwise privileged information for the benefit of all persons interested in the estate.

EV66.06   Subsection (4): responsibilities

The rights of a personal representative or a successor in title to property of a privilege holder are set out in s 66(2). The *responsibilities* of such a person are (in contrast to the framework of s 66(1)) set out in a separate subsection, s 66(4). If there is a justification for this break with the framework adopted by s 66(1) it may be that, as mentioned earlier, s 66(4) suddenly introduces the confusing qualifier of a personal representative *of a deceased person* (not found in s 66(2)).

The power of a joint holder of a privilege to prevent disclosure by a personal representative or successor in title of a privilege holder, set forth in s 66(4), matches the power granted to a joint holder of a privilege by s 66(1)(c) to prevent disclosure by another holder of the privilege. As with s 66(1)(c), a substantial uncertainty is introduced into s 66(4) by the concept of a person having a "legitimate interest" also

---

819   New Zealand Law Commission, *Evidence Law: Privilege*, NZLC PP23, Wellington, 1994, para 180.

being entitled to prevent disclosure by a representative or successor of a privilege holder.

67 Powers of Judge to disallow privilege

(1) A Judge must disallow a claim of privilege conferred by any of sections 54 to 59 and 64 in respect of a communication or information if satisfied there is a prima facie case that the communication was made or received, or the information was compiled or prepared, for a dishonest purpose or to enable or aid anyone to commit or plan to commit what the person claiming the privilege knew, or reasonably should have known, to be an offence.

(2) A Judge may disallow a claim of privilege conferred by any of sections 54 to 59 and 64 in respect of a communication or information if the Judge is of the opinion that evidence of the communication or information is necessary to enable the defendant in a criminal proceeding to present an effective defence.

(3) Any communication or information disclosed as the result of the disallowance of a claim of privilege under subsection (2) and any information derived from that disclosure cannot be used against the holder of the privilege in a proceeding in New Zealand.

EV67.01   Subsection (1): improper purpose

Section 67 sets out two occasions when a claim of privilege may (or must: s 67(1)) be disallowed.

Section 67(1) sets out the first of these two occasions. The judge *must* disallow a claim of privilege if the privileged occasion was used for what we may refer to as either a dishonest purpose or a criminal purpose. Section 67(1) is based on the common law "crime/fraud" exception to privilege.[820]

Although the common law cases focused on legal professional privilege (now covered by ss 54-56), s 67(1) applies to all privileges dealt with in ss 54-59 and 64.

Accordingly, no privilege would exist under s 57 if the purpose of the settlement negotiations was to defraud the Inland Revenue Department.

It is difficult to construct an example of an otherwise privileged communication to a minister of religion (s 58) that is made for a dishonest purpose or in furtherance of an offence.

Section 33(2) of the Evidence Amendment Act (No 2) 1980, the precursor to s 59 (privilege for information obtained by medical practitioners and clinical psychologists), denied privilege for communications made for a criminal purpose.[821]

If an informer (s 64) knowingly provided false information alleging the commission of a crime by another person, this could amount to an offence under s 24 of the

---

820   The common law "crime/fraud" exception to privilege is discussed in *R v Cox and Railton* (1884) 14 QBD 153. See also, *Adams on Criminal Law — Evidence*, EC20.09(11).

821   *Adams on Criminal Law — Evidence*, EC.20.12(9).

Summary Offences Act 1981. The result would be a disallowance of the privilege under s 67(1).[822]

The privilege against self-incrimination is exempted from the operation of s 67(1). This exemption is probably based on the peculiar nature of this privilege, which is a right to refuse to disclose information. Presumably, the legislature sought to avoid the argument that the privilege cannot be successfully claimed if the motivation for refusing to disclose information was the "dishonest" or "criminal" purpose of avoiding a rightful conviction. See, however, the discussion of s 51(3)(b)(ii).[823]

(1)   Prima facie case

The judge is required to disallow the claim of privilege once he or she is satisfied there is a prima facie case that the improper purpose existed. This "prima facie" standard is in accord with the common law.[824]

EV67.02   Dishonest purpose

Although most common law judgments refer to the "crime/fraud exception" to privilege, authorities such as *R v Cox & Railton*[825] also recognise *dishonesty* as sufficient to destroy privilege. As was the case at common law, s 67(1) operates to destroy privilege in cases that may not involve the intention to commit a crime. A "dishonest purpose" is sufficient.

The Act makes no attempt to define a "dishonest purpose". It is likely that the approach of *Crescent Farm (Sidcup) Sports Ltd v Sterling Offices Ltd*[826] will continue to be followed. Privilege will not be destroyed merely because the purpose amounted to a civil wrong. Dishonesty must be present, although this will include "all forms of fraud and dishonesty such as fraudulent breach of trust, fraudulent conspiracy, trickery and sham contrivances".[827] This necessarily leaves some flexibility, but it would not support the view of the High Court of Australia in *Attorney-General (NT) v Kearney*[828] that an intentional abuse of a statutory power is a sufficiently improper purpose to destroy privilege.[829]

(1)   Whose dishonest purpose?

Section 67(1) does not require that, to destroy privilege, the dishonest purpose must be that of any specific person. In particular, the dishonest purpose need not be that of the person who would otherwise be the privilege holder. It is possible to imagine cases where the privilege holder was used as a dupe by the person having the dishonest

822   See, generally, *R v Strawbridge* [2003] 1 NZLR 683 (CA).
823   See EV51.08.
824   *Morgan & Banks Ltd v Gemini Personnel Ltd* [2001] 1 NZLR 672 (CA), 679.
825   *R v Cox & Railton* (1884) 14 QBD 153, 171.
826   *Crescent Farm (Sidcup) Sports Ltd v Sterling Offices Ltd* [1972] Ch 553.
827   *Crescent Farm (Sidcup) Sports Ltd v Sterling Offices Ltd* [1972] Ch 553, 565. See similarly *Gemini Personnel Ltd v Morgan & Banks Ltd* [2001] 1 NZLR 14, para 68, per Laurenson J.
828   *Attorney-General (NT) v Kearney* (1985) 158 CLR 500; 61 ALR 55 (HCA).
829   See *Adams on Criminal Law — Evidence*, EC20.09(11).

purpose. Section 67(1) still requires the judge to disallow the privilege in such a case. Contrast the following discussion of a *criminal* purpose.

EV67.03   Criminal purpose

In addition to dishonesty, s 67(1) destroys privilege if the "communication was made or received, or if the information was … prepared to enable … anyone to commit or plan to commit what the person claiming the privilege knew or reasonably should have known, to be an offence". This wording distinguishes s 67(1)'s handling of a criminal purpose from its treatment of a dishonest purpose.

(1)   Whose criminal purpose?

Section 67(1) negates privilege even when the person claiming the privilege is not the person who plans to commit the offence. But what is the necessary extent of the involvement of the person claiming the privilege? The example of money laundering, suggested by *Francis & Francis (a firm) v Central Criminal Court*,[830] is instructive.

Assume that a drug trafficker makes use of an innocent dupe (D) as a means of laundering money. D consults a solicitor to assist in purchasing property with the ill-gotten money provided by the trafficker. Does s 67(1) destroy the legal advice privilege which would otherwise arise under s 54? The answer depends on whether, in the particular circumstances of the case, D "reasonably should have known" that the transaction amounted to the offence of money laundering.

The introduction of this test could lead to a different result than in *Francis* itself, where the House of Lords held that privilege was destroyed regardless of D's state of mind. Under the common law as declared by their Lordships, the criminal intention of the drug trafficker providing the funds was sufficient to destroy the privilege. However, under s 67(1), the judge will not be required to disallow the privilege if it is concluded that D should not reasonably have known that the transaction amounted to an offence.

The earlier discussion of a *dishonest* purpose suggested that, in that context, the money laundering example *would* lead to a disallowance of the privilege. Section 67(1) does not require that the person claiming the privilege "reasonably should have known of the dishonest purpose" as a prerequisite to disallowance of the privilege.

EV67.04   Subsection (2): enabling the presentation of an effective defence

In contrast to s 67(1), when the prerequisites set by s 67(2) exist, the judge is not required to disallow a claim of privilege. He or she has a discretion to do so when this is necessary to enable the defendant in a criminal proceeding to present an effective defence. The Act offers no guidance as to how that discretion should be exercised.

There is no obvious explanation why the distinction was drawn between the judge being "satisfied" in s 67(1) and being "of the opinion" in s 67(2).

---

830   *Francis & Francis (a firm) v Central Criminal Court* [1988] 3 All ER 775 (HL)`.

As with s 67(1), most of the privileges recognised by the Act are subject to disallowance under s 67(2). However, it is difficult to imagine realistic examples where s 67(2) could apply to certain of the privileges governed by ss 54-59 and 64. For instance, it is not easy to think of a case where the privilege protecting settlement negotiations (s 57) should be disallowed in order to permit a defendant in a criminal proceeding to present an effective defence.

As is also the case with s 67(1), the privilege against self-incrimination is specifically exempted from the operation of s 67(2). This means that a judge has no power to force someone to incriminate themselves, even when this would enable another person to present an effective defence in a criminal proceeding.

(1)   Change from the common law

Section 67(2) embodies a concept known to the common law as the "innocence at stake" exception to privilege. This exception was uncontroversial insofar as concerned the common law informer's privilege.[831] However, the weight of authority refused to allow this exception to override legal professional privilege.[832]

Past consideration of the common law "innocence at stake" exception focused on legal professional privilege in the following context. In a privileged communication, A admits to his solicitor that A committed the crime for which B has been charged. Somehow learning of this communication, B attempts to force A's solicitor to give evidence of the privileged admission of guilt made by A. In contrast to the common law, s 67(2) grants to a judge the power to require the solicitor to give evidence of A's admission, despite the fact that it is protected by the privilege protecting communication with a legal adviser (s 54).[833]

EV67.05   Subsection (3): derivative use immunity

To offset the dramatic effect of s 67(2), s 67(3) grants what North American jurisprudence has labelled a "derivative use immunity". The operation of this derivative use immunity can be demonstrated in the context of the example just discussed of forced testimony from a solicitor of a client's (A's) admission of guilt.

If A was subsequently charged with the crime, evidence of A's admission would be inadmissible for the prosecution at the trial of that charge. Likewise inadmissible would be "any information derived from" the disclosure forced from the solicitor. Thus, if the police based their investigation of A's guilt on the foundation of the disclosure forced from the solicitor, all subsequently acquired evidence of A's guilt would be inadmissible against A.

(1)   Broad version of immunity

Section 67(3) is drafted in terms which make its operation remarkably wide. The subsection aims to protect the privilege holder against any detrimental *use* of the

---

831   *R v De Bruin* 4/8/03, O'Regan J, HC Auckland T021790; *Adams on Criminal Law —
      Evidence*, EC20.17(8).

832   *R v King* [2007] 2 NZLR 137; (2005) 23 CRNZ 201.

833   See *Adams on Criminal Law — Evidence*, EC20.09(13).

disclosed communication or information in any subsequent proceedings, be they characterised as civil or criminal. This prohibition passes beyond mere use as evidence.

Section 67(3) is thus even broader in scope than the other example of derivative use immunity in the Act, s 63(3).[834]

EV67.06   Termination of privilege

The Act contains no provision which would result in termination of a privilege because of a change in the circumstances which gave rise to the privilege. Subsequent conduct on the part of a privilege holder may amount to a waiver, as discussed under s 65. However, there is no obvious source for argument that a privilege will lapse merely because time passes and circumstances change.

The issue is most likely to be raised in relation to the privilege for settlement negotiations or mediation (s 57) and the privilege for preparatory material for a proceeding (s 56). Although it was often said at common law in relation to the privilege protecting communications with legal advisers (s 54) that "once privileged, always privileged", the issue may be approached from a different perspective insofar as the privileges protecting settlement negotiation or preparatory materials are concerned. In both of these cases it might be argued that the privileges should cease when the litigation with which they were connected reaches its termination.

Insofar as concerns the preparatory materials privilege, in *Blank v Minister of Justice*[835] the Supreme Court of Canada held that, at common law, the privilege ends with the end of the litigation with which the privilege was connected. However, it is doubtful if a similar result can be reached under the Act. Sections 10 and 12 of the Act are unlikely to provide sufficient leeway to add a termination gloss on any of the privileges. It seems that under the Act, the rule of once privileged, always privileged is of universal application.

Confidentiality

EV68.Intro.01   Confidentiality

Sections 68-70 grant to a judge a discretion to protect confidentiality in various circumstances.

It is true that the privileges created in the preceding sections likewise protect confidentiality. However, the distinguishing feature of a privilege is that, beyond the specific exceptions dealt with in s 67, there is no room for a judge to deny the protection granted by a privilege on the basis that the judge considers that some competing public interest is more important. Under ss 68-70, such a weighing up process is an integral part of the decision whether or not to protect confidentiality.

---

834   See EV63.04.
835   *Blank v Minister of Justice* [2006] SCC 39 (SCC). *Blank* was accepted by Randerson J in the pre-2006 Act decision of *Snorkel Elevating Work Platforms Ltd v Thompson* [2007] NZAR 504, para 13.

---

68   Protection of journalists' sources

(1)   If a journalist has promised an informant not to disclose the informant's identity, neither the journalist nor his or her employer is compellable in a civil or criminal proceeding to answer any question or produce any document that would disclose the identity of the informant or enable that identity to be discovered.

(2)   A Judge of the High Court may order that subsection (1) is not to apply if satisfied by a party to a civil or criminal proceeding that, having regard to the issues to be determined in that proceeding, the public interest in the disclosure of evidence of the identity of the informant outweighs—

     (a)   any likely adverse effect of the disclosure on the informant or any other person; and

     (b)   the public interest in the communication of facts and opinion to the public by the news media and, accordingly also, in the ability of the news media to access sources of facts.

(3)   The Judge may make the order subject to any terms and conditions that the Judge thinks appropriate.

(4)   This section does not affect the power or authority of the House of Representatives.

(5)   In this section,—

informant means a person who gives information to a journalist in the normal course of the journalist's work in the expectation that the information may be published in a news medium

journalist means a person who in the normal course of that person's work may be given information by an informant in the expectation that the information may be published in a news medium

news medium means a medium for the dissemination to the public or a section of the public of news and observations on news

public interest in the disclosure of evidence includes, in a criminal proceeding, the defendant's right to present an effective defence.

EV68.01   Journalist's informant

Section 68(1) purports to protect the identity of a journalist's informant if the journalist has promised not to disclose the informant's identity.

EV68.02   Limited scope of protection

The protection granted by s 68(1) differs substantially from the protections which s 53 provides for privileges. Section 68(1) provides only that the journalist and his or her employer are *not compellable to disclose* the informant's identity. Disclosure from some source beyond that of the journalist or employer is not dealt with, although s 69 may be a possible source for protection in such cases.

EV68.03   Expectation of publication

Section 68(5) defines both "informant" and "journalist" in terms of the informant's expectation that the information he or she provides "may be published in a news medium". If there were no such expectation, there would be no protection under s 68. As discussed at EV69.03, it is unlikely that in a case not meeting one of the prerequisites set by s 68, a direction to protect the informant's identity would be made under s 69.

EV68.04   Normal course of work

Section 68(5) defines a journalist as a person "who *in the normal course of that person's work* may be given information by an informant". In the era of internet bloggers this aspect of the definition may be the subject of predictable disputes.

EV68.05   No protection if journalist wants to disclose

Section 68 is only relevant when the journalist or his or her employer does not want to disclose the informant's identity. Nothing in the section prevents the disclosure when the journalist or employer are willing to do so. This point is emphasised by the fact that s 52, which provides for directions protecting confidential matters (s 69) and matters of State (s 70), makes no reference to s 68. Section 68(1) merely grants a right for a journalist or his or her employer to refuse to disclose an informant's identity.

EV68.06   Subsection (2): judge can override protection

Despite the apparently absolute terms of s 68(1), s 68(2) grants to a Judge of the High Court the power to override the protection granted by the previous subsection. The judge can exercise this power if he or she is satisfied that the public interest in disclosure of the informant's identity outweighs the conflicting interests set forth in s 68(2)(a) and (b).

The concluding passage in s 68(2)(b) recognises that an order that a journalist disclose an informant's identity may have a negative effect in the future because potential informants may react to such an order by becoming more reluctant to communicate with journalists about sensitive facts.

EV68.07   Public interest

Section 68(2) limits the basis upon which the judge can order disclosure of an informant's identity. Only the *public* interest can justify disclosure. The private interests of the parties to a proceeding are not relevant unless it can somehow be argued that they embody the interest of the public. Such an argument is conceivable because the final definition in s 68(5) ensures that a *defendant's right to present an effective defence* in a criminal proceeding can be relied upon in arguing that the public interest justifies disclosure of the informant's identity.

EV68.08   Subsection (3): conditions

Section 68(3) grants to the judge a wide power to impose any terms and conditions on any order for disclosure. Although the Act does not repeat the more detailed provisions of the Law Commission's draft Code, there is no reason to doubt that, under the Act, the judge could follow the Code's suggestion and limit publication of the informant's identity. Likewise, it seems clear that the judge could order that the disclosure could not become a foundation for a defamation suit or other adverse consequences against the informant.

EV68.09   Subsection (4): Select Committee

Section 68(4) is included to cater for Australian authority, referred to by the Law Commission,[836] concerning a Parliamentary Select Committee's power to ascertain a journalist's sources. Section 68(4) ensures that the Act will not affect such power.

69   Overriding discretion as to confidential information

(1)   A **direction under this section** is a direction that any 1 or more of the following not be disclosed in a proceeding:

(a)   a confidential communication:

(b)   any confidential information:

(c)   any information that would or might reveal a confidential source of information.

(2)   A Judge may give a direction under this section if the Judge considers that the public interest in the disclosure in the proceeding of the communication or information is outweighed by the public interest in—

(a)   preventing harm to a person by whom, about whom, or on whose behalf the confidential information was obtained, recorded, or prepared or to whom it was communicated; or

(b)   preventing harm to—

(i)   the particular relationship in the course of which the confidential communication or confidential information was made, obtained, recorded, or prepared; or

(ii)   relationships that are of the same kind as, or of a kind similar to, the relationship referred to in subparagraph (i); or

(c)   maintaining activities that contribute to or rely on the free flow of information.

(3)   When considering whether to give a direction under this section, the Judge must have regard to—

(a)   the likely extent of harm that may result from the disclosure of the communication or information; and

(b)   the nature of the communication or information and its likely importance in the proceeding; and

(c)   the nature of the proceeding; and

---

836   LC *Evidence Code*, para C272.

(d)   the availability or possible availability of other means of obtaining evidence of the communication or information; and

(e)   the availability of means of preventing or restricting public disclosure of the evidence if the evidence is given; and

(f)   the sensitivity of the evidence, having regard to—

   (i)   the time that has elapsed since the communication was made or the information was compiled or prepared; and

   (ii)   the extent to which the information has already been disclosed to other persons; and

(g)   society's interest in protecting the privacy of victims of offences and, in particular, victims of sexual offences.

(4)   The Judge may, in addition to the matters stated in subsection (3), have regard to any other matters that the Judge considers relevant.

(5)   A Judge may give a direction under this section that a communication or information not be disclosed whether or not the communication or information is privileged by another provision of this subpart or would, except for a limitation or restriction imposed by this subpart, be privileged.

EV69.01   Protecting confidentiality

Section 69 grants a judge a discretion to prevent disclosure, in a proceeding,[837] of the confidential material listed in s 69(1). The section provides guidance for the exercise of this discretion, which involves the weighing up of various factors to determine if the public interest justifies protection of the confidential material.

Section 76 deals with confidentiality in the specific context of jury deliberations.

EV69.02   Change in the law

The precursor of s 69 was the well known s 35 of the Evidence Amendment Act (No 2) 1980. However, the new section alters the law in a variety of ways. One is that there no longer needs to be a "special relationship". The focus under s 69 is simply that of confidentiality. Most importantly, exercise of the discretion under s 69 is not dependent on the desire of the person in whom a confidence has been reposed. Section 69 permits a judge to protect confidentiality even in a case where the person to whom the confidence is imparted does not wish to preserve the confidence. This is emphasised by the powers to enforce s 69 that are found in s 52(2) and (4)(b).[838]

---

837   In *R v Stewart* 17/9/07, Panckhurst J, HC Christchurch CRI-2006-009-1151, para 20, Panckhurst J said that s 69 does not directly protect confidentiality at the inspection/discovery stage (but it is still sensible to assess a pre-trial request for disclosure in light of the confidentiality requirement set forth in s 69, if possible). The authors question that conclusion. Because s 4 defines a proceeding as including "(b) any interlocutory or other application to the court connected with that proceeding", the authors take the view that s 69 applies directly to a pre-trial application for disclosure of the sort that occurred in *Stewart*.

838   Contrast the treatment of s 68: see EV68.05.

Section 69 will be the obvious source for argument in cases where privilege existing under the earlier law (communication between spouses; communications with medical professionals in civil proceedings) have not been re-enacted.

(1)   Interested person

Section 52(2) permits a judge to give a direction under s 69 on the judge's own initiative or on the application of an "interested person". The Act gives no guidance as to who qualifies as an interested person. However, in view of the broad spectrum of interests sought to be protected by s 69(2) and (3), it is inevitable that a wide range of people will be able to apply under s 52(2). See the earlier discussion of that provision.[839]

(2)   Subsection (5): fall back when prerequisites to privilege not met

Section 69(5) makes it clear that a direction preventing disclosure of confidential material can be made under s 69(1) even though the circumstances fall short of establishing a privilege pursuant to one of the preceding sections of this Subpart of the Act. An example specifically referred by the Law Commission is medical privilege in civil proceedings.[840] Although s 32 of the Evidence Amendment Act (No 2) 1980 provided such a privilege, s 59 of the Act creates a privilege only in criminal proceedings. The Law Commission felt that it was acceptable that cases not falling within the narrow confines of s 59 could be catered for by s 69. That approach is in marked contrast to the earlier law: *C v Complaints Assessment Committee*.[841]

(3)   Concurrent privilege

Section 69(5) permits a direction protecting confidentiality even when the information would be concurrently protected by privilege. This provision must have been included out of an abundance of caution because, under s 52, the mechanics of protecting confidential information and privileged information will not differ in practice.

EV69.03   When prerequisites to s 68 not met

Section 69(5) deals only with cases where the prerequisites to a privilege are not present. It does not purport to control the right to apply for a direction protecting confidentiality when the prerequisites for a claim for protection of the identity of a journalist's informant under s 68 are not present. It is suggested that any such case should be determined solely with reference to s 68. As long as the case can be classed as one where the central issue is whether a journalist will be permitted to refuse to disclose an informant's identity, the outcome should stand or fall on the criteria set by s 68.

EV69.04   Confidentiality

Confidentiality is, of course, a prerequisite to the operation of s 69(1). The Act does not attempt to provide any definition of this core concept. Section 69(3)(f)(ii)

---

839   See EV52.05.
840   LC *Evidence Code*, 175.
841   *C v Complaints Assessment Committee* [2006] 3 NZLR 577 (SCNZ).

impliedly recognises that material may retain its quality of confidentiality even though it has been disclosed to other persons.

EV69.05   Subsection (2): public interest

Section 69(2) makes it clear that the weighing up process that determines if confidential material will be protected is concerned only with competing *public* interests. A private interest will not be relevant unless it can be argued to embody some wider public interest. However, the detailed provisions of s 69(2) and (3) make such an argument relatively easy to construct.

Section 69(2)(a) casts a wide net by permitting the judge to take into account potential harm to the person to whom a confidence has been communicated. Section 69(2)(b)(i) recognises a public interest in preventing harm to the particular relationship giving rise to the confidential communication etc in issue.

EV69.06   Right to present a defence

It is difficult to explain why s 69 contains no equivalent to the definition of "public interest" found in s 68(5) (protection of journalists' sources). Perhaps it was felt that a specific reference to "a defendant's right to present an effective defence" was not required for s 69 because the aim of that section is so broad. However, the strength of such an argument is undercut by the specific mention of victims of sexual abuse in s 69(3)(g).

It might be felt that s 8(2) can be called upon to assist the argument that a provision similar to s 68(5)'s recognition of the public interest of a defendant's right to present an effective defence can be implied into s 69. However, s 8(2) probably offers little assistance. Although that provision emphasises the right of the defendant to offer an effective defence, the specific focus of s 8(2) (balancing probative value against prejudicial effect) has no direct relevance to the enquiry dictated under s 69.

However, in view of the emphasis which s 6(b) places on the Bill of Rights Act, it is inconceivable that a defendant's right to present an effective defence, confirmed in s 25(e) of the Bill of Rights, would not be an important aspect of the public interest referred to in s 69(2).

EV69.07   Waiver/disallowing claims of confidentiality

Section 69(3)(f)(ii), obliquely, makes the point that earlier general provisions applicable to *privileges* (eg, ss 65 and 67) have no direct application to the protection of *confidentiality*. Although s 65 states that the protection of a privilege ends if the privilege is waived, no such express provision applies to confidentiality. Accordingly, s 69(3)(f)(ii) makes it clear that disclosure of confidential information to other persons does not amount to some form of "waiver". The extent of such a disclosure is merely one factor to be weighed up in the decision whether or not to protect the confidential information.

Section 67 requires or permits a judge to disallow a claim of privilege in certain circumstances. Although s 67(1) does not apply to s 69's protection of confidentiality, it will be difficult to argue that confidentiality should be protected even though the communication in question was made for a dishonest or criminal purpose. Inevitably, such a factor will be taken into account in a judge's determination whether or not to exercise the discretion provided by s 69.

As to s 67(2), see the above discussion of the "right to present a defence".[842]

EV69.08   Victims of sexual offending

In singling out the interests of victims of sexual offences, s 69(3)(g) will provide ammunition for prosecution arguments to resist disclosure of notes of counselling and medical treatment of victims following an alleged sexual offence.[843]

70   Discretion as to matters of State

(1)   A Judge may direct that a communication or information that relates to matters of State must not be disclosed in a proceeding if the Judge considers that the public interest in the communication or information being disclosed in the proceeding is outweighed by the public interest in withholding the communication or information.

(2)   A communication or information that relates to matters of State includes a communication or information—

   (a)   in respect of which the reason advanced in support of an application for a direction under this section is one of those set out in sections 6 and 7 of the Official Information Act 1982; or

   (b)   that is official information as defined in section 2(1) of the Official Information Act 1982 and in respect of which the reason advanced in support of the application for a direction under this section is one of those set out in section 9(2)(b) to (k) of that Act.

(3)   A Judge may give a direction under this section that a communication or information not be disclosed whether or not the communication or information is privileged by another provision of this subpart or would, except for a limitation or restriction imposed by this subpart, be privileged.

EV70.01   Overview

Section 70 grants to a judge a discretion to prevent disclosure of a communication or information that "relates to matters of State". Whether or not it is appropriate to exercise the discretion will depend on the conclusion the Judge reaches after weighing up the competing public interests referred to in s 70(1).

EV70.02   Public interest

In contrast to s 68 (journalists' sources), but similarly to s 69, s 70 contains no provision that the public interest in disclosure includes the defendant's right to present an effective defence in a criminal proceeding. However, as discussed under s 69,

---

842   See EV69.06.
843   See, generally, *Adams on Criminal Law*, Ch10.14.06(5).

s 6(b) should ensure that a defendant's right to present an effective defence will be a major component of the public interest weighed up by a judge under s 70.[844]

EV70.03   Relates to matters of State

Section 70(2) contains a partial definition of a communication or information that relates to matters of State. This refers directly to specific provisions of the Official Information Act 1982. All that is required to characterise a communication or information as a matter of State is that the person who applies to prevent disclosure *relies on an argument* based on the applicable subsection of the Official Information Act.[845] Of course, if such an argument has no basis because the communication or information could not reasonably raise the sort of policy issues reflected in the Official Information Act, there will be no hope that the weighing up process referred to in s 70(1) will favour a direction of non-disclosure.

(1)   Legislative shortcut

The incorporation of the provisions of the Official Information Act provides a streamlined method of defining "matters of State" for the purposes of s 70. However, the result is that the section provides potential protection from disclosure in situations which might have been thought to justify the more specific attention of the legislature.

Consider an example. Sections 110-119 of the Act contain detailed provisions governing testimony by anonymous witnesses. They were undoubtedly designed to protect the *safety of witnesses* in cases where the Act's very specific prerequisites are met.

The anonymous witnesses provisions, carried over from the Evidence Act 1908, were the result of extensive discussion of the issue by the courts, followed by detailed scrutiny by parliament. In contrast, s 70(2)(a) of the Act can now combine with s 6(d) of the Official Information Act to permit non-disclosure of a communication or information in order to protect the safety of *any* person. That broad result can be achieved without the need for any consideration of the sort of detailed factors that ss 110-119 require in the specific case of an anonymous witness.

A similar point can be made for numerous other examples. For instance, s 9(2)(b) of the Official Information Act could combine with s 70(2)(b) of the Act to permit non-disclosure of official information in order to protect a trade secret (despite the lack of any detailed statutory code).

EV70.04   Interested person

The earlier discussion of s 52(2) pointed out the near limitless class of potential "interested persons" who may apply under s 52(2) for a direction protecting a matter of State.[846]

---

844   See EV69.02.
845   This is because s 70(2)(a) and (b) require no more than that "the reason advanced in support of an application for a direction" of non disclosure is one of those set out in specific sections of the Official Information Act 1982.
846   See EV52.05.

EV70.05   Concurrent privilege

Section 70(3) is similar in effect to s 69(5). See discussion of that earlier provision.[847]

Part 3
Trial process

(s 71 to s 149)

Subpart 1—Eligibility and compellability

(s 71 to s 76)

71   Eligibility and compellability generally

(1)   In a civil or criminal proceeding,—

(a)   any person is eligible to give evidence; and

(b)   a person who is eligible to give evidence is compellable to give that evidence.

(2)   Subsection (1) is subject to sections 72 to 75.

EV71.01   All witnesses generally eligible and compellable

Any discussion of the handling of witnesses in trial proceedings must begin with two preliminary questions: who is eligible to give testimony and when may they be compelled to testify?

Section 71 makes it clear that, subject to certain exceptions set out in ss 72-75, all persons are both eligible and compellable to give evidence in civil and criminal proceedings. The provision thus eliminates any objections to a witness's testimony based on age or mental disability. Moreover, while witnesses (depending on their age) must still take an oath or make a promise to tell the truth under s 77,[848] s 71 abolishes common law tests of competence for children under 12 years of age and mentally disabled persons.[849] Finally, with respect to the prosecution's ability to call witnesses at a criminal trial, s 71 does away with the longstanding principle of non-compellability for the spouse of a defendant in a criminal case (a rule previously contained in s 5(6) of the Evidence Act 1908).[850]

EV71.02   Residual discretion under s 8

Declaring that all witnesses are eligible and compellable does not deal with the problem that some witnesses will, in fact, lack the basic testimonial capacities necessary to give rational and coherent testimony. As a matter of law, s 71 would not render such persons ineligible or non-compellable to testify at trial.

However, in *R v Tanner* — a criminal case dealing with the evidence of a 7-year-old child complainant — the Court of Appeal observed: "[I]f a young child is unable to

---

847   See EV69.02(3).
848   See EV77.01.
849   See *R v Tanner* 6/9/07, CA82/07; [2007] NZCA 391, para 25 (discussed at EV71.02).

give coherent evidence a Judge will still retain a discretion to exclude the testimony under s 8 of the Act (the general exclusion provision)".[851] The Court also noted that, while a decision to exclude evidence under s 8 may be made at any time, a pre-trial inquiry into a child's capacity to observe, remember or relate would "generally be preferable".[852] Nonetheless, *Tanner* makes clear that there is no longer any requirement for a judge to determine a child's understanding of the difference between lies and truth or of the importance of telling the truth.[853] Instead, pursuant to s 77(2), witnesses under 12 years must simply be: (a) "informed by the Judge of the importance of telling the truth and not telling lies" (s 77(2)(a)); and (b) "after being given that information, make a promise to tell the truth before giving evidence" (s 77(2)(b)).[854]

In addition to exclusion under s 8, the inability of a witness to give rational and coherent testimony could prompt a judicial ruling of inadmissibility on the ground of

---

850   See EV71.04. Likewise, the Act does not re-enact the marital communications privilege previously contained in s 29 of the Evidence Amendment Act (No 2) 1980. However, communications between spouses previously dealt with under s 29 can now be shielded from disclosure pursuant to the judicial discretion to protect confidential information contained in s 69 of the Act. See EV69.01. The Act did leave intact s 366(2) of the Crimes Act 1961, which states:

"366. Comment on failure to give evidence
.   .   .   .   .

"(2)   Where a person charged with an offence refrains from calling his wife or her husband, as the case may be, as a witness, no comment adverse to the person charged shall be made thereon."

For further discussion of s 366(2), see *Adams on Criminal Law*, CA366.06.

851   *R v Tanner* 6/9/07, CA82/07; [2007] NZCA 391, para 24. See EV8.01. However, any supposition that children lack the testimonial capacities of observation and recall is disputed by psychological studies of memory. Bearing in mind that all memory is fallible, research suggests that children are likely to be as accurate as adults regarding the *central* aspects of an event. Moreover, reporting errors for children tend to be those of omission rather than commission, so children can testify as accurately as adults given an absence of biased questioning. This is tacitly acknowledged in s 125(2) of the Act ("Judicial directions about children's evidence"). See EV125.03. See also reg 49 of the Evidence Regulations 2007 (dealing with judicial directions to a jury in a criminal proceeding about the evidence of children under the age of 6 years). For further discussion, see Bidrose and Goodman, "Testimony and Evidence: A Scientific Case Study of Memory for Child Sexual Abuse" (2000) 14 *Applied Cognitive Psychology* 197; New Zealand Law Commission, *Total Recall*, NZLC MP13, Wellington, 1999, Ch 4 ("Children's Memories").

852   *R v Tanner* 6/9/07, CA82/07; [2007] NZCA 391, para 24 (suggesting that, if required, a pre-trial inquiry would also facilitate the giving of expert evidence regarding a child's ability to give rational and coherent testimony in a proceeding). The same will be true with mentally disabled persons whose capacity to testify is at issue in a civil or criminal case. See, eg, *R v SJS* 10/8/06, CA498/05, para 25.

853   *R v Tanner* 6/9/07, CA82/07; [2007] NZCA 391, para 25. Compare the pre-2006 Act case of *R v Accused (CA245/90)* [1991] 2 NZLR 649 (CA). For discussion of the abolition of competence tests for children and other witnesses, see New Zealand Law Commission, *The Evidence of Children and Other Vulnerable Witnesses*, NZLC PP26, Wellington, 1996.

854   See EV71.03 and EV77.01.

---

irrelevance (s 7(2)).[855] Perceived deficits in testimonial capacity might also cause the evidence of the witness to be given less weight by the fact-finder in a civil or criminal trial.[856]

EV71.03   Oath or affirmation

Notwithstanding the general eligibility and compellability of witnesses under s 71, s 77(1) of the Act still requires the testimony of all witnesses over the age of 12 years to be given on oath or affirmation. Persons under 12 years must be informed by the judge of the importance of telling the truth and must promise to tell the truth before giving evidence (s 77(2)). Pursuant to reg 8 of the Evidence Regulations 2007, the same rules come into play when, under s 106 of the Act, video record evidence is offered as a alternative to the examination in chief of a complainant in a criminal proceeding.

For the form of the witness oath and other details related to oath taking, see the Oaths and Declarations Act 1957. While the circumstances under which it would occur are not specified, s 77(4) of the Act gives a judge the discretion to dispense with an oath, affirmation or promise to tell the truth that would otherwise be required of a witness under s 77(1) or (2). See further the discussions on ss 77 and 106.[857]

EV71.04   Elimination of spousal non-compellability: domestic violence cases

As noted at EV71.01 above, the elimination of spousal non-compellability in criminal proceedings represents s 71's most noteworthy modification to longstanding evidence law.[858] For a discussion of the impact of s 71 (and other provisions of the Act) on domestic violence prosecutions, see Optican and Sankoff, "The Evidence Bill 2005: A New Approach to Hearsay" [2005] NZLJ 446.

EV71.05   Excusing the witness from testifying

Witnesses who are otherwise compellable under s 71(1) of the Act can nonetheless be excused by a judge from testifying in criminal proceedings for "just cause" (s 352(1) of the Crimes Act 1961) or "sufficient cause" (s 20(5) of the

---

855   See EV7.01.

856   See EV7.04.

857   See, respectively, EV77.01 and EV106.01.

858   However, the Act did not repeal s 30(b) of the Alcoholism and Drug Addiction Act 1966. In the relevant part, it states:

> **"30. Evidence in proceedings**
>
> "In any proceedings under this Act (other than any prosecution for an offence)—
>
> •   •   •
>
> "(b)   The husband or wife of the applicant or alleged alcoholic shall be a competent but not compellable witness."

> Pursuant to s 5(1) of the Evidence Act, s 30(b) of the Alcoholism and Drug Addiction Act takes precedence over the absolute rule of spousal compellability envisaged by s 71. See EV5.01. The same would be true, in Court Martial proceedings for offences against the Armed Forces Discipline Act 1971, of the rules of non-compellability preserved for spouses and civil union partners under r 104 of the Armed Forces Discipline Rules of Procedure 1983 (SR 1983/236).

Summary Proceedings Act 1957).[859] Section 56B(1) of the Judicature Act 1908 allows a similar "just cause" exception to the compellability of a witness in a civil case.[860]

Pursuant to s 5(1) of the Act, the provisions cited above take precedence over s 71.[861] In practical if not legal effect, they may operate as a discretionary, judicially administered rule of witness non-compellability in civil and criminal trials. Nonetheless, in light of s 71's clear rule, it remains to be seen how judges will exercise their discretion to exempt a witness from testifying for just or sufficient cause.[862] Excusing a witness from giving evidence may also amount to a determination of non-compellability (s 16(2)(e)) that could have implications for application of the s 18 rule against hearsay.[863].

EV71.06 Eligibility and compellability versus privilege or confidentiality

Witnesses who are otherwise eligible and compellable in a civil or criminal proceeding may nonetheless be able to refuse to answer certain questions (or be prohibited from disclosing information) on the grounds of privilege or the protection of confidences. See the discussions of ss 51-70 (Subpart 8 of Part 2 of the Act).

72   Eligibility of Judges, jurors, and counsel

(1)   A person who is acting as a Judge in a proceeding is not eligible to give evidence in that proceeding.

(2)   A person who is acting as a juror or counsel in a proceeding is not eligible to give evidence in that proceeding except with the permission of the Judge.

(3)   In this section, **counsel** includes an employment advocate.

EV72.01 Eligibility of judges

In accordance with longstanding notions of forum neutrality, conflict of interest principles, and fair trial rights, s 72(1) states the obvious and necessary rule that a person "acting as Judge" in a civil or criminal proceeding is ineligible to give evidence in that proceeding.[864] Section 72(1) will not apply to any subsequent proceedings dealing with matters arising out of earlier proceedings over which the judge presided. However, while a judge will be eligible to testify in such cases, s 74(d) states that he or she cannot be compelled to give evidence "in respect of the Judge's conduct as a Judge".[865]

---

859   For further discussion of s 352(1) of the Crimes Act 1961, see *Adams on Criminal Law*, CA352.03-06.

860   For further discussion, see *McGechan on Procedure*, JS56B.01; HR497.10-13 (discussing r 497 of the High Court Rules ("Issue of subpoenas")).

861   See EV5.01.

862   See, eg, *R v Lologa* 19/7/07, Lang J, HC Auckland CRI-2005-092-7703.

863   See EV16.05.02.

864   See s 25(a) New Zealand Bill of Rights Act 1990 (the right of a criminal defendant to a fair and public hearing conducted by an independent and impartial court); *R v Fotu* [1995] 3 NZLR 129 (CA); *Auckland Casino Ltd v Casino Control Authority* [1995] 1 NZLR 142 (CA).

865   See EV74.03.

EV72.02   Eligibility of juror or counsel

Unless the judge gives permission, s 72(2) states that a person acting as a "juror or counsel" in a civil or criminal case will be ineligible to give evidence in that proceeding. If such individuals wish to give evidence in the hearing freely and without restriction, they will have to stop acting, or will not be allowed to act, in one of those capacities.[866] Section 72(2) will not apply to any subsequent proceedings dealing with matters arising out of earlier proceedings in which a person acted as a juror or counsel.

EV72.03   Judicial discretion

Section 72(2) allows a judge to grant jurors or counsel permission to give evidence in a civil or criminal proceeding in which they are involved. The circumstances in which this would be permitted are not elaborated on and should be exceptional.

(1)   Juror

For obvious reasons, a jury member who becomes a material witness in a proceeding should be automatically disqualified by the judge from any further involvement in the case. In this regard, and depending on the circumstances, s 374 of the Crimes Act 1961 permits a judge to proceed with a criminal trial after one or more jurors have been discharged and with less than the normal compliment of 12 jurors. While rarely employed, the same would be true with respect to juries in civil proceedings under s 54B of the Judicature Act 1908.

(2)   Counsel

An individual acting as his or her own counsel would not need judicial permission to testify in a criminal proceeding. Under s 354 of the Crimes Act 1961, which will take precedence over s 72(2) pursuant to s 5(1) of the Act,[867] an accused is entitled to make a "full defence ... by *himself* or by counsel".[868] In a civil trial, a litigant in person would undoubtedly be given judicial permission under s 72(2) to testify as a witness on his or her own behalf or, if called, on behalf of an adversary party in the case.[869]

As to the giving of evidence by counsel acting for parties in a civil or criminal trial, counsel might be permitted to testify regarding an uncontested matter arising in the middle of a hearing, or with respect to any other matter in the proceeding that does not implicate counsel's credibility as a witness.[870]

However, when acting counsel does testify in a proceeding, issues are likely to arise over whether the person should be allowed to continue his or her role as a legal representative in the case. In such circumstances, the decision to continue with or withdraw from a matter — either at counsel's own discretion or in the discretion of the trial judge — will require a careful appraisal of the depth and nature of counsel's

---

866   LC *Evidence Code*, para C295.

867   See EV5.01.

868   Emphasis added. See also s 25(e) of the New Zealand Bill of Rights Act 1990 (everyone charged with an offence has the right, in relation to the determination of the charge, "to be present at the trial and to present a defence").

869   See EV71.01.

870   See, eg, *Webb v Attewell* (1994) 100 BCLR (2d) 135 (BCCA).

involvement in the proceeding, the potential for hardship to the client, counsel's role as a witness, and any other matters involving the integrity of court processes and fair trial rights.[871]

EV72.04   Counsel includes employment advocate

For the avoidance of doubt, s 72(3) defines "counsel" to include employment representatives — whether lay or professional advocates — who appear in the Employment Relations Authority or Employment Court, but who are not qualified lawyers admitted as a Barrister and Solicitor of the High Court. Such definition seems at odds with the applicability of s 73(2) only to a "proceeding", as that term is defined in s 4(1) of the Act.[872]

73   Compellability of defendants and associated defendants in criminal proceedings

(1)   A defendant in a criminal proceeding is not a compellable witness for the prosecution or the defence in that proceeding.

(2)   An associated defendant is not compellable to give evidence for or against a defendant in a criminal proceeding unless—

    (a)   the associated defendant is being tried separately from the defendant; or

    (b)   the proceeding against the associated defendant has been determined.

(3)   A proceeding has been determined for the purposes of subsection (2) if—

    (a)   the proceeding has been stayed or, in a summary proceeding, the information against the associated defendant has been withdrawn or dismissed; or

    (b)   the associated defendant has been acquitted of the offence; or

    (c)   the associated defendant, having pleaded guilty to, or having been found guilty of, the offence, has been sentenced or otherwise dealt with for that offence.

(4)   In this section, **associated defendant**, in relation to a defendant in a criminal proceeding, means a person against whom a prosecution has been instituted for—

    (a)   an offence that arose in relation to the same events as did the offence for which the defendant is being prosecuted; or

---

871   Rule 8.06 of the New Zealand Law Society, *Rules of Professional Conduct for Barristers and Solicitors* (6th ed), Wellington, 2000, flatly states that: "A practitioner must not act as both counsel and witness in the same matter". Subsection (1) of the commentary to r 8.06 adds: "(1) If there is any reason for a practitioner to think that he or she may be required as a witness in a matter, the practitioner should decline to act as counsel". However, in keeping with s 72(2) of the Evidence Act, subsection (3) of the commentary to r 8.06 notes: "(3) If, having started to act as counsel, the practitioner finds it necessary to make an affidavit in respect of the matter concerned, then the practitioner must immediately retire from the position of counsel, unless the court, in the particular circumstances, directs that it is still appropriate for the practitioner to continue to act."

872   See EV4.35.01-03.

> (b)   an offence that relates to, or is connected with, the offence for which the defendant is being prosecuted.

EV73.01   General rule of defendant non-compellability

With regard to the defendant in a criminal proceeding, s 73 sets out the basic rule of non-compellability previously codified in s 5(1) of the Evidence Act 1908 and confirmed in s 25(d) of the New Zealand Bill of Rights Act 1990 (the right of an accused "not to be compelled to be a witness" at any hearing of the charge).[873] Pursuant to s 73(1), a defendant facing a criminal trial is not a compellable witness for either "the prosecution or the defence in that proceeding" (s 73(1)).

EV73.02   Compellability of associated defendants

(1)   Definition of "associated defendant"

As described below, the s 73(1) rule of non-compellability can change for a person who is an "associated defendant" in relation to "a defendant in a criminal proceeding" (s 73(4)).

Pursuant to s 73(4), an "associated defendant" is someone against whom a prosecution has been initiated for an offence: (a) arising out of the "same events" as the offence for which the defendant is being tried (s 73(4)(a)); or (b) "that relates to, or is connected with," the offence for which the defendant is being tried (s 73(4)(b)). According to the Law Commission, the two provisions encompass not only actual co-defendants in a criminal trial, but a broader class of persons charged with linked offending:[874]

> "[Section 73(4)(a)] of the definition makes a person an 'associated defendant' if he or she is charged with an offence that is the same as the one facing the defendant (whether jointly or separately charged), or with a different offence from that facing the defendant but arising in connection with the same events. [Section 73(4)(b)] covers related offences, an example being where a defendant is charged with the burglary of a building and the associated defendant is charged with receiving the goods stolen in that burglary."

(a)   *Associated defendant is a co-defendant*

If the "associated defendant" is actually a co-accused at the defendant's trial, the ordinary rule of non-compellability will apply. This follows from the prohibition in s 73(1) against a "defendant in a criminal proceeding" being a compellable witness for either "the prosecution or the defence" in that case.

(b)   *Associated defendant is not a co-defendant*

Pursuant to s 73(2), an associated defendant will be compellable for both the Crown and the defence in one of two distinct circumstances:

---

873   For a comprehensive discussion of s 25(d) of the New Zealand Bill of Rights Act 1990, see Rishworth, Huscroft, Optican, and Mahoney, *The New Zealand Bill of Rights*, Melbourne, Oxford University Press, 2003, Ch 23.

874   LC *Evidence Code*, para C297. See also LC *Evidence Reform*, para 340.

(i)   Where the associated defendant is being "tried separately" from the defendant (s 73(2)(a)); or

(ii)   Where the proceeding against the associated defendant has been "determined" (s 73(2)(b)).

For the avoidance of doubt, s 73(3) spells out when a proceeding will be "determined" for the purposes of s 73(2)(b):

(i)   Where the proceeding has been "stayed or, in a summary proceeding, the information against the associated defendant has been withdrawn or dismissed" (s 73(3)(a));

(ii)   Where the associated defendant has been "acquitted of the offence" (s 73(3)(b)); or

(iii)   Where the associated defendant has pled guilty or been convicted of the offence and "has been sentenced or otherwise dealt with for that offence" (s 73(3)(c)).

EV73.03   Privilege against self-incrimination

If the compellability of an associated defendant stems from being tried separately from the defendant in a criminal case (s 73(2)(a)), the privilege against self-incrimination — codified in s 60 of the Act — will undoubtedly permit the associated defendant to refuse to answer many, if not most, questions put to him or her at the defendant's trial. Indeed, because it applies to all specific demands for information "in the course of a proceeding" (s 60(1)(a)(i)), the privilege will be available whether the associated defendant is compelled to be a witness for the Crown or the defence, and regardless of whether the question is asked during examination in chief, cross-examination, or re-examination.

However, a different outcome may result if compellability is based on the fact that proceedings against the associated defendant have been "determined" pursuant to s 73(2)(b) and (3). In such circumstances, responding to questions at the defendant's trial may not place the associated defendant at any cognisable risk of further criminal prosecution — a requirement for asserting the privilege against self-incrimination under s 60(1)(b).[875]

EV73.04   Eligibility of criminal defendants and associated defendants

Section 73 speaks only to the *compellability* of a defendant or associated defendant to be a witness in a criminal case. It does not limit the *eligibility*[876] of such persons to testify voluntarily in criminal proceedings, whether for the defence (their own and/or that of an associated defendant) or on behalf of the prosecution.

However, depending on the circumstances, various common law rules of practice — which would still appear to be valid under s 12 of the Act[877] — may limit the

---

875   See EV60.04(3).
876   See EV71.01.
877   See EV12.01.

prosecution's ability to call a willing associated defendant to give evidence against the defendant in a criminal trial.[878] Likewise, with respect to criminal proceedings conducted before a jury, the voluntary testimony of an associated defendant may trigger a judicial warning about the reliability of such evidence pursuant to s 122. This will be particularly true where an associated defendant, whether an actual co-defendant or otherwise, "may have a motive to give false evidence that is prejudicial to a defendant" in a criminal case (s 122(2)(c)).[879]

74   Compellability of Sovereign and certain other persons

None of the following persons is compellable to give evidence:

(a)   the Sovereign:

(b)   the Governor-General:

(c)   a Sovereign or Head of State of a foreign country:

(d)   a Judge, in respect of the Judge's conduct as a Judge.

EV74.01   Non-compellability of the Sovereign and certain other persons

Section 74 reaffirms the common law rule that, for reasons related to the responsibilities or position of their office, certain New Zealand and foreign government officials are not compellable to give evidence in civil and criminal proceedings.

EV74.02   Sovereigns, Governor-General, and Heads of State

The list contained in s 74 is a limited one. It includes an absolute rule of non-compellability only for the New Zealand "Sovereign" (s 74(a)) and "Governor-General" (s 74(b)), as well as for the "Sovereign or Head of State of a foreign country" (s 74(c)).[880] Unless made non-compellable by some other enactment, which would take precedence over s 74 pursuant to s 5(1) of the Act,[881] all other New Zealand or foreign government officials will be obliged to give evidence in a civil or criminal case.[882]

---

878   For a discussion of this issue and of related matters dealing with the admissibility at a defendant's trial of an associated defendant's guilty plea, see *Adams on Criminal Law — Evidence*, EC10.06(4)(b); EC21.06(2)(b); EC21.06(6)(a). See also *R v O'Brien* [2001] 2 NZLR 145; (2000) 18 CRNZ 610 (CA).

879   See EV122.04(3).

880   In this regard, Sankoff notes: "In British constitutional theory, only subjects are compellable — the sovereign is not included in this general proposition ... The Queen cannot be a compellable witness since there is no process whereby to enforce her attendance. Only the Sovereign herself is exempt, and the governor general or lieutenant governor is still a subject of the Queen and thus compellable": Sankoff, *The Portable Guide to Witnesses*, Toronto, Thomson Carswell, 2006, 12. Section 74(b) modifies this common law position by creating a statutory rule of non-compellability for the New Zealand Governor-General.

881   See EV5.01.

EV74.03 Judges

Section 74(d) renders judges non-compellable to give evidence "in respect of [their] conduct as a Judge".[883] In matters unrelated to official judicial conduct, a judge will be compellable under the Act like any other witness (although, pursuant to s 72(1), not in any proceeding in which they are "acting as a Judge").[884]

EV74.04 Eligibility

Section 74 merely codifies a rule of *non-compellability*. Under s 71 of the Act, any of the persons named in the section will be *eligible* to give evidence in a civil or criminal proceeding if they so choose.[885]

75 Bank officer not compellable to produce banking records

(1) In any proceedings to which a bank is not a party, no officer of the bank is compellable—

     (a)   to produce any banking record of the bank, the contents of which can be proved under section 19; or

     (b)   to appear as a witness to prove the matters, transactions, and amounts recorded in those records.

(2) Subsection (1) is subject to any contrary order of a Judge made for a special reason.

(3) In this section, **bank** means—

     (a)   a registered bank within the meaning of section 2 of the Reserve Bank of New Zealand Act 1989:

     (b)   the Reserve Bank of New Zealand:

     (c)   any other person carrying on in New Zealand the business of banking.

---

882   See, eg, s 5(1) of the Diplomatic Privileges and Immunities Act 1968 (incorporating art 31(2) of the Vienna Convention on Diplomatic Relations 1961 and Optional Protocals, done at Vienna on 18 April 1961 ("A diplomatic agent is not obliged to give evidence as a witness")); s 4(1) of the Consular Privileges and Immunities Act 1971 (incorporating art 44 of the Vienna Convention on Consular Relations 1963 and Optional Protocals, done at Vienna on 24 April 1963 (setting out the conditions under which consular officials are liable to give evidence in judicial proceedings).

883   See EV72.01. In certain circumstances, judicial conduct can be the subject of a civil lawsuit for damages or other remedies. Section 74(d) would prevent the judge whose conduct was at issue in such a lawsuit from being compellable as a witness for the plaintiff. For a discussion of civil claims involving judicial conduct, see New Zealand Law Commission, *Crown Liability and Judicial Immunity: A Response to Baigent's Case and Harvey v Derrick*, NZLC R37, Wellington, 1997.

884   LC *Evidence Code*, para C298. See also EV72.01.

885   See EV71.01.

EV75.01 Non-compellability of bank officers

Section 75 re-enacts s 47C of the Evidence Act 1908. It provides a limited rule of non-compellability for bank officers otherwise compellable to give evidence in civil or criminal proceedings pursuant to s 71.[886]

Section 75(1)(a) provides that, in any proceeding where "a bank is not a party", bank officers cannot be compelled to produce banking records whose contents may be proven under the broad "business records" exception (s 19[887]) to the Act's prohibition on the admission of hearsay evidence (s 17[888]). Nor can a bank officer be compelled "to appear as a witness to prove the matters, transactions and amounts recorded in those records" (s 75(1)(b)).

EV75.02 "Bank", "banking record", and the "business of banking"

"Bank" is defined in s 75(3). As stated in s 75(3)(c), the "business of banking" will encompass building societies and other organisations that accept individual deposits but are not registered banks.[889] "Banking record" (s 75(1)(a)) is not defined. However, it is likely to mean any "business record" of the bank as that term is defined in s 16(1) of the Act.[890]

EV75.03 Policy

Like s 47C of the Evidence Act 1908, the aim of s 75 is "that the time of banking staff should be saved, by dispensing as far as possible with the production of the originals of their business records in Court, and their attendance in Court".[891] Similarly, and according to the parliamentary Select Committee that reported on the Act, "it [is] reasonable that a bank officer should not be compelled to appear in court in order to produce banking records of which they [are] unlikely to have specific personal knowledge".[892] Indeed, under the hearsay exception codified in s 47B of the Evidence Act 1908, and subject to certain safeguards, copies of banking records were admissible as "prima facie evidence ... of the matters, transactions, and accounts recorded in those records". Assuming its requirements can be satisfied,[893] the same result can now be achieved under s 19 — the "business records" exception to the Evidence Act's prohibition on hearsay evidence (s 17) — which s 75(1)(a) substitutes for s 47B of the Evidence Act 1908.

EV75.04 Judicial discretion

With respect to the circumstances set out in s 75(1), the rule of bank-officer non-compellability "is subject to any contrary order of a Judge made for a special reason" (s 75(2)). However, the Act is silent regarding the circumstances that will

---

886   See EV71.01.
887   See EV19.01.
888   See EV17.01.
889   See *United Dominions Trust Ltd v Kirkwood* [1966] 2 QB 431; [1966] 2 WLR 1083.
890   See EV16.02.01.
891   *Cross on Evidence* (8th NZ ed), 696.
892   *Select Committee Report on the Evidence Bill*, 9.
893   See EV75.05.

qualify as a "special reason" under s 75(2). Possible scenarios are where a bank officer has personal knowledge regarding transactions recorded in bank records that are relevant to civil or criminal proceedings, or where the bank officer's presence at trial is necessary to explain the records or clarify any relevant information they may contain. Evidence that a bank record had been altered, or was somehow unreliable, could also constitute a "special reason" for a bank officer to testify under s 75(2) (as well as impacting the admissibility of the record under s 19 of the Act and hence the applicability of s 75(1) at first instance).

EV75.05   Admissibility of banking records

When combined with the hearsay (business records) admissibility provision of s 19, the non-compellability rule of s 75 effectively eliminates a party's need or ability to call bank officers as witnesses where: (1) the proceeding does not involve the bank as a party; (2) there is no "special reason" to call the bank officer as a witness; and (3) the evidence sought by the party are merely banking records containing information or transactions relevant to the particular civil or criminal case. However, while s 75(1)(a) relieves bank officers from producing banking records whose contents can be admitted under s 19, a party will still need to offer evidence that, with respect to the documents in question, the requirements of s 19 have been satisfied.[894]

76   Evidence of jury deliberations

(1)   A person must not give evidence about the deliberations of a jury.

(2)   Subsection (1) does not prevent the giving of evidence about matters that do not form part of the deliberations of a jury, including (without limitation)—

     (a)   the competency or capacity of a juror; or

     (b)   any conduct of, or knowledge gained by, a juror that is believed to disqualify that juror from holding that position.

(3)   Subsection (1) does not prevent a person from giving evidence about the deliberations of a jury if the Judge is satisfied that the particular circumstances are so exceptional that there is a sufficiently compelling reason to allow that evidence to be given.

(4)   In determining, under subsection (3), whether to allow evidence to be given in any proceedings, the Judge must weigh—

     (a)   the public interest in protecting the confidentiality of jury deliberations generally:

     (b)   the public interest in ensuring that justice is done in those proceedings.

---

894   See EV19.01. See also *Adams on Criminal Law — Evidence*, EC10.06(1)(e) (discussing the admissibility of "business records" under s 3(1)(b) of the Evidence Amendment Act (No 2) 1980 (the predecessor to s 19 of the Evidence Act 2006)).

EV76.01   Overview

Section 76 prohibits the giving of evidence about the deliberations of a jury, in order to promote finality of verdicts and unencumbered discussion during deliberations. It therefore prohibits anything said or done during the time that the jury was performing its fact finding function.[895]

EV76.02   Content, not venue, important

The rule does away with any remnant of a distinction made at common law between impropriety inside or outside the jury room.[896] Section 76 makes it clear that it is not the venue that guides the operation of the prohibition, but the likely content of discussions. Therefore, deliberative conversations that take place outside of the jury room will be covered by s 76 unless the exception in s 76(3) applies.

EV76.03   Evidence not forming part of deliberations admissible

As the focus is on the performance of the fact-finding function, anything said or done in the jury room that was not concerned with that function may be admissible. To this end, s 76(2) provides that subs (1) "does not prevent the giving of evidence about matters that do not form part of the deliberations of a jury". Subsection (2) cites competence, capacity and disqualifying conduct as examples of matters concerning which evidence may be able to be given, but this is not an exhaustive list. Who is not competent or capable of being a juror is governed by ss 7 and 8 of the Juries Act 1981, and clearly capacity includes issues such as intellectual disability. Disqualifying conduct includes a juror making her own inquiries into the case.[897]

EV76.04   Subsection (3): exception to general prohibition

Subsection (3) contains an exception to the general prohibition in subs (1), whereby evidence about the deliberations of a jury may be given if the judge is satisfied that there are exceptional circumstances amounting to a sufficiently compelling reason to allow the evidence. This is a high standard to reach. An example of "circumstances so exceptional" that there may be "a sufficiently compelling reason" to allow evidence

---

895   Section 76 differs from both the draft legislation and the Law Commission's draft Code. The Law Commission proposed that evidence of juror deliberations should be allowed only if it was offered in order to establish that a juror acted in breach of his or her duty. The draft Bill contained a different public interest weighing than that found in the Act: the public interest in protecting the confidentiality of the jury deliberations was to be weighed against the public interest in avoiding or remedying any possible miscarriage of justice. Section 76 has a broader approach that "justice is done in those proceedings", which includes, but presumably is not limited to, avoiding a miscarriage of justice.

896   Older cases spoke of "prising open the door of the jury room", and protecting what went on in the jury room or jury box (see *R v Norton-Bennett* [1990] 1 NZLR 559; (1990) 5 CRNZ 496 (CA) for reference to some of these phrases). It has become clear that the content of the discussions is the overriding factor: *R v Norton-Bennett*; *R v Absolum* 21/8/03, CA118/03, para 8.

897   For an example, see New Zealand Law Commission, *Juries in Criminal Trials*, NZLC PP37, Wellington, 1999.

---

of deliberations could be where there is evidence that the jury used inappropriate methods of deliberation, such as the use of a Ouija board.[898]

Subpart 2—Oaths and affirmations

(s 77 to s 78)

77   Witnesses to give evidence on oath or affirmation

(1)   A witness in a proceeding who is of or over the age of 12 years must take an oath or make an affirmation before giving evidence.

(2)   A witness in a proceeding who is under the age of 12 years—

(a)   must be informed by the Judge of the importance of telling the truth and not telling lies; and

(b)   must, after being given that information, make a promise to tell the truth, before giving evidence.

(3)   Evidence given by a witness to whom subsection (2) applies must be treated in the same manner as if that evidence had been given on oath.

(4)   Despite subsections (1) and (2), a witness—

(a)   to whom either of those subsections applies may give evidence without taking an oath, or making an affirmation, or making a promise to tell the truth, with the permission of the Judge; and

(b)   if the Judge gives permission under paragraph (a), must be informed by the Judge of the importance of telling the truth and not telling lies, before the witness gives evidence; and

(c)   after being given the information referred to in paragraph (b), may give evidence which must be treated in the same manner as if that evidence had been given on oath.

EV77.01   Overview

Section 77 provides that a witness over the age of 12 years must take an oath or make an affirmation before giving evidence (s 77(1)).[899] Provisions for witnesses under 12 years are outlined in s 77(2) and (3), and an exception to the general requirements in s 77(1) and (2) is contained in s 77(4).

EV77.02   Confined to "proceedings"

Section 77 is limited to a witness in a proceeding — as defined by s 4, a proceeding must be conducted by a court. As such, s 77 does not govern proceedings other than those defined by s 4 (for example, tribunals are not included).[900]

---

898   *R v Young* [1995] 2 WLR 430 (CA).

899   The requirements in s 77 must be complied with for video record evidence: Evidence Regulations 2007, reg 8.

900   See EV4.35.01.

EV77.03   Witnesses under 12 years of age

Section 77(2) achieves in part the Law Commission's recommended abolition of the competence requirement, and the duty to test competence, for witnesses under 12 years of age. The Law Commission's draft Code prohibited the use of oaths, affirmations or promises for witnesses under 12 years. The Law Commission stated that "it makes little sense to allow a child to promise to tell the truth when no inquiry may be made into what that promise means to them".[901] By contrast, s 77(2) requires that children under 12 years promise to tell the truth unless s 77(4)(a) applies.

The requirement under s 77(2)(a) that the judge inform the witness under 12 years of the importance of telling the truth was included in order to ensure that the witness is aware of the solemnity of the occasion; the reference to "not telling lies" recognises that it may be easier to understand the concept of not telling lies than that of telling the truth.

EV77.04   Oaths and affirmations

There is no prohibition in s 77 on those under 12 years giving evidence on oath or making an affirmation, but s 77(2) assumes that younger witnesses will not do so. This is illustrated by the requirement that all witnesses in a proceeding who are under 12 years are informed of the importance of telling the truth and not telling lies, and then must make a promise to tell the truth.[902] Where a promise is made, an oath or affirmation would be redundant. Section 77(3) provides that evidence given by witnesses under 12 years must be treated in the same manner as if the evidence had been given on oath, which presupposes that a witness under 12 years will not take an oath or make an affirmation.

If a witness under 12 years wished to take an oath, it may be that the common law would apply by virtue of s 12. A child under 12 years would be able to give evidence under oath or affirmation if he or she is determined by the judge to be capable of understanding the nature and consequences of doing so.[903]

EV77.05   Subsection (4): evidence may be admitted without oath, affirmation or promise

Section 77(4) provides an exception to subss (1) and (2), whereby the judge can give permission to allow evidence where there has been no oath, affirmation or promise to tell the truth (s 77(4)(a)). Where evidence is allowed on this basis, the judge must inform the witness of the importance of telling the truth and not telling lies. Once this is done, s 77(4)(c) provides that the evidence be treated in the same manner as if it had been given on oath. There is no indication in s 77 regarding when permission under subs (4) should be given. However, it could possibly be used as an equivalent of subs (2) for adult witnesses, such as those with an intellectual disability.

---

901   LC *Evidence Reform*, para 352.

902   See *R v Tanner* 6/9/07, CA82/07; [2007] NZCA 391, para 23.

903   *R v Shelley* 10/8/06, CA498/05.

As s 77(4) applies to both child and adult witnesses, it may also be used where a child is unable to promise to tell the truth. Although s 77(4)(c) prevents the lack of oath having relevance, the manner in which the evidence is given may still affect the way that the evidence is treated, for example, where the tribunal of fact considers that the witness has limited understanding of the questions.

78 Interpreters to act on oath or affirmation

A person must either take an oath or make an affirmation before acting as an interpreter in a proceeding.

EV78.01 Overview

Section 78 codifies the previous law, which required a court interpreter to take an oath or make an affirmation.

The definition of interpreter in s 4 is "a person who provides communication assistance to a defendant or witness".[904] The Law Commission envisaged that the form of oath required under s 78 would be provided in regulations. Although this is not specifically provided for in s 201 (the provision in the Act related to the making of regulations), it is likely that it will be included in s 201(j), which governs communication assistance generally; or alternatively under s 201(o) (which provides for regulations regarding any matters contemplated by the Act or necessary for its administration or to give it full effect).

Subpart 3—Support, communication assistance, and views

(s 79 to s 82)

79 Support persons

(1) A complainant, when giving evidence in a criminal proceeding, is entitled to have 1 person, and may, with the permission of the Judge, have more than 1 person, near him or her to give support.

(2) Any other witness, when giving evidence in any proceeding, may with the permission of the Judge, have 1 or more support persons near him or her to give support.

(3) Despite subsections (1) and (2), the Judge may, in the interest of justice, direct that support may not be provided to a complainant or to a witness by—

    (a) any person; or

    (b) a particular person.

(4) A complainant or other witness who is to have a support person near him or her while giving evidence must, unless the Judge orders otherwise, disclose to all parties as soon as practicable the name of each person who is to provide that support.

---

904   See EV80.01 and EV4.24.01.

(5)   The Judge may give directions regulating the conduct of a person providing or receiving support under this section.

EV79.01   Rationale for allowing support persons

Section 79 provides for support persons for both complainants[905] and witnesses. The rationale is that having someone close by that the witness trusts will help him or her to give complete evidence.[906] Complete evidence is more likely to be useful evidence.[907]

EV79.02   Not limited to sexual cases

Section 79(1) extends the practice under the previous law of allowing complainants in sexual cases to have a support person near when they are giving evidence.[908] Section 79(1) is not limited to sexual cases; rather, it applies for complainants in all criminal proceedings.

EV79.03   Subsection (1): entitlement for complainants

Section 79(1) provides an entitlement to a support person for complainants.[909] This entitlement will apply regardless of the way in which evidence is given (for example, where a complainant gives evidence by closed-circuit television under s 105, a support person could be present in the room). If a complainant wishes to have more than one support person present, an application must be made to the judge.[910]

Section 375A(3)(b) of the Crimes Act 1961 requires the judge in a case of a sexual nature to advise the complainant of his or her right to request the presence of a support person. Section 375A(3)(b) has not been amended by the 2006 Act, and as such that section's requirements continue to apply only to complainants in sexual cases.

---

905   "Complainant" has been held to refer to the person involved in the offending, the alleged victim, who did or could have complained — the complainant is not necessarily the person who actually made the complaint: *A v Registrar of the District Court at Christchurch* (2006) 22 CRNZ 374; [2006] NZAR 195, paras 13-16, 21, 22.

906   LC *Evidence Reform*, 98.

907   It is, of course, open to the judge to direct the jury that the law permits support persons to be present, and that no adverse inference against the defendant should be drawn by the reason of the support person's presence: see *R v Russell* 2/11/07, Stevens J, HC Auckland CRI-2006-092-11084, para 19, for an example.

908   Crimes Act 1961, s 375A(3)(b).

909   Section 121 of the Intellectual Disability (Compulsory Care and Rehabilitation) Act 2003 also provides for support persons for care recipients.

910   Whether or not to grant permission for more than one support person is a matter of discretion for the judge. In *R v Russell* 2/11/07, Stevens J, HC Auckland CRI-2006-092-11084, the views of the witness were seen to be relevant. There, special consideration was given to the promotion of recovery for the complainant, allying the decision with the consideration in s 103 (particularly s 103(4)(b)(ii), see EV103.15). In *Russell*, the provision of a second, female, support person was seen to promote recovery of the complainant (paras 13-14).

EV79.04   Subsection (2): provision of support person discretionary for witnesses other than complainants

Section 79(2) provides that witnesses in both criminal and civil proceedings may apply to the judge to be able to have one or more support persons near. There is no limitation included in s 79 with regard to defendants in criminal cases, who may therefore apply to have a support person should they decide to give evidence. The Law Commission envisaged that the judge should consider some of the factors relevant to alternative ways of giving evidence under s 103(3) in deciding whether to allow a witness to have a support person.[911]

EV79.05   Judge can limit nature of support allowed

(1)   Subsection (3): Limits on who can support

Section 79(3) provides that the judge can direct "in the interests of justice" that support may not be provided to a complainant or witness. This may be a direction that no person will be allowed to support the complainant or witness, or that a particular person may not provide the support. The Law Commission gave the example of a public figure being vetoed because their support may affect the jury's assessment of the witness's veracity.[912] Therefore, the entitlement under s 79(1) may be withdrawn either fully or partially.

In considering the making of a direction under s 79(3), the judge will consider where the interests of justice lie — for example, in *R v E*,[913] the Court held that the mere presence of a mother may be inhibiting to a child complainant and can be one factor to consider. Whether or not the judge directs that a support person is replaced will depend on the availability of other suitable people.[914]

Section 79(3) can be exercised during the giving of evidence should there be an abuse of the process.

(2)   Subsection (5): regulation of witness and support person's actions

The function of support persons is to reduce stress and trauma for the witness. As implicitly indicated in s 79(1) and (2), support persons are allowed merely to "support" the witness, not to prompt or advise.[915] Section 79(5) allows the judge to give directions regulating the witness and/or their support person in furtherance of this desired function. For example, directions may relate to how close the support person can be to the witness or to how support persons can act.[916]

---

911   LC *Evidence Code*, para C308. See EV103.08-14.

912   LC *Evidence Reform*, 98.

913   *R v E* 11/9/07, CA308/06; [2007] NZCA 404.

914   *R v E* 11/9/07, CA308/06; [2007] NZCA 404, para 42-44.

915   LC *Evidence Code*, para C306.

916   Directions may prevent support persons from doing anything to distract the witness, or from reacting to the evidence given: *R v Russell* 2/11/07, Stevens J, HC Auckland CRI-2006-092-11084, para 17.

EV79.06   Subsection (4): disclosure of names of support persons

Section 79(4) requires that the names of support persons are disclosed to all parties. This will give other parties the opportunity to make submissions on suitability where the proposed support person has had any relevant prior involvement in the case.[917] The judge may order that disclosure is not required. For example, where there is a witness anonymity order in place by virtue of s 112, identification of the support person could lead to identification of the witness, and so the judge may rule that disclosure of the support person's name is not required, in order to protect identity of the witness.

80   Communication assistance

(1)   A defendant in a criminal proceeding is entitled to communication assistance, in accordance with this section and any regulations made under this Act, to—

    (a)   enable the defendant to understand the proceeding; and

    (b)   give evidence if the defendant elects to do so.

(2)   Communication assistance may be provided to a defendant in a criminal proceeding on the application of the defendant in the proceeding or on the initiative of the Judge.

(3)   A witness in a civil or criminal proceeding is entitled to communication assistance in accordance with this section and any regulations made under this Act to enable that witness to give evidence.

(4)   Communication assistance may be provided to a witness on the application of the witness or any party to the proceeding or on the initiative of the Judge.

(5)   Any statement made in Court to a Judge or a witness by a person providing communication assistance must, if known by the person making that statement to be false and intended by that person to be misleading, be treated as perjury for the purposes of sections 108 and 109 of the Crimes Act 1961.

EV80.01   Overview

Sections 80 and 81 govern the provision of communication assistance for both defendants and other witnesses. Section 80 anticipates regulations detailing procedures to be followed in the provision of communication assistance (see s 201(j)). These have not yet been enacted. Section 81 outlines when communication assistance will not need to be provided.

Section 4 defines communication assistance as "assistance that enables or facilitates communication" with persons who do not have sufficient proficiency in the English language to understand and give evidence, or who have a communication disability.[918] Communication assistance may include assistance such as provision of an interpreter, and any other mechanism or technological aid that can help witnesses

---

917   *R v E* 11/9/07, CA308/06; [2007] NZCA 404, para 42.
918   See EV4.05.01.

and defendants to give or understand evidence. [919] "Communication disability" is not defined in the Act.

Section 80(2) and (4) allow for communication assistance to be provided on application or on the initiative of the judge. An interpreter may be present during the recording of video evidence under the Evidence Regulations 2007.[920]

EV80.02   Defendants

Section 80(1) provides that the defendant in a criminal proceeding is entitled to communication assistance to enable understanding of the proceeding (regardless of whether the defendant gives evidence), and also to enable the defendant to give evidence should he or she elect to do so. This is in accordance with s 24(g) of the New Zealand Bill of Rights Act 1990, which provides that "everyone who is charged with an offence ... shall have the right to have the free assistance of an interpreter if the person cannot understand or speak the language used in court". The entitlement is subject to s 81(1), whereby communication assistance will not be provided should the judge consider that the defendant can understand the proceeding and/or understand and answer oral questions without the aid of communication assistance.

EV80.03   Witnesses other than defendants

Section 80(3) provides that a witness in both civil and criminal proceedings will be entitled to communication assistance. Unlike defendants, witnesses are entitled to communication assistance only to allow them to give evidence. The difference between s 80(1) and (3) reflects the requirements for a fair trial, whereby the defendant needs to understand what is being said in order to be able to participate in his or her own defence.

EV80.04   False statements treated as perjury

Section 80(5) is linked to the requirement that an interpreter takes an oath or makes an affirmation under s 78. If the interpreter makes a statement in court to a judge or a witness that he or she knows to be false, and intends to be misleading, it will be treated as perjury under ss 108 and 109 of the Crimes Act 1961. Section 108 requires that the witness makes an assertion "known to the witness to be false and being intended by him to mislead the tribunal". The reference in s 80(5) to a statement *to a witness* must be therefore be shown to have been intended to mislead *the tribunal* before the statement can be considered to constitute perjury.

81   Communication assistance need not be provided in certain circumstances

(1)   Communication assistance need not be provided to a defendant in a criminal proceeding if the Judge considers that the defendant—

     (a)   can sufficiently understand the proceeding; and

---

919   Section 14 of the Intellectual Disability (Compulsory Care and Rehabilitation) Act 2003 also provides for interpreters for care recipients where practicable.

920   Evidence Regulations 2007 (SR 2007/204), reg 7.

(b)   if the defendant elects to give evidence, can sufficiently understand questions put orally and can adequately respond to them.

(2)   Communication assistance need not be provided to a witness in a civil or a criminal proceeding if the Judge considers that the witness can sufficiently understand questions put orally and can adequately respond to them.

(3)   The Judge may direct what kind of communication assistance is to be provided to a defendant or a witness.

EV81.01   Overview

Section 81 limits s 80 by providing for instances where communication assistance need not be provided, and for judicial control of the kind of communication assistance allowed to be provided to a defendant or witness.

As the purpose of communication assistance is to aid in understanding the proceeding and in understanding and responding to questions put orally, it need only be provided when the defendant or witness is unable to understand the proceedings and/or the questions put to them. Section 81(1) and (2) allows the judge to refuse provision of communication assistance where he or she considers that a defendant can sufficiently understand the proceeding (s 81(1)) or where he or she considers that a defendant or witness can "sufficiently" understand questions put orally and "adequately" respond to them. This clearly focuses on oral questioning, which is the ordinary way of giving evidence.[921] There is no guidance in the Act regarding what level of understanding will be "sufficient" or on what would constitute an "adequate" response. It is to be presumed that such guidance is lacking in order to allow judges to decide those issues in light of the circumstances or the nature of the case. For example, in a criminal proceeding, a level of ability that constitutes sufficient understanding for a straightforward case of assault may not be sufficient for a complex fraud case.

82   Views

(1)   If, in any proceeding, the Judge considers that a view is in the interests of justice, the Judge may—

(a)   hold a view; or

(b)   if there is a jury, order a view.

(2)   A view may be held or ordered on the application of any party or on the Judge's own initiative.

(3)   If there is a jury, a view may be ordered to be held at any time before the jury retires, and the Judge may order a further view of the same place or thing during the jury's deliberations.

(4)   If there is not a jury, the Judge may hold a view at any time before judgment is delivered.

921   See EV83.01-02. Section 83 codifies the common law tradition of oral evidence in open court. For alternative ways of giving evidence, see EV102.01-EV106.03.

(5)   Information obtained at a view may be used as though that information had been given in evidence.

(6)   Every party, including the defendant in a criminal proceeding, and lawyers for the parties, is entitled to attend a view, but any party, or that party's lawyer, may waive that entitlement.

(7)   In this section, **view** means an inspection by the Judge or, if there is a jury, by the Judge and jury, of a place or thing that is not in the courtroom.

EV82.01   Overview

Section 82 re-enacts and amends s 28 of the Juries Act 1981 (which was repealed by s 215 of the Evidence Act 2006) and outlines when a view may be held, who is entitled to be present, and the use to which information gained from a view may be put. "View" is defined in s 82(7) as "an inspection of a place or thing that is not in the courtroom".

Section 82 applies to both civil and criminal proceedings but is not intended to hamper the effect of High Court and District Courts Rules providing for "inspection, observation and experimentation in civil proceedings".[922] The judge retains the discretion to hold a view "in the interests of justice".

Section 82 is restricted to views. The Law Commission considered that the use of visual aids in the giving of evidence could be dealt with under the court's inherent powers.[923] Demonstrations and reconstructions will be subject to ss 7 and 8.[924]

Section 82(2) allows for a view to be held or ordered on the judge's own initiative or on the application of any party. In criminal proceedings tried before a jury, a view may be ordered to be held before the jury retires and again during deliberations (s 82(3)).

One important clarification afforded by s 82 is who can and should be present at a view (s 82(6)). All parties and their lawyers are entitled to attend a view, but the entitlement may be waived.

EV82.02   Information gained from a view can be used as evidence

Under s 82(5), information obtained at a view may be used as though the information had been given in evidence. This represents a possible change from the common law position, depending on the circumstances in which views will be ordered under s 82(1). In *R v McGregor*,[925] two purposes of views were identified. First, a view can be held in order to "orient the jury within the overall framework of a case", thereby allowing them to follow the evidence and understand questions raised.[926] Secondly, a view can be held in order to assess a scene or situation. Before the 2006 Act, information yielded from a view conducted for the former purpose could not be used as part of the evidence at trial. Information gained from a view held to assess a scene

---

922   See High Court Rules, r 322, and District Courts Rules 1992, r 340.
923   LC *Evidence Reform*, para 375.
924   See EV25.01(4).
925   *R v McGregor* (1999) 16 CRNZ 606 (CA).
926   *R v McGregor* (1999) 16 CRNZ 606 (CA), para 24.

or situation could be used as though the information was given in court. The Act does not differentiate between these different purposes of views — provided that the judge orders a view in the "interests of justice" under s 82(1), all information gained at the view can be used as though it was given in evidence.

Subpart 4—Questioning of witnesses

(s 83 to s 101)

83   Ordinary way of giving evidence

(1)   The ordinary way for a witness to give evidence is,—

    (a)   in a criminal or civil proceeding, orally in a courtroom in the presence of—

        (i)   the Judge or, if there is a jury, the Judge and jury; and

        (ii)   the parties to the proceeding and their counsel; and

        (iii)   any member of the public who wishes to be present, unless excluded by order of the Judge; or

    (b)   in a criminal proceeding, in an affidavit filed in the court or by reading a written statement in a courtroom, if both the prosecution and the defendant consent to the giving of evidence in this form; or

    (c)   in a civil proceeding, in an affidavit filed in the court or by reading a written statement in a courtroom, if—

        (i)   rules of court permit or require the giving of evidence in this form; or

        (ii)   both parties consent to the giving of evidence in this form.

(2)   An affidavit or a written statement referred to in subsection (1)(b) or (c) may be given in evidence only if it—

    (a)   is the personal statement of the deponent or maker; and

    (b)   does not contain a statement that is otherwise inadmissible under this Act.

EV83.01   Ordinary way of giving evidence

Section 83(1)(a) codifies the ordinary mode of witness testimony in civil and criminal proceedings.[927] For explanation of the term "witness", see the discussion in s 4(1).[928]

The mode of testifying set out in s 83(1)(a) will be the normal and expected manner of witness testimony in civil and criminal trials. However, if both the prosecution and defence consent, the ordinary manner for a witness to give evidence in a criminal proceeding will also include evidence given in "an affidavit filed in the court or by

---

927   See *R v Accused (T4/88)* [1989] 1 NZLR 660 (CA), 664 (per Cooke P); *R v Teariki* (1999) 16 CRNZ 540; *Aeromotive Ltd v Page* 16/5/02, Harrison J, HC Hamilton CP31/99; *R v Wong* 1/5/06, Williams J, HC Auckland CRI-2005-004-15296; *R v MacLeod* 7/6/06, Williams J, HC Auckland CRI-2005-404-2389.

928   See EV4.46.01.

reading a written statement in a courtroom" (s 83(1)(b)). In a civil case, the same will be true if both parties consent (s 83(1)(c)(ii))[929] or — as provided by various provisions of the High Court Rules — if the "rules of court permit or require the giving of evidence in this form" (s 83(1)(c)(i)).[930] Accordingly, s 83 will not impact the current practice in civil proceedings of trial witnesses reading prepared briefs of evidence as a substitute for ordinary (oral) examination in chief (a procedure that is enshrined in rr 441A–441I of the High Court Rules).[931]

EV83.02   Policies underlying s 83

A seemingly unremarkable provision, s 83 actually codifies important and longstanding traditions at common law. As set out in s 83(1)(a)(iii), principles of "open justice" have always mandated that trial proceedings be accessible to members of the public.[932] And as reflected in s 83(1)(a)(i) and (ii), the physical presence of witnesses has always been considered a significant factor in adversarial court hearings.[933] Principled exceptions to s 83 have been recognised in the Evidence Act itself, other statutory directives, and existing case law.[934] Nonetheless, in most but certainly not all circumstances, the presentation and testing of evidence — as well as the integrity of civil and criminal trial processes — will be facilitated when the judge, jury, witnesses, lawyers and parties are all present and within sight of each other in open court.[935]

---

929   See, eg, r 500 of the High Court Rules:

> **"500. Evidence by affidavit by agreement**
> "(1)   In any proceeding heard by a Judge sitting without a jury, the parties may file an agreement signed by the parties, that the evidence, or any part of the evidence, shall be given by affidavit."

See also s 9 of the Evidence Act 2006, discussed at EV9.01.

930   See, eg, r 496 of the High Court Rules:

> **"496. Evidence to be given orally**
> "Except where otherwise directed by the Court or required or authorised by these rules or by any Act, disputed questions of fact arising at the trial of any proceeding shall be determined on evidence given by means of witnesses examined orally in open Court."

For a discussion of r 496 and its exceptions in civil proceedings, see *McGechan on Procedure*, HR496.01-03.

931   Pursuant to r 441F, evidence in chief in civil cases is usually given by a witness reading a written affidavit previously served on opposing parties in the case. See *McGechan on Procedure*, HR441A.01-HR441I.01. See also the discussion of ss 84 and 89 of the Act, respectively, at EV84.02 and EV89.05.

932   New Zealand Law Commission, *Access to Court Records*, NZLC R93, Wellington, 2006, 6.

933   See *Aeromotive Ltd v Page* 16/5/02, Harrison J, HC Hamilton CP31/99; *R v Kahui* 10/7/07, Williams J, HC Auckland CRI-2006-057-1135. See, however, *Churchill Group Holdings Ltd v Aral Property Holdings Ltd* 26/10/06, Williams J, HC Auckland CIV-2001-404-2302.

934   See EV83.04.

935   For examples of circumstances in which alternative modes of testifying were said to improve the cogency and reliability of a witness's evidence, see *R v Hekkenberg* 8/11/06, Gendall J, HC Nelson CRI-2005-042-4128; *R v Kahui* 10/7/07, Williams J, HC Auckland CRI-2006-057-1135; *R v E* 11/9/07, CA308/06; [2007] NZCA 404.

(1)   New Zealand Bill of Rights Act 1990

The mandate of s 83 is particularly important in criminal proceedings, where non-standard modes of witness testimony — or judicial orders excluding spectators from the courtroom — can implicate various provisions of the New Zealand Bill of Rights Act 1990.[936] These include the accused's right to: (a) "a fair and public hearing" (s 25(a)); (b) "be present at the trial and to present a defence" (s 25(e)); and (c) "examine witnesses for the prosecution" (s 25(f)).[937] In criminal proceedings, any judicial decision to modify the ordinary manner of witness testimony set out in s 83(1)(a) must be made with those rights in mind.[938]

EV83.03   Personal statement of deponent or maker

Under s 83(2), witnesses giving evidence by affidavits filed or statements read in court can do so only if the document "is the personal statement of the deponent or maker" (s 83(2)(a)); and "does not contain a statement that is otherwise inadmissible under this Act" (s 83(2)(b)).

Section 83(2) was added during Select Committee proceedings on the Evidence Act and is somewhat difficult to comprehend. Indeed, there seems little reason for s 83(2)(b) since, by definition, evidence that is "otherwise inadmissible under [the] Act" cannot be made admissible by inserting it into a written statement or affidavit intended for use in court. However, in this regard, and subject to a judicial determination that the meaning of an affidavit or written statement will remain clear, s 91 of the Act would permit a party to edit the inadmissible parts of any such document before employing it as witness testimony in a civil or criminal case.[939] Moreover, "with the written or oral agreement of all parties" (s 9(1)(a)) and in "any form or way" (s 9(1)(b)), s 9 allows a judge to admit evidence in a civil or criminal

---

936   This follows from application of s 6 of the New Zealand Bill of Rights Act 1990, which, to the extent possible, requires all legislative enactments to be read consistently with the rights set out in the Bill of Rights. See Rishworth, Huscroft, Optican, and Mahoney, *The New Zealand Bill of Rights*, Melbourne, Oxford University Press, 2003, Ch 4.

937   See also s 123(2) of the Evidence Act 2006 (requiring the judge in a criminal case to direct a jury that, when the law makes "special provision" for a witness to testify or be questioned in an alternative way, "the jury must not draw any adverse inference against the defendant because of that manner of giving evidence or questioning").

938   Relevant sections of the Bill of Rights related to fair trial processes will affect decisions under various provisions of the Evidence Act giving judges a discretion to permit alternative modes of witness testimony in criminal proceedings. See, eg, ss 103(4)(a)(ii), 107(4)(a)(ii), and 112(4)(c) of the Evidence Act 2006. For a discussion of the impact of the Bill of Rights on the judicial discretion to permit alternative modes of witness testimony in a criminal trial, see Rishworth, Huscroft, Optican, and Mahoney, *The New Zealand Bill of Rights*, Melbourne, Oxford University Press, 2003, 697-704. Fairness to parties in civil proceedings should likewise impact the judicial discretion to employ non-standard modes of witness testimony in a civil trial. See, eg, s 103(4)(a)(i) of the Evidence Act (providing that the judicial discretion to permit witnesses in civil proceedings to give evidence in an alternative way must take into account "(a) the need to ensure ... the fairness of the proceeding"). See also EV103.01.

939   See EV91.01.

---

proceeding that would not otherwise be admissible under the Act.[940] In such circumstances, s 83(2)(b) will not apply.

(1)   Policies underlying s 83(2)(a)

The ostensible reason for s 83(2)(a) is set out in the parliamentary debates accompanying passage of the Evidence Act. According to Christopher Finlayson MP[941]

> "[Section 83] deals with the questioning of witnesses and the ordinary way of giving evidence in criminal or civil proceedings. I particularly want to focus on civil proceedings, because the traditional way in which one gives evidence these days in a civil proceeding is to file what is called a written statement, or brief of evidence, in advance of a trial. The person giving evidence will read that evidence out and then be subjected to cross-examination.

> "The New Zealand Bar Association made a very powerful submission to the committee about the desirability of going back to the old practice of viva voce evidence being given by witnesses in civil proceedings because of the abuses that occur with briefs of evidence that, largely, are prepared by lawyers for their clients. There have been occasions where I have seen people read out briefs of evidence and they did not understand what they were saying or they could not pronounce the words. So we have added a new subclause (2) to [section 83] specifying that any statements made have to be the personal statements of the maker and must not contain statements that are otherwise inadmissible under the legislation.

> •   •   •   •   •

> "I think that should serve to remind practitioners that when they are doing these things—the briefs of evidence—the evidence is to be that of their witness, and they are not to prepare statements of evidence based on what they think the witness may think the evidence is. That kind of practice, as I said, is odious and needs to be stamped out."

Section 83(2)(a) reflects the laudable purpose of ensuring that, in the absence of viva voce testimony led by the calling party, a witness's brief of evidence in a civil proceeding incorporates testimony that would normally be expected during an ordinary (oral) examination in chief. However, as an overarching requirement of admissibility for affidavits or written statements otherwise acceptable under s 83, s 83(2)(a) is silent as to when, and based on what criteria, a document will be "personal" enough to be considered "the personal statement of the deponent or maker" (rather than being the statement of a lawyer involved in the case). Nor is any guidance offered as to exactly how judges might determine compliance with s 83(2)(a). Should a voir dire be held to ascertain whether a document is "the personal statement of the deponent or maker" — a possibility clearly contemplated under

---

940   See EV9.02.

941   Hansard, *Christopher Finlayson: Evidence Bill: Second Reading*, 14 November 2006 ((2006) 635 NZPD 6486) and 21 November 2006 ((2006) 635 NZPD 6651).

s 15 of the Act? [942] Such scenario seems unlikely and unnecessary, particularly since witnesses can be cross-examined in civil proceedings as to whether briefs of evidence actually set out their own version of events in the case. Indeed, in light of the availability of cross-examination to explore such issues, it is not clear why s 83(2)(a) should act as a barrier to the admission of written witness testimony taking the place of oral examination in chief.

(2)   Role for lawyers

It is probably unrealistic to assume that lawyers will have no input into crafting the briefs of evidence that typically substitute for the examination in chief of witnesses in civil proceedings. Section 83(2)(a) does not, in fact, prevent a lawyer from playing any such role. Like the determination regarding the "maker" of a hearsay statement pursuant to s 18 of the Act,[943] a trial judge will undoubtedly approach compliance with s 83(2)(a) as a question of fact in each particular case. Moreover, while s 83(2)(a) sets out criteria of admissibility directed to the court itself, in practical terms, the matter of personal authorship will arise only when an adversary party in civil proceedings raises such issue with regard to a witness's affidavit or written statement. Similarly, if an affidavit or written statement is tendered as witness testimony in a criminal case, the consent of the parties required under s 83(1)(b) will obviate any issues potentially arising under s 83(2)(a).

EV83.04   Alternatives and exceptions to the ordinary way of giving evidence

The ordinary way for a witness to give evidence set out in s 83(1) should be contrasted with the alternative methods of testimony set out in Subpart 5 of Part 3 of the Act (ss 102-120). Similarly, and subject to certain conditions, Subpart 1 of Part 4 of the Act provides for a New Zealand court to receive evidence and submissions by "video link or telephone conference" from Australia (s 168(1)).[944]

(1)   Additional statutory modification of s 83

As it does with every other provision of the Act, s 5(1) also renders s 83 subject to the express mandates of other statutes modifying the ordinary mode of witness testimony in civil and criminal proceedings.

For example, under s 185C of the Summary Proceedings Act 1957, and whether or not the accused consents, complainants in sexual abuse cases will usually give their evidence at preliminary hearings through written statements and without any opportunity for defence cross-examination.[945]

---

942   See the discussion of s 15 of the Act at EV15.01 (establishing rules for a voir dire procedure where, as a preliminary matter, evidence can be given "to prove the facts necessary for deciding whether some other evidence should be admitted in a proceeding …").

943   See EV16.03.01.

944   See also r 446ZC(1) of the High Court Rules (allowing a witness in a civil proceeding in New Zealand to give evidence from Australia by video link or telephone conference).

945   For discussion and application of s 185C, see *R v Accused (CA421/93)* [1994] 2 NZLR 54; (1993) 11 CRNZ 8 (CA); *A v Registrar of the District Court at Christchurch* (2006) 22 CRNZ 374; [2006] NZAR 195.

As applied in case law and under certain circumstances, s 376 of the Crimes Act 1961 and s 61(b) of the Summary Proceedings Act 1957 permit a criminal trial to proceed in the defendant's absence — a significant inroad into the s 83 requirement that courtroom witnesses give their evidence in the presence of the accused.[946]

Finally, while preserving the principle of open trials accessible to members of the public — a position codified in criminal cases by s 138(1) of the Criminal Justice Act 1985[947] — s 83(1)(a)(iii) specifically contemplates that third parties may be excluded from any proceeding (civil or criminal) by order of the court. In this regard, and subject to certain limits with respect to the media,[948] s 138(2) of the Criminal Justice Act 1985 permits judges to clear a criminal courtroom of spectators when "the interests of justice, or of public morality, or of the reputation of any victim of any alleged sexual offence or offence of extortion, or of the security or defence of New Zealand so require." Similarly, s 116(1)(a) of the Evidence Act allows a criminal trial to be "cleared of members of the public" when a judge considers it necessary to shield the identity of a criminal trial witness protected by an anonymity order under ss 110 or 112.

84   Examination of witnesses

(1)   Unless this Act or any other enactment provides otherwise, or the Judge directs to the contrary, in any proceeding—

(a)   a witness first gives evidence in chief; and

(b)   after giving evidence in chief, the witness may be cross-examined by all parties, other than the party calling the witness, who wish to do so; and

(c)   after all parties who wish to do so have cross-examined the witness, the witness may be re-examined.

---

946   Section 376 of the Crimes Act 1961 states:

"376. Presence of the accused

"(1)   Every accused person shall be entitled to be present in Court during the whole of his trial, unless he misconducts himself by so interrupting the proceedings as to render their continuance in his presence impracticable.

"(2)   The Court may permit the accused to be out of Court during the whole or any part of any trial on such terms as it thinks proper."

See also s 158 of the Summary Proceedings Act 1957. Section 61(b) of the Summary Proceedings Act 1957 permits a judge to proceed with the hearing of a summary offence if, after having received reasonable notice to attend, the accused does not personally appear. Pursuant to s 6 of the New Zealand Bill of Rights Act 1990, such provisions will be subject to s 25(e) of the Bill of Rights: the right of a criminal defendant "to be present at the trial and to present a defence". For further discussion of trial in absentia in New Zealand criminal proceedings, see Rishworth, Huscroft, Optican, and Mahoney, *The New Zealand Bill of Rights*, Melbourne, Oxford University Press, 2003, 685-687.

947   Subject to exceptions set out in s 138(2) and (3), s 138(1) of the Criminal Justice Act 1985 provides that "every sitting of any court dealing with any proceedings in respect of an offence shall be open to the public".

948   See s 138(3) of the Criminal Justice Act 1985.

(2)   If a witness gives evidence in an affidavit or by reading a written statement in a courtroom, it is to be treated for the purposes of this Act as evidence given in chief.

EV84.01   Order of examination

Section 84 confirms the right of parties to examine witnesses in civil and criminal cases and codifies the usual order in which witnesses are to be questioned at trial.[949] For explanation of the term "witness", see the discussion in s 4(1).[950]

Under s 84(1)(a), a witness will first give "evidence in chief". This is achieved by "examination in chief" (direct examination) — the process by which a party who has called a witness to give evidence on the party's behalf elicits evidence relevant to the proceedings and favourable to the examiner's case. As a general matter, examination in chief will be subject to the prohibition on leading questions contained in s 89 of the Act, as well as the prohibition on certain unacceptable questions set out in s 85.

Following examination in chief, s 84(1)(b) states that a witness may be "cross-examined" by all other parties in the case wishing to do so. "Cross-examination" is the process by which parties in a proceeding ask leading questions of an adverse witness to: (a) test and cast doubt on the accuracy of the evidence in chief given by the witness; and (b) elicit from the witness relevant facts favourable to the case of the cross-examining party. As a general matter, cross-examination will be subject to: (a) the cross-examination duties contained in s 92 of the Act; (b) limits on the cross-examination of friendly witnesses set out in s 93; (c) limits on the cross-examination of certain witnesses by parties in person under s 95; and (d) the prohibition on certain unacceptable questions codified in s 85. Pursuant to s 94, and subject to the veracity rules set out in s 37(1) and (4), a party may also cross-examine its own witness with leading questions following a judicial declaration that the witness is hostile.

Following the completion of all cross-examination, a witness may be "re-examined" under s 84(1)(c). "Re-examination" is the process by which a calling party seeks to deal with relevant issues of fact and veracity (credibility) raised within the scope of the witness's cross-examination. As a general matter, re-examination, and any further questioning of the witness following re-examination, will be controlled by the rules

---

949   See also s 25(f) of the New Zealand Bill of Rights Act 1990:

> **"25. Minium Standard of Criminal Procedure**
>
> "Everyone who is charged with an offence has, in relation to the determination of the charge, the following minimum rights:
>
> •   •   •   •   •
>
> "(4)   The right to examine the witnesses for the prosecution and to obtain the attendance and examination of witnesses for the defence under the same conditions as the prosecution:"

For a discussion of s 25(f) of the Bill of Rights, see Rishworth, Huscroft, Optican, and Mahoney, *The New Zealand Bill of Rights*, Melbourne, Oxford University Press, 2003, 690-706; Butler and Butler, *The New Zealand Bill of Rights Act: A Commentary*, Wellington, LexisNexis, 2005, 853-863.

950   See EV4.46.01.

codified in s 97 of the Act. It will also be subject to the prohibition on leading questions contained in s 89, as well as the prohibition on certain unacceptable questions set out in s 85.

EV84.02 Varying the order of examination

Section 84(1) provides that a trial judge may vary the order of examination in chief, cross-examination and re-examination if: (a) the Act (or any other enactment) requires it; or (b) in the court's discretion (the circumstances of which are left undefined). The Law Commission commentary to s 84(1) states:[951]

> "This rule codifies the usual order in which a witness gives evidence, subject to the court's inherent powers to regulate its own procedures. In multi-party cases, it is expected that the practice will continue of counsel agreeing on the order in which they cross-examine witnesses, and failing agreement, of counsel cross examining in the order in which the parties appear on the indictment or on the entituling in a civil proceeding."

However, with respect to cross-examination in civil cases, *McGechan on Procedure* notes:[952]

> "This order is subject to variation depending on the extent to which the various parties support or contest the relevant evidence in chief. Those supporting the evidence may be required to go first; those objecting it to follow."

Similarly, and as noted above,[953] a witness in a criminal proceeding called by a party and declared hostile by the court may, at first instance, be cross-examined by the calling party with leading questions pursuant to s 94 of the Act.

Section 84(2) states that, when a witness in a civil or criminal proceeding gives evidence for a calling party through an affidavit or by reading a written statement, such material is to be treated under the Act as "evidence given in chief" (the equivalent of a direct examination viva voce). Provided for in certain circumstances by s 83 of the Act, such practices are typically used in civil proceedings under Rule 441F of the High Court Rules.[954]

EV84.03 Order of witnesses

Section 84 refers only to the normal order of examining witnesses and not the order in which the witnesses themselves may be called to testify during a party's case. However, while it could be subject to judicial control in the interests of fairness, fair trial rights, or the appropriate conduct of proceedings, the sequence in which a party presents witnesses in a civil or criminal trial is generally their own decision.[955]

---

951   LC *Evidence Code*, para C319.

952   See *McGechan on Procedure*, HR487.04(2) (discussing *McKenzie v Robertson* [1940] NZLR 252).

953   See EV84.01.

954   Pursuant to r 441F, evidence in chief in civil cases is usually given by a witness reading a written affidavit previously served on opposing parties in the case. See *McGechan on Procedure*, HR441A.01-HR441I.01. See also the discussion of ss 83 and 89 of the Act, respectively, at EV83.01 and EV89.05.

For example, s 367 of the Crimes Act 1961 sets out the order in which the prosecution and the defendant in a criminal proceeding are to make their opening and closing addresses to the trier of fact. The provision says nothing about the order in which prosecution or defence witnesses may be called or examined. Nonetheless, s 367 makes it clear that, subject to the power of a court to permit further evidence after the close of a party's case under s 98 of the Evidence Act, the prosecution must present its witnesses in a criminal trial prior to any witnesses being called for the defence.[956]

85　　Unacceptable questions

(1)　　In any proceeding, the Judge may disallow, or direct that a witness is not obliged to answer, any question that the Judge considers improper, unfair, misleading, needlessly repetitive, or expressed in language that is too complicated for the witness to understand.

(2)　　Without limiting the matters that the Judge may take into account for the purposes of subsection (1), the Judge may have regard to—

　　(a)　　the age or maturity of the witness; and

　　(b)　　any physical, intellectual, psychological, or psychiatric impairment of the witness; and

　　(c)　　the linguistic or cultural background or religious beliefs of the witness; and

　　(d)　　the nature of the proceeding; and

　　(e)　　in the case of a hypothetical question, whether the hypothesis has been or will be proved by other evidence in the proceeding.

EV85.01　　Unacceptable questions

Section 85 gives the trial judge "a wide discretion to control the nature of ... questions and the manner in which they are put".[957] The discretion permits a judge simply to disallow an unacceptable question or, short of that, to direct that a witness is "not obliged to answer" the question posed (s 85(1)).

Section 85 replaces and extends s 14 of the Evidence Act 1908. Making no distinction between questions directed to veracity (credibility) or facts in issue, s 85 applies to all questioning of witnesses in civil and criminal proceedings and all phases of a witness's examination in court. However, s 85 will most typically be invoked to control cross-examination — whether of an adversary party witness cross-examined in the usual way (s 84(1)(b)), or a hostile witness examined by leading questions during the course of examination in chief (s 94).

955　　See, eg, *R v A* 27/9/06, Stevens J, HC Auckland CRI-2004-004-10735 (noting that, while it has been an accepted convention in criminal cases, there is no rule of law prohibiting a defendant from giving evidence after evidence has been given by witnesses called on the defendant's behalf).

956　　For a discussion of s 367 of the Crimes Act 1961, see *Adams on Criminal Law*, CA367.01-06.

957　　LC *Evidence Code*, para C320.

EV85.02   Types of unacceptable questions

The types of unacceptable questions listed in s 85(1) are wide-ranging. In like fashion, s 85(2) sets out a broad and non-exclusive list of factors guiding the judicial discretion to categorise questions as falling within s 85(1). The provision allows a trial judge to manage questioning based on a witness's individual characteristics, but also encompasses judicial controls on witness examination grounded in the orderly conduct of trials and the rational ascertainment of facts. Taken together, s 85(1) and (2) will therefore embrace questions that are: (a) objectionable in respect of a specific witness; (b) improper in a more general sense; or (c) unacceptable in light of the particular conduct of the proceeding or the nature and circumstances of the case.

EV85.03   Exercise of judicial discretion

Section 85 implicitly accepts the notion of party freedom in the examination of witnesses during civil and criminal trials. Nonetheless, and as noted by the Law Commission, the provision recognises that "what is an acceptable question for one witness may not be for another".[958] Indeed, a principal aim of s 85 is "to enable the judge to ensure that no party or witness is unfairly disadvantaged by the way he or she is questioned".[959] Accordingly, s 85 establishes the trial judge as a protector of witnesses — particularly vulnerable ones — a function in line with many other provisions of the Act.[960] Section 85 will, for example, work in tandem with s 95(6). That provision permits judges to control the form and substance of questions put to certain witnesses by a lawyer — or a court appointed third party — where a "[criminal] defendant or party to a proceeding" is "precluded from personally cross-examining" the witness pursuant to s 95(1) or (2) (s 95(5)).[961]

(1)   Protection of witnesses during examination

The witness-protective function of s 85 is made clear by several of the factors listed in s 85(2) to guide the exercise of judicial discretion under s 85(1). The significance attached to a witness's "cultural background or religious beliefs" is of particular note (s 85(2)(c)). By way of example, the Law Commission discussed how s 85 might be applied to the cross-examination of a Maori kaumatua (elder) in a civil or criminal case:[962]

> "The question-and-answer format is not the way Maori traditionally resolve disputes or discuss issues. Thus cross-examination of kaumatua can amount to an insult to their mana [honour], especially when questioning is directed at impeaching their credibility of exposing them to ridicule. While no sensible exceptions can be made for Maori or other cultural groups under the adversarial system, s 85(2)(c) will allow judges to exert some control over cross-

958   LC *Evidence Reform*, para 391.
959   LC *Evidence Code*, para C322.
960   See, eg, the discussion of the examination of child witnesses in *R v H (CA421/01)* (2002) 19 CRNZ 518 (CA) at EV100.02.
961   See EV95.03.
962   LC *Evidence Code*, para C323.

examination that may be culturally offensive. One way is to encourage counsel to state a possible position to which the kaumatua is invited to respond, instead of directly questioning a kaumatua."

The judicial managing of cross-examination can certainly be an appropriate response to a witness's personal characteristics, or to their cultural, ethnic or religious background. However, when exercising their discretion to control the nature and form of questioning under s 85, judges must be careful not to let the laudable goal of protecting witnesses undermine the purposeful rigour of cross-examination in a civil or criminal trial. Indeed, the parliamentary Select Committee that reviewed the Act removed a reference to "intimidating questioning" from the final version of s 85. As the Select Committee noted:

"There are other definitions of unacceptable questioning which protect the interests of the witness, and we consider that grounds to disallow a question because it is intimidating could lead to a loss of relevant information. Many legitimate lines of cross-examination will be intimidating to some witnesses and we consider that the other protections in [s 85] are sufficient to guide the Judge when deciding whether a question is unacceptable." [963]

Similarly, in *R v Thompson*, the Court of Appeal observed: "robust cross-examination is one of the many options open to counsel, who must be accorded wide discretion".[964] However, "[a]ggressive cross-examination will become improper when it is calculated to humiliate, belittle and break the witness".[965] The Court approved the statement of the High Court of Australia in *Wakeley v R*:[966]

"It is the duty of counsel to ensure that the discretion to cross-examine is not misused. That duty is the more onerous because counsel's discretion cannot be fully supervised by the presiding judge. Of course, there may come a stage when it is clear that the discretion is not being properly exercised. It is at that stage that the judge should intervene to prevent both an undue strain being imposed on the witness and an undue prolongation of the expensive procedure of hearing and determining a case. But until that stage is reached — and it is for the judge to ensure that the stage is not passed — the court is, to an extent, in the hands of cross-examining counsel."

EV85.04   Hypothetical questions

While much of s 85 is new and, as mentioned above,[967] broadens s 14 of the Evidence Act 1908, s 85(2)(e) reflects an existing High Court practice note on the use of hypothetical questions in cross-examination.[968] The practice note states:

---

963   *Select Committee Report on the Evidence Bill*, 10.

964   *R v Thompson* [2006] 2 NZLR 577; (2005) 22 CRNZ 889 (CA), para 66 (affirmed by *Thompson v R* [2006] 2 NZLR 577; (2006) 22 CRNZ 981 (SC)).

965   *R v Thompson* [2006] 2 NZLR 577; (2005) 22 CRNZ 889 (CA), para 68.

966   *R v Thompson* [2006] 2 NZLR 577; (2005) 22 CRNZ 889 (CA), para 66 (citing *Wakeley v R* (1990) 93 ALR 79 (HCA), 86).

967   See EV85.01.

"Procedural Notes

"(Use of Hypothetical Questions in Cross-examination)

"On 19 August 1985 the Right Honourable the Chief Justice issued the following Procedural Notes on the use of hypothetical questions in cross-examination:

"The Judges of the High Court have agreed as a matter of policy to implement the following procedures when counsel endeavour to use hypothetical questions in cross-examination:

"1.   A question in cross-examination which invites an answer on the basis that a witness may give certain evidence will only be permitted if cross-examining counsel gives an assurance, or the question clearly indicates, that the suggested evidence will be adduced.

"2.   If the evidence indicated is not adduced, the presiding Judge may, in the case of a jury trial, point out the failure to do so, and its significance, in summing up."

Prior to allowing a hypothetical question during a witness's cross-examination, s 85 would enable the trial judge to ask cross-examining counsel for a representation that "the hypothesis has been or will be proved by other evidence in the proceeding" (s 85(2)(e)). If such representation does not satisfy the court, s 85(1) would permit the judge to disallow the question as "improper", "misleading" or "unfair". Section 14 of the Act, dealing with the provisional admissibility of evidence in civil and criminal proceedings, would likewise support such result.[969]

EV85.05   Expert witnesses

While it will mainly be relevant to cross-examination, the controls on hypothetical questions suggested by s 85(2)(e) would, like the other considerations in s 85, apply equally to a witness's examination in chief and re-examination. Indeed, particularly with respect to expert opinion evidence admissible under s 25(1) of the Act, hypothetical questions are liable to be posed in all phases of an expert witness's testimony.[970]

86   Restriction of publication

A person commits a contempt of court who prints or publishes,—

---

968   [1985] 1 NZLR 386. For an application of the practice note in a criminal case, see *R v Lintott* 25/9/95, CA168/95. See also r 10.02 of the New Zealand Law Society Rules of Professional Conduct for Barristers and Solicitors (1988). Rule 10.02 states:

> "Counsel must not in the course of making submissions or cross-examining a witness say or lead a witness to say anything that might mislead the court. In particular, counsel must not make any statement to the court or put any proposition to a witness that is not supported by reasonable instructions, or that lacks factual foundation by reference to the information available to the court."

969   See EV14.01.
970   See EV25.05(3).

(a)   without the express permission of the Judge, any question that is disallowed by the Judge, or any evidence given in response to a question of that kind; or

(b)   any question, or any evidence given in response to a question, that the Judge has informed a witness he or she is not obliged to answer and has ordered must not be published.

EV86.01   Restricted publication of questions or answers

Section 86 essentially restates s 15 of the Evidence Act 1908.

Under s 86(a), it is contempt of court to "print or publish" any question disallowed by a judge in court proceedings, or any evidence given in response to a prohibited question, unless the judge gives express permission.[971]

Section 86(b) provides a similar rule for any question that a judge has informed a witness he or she does not have to answer — or any evidence given in response to such a question — and that the judge has ordered must not be published.

Questions or answers subject to s 86 will typically be those caught by s 85. When a judge simply disallows a question under s 85(1), s 86(a) will apply. Section 86(b) will be relevant when a witness is instructed that, pursuant to s 85(1), they may answer a question at their option. Whether the witness chooses to respond to a question after receiving such judicial advice, s 86(b) makes it contempt of court to print or publish the question, or the witness's answer to the question, if the judge has directed that no such disclosure take place.

EV86.02   Scope and purpose of s 86

The principal concern of s 86 is the protection of witnesses and the public interest.[972] Accordingly, the provision can apply to questions put, or answers given, during examination in chief, cross-examination or re-examination in a civil or criminal trial. Equally, the prohibition on printing or publishing suggests a broad scope for s 86. The provision will limit not only routine media reporting, but also any oral or written transmission of the restricted information from one party to another. Finally, the exercise of judicial discretion under s 86 "is not intended to limit the operation of other statutory provisions that allow a judge to order that evidence not be published".[973] An example would be the broad powers given to courts to forbid the publication of evidence in criminal proceedings under s 138(2)(a)(i) of the Criminal Justice Act 1985.[974]

---

971   The penalties available for breaching s 86 in the District Court are contained in s 206 of the Summary Proceedings Act 1957 ("Contempt of Court"). For a discussion of the inherent jurisdiction of the High Court to punish for criminal contempt not committed in the face of the court, see Ellis J, "Contempt of Court" (Part II) in Sir Robin Cooke et al (eds), *The Laws of New Zealand* (1993).

972   See *Taylor v NZ Newspapers Ltd (No 3)* [1938] NZLR 212 (SC, Auckland).

973   LC *Evidence Code*, para C324.

87   Privacy as to witness's precise address

(1)   In any proceeding, the precise particulars of a witness's address (for example, details of the street and number) may not, without the permission of the Judge, be—

(a)   the subject of any question to a witness or included in any evidence given; or

(b)   included in any statement or remark made by a witness, lawyer, officer of the court, or any other person.

(2)   The Judge must not grant permission under subsection (1) unless satisfied that the question to be put, the evidence to be given, or the statement or remark to be made, is of sufficient direct relevance to the facts in issue that to exclude it would be contrary to the interests of justice.

(3)   An application for permission under subsection (1) may be made before or after the commencement of any hearing, and is, where practicable, to be made and dealt with in chambers.

(4)   Nothing in subsection (1) applies in a criminal proceeding if it is necessary to disclose the particulars in the charge in order to ensure that the defendant is fully and fairly informed of the charge.

EV87.01   Admissibility of evidence of witness's address

This is a re-enactment and extension of s 23AA of the Evidence Act 1908 which applied to complainants in cases of a sexual nature, and provided that their address and occupation should not be stated in court, except with leave of the judge. Section 23AA(3) provided that the information could only be given if "of such direct relevance to the facts in issue that to exclude it would be contrary to the interests of justice" — the same test as in s 23A of the Evidence Act 1908 (now found in s 44 of the Evidence Act 2006).[975]

Although s 87(1) gives some guidance on what amounts to "precise particulars of a witness's address" (details of the street and number), this is expressly by way of example only. It is possible to imagine cases where these interests could be prejudiced by a disclosure of even the name of the town or community where the witness lived.

---

974   Section 138(2)(a)(i) of the Criminal Justice Act 1985 provides:

"(2)   Where a court is of the opinion that the interests of justice, or of public morality, or of the reputation of any victim of any alleged sexual offence or offence of extortion, or of the security or defence of New Zealand so require, it may make any one or more of the following orders:

"(a)   An order forbidding publication of any report or account of the whole or any part of—

"(i)   The evidence adduced ..."

975   See EV44.01.

Section 87 is another example of a provision where the context requires that the definition of "witness" include a future testifier.[976] This is because, in referring to "witnesses", it is clear that s 87 intends to prohibit disclosure of the address of a person who is scheduled to give evidence *at a later point in the proceeding*.

As a "witness" is a person who gives evidence and is able to be cross-examined,[977] s 87 seems to also apply to a defendant in a criminal proceeding who elects to testify.

EV87.02   Subsection (2): extension of limitation to cover statements and remarks

The Law Commission stated that the "intention of [the] section is to protect the safety and privacy of witnesses when they give evidence in open court, by not allowing evidence of or statements and questions about the particulars of a witness's address, except with the judge's permission."[978] However, the Act's version of the section is significantly wider in scope than this rationale suggests. The Code's version of s 87(1) stated:

"(1)   Except with the permission of the judge,

    "(a)   no question can be put to any witness and no evidence can be given; and

    "(b)   no statement or remark can be made in court by a witness, lawyer, officer of the court of any other person involved in the proceeding

    as to the precise particulars of a witness's address (for example, by asking or referring to details of the street and number)."

The changes in drafting have widened the effect of s 87 considerably — and perhaps unintentionally. In the Cabinet Paper dealing with the trial process provisions, the Associate Minister of Justice proposed that in order to "preserve a witness's privacy and safety … I propose that a witness's address shall not be disclosed in *open court*, except with the permission of the judge."[979] In commenting on the clause in the Bill, which was enacted unamended, the Ministry of Justice stated: "In all other cases, not just sexual cases, the address of the witness is not generally relevant, and leave should be sought if it is to be *stated in court*."[980] Both these statements indicate it was the intention of the reform only to extend the current provision to all witnesses (whether in criminal or civil proceedings), not to extend the need for leave to all "statements" and "remarks" in any proceeding.

(1)   Comparison with scope of s 88

Section 88(1)(b) retained the Law Commission's drafting and refers only to statements or remarks "made in court" by a limited range of people. Section 87(1) however is only limited by the reference to "in any proceeding" and includes remarks

---

976   See also EV4.46.02.
977   See EV4.46.01.
978   LC *Evidence Code*, para C325.
979   *Cabinet Paper 4*, para 18 (emphasis added).
980   *Departmental Report* (EV/MOJ/2), 13 (emphasis added).

by "any other person" — could this include a member of the public sitting in the court?

EV87.03   A changed admissibility test?

The standard for admissibility in s 87(2) has also changed from the Code — the phrase used in ss 87 and 88 is that the evidence must be of "*sufficient* direct relevance" as opposed to "such" direct relevance. The change was explained by Parliamentary Counsel because "from a plain drafting perspective, 'such' is not a favoured term" and that there is no difference between "such" and "sufficient".[981] The submitters concerned about the change (including the New Zealand Law Society) did not want the standard to be viewed as different or lower than under the previous sections (ss 23A and 23AA):[982]

> "If it is intended to provide a lower standard of relevance (as a natural reading of the words implies), then the Society sees no justification for that reform. If a different standard is not intended then, to avoid future argument, the 'such direct relevance' wording should be carried through to [ss 87 and 88]."

That a difference in interpretation may be the result of a change in wording is more likely given the retention of "*such* direct relevance" in s 44 of the Act.[983]

(1)   Satisfying admissibility test

It is impossible to anticipate all potential occasions in which a judge would be justified in granting permission to disclose a witness's address. One obvious example would be where the importance of the witness's evidence is derived from an observation he or she made from a window in his or her home. The ability of opposing parties to investigate the reliability of that observation may depend on their ability to go to the actual location and observe any potential impediments to the reported observation. Information about where the offence actually occurred may or may not need disclosure of the witness's address (at least in open court) unless it is material. It may be that the granting of permission should, under s 87, be connected to the stage in the proceeding (and perhaps the nature of the proceeding) that the address of the witness is sought to be disclosed.

EV87.04   Practical implications of s 87

In the words of the authors of the New Zealand Law Society seminar on the Evidence Act 2006:[984]

> "In practical terms, counsel will now need to identify instances where a witness's address is directly relevant to the facts in issue. It may be prudent to make a pre-trial application seeking that such evidence be allowed. Care will also need to be exercised by counsel not to inadvertently mention details of addresses in openings. The common practice of asking a witness an open-

---

981   *Departmental Report* (EV/MOJ/2), 13.
982   NZLS *Submission on the Evidence Bill*, 39.
983   See EV44.01.
984   Burston and Verrall, "Questioning of Witnesses" in NZLS *Intensive: Evidence Act 2006*, 120.

ended question as to where they reside may need to be replaced by asking a leading question which would not elicit detail of the witness's address."

Conformity with the requirements of s 87 will also require some witness education — even the witness cannot elect to offer evidence of their own address unless the judge gives permission.

The reference in s 87(3) to an application in "chambers" means an occasion when the courtroom is closed to the public. The preference for an application to be made in chambers, contained in s 87(3), ensures that any disclosure of the witness's address, which occurs as part of the application itself, will not necessarily be disclosed to the public.

A possible example of s 87(4) is a charge of burglary where the complainant will be a witness for the prosecution. (This subsection was added before the Bill was introduced.) See, however, s 331 of the Crimes Act 1961, which states that a count in an indictment need not describe anything with precision.

EV87.05   Victims' Rights Act 2002

In cases where a victim is not a witness, s 16 of the Victims' Rights Act 2002 applies to control the disclosure of a victim's address. In cases where a victim is a witness, s 5(1) may mean s 16 takes priority — although presumably it is open to the judge to grant leave on the same basis as in s 87.

---

88   Restriction on disclosure of complainant's occupation in sexual cases

(1)   In a sexual case, except with the permission of the Judge,—

> (a)   no question may be put to the complainant or any other witness, and no evidence may be given, concerning the complainant's occupation; and

> (b)   no statement or remark may be made in court by a witness, lawyer, officer of the court, or any other person involved in the proceeding concerning the complainant's occupation.

(2)   The Judge must not grant permission under subsection (1) unless satisfied that the question to be put, the evidence to be given, or the statement or remark to be made, is of sufficient direct relevance to the facts in issue that to exclude it would be contrary to the interests of justice.

(3)   An application for permission under subsection (1) may be made before or after the commencement of any hearing, and is, where practicable, to be made and dealt with in chambers.

EV88.01   Prohibition on evidence of complainant's occupation in sexual cases

Section 88 applies only in a sexual case as defined by s 4. In the circumstances outlined in s 88(1), disclosure of the complainant's occupation is prohibited except with permission by the judge. It is a much closer re-enactment of s 23AA of the Evidence Act 1908 than s 87, and is consistent with the Law Commission's draft Code provision, which relates the bar on this information to disclosure in open court.[985] The prohibition in s 88(1)(b) covers only statements or remarks made *in court* by a person *involved in the proceeding*.

EV88.02   Admissibility test: "sufficient direct relevance"

As discussed at EV87.03, the admissibility standard has been changed to one requiring "sufficient" rather than "such" direct relevance. Evidence of a complainant's occupation may be sufficiently relevant if offered in order to explain the circumstances in which the complainant and the accused first met. One example where the standard for admissibility might be met is where the complainant was a sex worker and this fact had particular relevance to the defence raised by the defendant. This however could not amount to the offering of reputation evidence.[986]

89   Leading questions in examination in chief and re-examination

(1)   In any proceeding, a leading question must not be put to a witness in examination in chief or re-examination unless—

(a)   the question relates to introductory or undisputed matters; or

(b)   the question is put with the consent of all other parties; or

(c)   the Judge, in exercise of the Judge's discretion, allows the question.

(2)   Subsection (1) does not prevent a Judge, if permitted by rules of court, from allowing a written statement or report of a witness to be tendered or treated as the evidence in chief of that person.

EV89.01   General prohibition on leading questions

Section 89 codifies the common law rule that, subject to certain exceptions, leading questions are not permitted during the examination in chief (direct examination) or re-examination of a witness in civil or criminal proceedings. For the definition of a "leading question", see the discussion under s 4(1).[987]

EV89.02   Preliminary matters and party consent

The goal of examination in chief and re-examination is to draw out the witness's own recollections and to permit the trier of fact to judge the quality and credibility of the witness's testimony. Thus, it is very important that such evidence be given in the words of the witness and not that of the examiner. Accordingly, the prohibition against leading questions in examination in chief and re-examination will be applied most stringently with respect to facts that are, or might be, in contention at trial. Indeed, s 89(1)(a) permits (and anticipates) leading questions with regard to the introductory parts of a witness's testimony (such as name, age and occupation), or with respect to

---

985   The initial rationale for the section can be found in Young, *Rape Study: A Discussion of Law and Practice*, Volume 1, Wellington, Department of Justice, 1983, 127, in which complainants who were interviewed as part of the study asked for further protection of their identity, and "objected to the fact that they were often asked in their evidence in chief to give not only their full name but also their address and place of employment".

986   See the discussion of the bar on reputation evidence by s 44(2) at EV44.02.

987   See EV4.28.01.

undisputed matters in the proceeding. Likewise, s 89(1)(b) makes it clear that leading questions will be acceptable during a witness's examination in chief or re-examination if "all other parties" in the proceeding consent.

EV89.03   Judicial discretion

In addition to the exceptions codified in s 89(1)(a) and (b), s 89(1)(c) gives trial judges a general (and unguided) discretion to allow leading questions during a witness's examination in chief or re-examination. Such discretion might be exercised, for example, when the leading questions are used to draw a witness's attention to a particular person or object for the purpose of identifying that individual or thing. Similarly, it will not normally be objectionable for a lawyer to use leading questions to focus a witness's mind on a particular point, suggest a subject for testimony, or, in some limited circumstances, to jog the memory of a forgetful witness.

Pursuant to s 89(1)(c), a judge may also permit leading questions to assist counsel in the examination in chief of very young persons, persons with difficulty speaking English, and persons who are unusually timid or of limited intelligence. In the pre-Evidence Act case *R v E*, [988] the Court of Appeal applied such discretion to objections directed at the admissibility of an evidential videotape substituting for the examination in chief of a child complainant in a sexual assault case (a mode of trial testimony now permitted under s 105(1)(a)(iii) of the Act and controlled by s 106 along with Part 1 of the Evidence Regulations 2007). Responding to a defence complaint that the interviewer had elicited the child's responses through leading questions, Glazebrook J wrote: [989]

> "It is true that the interviewer asked leading questions ... but this was designed to give the girl a chance to retract, modify or embellish allegations already made and to correct any errors of understanding on the part of the interviewer. This is a perfectly proper interview technique. Strictly, leading questions are not allowable in examination-in-chief ... We consider, however, that leading questions may not be objectionable in an evidential interview of a child if they merely repeat what the child has previously said in the interview, are not used to excess and are employed solely to permit the child to provide clarification, correction or elucidation. In the circumstances of this case, we do not consider that the questions in the evidential interview exceeded proper bounds.

> "We are conscious that there are some cases and commentators which suggest that leading questions may be allowable where young children are concerned — see *R v Lewis* [1991] 1 NZLR 409 at 411 (CA), *R v Guptill* (1994) 11 CRNZ 299 (CA) and Casey, *Garrow and Casey's Principles of the Law of Evidence* (8th ed 1996) at [26.4]. Given what is now known about the importance of using open-ended questions when interviewing children, these authorities should be treated with caution. We note, in any event, that under

---

988   *R v E* 11/9/07, CA308/06; [2007] NZCA 404.
989   *R v E* 11/9/07, CA308/06; [2007] NZCA 404, paras 24-25.

s 89 of the Evidence Act 2006, there is no exception to the prohibition of leading questions where a child is being questioned ..."

R v E makes it clear that, when permitting leading questions during examination in chief or re-examination pursuant to s 89(1)(c), a trial judge must ensure that the questions are genuinely necessary to elicit reliable testimony and are not merely an indirect method for the lawyer to supply answers to a suggestible witness. Moreover, the Law Commission has suggested:[990]

> "The problems associated with examining witnesses who are very young, frightened, or intellectually disabled, or who are not fluent in English, are best addressed by allowing them to give evidence in an alternative way [see Subpart 5 of Part 3 of the Act (ss 102-107)], to have a support person close by for emotional support [s 79], or by providing them with communication assistance [s 81]."

EV89.04   Leading questions on cross-examination

As the central purpose of cross-examination is to probe the truth of the witness's testimony — and because there is less danger that an adverse witness will adopt the question's implicit answer as their own — leading questions are both permitted and expected in the cross-examination of witnesses by opposing parties in a civil or criminal case. By excluding cross-examination from the scope of its prohibition on leading questions, s 89 recognises this longstanding mode of adversarial trial practice. Similarly, and reflecting the common law view, s 94 of the Act provides that, to the extent authorised by the court, a witness called by a party and declared hostile by a judge may be cross-examined (impeached by leading questions) during both examination in chief and re-examination.[991]

EV89.05   Briefs of evidence

For the avoidance of doubt in civil proceedings, s 89(2) makes it clear that s 89(1) will not impact the current practice of trial witnesses reading prepared briefs of evidence as a substitute for ordinary (oral) examination in chief. Such procedure is enshrined in rr 441A-441I of the High Court Rules and, subject to certain controls, is specifically provided for in s 83(1)(c)(i) of the Act.[992] In like fashion, s 84(2) provides that, when a witness in a civil or criminal proceeding gives evidence for a calling party through an affidavit or by reading a written statement, such material is to be treated under the Act as "evidence given in chief" (the equivalent of a direct examination in court viva voce).

---

990   LC *Evidence Code*, para C329.
991   See EV94.02.
992   Pursuant to r 441F, evidence in chief in civil cases is usually given by a witness reading a written affidavit previously served on opposing parties in the case. See *McGechan on Procedure*, HR441A.01-HR441I.01. See also the discussion of ss 83 and 84 of the Act, respectively, at EV83.01 and EV84.02.

90   Use of documents in questioning witness or refreshing memory

(1)   A party must not, for the purpose of questioning a witness in a proceeding, use a document that has been excluded under section 29 or 30.

(2)   A witness must not consult a document that has been excluded under section 29 or 30 while giving evidence.

(3)   If when questioning a witness a party proposes to use a document or to show a document to the witness, that document must be shown to every other party to the proceeding.

(4)   If a witness proposes to consult a document while giving evidence,—

    (a)   that document must be shown to every other party to the proceeding; and

    (b)   that document may not be consulted by that witness—

        (i)   without the prior leave of the Judge or the consent of the other parties; or

        (ii)   if the purpose of consulting that document is to refresh his or her memory while giving evidence, except in accordance with subsection (5).

(5)   For the purposes of refreshing his or her memory while giving evidence, a witness may, with the prior leave of the Judge, consult a document made or adopted at a time when his or her memory was fresh.

(6)   Subsection (5) is subject to subsection (2).

EV90.01   Use of documents while giving evidence

Section 90 places various controls on the way a document may be employed during the questioning of a witness at trial (both by the questioner and the witness). It applies in civil and criminal proceedings, and whether questioning takes place during examination in chief, cross-examination, or re-examination.

Section 90 is supplemented by s 96 of the Act, which regulates cross-examination on the previous statements of witnesses (whether contained in a document or otherwise).[993] "Document" is defined broadly under s 4(1).[994]

EV90.02   Use of most inadmissible documents permissible

As originally conceived by the Law Commission, a document rendered inadmissible under the Evidence Act could not be used by a party when questioning a witness in a proceeding or consulted by a witness during questioning.[995] However, the Select Committee narrowed the scope of s 90 considerably.[996] In its final form, s 90(1) only prohibits a party from questioning a witness with a document that has been excluded from evidence under s 29 ("Exclusion of statements influenced by oppression") or

---

993   See EV96.01.
994   See EV4.11.01.
995   LC *Evidence Code*, para C330.
996   See *Select Committee Report on the Evidence Bill*, 10-11.

s 30 ("Improperly obtained evidence"). An identical prohibition applies to a witness who desires to "consult a document" while "giving evidence"[997] (s 90(2)). As a result, the class of documents actually caught by the prohibition in s 90 is relatively narrow. Indeed, the result of s 90(1) and (2) is that the Act contains no *general* prohibition on a party using an inadmissible document while questioning a witness in a proceeding, or a witness consulting any such inadmissible document while giving evidence.

EV90.03   Use versus admissibility of a document

Section 90 merely controls a party's "use" of a document while questioning a witness and a witness's ability to "consult" a document during questioning. It does not speak to the admissibility of the document in evidence, a process that will be controlled by any other relevant provision of the Act. In a different context, the distinction between *using* a document and *offering it into evidence* is similarly made in s 96(3).[998]

The Act does not define what it means for a questioner to "use" or a witness to "consult" a document. However, s 90(1) is most likely intended to prohibit the questioner from holding up, referring, pointing, alluding, reading, paraphrasing, or showing to a witness any document excluded from evidence under ss 29 or 30. Likewise, s 90(2) will forbid a witness giving evidence from examining, looking at, or checking any such document.

(1)   Eliciting evidence on cross-examination

Section 90(1) does not purport to control the use of documents not coming within the specific class referred to in that subsection, namely, documents that have been excluded under ss 29 or 30. All other classes of inadmissible documents may be "used" for the purpose of questioning a witness — unless some other provision of the Act prohibits such use.

Under the Act, no party can, of course, offer evidence of an inadmissible document. However, one common "use" of a document is as a device for cross-examination. Because of the definition of "offer evidence" under s 4(1), a party offers evidence of a document if evidence of the document is elicited by cross-examination.[999] The result is that, although s 90(1) only prohibits the use of one relatively small class of inadmissible documents, s 4(1) operates to prohibit the use of *any* inadmissible document in the common context of evidence elicited by cross-examination.

It is doubtful that the drafters of the Act intended such an anomaly. A possible solution, suggested in a different context by the pre-2006 Act case of *R v McKenzie*, might be to permit "cross-examination on the subject matter" of an inadmissible document (other than those caught by s 90(1)) without any "reference to its source".[1000] In such circumstances, a cross-examining party could claim to be "using" the document as opposed to "offering" it as evidence in the case.

---

997   "Giving evidence" is defined in s 4(1) of the Act: see EV4.17.01.
998   See EV96.05(1).
999   See EV4.29.01.
1000   *R v McKenzie* [2004] 1 NZLR 181 (CA), 188.

EV90.04   Scope of s 90

(1)   Defendant's statement in a criminal case

The s 90(1) limitation is narrow in scope. It applies merely to *documents* that have *actually been excluded* under ss 29 or 30 of the Act. Pursuant to those provisions, exclusion can only result when the prosecution attempts to offer the document in evidence against the defendant in a criminal proceeding.[1001] Practically speaking, this means that the most common class of documents caught by s 90(1) will be records of police interviews containing the statement of a defendant in a criminal case.[1002] To the extent they can meaningfully be used for the purpose of questioning a witness — and whether or not they are excluded under ss 29 or 30 — any *oral* statements made to police by a criminal suspect will not be subject to the prohibition of s 90(1).

Most police statements sought to be admitted by the prosecution at trial will, in fact, be contained in a document. However, there is no apparent policy justification for the distinction made in s 90(1) between the use of oral versus written statements excluded under ss 29 or 30.

(2)   Exclusion of unreliable statements under s 28

When offered by the prosecution, s 28 of the Act renders inadmissible in a criminal proceeding a previous statement made by the defendant — whether oral or contained in a document — if a judge determines it to be unreliable.[1003] However, s 90(1) only forbids a questioner from using a document that has been excluded from evidence under ss 29 or 30. In this regard, Burston and Verrall observe:[1004]

> "It seems odd that a statement excluded under s 28 on the grounds of unreliability is able to be used in questioning a witness [under s 90] ... Perhaps the answer is that the evidence arising out of such questioning would be excluded under [s 8(1)(a)] on the grounds that its probative value would be outweighed by the risk that the evidence would have an unfairly prejudicial effect."[1005]

Notwithstanding such comments, it is by no means clear that, with s 90 being inapplicable, s 8(1)(a) would inevitably exclude this class of unreliable evidence in every case. There appears to be no explanation in either the Select Committee Report or the legislative history of the Act explaining why exclusion of a document under s 28 was omitted from the limitations imposed by s 90(1).[1006]

1001   See EV29.01 and EV30.03.
1002   See, eg, *R v Ram* [2007] 3 NZLR 322 (CA), paras 65-69. *Ram* observes that the term "document" in s 90(1) is "very widely defined in s 4(1) [of the Act] and would clearly capture the video statement [of a defendant in a criminal case]" (para 67). See EV4.11.01. *Ram* also discusses s 15 of the Act, which, in a criminal trial, would control the admissibility of evidence given by a defendant at a voir dire proceeding to determine whether a statement should be excluded under ss 29 or 30. See EV15.01.
1003   See EV28.01.
1004   Burston and Verrall, "Questioning of Witnesses" in NZLS *Intensive: Evidence Act 2006*, 121.
1005   See EV8.01.
1006   See *Select Committee Report on the Evidence Bill*, 10-11.

(3)   Relationship between ss 90 and 31

An irreconcilable conflict exists between ss 90(1) and 31 of the Act.[1007]

In a criminal proceeding, s 31 anticipates that another party — most commonly a co-defendant — will be able to offer the written statement of a defendant into evidence even when, pursuant to ss 28-30, such a statement was ruled inadmissible by a judge upon being offered by the prosecution.[1008] Nonetheless, the import of s 31 is contradicted by the text of s 90(1). Section 90(1) would prevent a co-defendant from being able to "use" a document excluded under ss 29 or 30 for the purpose of questioning a witness. Moreover, a common "use" of a document when questioning a witness will be as part of the process of eventually offering that document into evidence. Section 90(1) will likewise block that course of action by preventing the co-defendant from "using" the document during questioning, even when such questioning is aimed at admitting the document as evidence pursuant to s 31.

There is no interpretive gloss that can be imposed on s 90(1) to solve this difficulty. It can only be addressed by Parliament through appropriate amendments to the Act. Indeed, in light of s 31, there seems little justification for applying the prohibition of s 90(1) both to the prosecution and the defence in a criminal case. There appears to be nothing in either the Select Committee Report or the legislative history of the Act discussing or dealing with any potential conflict between ss 90(1) and 31.[1009]

(4)   Civil proceedings

As discussed above,[1010] ss 29 and 30 only apply to evidence offered by the prosecution against the defendant in a criminal case. The sections do not require such evidence to be inadmissible in any other context, such as a subsequent civil trial. However, s 90 — which refers to the "use" or "consultation" of a document excluded by ss 29 or 30 — may render such documents inadmissible in *all* proceedings, including civil ones, and not just in those where any actual determination of inadmissibility has been made. If such interpretation of s 90 is correct, it would extend the practical operation of s 90(1) and (2) and be a rare instance of the Act's control of improperly obtained evidence in a civil case.[1011]

EV90.05   Showing the document to other parties

Section 90(3) requires a party to show a document to "every other party to the proceeding" if the party: (a) "proposes to use" the document when questioning a witness; or (b) "proposes ... to show a document" to a witness during questioning. There is no requirement that the document be shown to the witness himself or herself (see, however, the discussion of s 96(2)(a)).[1012] Similarly, s 90(3) imposes no obligation on a party to show the document to the trial judge. However, when a party

1007   See EV31.01.
1008   See EV28.02, EV29.01, and EV30.03.
1009   See *Select Committee Report on the Evidence Bill*, 10-11.
1010   See EV90.04(1).
1011   See EV30.02.
1012   See EV96.03(1).

uses a document to question a witness, most judges will insist on seeing what the witness and the parties to the proceeding actually have before them. See also the discussion of s 90(4)(b)(i) below.[1013]

(1)   Silent read method of cross-examination

In its commentary to the draft Evidence Code, the Law Commission noted the following:[1014]

> "Section [90(3)] is new. It is intended to discourage the practice of the 'silent read' [method of cross-examination] whereby, without disclosing the contents to anyone else in court, counsel hands a witness a written statement and asks the witness to read it silently [before answering further questions]. Under s [90(3)], if counsel shows a written statement to a witness under examination, … the statement must be shown to every other party."

The result of s 90(3) is that all parties in a proceeding will be aware of the contents of document that: (a) any party proposes to use in questioning a witness; or (b) proposes to show to a witness during questioning. If the document is admissible, any appropriate party may offer it into evidence at a suitable moment in the proceeding. If the document has been excluded from evidence under ss 29 or 30, any party will be able to object to its use in questioning the witness pursuant to s 90(1).

EV90.06   Witness consulting a document

Section 90(4)-(6) govern the process of a witness consulting a document while giving evidence in a civil or criminal proceeding.

Section 90(4)(a) and (b)(i) set out rules applicable to all occasions where a witness proposes to consult a document while giving evidence. Section 90(4)(a) requires the document to be "shown to every other party in the proceeding". Section 90(4)(b)(i) allows a judge to maintain some control over the documents consulted by a witness during party questioning.

The most common reason for a witness to consult a document while giving evidence is to refresh his or her memory. Section 90(4)(b)(ii) requires compliance with s 90(5) when a witness desires to consult a document as a memory refreshing tool.[1015] There are, however, other instances in which a witness may want to check a document while testifying. For example, either at the request of the witness or the instigation of the questioner, a witness may wish to consult a document that he or she has never seen before — such as a trial exhibit — if the witness believes that the document may have some relevance to the question being asked during a party's examination. Expert witnesses may also desire to consult various documents when giving evidence pursuant to s 25.[1016]

1013   See EV90.06.
1014   LC *Evidence Code*, para C331.
1015   See EV90.06(1).
1016   See EV25.05.

(1)   Section 90(5): refreshing memory while giving evidence

Section 90(5) only refers to a witness refreshing his or her memory while "giving evidence" (defined in s 4(1) of the Act[1017]). The provision makes no attempt to change earlier law imposing few controls on a witness refreshing his or her memory prior to testifying in a civil or criminal case.[1018]

(2)   Contemporaneity

With respect to the substance of a document used to refresh a witness's memory while giving evidence, s 90(5) requires the document to have been "made or adopted" by a witness "at a time when his or her memory was fresh". Whether or not this test is satisfied will be a factual question determined by the judge in each individual case.[1019] Indeed, leave of the judge is required before a witness can consult a document pursuant to s 90(5).

The prerequisite of contemporaneity codified in s 90(5) reflects the common law position prior to the 1995 High Court judgment in *Equiticorp Industries Group Ltd (in stat man) v R*.[1020] In *Equiticorp*, Smellie J considered that a contemporaneity test is unnecessary if the document stimulates the witness's actual recollection of the facts in question. *Equiticorp* concluded that, if a witness truly remembers relevant events, it should not matter what sort of material stimulated the witness's recall.

Section 90(5) fails to incorporate the reasoning behind *Equiticorp*. With respect to a witness consulting a document to refresh his or her memory while giving evidence, contemporaneity is now a universal requirement under the Act.

(3)   Section 90(6): refreshing memory with an inadmissible document

As discussed above,[1021] s 90(2) only forbids a witness giving evidence from consulting a document excluded under ss 29 or 30. Section 90(6) simply confirms the precedence of s 90(2) when a witness consults a document for the purpose of refreshing memory under s 90(5).

(4)   Admissibility of documents used to refresh memory under s 35

Section 90(5) governs the *process* of a witness refreshing memory while giving evidence as opposed to the *admissibility* of any such document. Where a witness's memory is *not refreshed* after consulting a document pursuant to s 90(5), the document may itself become admissible in evidence — for all purposes — under s 35(3).[1022]

1017   See EV4.17.01.
1018   See *Adams on Criminal Law — Evidence*, EC13.02.
1019   See *Adams on Criminal Law — Evidence*, EC13.03. For discussion of who is the "maker" of a
           statement under s 16 of the Act, which will also be relevant to the phrase "made or adopted"
           by the witness as used in s 90(5), see EV16.03.01. See also *Adams on Criminal Law —
           Evidence*, EC10.06(1)(g).
1020   *Equiticorp Industries Group Ltd (in stat man) v R* [1995] 3 NZLR 243 (HC). See *Adams on
           Criminal Law — Evidence*, EC13.03(1).
1021   See EV90.02.
1022   For further discussion of s 35(3), see EV35.04(1).

91   Editing of inadmissible statements

(1)   If a statement is determined by the Judge to be inadmissible in part in a proceeding, a party who wishes to use an admissible part of the statement may, subject to the direction of the Judge, edit the statement by excluding any part of it that is inadmissible.

(2)   A party may not edit a statement under subsection (1) unless, in the opinion of the Judge, the inadmissible parts of the statement can be excluded without obscuring or confusing the meaning of the admissible part of the statement.

EV91.01   Editing of inadmissible statements

Section 91 allows a party to "use an admissible part of a statement" in a civil or criminal proceeding where another portion of the statement has been "determined by the Judge to be inadmissible" (s 91(1)).

Subject to "the direction [agreement] of the Judge", the party must first "edit the statement by excluding any part of it that is inadmissible" (s 91(1)). However, such editing process may take place only if, "in the opinion of the Judge, the inadmissible parts of the statement can be excluded without obscuring or confusing the meaning of the admissible part of the statement" (s 91(2)). The satisfaction of s 91(2) will likely depend on: (a) the nature of the statement; (b) the nature and extent of the relevant excisions; (c) the purpose for which the statement will be used by the party in the proceeding; and (d) if the trial involves a jury, the potential for juror misunderstanding regarding the import and relevance of the statement (a matter raising the issue of whether the partial use of the statement will unfairly prejudice any party or otherwise operate unfairly in the proceeding).[1023] The procedure envisaged by s 91 will obviously require application to a court prior to the statement being used by a party in a civil or criminal trial.

EV91.02   Examining witnesses

Provided the test of s 91(2) is met, s 91(1) will allow "the inadmissible portions of a statement to be removed, so that the remaining parts may be used in examining a witness."[1024] However, while a helpful tool for witness questioning, s 91 may be resorted to infrequently in civil and criminal trials. The reason is that statements under the Act are likely to be ruled admissible or inadmissible in their entirety, rather than being "determined by the Judge to be inadmissible in part" (s 91(1)). In such cases, s 91 will be inapposite, despite its potentially broad scope. Indeed, unlike the narrower class of "documents" referenced in s 90, the term "statement" in s 91 would encompass all manner of declarations and assertive conduct made by anyone. See further the discussion of "statement" in s 4(1).[1025]

1023   See EV8.01.
1024   LC *Evidence Code*, para C333.
1025   See EV4.41.01.

EV91.03   Use versus admissibility

As in s 90, the reference to the "use" of a statement in s 91 must be distinguished from the statement's actual admissibility under the Act (that is, from whether it is actually offered as evidence by a party in the case).[1026] However, since s 91 refers to a party's ability to use the "admissible part" of an otherwise inadmissible statement, the distinction between "use" and "admissibility" in the provision may be of little practical concern. While clearly referring to the "use" of a partially admissible statement, s 91(1) does not, in fact, purport to restrict such a statement from being offered as evidence by a party in a civil or criminal case.

EV91.04   Co-defendant statements

One area where s 91 appears to incorporate common law principles involves the editing of any out-of-court statements made by a defendant in a criminal case that implicates a co-defendant when offered as evidence at trial.

Section 27(1) of the Evidence Act codifies the general common law rule that "evidence offered by the prosecution in a criminal proceeding of a statement made by a defendant is admissible against that defendant but not against a co-defendant in the proceeding". In the course of a joint trial, and unless the exceptions codified in s 12A of the Act apply, the "usual practice" will be for a judge to direct the jury that the out-of-court statements offered by the prosecution against defendant A will not be evidence against co-defendant B.[1027] However, where A's statement implicates B — or contains material that is unfairly prejudicial to B's defence — there will be a risk that the jury will use A's evidence against B despite the court's direction. In such circumstances, and at B's request, a trial judge will have the discretion "to have such passages edited from A's statement on the basis of this risk".[1028]

The common law practice of editing the out-of-court statement by one defendant in the interests of a co-defendant will now be permissible under s 91 of the Act. However, in the pre-2006 Act decision of *R v Naea*, Winkelmann J suggested that the discretion to edit should be "exercised sparingly" and as a "rare" exception to the normal practice of directing a trial jury regarding the evidential use of co-defendant statements at trial. [1029] In deciding whether to edit a co-defendant's statement or warn the jury, courts will need to balance the relevant factors in favour of editing against the likely effectiveness of firm jury instructions.[1030] Citing the judgment of Penlington J in *R v Hanifah*, Winkelmann J set out the relevant factors for a trial judge to consider: [1031]

1026   See EV90.03.

1027   *R v Naea (No 12)* 9/7/07, Winkelmann J, HC Auckland CRI-2006-92-4989, para 8.

1028   *R v Naea (No 12)* 9/7/07, Winkelmann J, HC Auckland CRI-2006-92-4989, para 9.

1029   *R v Naea (No 12)* 9/7/07, Winkelmann J, HC Auckland CRI-2006-92-4989, paras 11-12. See also *R v Hanifah* [2002] 3 NZLR 555 (HC), 559. See, eg, *R v Hartley* [2007] 3 NZLR 299 (CA), paras 60-62 (approving the approach of the Privy Council in *Lobban v R* [1995] 2 All ER 602 (PC) that, if a statement made by a defendant was relevant to his or her defence, it could not be edited by a trial judge for the benefit of a co-defendant).

1030   *R v Naea (No 12)* 9/7/07, Winkelmann J, HC Auckland CRI-2006-92-4989, para 15. See also *R v Hanifah* [2002] 3 NZLR 555 (HC), 556.

"Whether a Court will edit will depend on all the circumstances of the particular trial. Such matters as the allegations made by the prosecution, the defence to be mounted, the stage of the trial, and the contents of the statements involved, will be relevant considerations. A Court will also take into account such matters as:

"(a)　The nature and extent of the editing sought;

"(b)　The risk of throwing suspicion on others not otherwise at risk;

"(c)　The possibility of a change in the statement being edited or that it might be more difficult to follow after editing;

"(d)　The risk of unfair treatment to other accused who, although unnamed, are nevertheless identifiable;

"(e)　The risk that there will be an editing-out of details which otherwise add to the credibility of the statements against the accused who made them; and

"(f)　The potential difficulties of cross-examination should the maker of an edited statement later choose to give evidence."

In the scenario described above, the factors listed in *Naea* will provide a gloss on the exercise of the judicial discretion to edit a co-defendant's out-of-court statement pursuant to s 91. Indeed, each of those considerations can fit within an overall judicial determination as to whether "the inadmissible parts of the statement can be excluded without obscuring or confusing the meaning of the admissible part of the statement" (s 91(2)). In *Hanifah*, Penlington J also noted the need to maintain fairness in the trial proceedings, "not only to all the accused but also to the Crown"[1032] — a position that finds support in the principles governing the general exclusion of evidence under s 8 of the Act. Penlington J went on to observe that, "[i]f there is a real risk of prejudice as a result of allegations made in out-of-court statements by one accused against another, then the remedy is severance of trials".[1033]

92　Cross-examination duties

(1)　In any proceeding, a party must cross-examine a witness on significant matters that are relevant and in issue and that contradict the evidence of the witness, if the witness could reasonably be expected to be in a position to give admissible evidence on those matters.

(2)　If a party fails to comply with this section, the Judge may—

(a)　grant permission for the witness to be recalled and questioned about the contradictory evidence; or

---

1031　*R v Naea (No 12)* 9/7/07, Winkelmann J, HC Auckland CRI-2006-92-4989, para 13 (citing *R v Hanifah* [2002] 3 NZLR 555 (HC), 556).

1032　*R v Hanifah* [2002] 3 NZLR 555 (HC), 556.

1033　*R v Hanifah* [2002] 3 NZLR 555 (HC), 559.

(b)   admit the contradictory evidence on the basis that the weight to be given to it may be affected by the fact that the witness, who may have been able to explain the contradiction, was not questioned about the evidence; or

(c)   exclude the contradictory evidence; or

(d)   make any other order that the Judge considers just.

EV92.01   Cross-examination duties

Section 92 codifies a particular version of a party's common law duty "to put the case" to witnesses on cross-examination.[1034]

Section 92(1) provides that a party must cross-examine adversary party witnesses on certain key matters in a civil or criminal proceeding. Based on the language of that provision, the duty to cross-examine will arise when four conditions are present:

(i)   The topic of cross-examination must deal with "significant matters" in the proceeding;

(ii)   The matters must be "relevant" and "in issue" in the proceeding;

(iii)   The matters must "contradict the evidence of the witness"; and

(iv)   The witness may "reasonably be expected to be in a position to give admissible evidence on those matters".

The satisfaction of these conditions will be a legal question for the judge on the facts and circumstances of a particular case. Indeed, it is foreseeable that the applicability of s 92 will change as a trial progresses and evidence is actually heard. On the other hand, various discovery and disclosure obligations imposed in civil and criminal proceedings — in addition to any relevant pre-trial hearings — should help clarify for the parties the matters likely to be caught by s 92.

EV92.02   Scope and extent of cross-examination duties

(1)   Submissions of counsel and challenges to veracity

Section 92(1) draws no distinction between parties or witnesses and, when it applies, imposes the duty to cross-examine equally in civil and criminal trials.

However, in all cases, the provision appears to focus on "the contradictory *evidence*" that has been or will be presented by a party in a proceeding (s 92(2)(a)-(c)).[1035] Nonetheless, the Law Commission has suggested that s 92 can be triggered when, at the close of a civil or criminal trial, a party's *submissions* to a judge or jury will contradict the evidence of an adversary party witness.[1036] Such a conclusion is not obvious, and depends on whether the submissions of counsel fall within the definition of "significant matters that are relevant and in issue and that contradict the evidence of the witness" (s 92(1)).[1037]

1034   See *Adams on Criminal Law — Evidence*, EC3.08.
1035   Emphasis added.
1036   LC *Evidence Code*, para C334.

Likewise, the Law Commission has stated that "[c]hallenges to the witness's [veracity under s 37] should be put to the witness if the challenging party intends to call evidence on the witness's [veracity] subsequently".[1038] It is by no means clear that s 92 imposes a duty to cross-examine in such circumstances. Indeed, even when a witness's veracity will be challenged by evidence presented later in the proceeding, this does not, by itself, "*contradict* the *evidence* of the witness"[1039] — the test set out in s 92(1).

(2)   The extent of cross-examination

Section 92(1) says nothing about the extent of cross-examination required when the duty to cross-examine is triggered. However, s 92(2)(a) implies that, at a minimum, counsel must question an adversary party witness about "the contradictory evidence" that has been or will be called by the cross-examining party. Furthermore, s 92(2)(b) suggests that any required cross-examination should permit the witness "to explain the contradiction" — an obligation also imposed under s 96(2)(b) of the Act (regulating the cross-examination of a witness with a prior inconsistent statement).[1040]

Taken literally, s 92 appears to require cross-examination of adversary party witnesses on every item of evidence in a party's case that meets the four-part test of s 92(1). However, applied mechanically, such an approach could blunt the impact of cross-examination and operate unfairly to a party's control of adversarial questioning in a civil or criminal trial. Similarly, inflexible recourse to s 92 might implicate s 6(e) of the Act (avoiding "unjustifiable expense and delay"), as well as s 8(1)(b) (general exclusion of evidence that will "needlessly prolong the proceeding"). It is therefore likely that, as established in case law prior to its enactment, judges will enforce s 92 in a manner consistent with its underlying goals. As the Court of Appeal stated in *Guterriez v R*:[1041]

> "The decisions referred to lead to the conclusion, which we adopt, that the [duty to cross-examine] is simply one of fairness. Has a reasonable opportunity been given to enable the evidence in question to be properly assessed? It is the responsibility of prosecuting counsel or a prosecutor who proposes to attack the credibility of defence witnesses, including the defendant, to cross-examine in a way which makes it plain that the relevant evidence is challenged and gives the witness a fair opportunity to answer the challenge. Such cross-examination however may not be necessary if from what has gone before or from the circumstances of the case it is fairly made plain that the truthfulness of particular facts given in evidence is not accepted, and an adequate opportunity to meet the challenge has otherwise been afforded."

1037   However, for a judgment suggesting that the submissions of counsel can trigger s 92, see *R v Cox* 7/12/05, CA204/05, para 41 (discussed in a different context at EV92.03).

1038   LC *Evidence Code*, para C334.

1039   Emphasis added.

1040   See EV96.03(2).

1041   *Guterriez v R* [1997] 1 NZLR 192 (CA), 199. For further discussion of the common law approach, see *Adams on Criminal Law — Evidence*, EC3.08.

Similarly, in the civil proceeding of *Kennedy v Kennedy*, Allan J wrote:[1042]

> "The [duty to cross-examine] is founded upon considerations of basic fairness in the conduct of a trial. A witness or a party must not be ambushed. But if a witness is plainly upon notice that his or her account is not accepted and that the Court will be asked to prefer other evidence, then a failure to put to a witness the whole of an opposing party's case, is unlikely to attract the application of the rule, particularly in a simple case where the issues are limited. Where a party is on proper notice of the case he or she must meet, then in general it will be possible for counsel to ensure that a witness is able, in examination in chief, to give all the evidence which may be relevant to a credibility assessment of that witness."

The Law Commission has also stated that s 92 does not require cross-examining counsel to put "every aspect of his or her case in a robotic fashion to the witness, if it is clear from the pleadings or the prior conduct of the proceeding which of the witness's assertions are under challenge".[1043] Judges have taken a similar approach when applying r 441K of the High Court Rules, which imports a comparable duty of cross-examination in civil proceedings in the High Court. Consistent with s 92 of the Evidence Act, r 441K states that "[u]nless the parties ... otherwise agree, the rule in *Browne v Dunn* (1893) 6 R 57 (HL) (which provides that if the Court is to be asked to disbelieve a witness, the witness should be cross-examined) shall apply."[1044]

EV92.03   Breach of solicitor-client privilege

Section 92 imposes an affirmative obligation on parties to put certain matters to adversary party witnesses during cross-examination in civil and criminal proceedings. However, within that general obligation, various provisions of the Evidence may impose limits on the form and content of questioning mandated by s 92(1).

For example, in criminal cases, a breach of solicitor-client privilege may occur when, during cross-examination, a prosecutor asks the defendant why his or her counsel did not "put to" a Crown witness the version of events testified to by the defendant during examination in chief.[1045] In *R v Cox*, the Court of Appeal disapproved of such questioning because it deals with a privileged communication between a defendant and his or her legal adviser (a protection now codified in s 54 of the Evidence Act):[1046]

1042   *Kennedy v Kennedy* 12/2/07, Allan J, HC Auckland CIV-2006-419-809, para 28. See also *Granger v W Holliday & Sons Ltd* 15/10/07, Mallon J, HC Auckland CIV-2007-454-102, para 55.

1043   LC *Evidence Code*, para C334.

1044   For discussion of the flexible application of r 441K in High Court civil proceedings, see *Kennedy v Kennedy* 12/2/07, Allan J, HC Auckland CIV-2006-419-809 and the cases cited therein.

1045   See Mahoney, "Putting the case against the duty to put the case" [2004] NZ Law Rev 313, 336-338.

1046   *R v Cox* 7/12/05, CA204/05, paras 41-42. See also *R v McGregor* 27/8/07, CA209/07; [2007] NZCA 365; *R v Leef* 24/8/06, CA14/06.

"As a general proposition, we accept that Crown counsel ought not to have asked questions which invited an answer involving disclosure of privileged communications between the appellant and his lawyer. But we also recognise that there will be occasions where Crown counsel wishes to mention the failure to cross-examine in his or her closing address, and it would not be fair to a defendant to do this without having provided an opportunity for the defendant to explain the matter.

"In our view, the appropriate course is simply to ask the defendant whether he has ever previously told anyone about a matter he has stated in evidence. He should not be asked to explain why his counsel failed to put a matter in cross-examination. There may be many reasons for this, such as a judgement by counsel that the matter is of insufficient significance to justify doing so or an oversight by counsel: the defendant having made the statement for the first time in Court is another possible reason, but not the only one."

EV92.04   Remedies

Section 92(2) grants judges a broad discretion to remedy a party's violation of s 92(1). However, whether and to what extent a remedy is fashioned will be guided by the policies underlying the duty to cross-examine, as well as by the nature of the breach and its potential impact on accurate fact finding in a particular case. As previously discussed,[1047] the Law Commission has reiterated the following rationale for s 92:[1048]

"The requirement [imposed by s 92] is designed to give a witness fair opportunity to reply to contradictory evidence that the questioner intends to call later, and to do this in a way that avoids the unnecessary disruption or inconvenience of having to recall a witness after the witness has departed. The requirement also ensures that the court receives all available evidence on a disputed issue."

As outlined below, remedies for a party's breach of s 92 will be assessed by judges in light of these core aims.

(1)   No remedy

Provided there is no unfairness in the proceeding — and where the evidence presented has afforded adequate coverage to key matters at issue in a civil or criminal trial — a party's transgression of s 92(1) may attract no remedial action under s 92(2).[1049]

(2)   Recall of witnesses: s 92(2)(a)

In appropriate circumstances, s 92(2)(a) indicates that any party impacted by a questioning party's breach of s 92(1) can ask the trial judge for "the witness to be recalled and questioned about the contradictory evidence".[1050] Such questioning

---

1047   See EV92.02(2).
1048   LC *Evidence Reform*, para 401.
1049   See, eg, *Guterriez v R* [1997] 1 NZLR 192 (CA). See also *Kennedy v Kennedy* 12/2/07, Allan J, HC Auckland CIV-2006-419-809 and the cases cited therein.

would presumably take place — by the party requesting the recall and/or any other interested party in the case — in accordance with the normal rules for witness examination set out in Subpart 4 of Part 3 of the Act (ss 83-101). In this regard, and when it is in the "interests of justice" to do so, s 99(1) would allow a judge to recall a witness for questioning under s 92 even without a specific party request.[1051] Likewise, where "justice requires", a judge could independently question the recalled witness about the contradictory evidence pursuant to s 100(1).[1052]

Unlike s 99(1), s 92(2)(a) does not limit the judge's discretion to recall a witness only where required by the interests of justice. However, in light of the s 99(1) test, a court's decision to opt for recalling a witness under s 92(2)(a) is likely to be governed by what is necessary to do justice in the case. Recall is therefore most likely to occur where the contradictory evidence to be put to the witness deals with a central matter in the proceeding, and involves a subject on which the recalled witness has significant information to impart.[1053]

(3)   Weight: s 92(2)(b)

Short of recalling a witness, s 92(2)(b) would inevitably cause a judge to instruct a jury in accordance with the terms of that subsection. In a proceeding without a jury, s 92(2)(b) could likewise impact a judge's assessment of the weight to be accorded to a witness's testimony in a civil or criminal trial.[1054]

(4)   Exclusion: s 92(2)(c)

Exclusion of the contradictory evidence for a party's breach of s 92(1) is possible under s 92(2)(c). However, such a drastic cure should be used sparingly and only where no other remedy (such as recalling a witness under s 92(2)(b)) can fulfil the policies of fairness and full coverage of the issues underlying s 92.

(5)   Other remedies considered just: s 92(2)(d)

The Law Commission has stated that the discretionary remedies listed under s 92(2) are "not intended to limit the court's inherent power to control its own proceedings".[1055] This is made clear by the catchall provision of s 92(2)(d). As suggested in *Guterriez v R*, that subsection could allow a judge to order that a party in breach of their cross-examination duties under s 92(1) "not be allowed later to suggest that the witness be disbelieved".[1056] However, as Mallon J noted in *Granger*

1050   *Guterriez v R* [1997] 1 NZLR 192 (CA), 198.
1051   See EV99.01.
1052   See EV100.02.
1053   See, eg, *R v McNeill* (2000) 146 CCC (3d) 551 (Ont CA); *R v W (CA222/06)* 1/3/07, CA222/06; [2007] NZCA 34 (observing that, where the late recall of a Crown witness took place as a result of arguments made by defence counsel in his closing address, the trial judge could have instead opted to advise the jury that such arguments were not founded upon any question put to a witness in the case).
1054   *Granger v W Holliday & Sons Ltd* 15/10/07, Mallon J, HC Auckland CIV-2007-454-102, para 57.
1055   LC *Evidence Code*, para C335.
1056   *Guterriez v R* [1997] 1 NZLR 192 (CA), 198.

v W Holliday & Sons Ltd, such result is not inevitable and the "appropriate consequences will depend on what is just in the circumstances of this case".[1057]

93   Limits on cross-examination

If a party in any proceeding cross-examines a witness who has the same, or substantially the same, interest in the proceeding as the cross-examining party, the Judge may, in the interests of justice, limit the extent to which leading questions may be asked in that cross-examination.

EV93.01   Limits on cross-examination of friendly witnesses

For the definition of a "leading question", see the discussion under s 4(1).[1058]

The ability to employ leading questions in cross-examination is a means of disciplining an adverse witness and controlling the scope of the witness's answers to adversarial questioning. However, as s 93 suggests, there may be instances where a witness nominally on cross-examination "has the same, or substantially the same interest in the proceeding as the cross-examining party". This may occur when testifying co-defendants cooperate to present a joint defence in a criminal trial, or when parties joined as plaintiffs or defendants in multi-party litigation find themselves on the same side of a civil dispute. Similarly, and pursuant to the authority given by s 71 of the Act, a party in civil proceedings may find it necessary to call the adversary party as a witness. While the adverse party's counsel would be entitled to "cross-examine" his or her client pursuant to s 84(1)(b), such questioning would be "cross-examination in form only and not in fact".[1059]

EV93.02   Judicial discretion

In circumstances like those described above, the policies supporting the use of leading questions in cross-examination are not supported. To the contrary, and in order to shore up their own position in the trial, witnesses with a similar interest in the proceeding to the cross-examining party may be eager to assist that party through obedient answers to suggestive questioning. Faced with a potentially sham interrogation, s 93 gives a judge the discretion "to limit the extent to which leading questions may be asked of compliant witnesses in cross-examination".[1060] The discretion is to be exercised in the "interests of justice" and will not apply to witnesses who simply agree with propositions put to them by leading questions. Instead, the witness under cross-examination must share some actual "interest" (pecuniary,

---

1057   *Granger v W Holliday & Sons Ltd* 15/10/07, Mallon J, HC Auckland CIV-2007-454-102, para 57, Mallon J also noted that the "fairness rationale" underlying s 92 has "less force" with respect to a party's failure to cross-examine an expert witness appointed by the court under r 324 of the High Court Rules (para 61). His Honour observed: "The court appointed expert reports to the Court and is there to assist the Court. It is for the Court to decide what it makes of the report" (para 61).

1058   See EV4.28.01.

1059   *Advisory Committee's Note to United States Federal Rule of Evidence 611(c)* (1972) 56 FRD 183, 275.

1060   LC *Evidence Reform*, para 410.

proprietary or penal) in the outcome of the proceedings — although s 93 does not require the witness to be an actual party in the particular civil or criminal case.

In deciding whether to limit the use of leading questions "in the interests of justice", s 93 obliges a judge to consider what is fair to the cross-examining party given the individual circumstances of a civil or criminal trial. For example, the Law Commission has pointed out that, in multi-party litigation, "little purpose is served by repetitive cross-examination on behalf of parties who share a common interest".[1061] However, in criminal proceedings, co-defendants might be afforded a greater opportunity to elicit favourable responses from one another if a decision is made to take the stand. In exercising their discretion under s 93, judges should also bear in mind that leading questions on cross-examination are not used solely for the purpose of testing a witness's version of events. Indeed, even if a witness shares the same or substantially the same interest in the proceeding as the cross-examining party, leading questions may be useful and necessary in eliciting relevant facts from the witness favourable to the party's case.

EV93.03   General exclusion of evidence

The Law Commission has stated that the s 93 discretion "is not intended to derogate from the judge's general power to exclude evidence under s 8 [of the Act]".[1062] Undoubtedly, and pursuant to s 8, a court could control the admission of evidence generated by a witness on cross-examination to whom s 93 would also apply. Section 93 is, in fact, directed only to the *form* of questions put to witnesses with interests in a proceeding similar to the cross-examining party. It does not provide a general power of exclusion for a witness's answers given in response to cross-examination, whether the questions are asked in a leading manner or otherwise.

94   Cross-examination by party of own witness

In any proceeding, the party who calls a witness may, if the Judge determines that the witness is hostile and gives permission, cross-examine the witness to the extent authorised by the Judge.

EV94.01   General prohibition on party cross-examination of own witness

As provided for in s 89(1) of the Act, a party calling a witness is not generally permitted to examine the witness with leading questions.[1063] However, the bar on leading questions during examination in chief is a proxy for a more general prohibition, recognised at common law, against a calling party impeaching its own witness through cross-examination. The principal rational for such a prohibition is that, by calling a witness, the party effectively vouches for the veracity and accuracy of the witness and should have no need to discredit him or her. The rationale may be criticised on the grounds that parties often have no choice as to whom they call as

---

1061   LC *Evidence Reform*, para 409.
1062   LC *Evidence Code*, para C336.
1063   See EV89.01.

witnesses. Similarly, witnesses called by a party often fail to give the expected evidence for reasons of bias or animus toward the calling party's case.

EV94.02   Hostile witness

Section 94 recognises the reality of adversarial process by permitting the court to transform a witness's examination in chief into a cross-examination marked by leading questions. However, codifying existing common law rules, the provision states that a calling party may cross-examine its own witness only: (1) "to the extent authorised by the Judge"; and (2) with the judge's permission following a determination that the witness is "hostile" (s 94).[1064]

For the meaning of "witness" and "hostile" witness, see the discussion in s 4(1).[1065].

EV94.03   Cross-examination of a hostile witness

The cross-examination contemplated under s 94 may consist of leading questions designed to contest the accuracy of any factual narrative offered by a hostile witness or to challenge the witness's veracity (credibility).

(1)   Challenges to veracity

Provided the witness is declared hostile under s 94, s 37(4) of the Act makes it clear that a party may challenge the veracity of its own witness pursuant to the veracity rules of s 37 (which themselves require that any evidence offered under s 37 be "substantially helpful" in assessing the hostile witness's veracity (s 37(1)). Section 37 would thus permit a party to call evidence from other witnesses challenging the veracity of a hostile witness. However, in place of a standard (non-impeaching and non-leading) direct examination, ss 37 and 94 will also allow evidence challenging veracity to be presented by the calling party through cross-examination of the hostile witness directly (such cross-examination proceeding by leading questions as permitted under s 89).

(2)   Re-examination

Sections 89 and 94 of the Act contemplate that, to the extent re-examination is allowed under s 97 and with permission of the judge, a calling party questioning a hostile witness may re-examine the witness in a manner similar to the cross-examination permitted during the witness's examination in chief.[1066]

(3)   Unfavourable witnesses

Should a witness testify unfavourably to a calling party and not be declared hostile by the court, challenges to the witness' veracity would not be permitted under the truthfulness rules of s 37(4) and cross-examination with leading questions would not be allowed under ss 89 and 94. On the other hand, nothing in those provisions forbids a party from calling *other* evidence to contradict the testimony of an unfavourable witness on facts in issue in the case. Such practice was previously allowed with

---

1064   See, eg, *R v Shaw* 22/11/05, CA159/05, para 67 (leave of the court is required for a party to treat their own witness as hostile and to cross-examine the witness with leading questions).
1065   See, respectively, EV4.46.01 and EV4.21.01-04

unfavourable (albeit non-hostile) witnesses under s 9 of the Evidence Act 1908 and is specifically preserved in s 37(4)(b) of the new Act.[1067]

EV94.04   Judicial authorisation

Section 94 states that a calling party may cross-examine a hostile witness only "to the extent authorised by the judge". Such provision should be read as permitting restraints on the cross-examination of a hostile witness in addition to any other restrictions already provided for in the Act (such as s 37(1)[1068]). In this regard, s 96 of the Act provides specific controls on the manner in which a calling party may introduce the previous statements of a hostile witness during cross-examination permitted by the court.[1069]

Unlike the explicit restrictions on cross-examination set out in other provisions of the Act, s 94 is silent as to the circumstances in which a judge would or should impose supplemental limits on the scope of a hostile witness's cross-examination by a calling party.

Prior to passage of the Act, judges often raised objections in criminal proceedings when prosecutors called a known hostile witness to the stand for the sole purpose of introducing the witness's prior inconsistent statements into evidence.[1070] While such statements constituted hearsay inadmissible for their truth under existing evidential rules, s 4(1) of the Act now defines the previous, out-of-court declarations of a testifying witness as non-hearsay statements admissible to prove the truth of their contents.[1071] Accordingly, the Act's description of hearsay removes a principal justification for restricting the cross-examination of prosecution witnesses known to be hostile before trial.[1072]

1066   See, eg, the pre-2006 Act case of *R v Webb* 3/7/96, Moran J, HC Christchurch T27/96. In *Webb*, a Crown witness (T) was declared hostile and, upon being cross-examined by the defence, gave evidence favourable to the defendant. The Crown then sought and was granted leave to re-examine the witness with leading questions. "The HC noted that authority on whether a party who has obtained leave to treat his witness as hostile has a right to re-examine him is scant and held that: (i) the matter is within the discretion of the trial Judge and how it is exercised will depend on the circumstances of the case; and (ii) here T was a Crown witness only in the sense that the Crown had called him, in every other respect he was a defence witness and fairness and balance dictated that the Crown should be permitted to re-examine him upon apparent contradictions and new material raised in the cross-examination by [the] defence; and (iii) having permitted re-examination, no useful purpose would be served by restricting the Crown to non-leading questions — a course which would have invited a further hostility ruling": 19 *The Capital Letter* 35, 7. Cf *R v Pohutuhutu* 18/9/87, Williamson J, HC Christchurch T21/87.

1067   See EV37.13. For further discussion of the common law distinction between "hostile" and "unfavourable" witnesses, see *Adams on Criminal Law — Evidence*, EC11.05.

1068   See EV94.03(1).

1069   See EV96.01.

1070   See *R v O'Brien* [2001] 2 NZLR 145; (2000) 18 CRNZ 610 (CA); *Commerce Commission v Gltrap City Ltd* 19/9/00, Glazebrook J, HC Auckland CP88/94, paras 10-15; *R v Schriek* [1997] 2 NZLR 139; (1996) 14 CRNZ 449 (CA), 145; 455. See also the discussion in *Adams on Criminal Law — Evidence*, EC11.10.

1071   See EV4.20.01.

1072   LC *Evidence Reform*, para 413.

Notwithstanding the example above, s 94 preserves a fundamental judicial control over the cross-examination of hostile witnesses by a calling party. In doing so, it permits judges to allow only such questioning as is necessary in the interests of justice and required by the concrete circumstances of a civil or criminal case. As the Court of Appeal stated in the pre-2006 Act decision of *R v O'Brien*:[1073]

> "It is sometimes assumed that a declaration of hostility entitles the party in whose favour the declaration is made to cross-examine the witness generally. There is, however, no right of general cross-examination following a determination that the witness is hostile ... A passage from *Stephen's Digest of the Law of Evidence*, approved in *R v Prefas and Pryce* (1986) 86 Cr App R 111 is helpful in this respect: see also *R v Thompson* (1976) 64 Cr App R 96. *Stephen's* states that the Judge may permit the examination of the hostile witness by the party calling him to be conducted in the manner of cross-examination 'to the extent to which the Judge considers necessary for the purpose of doing justice'."

See *R v Herewini*[1074] for an example of judicial discretion exercised under s 94. In *Herewini*, Stevens J found a prosecution witness to be hostile pursuant to ss 4(1) and 94 of the Act. A key factor in that determination was a discrepancy between the witness's trial testimony and her formal, pre-trial statement to the police. As the inconsistency concerned a particularly material matter in the proceeding, Stevens J authorised the prosecution to cross-examine the witness "on her signed deposition testimony".[1075] Further, his Honour ruled that such cross-examination should begin at the point where the witness's pre-trial statement diverged from her testimony in court.[1076]

95 Restrictions on cross-examination by parties in person

(1) A defendant in a criminal proceeding that is a sexual case or a proceeding concerning domestic violence or harassment is not entitled to personally cross-examine—

    (a) a complainant:

    (b) a child (other than a complainant) who is a witness, unless the Judge gives permission.

(2) In a civil or criminal proceeding, a Judge may, on the application of a witness, or a party calling a witness, or on the Judge's own initiative, order that a party to the proceeding must not personally cross-examine the witness.

1073   *R v O'Brien* [2001] 2 NZLR 145; (2000) 18 CRNZ 610 (CA), para 30. See also *Commerce Commission v Gltrap City Ltd* 19/9/00, Glazebrook J, HC Auckland CP88/94, paras 31-38; *R v Schriek* [1997] 2 NZLR 139; (1996) 14 CRNZ 449 (CA), 145; 455.

1074   *R v Herewini* 15/8/07, Stevens J, HC Rotorua CRI-2006-063-3151.

1075   *R v Herewini* 15/8/07, Stevens J, HC Rotorua CRI-2006-063-3151, para 21.

1076   *R v Herewini* 15/8/07, Stevens J, HC Rotorua CRI-2006-063-3151, para 21.

(3)   An order under subsection (2) may be made on 1 or more of the following grounds:

    (a)   the age or maturity of the witness:

    (b)   the physical, intellectual, psychological, or psychiatric impairment of the witness:

    (c)   the linguistic or cultural background or religious beliefs of the witness:

    (d)   the nature of the proceeding:

    (e)   the relationship of the witness to the unrepresented party:

    (f)   any other grounds likely to promote the purpose of the Act.

(4)   When considering whether or not to make an order under subsection (2), the Judge must have regard to—

    (a)   the need to ensure the fairness of the proceeding and, in a criminal proceeding, that the defendant has a fair trial; and

    (b)   the need to minimise the stress on the complainant or witness; and

    (c)   any other factor that is relevant to the just determination of the proceeding.

(5)   A defendant or party to a proceeding who, under this section, is precluded from personally cross-examining a witness may have his or her questions put to the witness by—

    (a)   a lawyer engaged by the defendant; or

    (b)   if the defendant is unrepresented and fails or refuses to engage a lawyer for the purpose within a reasonable time specified by the Judge, a person appointed by the Judge for the purpose.

(6)   In respect of each such question, the Judge may—

    (a)   allow the question to be put to the witness; or

    (b)   require the question to be put to the witness in a form rephrased by the Judge; or

    (c)   refuse to allow the question to be put to the witness.

(7)   Subsection (1) overrides section 354 of the Crimes Act 1961.

EV95.01   Comparison with s 23F

Section 95 is an extension of s 23F of the Evidence Act 1908, which operated only to prevent the cross-examination by the defendant personally of child or "mentally handicapped" complainants in cases of a sexual nature. Section 23F(3) provided the following guidance as to how cross-examination should proceed in the case of unrepresented defendants:

"(3)   Where an accused is not represented by counsel, the accused may put questions to the complainant (whether by means of an appropriate video link or otherwise as the Judge may direct) by stating the questions to a person, approved by the Judge, who shall repeat the questions to the complainant."

(1) The intended scope of the bar in s 95(1)

Section 95(1) extends the bar to other groups of witnesses, but its precise scope, as a result of drafting and policy changes during the legislative process is unclear. The Law Commission's original proposal was to retain the bar in s 23F (relating only to the cross-examination of child complainants in cases of a sexual nature), and give express discretion to control personal cross-examination in all other cases, on the basis that extending the bar to all complainants in sexual cases would be expensive and also ineffective in some cases. The Law Commission was of the view that use of alternative ways of giving evidence (for example, the use of CCTV so that the complainant is physically separated from the defendant) may be "more valuable".[1077] However, the majority of submissions on the proposals in the discussion paper favoured extension of the bar to all complainants in sexual cases.[1078]

Section 220 of the draft Code provided:

"(1) Notwithstanding s 354 of the Crimes Act 1961, a defendant in a criminal proceeding is not entitled to personally cross-examine

"(a) a complainant in a sexual case; or

"(b) a complainant in a proceeding involving domestic violence; or

"(c) a child who is a witness in a sexual case or a proceeding involving domestic violence."

This approach was supported in the relevant Cabinet Paper: "I propose that a defendant in a criminal proceeding shall not be entitled to personally cross-examine a complainant or child witness in a sexual case or a case involving domestic violence".[1079] However the drafting was amended in the Bill on the basis of advice from the Crown Law Office:[1080]

"[A] mandatory restriction on all child witnesses is inconsistent with the Bill of Rights Act. To avoid this inconsistency the Bill prevents personal cross-examination of child witnesses in particular cases unless the judge gives permission."

This change explains the wording of s 95(1)(b), which does not operate as a total bar, as compared to s 95(1)(a), which does. The Cabinet Papers do not, however, indicate any other change in policy from the Law Commission's draft.

The clause in the Bill was further amended in Select Committee by adding the words "or harassment", as the Committee was of the view that is was "appropriate to treat harassment cases in a similar way to domestic violence and sexual cases."[1081]

1077 See New Zealand Law Commission, *The Evidence of Children and Other Vulnerable Witnesses*, NZLC PP26, Wellington, 1996, para 180.

1078 LC *Evidence Reform*, para 415.

1079 *Cabinet Paper 4*, para 24.

1080 Ministry of Justice, *Letter of Advice to the Minister of Justice*, 8 February 2005, 13.

"Harassment", "sexual case" and "domestic violence" are terms defined in s 4, as are "child" and "child complainant".

(2)   Total bar only applies in criminal proceedings

The failure to define "complainant" adds to the difficulty of interpreting the scope of s 95(1). If no change to the Law Commission's policy position was intended, then the bar only applies in the case of personal cross-examination by *an accused* of a *complainant* in a sexual case, a case concerning domestic violence, or a case concerning harassment.[1082] The difficulty with the drafting of the opening words of s 95(1) is that it is unclear whether the "proceeding concerning domestic violence or harassment" must also be "criminal proceedings" (notably the definition of "sexual case" in s 4 provides that it must be a "criminal proceeding").[1083]

If "complainant" is interpreted to mean the victim of a criminal offence, who is a witness in the trial of the accused for that offence, then with regard to s 95(1)(a), the proceedings must also be criminal in nature and would not apply to situations where an application for a protection order, for example, is being made under the Domestic Violence Act 1995. Such an interpretation is consistent with the original policy, suggested to be unchanged in this respect, behind the provision, and has recently been applied in *FU v RU*.[1084] In that case, Ronald Young J traversed the legislative history of s 95(1) and held that it did not apply to an application for a domestic protection order. However, in such cases a judge could still make a discretionary order under s 95(2).

The use of the word "proceeding" in s 95(1) presumably means any such bar applies at all stages of a proceeding (in the case of cross-examination of a complainant at any preliminary hearing or voir dire), but it will usually have most significance at the substantive hearing.

(3)   The scope of s 95(1)(b)

With regard to s 95(1)(b), the current drafting suggests that it relates to child witnesses in criminal proceedings that deal with sexual cases, domestic violence or harassment. It does not apply in *any* proceeding that involves domestic violence (and now harassment) in which a child is a witness, although there seems to be have been mixed views about its scope during the legislative process. In response to the submission from Victim Support that the section should include child witnesses to family violence, the Ministry of Justice said: "We note that sub-clause (1) ... specifically covers child witnesses in domestic violence *and* criminal cases."[1085]

The change in drafting of s 95(1)(b) was not accompanied by any guidance to the judge as to whether or not to grant permission for personal cross-examination in such

---

1081   *Select Committee Report on the Evidence Bill*, 11.
1082   LC *Evidence Reform*, para 418 — assume that the use of the word "defendant" in this discussion means the accused.
1083   See EV4.40.01.
1084   *FU v RU* 1/10/07, Ronald Young J, HC Napier CIV-2007-441-761.
1085   *Departmental Report* (EV/MOJ/2), 16.

a situation. It is suggested that the relevant grounds from s 95(2) could be referred to. The Ministry of Justice stated, however, that by including the reference to child witnesses "in sub-clause (1) rather than relying solely on sub-clause (2) signals that it should only be in exceptional circumstances that such permission would be granted."[1086]

EV95.02   General discretion to prevent cross-examination by a party: grounds in s 95(3)

Section 95(2) gives the judge power to prohibit cross-examination in person of any witness by any party to any civil or criminal proceeding.

Section 95(3) sets out the grounds upon which the judge can order such a prohibition. Although these are the only grounds, they are widely drawn. This is particularly true of s 95(3)(f), which simply refers back to the purpose of the Act (s 6). This, said the Law Commission, "allows the judge to base a decision on grounds not precisely anticipated by the Code's provisions, but justified by the purpose of the Code".[1087] As noted in the commentary to s 6(b),[1088] this is one section in which a witness's substantive, as opposed to procedural, rights under the New Zealand Bill of Rights Act 1990 may be argued as being relevant to the exercise of judicial discretion — although see the discussion of s 95(3)(c) below.

Section 95(3)(a) would seem to include *old* age and *lack of* maturity.[1089]

Section 95(3)(b) now includes the addition of "psychological" impairment to the list proposed by the Law Commission.[1090] The Law Commission had used the term "disability" rather than "impairment" — but either term was viewed as preferable to the Evidence Act 1908's use of "mentally handicapped". The Law Commission stated: "'Psychiatric disability' is intended to cover not only those people suffering from the long-term effects of mental illness, but also those in the acute phase of any mental illness."[1091]

"Religious beliefs" was added to s 95(3)(c) by the Select Committee on the basis that "there is often a complex interrelationship between religious beliefs and cultural practices and including a witness's religious beliefs would obviate the need for a court to distinguish between religious beliefs and cultural practices".[1092] It was also seen as important to make the same amendment to s 95(3) as had been made to s 103(3)(e).[1093]

The reference to "cultural practices" in the Law Commission's draft was, however, directed at a very particular kind of example:[1094]

1086   *Departmental Report* (EV/MOJ/2), 17.

1087   LC *Evidence Code*, para C348.

1088   See EV6.03.

1089   LC *Evidence Code*, para C343.

1090   No explanation of this addition to the Bill prior to introduction is included in the Cabinet Papers or Ministerial advice.

1091   LC *Evidence Code*, para C344.

1092   *Select Committee Report on the Evidence Bill*, 11.

1093   *Departmental Report* (EV/MOJ/2), 18.

"The phrase 'cultural background' is intended to capture those witnesses who because of their cultural background may be particularly ill-equipped to answer a defendant directly — for example, a young witness giving evidence against a person to whom, in the witness's culture, obedience is generally owed, such as a person of chiefly status in a Pacific Island community."

It may also not be culturally appropriate for personal cross-examination of a kaumatua in some contexts.[1095] It is less easy to see the relevance of religious beliefs to a decision about whether a party should personally cross-examine a witness.

The Law Commission also said of the earlier form of s 95(3)(c): "'Linguistic background' refers to anyone who speaks a language other than English — the language of the court system."[1096] Whether a bar on personal cross-examination is the best option for such witnesses, however, will depend on the circumstances of the case. Section 80 may instead be utilised by such a witness.[1097]

An example of a situation which might raise s 95(3)(d) is a "criminal case involving a history of harassment".[1098]

In s 95(3)(e), the expression "the relationship of the witness to the unrepresented party" is intended "to capture those situations where a prior relationship of some kind, especially one involving unequal power, existed between the witness and unrepresented party (which would include the defendant in a criminal trial)".[1099] This means an applicant seeking a protection order may seek not to be personally cross-examined by the respondent, although there is no absolute bar on personal cross-examination in such proceedings.[1100]

(1)   Subsection (4): factors to consider in exercising the discretion

Section 95(4) provides broad guidelines that the judge must consider in determining whether to grant an order prohibiting cross-examination by a party acting in person under s 95(2). Section 95(4)(a) is arguably unnecessary, in view of the combined operation of ss 95(3)(f) and 6(b) and (c). An onerous requirement is placed on the judge by the introductory phrase in s 95(4). He or she *must* have regard to the broad range of factors referred to in s 95(4)(c), namely *any* factor that is relevant to the just determination of the proceeding.

EV95.03   Subsection (5): cross-examination must be undertaken by another person

The opening words of s 95(5) recognise that this subsection applies in all the circumstances in which the earlier portions of s 95 prevent personal cross-examination by a defendant *or any party* to a proceeding. It therefore appears to be

---

1094   LC *Evidence Code*, para C345.
1095   See also EV85.03.
1096   LC *Evidence Code*, para C345.
1097   See EV80.01.
1098   LC *Evidence Code*, para C346.
1099   LC *Evidence Code*, para C347.
1100   See EV95.01(2).

a legislative oversight carried through from the Bill that s 95(5)(a) and (b) refer only to *defendants*, rather than any party.

This subsection contains a further change from the Law Commission's draft (which also occurred prior to the Bill being introduced) with the addition to s 95(5)(b) of the words "and fails or refuses to engage a lawyer for the purpose specified by the Judge". The ability for the judge to ask the questions instead of the accused or any party was removed at Select Committee stage by the striking out the words "the Judge or" before the final words of s 95(5)(b), although no explanation for the change was given in the Select Committee's Report.

The issue of who pays for the appointed person is not specifically dealt with (contrast s 115(3)). It may be the subject of regulations passed pursuant to s 201(o). Although it is likely that the "person" appointed by the judge under s 95(5)(b) will be a lawyer, this is not mandatory.

Because s 95(6) refers back to s 95(5) by speaking of "each such question", the same legislative oversight referred to above affects s 95(6). Section 95(6)(b) gives the judge the ultimate control of the questions proposed by the defendant and which the defendant may have ordered his or her representative, engaged or appointed under s 95(5), to ask.

EV95.04   Warning

See s 123(1)(b) (an extension to s 23H of the Evidence Act 1908) for the jury warning required when the defendant has been prevented from personally cross-examining a witness in a criminal proceeding.[1101]

96   Cross-examination on previous statements of witnesses

(1)   A party who cross-examines a witness may question the witness about a previous statement made by that witness without showing it or disclosing its contents to the witness if the time, place, and other circumstances concerning the making of the statement are adequately identified to the witness.

(2)   If a witness does not expressly admit making the statement and the party wishes to prove that the witness did make the statement,—

(a)   the party must show the statement to the witness if it is in writing, or disclose its contents to the witness if the statement was not in writing; and

(b)   the witness must be given an opportunity to deny making the statement or to explain any inconsistency between the statement and the witness's testimony.

(3)   If a document is used by a defendant for the purpose of cross-examining a witness but is not offered as evidence by that defendant, the following rights of the defendant are not affected:

(a)   the defendant's right to make a no-case application; and

1101   See EV123.01.

(b)　　the defendant's rights in relation to the order of addressing the court.

EV96.01　Cross-examination about a previous statement

Section 96 combines and recasts ss 10 and 11 of the Evidence Act 1908. Sections 10 and 11 gave rise to a substantial body of case law, much of which will remain relevant under the new Act and need not be repeated here.[1102]

In civil and criminal proceedings, s 96(1) and (2) set out conditions governing a party's: (a) cross-examination of a witness about a previous statement; and (b) ability to prove that statement. The definition of "statement" and "previous statement" are contained in s 4(1).[1103] While it will mainly apply to cross-examination on a witness's previous *inconsistent* statements, s 96 is not restricted to assertions of that type.

According to the Law Commission, "[t]he purpose of s 96(1) and (2) is to state clearly at what stage and in what circumstances a previous statement must be shown to a witness who is being cross-examined on it".[1104]

EV96.02　Procedure for cross-examination under s 96(1)

Section 96(1) provides that a witness can be cross-examined about a previous statement, whether in oral or documentary form, without either being shown the statement or having its contents disclosed by the cross-examiner (although the questioner may do so if he or she wishes). However, in order to question a witness about a previous statement in this fashion, the cross-examiner must "adequately identify" to the witness "the time, place and other circumstances concerning the making of the statement" (s 96(1)). Aimed at protecting witnesses under cross-examination and treating them fairly (a policy imperative under s 6(c) of the Act),[1105] the satisfaction of these conditions will be a legal question for the trial judge.[1106]

EV96.03　Proving the previous statement under s 96(2)

Section 96(1) is a rule of general applicability governing cross-examination on any previous statement of a witness. In particular, it applies whether or not the cross-examining party wishes to prove the making of the statement that is the subject of questioning. However, if a party who adopts the form of questioning described in s 96(1) does desire to prove that the witness made the statement — and where the witness does not "expressly admit" making the statement after being asked (s 96(2)) — the additional requirements of s 96(2)(a) and (b) will apply.[1107]

1102　For a thorough discussion of case law interpreting and applying ss 10 and 11 of the Evidence Act 1908, see *Adams on Criminal Law — Evidence*, EC11.13.

1103　See, respectively, EV4.41.01 and EV4.34.01.

1104　LC *Evidence Code*, para C353.

1105　LC *Evidence Reform*, para 424.

1106　See *Adams on Criminal Law — Evidence*, EC11.13(1)(a).

1107　By permitting proof of the previous statement where the witness does not "expressly admit" having made it, s 96 anticipates such evidence when the witness "equivocates on the issue". *Adams on Criminal Law — Evidence*, EC11.13(1)(b).

(1)   Showing the statement to the witness or disclosing its contents

Where a witness does not "expressly admit" making a previous statement (s 96(2)), s 96(2)(a) requires the cross-examining party who wishes to prove that it was made to show the previous statement to the witness — if in writing — or to disclose its contents to the witness otherwise.

(2)   Opportunity to deny making the statement or to explain contradiction

Once the requirement of s 96(2)(a) has been satisfied, the witness must be afforded one of two additional opportunities under s 96(2)(b).

The first is the chance to deny making the previous statement after it has been shown to the witness or its contents disclosed — an obligation that will apply to all types of previous statements sought to be proved in compliance with s 96(2).

However, when the previous statement is a prior *inconsistent* statement, s 96(2)(b) requires the witness to be given the chance "to explain any inconsistency between the statement and the witness's testimony". Like the requirements set out in s 96(1), the policy justification for this prong of s 96(2)(b) is fairness to the witness on cross-examination.[1108] The subsection also promotes full coverage of the issues in a proceeding, a rationale that also underlies the duty to cross-examine certain witnesses imposed by s 92.[1109]

(3)   Proof of the previous statement

Assuming it is desired and necessary, s 96 does not specify when or how a party may prove the witness's previous statement once the conditions of s 96(2) have been satisfied. Presumably, the opportunity to do so can take place after cross-examination of the witness has been completed, and will depend on any applicable rules in the Act governing when and how a party may offer such proof.

EV96.04   Relationship with other rules of admissibility

While placing certain restrictions on a party's ability to cross-examine a witness on previous statements and prove those statements at trial, s 96 does not guarantee the admissibility of previous statements that comply with its rules. Indeed, despite conformity with s 96, there may be other provisions in the Act that limit a party's ability to admit previous statements as evidence in civil or criminal proceedings. Examples are given below.

(1)   Use of documents in questioning witnesses: (s 90)

Section 96 must be read in conjunction with s 90, which deals with a party's "use" of a "document" (s 90(1)) when questioning witnesses in civil or criminal proceedings.[1110]

If cross-examination of a witness under s 96(1) can be characterised as a party "using" a previous statement contained in a "document" (as that term is defined in

---

1108   LC *Evidence Reform*, para 424. See the discussion at EV96.02.
1109   See EV92.02(2).
1110   See EV90.03.

s 4(1)[1111], s 90 will obligate the cross-examiner to show the document "to every other party in the proceeding" (s 90(3)). However, as made clear by s 96(1), the statement need not be shown, or its contents disclosed, to the witness himself or herself.

Section 90(1) prohibits a party from using a document to question a witness in a criminal proceeding where the document has been excluded from evidence under s 29 (statements influenced by oppression) or s 30 (improperly obtained evidence).[1112]

(2)   Previous consistent statements (s 35)

While a cross-examiner is unlikely to want to prove the previous *consistent* statement of a witness under s 96(2), s 35 of the Act would limit the circumstances under which such a statement would be admissible as evidence in a civil or criminal case.[1113]

(3)   Hearsay (ss 16-22)

Since s 96(2) deals with proving the previous statement of a "witness", the statement will not be considered a "hearsay statement" as that term is defined in s 4(1) (which, among other conditions, classifies a hearsay statement as one "made by a person *other than* a witness …").[1114] Accordingly, the previous statement need not meet the applicable prerequisites for admitting hearsay evidence in a civil or criminal proceeding under ss 16-22.

(4)   Veracity (previous inconsistent statements) (s 37)

Provided it is "substantially helpful" in assessing veracity (s 37(1)), s 37 would allow a party to offer evidence about a witness's veracity in the form of a prior inconsistent statement (s 37(3)(c)).[1115] Accordingly, where the focus of cross-examination under s 96 is a previous inconsistent statement used to attack veracity, the s 37 test of substantial helpfulness will also apply.

However, as discussed in EV96.04(3) above, any prior statement of a witness is classified as non-hearsay under s 4(1) of the Act. The result is that, in most cases, prior inconsistent statements subject to s 96 will be offered for the truth of their contents and not for the purpose of undermining a witness's veracity. In such circumstances, and despite having an incidental impact on veracity, s 37 will not apply. Instead, admissibility of the prior inconsistent statement will be governed by the relevance rule of s 7, along with any other applicable rules of inclusion or exclusion under the Act.[1116]

(5)   Statements that are neither consistent nor inconsistent

In certain circumstances, a cross-examiner may wish to question a witness about a previous statement that is neither consistent nor inconsistent with the witness's

---

1111   See EV4.11.01.
1112   See EV90.02.
1113   See EV35.01.
1114   See EV4.20.01. Emphasis added.
1115   See EV37.08.
1116   See EV37.09.

evidence in the proceeding. While s 96 would still set out conditions governing cross-examination on such a statement and further proof of its making, admissibility will be managed by the relevance rule of s 7, along with any other applicable rules of inclusion or exclusion under the Act.

EV96.05   Defendant's rights: no-case application and order of address

(1)   Scope of s 96(3)

Section 96(3) is narrow in its scope. The provision applies only to a *defendant* who *uses* a "document" (defined in s 4(1)[1117]) to cross-examine a witness without actually *offering* it as evidence in the case (a distinction also drawn in s 90 of the Act).[1118] However, unlike s 96(1) and (2), s 96(3) applies to the use of *any* document on cross-examination and is not restricted to documents that incorporate the witness's previous statements.

(2)   Application in civil and criminal proceedings?

By its plain terms, s 96(3) makes no distinction between civil and criminal proceedings. Nonetheless, there is good reason to conclude that it was meant to apply only to defendants in civil trials. Indeed, under ss 347(3) and 367(3) of the Crimes Act 1961 — which take priority over s 96 pursuant to s 5(1) of the Evidence Act[1119] — a criminal defendant *always* has the right to: (a) make a "no-case" application (s 347(3)); and (b) address a jury following the prosecution's closing address (s 367(3)). Moreover, it is only in civil proceedings that a defendant loses the right to give the last address if the defendant offers evidence at trial.[1120] Accordingly, s 96(3)(b) can only potentially have impact in a civil case.

Under r 477(a) of the High Court Rules and r 481(a) of the District Courts Rules 1992, a defendant in a civil case may ask the judge to dismiss the plaintiff's claim on the grounds that "no reasonable cause of action is disclosed". Assuming that this judicial discretion can be exercised at any point during a civil proceeding, s 96(3)(a) simply re-iterates what a defendant is already entitled to under existing law. Indeed, there is nothing in r 477 or r 481 to suggest that a "no-case" application is in any way limited by the defence offer of evidence in a civil case.[1121]

97   Re-examination

(1)   On re-examination, a witness—

   (a)   may be questioned about matters arising out of evidence given by the witness in cross-examination, including any qualification in cross-examination of evidence given by the witness in examination in chief; but

---

1117   See EV4.11.01.
1118   See EV90.03.
1119   See EV5.01.
1120   See *McGechan on Procedure*, HR487.06 (discussing r 487 of the High Court Rules).
1121   See *McGechan on Procedure*, HR477.03 (discussing r 477 of the High Court Rules) and *District Courts Procedure* (looseleaf), Wellington, Brookers Ltd, 1995, DR481.04 (discussing r 481 of the District Courts Rules 1992).

(b)   may not be questioned about any other matter, except with the permission of the Judge.

(2)   If permission is given by the Judge under subsection (1), the Judge—

(a)   must allow other parties to cross-examine the witness on the additional evidence given; and

(b)   may allow further re-examination on matters arising out of that cross-examination.

EV97.01   Nature and scope of re-examination

At the conclusion of examination in chief and cross-examination, s 84(1)(c) of the Act provides for re-examination of witnesses in civil and criminal proceedings. Section 97 codifies existing law and practice related to the nature and scope of re-examination permitted under s 84.

Re-examination effectively provides a second opportunity for a calling party to question its own witness. However, since a party should normally use examination in chief to place before a court the relevant information possessed by the witness, s 97 generally limits re-examination to "matters arising out of evidence given by the witness in cross-examination, including any qualification in cross-examination of evidence given by the witness in examination in chief" (s 97(1)(a)). This limitation is intended to discourage a party from "intentionally leaving until re-examination evidence that should have been led in examination in chief".[1122] Indeed, in *R v E*, the Court of Appeal observed:[1123]

> "The primary purpose of re-examination is to allow counsel to clarify or explain areas of ambiguity or uncertainty which have emerged in answers in cross-examination — see Richardson *Archbold Criminal Pleading, Evidence & Practice* (2007) at [8-247]. It is not meant to provide the Crown with an opportunity to restate its case or to plug holes opened in cross-examination."

EV97.02   Leave to re-examine on new matters

As codified, s 97 contemplates that re-examination will generally be employed to allow a witness to explain or qualify evidence given in cross-examination that is either adverse to the calling party's case or damaging to the witness's veracity. However, under s 97(1)(b), new matters can be raised in re-examination with leave of the judge. The Law Commission has suggested that such leave might be granted if, for example, "a question has not been asked in examination in chief because of counsel's oversight, provided that it does not prejudice another party".[1124] However, if the judge does permit a new matter to be raised in re-examination under s 97(1)(b), the judge: (a) "must allow" the other parties in a proceeding to cross-examine the witness on the additional evidence (s 97(2)(a)); and (b) "may allow" further re-examination by the

---

1122   LC *Evidence Reform*, para 428.
1123   *R v E* 11/9/07, CA308/06; [2007] NZCA 404, para 72.
1124   LC *Evidence Reform*, para 428.

calling party on matters arising out of such additional cross-examination (s 97(2)(b)).

EV97.03   Leading questions

Pursuant to s 89 of the Act, and subject to certain exceptions, a "leading question" (defined in s 4(1)[1125]) should not to be put to a witness on re-examination.[1126] However, see EV94.03(2) for a discussion of the use of leading questions during the re-examination of a "hostile" witness (defined in s 4(1)[1127]) under s 94.

---

98   Further evidence after closure of case

(1)   In any proceeding, a party may not offer further evidence after closing that party's case, except with the permission of the Judge.

(2)   In a civil proceeding, the Judge may not grant permission under subsection (1) if any unfairness caused to any other party by the granting of permission cannot be remedied by an adjournment or an award of costs, or both.

(3)   In a criminal proceeding, the Judge may grant permission to the prosecution under subsection (1) if—

(a)   the further evidence relates to a purely formal matter; or

(b)   the further evidence relates to a matter arising out of the conduct of the defence, the relevance of which could not reasonably have been foreseen; or

(c)   the further evidence was not available or admissible before the prosecution's case was closed; or

(d)   for any other reason the interests of justice require the further evidence to be admitted.

(4)   In a criminal proceeding, the Judge may grant permission to a defendant under subsection (1) if the interests of justice require the further evidence to be admitted.

(5)   The Judge may grant permission under subsection (1),—

(a)   if there is a jury, at any time until the jury retires to consider its verdict:

(b)   in any other proceeding, at any time until judgment is delivered.

EV98.01   Further evidence after the close of a party's case

For both civil and criminal proceedings, s 98 codifies the common law position on a party's ability to offer further evidence after closing its case. The basic rule, reflected in s 98(1), is that a party must lead all evidence before its case ends, "except with the permission of the Judge" (s 98(1)).[1128]

1125   See EV4.28.01.

1126   See EV89.01. See also *R v E* 11/9/07, CA308/06; [2007] NZCA 404, paras 72-73.

1127   See EV4.21.01-04.

As suggested by the various terms of s 98, a party may have diverse reasons for seeking to adduce further evidence after closing its case. Indeed, in some circumstances, other provisions of the Act anticipate that a judge will give permission for additional evidence to be called. Section 99 provides one such example ("Witnesses recalled by the judge"[1129]), along with s 92 ("Cross-examination duties"). Section 92 permits a judge to recall a witness for questioning where a party has failed to cross-examine him or her on certain key matters in the proceeding about which the witness could "reasonably be expected … to give evidence" (s 92(2)(a)).[1130]

Another example given by the Law Commission involves s 35(2), which, in the relevant part, allows a party to offer evidence of a witness's prior consistent statement "to respond to a challenge to the witness's veracity or accuracy, based … on a claim of recent invention on the part of the witness".[1131] The Law Commission suggested that, in criminal proceedings, the Crown should be permitted to adduce further evidence of a witness's prior consistent statement where, following completion of the Crown's case, the defence calls evidence challenging the witness's testimony as a recent invention.[1132] Given the triggering mechanism in s 35(2), such "rebuttal evidence" is clearly appropriate under s 98 since the prior consistent statement would not have been "admissible before the prosecution's case was closed" (s 98(3)(c)).

EV98.02   Exercise of judicial discretion

Section 98 gives all parties in civil and criminal trials the chance to obtain judicial permission to call further evidence after closing their case. However, the grounds for doing so, and the likelihood of permission being granted, will change depending on the nature and circumstances of the proceeding and which party is seeking leave.

(1)   Subsection (2): civil proceedings

Reflecting the relative flexibility of the conduct of civil trials (which will almost always be held without a jury), the least restraints are put on courts under s 98(2). It allows judges to exercise their discretion to permit further evidence in civil proceedings "unless any unfairness caused to any other party" by granting permission "cannot be remedied by an adjournment or an award of costs" (s 98(2)). According to the Law Commission, "[s]uch unfairness might exist if the defendant could no longer call a previously available witness to meet … new evidence offered by the plaintiff".[1133] Nonetheless, the Law Commission's view was that, in most civil trials, a judge should permit a party to call further evidence under s 98(2). This will be particularly true regarding material offered by a plaintiff in response to defence evidence that could not reasonably have been anticipated in the plaintiff's case.[1134]

1128   See LC *Evidence Code*, para C358.
1129   See EV99.01
1130   See EV92.04(2).
1131   See EV35.04.
1132   See LC *Evidence Code*, para C358.
1133   See LC *Evidence Reform*, para 433.

(2)　　Subsection (4): criminal proceedings: defence

With respect to criminal proceedings, s 98 distinguishes between applications to present further evidence made by the defendant and the prosecution.

Defence requests are governed by s 98(4), which allows a judge to "grant permission to a defendant under subsection (1) if the interests of justice require the further evidence to be admitted". The lack of any additional qualification in s 98(4) reflects the fundamental concern in criminal proceedings that the accused receive a fair trial.[1135] By way of example, the Law Commission noted:[1136]

> "When defence evidence has been omitted because of counsel's oversight, it will normally be in the interests of justice to allow the evidence, but much may depend on the stage in the trial when the application is made".

(3)　　Subsection (3): Criminal proceedings: prosecution

The test for permitting a criminal defendant to offer further evidence after the close of his or her case under s 98(4) should be compared with the more restrictive standards imposed on the prosecution pursuant to s 98(3). As set out by the Court of Appeal in *R v Timutimu*, s 98(3) reflects the established common law approach:[1137]

> "[The] general principle is that all evidentiary material to be relied upon by the prosecution probative of guilt must be adduced before the close of its case: *R v Lee* [1976] 2 NZLR 171 (CA). Its rationale is fairness to the accused, so that he or she has an adequate opportunity to know the Crown case and plan a defence accordingly: *R v Chin* (1985) 157 CLR 671. Nevertheless, the Court has an inherent jurisdiction to allow the Crown to call further evidence at a later stage. The discretion is to be used sparingly and in such a way as to strike the appropriate balance of justice between the Crown and the defence. The two recognised categories of exception are, first, situations involving purely formal issues and, second, where issues have arisen unforeseeably or ex improviso. The discretion will be exercised rarely outside these two exceptions: *R v Francis* (1990) 91 Cr App R 271 at 275-276."

The "two recognised categories of exception" referred in *Timutimu* are effectively enshrined in s 98(3)(a) and (b).

1134　See LC *Evidence Reform*, para 433. See also LC *Evidence Code*, para C359; *Equiticorp Industries Group Ltd (in stat man) v Hawkins* [1996] 2 NZLR 82; (1995) 9 PRNZ 313 (HC). However, given the full discovery available in civil proceedings and the pre-trial exchange of witness briefs of evidence, a plaintiff will be surprised by defence proof at trial only in rare circumstances. See rr 293 and 441A-441Q of the High Court Rules.

1135　A criminal defendant's right to a fair trial is codified in s 25(a) of the New Zealand Bill of Rights Act 1990 and is reflected in various provisions of the Evidence Act 2006. See, eg, ss 8(2), 95(4)(a), 103(4)(a)(ii), and 112(4)(c).

1136　LC *Evidence Reform*, para 435.

1137　*R v Timutimu* 30/11/06, CA236/06, para 12. See also *R v Timutimu* 4/5/06, Winkelmann J, HC Auckland CRI-2004-92-14159, para 14 (discussing the relevant considerations when a court contemplates a prosecution request to present further evidence after the close of its case); *Adams on Criminal Law*, Ch5.15.

(a)   Subsection (3)(a): formal matters

As for examples of further evidence relating to a "purely formal matter" (s 98(3)(a)), the Law Commission referred to "formal evidence that the Attorney-General has given the necessary consent to a prosecution under s 144A of the Crimes Act 1961 (sexual conduct with children outside New Zealand)".[1138]

Another example is provided by *Murray v Ministry of Transport*,[1139] a drink-driving prosecution where, following the close of its case, the Crown was permitted to call evidence that the accused's blood sample was forwarded to a private analyst in accordance with the technical requirements of s 58B of the Transport Act 1962 (now s 74 of the Land Transport Act 1998).

The outcome reached in *Murray* should be compared with the result of *R v Rankin*.[1140] *Rankin* involved a prosecution for possession of pseudoephedrine with the intent to manufacture methamphetamine. Following the close of its case, Lang J refused to allow the prosecution to call further expert evidence establishing that pseudoephedrine could, in fact, be used in this type of manufacture. The Court noted that the defence had been structured around the prosecution's omission, and that the prosecution's failure to call the evidence in its original presentation was a fundamental rather than formal defect in proving the offence charged.[1141] *Rankin* suggests that, when considering whether to allow prosecutors to adduce further evidence under s 98(3), a key consideration for judges will be prejudice to the substance of the defence offered in response to the prosecution evidence initially presented in the case.

(b)   Subsection (3)(b): unforeseen matters

As indicated by common law decisions preceding the Act, most requests by the prosecution to admit evidence after the close of its case will be made under s 98(3)(b). This subparagraph targets evidence offered by the Crown to rebut unexpected material presented by the defence. According to the Law Commission, s 98(3)(b) confirms that prosecution rebuttal evidence need not be limited to matters "no human ingenuity" could have anticipated.[1142] Instead, the provision requires only that "the further evidence relates to a matter arising out of the conduct of the defence, the relevance of which could not *reasonably have been foreseen*" (s 98(3)(b)).[1143]

Whether it is reasonably foreseeable that the prosecution will have to answer some aspect of the defence case can only be decided on the facts and circumstances of each proceeding. However, decided judgments suggest that judicial permission to offer further evidence under s 98(3)(b) will be most appropriate where: (1) the prosecution had no advance warning of the defence evidence sought to be rebutted; (2) the rebuttal evidence deals with a significant matter in the trial (whether relevant to the facts in

---

1138   LC *Evidence Code*, para 360.
1139   *Murray v Ministry of Transport* [1984] 1 NZLR 610 (CA).
1140   *R v Rankin* 20/9/06, Lang J, HC Auckland CRI-2006-404-2851.
1141   *R v Rankin* 20/9/06, Lang J, HC Auckland CRI-2006-404-2851, paras 22-25.
1142   LC *Evidence Code*, para 360.
1143   Emphasis added.

issue or the veracity of a witness called by the prosecution or the defence); and (3) allowing evidence in rebuttal will serve the interests of justice by challenging potentially false defence testimony or otherwise helping the jury assess the merits of the defence case.[1144]

(c)   Subsection (3)(c): further evidence not available or admissible

Section 98(3)(c) provides two bases for the prosecution to admit further evidence after the close of its case.

As discussed at EV98.01 above, the Law Commission's reference to s 35(2) of the Act provides a good example of proof that might not be "admissible" before the prosecution's case is closed (s 98(3)(c)).

As to further evidence not "available" to the Crown before the end of its case (s 98(3)(c)), *McNicholl v Police* suggests that a judge should not allow prosecutors to offer rebutting material where, for tactical reasons, the Crown "holds back the detail" of such evidence to see whether the accused "[persists] in the allegations" to which the rebutting evidence relates or "[gives] any further details in support of them".[1145]

(d)   Subsection (3)(d): interests of justice

Notwithstanding the more specific circumstances set out in s 98(3)(a)-(c), s 98(3)(d) gives judges the discretion to permit the prosecution to re-open its case where "the interests of justice require the further evidence to be admitted." However, by comparison with defence applications to adduce further evidence pursuant to s 98(4), the particular circumstances listed in s 98(3)(a)-(c) suggest a more restrictive judicial attitude toward prosecution requests under s 98(3)(d). Indeed, consistent with the approach outlined in *R v Timutimu*,[1146] the Law Commission notes that s 98(3)(d) was added "to avoid injustice in *exceptional circumstances* that do not fit within [subparagraphs] (a)-(c)".[1147]

Timutimu itself provides a good example of when judicial permission to re-open the prosecution case will be appropriate under s 98(3)(d). The Court of Appeal approved a High Court decision allowing the Crown to call further witnesses aimed at remedying defects in the "chain of custody" of evidence central to the prosecution.[1148] According to Harrison J, there was no prejudice to the accused in admitting the testimony, a step that would have been undertaken in the Crown's initial

---

1144   See, eg, *R v Wickremasinghe (Reasons for Ruling No 3)* 6/3/03, Chambers J, HC Auckland T013408; *R v Nuku* 21/10/04, CA287/04; *R v Prangley* 25/7/06, Heath J, HC Auckland CRI-2005-055-1664; *R v W (CA222/06)* 1/3/07, CA222/06; [2007] NZCA 34 (observing that, where the late recall of a prosecution witness took place as a result of arguments made by defence counsel in his closing address, the trial judge could have instead opted to advise the jury that such arguments were not founded upon any question put to a witness in the case).

1145   *McNicholl v Police* (1989) 5 CRNZ 82, 84. See also *R v Sweeney* 3/11/88, CA61/88.

1146   *R v Timutimu* 30/11/06, CA236/06. See EV98.02(3).

1147   Emphasis added. LC *Evidence Reform*, para 434.

1148   *R v Timutimu* 30/11/06, CA236/06, para 9.

---

presentation but for a misunderstanding between counsel for the prosecution and the defence.[1149]

EV98.03   Time for further evidence

If the matter is being tried with a jury, permission from the judge to offer further evidence after the close of a party's case can be sought "at any time until after the jury retire to consider their verdict" (s 98(5)(a)).[1150] In all other proceedings, permission will be available "until judgment is delivered" in the case (s 98(5)(b)). Such time limits parallel those applying under s 99, a related provision dealing with the judicial discretion to recall witnesses in civil and criminal trials "in the interests of justice" (s 99(1)).[1151]

99   Witnesses recalled by Judge

(1)   In any proceeding, the Judge may recall a witness who has given evidence if the Judge considers that it is in the interests of justice to do so.

(2)   The Judge may recall a witness under subsection (1),—

      (a)   if there is a jury, at any time until the jury retires to consider its verdict:

      (b)   in any other proceeding, at any time until judgment is delivered.

EV99.01   Recall of witnesses by the judge

In civil cases, the traditional (common law) view was that the judge could call a witness, but "only with the consent of the parties".[1152] In criminal proceedings, judges had an inherent jurisdiction to call witnesses, although such power was to be "exercised only sparingly and where the interests of justice clearly so [required]".[1153]

Section 99 gives judges a more limited discretion than existed at common law. A court has the power only to *recall* (not call) witnesses in civil and criminal proceedings, provided "the Judge considers that it is in the interests of justice to do so" (s 99(1)).

EV99.02   Statutes permitting judges to call witnesses

In certain circumstances, statutes may grant specific powers to judges to call witnesses in various types of proceedings.[1154] Under s 368(2) of the Crimes Act 1961, a court also has the power to require the prosecution in a criminal case to call a witness whom

---

1149   *R v Timutimu* 30/11/06, CA236/06, para 20. Compare the result in *R v Rankin* 20/9/06, Lang J, HC Auckland CRI-2006-404-2851, discussed at EV98.02(3)(a).

1150   See, eg, *R v W (CA222/06)* 1/3/07, CA222/06; [2007] NZCA 34.

1151   See EV99.05.

1152   *Cross on Evidence* (8th NZ ed), 233.

1153   *Adams on Criminal Law*, CA368.03; Ch5.16.02 (citing *R v Bishop* [1996] 3 NZLR 399 (CA), 401). See *R v Tumarae* 27/9/06, Winkelmann J, HC Rotorua CRI-2006-463-67; *R v S* 17/9/07, Panckhurst J, HC Christchurch CRI-2006-009-1151.

1154   Examples include: s 199(1) of the Children, Young Persons, and Their Families Act 1989; s 78 of the Protection of Personal and Property Rights Act 1988; s 23 of the Mental Health (Compulsory Assessment and Treatment) Act 1992; and s 82 of the Domestic Violence Act 1995.

the court believes should be called. However, such power is to be exercised only in rare cases and where required by the interests of justice.[1155]

Specific statutory provisions allowing judges to call witnesses in a proceeding will take precedence over s 99 pursuant to s 5(1) of the Evidence Act.[1156] Apart from such statutes, s 99 would appear to eliminate the common law power of judges to call witnesses in civil and criminal proceedings.[1157]

EV99.03   Exercise of judicial discretion

According to the Law Commission — and by contrast with the common law power of judges to call witnesses in a proceeding — the judicial power of recall codified in s 99 "is a lesser intrusion into party freedom" to decide what evidence to present in a civil or criminal case.[1158] Moreover, in obeisance to party freedom in the presentation of evidence, the Law Commission expected that "a judge's discretion to recall a witness will be exercised sparingly", a view consistent with the common law.[1159] Indeed, on the plain terms of s 99(1), recall will only be permitted when required by "the interests of justice". This is a high standard, suggesting that further evidence from a witness is necessary to: (a) ensure trial fairness; (b) prevent a miscarriage of justice; or (c) allow the judge or jury to render a reasoned and appropriate verdict on the facts of the case.

Section 99 is silent as to the specific circumstances in which judges might exercise their discretion to recall witnesses in the interests of justice. Possible situations could involve important but unexpected turns of evidence in a proceeding, or developments suggesting that witnesses who have already testified should be recalled to deal with significant and newly revealed facts.[1160] A noteworthy jury question transmitted to the judge under s 101 of the Act might also necessitate recalling a witness to respond to the enquiry.[1161] In summary (judge alone) proceedings, the course of evidence may cause a judge to seek further testimony from a witness to deal with a substantial matter for decision in the case.

(1)   Cross-examination duties

Perhaps the most likely scenario implicating the recall of a witness under s 99 will involve a party's cross-examination duties under s 92.[1162]

1155   See *Adams on Criminal Law*, CA368.02; Ch5.16.03. See, eg, *R v Wilson* [1997] 2 NZLR 500; (1996) 14 CRNZ 607; *R v S* 17/9/07, Panckhurst J, HC Christchurch CRI-2006-009-1151; *Tassell v Police* 7/12/06, Lang J, HC Rotorua CRI-2006-463-69 (finding no prejudice to the accused when the Crown failed to call the arresting officer as a witness in its case).
1156   See EV5.01.
1157   See EV99.01 above.
1158   LC *Evidence Reform*, para 438.
1159   LC *Evidence Code*, para C362.
1160   See, eg, *R v Ellis (No 15)* 27/5/93, Williamson J, HC Christchurch T9/93 (allowing the defence to recall a Crown witness for further cross-examination in order to put several new matters to the witness omitted during the initial cross-examination).
1161   See EV101.01.
1162   See EV92.04(2).

A codification of the common law duty to "put the case"[1163] of an adversary party to a witness under cross-examination, s 92(1) requires a party to "cross-examine a witness on substantial matters of the party's case that contradict the evidence of the witness if the witness is, or might be, in a position to give admissible evidence on those matters." If a party fails to comply with that section, the judge has, among other options, the discretion to "grant permission for the witness to be recalled and questioned about the contradictory evidence" (s 92(2)(a)). Unlike s 99(1), s 92(2)(a) does not limit the judge's discretion to recall a witness only where required by the interests of justice. However, in light of the s 99(1) test, a court's decision to opt for recalling a witness under s 92(2)(a) is likely to be governed by what is necessary to do justice in the case. Recall is therefore most likely to occur where the contradictory evidence to be put to the witness deals with a central matter in the proceeding, and involves a subject on which the recalled witness has significant information to impart.[1164]

EV99.04   Examination by the parties

Section 99 presumably covers decisions to recall a witness made by the judge himself or herself, or made by the judge at the request of one or more of the parties to the proceeding. Nonetheless, a witness recalled under s 99 should still be considered the witness of the party that first called him or her to the stand. As a result, a judge should permit questions to be put to a recalled witness by the parties in the usual way (that is, through examination in chief, cross-examination and re-examination as provided for by ss 84, 89, and 97). Pursuant to s 100(1), a witness recalled by a judge may also be subject to judicial questioning if "justice requires".[1165]

EV99.05   Time for recalling witnesses

Section 99 provides fixed time limits within which the judicial recall of a witness may take place. When the case is being tried with a jury, recalling a witness is permitted "at any time until the jury retire to consider their verdict" (s 99(2)(a)).[1166] In summary (judge alone) proceedings, recall may occur "at any time until judgment is delivered" in the case (s 99(2)(b)). These limits coincide with the time limits for the discretionary admission of further evidence after the close of a party's case under s 98(1) and (5).[1167]

100   Questioning of witnesses by Judge

(1)   In any proceeding, the Judge may ask a witness any questions that, in the opinion of the Judge, justice requires.

1163   LC *Evidence Reform*, para 401.
1164   See EV92.04(2). See also, eg, *R v McNeill* (2000) 144 CCC (3d) 551 (Ont CA); *R v W (CA222/06)* 1/3/07, CA222/06; [2007] NZCA 34 (observing that, where the late recall of a Crown witness took place as a result of arguments made by defence counsel in his closing address, the trial judge could have instead opted to advise the jury that such arguments were not founded upon any question put to a witness in the case).
1165   See EV100.01.
1166   See, eg, *R v W (CA222/06)* 1/3/07, CA222/06; [2007] NZCA 34.
1167   See EV98.03.

(2)   If the Judge questions a witness,—

    (a)   every party, other than the party who called the witness, may cross-examine the witness on any matter raised by the Judge's questions; and

    (b)   the party who called the witness may re-examine the witness.

EV100.01   Judicial questioning of witnesses

Section 100 codifies the existing practice of permitting judges in civil and criminal proceedings to ask their own questions of witnesses. However, the provision makes it clear that a judge should question a witness only when necessitated by the requirements of justice (s 100(1)). Accordingly, s 100 reminds judges that they are not advocates, and must remain a neutral and impartial arbiter at trial.

EV100.02   Interests of justice

Existing case law — including, in criminal proceedings, decisions explicating the fair trial provision of s 25(a) of the New Zealand Bill of Rights Act 1990 — will guide the exercise of judicial discretion under s 100(1).[1168] As a result, judges will generally be entitled to "put questions to a witness in order to clarify an obscure answer or to resolve possible misunderstandings of any question by a witness [or] to remedy an omission of counsel, by putting questions which the Judge thinks ought to have been asked in order to bring out or explain a relevant matter".[1169] However, the nature and scope of judicial questioning must not suggest to an impartial observer, fully apprised of all the relevant facts, that there is a "real danger" that "the [court] would not discharge its task impartially as between the litigants".[1170] Indeed, s 100 will not permit judicial questioning of witnesses that causes a court to lose the appearance of neutrality required by law, or that creates a "real danger that the trial was unfair".[1171]

As the requirements of justice referred to in s 100(1) will differ with the facts of each proceeding, the line between acceptable and non-acceptable judicial questioning of

---

1168   Section 25(a) of the New Zealand Bill of Rights Act 1990 provides that anyone tried for a criminal offence has the right to a "fair and public hearing by an independent and impartial court". For discussion of the case law related to s 25(a) and judicial questioning in criminal trials, see Rishworth, Huscroft, Optican, and Mahoney, *The New Zealand Bill of Rights*, Melbourne, Oxford University Press, 2003, 673-675.

1169   *R v Darlyn* (1946) 88 CCC 269 (BCCA), 277 (cited with approval in *Brouillard v R* [1985] 1 SCR 39 (SCC)). See, eg, *R v Yorston* 21/12/06, CA195/06, para 26 (interventions by trial judge were "necessary to prevent an irrelevant or objectionable or potentially dangerous line of questioning" by accused's counsel and did not result in an unfair trial); *E H Cochrane Ltd v Ministry of Transport* [1987] 1 NZLR 146 (CA), 150 (judicial questioning can be constructive in "clarifying issues or eliminating irrelevancies").

1170   Rishworth, Huscroft, Optican, and Mahoney, *The New Zealand Bill of Rights*, Melbourne, Oxford University Press, 2003, 673 (citing *Auckland Casino Ltd v Casino Control Authority* [1995] 1 NZLR 142 (CA), 149). See also *R v Fotu* [1995] 3 NZLR 129 (CA); *R v Loumoli* (1995) 13 CRNZ 7 (CA); *R v Parata* (2001) 19 CRNZ 352 (CA), 360.

1171   *R v Parata* (2001) 19 CRNZ 352 (CA), 360. See also *R v H (CA421/01)* (2002) 19 CRNZ 518 (CA); *Tassell v Police* 7/12/06, Lang J, HC Rotorua CRI-2006-463-69 (self-represented defendant in a criminal case did not get a fair trial when the judge took over the questioning of a defence witness and the accused did not have an opportunity to question the witness himself).

---

witnesses may sometimes be difficult to draw. This will be particularly true in criminal trials. In *R v H (CA421/01)*, the Court of Appeal stated:[1172]

> "Intervention by a judge in performing the legitimate and important role of assisting a jury in a criminal trial can have the incidental effect of advancing the case of the Crown or defence to some extent. That consequence of clarification of evidence is often inevitable and is not in itself objectionable. What the judge is, however, bound to do is to refrain from stepping outside the limits of the judicial role ... As well, while acting within the legitimate scope of the judicial role, the judge must not act in a manner which reasonably gives rise to an impression there is a lack of neutrality in the judge's conduct of the trial ...

> "Particular difficulties can arise from judicial intervention in the course of cross-examination in a criminal trial. The judge may give the impression of criticism of the conduct of the cross-examination of a particular witness by counsel. This can equally apply to prosecution as well as to defence counsel. In such a case the judge's own questions, especially if asked in more neutral terms than those of counsel, may also indicate the judge is impressed with the witness, reinforcing the credibility of the witness in the eyes of the jury. There is a risk also that frequent interventions may have a detrimental effect on the efficacy of cross-examination of important witnesses. Sometimes they can seriously interfere with the legitimate designs of counsel to weaken the adversary's case by a structured and planned cross-examination. In general, while cross-examination is being competently undertaken, it is prudent for a judge to interrupt only to the extent necessary to clarify matters in the evidence the jury may misunderstand: *R v Sharp* [1993] All ER 225, 235 (CA); *R v M* (1991) 7 CRNZ 439, 444 (CA)."

However, as noted by Lamar J in the Supreme Court of Canada's decision in *Brouillard v R*, "it is clear that judges are no longer required to be as passive as they once were ... We now not only accept that a judge may intervene in the adversarial debate, but also believe that it is sometimes essential for him to do so for justice to be done".[1173] Moreover, the level of acceptable judicial intervention may change given the characteristics of the witness and/or the nature of the issues in the case.

For example, more active judicial questioning may be particularly appropriate in child custody proceedings where the court must decide the best interests of the child.[1174] Similarly, in *R v H (CA421/01)*, the Court of Appeal observed:[1175]

1172   *R v H (CA421/01)* (2002) 19 CRNZ 518 (CA), para 34. See *Adams on Criminal Law*, Ch5.27.02.
1173   *Brouillard v R* [1985] 1 SCR 39 (SCC), para 17.
1174   See *Cundy v Irving* (1998) 106 BCAC 5 (BCCA).
1175   *R v H (CA421/01)* (2002) 19 CRNZ 518 (CA), para 35. Pursuant to s 85 of the Act, a judge may disallow a question put to a witness where, because of the witness's "age or maturity" (s 85(2)), the question is "expressed in language that is too complicated for the witness to understand" (s 85(1)). See EV85.01-03.

"In the case of a child witness the judge has the further particular responsibility to ensure questions put by counsel, including cross-examining counsel, are clear and appropriate for a child of that age and development, so that the child witness understands them. Nevertheless, the legitimate desire to assist a child witness to understand and be able to respond to questions does not permit the judge to take over the role of counsel in the adversary system."

EV100.03   Further questioning by parties

In the interests of party fairness, s 100(2)(a) provides that, if the trial judge questions a witness, every party, other than the party who called the witness, "may cross-examine the witness on any matter raised by the judge's questions". Similarly, s 100(2)(b) states that the calling party may re-examine the witness — presumably on matters arising out of any judicial questioning during cross-examination or adversarial party cross-examination triggered under s 100(2)(a). See further the discussion of re-examination under s 97.[1176]

101   Jury questions

(1)   If a jury wishes to put a question to a witness in a proceeding,—

     (a)   the jury must first inform the Judge of the question; and

     (b)   the Judge must determine—

         (i)   whether and how the question should be put to the witness; and

         (ii)   if the question is to be put to the witness, whether the parties may question the witness about matters raised by the question.

(2)   If a question from the jury is put to a witness, then, subject to any determination made by the Judge under subsection (1)(b)(ii),—

     (a)   every party, other than the party who called the witness, may cross-examine the witness on any matter raised by the jury's question; and

     (b)   the party who called the witness may re-examine the witness.

EV101.01   Jury questions

When sitting with a jury, s 101 grants judges the discretion to allow jury members to put a question to a witness on the stand.

The regulated process set out in s 101 requires the jury to inform the judge that they wish to put a question to a witness in a civil or (as is most likely to be the case) criminal proceeding (s 101(1)(a)). The judge must then determine: (a) "whether and how the question should be put to the witness" (s 101(1)(b)(i)); and (b) if the question is put to the witness, whether the parties in the case "may question the witness about matters raised by the question" (s 101(1)(b)(ii)). If the jury's question is put to the witness, and the judge permits the parties to question the witness about the matters raised by the question, "every party, other than the party who called the witness, may cross-

---

1176   See EV97.01.

examine the witness on any matter raised by the jury's questions" (s 101(2)(a)). The party who called the witness may then re-examine the witness (s 101(2)(b)). However, pursuant to s 97 of the Act, such re-examination will generally be limited to the scope of the matters raised in cross-examination allowed under s 101(2)(a).[1177]

EV101.02   Exercise of judicial discretion

In line with overseas studies, research by the New Zealand Law Commission has concluded that, "if properly controlled, jury questions would promote the rational ascertainment of facts, which is one of the primary purposes of the [Evidence Act 2006]".[1178] Accordingly, s 101 leaves it to judicial discretion as to whether and how a jury question will be put to a testifying witness, and the extent to which the non-calling parties may question the witness about the matters raised by the question. The provision gives no guidance as to the manner in which such discretion should be exercised. However, to the extent applicable, a judge will likely consider the following points:

(a)   The relevance and significance of the jury question to the issues in the proceeding;

(b)   The extent to which the question raises a new matter related to the witness's evidence or seeks to clarify the witness's existing testimony;

(c)   Whether the matters raised in the jury question are, in some fashion, likely to be dealt with by the parties in the course of the trial;

(d)   Whether the jury question should be put to the witness by the judge or counsel for a party to the case;

(e)   The clarity and coherence of the jury question, the likelihood of jurors being confused or misinformed by the witness's response, and the possibility of the question generating an answer made inadmissible by some other provision of the Act; and

(f)   Whether a witness's response to the question is likely to encourage further jury questioning and the desirability of allowing such questioning in the proceeding.

EV101.03   Advice to juries

Section 101 is silent as to whether and how juries should be told of their ability to ask questions of witnesses under the Act. In its 2001 report, *Juries In Criminal Trials*, the Law Commission determined that "juries should be routinely advised of their right to submit questions to the Judge, which the Judge may then put to the witness."[1179] However, while case law has always accepted the idea of jury questioning of

---

1177   See EV97.01.

1178   New Zealand Law Commission, *Juries in Criminal Trials*, NZLC R69, Wellington, 2001, para 360. See also LC *Evidence Reform*, para 444.

1179   Ministry of Justice Criminal Practice Committee, *Guide to Jury Trial Practice*, Wellington, 2003, para 58 (citing New Zealand Law Commission, *Juries in Criminal Trials*, NZLC R69, Wellington, 2001, para 368).

witnesses, it has not looked favourably on judicial advice or procedures designed to encourage the practice.[1180] In its 2003 *Guide to Jury Trial Practice*, the Ministry of Justice Criminal Practice Committee agreed that jurors should be informed of their ability to put questions to a witness in a criminal case.[1181] Nonetheless, the Committee concluded:[1182]

> "The jury should be told that it is not certain that any question they want put will actually be asked because evidence is for counsel. The process for asking questions must be formal, to ensure that it remains controlled and is only used where necessary and appropriate."

The Committee also proposed the following method for dealing with jury questions in criminal proceedings:[1183]

> "(a)   The Judge in his or her opening remarks should advise the jury that they may ask questions during the trial, and that this should be done only for the purpose of clarifying what has been said, and advise them of the process to be followed. The process is that questions should be put in writing and given to the Judge who might or might not put it to the witness or give it to counsel to decide whether they want to put it to the witness. The jury should be advised that the rules of evidence prevent some questions from being asked, so they should not be concerned if their question is not put to the witness.

> "(b)   If the jury has a question, the foreman should write it down and give it to the court taker during an adjournment, and the court taker will then deliver it to the Judge.

> "(c)   The Judge may wish to where appropriate show the written question to counsel and hear their views on an appropriate response."

In its commentary on the Evidence Act, the Law Commission suggested that, when the jury alerts the judge that they wish to put a question to a witness, "[t]he judge is likely to alert counsel, because in many cases it will be appropriate for counsel to put the question".[1184]

EV101.04   Timing of jury questions

Presumably, the processes described above necessitate that, during the taking of testimony at trial, jurors will be given some opportunity to consider whether they

---

1180   See, eg, *R v Parata* (2001) 19 CRNZ 352 (CA), 359; *R v Lo Presti* [1992] 1 VR 696 (Vic SC), 701-702.

1181   Ministry of Justice Criminal Practice Committee, *Guide to Jury Trial Practice*, Wellington, 2003, para 58.

1182   Ministry of Justice Criminal Practice Committee, *Guide to Jury Trial Practice*, Wellington, 2003, para 58.

1183   Ministry of Justice Criminal Practice Committee, *Guide to Jury Trial Practice*, Wellington, 2003, para 59. See *R v Yorston* 21/12/06, CA195/06, for a discussion of other common law procedures devised for dealing with jury questions during a criminal trial that could be employed at a judge's discretion under s 101.

1184   LC *Evidence Code*, para 366.

wish to put a question (or questions) to a particular witness on the stand. Depending on the course of the proceedings, a judge would also have the power to recall witnesses to answer a jury question pursuant to s 99 of the Act.[1185] Jury questions might also be put to witnesses if a judge allows a party to re-open its case pursuant to s 98.[1186] However, by virtue of ss 98(5)(a) and 99(2)(a), no additional evidence is permitted and no witnesses may be recalled after the jury retires to consider its verdict.[1187] Accordingly, no jury questions may be put to witnesses once deliberations in a civil or criminal proceeding have commenced.

Subpart 5—Alternative ways of giving evidence

(s 102 to s 120)

102   Application

Sections 103 to 106 (which provide for alternative ways of giving evidence) are subject to the following provisions (which deal with specific situations):

(a)   section 107 (which relates to child complainants):

(b)   sections 108 and 109 (which relate to undercover police officers):

(c)   sections 110 to 119 (which relate to anonymous witnesses).

EV102.01   Overview

Section 102 is a reminder that when the witness in question fits within one of the three classes listed, the specified provisions of the Act relating to each must be followed.

General

103   Directions about alternative ways of giving evidence

(1)   In any proceeding, the Judge may, either on the application of a party or on the Judge's own initiative, direct that a witness is to give evidence in chief and be cross-examined in the ordinary way or in an alternative way as provided in section 105.

(2)   An application for directions under subsection (1) must be made to the Judge as early as practicable before the proceeding is to be heard, or at any later time permitted by the court.

(3)   A direction under subsection (1) that a witness is to give evidence in an alternative way, may be made on the grounds of—

    (a)   the age or maturity of the witness:

    (b)   the physical, intellectual, psychological, or psychiatric impairment of the witness:

    (c)   the trauma suffered by the witness:

1185   However, s 99(1) requires that any judicial recall of a witness be "in the interests of justice". See EV99.01.

1186   See EV98.01.

1187   See, respectively, EV98.03 and EV99.05.

(d)   the witness's fear of intimidation:

(e)   the linguistic or cultural background or religious beliefs of the witness:

(f)   the nature of the proceeding:

(g)   the nature of the evidence that the witness is expected to give:

(h)   the relationship of the witness to any party to the proceeding:

(i)   the absence or likely absence of the witness from New Zealand:

(j)   any other ground likely to promote the purpose of the Act.

(4)   In giving directions under subsection (1), the Judge must have regard to—

     (a)   the need to ensure—

         (i)   the fairness of the proceeding; and

         (ii)   in a criminal proceeding, that there is a fair trial; and

     (b)   the views of the witness and—

         (i)   the need to minimise the stress on the witness; and

         (ii)   in a criminal proceeding, the need to promote the recovery of a complainant from the alleged offence; and

     (c)   any other factor that is relevant to the just determination of the proceeding.

EV103.01   Extension of the availability of "alternative ways" of giving evidence to all witnesses in any proceedings

Sections 103-106 are an expansion of ss 23D-23E of the (now repealed) Evidence Act 1908. Those sections provided that young or "mentally handicapped" complainants in a sexual case could give evidence in another "mode" (by pre-recorded videotape or behind one-way glass, for example (s 23E)). Sections 103-106 of the Act expand the earlier regime by granting a power to the judge to permit *any* witness in *any* proceeding to give evidence in chief and be cross-examined in an alternative way. This includes a defendant in a criminal proceeding,[1188] and witnesses in civil proceedings.[1189] The "alternative ways" in which a witness may give evidence are set out in s 105.

EV103.02   The role of inherent jurisdiction under the Act

Prior to the introduction of the Act, there was some debate as to whether the court could rely on its inherent jurisdiction to allow witnesses other than those covered by the statutory regime to give evidence from behind a screen, for example. The case of *R v Moke & Lawrence* confirmed that in some cases other vulnerable witnesses, especially complainants could testify in a different "mode",[1190] although in relation to adult complainants this has usually only been via the provision of a screen, not by pre-recorded videotape.[1191] Just prior to the Act coming into effect, however, the Court

---

1188   See EV103.07.

1189   See also EV188.04.

1190   *R v Moke & Lawrence* [1996] 1 NZLR 363; (1995) 13 CRNZ 386 (CA).

of Appeal confirmed the decision of a trial judge that the evidential video of a 6-year-old child, who was witness to burglary and wounding with intent in his own home, could be played at trial:[1192]

> "We have no doubt that there is jurisdiction to permit evidence of child witnesses to be given otherwise that in the ordinary fashion and, in particular, in part through a video interview."

The Act no longer requires a court to resort to its inherent jurisdiction on making an order for any witness to give their evidence in chief in an alternative way. However, the answer is not so clear with regard to directions as to the way cross-examination and re-examination should proceed.

EV103.03   Pre-trial cross-examination under the Act

Although s 103(1) refers to cross-examination of a witness in an alternative way, it is arguable that the Act does not provide for *pre-trial* cross-examination. Section 105(1)(a)(iii) appears to recognise pre-trial cross-examination as part of the alternative way of giving evidence known as a "video record" (defined in s 4) which is made before the hearing of the proceeding. Section 106, which deals specifically with video record evidence, does not state explicitly that it is solely a means of offering a witness's examination in chief. However, s 105(2) seems to assume that in every case in which video record evidence is employed, further directions will be needed under s 103 as to the manner in which cross-examination and re-examination is to be conducted. Cross-examination could occur in either of the ways set forth in s 105(1)(a)(i) or (ii), but both of these alternative ways of giving evidence involve the witness testifying at the hearing itself. On the basis of the wording of these provisions, it is arguable that pre-trial cross-examination is not provided for in the Act.[1193]

In *R v Kereopa*,[1194] however, Heath J directed, pursuant to s 103(1), that a prosecution witness's evidence (including cross-examination) be taken by video record, on the basis that she was terminally ill and unlikely to be alive at the time of trial.

The Law Commission initially proposed that pre-trial cross-examination and re-examination should form part of the draft Code, in the case of child complainants or elderly witnesses.[1195] Although the wording of the Code left open the possibility of

---

1191   *R v Daniels* (1993) 10 CRNZ 165 (CA), 168; *R v Kahui* 10/7/07, Williams J, HC Auckland CRI-2006-057-1135, para 17.

1192   *R v Lewis* 28/11/06, CA311/06, para 10, contra *R v Paul* 21/9/05, MacKenzie J, HC Palmerston North CRI-2004-054-102, para 21.

1193   Section 201 does not exclude the possibility of pre-trial cross-examination. However, currently the only regulations made under s 201 of the Act that deal with the recording of video evidence apply to the evidential interviews of complainants. "This subpart applies to the video recording of a complainant's evidence if it is intended that the video record may be offered later as evidence in a criminal proceeding": Evidence Regulations 2007, reg 4.

1194   *R v Kereopa* 18/9/07, Heath J, HC Tauranga CRI-2007-087-411.

1195   New Zealand Law Commission, *The Evidence of Children and Other Vulnerable Witnesses*, NZLC PP26, Wellington, 1996, paras 144-155; draft ss 20-21.

pre-trial cross-examination by video record, the Law Commission did not recommend its use in its final report, due to the almost unanimous opposition from the defence bar.[1196] The Law Commission stated: "Until more is known about the experience of other jurisdictions with pre-trial cross-examination, the Law Commission does not recommend it."[1197]

Since the publication of the report and draft Code, there have been a number of other jurisdictions that have adopted or are conducting pilots on the use of pre-trial cross-examination.[1198] Most significantly, s 28 of the Youth Justice and Criminal Evidence Act 1999 (UK)[1199] provides for mandatory pre-trial cross-examination of all child witnesses who are "in need of special protection".[1200] Due to concerns expressed by the Criminal Bar Association, plans to implement pilots were deferred, and repeal of s 28 was even mooted following the presentation of an unsupportive report in 2004.[1201] In June 2007, however, a review of trial processes for young witnesses recommended the retention of s 28 "for use by the most vulnerable witnesses if this is the only way in which they would be able to give their evidence".[1202]

Given that there is now information from other jurisdictions available, it may be appropriate for New Zealand to consider the use of pre-trial cross-examination. Although it may well be possible for the practice to develop as part of an exercise of the inherent jurisdiction (s 11), because of the concerns of the profession and the argument that the Act does not provide statutory authority, it may be a matter best left for clear legislative regulation. The Law Commission was of the view that the provision of pre-trial cross-examination is consistent with the purposes of the Act and with the rationale of providing access to alternative ways for vulnerable witnesses.[1203]

EV103.04   Re-examination in an alternative way

Sections 103(1), 104, and 107(1) only provide for a witness to give *evidence in chief* and be *cross-examined* in an alternative way. No provision is made for re-examination of the witness in the same or any other alternative way. This appears to

---

1196   LC *Evidence Reform*, para 459.

1197   LC *Evidence Reform*, para 460.

1198   See Hoyano and Keenan, *Child Abuse Law and Policy Across Boundaries*, Oxford, Oxford University Press, 2007.

1199   Section 28 was based on the recommendations from The Home Office, *Report of the Advisory Group on Video Evidence*, London, 1989 and The Home Office, *Speaking Up for Justice*, London, 1998.

1200   Defined in the Act as those who are testifying about alleged sexual or violent offences, abduction or neglect (ss 21 and 35 of the Youth Justice and Criminal Evidence Act).

1201   See Birch and Powell, *Meeting the Challenges of Pigot: Pre-Trial Cross Examination under s 28 of the Youth Justice and Criminal Evidence Act 1999 — A Briefing Paper for the Home Office*, Nottingham, Nottingham University, 2004.

1202   Office for Criminal Justice Reform, *Improving the Criminal Trial Process for Young Witnesses: A Consultation Paper* London, 2007. For a commentary on this paper, see Hoyano, "The Child Witness Review: Much Ado about too Little" [2007] *Criminal Law Review* 849.

1203   New Zealand Law Commission, *The Evidence of Children and Other Vulnerable Witnesses*, NZLC PP26, Wellington, 1996, paras 144-155.

---

be due to a legislative oversight. Section 105(2) assumes that directions under s 103(1) can include the manner in which a witness is to be re-examined, but s 103(1) makes no mention of re-examination. It may be that s 105(2) will be relied upon as providing sufficient authority to give directions for re-examination to be conducted in an alternative way. However, that solution would only apply when the witness's evidence in chief has been given by a video record, as opposed to some other alternative way of giving evidence not mentioned in s 105(2). It may be tempting to suggest that a witness's "evidence in chief" under s 103(1) should be interpreted to include evidence given in re-examination. The problem with this suggestion is that s 84(1) draws a clear distinction between a witness giving evidence in chief and then being re-examined. Therefore, it must be concluded that s 103(1) gives no jurisdiction to direct that a witness be re-examined in an alternative way. To avoid this oversight, a judge may rely on his or her inherent powers (s 11) and direct that a witness be re-examined in the same alternative way in which he or she gave evidence in chief and was cross-examined.

EV103.05   Direction to give evidence in ordinary way

Section 103(1) provides that a direction can be made that a particular witness give evidence in chief and be cross-examined "in the ordinary way". This refers to s 83. An application for a witness to give evidence in the ordinary way may occur when some question is raised about the vulnerability or other characteristic of a potential witness and a party wishes to clarify the means by which the witness will give evidence. It may also be that the witness, although a child, may prefer to give evidence in the ordinary way. The views of witnesses and child complainants must be considered when the judge makes a decision as to how they will give evidence (ss 103(4)(b) and 107(4)(b)).

EV103.06   Witness

In requiring that an application be made as early as practicable before the proceeding is to be heard, s 103(2) clearly anticipates that the "witness" referred to in this Subpart includes a person who is scheduled to give evidence at some future point in the proceeding (see the discussion of "witness" in s 4).[1204]

EV103.07   Parties and defendants in criminal proceedings

There is no express provision stating that a "witness" for the purpose of s 103 does not include a party who will testify. The Law Commission was of the view that even a defendant in a criminal proceeding could apply under s 103 to give evidence in chief and be cross-examined in an alternative way, although this would be exceptional.[1205] Examples of cases where alternative ways of giving evidence have been made available to defendants include those when the safety of the defendant may be at risk.[1206] In such cases, a video link is used so the defendant is not required to physically be present in court (see s 105(1)(a)(ii)).

1204   See EV4.46.02.
1205   LC *Evidence Code*, para C371; LC *Evidence Reform*, para 454ff.

Although some of the various provisions in ss 103-106 appear to be based on the assumption that a party and the witness in question are separate people (for example, ss 103(3)(h), 104(a), and 105(1)(a)(i) and (c)), they are drafted as alternatives to other considerations or situations which may well apply to a defendant in a criminal proceeding. The amendment made in the legislative process to read "or some other specified person" in s 105(1)(a)(i)[1207] may well apply to a defendant (as a witness) who may find it too difficult to testify while being able to see the alleged victim, or members of the victim's family.[1208]

EV103.08   Grounds for directing how a witness is to give evidence

Section 103(3) sets out the grounds upon which a direction may be given that a witness is to give evidence in the ordinary or an alternative way. The grounds must be considered in tandem with the matters set out in s 103(4). Some of the grounds listed in s 103(3) are drafted with particular relevance to specific alternative ways of giving evidence as listed in s 105. For example, s 103(3)(i) is directed at the alternative way of giving evidence referred to in s 105(1)(a)(ii). In different contexts, some of the grounds also appear elsewhere in the Act, for example in ss 85(2) and 95(3).

EV103.09   Subsection (3)(c): intellectual, psychological, or psychiatric impairment

This ground takes the place of the inquiry into whether the complainant in a sexual case had a "mental handicap" under the Evidence Act 1908. This Act provides no special procedure or approach for witnesses with this type of impairment, as compared to child complainants — see s 107. The Law Commission, in their preliminary paper, articulated the reasons for this change:[1209]

> "On the face of it, this reduces the protection for intellectually disabled complainants because an application on their behalf in sexual cases will no longer be mandatory. The Law Commission believes that this approach is sustainable because: the distinction between child complainants and all other witnesses is clear and easy to draw; the identification of intellectually disabled witnesses may not always be straightforward, and a mandatory requirement may impose an unrealistic burden on the parties; dealing with intellectually disabled people and children as one group is inappropriate; and the capacities of people with intellectual disabilities vary significantly and should be assessed according to individual need, not as members of a group."

1206   New Zealand Law Commission, *The Evidence of Children and Other Vulnerable Witnesses*, NZLC PP26, Wellington, 1996, fn 144 (referring to the case of Martin Bryant in Tasmania); see also the recent reference to telephone conferencing as opposed to a court appearance for Graeme Burton (*Radio New Zealand Newswire*, 24 April 2007).

1207   Ministry of Justice, *Letter of Advice to the Minister of Justice*, 8 February 2005, 14.

1208   The issue as to whether defendants in criminal proceedings should be able to give evidence in an alternative way was not the subject of any submissions on this part of the Bill.

1209   New Zealand Law Commission, *The Evidence of Children and Other Vulnerable Witnesses*, NZLC PP26, Wellington, 1996, para 137.

Intellectual disability is therefore now one of the grounds for giving a direction, and requires an application from a party or on the judge's own initiative. There is no mandatory requirement that such a direction is sought.

EV103.10   Subsection (3)(c): trauma

It appears that s 103(3)(c) refers to any trauma suffered by the witness by virtue of the events about which the witness is to give evidence, rather than any trauma to be caused by the act of giving evidence. Although a witness may be traumatised by the process of giving evidence in the ordinary way, this can be taken into account under para (j), referring to the purposes of the Act in s 6 as helping "secure the just determination of proceedings" or "promoting fairness to parties and witnesses" (also specifically referred to in s 103(4)(a)(i)). The argument is that a witness who may be traumatised by the experience of giving evidence in the ordinary way (orally, in court) will not give the best evidence, hence not resulting in a "just determination".

EV103.11   Subsection (3)(d): intimidation

Section 103(3)(d) is framed broadly. The fact that a witness can be intimidated while giving evidence by someone other than a defendant in a criminal proceeding is implicit in s 105(1)(a)(i). Note, however, that a specific reference to "intimidating questions" in s 85 was removed by the Select Committee.[1210]

EV103.12   Subsection (3)(g) and (h): the nature of the evidence and the relationship of the witness to any party

These two grounds will be particularly relevant when considering the position of complainants in cases involving sexual offences and domestic violence.[1211] Given the abolition of spousal non-compellability, resort will no doubt be had to s 103: "Often the circumstances arising in such cases would provide sufficient justification to allow a spouse [or partner] to give evidence in an alternative way."[1212] The use of alternative ways may also be used as a way to mitigate the effects of personal cross-examination in cases where no absolute bar is imposed by s 95(1).

EV103.13   Subsection (3)(e): religious belief

The fact that s 105(1)(a) provides only a closed list of alternative ways of giving evidence should be emphasised in considering s 103(3)(e). It might be thought that this paragraph could be relied upon to justify a direction that a Muslim woman be entitled to testify while wearing the complete facial covering of a burqua, an issue

---

1210   See EV85.03(1).

1211   See, eg, *R v Hekkenberg* 8/11/06, Gendall J, HC Nelson CRI-2005-042-4128 (ordering that three non-complainant adult witnesses — daughters of the accused facing murder charges — be screened from him while giving testimony in order to ensure their ability to give cogent evidence and due to the fear of their father as a result of alleged extensive historical abuse). See also *R v Kahui* 10/7/07, Williams J, HC Auckland CRI-2006-057-1135, para 10 (permitting an adult complainant in a sexual assault case to be screened from the defendant when giving testimony to ensure that the complainant "can give her evidence in a manner which will best place the issues in the trial before the jury for its decision").

1212   Gordon, Morgan QC, Morris, and Williams, "The Criminal Trial Process" in NZLS *Intensive: Evidence Act 2006*, 206.

that arose while the Evidence Bill was in the drafting process. Although this is presumed to be the reason for the addition of the reference to the ground of "religious belief" (it was not a ground contained in the draft Code which referred only to "cultural background"),[1213] no explanation of the addition is contained in any of the relevant Cabinet Papers. However, if this was the reason for the addition, none of the alternative ways listed in s 105 encompass a direction that would allow a witness to testify with their face covered in this way. The resolution of the concern of a Muslim woman may well have to be addressed as it was prior to the Act — by use of a screen which allowed the witness's face to be seen by the judge, the lawyers, and female court staff, but by no-one else.[1214]

EV103.14   Subsection (3)(i): the absence or likely absence of the witness from New Zealand

This ground makes it clear that the directions under s 103 can be made in cases where the witness is not "vulnerable". The ability for the court to order that evidence be given from a witness who is overseas or in another part of the country (see also s 168) is related to the definition of "unavailable" in s 16. If a person can be a witness, even though out of the country or bed-ridden, through use of a video link for example, they will not be considered "unavailable" for the purposes of the exception to the hearsay rule (s 18).

EV103.15   Subsection (4): mandatory considerations

The judge must also consider the matters set out in s 103(4). The broad requirement placed on the judge by s 103(4)(c) imposes quite an onerous duty — to consider *any* matter which is relevant to the just determination of the proceeding (which is also repetitious of s 103(3)(j)). It is not easy to understand why it was considered necessary to include both s 103(4)(a)(i) and (ii). This is a change in drafting from the Code, which instead provided: "and in particular in a criminal proceeding, that the defendant has a fair trial." Both aspects of the need to ensure fairness are also contained in s 6(b) and (c), s 6(b) referring specifically to the rights affirmed by the New Zealand Bill of Rights Act 1990. In this context, s 25(e) and (f) have particular relevance.[1215]

That fairness to witnesses also should be considered when deciding to direct on the use of alternative ways was recognised before the Act came into force:[1216]

> "It remains to be said that in the determination to ensure our criminal trial process is as fair as possible, fairness to all accused should predominate since they, of course, have most to lose. But fairness to an accused is not the only criterion. The fairness of a criminal trial is fairness on all its bearings, including fairness to a complainant. The community, too, has a deep interest in trials

---

1213   See also the discussion of this ground at LC *Evidence Reform*, para 458.
1214   *New Zealand Herald*, 18 January 2005.
1215   See the discussion of the consideration of fairness to the defendant in a criminal case in New Zealand Law Commission, *The Evidence of Children and Other Vulnerable Witnesses*, NZLC PP26, Wellington, 1996, 51-53 and further at EV83.02(1).
1216   *R v Kahui* 10/7/07, Williams J, HC Auckland CRI-2006-057-1135, para 15.

being fair so that the guilt or innocence of those of crimes can be best assesses. That includes witnesses being able to give evidence in manner which best presents the issues in a trial to the jury or judge."

The New Zealand Law Society, in its submission to the Select Committee, recommended the removal of s 103(4)(b)(ii) on the basis that it "is putting the cart before the horse to require a Judge to have regard to the need to promote recovery of a complainant from an alleged offence prior to the defendant's guilt being proved."[1217] Wording such as "the importance of promoting the recovery of the complainant from the offence, if it occurred" may have better expressed the relevant consideration.[1218] Many judges may feel ill equipped to assess the extent to which any particular alternative way of giving evidence listed in s 105 will achieve the aim stated in s 103(4)(b)(ii). In such a case the judge may call for a report under s 104(b).

104   Chambers hearing before directions for alternative ways of giving evidence

If an application for directions is made under section 103, before giving any directions about the way in which a witness is to give evidence in chief and be cross-examined, the Judge—

(a)   must give each party an opportunity to be heard in chambers; and

(b)   may call for and receive a report, from any person considered by the Judge to be qualified to advise, on the effect on the witness of giving evidence in the ordinary way or any alternative way.

EV104.01   Restrictions when judge acts on own initiative

The opening phrase of s 104 seems to limit the section's operation, so that the right to be heard given to the parties by s 104(a) does not apply when, pursuant to s 103(1), the judge of his or her own initiative directs that a witness is to give evidence in an alternative way. This may well be the unintentional result of a drafting change that was not identified as a policy change in any of the relevant Cabinet Papers.

The draft Code's version of this section provided that "the judge must give each party an opportunity to be heard in chambers" before giving "any directions about the way in which a witness is to give evidence." The commentary to the draft provision stated: "the right of each party to be heard under s 104(1) relates to the decision on whether the application should be granted and, if so, to the terms of the directions."[1219] That the parties should be heard on a decision to give directions, even when done at the judge's own initiative, seems axiomatic.

The same drafting issue arises in relation to the report referred to in s 104(b). The section does not seem to authorise the obtaining of such a report when the judge acts on his or her own initiative in raising the issue of a witness giving evidence in an

---

1217   NZLS *Submission on the Evidence Bill*, 42.
1218   The authors are grateful to the late Judge Murray Abbott for this point.
1219   LC *Evidence Code*, para C373.

alternative way. However, in such a case a judge would likely rely on his or her inherent powers, under s 11, to order such a report.

EV104.02   Qualifications of person making report

The person giving the report referred to in s 104(b) must only meet the standard set out in that subsection. He or she need only be considered by the judge to be "qualified to advise" on the matters referred to in s 104(b). However, under the similar provision in the earlier legislation, Fisher J pointed out in *R v Teariki*[1220] that the person providing the report is giving expert opinion evidence and thus must be duly qualified as an expert witness. Fisher J held that for this reason, a report in the form of an affidavit by the mother of a young complainant should not have been accepted in evidence. Under the Act, a similar result is likely. See s 4's definition of "expert evidence"[1221] and the substantial helpfulness test in s 25(1).[1222]

According to the Law Commission: "The decision as to who is qualified to provide a report is one for the judge, who may or may not choose to hear submissions from counsel on the point. The parties will have a right to be heard on the substance of any report received by the judge, but not on the choice of who should be asked to provide it."[1223]

105   Alternative ways of giving evidence

(1)   A Judge may direct, under section 103, that the evidence of a witness is to be given in an alternative way so that—

     (a)   the witness gives evidence—

         (i)   while in the courtroom but unable to see the defendant or some other specified person; or

         (ii)   from an appropriate place outside the courtroom, either in New Zealand or elsewhere; or

         (iii)   by a video record made before the hearing of the proceeding:

     (b)   any appropriate practical and technical means may be used to enable the Judge, the jury (if any), and any lawyers to see and hear the witness giving evidence, in accordance with any regulations made under section 201:

     (c)   in a criminal proceeding, the defendant is able to see and hear the witness, except where the Judge directs otherwise:

     (d)   in a proceeding in which a witness anonymity order has been made, effect is given to the terms of that order.

(2)   If a video record of the witness's evidence is to be shown at the hearing of the proceeding, the Judge must give directions under section 103 as to the manner in which cross-examination and re-examination of the witness is to be conducted.

1220   *R v Teariki* (1999) 16 CRNZ 540.

1221   See EV4.15.01.

1222   See EV25.02.

1223   LC *Evidence Code*, para C373.

(3)   The Judge may admit evidence that is given substantially in accordance with the terms of a direction under section 103, despite a failure to observe strictly all of those terms.

EV105.01   Closed list of alternatives

Section 105(1)(a) sets out the possible alternative ways by which a witness may be directed under s 103(1) to give evidence in chief and be cross-examined. It is important to recognise that this is a *closed list* of possible alternative ways, even though it is drafted in a way that accommodates "new ways of giving evidence that advancing technology may make possible."[1224] Rather than listing the various ways of giving evidence that is permissible under this part of the Act, s 105 sets out the requirements of any alternative ways.

EV105.02   Screening

The possibility referred to in s 105(1)(a)(i) will often involve the simple expedient of the witness giving evidence behind a screen. This subparagraph also recognises that a person other than the defendant in a criminal proceeding may intimidate a witness. The fact that the witness is unable to see "the defendant or some other specified person" may appear to make it inevitable that the defendant or other person will not be able to see the witness in such a case. However, s 105(1)(c) assumes that the general rule in a criminal proceeding is that the defendant must be able to see and hear the witness. This can be achieved by a variety of means, including a one-way mirror or glass (as was specifically referred to in s 23E(1)(c) of the Evidence Act 1908).

Section 105(1)(c) provides for a direction that the defendant shall not be able to see or even *hear* the witness giving evidence. Concerns about this provision were raised by the New Zealand Law Society who were of the view that "the defendant when present in Court should always be able to hear the evidence being given against him or her unless he or she forfeits that right by misconducting themselves so as to bring section 376 of the Crimes Act into play."[1225] No change was made to the section, presumably because the Select Committee accepted the Ministry of Justice's view: "While it may be extremely rare, the situation where the defendant is unable to hear the [witness] may arise. For example, if the witness has an anonymity order and a distinctive voice, the Judge may direct that the witness's voice is disguised in some way."[1226]

Section 105(1)(b) appears to assume a rule that, when a defendant is represented by a lawyer, at least the defendant's lawyer (and the other persons referred to in the subsection) must be able to see and hear the witness.

EV105.03   Video record

"Video record" is defined in s 4.[1227]

1224   LC *Evidence Code*, para C376.
1225   NZLS *Submission on the Evidence Bill*, 43.
1226   *Departmental Report* (EV/MOJ/2), 23.
1227   See EV4.43.01.

Section 105(1)(a)(iii) is given substance by s 106. The discussion at EV103.03 suggested that the effect of s 105(2) is that a video record can only contain the witness's evidence in chief. The Act arguably makes no provision for pre-trial cross-examination or re-examination. This subparagraph only refers to video records "made before the hearing of the proceeding". Although it would be unusual, presumably it could be that a video record of a witness's evidence is made *during* the hearing of the proceeding (perhaps when the witness cannot attend court and a suitable video link is not available). Section 105 does not accommodate such a situation (and it maybe that regulations made under s 201 may ultimately prevent it), however, it could be a situation dealt with by way of s 11.

EV105.04   Directions as to which alternative way should be employed

The Act does not prioritise the various ways that evidence may be given, although the focus will no doubt remain on what measure is most effective to ensure the witness gives the best evidence, which will enhance the "truth finding process".[1228] This may mean that for adult complainants in cases involving sexual abuse or domestic violence, giving evidence in a way that means they cannot see the defendant will meet their particular concerns. The evidence of young children may, however, be more reliable when recorded as soon as practicable after the event,[1229] so the use of pre-recorded video tape may be the best way to achieve the admission of the best evidence, which may also have the effect of reducing stress for a young witness. As discussed at EV103.15, if a judge is unsure which way of giving evidence will best respond to the needs of the particular witness, a report may be called for from a person who is "qualified to advise" (s 104(b)).

It may also be argued that early recording of relevant evidence enhances its reliability, regardless of the age of the witness or the circumstances of the case. As recently pondered by Williams J:[1230]

> "The norm [of requiring witnesses to be physically present in the court room] appears to be one of very long standing, but whether there is empirical evidence to support it is unknown. Such would be a fascinating study, as would the question as to whether the norm remains the optimum means of conducting

1228   *R v L* [1993] 4 SCR 419 (SCC); see also New Zealand Law Commission, *The Evidence of Children and Other Vulnerable Witnesses*, NZLC PP26, Wellington, 1996, paras 101-121.

1229   New Zealand Law Commission, *The Evidence of Children and Other Vulnerable Witnesses*, NZLC PP26, Wellington, 1996, paras A1-A12.

1230   *R v Kahui* 10/7/07, Williams J, HC Auckland CRI-2006-057-1135, para 13. Research that considers fact-finders' ability to accurately assess credibility clues due to a witness's physical presence in the courtroom indicates that there is a "no better than chance" likelihood of making accurate assessments of veracity on the basis of witness demeanour: Stromwall and Granhag, "How to detect deception? Arresting the beliefs of police officers, prosecutors and judges" (2003) 9(1) *Psychology, Crime and Law* 19; Orcutt, Goodman, Tobey, Batterman-Faunce, and Thomas, "Detecting deception in children's testimony: Factfinders' abilities to reach the truth in open court and closed-circuit trials" (2001) 18(4) *Law and Human Behaviour* 339. See also New Zealand Law Commission, *Evidence Law: Character and Credibility: A Discussion Paper*, NZLC PP27, Wellington, 1997, para 115ff.

trials in an era of widespread digital cameras, mobile phones with camera facilities, email and the internet."

EV105.05   Facilitating alternative ways of giving evidence

Section 105(1)(b)-(d) should not be seen as adding to the closed list of alternative means of giving evidence set out in s 105(1)(a). The regulations referred to in s 105(1)(b) will be promulgated pursuant to s 201. Those already promulgated do not cover all matters regulating the use of video records, just "the video recording of a complainant's evidence if it is intended that the video record may be offered later as evidence in a criminal proceeding".[1231] Section 105(1)(d) recognises that as long as the terms of an existing witness anonymity order granted under ss 110-118 are adhered to, they can be supplemented by directions that the witness is to give evidence in an alternative way.

There is no requirement that the judge's directions under s 105(2) must be that the witness is to be cross-examined or re-examined in an *alternative way*. Section 103(1) anticipates the possibility of a direction that the witness give evidence in the ordinary way, as per s 83.

EV105.06   No re-enactment of s 23E(4) of the Evidence Act 1908

This section provided that where a complainant gave evidence from behind a partition or closed-circuit television, the judge could also direct that the questions to be put to the complainant "shall be given through an appropriate audiolink to a person, approved by the Judge, placed next to the complainant, who shall repeat the question to the complainant." It seems likely that this provision was previously considered necessary to ensure that a complainant could properly hear the question that was asked, due to the type of technology in use when the section was enacted (s 23E(1)(d) actually refers to the evidence of the complainant who is behind a partition being given through an audiolink). If the situation arises under the Act where a witness cannot hear the questions well enough, communication assistance may be required (s 80(3)). If a witness has concerns about who is asking the question, this may be considered under s 95, if relevant.

EV105.07   Breach of terms of a direction

Section 105(3) assumes that evidence that does not comply with a direction given under s 103(1) can be excluded, and this is so whether the variation from the direction was substantial or not. It is a matter for the judge's discretion. See similarly s 106(8), which applies to a video record.

EV105.08   Jury warning

For the special jury warning required when any witness gives evidence in an alternative way in a criminal proceeding, see s 123(1)(a).

1231   Evidence Regulations 2007, reg 4.

106   Video record evidence

(1)   In a criminal proceeding tried on indictment, the video record evidence of a witness that is to be offered as an alternative way of giving evidence at the trial—

(a)   must, if a video record of that witness's evidence was offered in evidence at the preliminary hearing, include the same video record; and

(b)   may include a video record made after the preliminary hearing.

(2)   A video record offered as an alternative way of giving evidence must be recorded in compliance with any regulations made under this Act.

(3)   A video record that is to be offered as an alternative way of giving evidence in a proceeding must be offered for viewing by all parties or their lawyers before it is offered in evidence, unless the Judge directs otherwise.

(4)   A copy of any video record that is to be offered as an alternative method of giving evidence in a proceeding—

(a)   must be given to the lawyer for each party before it is offered in evidence, unless the Judge directs otherwise; and

(b)   must be dealt with in accordance with any requirements set out in regulations made under section 201 concerning the custody or return of copies of video records, or prohibiting or restricting their copying.

(5)   All parties must be given the opportunity to make submissions about the admissibility of all or any part of a video record that is to be offered as an alternative way of giving evidence.

(6)   If any party indicates that the party wishes to object to the admissibility of all or any part of a video record that is to be offered as an alternative way of giving evidence, that video record must be viewed by the Judge.

(7)   The Judge may order to be excised from a video record offered as evidence any material that, if the evidence were given in the ordinary way, would or could be excluded in accordance with this Act.

(8)   The Judge may admit a video record that is recorded and offered as evidence substantially in accordance with the terms of any direction under this subpart and the terms of regulations referred to in subsection (2), despite a failure to observe strictly all of those terms.

Editorial Note: Evidence Amendment Bill (No 2) 2007

Section 106 may be amended by the Evidence Amendment Bill (No 2) 2007 which, if passed, will repeal subsection (4) and substitute the following subsection:

"(4)   A copy of any video record that is to be offered as an alternative method of giving evidence in a proceeding must be dealt with in accordance with any requirements set out in regulations made under section 201 concerning the custody or return of copies of video records, or prohibiting or restricting their copying."

EV106.01   Use of video records not limited to indictable proceedings

Although s 106(1) refers to indictable proceedings, this should not be taken to be a limitation on the power under s 103(1) to direct that evidence be given in an alternative way. Section 106(1) is designed solely to deal with the issues raised by video records and preliminary hearings and these issues only arise in indictable proceedings. Directions under s 103 may be given in summary or indictable proceedings as well as civil proceedings.

"Video record" is defined in s 4.

EV106.02   Use of a video record made after a preliminary hearing

Section 106(1)(b) allows for video interviews of a witness that have been obtained after a preliminary hearing to be offered at trial. Under the previous provision (s 23E(1)(a) of the Evidence Act 1908) only video records that were produced at the preliminary hearing could be used at trial.[1232] Under the Act, a video record can now be used at trial if the need to do so only becomes apparent after the preliminary hearing:[1233]

> "This will enable video-recorded evidence to be offered if initial expectations that a witness will be able to give evidence in the ordinary way are not subsequently borne out. If for any reason a witness whose evidence has been video-recorded later becomes unavailable for cross-examination, the evidence is hearsay and must comply with the hearsay rules."

EV106.03   Regulations

Subsections (3) and (4) both anticipate regulations governing the process of offering evidence through a video record (see s 201). The New Zealand Law Society was concerned about the use of the words "unless the Judge directs otherwise" in s 106(3) on the basis that for "the purpose of preparation for trial the defence should be entitled to a copy of a video record to be offered in evidence against the defendant. The privacy interests of the compliant can be adequately protected by statutory conditions as to counsel not further copying the video record, retaining it in counsel's custody, and returning the copy to the court at the conclusion of the proceedings".[1234] The Select Committee did not recommend that change but did add s 106(4) (which may be amended):[1235]

> "We are mindful of the risk to confidentiality that video records may create, so we recommend that regulations be made governing the copying, custody, and return of copies of video records.

> "We consider that the behaviour of lawyers is controlled by their professional rules of conduct and ethics and we believe that the New Zealand Law Society

---

1232   Gordon, Morgan QC, Morris, and Williams, "The Criminal Trial Process" in NZLS *Intensive: Evidence Act 2006*, 206; see also *Cross on Evidence* (8th NZ ed), para 7.10.

1233   LC *Evidence Code*, para C379.

1234   NZLS *Submission on the Evidence Bill*, 45.

1235   See Editorial Note relating to the Evidence Amendment Bill (No 2) 2007 above.

has a responsibility to maintain adequate standards for conduct of lawyers. This will ensure that lawyers can pursue the interests of their clients and protect the interests of vulnerable witnesses with clear guidelines."[1236]

For the regulations dealing with copying of and access to video records, see regs 14-20 of the Evidence Regulations 2007.

Section 106(6) differs from the previous provision, s 23E(2) of the Evidence Act 1908, in that the judge is only required to view a video record if there is an objection to the admissibility of all or part of it. This change was not recommended by the Law Commission, and was objected to by the New Zealand Law Society.[1237] The Ministry of Justice stated that the change was made "because [the requirement for the judge to view the video record in all cases] can be seen as an unduly onerous task and of limited value where no objection to the evidence is to be made. The obligation to challenge inadmissibility is on counsel."[1238]

Section 106(8) is similar to s 105(3). The Law Commission stated that "current case law requires 'substantial but not slavish' compliance with the regulations."[1239] Prior decisions relating to this issue will remain relevant under the Act.[1240]

Directions about child complainants' evidence

107 Directions about way child complainants are to give evidence

(1) In a criminal proceeding in which there is a child complainant, the prosecution must apply to the court in which the case will be tried for directions about the way in which the complainant is to give evidence in chief and be cross-examined.

(2) An application for directions under subsection (1) must be made to the court as early as practicable before the case is to be tried, or at any later time permitted by the court.

(3) When an application is made for directions under subsection (1), before giving any directions about the way in which the complainant is to give evidence in chief and be cross-examined, the Judge—

(a) must give each party an opportunity to be heard in chambers; and

(b) may call for and receive a report, from any persons considered by the Judge to be qualified to advise, on the effect on the complainant of giving evidence in the ordinary way or any alternative way.

(4) When considering an application under subsection (1), the Judge must have regard to—

(a) the need to ensure—

(i) the fairness of the proceeding; and

1236 *Select Committee Report on the Evidence Bill*, 12.
1237 NZLS *Submission on the Evidence Bill*, 45-46.
1238 *Departmental Report* (EV/MOJ/2), 25.
1239 LC *Evidence Code*, para C381.

> > (ii)   that there is a fair trial; and
>
> (b)   the views of the complainant and—
>
> > (i)   the need to minimise the stress on the complainant; and
> >
> > (ii)   the need to promote the recovery of the complainant from the alleged offence; and
>
> (c)   any other factor that is relevant to the just determination of the proceeding.

EV107.01   Mandatory directions for all child complainants

Section 107 broadens the requirements previously contained in s 23D of the Evidence Act 1908 by requiring the prosecution to apply for directions as to the way in which a child complainant is to give evidence in *any* criminal proceeding, not merely sexual cases.

The clear purpose of s 107 is to raise the issue of whether the child complainant is to give evidence in one of the alternative ways provided for by s 105(1)(a) (or whether they will give evidence in the "ordinary way").[1241]

Section 4 defines a "child" as a person under the age of 18 years.

EV107.02   Re-examination and pre-trial cross-examination

See the discussion at EV103.03, which is similar to s 107(1).

EV107.03   The grounds of making an order under s 107

Section 107(3) is similar to s 104. See the discussion of that earlier provision.

Section 107(4) is similar to s 103(4). The reference to taking into account the views of the complainant (changed from "wishes" by the Select Committee) was included by the Law Commission as being "in keeping with New Zealand's obligations under the United Nations Convention on the Rights of the Child, and is supported by research suggesting it is helpful for children to feel they have some control over the process."[1242]

Section 107(4)(c) contains the phrase "any other factor that is relevant to the just determination of the proceeding". This will allow the judge to also consider the factors in s 103(3) which may be relevant to the particular situation and may well impact on the complainant's ability to give the most reliable evidence.

1240   *Adams on Criminal Law — Evidence*, EC17.10.

1241   See EV83.01.

1242   LC *Evidence Code*, para C370. See also New Zealand Law Commission, *The Evidence of Children and Other Vulnerable Witnesses*, NZLC PP26, Wellington, 1996, para 134. The United Nations Convention on the Rights of the Child is reproduced in Schedule 2 to the Children's Commissioner Act 2003.

Giving of evidence by undercover police officers

108 Undercover police officers

(1) This section and section 109 apply in any case where a person is being, or is to be, proceeded against by indictment—

(a) for any offence that is punishable by imprisonment for life or for a term of at least 7 years; or

(b) for any other offence against any provisions of the Misuse of Drugs Act 1975, except sections 7 and 13; or

(c) for an offence against section 98A of the Crimes Act 1961; or

(d) for conspiracy to commit, or for attempting to commit, an offence described in paragraph (a) or (b).

(2) If, in any proceeding to which this section applies, it is intended to call an undercover police officer as a witness for the prosecution, the Commissioner of Police may, at any time before an indictment is presented, file in the court in which the proceedings are to be held a certificate signed by the Commissioner stating, in respect of that witness, the following particulars:

(a) that during the period specified in the certificate the witness was a member of the police and acted as an undercover police officer:

(b) that the witness has not been convicted of any offence or (as the case may require) that the witness has not been convicted of any offence other than the offence, or offences, described in the certificate:

(c) that the witness has not been found guilty of an offence of misconduct or neglect of duty under the Police Act 1958, or (as the case may require) that the witness has not been found guilty of any offence of that kind except the offence or offences described in the certificate.

(3) If, to the knowledge of the Commissioner of Police, the credibility of the witness in giving evidence in any other proceeding has been the subject of adverse comment by the Judge, the Commissioner must also include in the certificate a statement of the relevant particulars.

(4) It is sufficient for the purposes of subsections (2) and (3) if the certificate includes a statement of the nature of any offence or comment referred to in the certificate and the year in which the offence was committed or the comment was made, and it is not necessary to include the venue or precise date of the proceedings or any other particulars that might enable the true name or true address of the witness to be discovered.

(5) In this section and in section 109, **undercover police officer**, in relation to any proceeding to which this section applies, means a member of the police whose identity was concealed for the purpose of any investigation relevant to the proceedings.

Compare: 1908 No 56 s 13A(1)-(5)

EV108.01   Subsection (1): section applies to limited offences

Sections 108 and 109 re-enact, and are almost identical to, s 13A of the Evidence Act 1908, which was introduced in 1986. There is some rearrangement of subsections, and s 108 covers what was s 13A(1)-(5). As is the case with ss 110-119, ss 108 and 109 have not been redrafted in line with the terminology of the Evidence Act 2006.

In re-enacting s 13A of the Evidence Act 1908, ss 108 and 109 provide immunity to undercover officers from disclosure of their identity in cases tried indictably where the offence is punishable for a term of at least 7 years (s 108(1)(a)), for certain offences under the Misuse of Drugs Act 1975 (s 108(1)(b)) and for offences of conspiracy or attempt to commit any offence under s 108(1)(a) or (b). The only substantive change made by s 108 is the addition of the offence of participation in an organised criminal group (s 98A of the Crimes Act 1961) to the qualifying offences in s 108(1).

EV108.02   Rationale for protection of identity

Section 13A of the Evidence Act 1908 was enacted in response to the case of *R v Hughes*,[1243] where the Court of Appeal held that undercover officers could be required to disclose their true identities in a proceeding. The majority of the Court was concerned that, if an officer's real name was not revealed, the defendant could not realistically raise issues affecting the officer's credibility.

It has been held that the provision of anonymity orders can be compatible with the right to a fair trial,[1244] but there is tension between that right and the protection of witnesses:[1245]

> "Any limitation on the ability of an accused person to cross-examine prosecution witnesses may impact on the right to a fair trial. Yet, if offenders are able to avoid punishment by intimidating potential witnesses into silence, the integrity of the criminal justice system will be undermined and the law will fall into disrepute."

However, once an officer has been compelled to reveal his or her true identity, he or she can be of limited use as undercover officers in the future, and may be in danger of retaliation by those they knew undercover.

Sections 108 and 109 attempt to satisfy the need to protect undercover officers whilst also satisfying s 25(a) (the right to a fair and public hearing) and s 25(f) (the right to examine witnesses for the prosecution) of the New Zealand Bill of Rights Act

---

1243   *R v Hughes* [1986] 2 NZLR 129; (1986) 2 CRNZ 18 (CA).

1244   *R v Davis* [2006] 1 WLR 3130 (CA).

1245   New Zealand Law Commission, *Evidence Law: Witness Anonymity*, NZLC R42, Wellington, 1997, para 4. See also *R v Hughes* [1986] 2 NZLR 129; (1986) 2 CRNZ 18 (CA); *S v Pastoors* 1986 (4) SA 222 (W); Beresford, "The new Zealand approach to witness anonymity and the right to a fair trial" (2000) 7 Canta LR 465.

1990.[1246] The same tensions apply in regard to witness anonymity orders under ss 110 and 112.

EV108.03   Commissioner of Police to issue certificate

If the offence is one to which s 108(1) applies, then under s 108(2), the Commissioner of Police may sign and file a certificate confirming that the witness acted as an undercover officer. The purpose of the certificate is to outline any facts that may affect the undercover officer's credibility. To this end, the certificate should state any offences for which the officer has been convicted, including any offences of misconduct or neglect of duty under the Police Act 1958, and any adverse comment regarding the credibility of the witness made by the judge in any other proceeding (s 108(3)). Under s 109(4), a copy of the certificate must be served on the defendant at least 14 days before the witness is to give evidence.

109   Effect of certificate under section 108

(1)   If, in any proceeding to which section 108 applies, the Commissioner of Police files a certificate under section 108 relating to any witness, the following provisions apply:

     (a)   if a witness is subsequently called for the prosecution and states that, during the period specified in the certificate, he or she was a member of the police and acted as an undercover police officer under the name specified in the certificate, it must be presumed, in the absence of proof to the contrary, that the certificate has been given in respect of that witness:

     (b)   it is sufficient if the witness is identified by the name by which the witness was known while acting as an undercover police officer, and, except if leave is given under paragraph (d), the witness must not be required to state his or her true name or address, or to give any particulars likely to lead to the discovery of that name or address:

     (c)   except if leave is given under paragraph (d), no lawyer, officer of the court, or other person involved in the proceeding may state in court the true name or the address of the witness, or give any particulars likely to lead to the discovery of that name or address:

     (d)   no evidence may be given, and no question may be put to the witness, or to any other witness, relating directly or indirectly to the true name or the address of the witness, except by leave of the Judge:

     (e)   on an application for leave under paragraph (d), the certificate is, in the absence of evidence to the contrary, sufficient evidence of the particulars stated in it.

1246   Optican and Rishworth, "Minimum Standards of Criminal Procedure for Trial, Sentencing and Appeals" in Rishworth, Huscroft, Optican, and Mahoney, *The New Zealand Bill of Rights*, Melbourne, Oxford University Press, 2003, 695-697.

(2)   The Judge may not grant leave under subsection (1)(d) unless the Judge is satisfied—

       (a)   that there is some evidence before the Judge that, if believed by the jury, could call into question the credibility of the witness; and

       (b)   that it is necessary in the interests of justice that the defendant be enabled to test properly the credibility of the witness; and

       (c)   that it would be impracticable for the defendant to test properly the credibility of the witness if the accused were not informed of the true name or the true address of the witness.

(3)   An application for leave under subsection (1)(d)—

       (a)   may be made from time to time and at any stage of the proceeding; and

       (b)   must, where practicable, be made and dealt with in chambers; and

       (c)   if the application is made during the trial before a jury, must be dealt with and determined by the Judge in the absence of the jury.

(4)   If the Commissioner of Police gives a certificate under section 108 in respect of any witness, the Commissioner must serve a copy of the certificate on the defendant, or on any lawyer acting for the defendant, at least 14 days before the witness is to give evidence.

Compare: 1908 No 56 s 13A(6)-(9)

EV109.01   Overview

Once the provisions of s 108 are complied with, protection of an undercover officer's identity and place of residence is automatic. As such, s 109 provides that undercover officers may testify under their cover name and no question or evidence may be given that may lead to the discovery of the true identity or address of the witness, except if leave is given under s 109(1)(d).

Section 109(2) provides that leave to give evidence or put questions relating to the true name and address of the witness will only be granted under s 109(1)(d) where the judge is satisfied that there is evidence that could call into question the credibility of the witness, that it is necessary in the interests of justice that the defendant "be enabled to test properly the credibility of the witness", and that this can be achieved only by knowing the true identity of the witness.

Giving of evidence by anonymous witnesses

EV110.Intro.01   Overview of ss 110-119

Sections 110-119 re-enact ss 13B-13J of the Evidence Act 1908, which were introduced in 1997[1247] in response to the decision in *R v Hines*.[1248] In *Hines*, a majority of the Court of Appeal decided that the balancing of competing public interests in

---

1247   See Evidence (Witness Anonymity) Amendment Act 1997.

1248   *R v Hines* (1997) 15 CRNZ 158.

---

enabling protection of identity for witnesses who have fear for their safety should be a task performed by Parliament rather than by the courts. There was (and is) little statistical information on witness intimidation upon which to base a continued need for the provisions in the 2006 Act.[1249]

In the 2006 Act, there is some re-ordering of the earlier sections (for example, s 13B has been split to form ss 110 and 111) and some changes in terminology, but the sections otherwise have changed little from their previous enactment. Section 13F has become s 123(1)(c) of the 2006 Act.[1250]

Sections 110-119 apply only in criminal proceedings, but it is open to the court to exercise its inherent jurisdiction to make an order preserving anonymity in civil proceedings.[1251] In criminal proceedings, protection can be provided outside of the Act where a judge exercises the inherent jurisdiction of the court.[1252]

EV110.Intro.02 Provision applicable only in indictable proceedings

This part of the Act prevents disclosure of a witness's identity in exceptional circumstances, in both criminal pre-trial and trial proceedings by indictment. The restriction to indictable proceedings signals that the protection of witnesses, and the attendant impact on the defendant's rights, should only be contemplated in serious cases. In more minor cases, the public interest in allowing the proceedings to continue by protecting the identity of a witness will not be able to override the rights of the defendant to know who will give evidence against him or her.[1253] As under the pre-2006 Act law, in each case the judge will have to carefully assess, with the aid of s 110(4) and (5) (or s 112(4) and (5)), what the impact on the pre-trial hearing and trial will be should an order be made. In this way, the 2006 Act upholds the Law Commission's initial view that the granting of witness anonymity orders is a power that "must be most carefully circumscribed, to avoid a distortion of our system that, being more insidious, is even more dangerous than witness intimidation."[1254]

EV110.Intro.03 "Identity"

"Identity" is not defined in the 2006 Act. However, it is clear from the cases under s 13B and 13C of the Evidence Act 1908 that the concept of "identity" incorporates all of the aspects of identity outlined in ss 110-119: name, address, occupation and appearance[1255] (as evidenced by the ability to alter the mode of evidence under s 116). That a defendant already knows one aspect of a witness's identity does not necessarily preclude an order being made to prevent disclosure of the other aspects.[1256] The decision should be based on the particular facts of each case.[1257]

1249 New Zealand Law Commission, *Witness Anonymity: A Discussion Paper*, NZLC PP29, Wellington, 1997, para 18; LC *Evidence Reform*, 12.
1250 See also s 87, which protects questioning or evidence about a witness's address.
1251 *Withey v Attorney-General* 18/5/98, Greig J, HC Palmerston North CP10/95.
1252 *R v Dunnill* [1998] 2 NZLR 341; (1998) 17 CRNZ 594.
1253 See EV108.02.
1254 New Zealand Law Commission, *Witness Anonymity: A Discussion Paper*, NZLC PP29, Wellington, 1997, para 66.
1255 *R v Dunnill* [1998] 2 NZLR 341; (1998) 17 CRNZ 594.

EV110.Intro.04   Not a guaranteed protection of identity

It is clear that the provisions in this part of the Act cannot provide a failsafe method of protection of identity, and that any particulars ordered not to be disclosed during proceedings may in some circumstances be able to be otherwise obtained. However, the provisions do offer significant protection for witnesses who have a reasonable fear for safety and security should they be identified during the committal hearing or trial.

110   Pre-trial witness anonymity order

(1)   This section and section 111 apply if a person is charged with an offence and is to be proceeded against by indictment.

(2)   At any time after the person is charged, the prosecution or the defendant may apply to a Judge for an order—

    (a)   excusing the applicant from disclosing to the other party prior to the preliminary hearing the name, address, and occupation of any witness, and (except with leave of the Judge) any other particulars likely to lead to the witness's identification; and

    (b)   excusing the witness from stating at the preliminary hearing his or her name, address, and occupation, and (except with leave of the Judge) any other particulars likely to lead to the witness's identification.

(3)   The Judge must hear and determine the application in chambers, and—

    (a)   the Judge must give each party an opportunity to be heard on the application; and

    (b)   neither the party supporting the application nor the witness need disclose any information that might disclose the witness's identity to any person (other than the Judge) before the application is dealt with.

(4)   The Judge may make the order if he or she believes on reasonable grounds that—

    (a)   the safety of the witness or of any other person is likely to be endangered, or there is likely to be serious damage to property, if the witness's identity is disclosed before the trial; and

    (b)   withholding the witness's identity until the trial would not be contrary to the interests of justice.

(5)   Without limiting subsection (4), in considering the application, the Judge must have regard to—

    (a)   the general right of a defendant to know the identity of witnesses; and

    (b)   the principle that witness anonymity orders are justified only in exceptional circumstances; and

---

1256   *R v Dunnill* [1998] 2 NZLR 341; (1998) 17 CRNZ 594, 347; 598.
1257   See EV110.04.

      (c)   the gravity of the offence; and

      (d)   the importance of the witness's evidence to the case of the party who wishes to call the witness; and

      (e)   whether it is practical for the witness to be protected prior to the trial by any other means; and

      (f)   whether there is other evidence that corroborates the witness's evidence.

(6)   A pre-trial witness anonymity order may be made by—

      (a)   a District Court Judge who holds a warrant under the District Courts Act 1947 to conduct trials on indictment:

      (b)   if the preliminary hearing is held in a Youth Court, a Judge referred to in section 274(2)(a) of the Children, Young Persons, and Their Families Act 1989:

      (c)   a High Court Judge.

Compare: 1908 No 56 s 13B(1)–(5), (7)

EV110.01   Section 110: pre-trial order

Under s 110, the prosecution or defendant may apply to a judge for an order that excuses the applicant from disclosing the name, address, occupation or other information likely to lead to the witness's identification prior to a preliminary hearing. An order may also be granted that excuses the witness from stating any identifying information at a preliminary hearing. Section 110 provides that the judge should make a pre-trial order where he or she believes on reasonable grounds that withholding the identity of the witness is not contrary to the interests of justice, and that the safety of the witness or another person is likely to be endangered or that there is likely to be serious damage to property if the witness's identity is disclosed.

EV110.02   Subsection (4)(a): "likely"

Under both s 110 and s 112, "likely" means that there is a real risk that the endangerment or damage will happen — this was the meaning ascribed to the term under s 13C of the Evidence Act 1908.[1258]

EV110.03   Damage to persons or property may qualify for protection

Prior to the passage of the 2006 Act, the government were advised that serious damage to property, absent any link to endangerment of persons, may not be compliant with the New Zealand Bill of Rights Act 1990[1259] (damage to property in the Evidence (Witness Anonymity) Amendment Act 1997 was added by the Select Committee). This is because a risk of damage to property alone arguably does not justify a restriction of the defendant's right to question the witness in the usual way. However, serious damage to property unaccompanied by endangerment to life remains a

---

1258   *R v Atkins* [2000] 2 NZLR 46; (2000) 17 CRNZ 581 (CA), 53; 587.

1259   Office of the Minister of Justice, *Evidence Bill: Changes to Policy Decisions and Approval for Introduction*, Cabinet Paper (CAB/100/2002/1), March 2005, paras 32-37.

sufficient basis for the exercise of the judge's discretion to order witness anonymity under both s 110 and s 112. Any Bill of Rights Act compliance issue therefore remains unresolved.

EV110.04   Subsection (5): factors that must be considered

Section 110(5) outlines a non-exhaustive list of factors that the judge must have regard to in deciding whether to grant a witness anonymity order. These include the provision that such orders are "justified only in exceptional circumstances".[1260] The issues covered by s 110(5) illustrate the tension between the right to a fair trial and the protection of witnesses from intimidation even at the pre-trial stage, and this tension is present even more clearly in s 112 where the order is made for trial.

111   Effect of pre-trial witness anonymity order

If a pre-trial witness anonymity order is made under section 110,—

(a)   the party who applied for the order must give the Judge the name, address, and occupation of the witness; and

(b)   during the course of the preliminary hearing, no lawyer, officer of the court, or other person involved in the preliminary hearing may disclose the name, address, or occupation of the witness, or any other particulars likely to lead to the witness's identification; and

(c)   during the course of the preliminary hearing,—

    (i)   no oral evidence may be given, and no question may be put to any witness, if the evidence or question relates to the name, address, or occupation of the witness who is subject to the order; and

    (ii)   except with leave of the Judge, no oral evidence may be given, and no question may be put to any witness, if the evidence or question relates to any other particulars likely to lead to the identification of the witness who is subject to the order; and

(d)   no person may publish, in any report or account relating to the proceeding, the name, address, or occupation of the witness, or any other particulars likely to lead to the witness's identification.

Compare: 1908 No 56 s 13B(6)

EV111.01   Overview

Section 111 re-enacts s 13B(6) of the Evidence Act 1908 and outlines the effect of a pre-trial witness anonymity order under s 110. If an order is granted under s 110, then no one involved in the preliminary hearing may disclose the witness's name, address, occupation, or other identifying information. In addition, no evidence may be given or questions put that relate to the witness's name, address or occupation. Questions

---

1260   See s 110(5)(b), "exceptional circumstances" has been deemed to be something "quite out of the ordinary": *Police v Kelly* [1999] DCR 634, citing *Awa v Independent News Auckland Ltd (No 2)* [1996] 2 NZLR 184; (1996) 9 PRNZ 289.

or evidence relating to other particulars likely to lead to identification of the witness may only be given with the leave of the judge.

112   Witness anonymity order for purpose of High Court trial

(1)   This section and section 113 apply if a person is charged with an indictable offence and is committed to—

    (a)   the High Court for trial; or

    (b)   a District Court for trial and is the subject of an application under section 28J of the District Courts Act 1947 to transfer the proceeding to the High Court.

(2)   At any time after the person is committed for trial, the prosecution or the accused may apply to a High Court Judge for a witness anonymity order under this section.

(3)   The Judge must hear and determine the application in chambers, and—

    (a)   the Judge must give each party an opportunity to be heard on the application; and

    (b)   neither the party supporting the application nor the witness need disclose any information that might disclose the witness's identity to any person (other than the Judge) before the application is dealt with.

(4)   The Judge may make a witness anonymity order if satisfied that—

    (a)   the safety of the witness or of any other person is likely to be endangered, or there is likely to be serious damage to property, if the witness's identity is disclosed; and

    (b)   either—

        (i)   there is no reason to believe that the witness has a motive or tendency to be dishonest, having regard (where applicable) to the witness's previous convictions or the witness's relationship with the accused or any associates of the accused; or

        (ii)   the witness's credibility can be tested properly without disclosure of the witness's identity; and

    (c)   the making of the order would not deprive the accused of a fair trial.

(5)   Without limiting subsection (4), in considering the application, the Judge must have regard to—

    (a)   the general right of a defendant to know the identity of witnesses; and

    (b)   the principle that witness anonymity orders are justified only in exceptional circumstances; and

    (c)   the gravity of the offence; and

    (d)   the importance of the witness's evidence to the case of the party who wishes to call the witness; and

(e)   whether it is practical for the witness to be protected by any means other than an anonymity order; and

(f)   whether there is other evidence that corroborates the witness's evidence.

Compare: 1908 No 56 s 13C(1)-(5)

EV112.01   Overview

Section 112 provides for a witness anonymity order to be made in exceptional circumstances, bearing in mind the defendant's right to a fair trial.[1261] Section 112 governs the granting of witness anonymity orders for the purpose of a trial in an indictable criminal proceeding. If an order is granted under s 112, the trial must be heard in the High Court. Only Judges of the High Court are able to grant orders under the section because of the exceptional nature of such orders, and in order to preserve consistency of approach.[1262] It is clear that the power to grant a witness anonymity order is one that should be used in moderation, and that an overall assessment of the case should be made before finding that the circumstances are indeed exceptional.[1263]

EV112.02   Subsection (4)(a): judge must be "satisfied" of danger to persons or property

The judge must be "satisfied"[1264] — which does not carry any particular onus of proof — that if the identity of the witness is disclosed the safety of the witness or another person will be endangered, or that there is likely to be serious damage to property. This does not necessarily require evidence of actual threats, and the likely endangerment or damage need not come from the defendant directly.

EV112.03   Subsection (4)(b): witness credibility must be able to be tested

Unlike the procedure under s 110 for a pre-trial order, the judge must be satisfied under s 112 that the credibility of the witness will be able to be tested without disclosing his or her identity (s 112(4)(b)(ii)), or that there is no reason to believe that the witness is (or has a motive to be) untruthful (s 112(4)(b)(i)). The judge does not have to assess the witness's truthfulness, but must simply be "satisfied" that there is no evidence that raises doubt as to truthfulness, such as any relationship with the accused or previous convictions.

EV112.04   Judge has responsibility to ensure fair trial

Section 112(4)(c) reflects the responsibility of the judge to ensure a fair trial by providing that he or she should be "satisfied" that making a witness anonymity order will not deprive the defendant of a fair trial.[1265]

1261   See EV108.02 and EV110.Intro.02.
1262   New Zealand Law Commission, *Evidence Law: Witness Anonymity*, NZLC R42, Wellington, 1997, para 20.
1263   *R v Atkins* [2000] 2 NZLR 46; (2000) 17 CRNZ 581 (CA), para 30.
1264   Unlike s 110, where he or she must "believe on reasonable grounds".
1265   See EV108.02 and EV110.Intro.02.

EV112.05　Inconsistency of terminology

Section 112(4)(c) refers to "an accused" rather than "a defendant", but it is to be assumed that this is an oversight when changing the terminology of the 1908 Act to the 2006 Act.

EV112.06　Appeals against decision on provision of order

Appeals against the making of an anonymity order, or against a refusal to make an anonymity order under ss 112 and 113 are governed by s 379A(1)(f) of the Crimes Act 1961.

113　Effect of witness anonymity under section 112

If a witness anonymity order is made under section 112,—

(a)　the party who applied for the order must give the Judge the name, address, and occupation of the witness; and

(b)　the witness may not be required to state in court his or her name, address, or occupation; and

(c)　during the course of the trial no lawyer, officer of the court, or other person involved in the proceeding may disclose—

　　(i)　the name, address, or occupation of the witness; or

　　(ii)　except with leave of the Judge, any other particulars likely to lead to the witness's identification; and

(d)　during the course of the trial—

　　(i)　no oral evidence may be given, and no question may be put to any witness, if the evidence or question relates to the name, address, or occupation of the witness who is subject to the order; and

　　(ii)　except with leave of the Judge, no oral evidence may be given, and no question may be put to any witness, if the evidence or question relates to any other particulars likely to lead to the identification of the witness who is subject to the order; and

(e)　no person may publish, in any report or account relating to the proceedings, the name, address, or occupation of the witness, or any other particulars likely to lead to the witness's identification.

Compare: 1908 No 56 s 13C(6)

EV113.01　Overview

For s 113, the effect of an order made under s 112 is the same as that of pre-trial orders under s 111.[1266]

1266　See EV111.01.

114 Trial to be held in High Court if witness anonymity order made

(1) If an application to transfer a proceeding to the High Court is made under section 28J of the District Courts Act 1947 and a witness anonymity order is made under section 112 in that case before the application is dealt with, the Judge considering the application must transfer the proceeding to the High Court.

(2) In any other case where a witness who may be called to give evidence in a criminal trial is the subject of a witness anonymity order made under section 112, the trial must be held in the High Court.

(3) This section has effect despite anything in sections 28A and 28J of the District Courts Act 1947.

Compare: 1908 No 56 s 13A

EV114.01 Overview

Where a defendant charged with an indictable criminal offence is committed to the District Court, any application for a witness anonymity order can only be considered under s 112 if there is an application to transfer the proceeding to the High Court. If a witness anonymity order is made under s 112 before the transfer application is dealt with, s 114 provides that the proceeding must be transferred to the High Court. Section 114(2) reiterates that the trial must be heard in the High Court wherever a witness subject to an anonymity order may be called to give evidence. This reflects the desire to restrict the granting of orders to serious criminal offences.

115 Judge may appoint independent counsel to assist

(1) For the purposes of considering an application for a witness anonymity order under section 112, the Judge may appoint an independent counsel to assist the Judge and, without limiting the directions the Judge may give, the Judge may direct the independent counsel to—

(a) inquire into the matters referred to in section 112(4)(a) and (b) and any other matters the Judge thinks relevant; and

(b) report the counsel's findings to the Judge.

(2) The party who applied for the witness anonymity order must make available to the independent counsel all information relating to the proceeding that is in the party's possession.

(3) Fees for professional services provided by counsel appointed under this section, and reasonable expenses incurred,—

(a) may be determined in accordance with regulations made under section 201; and

(b) are payable from money appropriated by Parliament for the purpose.

(4) The bill of costs submitted by a counsel appointed under this section must be given to the Registrar of the High Court in which the proceeding was heard, and the Registrar may tax the bill of costs.

(5)   If the counsel is dissatisfied with the decision of the Registrar as to the amount of the bill, the counsel may, within 14 days after the date of the decision, apply to a Judge of the court to review the decision, and the Judge may make any order varying or confirming the decision that the Judge considers fair and reasonable.

Compare: 1908 No 56 s 13E

EV115.01   Overview

Section 115 gives the judge discretion to appoint independent counsel when considering an application under s 112. The section provides that the judge may ask the independent counsel to inquire into matters relevant to establishing whether the safety of the witness or other person is likely to be endangered, or property likely to be seriously damaged, if the witness's identity is disclosed. Independent counsel can also make inquiries regarding the honesty of the witness, and any other relevant matter. To aid efficiency and accuracy of the process, the party who applies for the witness anonymity order must make all information they have that relates to the proceeding available to the independent counsel under s 115(2).

The appointment of independent counsel safeguards the interests of the party against whom anonymous evidence will be given. As this is usually the defendant, the function of s 115 is to "compensate as far as practicable for the disadvantage to the defence occasioned by the order,"[1267] given that the ability of the defendant to raise issues regarding the claims and credibility of the witness will be severely reduced both at the time the application is considered (see s 112(3)(b)) and, if the order is made, at trial. In other words, the appointment of independent counsel should reduce the risk of injustice inherent in an encroachment on the right of the defendant to "face accusers" and cross-examine all witnesses for the prosecution (see discussion regarding the tension inherent in witness anonymity provisions).[1268]

116   Judge may make orders and give directions to preserve anonymity of witness

(1)   A Judge who makes an order under section 110 or 112 may, for the purposes of the preliminary hearing or trial (as the case may be), also make any orders and give any directions that the Judge considers necessary to preserve the anonymity of the witness, including (without limitation) 1 or more of the following directions:

     (a)   that the court be cleared of members of the public:

     (b)   that the witness be screened from the defendant:

     (c)   that the witness give evidence by closed-circuit television or by video link.

1267   New Zealand Law Commission, *Witness Anonymity: A Discussion Paper*, NZLC PP29, Wellington, 1997, para 71.

1268   See EV108.02.

(2)   In considering whether to give directions concerning the mode in which the witness is to give his or her evidence at the preliminary hearing or trial, the Judge must have regard to the need to protect the witness while at the same time ensuring a fair hearing for the defendant.

(3)   This section does not limit—

(a)   section 206 of the Summary Proceedings Act 1957 (which confers power to deal with contempt of court); or

(b)   section 138 of the Criminal Justice Act 1985 (which confers power to clear the court); or

(c)   any power of the court to direct that evidence be given, or to permit evidence to be given, by a particular mode.

Compare: 1908 No 56 s 13G

EV116.01   Overview

Section 116 provides that where either a pre-trial or trial witness anonymity order is given, the judge may also make any orders necessary to protect the anonymity of the witness. Possible directions are outlined in s 116(1), but these are not exhaustive. As in other provisions regarding alternative modes of giving evidence,[1269] and under ss 110 and 112, the judge must have regard to protecting the witness and also ensuring that the hearing is fair (s 116(2)).[1270] The terms of a witness anonymity order will have precedence over the general provision governing alternative ways of giving evidence.[1271] However, directions as to alternative ways of giving evidence can supplement the terms of a witness anonymity order and may be utilised in order to give full effect to it.

117   Variation or discharge of witness anonymity order during trial

At any time before a witness gives evidence during a trial, a High Court Judge may, on his or her own motion or on the application of either party, vary or discharge a witness anonymity order made for the purposes of the proceeding under section 112.

Compare: 1908 No 56 s 13H

EV117.01   Overview

This section applies to witness anonymity orders made for the purpose of a trial under s 112. Variation or discharge may result from issues reported to the judge by an independent counsel appointed under s 115, or for any other reason raised by either party. Variation may include the addition of extra provisions to preserve anonymity under s 116. Variation or discharge can only take place under s 117 *before* a witness gives evidence. This means that witnesses will not begin giving evidence and then

---

1269   See EV103.15.

1270   However, see *R v Atkins* [2000] 2 NZLR 46; (2000) 17 CRNZ 581 (CA), where extensive measures were taken to protect witnesses, including voice and image distortion. The Court of Appeal held that any adverse inferences could be lessened by firm direction from the trial judge.

1271   See s 105(1)(d) and EV105.05.

have their identity revealed if an order is discharged; instead, witnesses will know prior to giving evidence whether they will have protection, and what form that protection will take.

118 Witness in police witness protection programme

If, at any time after the events that are the subject of a charge, a witness under a police witness protection programme assumes a new identity, the witness may not be required in any proceeding concerning the charge to disclose his or her assumed name or any particulars likely to disclose his or her new identity.

Compare: 1908 No 56 s 13I

EV118.01   Overview

Undoubtedly, disclosure of assumed names and new identities would undermine the expensive and difficult process of witness protection. Section 118 protects witnesses who are in a witness protection programme from disclosing anything likely to indicate their new identity.

119 Offences

(1)   A person commits an offence and is liable on conviction on indictment to a term of imprisonment not exceeding 7 years who, with knowledge of a pre-trial witness anonymity order made under section 110, intentionally contravenes section 111(b) or (d).

(2)   A person commits an offence and is liable on conviction on indictment to a term of imprisonment not exceeding 7 years who, with knowledge of a witness anonymity order made under section 112, intentionally contravenes section 113(c) or (e).

(3)   If a person contravenes section 111(b) or (d) or 113(c) or (e), and that contravention does not constitute an offence against subsection (1) or (2) of this section, the person commits an offence and is liable on summary conviction,—

(a)   in the case of an individual, to a fine not exceeding $2,000:

(b)   in the case of a body corporate, to a fine not exceeding $10,000.

(4)   Nothing in this section limits the power of any court to punish any contempt of court.

Compare: 1908 No 56 s 13J

EV119.01   Overview

As a witness anonymity order is given only in exceptional circumstances, where the safety of the witness is endangered (or serious damage to property is likely), it was the Law Commission's view that a more adequate deterrent penalty was required than that available for contempt of court[1272] (see s 401 of the Crimes Act 1961). Section

---

1272   New Zealand Law Commission, *Witness Anonymity: A Discussion Paper*, NZLC PP29, Wellington, 1997, para 70.

119 provides for penalties for breach of a witness anonymity order made under either s 110 or s 112, and re-enacts s 13J of the Evidence Act 1908. The penalty in s 119(1) and (2) are commensurate with the penalty for perverting the course of justice (s 117(d) of the Crimes Act 1961).

Section 119(3) provides for summary punishment where the knowledge and intention required under subss (1) and (2) are not present, both for individuals and bodies corporate.

Signature of statements by assumed name

120   Persons who may sign statements by assumed name

(1)   A deposition or other written statement of evidence given by an undercover police officer may be given and signed in the name by which the officer was known during the relevant investigation.

(2)   A deposition or other written statement given by a witness who is the subject of an application for an anonymity order made under section 112, or who is the subject of an anonymity order made under section 110 or 112, may be given and signed by the witness using the term "witness" followed by an initial or mark.

(3)   This section overrides any contrary provision in this Act or any other enactment.

Compare: 1957 No 87 s 178A

EV120.01   Overview

Section 120 substantially re-enacts s 178A of the Summary Proceedings Act 1957. It allows for undercover police officers and witnesses subject to anonymity orders under s 110 or s 112 to sign a statement under an assumed name (undercover officers) or initial or mark (anonymous witnesses). The section will act to prevent disclosure of the identity of these classes of witnesses should their statements be disclosed to the defendant.

Subpart 6—Corroboration, judicial directions, and judicial warnings

(s 121 to s 127)

EVPt3Sub6.01   Overview

With one exception, Subpart 6 of Part 3 applies to criminal proceedings only. The exception is s 125(2) with regard to children's evidence.

121   Corroboration

(1)   It is not necessary in a criminal proceeding for the evidence on which the prosecution relies to be corroborated, except with respect to the offences of—

(a)   perjury (section 108 of the Crimes Act 1961); and

(b)   false oaths (section 110 of the Crimes Act 1961); and

(c)   false statements or declarations (section 111 of the Crimes Act 1961); and

(d)   treason (section 73 of the Crimes Act 1961).

(2)   Subject to subsection (1) and section 122, if in a criminal proceeding there is a jury, it is not necessary for the Judge to—

      (a)   warn the jury that it is dangerous to act on uncorroborated evidence or to give a warning to the same or similar effect; or

      (b)   give a direction relating to the absence of corroboration.

EV121.02   Corroboration not generally required

Section 121(1) confirms the approach under the previous law that, for the majority of offences, evidence need not be corroborated in criminal proceedings (see ss 12B and 23AB of the Evidence Act 1908). The offences requiring corroboration are set out in s 121(1)(a)-(d).[1273]

In drafting the Evidence Code version of s 121, the Law Commission followed the approach of the Evidence Law Reform Committee's *Report on Corroboration* (1984), which took the view that a corroboration requirement added nothing to the trier of fact's evaluation of the evidence in most cases.[1274]

EV121.03   Offences requiring corroboration

The offences listed in s 121(1)(a)-(d) are exceptions to the general view that corroboration adds little to the fact-finding task. Perjury and related offences were justified as exceptions by the Law Commission in order to protect witnesses from "vexatious accusations of lying on oath. It is thought that making it too easy to prosecute someone for perjury might discourage people from giving evidence, which is undesirable."[1275] Presumably the view is that even truthful witnesses would be discouraged should they risk easy accusations of perjury. The justification for treason as an excepted offence is perhaps more questionable. The Law Commission adopted the argument of the Evidence Law Reform Committee's *Report on Corroboration* (1984) that corroboration is necessary where treason is charged, because of the risk that dominant political parties could obtain false testimony of treason in order to get rid of troublesome opponents. This concern appears less realistic in the current political climate, over 20 years after the Evidence Law Reform Committee's report.[1276]

EV121.04   No warning or direction generally required

Section 121(2) provides that there is no requirement for either a general warning to the jury about the dangers of relying on uncorroborated evidence, or a direction relating to the absence of corroboration.

EV121.05   Prohibition of warning in cases involving child complainants

Section 125(1) prohibits such a warning in cases involving child complainants where the warning would not have been given had the complainant been an adult.

1273   See also Crimes Act 1961, ss 75 and 112.
1274   Evidence Law Reform Committee, *Report on Corroboration*, Wellington, 1984.
1275   LC *Evidence Reform*, 123.
1276   Evidence Law Reform Committee, *Report on Corroboration*, Wellington, 1984.

EV121.06   Section 121 subject to s 122

Section 121(2) is subject to the need for corroboration for the offences outlined in s 121(1)(a)-(d), and to s 122, which allows the judge to warn the jury about unreliable evidence. If the judge is of the opinion that uncorroborated evidence may be unreliable, he or she may warn the jury of the need for caution, notwithstanding the general provision in s 121(2). This would not necessarily take the form of the warning envisaged under s 121(2)(a) and (b), but could do so.

122   Judicial directions about evidence which may be unreliable

(1)   If, in a criminal proceeding tried with a jury, the Judge is of the opinion that any evidence given in that proceeding that is admissible may nevertheless be unreliable, the Judge may warn the jury of the need for caution in deciding—

    (a)   whether to accept the evidence:

    (b)   the weight to be given to the evidence.

(2)   In a criminal proceeding tried with a jury the Judge must consider whether to give a warning under subsection (1) whenever the following evidence is given:

    (a)   hearsay evidence:

    (b)   evidence of a statement by the defendant, if that evidence is the only evidence implicating the defendant:

    (c)   evidence given by a witness who may have a motive to give false evidence that is prejudicial to a defendant:

    (d)   evidence of a statement by the defendant to another person made while both the defendant and the other person were detained in prison, a police station, or another place of detention:

    (e)   evidence about the conduct of the defendant if that conduct is alleged to have occurred more than 10 years previously.

(3)   In a criminal proceeding tried with a jury, a party may request the Judge to give a warning under subsection (1) but the Judge need not comply with that request—

    (a)   if the Judge is of the opinion that to do so might unnecessarily emphasise evidence; or

    (b)   if the Judge is of the opinion that there is any other good reason not to comply with the request.

(4)   It is not necessary for a Judge to use a particular form of words in giving the warning.

(5)   If there is no jury, the Judge must bear in mind the need for caution before convicting a defendant in reliance on evidence of a kind that may be unreliable.

(6)   This section does not affect any other power of the Judge to warn or inform the jury.

EV122.01   Overview

Section 122 is primarily concerned with trials by jury. The section applies only to criminal proceedings. It provides in subs (1) that the judge *may* warn the jury about evidence that he or she thinks may be unreliable; and in subs (2) that the judge *must consider* doing so whenever certain classes of evidence are given. Its scope is very broad.

Section 122 therefore confirms that reliability is not generally a requirement of admissibility. However, certain admissibility rules, such as ss 18 and 25, have as their mainstay an evaluation of reliability before admissibility is allowed; and s 8(1)(a) would act to exclude very unreliable evidence where its probative value is outweighed by the risk that the evidence will have an unfairly prejudicial effect on the proceeding.

EV122.02   Subsection (1): discretionary not mandatory

Where the judge is of the opinion that admissible evidence may be unreliable, s 122(1) permits him or her to warn the jury of the need for caution in deciding both whether to accept the evidence and the weight to give to it.[1277]

The Act allows for discretion to be exercised in every case, not just where there is a certain class of evidence under s 122(2) or where a party requests the giving of a warning under s 122(3). It is questionable what s 122(2) adds to s 122(1) apart from a requirement that the judge takes extra care to focus his or her mind on the need for a warning where certain kinds of evidence are given.

(1)   Focus on evidence relating to the defendant's guilt

It appears that a general warning under s 122(1) may apply to evidence from all parties — defendant, co-defendant or prosecution. However, the overall focus of the section is evidence relating to the defendant's guilt (from either the prosecution or a co-defendant) and protection of the defendant's due process rights. This is articulated in the self-warning reminder in s 122(5) and in s 122(2)(b)-(e), which focus on evidence from the prosecution or a co-defendant that may lead to the conviction of a defendant.

EV122.03   Timing of the warning

There is no requirement in s 122 that any warning be given at a particular time. The warning could be given in summing-up to the jury, or at the time the evidence is given. If the warning is given at the time of the evidence, and then repeated or referred to in the summing-up, this would potentially risk emphasising the evidence (and perhaps undermining the warning itself in some circumstances).

1277   The Law Commission recommended that the warning be mandatory. However, the Select Committee acted on submissions regarding the risk that a required warning would lead to argument about reliability in every case, thereby prolonging proceedings unnecessarily: *Select Committee Report on the Evidence Bill*, 12.

EV122.04   Subsection (2)

Section 122(2) requires the judge to *consider* giving a warning under s 122(1) whenever certain types of evidence that inherently carry the risk of unreliability are given (see s 122(2)(a)-(e)). The Act expands on the categories of evidence that are to be treated with caution from those found in the Law Commission's draft Code and the Bill.

As s 122(2) only requires that the judge *consider* giving a warning, where a judge exercises the discretion not to warn it will not be viewed as an error unless there is a reason beyond the fact that the evidence was in one of the categories in s 122(2). In other words, the concern cannot be general but must be particular. This is evidenced by s 122(2)(b), which envisages the defendant's statement to be the only evidence implicating her or him. If the fact of being in that category of evidence is enough alone to require a warning, it presumably would have been made mandatory for the judge to give a warning to treat the evidence with caution in every case where there was evidence of that type given.

(1)   Subsection (2)(a): hearsay: reliability standard

Section 122(2)(a) reflects the concern that hearsay evidence may be unreliable because the maker of the statement has not promised to tell the truth, and there can be no testing of the evidence under cross-examination. Section 122 assumes that unreliable evidence may still be admissible. However, s 18(1)(a) provides that a hearsay statement will be admissible only if the "circumstances relating to the statement provide a reasonable assurance that the statement is reliable". Section 122 therefore provides for hearsay evidence that is admissible as reliable under s 18, but that still leaves the judge of the opinion that the evidence may be unreliable under s 122. This appears to suggest the rather unsatisfactory conclusion that the "reasonable assurance of reliability" for the purposes of *admission* is a different reliability standard to that required in the tribunal of fact's decision regarding *acceptance* of the evidence.

(2)   Subsection (2)(b): confessions

Section 122(2)(b), which applies to confessions that are the only evidence implicating the defendant, acknowledges the risk that a defendant may falsely "confess". The admission of such statements requires that the circumstances in which the statement was made "were not likely to have affected its reliability". Section 122(2)(b) envisages a statement that is reliable enough to be admitted under s 28, but which still requires a warning because of potential unreliability under s 122. It is difficult to imagine such a case.

(3)   Motive to give false evidence

Evidence under s 122(2)(c) replaces s 12C of the Evidence Act 1908.[1278] Section 122(2)(d) was added by the Select Committee as a separate class of evidence but may also be an example of the type of evidence that could be covered by s 122(2)(c).[1279]

1278   *Adams on Criminal Law — Evidence*, EC21.06.

(4)   Delay between alleged offence and proceeding

Section 122(2)(e) is also a Select Committee addition. Section 122 requires the judge to be alert to the potential for unreliability inherent in certain types of evidence — the Law Commission view was therefore that while evidence of the type in s 122(2)(e) *may* be unreliable in some cases, the risk of unreliability is not *inherent* in cases where there is delay.[1280] The Select Committee disagreed — certainly it is accepted that delay can inhibit accurate and full memory recall. The debate around recovered memories — dubbed the "memory war" — is, however, still raging.[1281] Section 122(2)(e) could be seen to simply acknowledge that most memories will be affected by long delays — whether there is more risk of unreliability inherent in such evidence than in any other is, however, debateable. Certainly, a 10-year cut-off appears to be rather arbitrary.

EV122.05   Subsection (3)

Section 122(3) clarifies that a judge does not have to give a warning under s 122(1) merely because a party requests it.

123   Judicial directions about certain ways of offering evidence

(1)   The Judge must give the direction referred to in subsection (2) if, in a criminal proceeding tried with a jury,—

(a)   a witness offers evidence in an alternative way under this Part; or

(b)   the defendant is not permitted to personally cross-examine a witness; or

(c)   a witness offers evidence in accordance with a witness anonymity order.

(2)   The direction required by subsection (1) is a direction to the jury that—

(a)   the law makes special provision for the manner in which evidence is to be given, or questions are to be asked, in certain circumstances; and

(b)   the jury must not draw any adverse inference against the defendant because of that manner of giving evidence or questioning.

EV123.01   Overview

Section 123 is a more generally applicable version of s 23H(a) of the Evidence Act 1908. It requires the judge in criminal proceedings to direct the jury that the law makes special provision for the giving of evidence in certain circumstances, and that no adverse inferences should be drawn against the defendant where a witness has offered evidence in an alternative way (s 105), where a defendant has not been allowed to personally cross-examine a witness (s 95), or where a witness offers evidence in

---

1279   *Adams on Criminal Law — Evidence*, EC21.06(2).

1280   The Law Commission did not incorporate this type of evidence into the Code equivalent of s 122 because it considered that delay does not necessarily make evidence unreliable. Where reliability can be questioned, the general provision under s 122(1) was seen to suffice. See the discussion in LC *Evidence Reform*, para 476.

1281   Loftus and Davis, "Recovered Memories" (2006) 2 *Annual Review of Clinical Psychology* 469.

accordance with a witness anonymity order (s 112). The purpose of s 123 is to counteract any adverse effect on the defendant arising from the fact that evidence was given in any of the ways specified.

Where a witness offers evidence in one of the ways outlined in s 123(1), the judge is required to give the direction in s 123(2).

As the warning is specifically targeted to the jury, and must only be given in criminal proceedings tried with a jury, pre-trial witness anonymity orders under s 110 are not covered by s 123 (only s 112 trial witness anonymity orders will trigger the warning).

In common with s 122, there is no specific timing required for the giving of the warning. It could be given before the evidence listed in s 123(1), or as part of the summing up to the jury.

124　Judicial warnings about lies

(1)　This section applies if evidence offered in a criminal proceeding suggests that a defendant has lied either before or during the proceeding.

(2)　If evidence of a defendant's lie is offered in a criminal proceeding tried with a jury, the Judge is not obliged to give a specific direction as to what inference the jury may draw from that evidence.

(3)　Despite subsection (2), if, in a criminal proceeding tried with a jury, the Judge is of the opinion that the jury may place undue weight on evidence of a defendant's lie, or if the defendant so requests, the Judge must warn the jury that—

(a)　the jury must be satisfied before using the evidence that the defendant did lie; and

(b)　people lie for various reasons; and

(c)　the jury should not necessarily conclude that, just because the defendant lied, the defendant is guilty of the offence for which the defendant is being tried.

(4)　In a criminal proceeding tried without a jury, the Judge must have regard to the matters set out in paragraphs (a) to (c) of subsection (3) before placing any weight on evidence of a defendant's lie.

EV124.01　Overview

Section 124 provides for instruction to the jury about evidence suggesting that the defendant lied before or during a criminal proceeding (it is a matter for the jury to conclude whether the defendant actually did lie — as reflected in s 124(3)(a)). There is no obligation on the judge to do so unless he or she is "of the opinion that the jury may place undue weight on the evidence of a defendant's lie" or if the defendant requests that the warning is given.

The Law Commission's draft Code equivalent of s 124 was included in order to address the situation that "by default, the common law has been reformed so that in effect lies can only be relevant to credibility and never indicative of guilt".[1282] There is a tension in this area: while people who lie are not necessarily guilty, this does not mean that guilty people never lie. The Law Commission aimed for a reform that reflected and accommodated this tension, allowing for a lie to be indicative of guilt where appropriate. As guilty people sometimes do lie, this should be able to be part of the case against the defendant in many cases. The reform therefore treats lies as a form of circumstantial evidence, with the inference to be drawn from the lie a matter for the jury.

However, it is likely that many defendants will request that a s 124(3) warning is given, meaning that the direction will be given in the majority of cases where there is evidence suggesting that a defendant has lied. As s 124(2) states that the judge is not obliged to give a specific direction as to what inference the jury may draw from the evidence, where a warning under s 124(3) is given, the jury will be left to decide how they use the evidence of the lie, after hearing the guidance under subs (3).

(1)   Subsection (2): defendant's lie can be indicative of guilt

Unlike the previous law, where a defendant's lie could be relied upon as evidence of a lack of veracity, but could not usually be treated as evidence indicative of guilt,[1283] the Act provides that a proved lie by a defendant about a material matter can be taken into account as circumstantial evidence of guilt (and/or as going to veracity).

Section 124(2) allows evidence suggesting that a defendant has lied to be left to the jury without any specific direction from the judge as to the use to which the evidence can be put. The jury therefore decide what to make of the defendant's lie without guidance from the judge as to how or why a lie might help to prove guilt. Even where not directly connected to the alleged offending behaviour, the defendant's lie may damage the veracity of the defendant in the eyes of the jury.

The judge can still warn the jury that people may lie for reasons other than guilt and so (s 124(3)(c)) it should not be immediately concluded that a defendant's lie equates to guilt.

(2)   Subsection (3): warning necessary where jury may place undue weight on evidence that the defendant lied

Section 124(3) provides that a warning of the type in s 124(3)(a)-(c) is mandatory where the judge thinks that the jury may place undue weight on evidence of the defendant's lie, thereby drawing inferences that are not warranted; or where it is requested by the defendant. There is a danger that a warning could emphasise the defendant's lie, meaning that it could be counterproductive to warn in some cases, even when requested to do so by the defendant.[1284]

1282   LC *Evidence Reform*, 126.
1283   See, eg, *R v Gye* [1990] 1 NZLR 528; (1989) 5 CRNZ 245 (CA).
1284   *R v Hoko* (2003) 20 CRNZ 464 (CA).

(3)   Judge sitting alone

Section 124(4) is a reminder for judges sitting alone that they should take account of the matters in s 124(3)(a)-(c).

125   Judicial directions about children's evidence

(1)   In a criminal proceeding tried with a jury in which the complainant is a child at the time when the proceeding commences, the Judge must not give any warning to the jury about the absence of corroboration of the evidence of the complainant if the Judge would not have given that kind of a warning had the complainant been an adult.

(2)   In a proceeding tried with a jury in which a witness is a child, the Judge must not, unless expert evidence is given in that proceeding supporting the giving of the following direction or the making of the following comment:

(a)   instruct the jury that there is a need to scrutinise the evidence of children generally with special care; or

(b)   suggest to the jury that children generally have tendencies to invent or distort.

(3)   This section does not affect any other power of the Judge to warn or inform the jury about children's evidence exercised in accordance with the requirements of regulations made under section 201.

EV125.01   Overview

Section 125(1) and (2) extend s 23H(b) and (c) of the Evidence Act 1908 to all criminal proceedings tried with a jury — the previous law was limited to sexual cases. Furthermore, s 125(2) also applies to civil proceedings. Section 125 provides that evidence given by children (defined under s 4 as person under the age of 18 years) should, in general, be treated in the same way as evidence given by adults. The general thrust of the section, then, is to prevent the differential treatment of child complainants and witnesses. Research has shown that children are no less capable than adults of reliably and accurately recalling material.[1285]

EV125.02   Subsection (1)

Section 125(1) prohibits the judge from giving warnings about the absence of corroboration where a warning would not have been given in the case of an adult complainant.

EV125.03   Subsection (2): no direction to scrutinise children's evidence with special care in most cases

Section 125(2) prohibits a direction or a comment (absent expert evidence to the contrary) that there is a need to scrutinise children's evidence with special care, or that children generally have a tendency to invent or distort. It applies to all child

---

1285   See Pipe, Lamb, Orbach, and Esplin, "Recent research on children's testimony about experienced and witnessed events" (2004) 24(4) *Developmental Review* 440.

witnesses, provided that they are under the age of 18 years at the time that they give evidence.

(1)   Expert may recommend a direction

Section 125(2) qualifies the prohibition on judicial direction or comment where expert evidence supports the giving of a direction. Although such evidence would need to satisfy the substantial helpfulness test under s 25, the qualification risks undermining the general thrust of s 125 and may result in a proliferation of expert opinion evidence where experts disagree.

It may be that the qualification insulates s 125(2) against potential changes in knowledge in the area, but these could be accommodated by expert evidence direct to the jury without any judicial instruction; or by changes to the regulations issued for subs (3), which would take precedence over subs (2).

EV125.04   Special direction for children under the age of 6 years

Section 125(3) provides that the prohibitions in subss (1) and (2) do not limit the judge warning or informing the jury about children's evidence in accordance with regulations made under s 201. The original Evidence Bill contained a qualification of s 125(2), allowing for a detailed special direction in respect of evidence given by children under 6 years of age.[1286]

The Select Committee substituted s 125(3) for the detailed requirements contained in the Bill. The more detailed requirements for child witnesses under 6 years of age have been set out in reg 49 of the Evidence Regulations 2007 which will allow easier amendment of the detail to incorporate scientific advances. There remains some arbitrariness to the age chosen. Unlike s 125(2), which focuses on unprompted evidence in belying a tendency to invent or distort, the regulation is intended to focus the trier of fact on the way the evidence was *obtained* from children at each stage of the investigation and trial. Regulation 49 provides:

> "**49. Warning or informing jury about very young children's evidence**
> "If, in a criminal proceeding tried with a jury in which a witness is a child under the age of 6 years, the Judge is of the opinion that the jury may be assisted by a direction about the evidence of very young children and how the jury should assess that evidence, the Judge may give the jury a direction to the following effect:
>
> "(a)   even very young children can accurately remember and report things that have happened to them in the past, but because of developmental differences, children may not report their memories in the same manner or to the same extent as an adult would:

1286   When the Law Commission's Code was drafted, some members of the judiciary opposed the inclusion of the qualification as requiring the judge to effectively give expert evidence. A number of submissions received by the Select Committee on the Bill were also concerned about the qualification, arguing that it set out a model direction which was too prescriptive and insensitive to changes in knowledge.

"(b)   this does not mean that a child witness is any more or less reliable than an adult witness:

"(c)   one difference is that very young children typically say very little without some help to focus on the events in question:

"(d)   another difference is that, depending on how they are questioned, very young children can be more open to suggestion than other children or adults:

"(e)   the reliability of the evidence of very young children depends on the way they are questioned, and it is important, when deciding how much weight to give to their evidence, to distinguish between open questions aimed at obtaining answers from children in their own words from leading questions that may put words into their mouths."

It is clear that suggestive questioning is a concern. The regulation focuses on the way evidence was obtained from child witnesses by investigators (and therefore generally by the prosecution). However, defence counsel may also lead or confuse children with questioning — s 85 may disallow some of these questions (s 85(2)(a) provides that the judge may have regard to the age and maturity of the witness in deciding whether to disallow certain questions[1287]) and the warning regarding leading questions in reg 49(e) could be used to address this.

As s 125 does not affect the power of the judge to warn or inform the jury about children's evidence under the regulations, the regulations will take priority even if in future they conflict with subs (2)(a) or (b).

126   Judicial warnings about identification evidence

(1)   In a criminal proceeding tried with a jury in which the case against the defendant depends wholly or substantially on the correctness of 1 or more visual or voice identifications of the defendant or any other person, the Judge must warn the jury of the special need for caution before finding the defendant guilty in reliance on the correctness of any such identification.

(2)   The warning need not be in any particular words but must—

(a)   warn the jury that a mistaken identification can result in a serious miscarriage of justice; and

(b)   alert the jury to the possibility that a mistaken witness may be convincing; and

(c)   where there is more than 1 identification witness, refer to the possibility that all of them may be mistaken.

1287   See EV85.02-03.

EV126.01   Overview

Because identification evidence carries an inherent risk of unreliability,[1288] the courts warn juries about the dangers of relying on eyewitness evidence in all criminal cases where it is a substantial part of the evidence in a case. Section 126 replaces the warning found in s 344D of the Crimes Act 1961, which was repealed by the s 215 of the Evidence Act 2006. However, much of the law developed under s 344D remains applicable. As s 126 governs jury trials only, the summary equivalent of s 344D, s 67A of the Summary Proceedings Act 1957, is unaffected by the Act.[1289]

Unlike s 344D, s 126 applies to both visual and voice identification. This will result in little practical change, as the practice prior to the Act was to give a warning in voice identification cases even though such a warning was not *required* under s 344D.[1290]

The Law Commission originally suggested a more detailed judicial direction than that contained in s 126, containing references to memory research. However, this approach was abandoned in favour of the simpler approach found in s 126, which still leaves room for judges to tailor the warning to each case. The commentary to the Code suggests some of the additional factors that may be included in a warning where appropriate, such as reference to witness confidence being a poor predictor of reliability, stress, lighting at the time of the offence, witness factors such as poor eyesight, own-race bias in identification and so on. All of these factors are relevant not only to jury deliberation as to the weight to be accorded to evidence, but also as to admissibility of identification evidence, as assessed by the judge under ss 45 and 46.[1291]

EV126.02   Subsection (2): no particular form of words required

The warning in s 126 (and its predecessor s 344D) has its roots in the English case of *R v Turnbull*.[1292] As in *Turnbull*, s 126 does not require any particular form of words for the warning. Under s 344D, it was assumed that the requirement was to convey the purpose and spirit of the warning to the jury, leaving a considerable amount of freedom for judges to tailor the warning to each case.[1293]

(1)   Subsection (2)(a): warning as to risk of serious miscarriage of justice

Section 126 introduces some changes to the warning as required under s 344D, and one important change is that judges will be required to warn the jury that mistaken identification can result in a "serious miscarriage of justice". Prior to the Act, the requirement was simply that judges inform the jury about the reasons for the warning,

1288   See EV45.01(1).
1289   Section 67A of the Summary Proceedings Act 1957 traditionally operated broadly in any event. It was not restricted to identification of the accused, for example. See *Adams on Criminal Law — Evidence*, EC7.04.
1290   See *R v Wickramasinghe* (1992) 8 CRNZ 478 (CA), *R v Waipouri* [1993] 2 NZLR 410; (1994) 9 CRNZ 330 (CA), and *Adams on Criminal Law — Evidence*, EC7.03(6).
1291   See EV45.04(2); EV45.05(1).
1292   *R v Turnbull* [1976] 3 All ER 549; (1976) 63 Cr App R 132; [1976] 3 WLR 445 (CA).
1293   *R v Mei* [1990] 3 NZLR 16; (1989) 4 CRNZ 580 (CA).

which would usually, *but not necessarily*, result in informing the jury that a serious miscarriage of justice could result.[1294]

(2)   Refers to identification of persons only

Under s 126, a warning is required where the case depends "wholly or substantially on the correctness of 1 or more visual or voice identifications of the defendant or any other person". This differs from s 344D, where only identification evidence of the defendant triggered the requirement for a warning.[1295] However, s 126 is restricted to identification of human beings, and so identification of animals or inanimate objects would not trigger the warning, although in some circumstances a warning similar to that in s 126 could be used.[1296]

(3)   Section 126 warning to be given in cases where s 45 does not apply

The s 45 admissibility inquiry will apply only to identifications of the defendant. In those cases where there is identification of some other person, a s 126 warning will still be required, and the admissibility inquiry will be governed by s 8(1)(a) (probative value of the evidence outweighs prejudicial effect on the proceeding). Therefore, as under the pre-2006 Act law, where the case depends wholly or substantially on identification evidence the judge will assess the quality of the identification evidence and identify any evidence which is capable of supporting it.[1297] It is up to the jury to ultimately decide whether other evidence actually does support the evidence of identification.

127   Delayed complaints or failure to complain in sexual cases

(1)   Subsection (2) applies if, in a sexual case tried before a jury, evidence is given or a question is asked or a comment is made that tends to suggest that the person against whom the offence is alleged to have been committed either delayed making or failed to make a complaint in respect of the offence.

(2)   If this subsection applies, the Judge may tell the jury that there can be good reasons for the victim of an offence of that kind to delay making or fail to make a complaint in respect of the offence.

1294   In *R v Kereopa* 18/9/07, Heath J, HC Tauranga CRI-2007-087-411, Heath J stated that the change in s 126(2) means that it is "more strongly in favour of an accused than the corresponding warning required, prior to 1 August 2007, by s 344D Crimes Act 1961" (para 16).

1295   Although a warning was usually given where identification of some other person was crucial in the case: see *R v P* (1991) 8 CRNZ 33 (CA).

1296   This was also the case under the pre-2006 Act law: see *R v Tokotaua* 7/5/93, CA432/92.

1297   Where the identification evidence is of poor quality and is unsupported, the case should be withdrawn from the jury. However, even where the quality of the identification evidence is poor, if there is evidence capable of supporting it then it may still be left to the jury so long as it is accompanied by a s 126 warning. If there is good quality identification evidence, the fact that it is unsupported will not preclude its admission, again accompanied by a s 126 warning. On assessment of other evidence in the case, see EV45.04(2); EV45.05(1).

EV127.01   Overview

Section 127 provides that a judge *may* tell the jury that there may be good reasons for the victim of a sexual offence to delay making or to fail to make a complaint, where there has been evidence, questions or comments that tend to suggest that the alleged victim delayed making or failed to make a complaint. This follows the approach of s 23AC of the Evidence Act 1908.

EV127.02   Relationship to previous law on recent complaint

Section 127 reflects the previous law on recent complaint evidence, which was seen to be an exception to the rule against previous consistent statements when the complaint was made "at the first reasonable opportunity".

The recent complaint exception is not replicated under the Act. Evidence of recent complaint will only be able to be given under the Act where it is necessary to "respond to a challenge to the witness's veracity or accuracy" (s 35(2)) and would not need to have been made at the "first reasonable opportunity". Section 23AC focused on failure to make a complaint in the sense that there was no consistent complaint made at the first reasonable opportunity, not that there was no complaint made at all (the latter situation being very rare in cases that proceed to trial). The very basis of s 127 is therefore questionable, as true failure to make a complaint will be rare, but failure to make a complaint at the first reasonable opportunity is irrelevant under the Act.

EV127.03   Discretionary warning in cases of delay

If delay has, in the opinion of the judge, damaged veracity, s 127(2) does not *require* that the judge tells the jury that there may be good reasons for delay — such direction is discretionary, not mandatory. The discretion in s 127 was retained in order to enable the judge to balance the competing interests in the case, and to make a decision based on the circumstances of each individual case. For example, if there is a delay of more than 10 years, the judge may give a warning under s 122(2)(e),[1298] notwithstanding s 127(2), a result which may be fairly common, given that many complainants will not disclose sexual abuse until a long period of time has elapsed.[1299]

EV127.04   Relationship to s 35

Section 127 is not particularly responsive to the new admissibility rule for previous consistent statements. For example, if there has been a complaint but it is held, pursuant to s 35(2), that there has been no "challenge to the witness's veracity or accuracy", then the previous consistent statement (the "recent complaint") will not be admissible. Suppose then that defence counsel tells the jury that it could be expected that a complainant in a sexual case would make a complaint soon after the incident (a "comment" under s 127(1)), and here no complaint has been admitted, a s 127 direction will not help to address the comment — there has been no failure to complain, and may not have been a delay either. If there was a delay in complaining,

---

1298   See *R v R* 19/7/07, Stevens J, HC Auckland CRI-2006-092-11084.
1299   See EV122.04(4).

the judge cannot comment on delay as envisaged by s 127 without referring to the previous complaint — and if this is not allowed under s 35(2), s 127 becomes difficult to apply. Presumably, the appropriate direction would be to tell the jury that just because they have not heard about a previous complaint there may well have been one — or alternatively that there is no requirement that there is an earlier complaint and the jury should not draw any inferences from the fact that no previous complaint was offered in evidence.

Subpart 7—Notice of uncontroverted facts and reference to reliable public documents

(s 128 to s 129)

128   Notice of uncontroverted facts

(1)   A Judge or jury may take notice of facts so known and accepted either generally or in the locality in which the proceeding is being held that they cannot reasonably be questioned.

(2)   A Judge may take notice of facts capable of accurate and ready determination by reference to sources whose accuracy cannot reasonably be questioned and, if the proceedings involve a jury, may direct the jury in relation to this matter.

EV128.01   Overview

Under s 128, notice of certain facts may be taken. Such facts may be accepted without the need for proof. The jury may take notice of facts under s 128(1), but may only do so under s 128(2) on the direction of the judge. It is assumed that, as at common law, facts that are noticed under s 128 will be proved and no other supporting evidence will be required. However, the provisions of s 128 are discretionary, and so where there is any doubt as to whether the facts will be judicially noticed, it will be wise to offer evidence to prove the fact concerned.

EV128.02   Only covers adjudicative facts

Section 128 is concerned only with adjudicative facts (not judicial notice of the law or legislative facts).[1300] The difference between adjudicative and legislative facts was commented on by the High Court of Australia in *Woods v Multi Sport Holdings Pty Ltd*:[1301]

> "An adjudicative fact is a fact in issue or a fact relevant to a fact in issue. A legislative fact is a 'fact which helps the court determine the content of law and policy and to exercise its discretion or judgment in determining what course of action to take'."

Provisions under the previous law for judicial notice of statutes and regulations are not re-enacted.

1300   New Zealand Law Commission, *Evidence Law: Documentary Evidence and Judicial Notice: A Discussion Paper*, NZLC PP22, Wellington, 1994, para 256ff.

1301   *Woods v Multi Sport Holdings Pty Ltd* (2002) 208 CLR 460; 186 ALR 145 (HCA), para 65. See also *Hansen v R* [2007] 3 NZLR 1; (2007) 23 CRNZ 104 (SC), para 230.

EV128.03   Generally and locally known facts

Section 128(1) concerns notice of facts known and accepted generally or in the locality (allowing for local knowledge to be judicially noticed even where the facts are not known in the general, national population).

EV128.04   Generally and locally known facts can be noticed by the jury

Section 128(1) envisages notice to be taken by the jury of generally accepted facts without direction or control from the judge — a rather controversial issue because jurors may use their own knowledge of the facts in preference to evidence admitted by the court. The Law Commission's view on the matter was that, although judges should not highlight the ability of the jury to take "judicial notice" of certain facts, and that jurors should in general confine themselves to the evidence, "legislating against judicial notice by the jury is unlikely to be effective. If during their deliberations juries decide to assume the existence of facts that have not been proved in evidence, little if anything can be done".[1302]

EV128.05   Facts that can be determined by reference to accurate sources: s 128(2)

Section 128(2) allows for notice of facts that are capable of "accurate and ready determination by reference to sources whose accuracy cannot reasonably be questioned". This subsection can be distinguished from s 128(1), as it only permits the jury to take notice of facts capable of accurate and ready determination when directed to do so by the judge. For example, the day on which a public event fell, such as Queen Elizabeth II's coronation, may not fit under s 128(1) but could be obtained by reference to accurate historical sources; tide tables and calendars are examples of accurate and ready sources.

129   Admission of reliable published documents

(1)   A Judge may, in matters of public history, literature, science, or art, admit as evidence any published documents that the Judge considers to be reliable sources of information on the subjects to which they respectively relate.

(2)   Subpart 1 of Part 2 (which relates to hearsay evidence) and subpart 2 of Part 2 (which relates to opinion evidence and expert evidence) do not apply to evidence referred to under subsection (1).

EV129.01   Overview

Section 129 replaces s 42 of the Evidence Act 1908. It allows admission of some hearsay and opinion evidence without the need to satisfy the admissibility rules in s 18 and ss 24 or 25. Section 129 codifies the common law exception to the hearsay rule that admitted accredited histories, scientific works and maps in order to prove facts of a public nature.

1302   LC *Evidence Reform*, 131.

Section 129(1) is permissive, not mandatory. The focus of the section is the reliability of such documents; hence the provision in s 129(2) that the opinion and hearsay rules do not apply to evidence that is admitted under s 129(1).

Provided that they are considered by the judge to be reliable sources of information, any published documents concerned with public history, science, literature or art may suffice. This is potentially very wide (see the definition of document in s 4).[1303]

Subpart 8—Documentary evidence and evidence produced by machine, device, or technical process

(s 130 to s 149)

General and special rules

130   Offering documents in evidence without calling witness

(1)   A party may give notice in writing to every other party that the party proposes to offer a document (whether or not a public document), a copy of which is attached to the notice, as evidence in the proceeding without calling a witness to produce the document.

(2)   A party who on receiving a notice wishes to object to the authenticity of the document to which the notice refers, or to the fact that it is to be offered in evidence without being produced by a witness, must give a notice of objection in writing to every other party.

(3)   If no party objects to a proposal to offer a document as evidence without calling a witness to produce it, or if the Judge dismisses an objection to the proposal on the ground that no useful purpose would be served by requiring the party concerned to call a witness to produce the document,—

    (a)   the document, if otherwise admissible, may be admitted in evidence; and

    (b)   it will be presumed, in the absence of evidence to the contrary, that the nature, origin, and contents of the document are as shown on its face.

(4)   A party must give notice of a proposal to offer a document without calling a witness to produce it—

    (a)   in sufficient time before the hearing to provide all the other parties with a fair opportunity to consider the proposal; or

    (b)   within the time, whether before or after the commencement of the hearing, that the Judge allows and subject to any conditions that the Judge imposes.

(5)   A party must give notice of objection to a proposal to offer a document without calling a witness to produce it—

    (a)   in sufficient time before the hearing to provide all the other parties with a fair opportunity to consider the notice; or

---

1303   See EV4.11.01.

(b)   within the time, whether before or after the commencement of the hearing, that the Judge allows and subject to any conditions that the Judge imposes.

(6)   The Judge may dispense with the requirement for a party to give notice under subsection (1) or (2) subject to any conditions that the Judge imposes.

(7)   This section is subject to sections 131 and 132.

EV130.01   The effect of this new process

Section 130 sets out a *procedure* by which a party will be able to offer a document in evidence without calling a witness to produce the document. Such a process is new, and is intended "to simplify the process of producing documents in evidence."[1304] However, given the practices that already existed in civil proceedings before the Act,[1305] s 130 will appear more novel in criminal proceedings. The effect of the section is that if no other party objects, or the judge dismisses the objection, the document will be admitted (subject to any applicable admissibility requirements — for example, the hearsay rule) "and will be presumed to be what it purports to be and to contain what it purports to contain on its face."[1306]

EV130.02   Notice

Section 130 operates on the basis of written notices to all parties in the proceeding. The party wishing to offer a document without calling a witness to produce it must give notice pursuant to s 130(1), attaching a copy of the document. The notice requirement will therefore entail pre-trial disclosure on the part of the defence in criminal proceedings, if they wish to take advantage of the procedure.[1307] The notice must be sent within the time set out in s 130(4). The Law Commission rejected suggestions that a specific time should be included.[1308]

In the words of the Law Commission:[1309]

> "The notice requirement is in addition to any disclosure that occurred during discovery ... Compliance should be a simple matter. For instance, parties may indicate by reference to the list of documents provided at discovery which documents will be produced in this way."

Section 130(6) allows the judge to dispense with the requirement for a notice or for a notice of objection. The judge may impose conditions as the price for such

---

1304   LC *Evidence Code*, para C410.
1305   See, for example, r 4410 of the High Court Rules, which deals with the consequences of incorporating a document in a common bundle (enacted as s 132 of the Act).
1306   LC *Evidence Code*, para C410.
1307   LC *Evidence Reform*, para 519.
1308   LC *Evidence Reform*, para 518: "Reference to 'sufficient time' to enable other parties to respond will enable a judge to set a timetable in any particular case. It will also avoid conflict with other time limits in other legislation such as the High Court Rules and District Court Rules." The New Zealand Law Society expressed the view that a "statement of the rights and consequences associated should be provided for in the notice that is to be given." (NZLS *Submission on the Evidence Bill*, 49) Presumably this could be done by way of reference to the section.
1309   LC *Evidence Code*, para C411.

dispensation. The Law Commission pointed out that the judge's ability to impose conditions under s 130(6) enables the judge to develop a specific regime for a particular case — for example, a complex case with a large volume of documents.[1310]

EV130.03   Objections

Objections to the proposal to offer the document in this way may be based on either of the two grounds set out in s 130(2). These are (a) the authenticity of the document, or (b) the proposal to offer it without calling a witness to produce the document. The party who objects must give written notice of their objection to every other party, under s 130(2). Although it is not stated expressly, it is probable that the notice must state which of the two grounds of objection set out in s 130(2) is relied upon or if both are relied upon. The notice of objection must be sent within the time set out in s 130(5).

EV130.04   Objections and admissibility

Section 130(3) permits the judge to dismiss an objection that has been made under s 130(2). The one ground upon which the judge can take this step is if no useful purpose would be served by requiring a witness to be called to produce the document. It is unlikely that the judge would dismiss an objection that raised a legitimate concern over the authenticity of the document. In such a case there will need to be a witness to produce the document and deal with the concerns that have been raised.

The ground for dismissing an objection was proposed by the New Zealand Law Society because the Law Society was concerned that the section did not provide any clear direction as to when a judge might dismiss an objection:[1311]

> "The intention of the [section] should be to facilitate the proof of formal, non-controversial documents, where no useful purpose would be served by requiring a competent witness to attend Court. The clause should not have any wider application. For example, it should not operate to admit a document into evidence where authenticity is disputed and a witness can be called to prove the document. The judge should not be entitled to dismiss the objection on broad unspecified grounds."

The Ministry of Justice agreed with this statement of the section's purpose.[1312]

Section 130(3)(a) confirms that even where no objection is made under s 130(2) or where the judge dismisses any such objection, the document may still be inadmissible (for example, the hearsay provisions could apply to render inadmissible a document which met the specific criteria for being offered as evidence under s 130).

EV130.05   Authenticity

Section 130(2) permits a party to object to the authenticity of a document that another party proposes to offer without calling a witness to produce the document. The Act does not define the concept of "authenticity". However, it is likely that the matters

---

1310   LC *Evidence Code*, para C413.
1311   NZLS *Submission on the Evidence Bill*, 49.
1312   *Departmental Report* (EV/MOJ/2), 35; *Select Committee Report on the Evidence Bill*, 13.

presumed by s 130(3)(b) are meant to summarise the concept, namely that the "nature, origin and contents of the document are as shown on its face".

This suggestion is borne out by the additions made by the Select Committee to ss 138(2), 140(3), 141(2), 142(2), and 143(4). Each of these additions give a discretion to the judge to decide not to apply the presumption (or the rule in the case of s 140(3)) otherwise stated in each of those sections. All of these presumptions (or rules) can be characterised as dealing with the same general matters that are described in s 130(3)(b).

EV130.06   "Evidence to the contrary"

The surprising effect of s 130(3)(b) appears to be that even where a party has not objected to a proposal made under s 130(1) or where a party's objection has been dismissed by the judge, the party may still offer "evidence to the contrary" challenging the authenticity of the document after it has been admitted under s 130(3)(a).

The Act contains no guidance as to what amounts to "evidence to the contrary" sufficient to rebut the presumption of authenticity stated in s 130(3)(b). Nor is there any guidance on the effect of the presumption being successfully rebutted. Some guidance on these issues may be derived from earlier authorities.[1313]

EV130.07   Effect of rebutting the presumption of authenticity

It is suggested that in a case where evidence to the contrary successfully rebuts the effect of the presumption set forth in s 130(3)(b), the result is not to rob the document of all evidential value. Certainly, opposing parties will be able to argue that the document may not be authentic. However, the party who offered the document in evidence should still be able to offer other evidence that the document is indeed authentic.

With the presumption playing no role, the issue of authenticity is a matter for the judge to decide on the basis of the available evidence, as with all the other contested issues in the case. Of course, if the party who is relying on the document offers no evidence supporting its authenticity after "evidence to the contrary" has rebutted the effect of the presumption, the judge may find it difficult to rule in favour of the document's authenticity. (Contrast the discussion at EV141.04 of the process of rebutting a presumption, which remains in effect until the contrary is *proved*.)

EV130.08   Special provisions in civil proceedings

Section 130(7) recognises that the effect of ss 131 and 132 will be to admit the classes of documents referred to in those sections without those documents having been

---

1313   *Adams on Criminal Law — Evidence*, EC1.08(3)-(4). Note also that in its original work on documentary evidence, the Law Commission proposed that this type of presumption, rebutted by "evidence to the contrary", should only be enacted in relation to the ordinary operation of machines (now s 137 of the Act) and the Law Commission discussed how the presumption would operate in that specific context (New Zealand Law Commission, *Evidence Law: Documentary Evidence and Judicial Notice: A Discussion Paper*, NZLC PP22, Wellington 1994, paras 139-151). The Law Commission viewed this presumption as one that operates to shifts the evidential burden (para 63).

produced by a witness. Section 130(7) ensures that the general regime established by s 130 for offering a documents as evidence without calling a witness is not applicable in cases where ss 131 and 132 apply. In such cases, the requirements of notices under s 130 will have no application.

131   Admission of depositions

In a civil proceeding a party may, on any terms that the Judge directs and subject to any exclusion that the Judge considers just, give in evidence any depositions that have been taken—

(a)   in New Zealand under the direction of a Judge; or

(b)   overseas in accordance with the provisions of this Act and any rules of court.

EV131.01   Overview

Section 131 was added to the Evidence Bill by the Select Committee in order to "parallel the appropriate High Court Rule".[1314] See rr 369-381 of the High Court Rules. See the discussion of s 130(7).[1315]

132   Documents required to be discovered or included in common bundle

(1)   This section applies only to a civil proceeding.

(2)   A document in a common bundle is received in evidence when the relevant conditions set out in rules of court have been complied with.

(3)   A document required by rules of court to be included in a party's affidavit or list made for the purposes of discovery but which has not been so included, may be produced in evidence at the hearing only with—

    (a)   the consent of the other party; or

    (b)   the leave of the Judge.

(4)   Each document contained in the common bundle is subject to presumptions as to nature and origin that—

    (a)   are specified in rules of court; and

    (b)   are rebuttable in circumstances and in the manner set out in those rules.

EV132.01   Overview

Section 132 was added to the Evidence Bill by the Select Committee for the same reason referred to under s 131. See rr 441N, 441O, and 441P of the High Court Rules.[1316] See also the discussion of s 130(7).[1317] Its purpose is to ensure that a party

1314   *Select Committee Report on the Evidence Bill*, 2.
1315   See EV130.08.
1316   See discussion of the rules in Jagose, Katz, and McCall, "Documentary Evidence and Cross-Border Evidence Issues" in NZLS *Intensive: Evidence Act 2006*, 234-235.
1317   See EV130.08.

includes all relevant documents in its list of documents, or risk not being able to produce a non-discovered document.

133   Summary of voluminous documents

(1)   A party may, if notice is given to all other parties in sufficient time before the hearing and with the permission of the Judge, give evidence of the contents of a voluminous document or a voluminous compilation of documents by means of a summary or chart.

(2)   A party offering evidence by means of a summary or chart must, if the Judge so directs on the request of another party or on the Judge's own initiative, either—

(a)   produce the voluminous document or voluminous compilation of documents for examination in court during the hearing; or

(b)   make it available for examination and copying by other parties at a reasonable time and place.

EV133.01   Summaries or charts

The effect of s 133, which applies in any proceeding, is that evidence of the contents of a voluminous document or of a voluminous compilation of documents (see the definition of "document" in s 4) can be given by a mere *summary* of that document or compilation or by a *chart*. This is a change to the law before the 2006 Act, which provided that a summary is no evidence and that the entries in the summary must be independently proved by other evidence.[1318]

EV133.02   No express right to check accuracy

Opposing parties will normally want to check the accuracy of the summary or chart offered under s 133. Section 133 provides no guaranteed right to do so. However, it is likely that before granting the necessary permission to give evidence of the summary or chart under s 133(1), the judge will rely on s 133(2)(b) to require that opposing parties be given the opportunity to check its accuracy.

EV133.03   Examination in court or elsewhere

Section 133(2) is drafted in a way which appears to grant power to the judge to order either an examination of the voluminous document in court (s 133(2)(a)) or at another place (s 133(2)(b)), but not both. It is hoped that the provision will be interpreted to allow the judge to direct the occurrence of both paras (a) and (b) in appropriate cases. The Law Commission accepted that the judge would have power to make both of the directions referred to in s 133(2).[1319]

EV133.04   Timing of notice

Section 133(1) requires that the party proposing to offer evidence of the summary or chart gives notice of their intention "in sufficient time before the hearing". This begs the question: sufficient time for what? Although numerous possible answers may be

---

1318   *R v Menzies* [1982] 1 NZLR 40 (CA); *R v Moroney* 26/5/93, CA448/92.
1319   LC *Evidence Code*, para C415.

proposed, it is suggested that the preferable one is: in sufficient time to allow other parties to examine and copy (as referred to in s 133(2)(b)) and to do so in sufficient time to argue before a judge whether the summary or chart will be admitted into evidence. This will usually require checking the summary or chart against the "voluminous document" or "voluminous compilation" so "sufficient time" will relate to the time needed to undertake this comparison. (Compare the more specific timing of the notices required by s 135(1)(a) and s 22(4).)

EV133.05   Comparable overseas legislation and admissibility

Section 133 is based on r 1006 of the Federal Rules of Evidence (US).[1320] One difference is that the US rule only applies when the voluminous material "cannot conveniently be examined in court"; a similar phrase is also contained in s 50 of the Evidence Act 1995 (Aust).[1321] This prerequisite is not expressed in s 133. The Act contains no criteria to determine when a document is "voluminous".

The commentary to the US rule makes the point that:[1322]

> "Before offering a summary under Rule 1006, the proponents will have to lay a proper foundation for the admission of the originals. Once the originals are authenticated, the summary must be authenticated. If the data or material that is used as the basis for a summary or chart would not be accepted at trial (even through the testimony of an expert) … the summary or chart itself is not admissible in evidence."

Section 133 however, says nothing about the admissibility of the voluminous document, which must therefore be a separate question. If the document or compilation is inadmissible, then the summary will also be inadmissible unless admitted by consent.[1323] If only some of the documents in the compilation are inadmissible, the judge may have to order the summary to be rectified in situations where the inadmissible documents affect the meaning of the chart or summary.

134   Admission of documents discovered in civil proceedings

In a civil proceeding, wherever a party is permitted under rules of court to inspect a document,—

(a)   the requirement to prove the authenticity of the document may be dispensed with in circumstances described in those rules; and

(b)   the procedure to be adopted by a party seeking to require proof of the authenticity of the document is that set out in those rules; and

---

1320   LC *Evidence Code*, para C415; see also New Zealand Law Commission, *Evidence Law: Documentary Evidence and Judicial Notice: A Discussion Paper*, NZLC PP22, Wellington 1994, 118 (s 6 of the draft Code).

1321   Odgers, *Uniform Evidence Law* (5th ed), Sydney, Thomson Lawbook Co, 2002, 118.

1322   See also New Zealand Law Commission, *Evidence Law: Documentary Evidence and Judicial Notice: A Discussion Paper*, NZLC PP22, Wellington 1994, para 217.

1323   See EV9.01.

(c)   the production of secondary evidence to prove the authenticity of the document may be permitted in circumstances described in those rules.

Compare: HCR 314

EV134.01   Overview

Section 134 was added to the Evidence Bill by the Select Committee for the reason set out at EV131.01. See r 314 of the High Court Rules which deals with an "admission as to authenticity" through the inspection of a document specified in an affidavit sworn under rr 294-299 of the High Court Rules. The admission as to authenticity is no more than an admission that the document is genuine and what it appears to be, not that the contents of the document are accurate.[1324]

135   Translations and transcripts

(1)   A party may offer a document that purports to be a translation into English of a document in a language other than English, or a translation into Maori of a document in a language other than Maori, if—

(a)   notice is given to all other parties in sufficient time before the hearing to provide those other parties with a fair opportunity to scrutinise the translation; and

(b)   all other requirements prescribed in regulations made under section 201 concerning that document are satisfied.

(2)   The translation is presumed to be an accurate translation, in the absence of evidence to the contrary.

(3)   A party, if notice is given to all other parties in sufficient time before the hearing to provide those other parties with a fair opportunity to scrutinise the transcript and all other prescribed requirements referred to in subsection (1)(b) are satisfied, may offer a document that purports to be a transcript of information or other matter that is recorded—

(a)   in a code (including shorthand writing or programming code); or

(b)   in a way that is capable of being reproduced as sound or script.

(4)   A party who offers a transcript of information or other matter in a sound recording under subsection (3) must play all or part of the sound recording in court during the hearing if—

(a)   the sound recording is available; and

(b)   the Judge so directs, either on the application of another party or on the Judge's own initiative.

1324   See further discussion in Jagose, Katz, and McCall, "Documentary Evidence and Cross-Border Evidence Issues" in NZLS *Intensive: Evidence Act 2006*, 229.

EV135.01   Translation into English or Maori

Section 135 deals with two distinct classes of "translations and transcripts" (neither term is defined in the Act). Subsections (1) and (2) offer a means of obtaining a *presumption of accuracy* for a document which purports to be a translation into English or Maori. Subsections (3) and (4) set out the conditions under which a transcript of otherwise incomprehensible recorded material can be offered in evidence.

The Act contains no general impediment to the admissibility of translations of documents into languages other than English or Maori. They could be admitted as part of expert opinion evidence or in other ways if relevant. The same can be said of translations into English or Maori that do not comply with the requirements set by s 135(1).

EV135.02   Presumption of accuracy

The special feature of documents fitting within s 135(1) is that they will be presumed to be an accurate translation under s 135(2), "in the absence of evidence to the contrary". The original wording of this rebuttal of the presumption of accuracy was "unless evidence sufficient to raise doubt about the presumption is offered".[1325] See also s 130(3)(b).

EV135.03   Other rules of admissibility

The Law Commission pointed out that s 135(1) and (2) do not concern general rules of admissibility. Even if the document meets all the requirements set by s 135, it may be rendered inadmissible by some other rule in the Act.[1326]

One of the reasons given by the Select Committee for adding the requirement for compliance with regulations, per s 135(1)(b) (see also s 135(3)), was because the regulations enacted pursuant to s 201(n) would ensure that translations are accepted only if the original document satisfies the Act's general requirements for admissibility.[1327]

EV135.04   The notice requirement

The added requirement of compliance with regulations by the Select Committee was included in response to the New Zealand Law Society submission that the party "receiving the notice should always be given sufficient information about the interpreter, particularly with respect to qualifications and experience, and the time

---

1325   LC *Evidence Code*, 262 (s 119(2) of the draft Code). Note that s 137 was initially proposed as an adaptation of s 146 of the Evidence Act 1995 (Aust), which includes the phrase "unless evidence is sufficient to raise a doubt about the presumption is adduced". The wording was changed prior to the Bill: "Although the Law Commission stated its intention to have a lower standard than 'evidence to the contrary', [LC *Evidence Code*, para C420] it is unclear whether their formulation achieves this. Absence of evidence to the contrary is a commonly understood approach which is appropriate in these circumstances.": Ministry of Justice, *Letter of Advice to the Minister of Justice*, 8 February 2005.

1326   LC *Evidence Code*, para C416.

1327   *Select Committee Report on the Evidence Bill*, 14.

and place of the translation, as to be able to determine the reliability of it. If there is no onus on the offering party to do so, the clause lacks utility."[1328] The New Zealand Law Society recommended that the certification or verification process required in relation to Maori translations by the High Court Rules should be followed for notices under the Act. The Ministry of Justice agreed, recommending to the Select Committee that: "additional requirements relating to the translation of documents or transcripts … be imposed by regulations."[1329]

To date, no regulations have been enacted under s 201(n) to deal with notice requirements or the issue of admissibility of translations.[1330]

EV135.05   "Purports to be"

Some meaning must be ascribed to the requirement in s 135(1) that the document in question "purports to be" a translation into English or Maori of another document. The benefit of the presumption in s 135(2) will not be available if the document does not in some manner "purport" to be a translation. This curious limitation would not apply if the drafting technique employed in s 137(2) had been employed in s 135(1). Section 137(2) refers to a document "that was or purports to have been" (displayed, etc). Presumably, a document will "purport to be a translation" for the purpose of s 135(1) if it is merely entitled "Translation".[1331]

EV135.06   Transcript of recorded material

Section 135(3) differs from s 135(1) and (2) because it is not aimed at laying the foundation for a presumption of accuracy. It does no more than permit a party to offer in evidence a document purporting to be a transcript of the "information or other matter" that has been recorded in the ways set out in s 135(3)(a) and (b). In this way, the rule changes the previous law which provided that a transcript was to be used only as an aid to the interpretation of a recording and not in substitution for it.[1332]

The Law Commission said that the phrase "a transcript of information or other matter" was "deliberately wide in order to include matter not consisting in words — for example, figures, symbols, music and other sounds, such as radar blips".[1333] This clarifies that the "transcript" dealt with in s 135(3) is essentially a "translation" into English (or Maori) of what would otherwise be unrecognisable material as described in s 135(3)(a) and (b). Although s 135(3) does not actually specify that the recorded material must be incomprehensible without the transcript, it can be assumed that this will be the usual application of this provision.

1328   NZLS *Submission on the Evidence Bill*, 49.
1329   *Departmental Report* (EV/MOJ/2), 36.
1330   See EV135.07.
1331   See also the discussion at EV138.03.
1332   Jagose, Katz, and McCall, "Documentary Evidence and Cross-Border Evidence Issues" in NZLS *Intensive: Evidence Act 2006*, 230, citing *R v Taylor* [1993] 1 NZLR 647.
1333   LC *Evidence Code*, para C417.

With regard to the transcripts referred to in s 135(3), the notice requirement will enable "opposing parties to apply to have the sound recording played in whole or in part if the accuracy of the transcript is in doubt."[1334]

EV135.07   Transcript inadmissible if not offered in compliance with s 135(3)

An argument could be made that unless there is compliance with s 135(3) and (4), a transcript of the sort described in s 135(3) is not admissible. This is because the only purpose served by s 135(3) is to render the transcript admissible. There is no additional purpose to match the presumption of accuracy applicable to translations by s 135(2).

The contrary argument would be that the transcript may still be admissible if it is supported by expert opinion evidence confirming its accuracy. Lack of compliance with s 135(3) and (4) means only that the specific route to admissibility provided by these provision is not available.

The Law Commission was seemingly of the view that s 135(3) was a procedural requirement and not one that determined admissibility. The Law Commission stated that the "transcript will still only admissible only if the information it transcribes is admissible".[1335]

(1)   Relationship with s 137(2)

Because of the prerequisites to admissibility set by s 135(3), a party may wish to consider if s 137(2) is an alternative basis for admissibility in a particular case. The latter provision appears to provide an easier route to admissibility.

The two provisions have obvious similarities. Both focus on "information or other matter" that is *recorded* (s 135(3)) or *stored* (s 137(2)) in the particular ways described by each.

The substantial point of difference between s 135(3) and s 137(2) is that the transcript dealt with by s 135(3) appears to involve the work of a human expert, who "translates" into English the recorded matters. In contrast, the document rendered admissible by s 137(2) is one that "purports to have been displayed, retrieved, or collated" by *use* of the machine, device or technical process with which s 137(2) is concerned. To justify the ease with which the evidence can be offered under s 137(2) when compared to s 135(3) and (4), it is suggested that the machine, device, or technical process referred to in s 137(2) must itself display, retrieve, or collate the document without the need for any human expert "translation" of the sort dealt with in s 135(3).

EV135.08   Prescribed requirements

Section 135(3) requires compliance with the regulations referred to in s 135(1)(b). This must assume that the same set of eventual regulations will apply to translations under s 135(1) and transcripts under s 135(3). This may not be a safe assumption, given the different aims of the two provisions. The actual regulation making power

---

1334   LC *Evidence Code*, para C417.
1335   LC *Evidence Code*, para C417.

under s 201(n) refers only to the translation of documents into English or Maori, as dealt with by s 135(1) and (2).

EV135.09   Sound recording

The requirement set forth in s 135(4) relates only to sound recording. Presumably, the reason that the obligation contained in s 135(4) is limited in this way is because playing any other form of recording referred to in s 135(3) would be unintelligible if played for the fact-finder.

136   Proof of signatures on attested documents

(1)   The signature, execution, or attestation of a document (including a testamentary document) that is required by law to be attested may be proved by any satisfactory means.

(2)   An attesting witness need not be called to prove that the document was signed, executed, or attested (whether by handwriting, digital means, or otherwise) as it purports to have been signed, executed, or attested.

EV136.01   Overview

Section 136 of the Act removes any requirement to call an attesting witness (even for the purpose of proving the valid witnessing of a will or testamentary document — see s 5 of the Evidence Amendment Act 1945) and allows attestation to be proved "by any satisfactory means". "[Section 136] completes a process which does away with the previous common law rules on attestation."[1336]

137   Evidence produced by machine, device, or technical process

(1)   If a party offers evidence that was produced wholly or partly by a machine, device, or technical process (for example, scanning) and the machine, device, or technical process is of a kind that ordinarily does what a party asserts it to have done, it is presumed that on a particular occasion the machine, device, or technical process did what that party asserts it to have done, in the absence of evidence to the contrary.

(2)   If information or other matter is stored in such a way that it cannot be used by the court unless a machine, device, or technical process is used to display, retrieve, produce, or collate it, a party may offer a document that was or purports to have been displayed, retrieved, or collated by use of the machine, device, or technical process.

EV137.01   Overview

Section 137 has two distinct functions. Subsection (1) provides a presumption of accuracy for evidence produced by a machine, device or technical process. Subsection (2) permits a party to offer evidence, in certain circumstances, of a

---

1336   *Departmental Report* (EV/MOJ/2), 36; LC *Evidence Code*, para C418.

"document" (widely defined by s 4) "that was or purports to have been displayed ... by use of a machine ...".

EV137.02   Section promotes use of new technology

The general words "machine, device or technical process" were intended by the Law Commission to encompass future technological developments.[1337] The specific example of "scanning", added to s 137(1) by the Select Committee in response to a submission from the Bankers' Association, reinforces the legislative intention for this provision to promote the use of evidence produced by modern technological methods. The phrase "technological process" was intended to cover chemical or other process that might not "aptly be described as carried out by a machine or device."[1338]

(1)   Presumption of accuracy

Section 137(1) is based on a common law presumption that has assumed additional importance in respect of computer-generated evidence.[1339]

One of the prerequisites for the presumption contained in s 137(1) is that the machine, device, or technical process must be "of a kind that ordinarily does what a party asserts it to have done". This is a matter which itself must be proven, although the topic is of the sort that has the potential to be judicially noticed under s 128(1).

It is likely that the limitation of "ordinarily" is meant to reflect the approach of the common law and render the presumption inapplicable to a newly invented machine, device, or technical process. However, it could be argued that even in the case of a prototype, it is possible to prove that extensive testing has shown that the prototype machine, device, or technical process "ordinarily does what the party asserts to have done",[1340] thereby obtaining the advantage of the presumption.

(2)   Presumption rebutted by evidence to the contrary

See also the discussion at EV130.06 and EV135.02.

The focus of the evidence to the contrary would be that, despite the assertion of the party who offered the evidence produced by the machine, device, or technical process, on the particular occasion in question the machine did not do what that party asserted it did. The Law Commission said of this process:[1341]

> "When the presumption is successfully challenged, in addition to evidence on the workings of the class of machines to which the particular machine belongs, the proponent will also have to offer evidence that the particular machine was reliable and was properly operated on the occasion in question. This will enable

---

1337   LC *Evidence Code*, para C419.
1338   LC *Evidence Code*, para C419; see also New Zealand Law Commission, *Evidence Law: Documentary Evidence and Judicial Notice: A Discussion Paper*, NZLC PP22, Wellington 1994, para C73.
1339   *Adams on Criminal Law — Evidence*, EC1.08(1)(d); see also Jagose, Katz, and McCall, "Documentary Evidence and Cross-Border Evidence Issues" in NZLS *Intensive: Evidence Act 2006*, 231-234.
1340   By the use of expert evidence (s 25).
1341   LC *Evidence Code*, para C420.

the fact-finder to infer what would otherwise be presumed: ie, that on the occasion in question, the machine did what it ordinarily does."

EV137.03   Scope of s 137(2)

Section 137(2) creates no presumption. It carries none of the prerequisites to admissibility required by the closely associated s 135(3). See the discussion at EV135.07(1) for a comparison of that provision and s 137(2).

Section 137(2) requires only that the information or other matter be *stored* in such a way that it cannot be used by the court unless a machine, device, or technical process is used to display, retrieve, produce, or collate it (for example, by printing it onto paper).[1342] There is no requirement that the storage referred to is in any particular form, although it is difficult to imagine many cases where the storage involved would not concurrently fit within the class of *recordings* set out in s 135(3).

It is difficult to understand the way the term "produce" is used in the drafting of s 137(2). It appears in s 137(2)'s description of the class of information or other matter to which the subsection applies. However, it is not part of the otherwise identical list of processes set out in the second half of the subsection that describes how the document is created for the court's use. Surely a party is still able to offer a document *produced* by use of the machine, device, or technical process.

EV137.04   "Purports to have been"

Unlike provisions such as s 135(1), s 137(2) does not refer only to a document that "purports to be" of a particular class. Section 137(2) applies if the document "was or purports to have been displayed ... by use of the machine ...".

If a party asserts that the document *was* displayed etc, this will have to be proven, presumably by a witness who observed this occurrence. Similarly, when a party chooses the option that the document "purports to have been" displayed etc, this is still a prerequisite which must be proven before a party can obtain the benefit offered by s 137(2). However, it is not easy to envision the sort of evidence which will be admissible to prove that a document "purports to have been" "displayed ... by a machine". One possibility could be a (hearsay) heading to that effect on the document itself.

138   Authenticity of public documents

(1)   Subsection (2) applies to a document that purports to be a public document, or a copy of or an extract from or a summary of a public document, and to have been—

    (a)   sealed with the seal of a person or a body that might reasonably be supposed to have the custody of that public document; or

    (b)   certified to be such a copy, extract, or summary by a person who might reasonably be supposed to have the custody of that public document.

1342   LC *Evidence Code*, para C422.

(2)   If this subsection applies, the document is presumed, unless the Judge decides otherwise, to be a public document or a copy of the public document or an extract from or summary of the public document and may be offered in evidence to prove the truth of its contents.

(3)   Subpart 1 of Part 2 (which relates to hearsay evidence) does not apply to evidence offered under this section.

EV138.01   Public documents presumed authentic

Section 138 provides an unprecedented form of presumption of the authenticity of a document which purports to be a public document (or a copy of or an extract from, or a summary of a public document) if either of the prerequisites set by s 138(1)(a) or (b) are met. "Public document" and "copy" are defined in s 4.

EV138.02   Contrast with s 13

The discussion of s 13 emphasised that that section permits the judge to draw an inference as to the authenticity of a wide class of documents. However, a party who is relying on s 13 can never be certain as to whether or not the judge will draw such an inference. The benefit offered by a provision such as s 138 is to provide a means of obtaining a *presumption of authenticity* for the specific class of documents dealt with by the section.

EV138.03   "Purports to be"

The presumption of authenticity in s 138(2) is only available for a document that "purports to be" a public document, as described in s 138(1). Unlike similar provisions such as s 135(1) or s 137(2), the purpose of the phrase "purports to be" in s 138(1) is easy to grasp. There would be no need to provide a presumption of authenticity for a document that *is* (rather than merely "purports to be") a public document.

Section 138(1) goes on to impose further prerequisites to the operation of the presumption of authenticity. The purported public document (or copy, extract or summary thereof) must also "purport to have been" sealed or certified in the ways specified in s 138(1)(a) or (b). For the same reason discussed above, the use of "purports to be" is sensible in this context as well.

Because the definition of "public document" in s 4 covers a wide range of documents from foreign jurisdictions, there may be cases where a judge will require some evidence to assist the judge making the "reasonable suppositions" required by s 138(1)(a) or (b).

EV138.04   Unprecedented presumption

Until the Evidence Bill reached the Select Committee, the presumptions contained in ss 138(2), 141(2), 142(2), and 143(4) used the standard legislative formula that the presumption would apply unless "the contrary is proved".

However, in the case of each of these provisions (see similarly s 140(3)) the Select Committee introduced the unprecedented concept that the presumption would apply unless "the Judge decides otherwise". In justifying these alterations to the Evidence Bill, the Select Committee spoke in terms of authenticity as follows:[1343]

"Presumptions as to authenticity of documents

"We recommend that there be judicial discretion to depart from the evidentiary presumptions contained in [sections 138, 140, 141, 142 and 143]. Without such a discretion the court would be bound to accept as authentic a wide variety of certificates and documents in the absence of evidence to the contrary. In some cases it would be difficult or impossible for an opponent to prove a lack of authenticity."

These changes were in response to the New Zealand Law Society's submission that a judge must retain a discretion to exclude the evidence *for good cause*, citing in support the example of the Nigerian Bank scams.[1344]

The Select Committee's concern with the difficulty or impossibility of an opponent proving the lack of authenticity could perhaps have been allayed if the Select Committee had turned to the common legislative device of permitting (mere) "evidence to the contrary" to rebut the presumption.[1345] However, the Select Committee's solution does not even impose *this* lesser onus on the party who wishes to contest authenticity.

These sections of the Evidence Act (ss 138(2)-143(4)) have therefore introduced a unique form of presumption into the law. The judge appears to have been given an unfettered discretion to disregard the presumption whenever something does not "feel right". There need be neither proof nor even any evidence that the document in question is not authentic. The judge can still decide not to apply the presumption.

1343   *Select Committee Report on the Evidence Bill*, 13.
1344   NZLS *Submission on the Evidence Bill*, 52. The Nigerian Advance Fee Scheme (also known internationally as "4-1-9" fraud after the section of the Nigerian penal code which addresses fraud schemes) is generally targeted at small and medium sized businesses, as well as charities. This global scam involves the receipt of an unsolicited letter purporting to come from someone who claims to work for the Nigerian Central Bank or from the Nigerian Government. (The Central Bank of Nigeria denies all connection to those who promote this scheme.) In the letter, a Nigerian claiming to be a senior civil servant will inform the recipient that he is seeking a reputable foreign company into whose account he can deposit funds ranging from $10-$60 million which the Nigerian government overpaid on some procurement contract. The goal is to delude the recipient into thinking that he or she has been singled out to participate in a very lucrative arrangement. The recipient is reassured of the authenticity of the arrangement by forged or false documents bearing apparently official Nigerian government letterhead, seals, as well as false letters of credit, payment schedules and bank drafts. Once the recipient becomes confident of the potential success of the deal, something goes wrong. The recipient is then pressured or threatened to provide one or more large sums of money to save the venture. For example, an official will demand an unforeseen fee to the Nigerian government that will have to be paid before the money can be transferred. Each fee paid is described as the very last fee required. The scheme may be stretched out over many months. See also EV142.01.
1345   See EV130.06.

EV138.05   Hearsay

When the presumption of authenticity operates, s 138(2) says expressly that the public document may be offered in evidence to prove the truth of its contents. Section 138(3) ensures that the hearsay rule will not stand in the way of this process.

139   Evidence of convictions, acquittals, and other judicial proceedings

(1)   Evidence of the following facts, if admissible, may be given by a certificate purporting to be signed by a Judge, a registrar, or other officer having custody of the relevant court records:

    (a)   the conviction or acquittal of a person charged with an offence and the particulars of the offence charged and of the person (including the name and date of birth of the person if the person is an individual, and the name and date and place of incorporation of the person if the person is a body corporate):

    (b)   the sentencing by a court of a person to any penalty or other disposition of the case following a plea or finding of guilt, and the particulars of the offence for which that person was sentenced or otherwise dealt with and of the person (including the name and date of birth of the person if the person is an individual, and the name and date and place of incorporation of the person if the person is a body corporate):

    (c)   an order or judgment of a court and the nature, parties, and particulars of the proceeding to which the order or judgment relates:

    (d)   the existence of a criminal or civil proceeding, whether or not the proceeding has been concluded, and the nature of the proceeding.

(2)   A certificate under this section is sufficient evidence of the facts stated in it without proof of the signature or office of the person appearing to have signed the certificate.

(3)   The manner of proving the facts referred to in subsection (1) authorised by this section is in addition to any other manner of proving any of those facts authorised by law.

(4)   Subsection (5) applies if—

    (a)   a certificate under this section is offered in evidence in a proceeding for the purpose of proving the conviction or acquittal of a person, or the sentence by a court of a person to a penalty, or an order made by a court concerning a person; and

    (b)   the name of the person stated in the certificate is substantially similar to the name of the person concerning whom the evidence is offered.

(5)   If this subsection applies, it is presumed, in the absence of evidence to the contrary, that the person whose name is stated in the certificate is the person concerning whom the evidence is offered.

(6)   Subpart 1 of Part 2 (which relates to hearsay evidence) does not apply to evidence offered under this section.

EV139.01   Introduction

Section 139 provides a convenient method of offering evidence of the matters contained in s 139(1)(a)-(d). It is a revision and extension of s 27 of the Evidence Amendment Act (No 2) 1980.[1346] Because the certificate which is offered in evidence will necessarily contain hearsay statements of those matters, s 139(6) ensures that the hearsay provisions in the Act do not frustrate the purpose of s 139(1), however the evidence of the facts must be otherwise admissible — that is, s 139 is not an admissibility rule except insofar as s 139(6) excludes the operation of the hearsay rules.[1347] (See also the associated discussion of ss 47-50.)[1348]

EV139.02   Purporting to be signed

Section 139(2) emphasises that s 139(1) operates to admit a certificate "purporting to be signed" by any of the officials listed in s 139(1). "The certificate will in itself be sufficient to prove the existence of [the conviction]. It will not be necessary to prove the signature or office of the signatory."[1349] Although the certificates listed in s 139(1)(a)-(d) are admitted as evidence even though they do no more than "purport to be signed" by the appropriate official, it remains up to the judge to determine whether to act on the evidence. Any suspicion by the judge that the signature on the certificate is not valid would inevitably result in the judge placing little or not weight on the evidence offered under s 139(1).

EV139.03   Other methods of proof

Section 139(3) recognises other methods of proving the matters referred to in s 139(1). One other relevant provision of the sort envisioned by s 139(3) is s 71 of the Summary Proceedings Act 1957 ("Criminal Records"), which has not been repealed by the Act. See also s 140 of the Act.

EV139.04   Presumption of identity

Sections 139(4) and (5) create a presumption to deal with an issue often raised in criminal proceedings where the defence makes no admission that the defendant is the same person who is named in the certificate which has been offered in evidence under s 139(1). Because the presumption also operates in the case of an acquittal, it will not only be the prosecution who will want to rely on the presumption of identity created by ss 139(4) and (5). Additionally, ss 47-49 make it clear that evidence proven by the means provided by s 139 may be admissible in civil or criminal proceedings. The presumption will be of assistance in this context as well.

1346   *Cash for Scraps Ltd v Auckland Regional Council* 9/10/07, Cooper J, HC Auckland CIV-2006-404-4270, para 87.

1347   LC *Evidence Reform*, para 531.

1348   Discussion of ss 47-50 can also be found in Jagose, Katz, and McCall, "Documentary Evidence and Cross-Border Evidence Issues" in NZLS *Intensive: Evidence Act 2006*, 235-236.

1349   LC *Evidence Code*, para C427.

The presumption created by ss 139(4) and (5) operates "in the absence of evidence to the contrary", not evidence *proving* the contrary. Once evidence as to the contrary exists, the presumption is negated.[1350]

140   Proof of conviction by fingerprints

(1)   A certificate is admissible in evidence to prove the identity of a person alleged to have been convicted in a country of an offence if—

    (a)   the certificate purports to be signed by a fingerprint examiner; and

    (b)   copies of the fingerprints of the person are exhibited or shown on the certificate; and

    (c)   the certificate certifies that those copies are copies of the fingerprints of a person who was convicted in the fingerprint examiner's country of the offence of which particulars are given.

(2)   Subsection (3) applies to a certificate that—

    (a)   purports to be signed by a fingerprint examiner; and

    (b)   certifies that the copies of the fingerprints that are exhibited or shown on the certificate made under subsection (1) and the fingerprints of the person in respect of whom a conviction is sought to be proved (a copy of which is exhibited or shown on the certificate made under this subsection) are the fingerprints of the same person.

(3)   A certificate to which this subsection applies is, unless the Judge decides otherwise, evidence that the person in respect of whom the conviction is sought to be proved was convicted of the offence of which particulars were given in the certificate made under subsection (1).

(4)   The manner of proving a conviction authorised by this section is in addition to any other manner of proving the conviction authorised by law.

(5)   The Governor-General may, by Order in Council, declare that certificates purporting to be made by specified persons or classes of persons in any country other than New Zealand, Australia, United Kingdom, or Canada in respect of convictions for offences committed in that country and to the same effect as certificates under subsection (1) are evidence as if they had been made under subsection (1).

(6)   In this section, **fingerprint examiner** means a fingerprint examiner who is—

    (a)   a member or employee of the police; or

    (b)   a member or employee of a police force in the United Kingdom; or

    (c)   a member or employee of a police force of Australia or the police force of a State or territory of Australia; or

---

1350   See also EV130.06.

     (d)   a member or employee of a police force of Canada or the police force of a Province or territory of Canada.

(7)   Subpart 1 of Part 2 (which relates to hearsay evidence) and Subpart 2 of Part 2 (which relates to opinion and expert evidence) do not apply to evidence offered under this section.

EV140.01   Introduction

Section 140 is largely a re-enactment of s 12A of the Evidence Act 1908. Case law under that section will therefore remain relevant.[1351] Unlike s 139, s 140 is limited to evidence of a person's conviction for an offence. It is also not an admissibility provision — it merely creates a mechanism for proving a fact if it is relevant and otherwise admissible.

The identity of a person alleged to have been convicted of an offence in New Zealand or in a foreign jurisdiction may be in issue in civil or criminal proceedings in New Zealand. For example, even in a case where the presumption of identity created by s 139(4) and (5) was available, the identity of the convicted person may remain in issue because "evidence to the contrary", offered under s 139(5), has rebutted the presumption.

Section 140 provides a method of proving the identity of the convicted person through the certificate of a "fingerprint examiner" (referred to as a "fingerprint expert" in s 12A). The section also permits the certificate of a fingerprint examiner to match the fingerprints of the convicted person with the fingerprints of the person in respect of whom the conviction is sought to be proved in the current civil or criminal proceedings.

EV140.02   Foreign convictions

The conviction referred to in the certificate can be a conviction in a foreign country as well as one in New Zealand. However, the effect of s 140(1)(c) and (6) is that the section applies only to certificates from fingerprint examiners from Australia, the UK, and Canada (not EU countries or the US).[1352] To date, no Orders in Council have been passed pursuant to s 140(5) to include certificates from fingerprint examiners in any other countries.

EV140.03   Hearsay and opinion

The certificates give the fingerprint examiner's opinion that based on identical fingerprints, the person who was convicted and the person in respect of whom the conviction is sought to be proved, are the same person. This is both a hearsay statement and expert opinion evidence. Accordingly, s 140(7) renders inapplicable both the hearsay and expert evidence provisions of the Act which otherwise might allow objections to the certificates. A certificate issued under s 140(1) is therefore admissible to prove the truth of its contents.[1353]

1351   *Cross on Evidence* (8th NZ ed), para 21.10.
1352   See further commentary on this point in *Cross on Evidence* (online), EVA140.4.
1353   LC *Evidence Code*, para C429.

EV140.04   "Unless the Judge decides otherwise"

Section 140 does not provide a presumption. It simply renders admissible the certificates referred to in s 140(1) and (2) and permits them to be used to match the identity of the convicted person with the person whose status as a convicted person is in issue in a New Zealand proceeding.

However, s 140(3) adds the qualification that the pertinent certificate will stand as evidence of the crucial matching of identity "unless the Judge decides otherwise". Similarly with the presumption discussed under s 138(2), the effect of s 140(3) is to give the judge an unfettered discretion to reject the certificates as evidence even though there is no "evidence to the contrary" questioning its authenticity. This is unprecedented. No such provision was contained in s 12A of the Evidence Act 1908.

EV140.05   "Purports to be signed"

One example where the judge might act under s 140(3) and "decide otherwise", thereby rejecting the certificate as evidence, is where the judge had some suspicion about the signature on the certificate. In common with numerous other provisions in this Subpart, s 140(1)(a) requires only that the certificate "purports to be" signed by a fingerprint examiner.[1354]

141   New Zealand and foreign official documents

(1)   Subsection (2) applies to a document that purports—

     (a)   to have been printed in the *Gazette* ; or

     (b)   to have been printed or published by authority of the New Zealand Government; or

     (c)   to have been printed or published by the Government Printer; or

     (d)   to have been printed or published by order of or under the authority of the House of Representatives.

(2)   If this subsection applies, the document is presumed, unless the Judge decides otherwise, to be what it purports to be and to have been so printed and published and to have been published on the date on which it purports to have been published.

(3)   Subsection (4) applies to a document that purports—

     (a)   to have been printed or published in a government or official gazette (by whatever name called) of a foreign country; or

     (b)   to have been printed or published by the government or official printer of a foreign country; or

     (c)   to have been printed or published by the authority of the legislative, executive, or judicial branch of the government of a foreign country; or

     (d)   to have been printed or published by an international organisation.

1354   See also EV135.05, EV137.04, and EV138.03.

(4)   If this subsection applies, the document is presumed, unless the contrary is proved, to be what it purports to be and to have been printed or published in the manner provided in subsection (3) and to have been published on the date on which it purports to have been published.

(5)   Subpart 1 of Part 2 (which relates to hearsay evidence) does not apply to evidence offered under this section.

EV141.01   Introduction

The Law Commission said that ss 141-143 replace some 29 sections of the Evidence Act 1908 (and its subsequent amendments) "which are complicated and difficult to relate to each other".[1355]

EV141.02   Presumptions of authenticity

Sections 141-143 contain various presumptions rather than admissibility rules. The presumptions are intended to assist or facilitate the admission of documentary evidence or the proof of particular facts.[1356]

Section 141 provides two different forms of presumption of authenticity for "official documents". The form of presumption depends on whether the documents are New Zealand official documents or foreign official documents.

The Act does not contain any express definition of "official documents" but the heading of s 141 combines with s 141(1) and (3) to justify the reference to New Zealand and foreign "official documents".

Section 141(3)'s references to a foreign country must be read in the light of s 4's broad definition of "country".

EV141.03   Two presumptions

The first presumption of authenticity is contained in s 141(2). It applies to the New Zealand official documents described in s 141(1).

The second presumption is contained in s 141(4) and applies to the foreign official documents described in s 141(3).

The presumptions in s 141(2) and (4) are similar in effect except for the startling difference that only s 141(2) contains the Select Committee's grant of an unfettered power to the judge to negate the effect of the presumption. See the comments on the similar provision at EV138.04.

The Select Committee's justification referred to in the discussion at EV138.04 would seem to apply equally to s 141(4). There is, therefore, no easy way to understand the Select Committee's lack of consistency.

1355   LC *Evidence Code*, para C432.
1356   LC *Evidence Code*, para C432. For a discussion of the role of presumptions, see New Zealand Law Commission, *Evidence Law: Documentary Evidence and Judicial Notice: A Discussion Paper*, NZLC PP22, Wellington 1994, paras 68-78.

Section 141(4) requires that the opposing party *prove* the lack of authenticity — precisely the process that the Select Committee believed could on occasion be an impossible burden. Indeed, the burden imposed on the opposing party by s 141(4) is even more surprising because it requires proof to the contrary in regard to *foreign* official documents, while granting the judge an unfettered discretion to reject the authenticity of a New Zealand official document under s 141(2). The distinction is incomprehensible because it should be easier for a party to marshal evidence attacking the authenticity of New Zealand official documents than would be the case with foreign official documents.

EV141.04   Unless the contrary is proved

The presumption created by s 141(4) must be contrasted with the class of presumption discussed at EV130.06. The type of presumption created by s 141(4) requires the judge to accept the presumed fact regardless of the mere existence of "evidence to the contrary". However, once the contrary has been proved, there is nothing further to consider. The judge has accepted that the presumed fact does not exist. This is precisely because the contrary has been proved to the judge's satisfaction.

EV141.05   Standard of proof

With few exceptions (eg, ss 28-30 and 45-46) the Act does not provide guidance on the applicable standard of proof. Accordingly, in determining the standard of proof to apply to a provision such as s 141(4) ("unless the contrary is proved") reference will have to be made to the law outside the Act. (See the discussion at EV12.02 as to whether the absence of a specific reference to the requisite standard of proof amounts to a "gap" regarding "the admission of any particular evidence".)

The general proposition is that liability must be proven beyond reasonable doubt in criminal proceedings and on the balance of probabilities in civil proceedings.[1357] However, there are numerous intricacies wrapped up in that proposition.[1358]

142   Notification of acts in official documents

(1)   Subsection (2) applies if the doing of an act by the Governor-General or the House of Representatives, or by a person authorised to do the act by the law of New Zealand, is notified or published in—

     (a)   the *Gazette* ; or

     (b)   a document that was printed or published by authority of the New Zealand Government; or

     (c)   a document that was printed or published by the Government Printer; or

     (d)   a document that was printed or published by order of or under the authority of the House of Representatives.

1357   New Zealand Law Commission, *Evidence Law: Documentary Evidence and Judicial Notice: A Discussion Paper*, NZLC PP22, Wellington 1994, para 90.

1358   *Adams on Criminal Law — Evidence*, EC2.

(2)   If this subsection applies, it is presumed, unless the Judge decides otherwise, that the act was done and that it was done on the date (if any) that appears in the *Gazette* or document.

(3)   Subsection (4) applies if the doing of an act by a foreign legislature or a person authorised to do the act by the law of a foreign country is notified or published in—

    (a)   a government or official gazette (by whatever name called) of a foreign country; or

    (b)   a document that was printed or published by the government or official printer of a foreign country; or

    (c)   a document that was printed or published by the authority of the legislative, executive, or judicial branch of the government of a foreign country.

(4)   If this subsection applies, it is presumed, unless the contrary is proved, that the act was done and that it was done on the date (if any) that appears in the government or official gazette (however described) or other document.

(5)   If the doing of an act by an international organisation is notified or published in a document that was printed or published by the international organisation, it is presumed, unless the contrary is proved, that the act was done and that it was done on the date (if any) that appears in the document.

(6)   Subpart 1 of Part 2 (which relates to hearsay evidence) does not apply to evidence offered under this section.

EV142.01   Presumption that acts were performed

Section 142(1) is an adaptation of s 46 of the Evidence Act 1908. Section 142 creates three separate presumptions that *acts* were performed when those acts have been notified or published in the ways set out in the section. The section does not contain presumptions *about* documents, but was placed in this part of the Act because the presumptions have a direct relationship to documents offered in evidence.[1359] The three presumptions relate to acts done by specified persons or governmental bodies of New Zealand (s 142(2)), a foreign country (s 142(4)), or an international organisation (s 142(5)).

Section 140 does not deal with the issue of the authenticity of a document. Nonetheless, the reasoning applied by the Select Committee to that issue was relied upon by the Committee to justify their addition to s 142(2) of the unfettered discretion for the judge to reject the presumed fact that an act was done in a New Zealand context. The judge's power to do so is not dependent on the existence of any evidence to the contrary.[1360]

1359   LC *Evidence Code*, para C435.
1360   See also EV138.04.

As was discussed in the broadly similar circumstances dealt with by s 141, there is no readily understandable reason why the Select Committee did not apply the same approach taken to s 142(2) to either of the presumptions created by s 142(4) or (5). In both these cases, dealing with acts in a foreign country or an international organisation, the party opposing the effect of the presumption must *prove the contrary*, before the judge can reject the effect of the presumption and conclude that the act did not occur. This difference in approach also seems at odds with the submissions received on this provision, in which the New Zealand Law Society, for example, was particularly concerned with the recent scams originating in Nigeria where reliance was placed on documents allegedly issued by the Nigerian Government.[1361]

EV142.02   Accuracy and lawfulness

Section 142 covers a wide variety of publications but it does not presume the accuracy of the facts mentioned in those publications.[1362] As the Law Commission noted, unlike s 46 of the Evidence Act 1908, s 142 "does not explicitly presume the lawfulness of the action notified or published in the official publication ... [such a presumption] does not add anything to the common law presumption of the regularity of official acts and is best considered as a matter of substantive administrative law."[1363]

143   Presumptions as to New Zealand and foreign official seals and signatures

(1)   Subsection (4) applies to the imprint of a seal that appears on a document and purports to be the imprint of the Seal of New Zealand, or the former Public Seal of New Zealand, or 1 of the seals of the United Kingdom on a document relating to New Zealand, or the seal of a foreign country.

(2)   Subsection (4) applies to the imprint of a seal that appears on a document and purports to be the imprint of the seal of a body (including a court or tribunal) exercising a function of a public nature under the law of New Zealand or the law of a foreign country.

(3)   Subsection (4) applies to the imprint of a seal that appears on a document and purports to be the imprint of the seal of a person holding a public office or exercising a function of a public nature under the law of New Zealand or the law of a foreign country.

(4)   If this subsection applies to the imprint of a seal that appears on a document, the imprint is presumed, unless the Judge decides otherwise, to be the imprint of that seal and the document is presumed, unless the contrary is proved, to have been sealed as it purports to have been sealed.

(5)   A document that purports to have been signed by a person as the holder of a public office or in the exercise of a function of a public nature under the law of

---

1361   NZLS *Submission on the Evidence Bill*, 52; see further the discussion of s 138(2) at EV138.04.

1362   LC *Evidence Code*, para C437.

1363   LC *Evidence Code*, para C438.

New Zealand, or the law of a foreign country, is presumed, unless the contrary is proved, to have been signed by that person acting in an official capacity.

EV143.01   Presumption of valid sealing or signature

Section 143 provides two different forms of presumptions of authenticity. The first, contained in s 143(4), presumes the authenticity of seals imprinted on the documents described in s 143(1)-(3). This presumption applies "unless the Judge decides otherwise". See the discussion at EV138.04 regarding this unprecedented form of presumption. Section 143(5) creates a presumption of authenticity of a signature appearing on the class of document described in that subsection. The presumption operates until the contrary is proved. See the general discussion of this form of presumption at EV141.03.

Section 143(4) and (5) draw the same distinction between forms of presumptions as was discussed (and questioned) at EV141.03 and EV142.01. No reason for the distinction is apparent.

144   Evidence of foreign law

(1)   A party may offer as evidence of a statute or other written law, proclamation, treaty, or act of State, of a foreign country—

    (a)   evidence given by an expert; or

    (b)   a copy of the statute or other written law, proclamation, treaty, or act of State that is certified as a true copy by a person who might reasonably be supposed to have the custody of the statute or other written law, proclamation, treaty, or act of State; or

    (c)   any document containing the statute or other written law, proclamation, treaty, or act of State that purports to have been issued by the government or official printer of the country or by authority of the government or administration of the country; or

    (d)   any document containing the statute or other written law, proclamation, treaty, or act of State that appears to the Judge to be a reliable source of information.

(2)   In addition, or as an alternative, to the evidence of an expert, a party may offer as evidence of the unwritten or common law of a foreign country, or as evidence of the interpretation of a statute or other written law or a proclamation of a foreign country, a document—

    (a)   containing reports of judgments of the courts of the country; and

    (b)   that appears to the Judge to be a reliable source of information about the law of that country.

(3)   A party may offer as evidence of a statute or other written law of a foreign country, or of the unwritten or common law of a foreign country, any publication—

(a)   that describes or explains the law of that country; and

(b)   that appears to the Judge to be a reliable source of information about the law of that country.

(4)   A Judge is not bound to accept or act on a statement in any document as evidence of the law of a foreign country.

(5)   A reference in this section to a statute of a foreign country includes a reference to a regulation, rule, bylaw, or other instrument of subordinate legislation of the country.

(6)   Subpart 1 of Part 2 (which relates to hearsay evidence) does not apply to evidence offered under this section.

EV144.01   Introduction

Section 144 amalgamates and expands ss 39–41 of the Evidence Act 1908.

EV144.02   Expert evidence of foreign law

Section 144(1)(a) recognises the availability of expert evidence as a means of proving the various categories of foreign law listed in the opening phrase of s 144(1). Nothing in s 144 renders the opinion and expert evidence rules inapplicable to the section. Accordingly, evidence offered under s 144(1)(a) must still comply with the substantial helpfulness test in s 25(1).[1364]

EV144.03   Expert evidence not always required

Although it is usual for a party to offer evidence from an expert in attempting to prove foreign law, *Dymocks Franchise Systems (NSW) Pty Ltd v Todd*[1365] confirms that this is not always a necessity. The various forms of documentary evidence set out in s 144 could be relied upon in an appropriate case in the absence of evidence from an expert. However, the Privy Council in *Dymocks* also recognised that evidence from an expert will be a virtual necessity in a case where there is some uncertainty as to the current state of that foreign law.[1366]

EV144.04   Foreign law is a question of fact

Although s 144 recognises a broad spectrum of documents that may be relied upon as evidence of foreign law, s 144(4) makes it clear that the issue remains one for the judge to decide by weighing up the evidence available.[1367] This is in keeping with s 19C of the Judicature Act 1908. The issue of foreign law is a matter of fact, yet it is an issue for the judge to determine even if the trial is conducted before a jury.

1364   LC *Evidence Code*, para C405. See also s 61(1)(b).

1365   *Dymocks Franchise Systems (NSW) Pty Ltd v Todd* [2004] 1 NZLR 289 (PC).

1366   *Dymocks Franchise Systems (NSW) Pty Ltd v Todd* [2004] 1 NZLR 289 (PC), para 54.

1367   "The judge's acceptance or otherwise is likely to depend, among other things, on how familiar the judge is with the legal system of the jurisdiction and thus whether the judge is able to understand the statements in their context and to assess how authoritative the publication may be.": LC *Evidence Code*, para C404

EV144.05   Failure to prove foreign law

The Law Commission stated that the Act was not intended to alter the existing approach that in the absence of evidence of foreign law, a judge will simply apply New Zealand law to the issue being litigated.[1368]

EV144.06   Purporting to be signed

Unlike various preceding provisions (ss 135, 137, 138, and 143), s 144(1)(b) does not refer to a certificate that "purports to be signed" by the person described in that provision. The result must be that the certificate is only admissible for the purpose of s 144(1) if the judge is satisfied that the certificate is indeed the certificate the person described. Compare s 144(1)(c).

Special rules applying where no requirement for legalisation of foreign public document

EV145.Intro.01   No requirement for legalisation of foreign public documents

Sections 145-147 were first enacted in the Evidence Amendment Act 2000 which allowed New Zealand to become a party to the Hague Convention abolishing the Requirement of Legalisation for Foreign Public Documents. The Law Commission in the 1999 report did therefore not consider these sections. The Law Commission, did, however, recommend that other matters relating to the taking of evidence overseas be gathered together in a separate statute, pending review.[1369]

"Legalisation" can be a time-consuming and laborious process by which matters related to the authenticity of documents must be certified by diplomatic or consular agents of the country in which the documents are to be produced. Parties to the Convention are required to exempt from the legalisation process certain public documents executed in the territory of one Party to the Convention to be produced in the territory of another Party. Legalisation may be replaced, if some formality is desired, by attaching to the relevant document a certificate issued by a competent authority of the foreign state.[1370]

EV145.Intro.02   Public document

Section 4 confirms that ss 145-147 utilise the particular definition of "public document" set out in s 145. The detailed definition of "public document" in s 4 applies elsewhere in the Act. The s 145 definition relates to the documents covered by the Convention, which does not apply to documents executed by diplomatic or consular agents or documents dealing with commercial or customs operations.[1371]

1368   LC *Evidence Code*, para C403.
1369   LC *Evidence Reform*, paras 505-506.
1370   New Zealand's "competent authority" is the Department of Internal Affairs. See Jagose, Katz, and McCall, "Documentary Evidence and Cross-Border Evidence Issues" in NZLS *Intensive: Evidence Act 2006*, 238.
1371   Jagose, Katz, and McCall, "Documentary Evidence and Cross-Border Evidence Issues" in NZLS *Intensive: Evidence Act 2006*, 238.

EV145.Intro.03   Producing foreign public documents to an "authority"

Sections 145-147 provide a streamlined method for authenticating "foreign public documents" (as defined in s 145) which are produced to a New Zealand authority.

By focusing on the *production* of foreign public documents to a "New Zealand authority" as defined by s 143, it is clear that ss 145-147 will operate in a context far broader than the rest of the Act. As a general proposition, the Act governs *proceedings*, which s 4 defined as being restricted to *court* proceedings. Sections 145-147 have the wider aim of ensuring acceptance by all "New Zealand authorities" of foreign public documents.

EV145.Intro.04   Authenticity

By means of a "Convention certificate" (as defined in s 145), the matters set out in s 145's definition of "legalisation" are to be accepted unless, per s 147(3), "the contrary is proved". For the operation of this class of presumption, see the discussion at EV141.03. The streamlined method for authentification set out in ss 145-147 is available only for "public documents" that were executed in a "foreign country" (defined by s 4) that did not raise an objection to New Zealand's accession to the Hague Convention referred to above. This is clear from para (b) of the definition of "foreign public document" in s 145. The issue of whether a particular country did raise an objection to New Zealand's accession to the Convention is itself the subject of the presumption in s 146.

145   Interpretation

In this section and sections 146 and 147,—

Convention means the Hague Convention Abolishing the Requirement of Legalisation for Foreign Public Documents, done at The Hague on 5 October 1961

Convention certificate means a certificate issued under the Convention in relation to a foreign public document by the competent authority of the State from which the foreign public document emanates

foreign public document means a public document that—

(a)   has to be produced in New Zealand; and

(b)   was executed in a foreign country that—

    (i)   is a contracting State under the Convention; and

    (ii)   did not raise an objection to New Zealand's accession to the Convention

legalisation means the formality by which New Zealand's diplomatic or consular agents certify, in relation to a public document that has to be produced in New Zealand and that was executed in a foreign country,—

(a)   the authenticity of the signature on the public document; and

(b)   the capacity in which the person signing the public document has acted; and

(c)   where appropriate, the identity of the stamp or seal that the public document bears

New Zealand authority means any person in New Zealand (including any court, any person acting judicially, and any person exercising a power or performing a function under a New Zealand law) to whom a foreign public document has to be produced

public document —

(a) includes any of the following documents:

   (i) a document emanating from an authority or from an official connected with the courts or tribunals of a State, including a document emanating from a public prosecutor, a clerk of a court, or a process server; and

   (ii) an administrative document (other than an administrative document dealing directly with commercial or customs operations); and

   (iii) a notarial act; and

   (iv) an official certificate that is placed on a document signed by a person in the person's private capacity (for example, an official certificate recording the registration of a document or the fact that the document was in existence on a certain date, or an official or notarial authentication of a signature); but

(b) does not include a document executed by a diplomatic or consular agent.

Compare: 1908 No 56 s 45A; 2000 No 62 s 3

146 Foreign public documents: certificates as to contracting States under Convention

A certificate purporting to be signed by the Secretary of Foreign Affairs and Trade, and stating that a country is a contracting State under the Convention that did not raise an objection to New Zealand's accession to the Convention, is sufficient evidence of those matters, unless the contrary is proved.

Compare: 1908 No 56 s 45B; 2000 No 62 s 3

147 Foreign public documents: Convention certificates sufficient authentication of certain matters

(1) A Convention certificate placed on, or attached to, a foreign public document is the only formality that a New Zealand authority may require, in relation to the document, as evidence or certification of—

   (a) the authenticity of the signature on the document; and

   (b) the capacity in which the person signing the document has acted; and

   (c) where appropriate, the identity of the seal or stamp that the document bears.

(2) If a foreign public document is not subject to a requirement of legalisation, no New Zealand authority may require, in relation to the document, a Convention certificate as evidence or certification of the matters referred to in paragraphs (a) to (c) of subsection (1).

(3)   A New Zealand authority must accept, in relation to a foreign public document, a Convention certificate placed on, or attached to, the document as sufficient evidence or certification of the matters referred to in paragraphs (a) to (c) of subsection (1), unless the contrary is proved.

(4)   Subsection (3) does not prevent a New Zealand authority from accepting, in relation to a foreign public document, a lesser formality than a Convention certificate placed on, or attached to, the document as evidence or certification of the matters referred to in paragraphs (a) to (c) of subsection (1).

Compare: 1908 No 56 s 45C; Foreign Evidence Act 1994 (Aust) ss 37-39; 2000 No 62 s 3

Special rules relating to public documents admissible under Australian law

EV148.Intro.01   New Zealand court to apply Australian law

Sections 148 and 149 are slightly altered versions of ss 9 and 10 of the Evidence Amendment Act 1990. The Law Commission was of the view that s 10 could be contained in a separate Act dealing with evidence from overseas and the content of s 9 was adequately dealt with by the terms of s 141. These sections were therefore not re-drafted by the Law Commission along with the other sections in this Subpart, which may explain the difference in wording discussed below.

EV148.Intro.02   Not restricted to "proceedings"

The operation of ss 148 and 149 differ from much of the remainder of the Act by not being restricted to "proceedings", a term defined by s 4 to be restricted to *court* proceedings.[1372] Sections 148 and 149 should therefore apply to any New Zealand court, tribunal, or other authority that is faced with an issue of the admissibility in evidence of the classes of "documents" dealt with by the two sections.

Sections 148 and 149 require the New Zealand authority to apply the Australian rules of admissibility referred to in the two sections, and to admit documents when they would be admissible under Australian law.

EV148.Intro.03   Public documents

Section 148 applies to "public documents", which are partially defined by s 148(4). This is curious because the definition in s 4 of "public document" makes no allowance for this specific definition in s 148(4). Paragraph (b) of the s 4 defintion does so in the case of the separate definition of "public document" applicable to ss 145-147. The issue may not be of great practical importance because it is likely that the definition in s 148(4) is compatible with s 4's wide general definition of "public document".

EV148.Intro.04   Australian law

Section 148 makes no attempt to list the wide variety of Australian Acts (s 148(1) and (2)) or other laws (s 148(3)) which operate to admit public documents into evidence. The section merely provides that when a public document is admissible

---

1372   See EV4.35.01.

under Australian law, it is thereby rendered admissible in New Zealand. The issue of when Australian law provides for admissibility of public documents would need to be proven by evidence (s 144) or, if appropriate, "noticed" under s 128.[1373]

148   Evidence of public documents by reference to Australian law

(1)   A public document that is admissible in evidence under an Australian Act is admissible in evidence to the same extent and for the same purpose if it appears to be sealed, stamped, signed, signed and sealed, or signed and stamped in accordance with that Act.

(2)   A certified copy of, or a certified extract from, a public document that is admissible in evidence under subsection (1) is also admissible in evidence.

(3)   Despite subsection (1), a public document that is admissible in evidence under Australian law, to any extent or for any purpose, without proof of—

(a)   the seal, stamp, or signature that authenticates it; or

(b)   the judicial or official character of the person who appears to have signed it—

is admissible in evidence to the same extent and for the same purpose without such proof.

(4)   In this section, **public document** means an official or public document; and includes a certificate, an entry in a register, and a record of any proceedings.

Compare: 1990 No 46 s 9

149   Evidence of other public documents

A copy of, or an extract from, an Australian document that is, by reason of its public nature, admissible in evidence in Australia merely on its production from the proper custody, is admissible in evidence if—

(a)   the copy or extract is proved to be an examined copy or extract; or

(b)   the copy or extract appears to be signed or certified as a true copy or extract by the person who has custody of the document and that person also certifies that he or she has custody of it.

Compare: 1990 No 46 s 10

Part 4
Evidence from overseas or to be used overseas

(s 150 to s 200)

EVPt4.01   Evidence from overseas or to be used overseas

As indicated by its title, Part 4 of the Act regulates the process of obtaining evidence from overseas sources for use in a New Zealand proceeding, as well as obtaining evidence from a source in New Zealand for use in an overseas proceeding. To a large

---

1373   See, generally, Heydon, *Cross on Evidence* (7th Aus ed), Sydney, LexisNexis Butterworths, 2004, 1070-1076.

extent, this Part of the Act merely restates previously existing provisions contained in various amendments to the Evidence Act 1908. Other relevant statutes remain intact. Notably, Part 1A of the Judicature Act 1908 is unaffected. That Part of the Judicature Act facilitates trans-Tasman litigation involving various proceedings under the Commerce Act 1986 or the Trade Practices Act 1974 (Aust). Likewise, the Mutual Assistance in Criminal Matters Act 1992 continues in force.[1374] That Act provides for evidence obtained overseas to be admitted in a New Zealand criminal proceeding. It also provides for bringing witnesses from overseas to give evidence in a New Zealand criminal proceeding and for New Zealand to assist foreign jurisdictions to obtain evidence from New Zealand for use in a foreign criminal proceeding.

Subpart 1—Proceedings in Australia and New Zealand

(s 150 to s 181)

EVPt4Sub1.01   Proceedings in Australia and New Zealand

Sections 150-181 reflect the commitment of the New Zealand and Australian governments to strengthen the ties between their legal systems. The Subpart is a near verbatim repeat of the Evidence Amendment Act 1994. The special provisions for trans-Tasman litigation assistance contained in this Subpart are unaffected by subsequent provisions in the Act which apply to other jurisdictions. See ss 183 and 191.[1375]

(1)   Summary of provisions

This Subpart allows a subpoena issued by a New Zealand or Australian court to have the standard, coercive effect of a fully domestic subpoena, even though it is directed at and served upon a person who is in the other jurisdiction. This means, for example, that subject to various restrictions, a litigant in a New Zealand proceeding who follows the Subpart's procedures can serve a subpoena on an Australian resident and force him or her to travel to New Zealand in order to testify at trial. Failure to comply with the subpoena permits the commencement of enforcement proceedings.

(2)   Video link and telephone conference

By virtue of the definitions contained in ss 150 and 151 of an "Australian subpoena", "New Zealand subpoena", and a "specified proceeding", the ability of litigants to obtain a subpoena under this part is limited. It is not possible in a "specified proceeding" which, most importantly, means that it is not possible in a *criminal proceeding*.[1376] However, the effect of ss 168-180 is that evidence for a criminal

---

1374   See EV192.06.

1375   See EV183.01.

1376   The Trans-Tasman Working Group recommended extending the provisions of the Evidence Amendment Act 1994 (which is now contained in this Subpart of the Evidence Act 2006) to allow the service of subpoenas in criminal proceedings with the leave of a judge. See Attorney-General's Department (Australia) and Ministry of Justice (New Zealand), *Trans-Tasman Court Proceedings and regulatory Enforcement: A Report by the Trans-Tasman Working Group* (2006), 25 (recommendation 10).

proceeding in either jurisdiction can be obtained from the other jurisdiction by means of a video link or telephone conference where a witness is willing.

The effect of ss 168-180 is that evidence may be given, and counsel may make submissions by video link or telephone.[1377] The use of video link and telephone technology reduces the need for witnesses to travel to the other country to give evidence, thereby reducing cost and inconvenience.

(3)   Leave required

Regardless of the level of the New Zealand court in which the proceedings have been commenced, s 154(1) requires that a High Court Judge must grant leave before a New Zealand subpoena can be served on a witness in Australia. The section gives guidance for the exercise of a judge's discretion in determining whether or not to grant leave.

The Act does not purport to govern the issuance of a subpoena by an Australian Court. There is, therefore, no attempt to impose a requirement that any particular court grant leave before an "Australian subpoena" is issued.

(4)   Setting aside subpoenas

The Act allows a witness on whom a New Zealand subpoena has been served to apply to the High Court to set the subpoena aside. Section 160 sets out a non-exhaustive list of grounds upon which this could take place.

The Act does not purport to grant to a New Zealand court the power to set aside an Australian subpoena. However, ss 164 and 165 set out grounds upon which the person who is the subject of an Australian subpoena is not required to comply with it — or whose failure to comply may be excused by the High Court.

EVPt4Sub1.02   Tribunals

The definitions of a "New Zealand court" and an "Australian court", which can issue subpoenas under this Subpart, anticipate that the definitions may eventually extend to include tribunals. To the same effect is the definition of a "Judge". However, this can only occur when the Minister of Justice declares a particular tribunal to come within the definitions. No such declaration has yet occurred and none was ever made under the prior legislation, the Evidence Amendment Act 1994.

In *Plumley v Ellis*,[1378] Barker J concluded that under the Evidence Amendment Act 1994, a New Zealand subpoena could be issued to require an Australian witness to appear at a New Zealand *arbitration*.[1379]

1377   Although the provisions enable the making of submissions by telephone or video link, the Trans Tasman Working Group was not aware of any instances where counsel had done so, see Attorney-General's Department (Australia) and Ministry of Justice (New Zealand), *Trans-Tasman Court Proceedings and regulatory Enforcement: A Report by the Trans-Tasman Working Group* (2006), 21. A series of recommendations to enable more extensive use of technology are contained in the report.

1378   *Plumley v Ellis* [1997] 2 NZLR 579; (1997) 10 PRNZ 492.

EVPt4Sub1.03   Interlocutory proceedings and Rules of Court

Notwithstanding the fact that s 5(2) grants the Act a general priority over the rules of court, s 154(6) makes the issuance of a New Zealand subpoena subject to the applicable rules of court. As confirmed by *European Stone Surfaces Ltd v Italian Surfaces NZ Ltd*,[1380] the applicable rules of court are rr 497 and 502A-502J of the High Court Rules. In *A v Bottrill*,[1381] Young J held that the result of the operation of r 497 was that a New Zealand subpoena could not be issued to compel a witness to testify in an *interlocutory proceeding*.

Interpretation and application

150   Interpretation

In this subpart, unless the context otherwise requires,—

Australian court includes a tribunal declared by the Minister of Justice under section 152 to be an Australian court

Australian subpoena means a subpoena issued by an Australian court in a proceeding other than a specified proceeding

document has the meaning given to it by section 4

expenses, in relation to a subpoena, includes the reasonable costs, necessary for the purposes of complying with the subpoena, of—

(a)   travel to and from, and accommodation at, the place at which compliance with the subpoena is required; and

(b)   finding, collating, and producing a document or thing necessary for the purposes of complying with the subpoena

Federal Court means the Federal Court of Australia

High Court means the High Court of New Zealand

Judge, in relation to an Australian court, includes a Judicial Registrar, Magistrate, Master, and a member of a tribunal

New Zealand court includes a tribunal declared by the Minister of Justice under section 152 to be a New Zealand court

New Zealand subpoena means a subpoena issued by a New Zealand court in a proceeding other than a specified proceeding

prescribed means prescribed by rules or regulations made under section 199 or 200

1379   The vast majority of the provisions of the Evidence Act 2006 apply only in a "proceeding", which is defined in s 4 as a proceeding conducted by a *court*. Accordingly, even though a witness is compelled under Subpart 1 of Part 4 of the Act to appear at an arbitration (or a tribunal, if a declaration is made of the sort envisioned in s 150's definition of "New Zealand court") the provisions of the Act will not apply to that arbitration (or to the hearing conducted by the tribunal).

1380   *European Stone Surfaces Ltd v Italian Surfaces NZ Ltd* (2006) 18 PRNZ 165, para 7.

1381   *A v Bottrill* (1999) 14 PRNZ 94.

subpoena—

(a)   means a process that requires a person to do one or both of the following:

    (i)   give evidence; or

    (ii)   produce a document or thing; but

(b)   does not include a process that requires a person to produce a document in connection with discovery and inspection of documents

tribunal—

(a)   means a person or body authorised under New Zealand law or a law of the Commonwealth of Australia or a State or territory of Australia, as the case may be, to take evidence on oath or affirmation; but

(b)   does not include a court or a person exercising a power conferred on the person as a Judge, Magistrate, or officer of a court

witness, in relation to a subpoena, means the person to whom the subpoena is addressed.

Compare: 1994 No 31 s 2

151   Meaning of specified proceeding

In this subpart, **specified proceeding** means a proceeding—

(a)   in respect of which a person is seeking an order under the Convention on the Civil Aspects of International Child Abduction signed at the Hague on 25 October 1980; or

(b)   relating to the status or property of a person under a disability; or

(c)   that is a criminal proceeding.

152   Power of Minister of Justice in relation to certain tribunals

For the purposes of this subpart, the Minister of Justice may, by notice in the *Gazette*, declare—

(a)   any New Zealand tribunal to be a New Zealand court:

(b)   any tribunal of the Commonwealth of Australia or of a State or a territory of Australia to be an Australian court.

Compare: 1994 No 31 s 3

153   Act not to apply to certain proceedings in High Court of New Zealand and Federal Court of Australia

Nothing in this subpart applies in relation to any proceedings to which Part 1A of the Judicature Act 1908 applies.

Compare: 1994 No 31 s 4

Service of and compliance with New Zealand subpoenas in Australia

154   Service of New Zealand subpoenas in Australia

(1)   A New Zealand subpoena may, with the leave of a Judge of the High Court, be served on a witness in Australia.

(2)   In determining whether to grant leave the Judge must, in addition to any other matter that the Judge considers relevant, have regard to—

(a)   the significance of the oral evidence to be given, or the document or thing to be produced, or both; and

(b)   whether the oral evidence to be given, the document or thing to be produced, or both could be obtained without significantly greater expense by other means and with less inconvenience to the witness.

(3)   The Judge may grant leave subject to any conditions that the Judge thinks fit, and must impose a condition that the New Zealand subpoena is not to be served after a specified date.

(4)   The Judge must not grant leave if the subpoena is addressed to a witness who has not attained the age of 18 years.

(5)   The Judge may give directions as to service.

(6)   This section is subject to the applicable rules of court.

Compare: 1994 No 31 s 5

155   New Zealand subpoena may require evidence to be given in New Zealand or Australia

A New Zealand subpoena served on a witness in Australia may require the witness to give evidence or produce a document or thing or both at a place in New Zealand or Australia.

Compare: 1994 No 31 s 6

156   Service of subpoena

(1)   A New Zealand subpoena served on a witness in Australia must be served in accordance with New Zealand law.

(2)   The subpoena must not be served in Australia unless it is accompanied by—

(a)   a copy of the order granting leave to serve the subpoena; and

(b)   a statement in the prescribed form that—

(i)   sets out the rights and obligations of the witness in relation to the subpoena; and

(ii)   includes information about the way in which an application may be made to have the subpoena set aside.

(3)   Subsection (1) is subject to any directions as to service imposed under section 154(5).

Compare: 1994 No 31 s 7

157   Expenses

(1)   A witness on whom a New Zealand subpoena has been served in Australia is not required to comply with the subpoena unless, at the appropriate time, allowances and travelling expenses or vouchers in substitution for allowances and travelling

expenses sufficient to meet the witness's reasonable expenses of complying with the subpoena are paid or given to the witness.

(2)   Subsection (3) applies to a witness on whom a New Zealand subpoena has been served in Australia that requires the witness to produce documents or things, but does not require the witness to give oral evidence.

(3)   A witness to whom this subsection applies who elects to comply with the subpoena by producing the documents or things at an Australian court, is not required to comply with the subpoena unless, at the appropriate time, expenses sufficient to meet the witness's reasonable expenses of producing the documents or things to an Australian court and the expenses of transmitting the documents or things to the New Zealand court that issued the subpoena are paid or given to the witness.

(4)   In this section, the **appropriate time** means the time of service of the subpoena or at some other reasonable time before the witness is required to comply with it.

Compare: 1994 No 31 s 8

158   Payment of additional amounts to witness

(1)   A witness who has complied with a New Zealand subpoena that was served on the witness in Australia is entitled to be paid any reasonable expenses incurred by the witness in complying with the subpoena in addition to any expenses paid or given to the witness under section 157.

(2)   The expenses must be paid by the person who obtained the subpoena or, if the subpoena was issued under a direction of a New Zealand court, by the Crown.

(3)   Any money required to be paid by the Crown under subsection (2) must be paid out of the Crown bank account.

(4)   The court which issued the subpoena may, on the application of the person by whom the subpoena was obtained or the witness, make an order—

        (a)   specifying the amount to which the witness is entitled under this section; and

        (b)   requiring the person who obtained the subpoena or the Crown, as the case may be, to pay the amount to the witness.

(5)   An order made under subsection (4) by a court which does not have the power to enforce its orders may be filed in any District Court and when filed, is enforceable as a judgment of the District Court.

Compare: 1994 No 31 s 9

159   Subpoenas for production

(1)   A New Zealand subpoena that requires a witness in Australia to produce documents or things, but does not require the witness to give oral evidence, must state that the witness may comply with the subpoena by producing the documents or things at any registry of an Australian court not later than 10 days before the

date specified in the subpoena as the date on which the documents or things are required for production in the New Zealand court.

(2)   For the purposes of subsection (1), **registry**, in relation to an Australian court, means a registry of an Australian court authorised by a law of the Commonwealth of Australia to receive such documents or things.

Compare: 1994 No 31 s 10

160   Setting aside of subpoena served in Australia

(1)   A witness on whom a New Zealand subpoena is served in Australia may apply to the High Court to set the subpoena aside.

(2)   The High Court must set the subpoena aside if—

(a)   the subpoena requires the witness to attend at a sitting of a New Zealand court and the High Court is satisfied that—

(i)   the witness does not have, and cannot by the exercise of reasonable diligence within the time required for compliance obtain, the necessary travel documents; or

(ii)   the witness is liable to be detained in New Zealand for the purpose of serving a sentence; or

(iii)   the witness is liable to prosecution for an offence, or is being prosecuted for an offence, in New Zealand; or

(iv)   the witness is liable to the imposition of a civil penalty in civil proceedings in New Zealand, not being proceedings for a pecuniary penalty under the Commerce Act 1986; or

(b)   the witness is subject to a restriction on his or her movements, imposed by law or by order of a court, that would prevent the witness complying with the subpoena.

(3)   Without limiting subsection (1), the High Court may set the subpoena aside if it is satisfied that—

(a)   the evidence of the witness could be obtained satisfactorily without significantly greater expense by other means; or

(b)   compliance with the subpoena would cause hardship or serious inconvenience to the witness; or

(c)   in the case of a subpoena that requires a witness to produce documents or things, whether or not it also requires the witness to give oral evidence,—

(i)   the documents or things should not be taken out of Australia; and

(ii)   satisfactory evidence of the contents of the documents or evidence of the things can be given by other means.

(4)   An application to set aside a subpoena under subsection (1) must be filed in the office of the High Court in which leave to serve the subpoena was given, together with any affidavit setting out facts on which the applicant relies.

(5)   The Registrar of the High Court in which the application is filed must ensure that a copy of the application and any affidavit setting out facts on which the applicant relies is served on the solicitor on the record for the person who obtained leave to serve the subpoena, or if there is no solicitor on the record, on that person.

Compare: 1994 No 31 s 11

161   Failure to comply with subpoena

If a witness fails to comply with a New Zealand subpoena served in Australia, the court which issued the subpoena may, on the application of a party to the proceedings in which the subpoena was obtained, or of its own motion, give a certificate in the prescribed form stating that—

(a)   a Judge of the High Court has given leave to serve the subpoena issued by the court giving the certificate; and

(b)   the witness failed to comply with the subpoena.

Compare: 1994 No 31 s 12

162   Other powers not affected

Nothing in sections 154 to 161 limits or affects any other powers of a New Zealand court.

Compare: 1994 No 31 s 13

Service of and compliance with Australian subpoenas in New Zealand

163   Service of Australian subpoenas in New Zealand

(1)   An Australian subpoena may be served on a witness in New Zealand.

(2)   The subpoena must be accompanied by—

(a)   a copy of the order of the Judge of the Federal Court, or of the order of the Judge of the Family Court of Australia, or the order of the Judge of a Supreme Court of a State or a territory of Australia, as the case may be, by whom leave was granted to serve the subpoena in New Zealand; and

(b)   a statement setting out the rights and obligations of the witness, including information about the way in which an application may be made to the appropriate Australian court to have the subpoena set aside.

Compare: 1994 No 31 s 14

164   Compliance with Australian subpoena

(1)   A witness served with an Australian subpoena must comply with the subpoena.

(2)   Despite subsection (1) a witness served with an Australian subpoena is not required to comply with the subpoena if—

(a)   the subpoena is not served on the witness in accordance with section 163 and the law and rules that apply to the issue and service of the subpoena in the Australian court that issued it; or

(b)   allowances and travelling expenses or vouchers in substitution for allowances and travelling expenses sufficient to meet the witness's reasonable expenses of complying with the subpoena are not given or paid to the witness at the appropriate time; or

(c)   the witness is under the age of 18 years.

(3)   In this section the **appropriate time** means the time of service of the subpoena or at some other reasonable time before the witness is required to comply with it.

Compare: 1994 No 31 s 15

165   Failure of witness to comply with Australian subpoena

(1)   The High Court may, on receiving from the Australian court which issued the Australian subpoena a certificate stating that the witness has failed to comply with the subpoena, issue a warrant requiring any member of the police to arrest the witness and to bring him or her before the High Court.

(2)   The High Court may, on the appearance of the witness before the court, impose a fine not exceeding $10,000 unless the court is satisfied that the failure to comply with the subpoena should be excused.

(3)   In determining whether the failure to comply with the subpoena should be excused, the High Court may have regard to—

(a)   any matters that were not brought to the attention of the Australian court which granted leave to serve the subpoena, if the High Court is satisfied that—

(i)   the Australian court would have been likely to have set aside the subpoena if those matters had been brought to the attention of that court; and

(ii)   the failure to bring those matters to the attention of the Australian court was not due to any fault on the part of the witness or was due to an omission of the witness that should be excused; and

(b)   any matters to which the High Court would have regard if the subpoena had been issued by the High Court.

(4)   For the purposes of this section, a certificate under the seal of an Australian court stating—

(a)   that leave to serve the subpoena was granted by a Judge of the Federal Court or a Judge of the Family Court of Australia or a Judge of a Supreme Court of an Australian State or a territory; and

(b)   that the witness failed to comply with the subpoena—

is sufficient evidence of the matters stated in it unless the witness establishes to the satisfaction of the High Court that the witness did in fact comply with the subpoena.

(5)   Without limiting subsection (3), no finding of fact made by the Federal Court or by the Family Court of Australia or by a Supreme Court of an Australian State or a territory on an application to have the subpoena set aside may be challenged by any person alleged to have failed to comply with the subpoena unless the court was deliberately misled in making those findings of fact.

Compare: 1994 No 31 s 16

166   Transmission of documents or things to Australian court

(1)   The Registrar holding office at the registry of the High Court at which a document or thing is produced in compliance with an Australian subpoena must, on payment of the appropriate sum, accept the document or thing, and,—

(a)   as soon as practicable, inform the Registrar of the Australian court that issued the subpoena, by facsimile or similar means of communication, that the document or thing has been produced; and

(b)   send the document or thing, without delay, to the Australian court before the date on which it is required to be produced to that court.

(2)   In this section **the appropriate sum** in relation to a document or thing required to be produced in compliance with an Australian subpoena means a sum that is sufficient to send the document or thing to the Australian court that issued the subpoena by a means that will ensure it is received by the court before the date on which it is required to be produced.

Compare: 1994 No 31 s 17

167   Other powers to serve subpoenas not affected

Nothing in this Act limits or affects any right or power conferred by or under a law of the Commonwealth or a State or a territory of Australia to serve a subpoena in New Zealand on an Australian citizen.

Compare: 1994 No 31 s 18

Video link and telephone conferences in New Zealand proceedings

168   New Zealand court may receive evidence and submissions by video link and telephone conference from Australia

(1)   On the application of a party to a proceeding before a New Zealand court, the court may, if it is satisfied that the necessary facilities and equipment are available, or can reasonably be made available, and that evidence or submissions in the proceeding could more conveniently be given or made from Australia, direct that evidence be given from Australia, or submissions be made from Australia, by video link or telephone conference.

(2)   Unless the New Zealand court otherwise orders, the costs incurred in giving evidence or making submissions by video link or telephone conference and transmitting the evidence or submissions, in accordance with a direction given under subsection (1), must be paid by the applicant.

(3)   The New Zealand court may make an order specifying the amount payable by a party under subsection (2), and requiring the party to pay that amount.

(4)   An order made under subsection (3) by a court which does not have the power to enforce its orders may be filed in any District Court and, when filed, is enforceable as a judgment of the District Court.

Compare: 1994 No 31 s 19

169   Powers of New Zealand court in Australia

For the purposes of the taking of evidence or the receiving of submissions by video link or telephone conference from Australia under section 168, the New Zealand court may exercise in Australia all its powers which it is permitted to exercise in Australia under Australian law.

Compare: 1994 No 31 s 20

170   Evidence and submissions by video link

Evidence must not be given or submissions made by video link from Australia unless the courtroom or other place where the New Zealand court is sitting in New Zealand and the place where the evidence is to be given or the submissions are to be made in Australia are equipped with video facilities that—

(a)   enable persons present at the place where the court is sitting in New Zealand to see and hear the person giving evidence or making the submissions in Australia; and

(b)   enable persons present at the place where the evidence is given or the submissions are made in Australia to see and hear persons at the place where the court is sitting in New Zealand.

Compare: 1994 No 31 s 21

171   Evidence and submissions by telephone

Evidence must not be given or submissions made by telephone conference from Australia unless the courtroom or other place where the New Zealand court is sitting in New Zealand and the place where the evidence is to be given or the submissions are to be made in Australia are equipped with telephone conference facilities that—

(a)   enable persons present at the place where the court is sitting in New Zealand to hear the person giving evidence or making the submissions in Australia; and

(b)   enable persons present at the place where the evidence is given or the submissions are made in Australia to hear persons at the place where the court is sitting in New Zealand.

Compare: 1994 No 31 s 22

172   Rights of Australian counsel

A person who is entitled to practise as a barrister, or a solicitor, or both in a Supreme Court of a State or a territory of Australia from which evidence is to be given or submissions made by video link or telephone conference to a New Zealand court, is entitled to practise as a barrister, or solicitor, or both in relation to—

(a) the examination, cross-examination, or re-examination of a witness in Australia whose evidence is being given by video link or telephone conference in the proceeding before the New Zealand court; and

(b) the making of submissions by video link or telephone conference from Australia in the proceeding before the New Zealand court.

Compare: 1994 No 31 s 23

Video link and telephone conferences in Australian proceedings

173 Australian court may take evidence and receive submissions by video link or telephone conference in New Zealand

An Australian court may take evidence or receive submissions from a person in New Zealand by video link or telephone conference for the purposes of a proceeding before that court.

Compare: 1994 No 31 s 24

174 Powers of Australian court

(1) For the purposes of taking evidence from a witness in New Zealand or hearing submissions from a person in New Zealand, an Australian court may exercise in New Zealand any of its powers, except its powers to—

(a) punish for contempt; and

(b) enforce or execute its judgments or process.

(2) Subject to subsection (1), the Australian law that applies to the proceeding in Australia also applies to the practice and procedure of the Australian court in taking evidence or receiving submissions from a person in New Zealand.

Compare: 1994 No 31 s 25

175 Orders of Australian court

(1) Without limiting section 174, the Australian court may, by order,—

(a) direct that the hearing or any part of the hearing be held in private; or

(b) require any person to leave the place where the evidence is or is to be given or the submissions are or are to be made; or

(c) prohibit or restrict the publication of evidence or the name of any party or of any witness.

(2) An order made under subsection (1) may be enforced by a Judge of the High Court who, for that purpose, has and may exercise the powers, including the power to punish for contempt, that would have been available to enforce the order if it had been made by that Judge.

Compare: 1994 No 31 s 26

176 Place where evidence given part of Australian court

For the purposes of sections 174 and 175, the place in New Zealand where the evidence is given or the submissions are made in a proceeding before an Australian court are deemed to be part of that court.

Compare: 1994 No 31 s 27

177 Privileges, protections, and immunities of Judges, counsel, and witnesses in Australian proceedings

(1) A Judge of an Australian court has, in relation to the taking of evidence or the making of submissions by video link or telephone conference from a person in New Zealand, all the privileges, protections, and immunities of a Judge of the High Court.

(2) A person appearing as a barrister, a solicitor, or both has, in relation to the taking of the evidence or the making of the submissions, all the privileges and immunities of counsel in the High Court.

(3) Every witness who gives evidence in a proceeding before an Australian court by video link or telephone conference from New Zealand has all the privileges and immunities of a witness in the High Court.

Compare: 1994 No 31 s 28

178 Power of Australian court to administer oaths in New Zealand

(1) An Australian court may, for the purpose of obtaining the evidence of a person in New Zealand by video link or telephone conference, administer an oath or affirmation in accordance with the practice and procedure of that court.

(2) Evidence given by a person on oath or affirmation administered by the Australian court under subsection (1) is, for the purposes of section 108 of the Crimes Act 1961 (which relates to perjury), deemed to have been given as evidence in a judicial proceeding on oath.

Compare: 1994 No 31 s 29

179 Contempt of Australian court

(1) Every person commits an offence who, in New Zealand, at a place where evidence is being given or submissions are being made by video link or telephone conference in a proceeding before an Australian court,—

(a) assaults—

(i) a person appearing as a barrister, or solicitor, or both in the proceeding; or

(ii) a witness in the proceeding; or

(iii) an officer of a New Zealand court giving assistance under section 180; or

(b) threatens or intimidates or wilfully insults—

(i) a Judge of the Australian court taking part in the proceeding; or

(ii)   a Registrar or officer of the Australian court taking part in, or assisting with, the proceeding; or

(iii)   a person appearing as a barrister, or solicitor, or both in the proceeding; or

(iv)   a witness in the proceeding; or

(c)   wilfully interrupts or obstructs the proceeding; or

(d)   wilfully and without lawful excuse, disobeys any order or direction of the Australian court in the course of the proceeding.

(2)   Every person who commits an offence against this section is liable on summary conviction to imprisonment for a term not exceeding 3 months or to a fine not exceeding $1,000, or to both.

Compare: 1994 No 31 s 30

180   Assistance to Australian court

An officer of a New Zealand court may, at the request of an Australian court,—

(a)   attend at the place in New Zealand where evidence is being or will be given or submissions are being or will be made by video link or telephone conference in a proceeding before the Australian court; and

(b)   take any action that the Australian court directs to facilitate the proceeding; and

(c)   assist with the administering by the Australian court of an oath or affirmation.

Compare: 1994 No 31 s 31

Enforcement of Australian orders

181   Enforcement of certain orders made by Australian court

(1)   Subsection (2) applies to an order made by an Australian Court under the Evidence and Procedure (New Zealand) Act 1994 of the Commonwealth of Australia for—

(a)   the payment of expenses incurred by a witness in complying with an Australian subpoena served on the witness in New Zealand; or

(b)   the payment of expenses incurred by a person in connection with the taking of evidence or the making of submissions from New Zealand by video link or telephone, as the case may be.

(2)   For the purposes of the Reciprocal Enforcement of Judgments Act 1934, an order to which this subsection applies is deemed,—

(a)   if the order was made by an Australian court that is a superior court, to be a money judgment of a superior court that had jurisdiction to make the order; or

(b)   if the order was made by an Australian court that is not a superior court, to be a money judgment of a specified inferior court that had jurisdiction to make the order.

(3)   Nothing in section 6 (except paragraphs (a), and (d) to (f) of subsection (1)) of the Reciprocal Enforcement of Judgments Act 1934 applies to an order referred to in subsection (1) of this section.

Compare: 1994 No 31 s 32

Subpart 2—Evidence for use in civil proceedings overseas and evidence for use in civil proceedings in High Court

(s 182 to s 189)

182   Interpretation

In this subpart, unless the context otherwise requires,—

civil proceeding means any proceeding other than a criminal proceeding

Hague Convention on Evidence Abroad means the Convention on the Taking of Evidence Abroad in Civil or Commercial Matters signed at the Hague on 18 March 1970

High Court means the High Court of New Zealand

Judge means a Judge of the High Court

request includes any commission, order, or other process issued by or on behalf of the requesting court

requesting court means any court or tribunal exercising jurisdiction in a country or territory outside New Zealand.

EV182.01   Interpretation

Section 182 is a definitional provision setting out the meanings of various terms used in Subpart 2 of Part 4 of the Act (ss 182-189) — which deals with New Zealand High Court processes for the taking of evidence to be used in civil proceedings overseas and vice versa.

EV182.02   Hague Convention on Evidence Abroad

According to the 2006 *Departmental Report for the Justice and Electoral Committee* prepared by the Ministry of Justice:[1382]

> "[Subpart 2 of Part 4 of the Evidence Act] will allow New Zealand to become a party to the [Convention on the Taking of Evidence Abroad in Civil or Commercial Matters signed at the Hague on 18 March 1970 (referred to in s 182 of the Act as the 'Hague Convention on Evidence Abroad')]. The Convention facilitates the taking of evidence overseas by overcoming differences between civil and common law systems. There are currently 43 parties to the Convention.

> "[Sections 184 to 187 ('Evidence for use in civil proceedings overseas')] are based on provisions of the Evidence (Proceedings in Other Jurisdictions) Act

---

1382   *Departmental Report* (EV/MOJ/3), 3. See also New Zealand Law Commission, *International Trade Conventions*, NZLC SP5, Wellington, 2000, Ch 6.

1975 (UK), which allowed the United Kingdom to join the Convention. Most Australian states have also followed this legislative model.

"These clauses will also continue to allow New Zealand courts to assist the taking of evidence for applicants in countries that are not parties to the Hague Convention."

Applying only to civil proceedings, Subpart 2 varies the schema established in ss 48-48J of the Evidence Act 1908 and Part 4 (ss 37-49) of the Evidence Amendment Act (No 2) 1980. Implementing and reflecting the Hague Convention on Evidence Abroad, ss 184-187 of the Act will apply to all foreign jurisdictions through the wide definition of a "requesting court" set out in s 182.

183 Relationship with subpart 1

This subpart does not affect the application or operation of subpart 1.

EV183.01 Relationship between Subparts 1 and 2 of Part 4

With minor modifications, Subpart 1 (ss 150-181) ("Proceedings in Australia and New Zealand: Interpretation and Application") of Part 4 of the Act ("Evidence from overseas or to be used overseas") carries over provisions introduced into the Evidence Act 1908 by the Evidence Amendment Act 1994. These rules: (1) allow a New Zealand court to summon a witness in Australia for civil proceedings in New Zealand and vice-versa; and (2) provide for a New Zealand court to receive evidence in any proceeding from a witness in Australia — by video link and telephone conference — and vice-versa.[1383]

Section 183 sets out the relationship between Subparts 1 and 2 of Part 4 of the Act by providing that Subpart 2 does not affect "the application or interpretation of subpart 1". As a result, the rules set out in Subpart 2 of Part 4 of the Act (ss 182-189) — which deal with New Zealand High Court processes for the taking of evidence to be used in civil proceedings overseas and vice-versa — will not impact or limit the specific subpoena and evidence taking procedures operating between Australia and New Zealand pursuant to Subpart 1 of Part 4.[1384]

Evidence for use in civil proceedings overseas

184 Application to High Court for assistance in obtaining evidence for civil proceedings in another court

The High Court or a Judge may exercise the powers conferred by section 185(1) if an application is made to the High Court or a Judge for an order for evidence to be obtained in New Zealand and the court or Judge is satisfied—

(a) that the application is made to implement a request issued by or on behalf of a requesting court; and

---

1383   See EVPt4Sub1.01-03.
1384   See also EV191.01.

(b)   that any requirements prescribed in rules or regulations made under section 200 as to the form of the application and the manner in which it must be made are satisfied; and

(c)   that the evidence to which the application relates is to be obtained for the purposes of civil proceedings which either have been instituted before the requesting court or whose institution before that court is contemplated.

EV184.01   Evidence for use in overseas civil proceedings

While dealing only with civil proceedings (foreign criminal proceedings now being handled under ss 192-98 of the Act), s 184 replaces and extends s 48A of the Evidence Act 1908 and s 39 of the Evidence Amendment Act (No 2) 1980. When its requirements are met, s 184 gives the High Court the jurisdiction to give effect to a request from a foreign court that evidence be taken in New Zealand for use in an overseas civil proceeding.

EV184.02   Requirements for High Court assistance to overseas court

The scope of the High Court's authority to give effect to an application for assistance from a foreign court is contained in s 185(1).[1385] To trigger the exercise of those powers, s 184 requires the High Court to be satisfied that any such application: (a) "is made to implement a request issued by or on behalf of a requesting court" (s 184(a)); (b) complies in form and manner with "any requirements prescribed in rules or regulations made under s 200" (s 184(b)); and (c) deals with evidence "to be obtained for the purposes of civil proceedings which either have been instituted before the requesting court or whose institution before that court is contemplated" (s 184(c)).

(1)   Definitions of "request", "requesting court", and "civil proceeding"

As used in ss 184 and 185, the definitions of "request", "requesting court", and "civil proceeding" are contained in s 182 of the Act.[1386]

(2)   Form and manner of request for assistance

As referenced in s 184(b), s 200 provides for the making of rules and regulations to carry out the provisions of Part 4 of the Act (including s 184). To date, no such rules or regulations have been promulgated under s 200.[1387] However, arts 1-6 of the Hague Convention on Evidence Abroad contain detailed measures regarding the form and content of "Letters of Request" for assistance in obtaining evidence in civil proceedings, as well as their appropriate method of transmission between "Contracting States" (countries that are parties to the Convention).[1388] As discussed at EV182.02, Subpart 2 of Part 4 of the Act is intended to make New Zealand a

---

1385   See EV185.02.
1386   See EV182.01.
1387   See EV200.01.
1388   See the Convention on the Taking of Evidence Abroad in Civil or Commercial Matters signed at the Hague on 18 March 1970 (referred to in s 182 of the Act as the "Hague Convention on Evidence Abroad").

Contracting State. Presumably, any regulations issued under s 200 will incorporate procedures set out in the Hague Convention for Letters of Request from an overseas court to the High Court for assistance in obtaining evidence for civil proceedings overseas.

(3) Instituted or contemplated civil proceedings overseas

Section 184(c) anticipates that the foreign court can make a request to the High Court for assistance in obtaining evidence during or before the actual commencement of any civil proceedings overseas. However, in order to meet the jurisdictional threshold of s 184, the proceeding must be a proceeding of the court that actually issues the request to the High Court.[1389] This follows from the language of s 184(c), which requires the foreign civil proceeding to be one already "*instituted before* the *requesting court* or whose *institution before that court is contemplated*".[1390] Accordingly, s 184 will exclude assistance for private foreign arbitration proceedings not conducted by an overseas court.[1391]

(4) Power of the New Zealand Solicitor-General

Rule 381 of the High Court Rules makes it clear that, where no agent in New Zealand promotes the application for assistance from the overseas requesting court to the High Court, the Solicitor-General is empowered to act. Rule 381 states:

> **"381. Application by Solicitor-General on letters of request from abroad**
> "Where, in any proceedings to which sections 182 to 187 of the Evidence Act 2006 apply, a letter of request is received in any office of the Court and it does not appear that the same is desired or intended to be carried into effect by an application to the Court made by the agent in New Zealand of a party to the proceedings, the Registrar shall transmit the same to the Solicitor-General, who may thereupon make such application and take such steps as may be necessary to give effect to the same."

185 Power of High Court to give effect to application for assistance

(1) If this section applies, the High Court or a Judge may—

    (a) order that any provision for the taking of evidence in New Zealand that the High Court or the Judge considers appropriate for giving effect to the request to which the application relates, be made:

    (b) include in that order a requirement for any specified person to do any specified thing that the High Court or the Judge considers appropriate for that purpose.

(2) An order under subsection (1) may include, without limitation, provision—

    (a) for the examination of witnesses, either orally or in writing at any agreed time or at any specified time and place:

1389   See, eg, *Re Intec USA, LLC* (2006) 18 PRNZ 222 (HC).
1390   Emphasis added.
1391   See, eg, *Re Intec USA, LLC* (2006) 18 PRNZ 222 (HC).

(b)   for the production of documents:

(c)   for the inspection, photographing, preservation, custody, or detention of any property:

(d)   for the taking of samples of any property and the carrying out of any experiments on or with any property:

(e)   for the medical examination of any person:

(f)   without limiting paragraph (e), for the taking and testing of samples of blood from any person.

(3)   An order under subsection (1) may not require any particular steps to be taken unless they are steps which can be required to be taken by way of obtaining evidence for the purposes of civil proceedings in the High Court (whether or not proceedings of the same description as those to which the application for the order relates).

(4)   Subsection (3) does not preclude the making of an order requiring a person to give evidence (either orally or in writing) otherwise than on oath if this is asked for by the requesting court.

(5)   An order under subsection (1) may not require a person—

(a)   to state what documents relevant to the proceedings to which the application for the order relates are or have been in the person's possession, custody, or power:

(b)   to produce any documents other than particular documents specified in the order as being documents appearing to the court making the order to be, or to be likely to be, in the person's possession, custody, or power and relevant to the proceedings.

(6)   A person who, pursuant to an order under subsection (1), is required to attend at any place, is entitled to the same conduct money and payment for expenses and loss of time as on attendance as a witness in civil proceedings before the High Court.

(7)   An order made under subsection (1) may be enforced in the same manner as if it were an order made by the High Court or Judge in proceedings pending in the High Court or before the Judge.

EV185.01   Powers of High Court to assist overseas court

Section 185 sets out the scope of the High Court's powers to give effect to an application for assistance from a foreign court under s 184.[1392]

EV185.02   Broad scope of assistance in obtaining evidence

As a general matter, the High Court has the power to make any order for the taking of evidence in New Zealand that the Court "considers appropriate for giving effect

---

1392   See EV184.02.

to the request to which the application relates" (s 185(1)(a)).[1393] For the avoidance of doubt, s 185(2) lists a broad and non-exclusive class of real and testimonial evidence that may be encompassed by a High Court order under s 185(1).

EV185.03   Limitations on High Court powers to obtain evidence

Despite the broad class of evidence encompassed by s 185, the High Court's power to make orders for assistance under s 185(1) will be subject to the limitations imposed by s 185(3) and (5).[1394]

(1)   Domestic civil proceedings

Notwithstanding a proper request for assistance from an overseas court under s 184, s 185(3) pegs the power of the High Court to make orders for the obtaining of evidence in New Zealand to steps that would be available in domestic civil proceedings in the High Court (regardless of how such proceedings might be described or titled). Accordingly, a foreign court will not be able to obtain evidence pursuant to an order under s 185 unless a comparable means exists for parties in New Zealand to secure such evidence in a High Court civil case.

(2)   Requests in the nature of discovery

Incorporating common law rulings under s 48A of the Evidence Act 1908 — the predecessor to s 184 of the Evidence Act 2006[1395] — s 185(5) makes it clear that requests for assistance from an overseas court under s 184 cannot be used to undertake general discovery in New Zealand from either the parties to the foreign civil proceeding or third parties.[1396] Instead, documents can only be ordered produced pursuant to s 185(2)(b) if: (a) they are "particular documents specified in the order"; and (b) it appears to the High Court that such documents are "likely to be" both "relevant to the proceedings" and within a person's "possession, custody, or power" (s 185(5)(b)).[1397]

In assessing whether the particularity standard of s 185(5)(b) has been met, case law under s 48A of the Evidence Act 1908 indicated that the principles to be applied were those related to a subpoena duces tecum.[1398] Such an approach means that documents ordered produced pursuant to s 185(2)(b) must, at first instance, be delivered to the

---

1393   See EV184.02.
1394   See also the discussion of s 186 at EV186.01.
1395   See EV184.01.
1396   See Turner, "Civil Procedure" [2004] NZ Law Rev 345, 355 (discussing *Perry v Molteno* (1999) 13 PRNZ 546 (HC); *FCA Investment Co v Nelson* 14/10/03, Heath J, HC Auckland CIV-2003-404-4287; *TT Jones v Creighton LLC* 23/7/03, Venning J, HC Rotorua CP2/03). See also *Re Intec USA, LLC* (2006) 18 PRNZ 222 (HC).
1397   For discussion of the phrase "possession, custody or power", see *FCA Investment Co v Nelson* 14/10/03, Heath J, HC Auckland CIV-2003-404-4287 (quoting *Lonrho Ltd v Shell Petroleum Co Ltd* [1980] 1 WLR 627 (HL), 635-636, per Lord Diplock). See also *Xuan v Wu* 14/10/03, Heath J, HC Auckland CIV-2002-404-1843; *Johansen v American International Underwriters (NZ) Ltd* [1997] 3 NZLR 765; (1997) 11 PRNZ 22 (HC).
1398   See *Perry v Molteno* (1999) 13 PRNZ 546 (HC); *FCA Investment Co v Nelson* 14/10/03, Heath J, HC Auckland CIV-2003-404-4287; *TT Jones v Creighton LLC* 23/7/03, Venning J, HC Rotorua CP2/03; *Re Intec USA, LLC* (2006) 18 PRNZ 222 (HC).

High Court rather than to the party to the oversees civil proceeding.[1399] It will then fall to the Court to decide "whether the documents produced should be provided to the parties to the litigation".[1400]

EV185.04   Procedures for examining witnesses

Section 185(2)(a) clearly provides for the examination of witnesses in New Zealand in order to obtain evidence for an overseas civil proceeding. Case law under s 48A of the Evidence Act 1908 suggested that such examination could be conducted pursuant to rr 369-376 of the High Court Rules.[1401] Section 185(3) indicates that this procedure will continue to be available for witness examination orders made under s 185(1).

In *Re Nattrass*[1402] — a case dealing with s 48A of the Evidence Act 1908 — the High Court ordered that, pursuant to Letters of Request from the Supreme Court of Hong Kong, witnesses in New Zealand could be examined for a pending Hong Kong criminal proceeding (a request now handled under s 192(1) of the Evidence Act 2006).[1403] Tompkins J noted:[1404]

> "Judicial and international comity requires that any request of a foreign court for evidence to be taken under [s 48A of the Evidence Act 1908] should be treated with sympathy and respect and complied with so far as the principles of English law permit."

In accordance with the wishes of the Supreme Court, the High Court ordered that that the Hong Kong trial judge be named as the person to preside over the examination in New Zealand, and that prosecution and defence counsel appearing in the Hong Kong proceeding be allowed to examine the New Zealand witnesses. Tompkins J also made "important points about the powers of a foreign examiner appointed pursuant to an application under s 48A [of the Evidence Act 1908]" and "the ability of overseas counsel to examine witnesses in New Zealand".[1405] Such observations should still be relevant to orders promulgated under s 185(2) of the Evidence Act 2006.

(1)   Evidence other than on oath

If the requesting (overseas) court (defined in s 182) asks for some type of alternative procedure, s 185(4) provides that, notwithstanding s 185(3), the High Court may make an order for a witness to give evidence in New Zealand "otherwise than on oath".

1399   See *Perry v Molteno* (1999) 13 PRNZ 546 (HC); *FCA Investment Co v Nelson* 14/10/03, Heath J, HC Auckland CIV-2003-404-4287.

1400   Turner, "Civil Procedure" [2004] NZ Law Rev 345, 352 (discussing *Perry v Molteno* (1999) 13 PRNZ 546 (HC)).

1401   See Turner, "Civil Procedure" [2004] NZ Law Rev 345, 355 (discussing *Re Nattrass* (1997) 10 PRNZ 335 (HC), 337 and *Perry v Molteno* (1999) 13 PRNZ 546 (HC)).

1402   *Re Nattrass* (1997) 10 PRNZ 335 (HC).

1403   See EV192.01.

1404   *Re Nattrass* (1997) 10 PRNZ 335 (HC), 337 (quoting *Seyfang v GD Searle & Co* [1973] QB 148; [1973] 1 All ER 290, per Cooke J)).

1405   Turner, "Civil Procedure" [2004] NZ Law Rev 345, 351.

EV185.05   Compensation for persons "required to attend" under s 185(1)

Section 185(6) provides that a person "required to attend at any place" pursuant to a High Court order under s 185(1) is entitled to the same compensation as someone who attends "as a witness in civil proceedings before the High Court".

In its December 2006 Consultation Paper, *Specific changes to the recovery of costs in the High Court Rules*, the Rules Committee discussed the current position regarding witness fees in civil proceedings under r 48H of the High Court Rules:[1406]

> "14.   Witnesses' fees and expenses used to be dealt with in the Third Schedule to the High Court Rules. It provided that witnesses' and interpreters' fees, allowances, and travelling expenses were to be calculated in accordance with the Witnesses and Interpreters Fees Regulations 1974.

> "15.   It has been determined that in civil proceedings expenses and disbursements, in particular witnesses' fees, are no longer recoverable under the Witnesses and Interpreters Fees Regulations: [see *Air New Zealand v Commerce Commission* (2005) 17 PRNZ 786 (HC), 802, and *Three Meade Street Ltd v Rotorua District Council* 21/11/05, Venning J, HC Rotorua CIV-2003-463-132].

> "16.   Currently Rule 48H governs the recovery of disbursements and expenses as expressly listed in the rule itself or the Third Schedule to the High Court Rules. However, witnesses' fees and allowances are not specifically provided for. Witnesses' fees can be recovered under the criteria set out in r 48H(1)(a). The Court must approve inclusion of witnesses' fees in a claim for disbursements: r 48H(2)(a)."

EV185.06   Enforcement of High Court order

With respect to its enforcement, s 185(7) gives an order made under s 185(1) the same status "as if it were" a High Court order made in domestic proceedings in New Zealand. See, however, EV186.01 for a discussion of the rules related to the non-compellability of witnesses in New Zealand otherwise subject to an examination order under s 185(1).

186   Privileges of witnesses

(1)   A person may not be compelled by an order under section 185(1) to give any evidence which the person could not be compelled to give—

    (a)   in civil proceedings in New Zealand; or

    (b)   in civil proceedings in the country or territory in which the requesting court exercises jurisdiction.

(2)   Subsection (1)(b) does not apply unless the person in question claims to be exempt from giving the evidence and the claim is either—

[1406]   Rules Committee, *Rules Committee Consultation Paper: Specific changes to the recovery of costs in the High Court Rules*, Wellington, 18 December 2006, paras 14-16. See also *McGechan on Procedure*, HR48H.02.

(a)   supported by a statement contained in the request (whether unconditionally or subject to conditions that are fulfilled); or

(b)   conceded by the applicant for the order under section 185(1).

(3)   If a claim is made by a person for exemption under subsection (2) but the High Court or a Judge is not satisfied that subsection (2) applies, the person may be required to give the evidence to which the claim relates but that evidence must not be transmitted to the requesting court if—

(a)   the High Court or a Judge refers the claim to the requesting court for consideration and determination; and

(b)   that court upholds the claim for exemption.

(4)   A person may not be compelled by an order under section 185(1) to give any evidence if the giving of that evidence would be prejudicial to the security of New Zealand and a certificate signed by the Attorney-General to the effect that it would be so prejudicial for that person to do so is conclusive evidence of that fact.

(5)   In this section **giving evidence** includes—

(a)   answering any question:

(b)   producing any document.

EV186.01   Privileges of witnesses

In the relevant part, s 186 repeats and extends ss 48D and 48H of the Evidence Act 1908. In certain situations, it permits a witness in New Zealand to resist giving evidence he or she would otherwise be compelled to provide pursuant to a High Court order under s 185(1). Section 195 of the Act creates comparable (but not identical) exemptions where evidence is sought from witnesses in New Zealand for foreign criminal proceedings.[1407]

EV186.02   Scope of s 186

Section 186(1) and (4) set out three separate circumstances[1408] under which a witness otherwise obliged to give evidence for use in an overseas civil proceeding cannot be compelled to do so pursuant to s 185(1).

For the avoidance of doubt, "giving evidence" in s 186 is defined to include: (a) "answering any question" (s 186(5)(a)); or (b) "producing any document" (defined broadly in s 4(1)[1409]) (s 186(5)(b)). See also the discussion at EV184.02(1) for the definitions of "request", "requesting court", and "civil proceeding" as used in s 186.

EV186.03   Exemption under foreign law

Questions of witness non-compellability under s 186(1)(b) will be settled by reference to the law of the overseas jurisdiction before whose court the civil proceeding will

---

1407   See EV195.01.
1408   See EV186.03-05.
1409   See EV4.11.01.

take place. Depending on the relevant foreign legal rules, this may include protections for witnesses not otherwise recognised under New Zealand law. See the discussion of s 61.[1410]

(1) Proving the exemption

Section 186(2) makes it clear that, where a person claims to be exempt from giving evidence under s 185(1) on the basis of overseas law, the claim must be: (a) "supported by a statement contained in the request (whether unconditionally or subject to conditions that are fulfilled)" (s 186(2)(a)); or (b) "conceded by the applicant for the order under section 185(1)" (s 186(2)(b)).

If not satisfied that the requirements of s 186(2) have been met, the High Court has several options under s 186(3). It may require the witness to give the evidence to which the claim of exemption relates (s 186(3)). However, s 186(3)(a) gives the High Court the power to refer any claim to the requesting (overseas) court "for consideration and determination". If the requesting court "upholds the claim for exemption" following referral (s 186(3)(b)), s 186(3) forbids the High Court from transmitting any of the exempted evidence overseas.

Section 186 does not specify the conditions under which the New Zealand High Court would itself determine a claim under s 186(2) or refer it for determination to the relevant overseas court pursuant to s 186(3). Presumably, referral will be preferred where the High Court cannot readily evaluate a claim of non-compellability under the laws of the foreign jurisdiction, or where the overseas court is simply better placed to consider the claim on the facts and circumstances of a particular case.

Section 144 of the Act, which deals with the manner in which a party may offer evidence in a New Zealand court of relevant foreign law, will undoubtedly be germane to various matters arising under s 186(2) and (3).[1411]

EV186.04   Exemption under New Zealand law

By contrast with s 186(1)(b), questions of non-compellability under s 186(1)(a) will be settled by reference to other provisions of the Evidence Act. Successful claims are likely to be rare since, as a general matter, s 71 makes most persons eligible and compellable witnesses in New Zealand civil and criminal proceedings.[1412] However, where relevant, s 186(1)(a) will encompass non-compellability based on three potential grounds.

(1) Status of witnesses

The status of a witness in New Zealand obliged to give evidence under s 185(1) may ground a claim for exemption under s 186(1)(a). See the discussion of ss 72-76.

1410   See EV61.03.
1411   See EV144.01.
1412   See EV71.01.

(2)   Privilege

An evidential privilege recognised in New Zealand civil proceedings may also ground a claim of exemption under s 186(1)(a). See the discussion of ss 51-67.

(3)   Judicial discretion to protect confidences

A successful claim under s 186(1)(a) could be based on the discretion vested in New Zealand judges to allow a witness to withhold certain confidential information from disclosure in domestic civil proceedings. See the discussion of ss 68-70.

EV186.05   Prejudice to the security of New Zealand

The bases of non-compellability incorporated in s 186(1)(a) are buttressed by the broader ground of New Zealand national interest contained in s 186(4).

Directed to the overall protection of New Zealand rather than the individual concerns of the witness, applications under s 186(4) are likely to be rare. However, where relevant, s 186(4) will prevent a judicial order under s 185(1) compelling an individual to give evidence for an overseas civil proceeding that "would be prejudicial to the security of New Zealand". Moreover, while not required to establish the type of prejudice to the New Zealand state referenced in s 186, "a certificate signed by the Attorney-General that it would be ... prejudicial for [a] person to [give such evidence] is *conclusive* evidence of that fact" (s 186(4)).[1413]

(1)   Comparison with s 195(2)

It is curious that the grounds of non-compellability set out in s 186(4) are narrower than those contained in s 195(2) of the Act — a parallel provision that renders a witness in New Zealand non-compellable to give evidence for use in overseas *criminal* proceedings[1414] if the evidence "would otherwise be prejudicial to the security *or sovereignty of New Zealand or would be likely to be prejudicial to the trading, commercial or economic interests of New Zealand*".[1415] Indeed, it seems difficult to understand why the kinds of national harms set out in s 195(2) should be so much broader than those recognised in s 186(4). The distinction between evidence taken in the High Court for overseas civil or criminal proceedings hardly justifies the disparity, particularly when various state interests could be implicated by the testimony of witnesses in New Zealand sought for any type of foreign case. Nor do any reports or briefing papers on the Act — either from the Ministry of Justice, Parliament or third parties — explain the substantive differences between ss 186(4) and 195(2).

EV186.06   Witnesses are eligible to testify voluntarily

Like s 71 of the Act, s 186 does not forbid witnesses in New Zealand from giving, if they so choose, the kinds of evidence that would be shielded from disclosure under s 186(1) or (4). It simply deals with the *compellability* of witnesses who wish to resist a High Court order issued pursuant to s 185(1). Likewise, and despite the important

---

1413   Emphasis added.
1414   See EV192.01.
1415   Emphasis added. See EV195.04.

national interest identified in s 186(4), the provision does not specifically permit the Crown to *prevent* a willing witness in New Zealand from providing evidence regarding such matters under s 185(1). Compare ss 48H and 48I of the Evidence Act 1908. Nonetheless, s 70(1) of the Act — which gives a judge the discretion to direct that certain communications or information relating to "matters of State" not be disclosed in a proceeding — would likely be interpreted as permitting a Crown application to prevent sensitive material from being obtained for a foreign civil case under s 185.[1416]

187   Orders not to bind the Crown or Crown servants

No order may be made under this subpart that is binding on the Crown or on any person in his or her capacity as an officer or servant of the Crown.

EV187.01   Orders cannot bind the Crown or Crown agents

Section 187 of the Act makes it clear that a New Zealand court has no jurisdiction to order the New Zealand Crown — or a Crown official — to provide evidence for use in overseas civil proceedings pursuant to ss 184-85.

EV187.02   Relevance of UK legislation

Section 187 effectively adopts the language of s 9(4) of the Evidence (Proceedings in Other Jurisdictions) Act 1975 (UK) — legislation permitting the UK to join the Hague Convention on Evidence Abroad. Accordingly, the interpretation and application of s 187 may be guided by English case law.

In *Re Pan American World Airways Inc and other's application*, the English Court of Appeal held that the jurisdictional limits set out in s 9(4) barred a judge from ordering a retired Crown scientist to give evidence — for use in an American court — on matters related to work done when he was an "officer or servant of the Crown".[1417] As Lord Donaldson of Lymington MR wrote:

> "Section 9(4), which operates at the time of the application for an order under the Act, looks back towards the time in relation to which the witness would give evidence if an order was made and not forward to the time at which he would do so ... The limiting words 'in his capacity as an officer or servant of the Crown' leave the court free to order a witness to give evidence notwithstanding that at the relevant time he was an officer or servant of the Crown, if the matters in respect of which he is to give evidence did not come to his notice in that capacity, for example, the civil servant who, when on holiday or at home, happens to witness a road traffic accident ... The whole of the evidence sought from Dr. Hayes relates to matters which came to his notice in his capacity as an officer or servant of the Crown and accordingly section 9(4) applies."[1418]

1416   See EV70.01.
1417   *Re Pan American World Airways Inc and other's application* [1992] 3 All ER 197 (CA), 203.
1418   *Re Pan American World Airways Inc and other's application* [1992] 3 All ER 197 (CA), 203.

The Court went on to observe:[1419]

> "Nothing in the Act or in the [Hague Convention on Evidence Abroad] prevents the Crown from facilitating the giving of evidence by its present or former officers or servants, subject to such conditions if any as it may deem appropriate, but the courts have no power to order anyone to give evidence in circumstances in which section 9(4) applies."

The same would be true in New Zealand under s 187 of the Evidence Act.

Procedure for taking evidence overseas for use in civil proceedings in High Court

188   Procedure for taking evidence outside New Zealand in civil proceedings in High Court

(1)   If at any stage of any civil proceeding in the High Court it appears necessary or desirable in the interests of justice, the High Court or a Judge may order that—

   (a)   any person named in the order be examined on oath, by interrogatories or otherwise, at any place outside New Zealand before any officer of the High Court, any overseas representative, or any other person named in the order by name or designation; and

   (b)   any deposition so taken be filed in the High Court; and

   (c)   any party to the proceeding be empowered to give that deposition in evidence in the proceeding, on any terms as the High Court or Judge may direct.

(2)   In any civil proceeding in the High Court, if the High Court or a Judge thinks fit, instead of making an order for the examination of a witness or person under subsection (1), the High Court or Judge may order that a Letter of Request be issued directed to any overseas court of competent jurisdiction for the examination of a witness or person named in the order.

(3)   If an order is made under subsection (2), a Letter of Request must be issued accordingly, and signed by a Judge or Registrar, and sealed with the seal of the High Court in a form—

   (a)   that the High Court or Judge approves or that is prescribed by rules of court or regulations made under section 200; or

   (b)   that is consistent with the requirements of any convention to which the country in which the overseas court is, is a party to (for example, the Hague Convention on Evidence Abroad).

(4)   Letters of Request must be transmitted to and from an overseas court through any channels—

1419   *Re Pan American World Airways Inc and other's application* [1992] 3 All ER 197 (CA), 203.

(a)   that are prescribed by rules of court or regulations made under section 200; or

(b)   that are consistent with the requirements of any convention to which the country in which the overseas court is, is a party to (for example, the Hague Convention on Evidence Abroad).

(5)   On the application of any opposite party, and on being satisfied that the party for whose benefit an order under subsection (1) or (2) was made is not proceeding with due diligence to implement the order and the delay is not the responsibility of any other person, the Judge may—

(a)   rescind the order; or

(b)   make any other order the Judge considers to be in the interests of justice.

(6)   This section does not limit sections 103 to 106.

Compare: 1980 No 27 s 46

EV188.01   Obtaining overseas evidence for New Zealand civil proceedings

With some revision, s 188 re-enacts the procedures for the taking of evidence in New Zealand civil proceedings from overseas witnesses set out in: (a) ss 44 and 46 of the Evidence Amendment Act (No 2) 1980; and (b) r 369 of the High Court Rules ("Order for examination of witness or for letters of request"). Indeed, with any necessary modification pursuant to s 5(2) of the Evidence Act,[1420] specific processes for overseas witness examinations contained in rr 369-380 of the High Court Rules will apply to evidence sought from such witnesses under s 188.[1421]

EV188.02   Procedures for obtaining overseas evidence

Complementing ss 184-187 of the Act — which establish High Court procedures for obtaining evidence in New Zealand to be used in overseas civil proceedings — s 188 sets out two mechanisms for the High Court to take evidence in New Zealand civil cases from a witness who is overseas. Either procedure can be used at "any stage of any civil proceeding in the High Court" and may be invoked when "it appears" to a High Court judge "necessary or desirable in the interests of justice" (s 188(1)).

(1)   Meaning of "civil proceeding" and "interests of justice"

"Civil proceeding" is defined in s 182 of the Act.[1422] However, s 188 gives no guidance regarding application of the "interests of justice" test contained in s 188(1). As detailed in case law considering r 369 of the High Court Rules, relevant considerations will likely include: (a) the ability, willingness or practicability of the witness coming to give evidence in New Zealand; (b) the significance of the witness's evidence to the issues in the case; (c) the relative expense involved in taking evidence abroad as compared with bringing the witness to New Zealand; (d) the extent to which the

---

1420   See EV5.02.

1421   For a discussion of rr 369-380 of the High Court Rules ("Evidence by deposition"), see *McGechan on Procedure*, HR369.01-HR380.01.

1422   See EV182.01.

credibility and demeanour of the witness will be relevant issues in the proceeding; (e) the desirability of cross-examining the witness and the extent to which cross-examination can take place in the overseas venue; and (f) the interests of the parties to the proceedings.[1423]

(2) Order for overseas examination

The first mechanism for taking overseas evidence — set out in s 188(1)(a) and appropriately used with a cooperative witness — permits the High Court to order that "any person ... be examined on oath, by interrogatories or otherwise, at any place outside New Zealand before any officer of the High Court, any overseas representative, or any other person named in the order by name or designation". The evidence taken from the overseas witness — referred to as a "deposition" — may then be ordered to be "filed in the High Court" (s 188(1)(b)). Under s 188(1)(c), a deposition taken pursuant to s 188(1)(a) can be given in evidence by "any party to the [New Zealand civil proceeding] ... on any terms as the High Court or Judge may direct". Subject to any justifiable exclusions based on the grounds of inadmissibility, the reception into evidence of depositions in civil proceedings is similarly provided for in s 131 of the Act[1424] and r 376 of the High Court Rules.[1425]

(3) Letter of request

Section 188(2) sets out the second mechanism by which the High Court can obtain the evidence of an overseas witness for use in New Zealand civil proceedings. While the procedure will most often be used in the case of an unwilling witness, s 188(2) permits the High Court to order that "a Letter of Request be issued directed to any overseas court of competent jurisdiction for the examination of a witness or person named in the order". Pursuant to s 188(3)(a) and (b), the Letter of Request must be issued, signed by a High Court judge or registrar, and sealed with the seal of the High Court in a form:

> "(a) that the High Court or Judge approves or that is prescribed by rules of court or regulations made under section 200; or

> "(b) that is consistent with the requirements of any convention to which the country in which the overseas court is, is a party to (for example, the Hague Convention on Evidence Abroad)."

The same conditions will apply to "any channels" through which the Letter of Request is transmitted "to and from an overseas court" (s 188(4)).

As referenced in s 188(3)(a) and (4)(a), s 200 provides for the making of rules and regulations to carry out the provisions of Part 4 of the Act (including s 188). However, to date, no such rules or regulations have been promulgated.[1426] Rules 378-380 of the High Court Rules provide specific procedures for the issuing of a Letter of Request

---

1423   See *McGechan on Procedure*, HR369.07-20. See also s 6 of the Evidence on Commission Act 1995 (NSW) (Australia).
1424   See EV131.01.
1425   See *McGechan on Procedure*, HR376.01.
1426   See EV200.01.

to an overseas jurisdiction by the High Court. Articles 1-6 of the Hague Convention on Evidence Abroad contain more detailed measures regarding the form and content of such letters, as well as their appropriate method of transmission between "Contracting States" (countries that are parties to the Convention).[1427] While Subpart 2 of Part 4 of the Act is intended to make New Zealand a Contracting State,[1428] s 188(3)(b) and (4)(b) require only that the Letter of Request from the High Court comply with any convention to which the country *receiving* the letter is a party.[1429]

EV188.03   Requirement of due diligence

Section 188(5) repeats r 369(2) of the High Court Rules.[1430] If a judicial order is made to take the testimony of an overseas witness pursuant to s 188(1) or (2), the party who obtained it must act with "due diligence to implement the order" (s 188(5)).

"Due diligence" is not defined in s 188. However, s 188(5) presumably requires a party to take concrete and expeditious steps to secure a witness's deposition evidence under s 188. If such measures do not take place, and delay becomes undue, any opposing party in the civil proceeding may apply to a High Court Judge under s 188(5) to: "(a) rescind the order; or (b) make any other order the Judge considers to be in the interests of justice" (s 188(5)(a)-(b)).

Applications under s 188(5) will not be appropriate where any delay in implementing the overseas witness examination order is "the responsibility of any other person", that is, a person other than the party for whose benefit the order was made (s 188(5)). This is most likely to be the case where an order is issued under s 188(2), and involves a Letter of Request from New Zealand to an overseas court invoking the administrative processes of that court.

EV188.04   Alternative modes of witness testimony under ss 103-106

Section 188(6) states (somewhat obscurely) that the power of the High Court to order the examination of an overseas witness in a New Zealand civil proceeding "does not limit the operation of ss 103-106" of the Act. These sections provide for modes of hearing evidence at trial other than the usual method of a person testifying live and in open court. Typically used with young, fearful or timid witnesses in domestic

---

1427   See the Convention on the Taking of Evidence Abroad in Civil or Commercial Matters signed at the Hague on 18 March 1970 (referred to in s 182 of the Act as the "Hague Convention on Evidence Abroad"). Rule 377 of the High Court Rules states:

> **"377. Letters of request where Convention exists**
> "Where a Convention is in force between the Sovereign of a country and the Sovereign of New Zealand or the Government of a country and the Government of New Zealand relating to the taking of evidence in that country for use in New Zealand, the provisions of rules 378 to 380 shall apply subject to any special provisions contained in the Convention."

   This rule would encompass Letters of Request from the High Court to any country that, like New Zealand, is also a party to the Hague Convention on Evidence Abroad. See EV182.02.

1428   See EV182.02.

1429   See *McGechan on Procedure*, HR377.01-HR380.01.

1430   See *McGechan on Procedure*, HR369.06

criminal trials, such alternative means of testimony are unlikely to be ordered for an overseas witness providing deposition evidence in a New Zealand civil case. On the other hand, s 188(6) probably means that, in addition to the deposition procedure set out in s 188, overseas witnesses in High Court civil proceedings may also avail themselves of the alternative modes of testimony established in ss 103-106. This would include testifying in a civil trial via video link, a procedure specifically contemplated under ss 103 and 105 of the Act, and well established in New Zealand civil proceedings under precedents of the High Court.[1431]

Offences

189   False statements

(1)   Every person commits an offence who, being required under subsection 185(1) to give evidence (either orally or in writing) otherwise than on oath, makes a statement—

(a)   which he or she knows to be false in a material particular; or

(b)   which is false in a material particular and which he or she does not believe to be true.

(2)   Every person who commits an offence against subsection (1) is liable on summary conviction to imprisonment for a term not exceeding 3 years.

EV189.01   Offence to make false statement

Section 189 creates the offence of making a false statement when an individual is required by a New Zealand High Court judge to give oral or written evidence (otherwise than on oath) for use in overseas civil proceedings pursuant to s 185(1).

EV189.02   Penalty

As set out in s 189(2), the penalty of up to 3 years' imprisonment parallels that under s 111 of the Crimes Act 1961 — which deals with making a false statement or declaration in official circumstances that "would amount to perjury if made on oath in a judicial proceeding".[1432] If made pursuant to a court order issued under s 185(1), false and misleading evidence given on oath could subject the mendacious

---

1431   See EV103.01. For pre-Evidence Act case law discussing the judicial discretion to allow non-standard modes of witness testimony in civil trials, see *Aeromotive Ltd v Page* 16/5/02, Harrison J, HC Hamilton CP31/99; *Ithaca v Guiness Peat Group Plc* 13/9/02, Paterson J, HC Auckland M1000-SD02; *Churchill Group Holdings Ltd v Aral Property Holdings Ltd* 26/10/06, Williams J, HC Auckland CIV-2001-404-2302. In *Churchill Group Holdings*, Williams J noted that, with respect to civil proceedings, r 496 of the High Court Rules "gives the Court power to determine all questions on 'evidence given by means of witnesses examined orally and in open Court'". However, as now provided for in s 105 of the Evidence Act 2006, case law has held this rule to encompass "the giving of evidence by video link" (para 14). See also *McGechan on Procedure*, HR496.02(2) (discussing the authorities reviewed in *Ithaca (Custodians) Ltd v Perry Corp* (2002) 16 PRNZ 773 (HC)); Turner, "Civil Procedure" [2004] NZ Law Rev 345, 355-358.

1432   See, eg, *Kwong v Department of Labour* 7/11/05, Venning J, HC Auckland CRI-2005-404-209. See also EV198.03.

declarant to a prosecution for "false oaths" under s 110 of the Crimes Act 1961 (providing for up to 5 years' imprisonment upon conviction).

EV189.03 Jury trial

While s 189(2) refers to liability on "summary conviction", defendants will be able to elect trial by jury pursuant to s 24(e) of the New Zealand Bill of Rights Act 1990 and s 66 of the Summary Proceedings Act 1957. This follows from application of s 5(1) of the Act and stems from the prescribed penalty under s 169 being greater than 3 months' imprisonment.[1433]

EV189.04 Elements of offence: materiality

In order to commit an offence under s 189, the individual giving evidence under s 185(1) must either: (a) know that they are making a false statement with respect to an issue that is material to the overseas proceedings (s 189(1)(a)); or (b) make a statement that is false in a material particular and which the individual does not believe to be true (s 189(1)(b)). The requirement of materiality in s 189(1) means that the false statement must "have a bearing on an issue in the case" and cannot be trivial or inconsequential in the context of the overseas civil proceedings. [1434]

Subpart 3—Evidence for use in overseas criminal proceedings

(s 190 to s 198)

190 Interpretation

In this subpart—

High Court means the High Court of New Zealand

Judge means a Judge of the High Court

overseas court means a court or tribunal exercising jurisdiction in any country outside New Zealand

overseas representative —

(a) means any Ambassador, High Commissioner, Commissioner, Minister, Counsellor, Chargé d'Affaires, Head of Mission, Consular Officer, or Pro-consul of any country other than New Zealand exercising jurisdiction in New Zealand; and

(b) includes any person lawfully acting for any of those officers and also includes any Diplomatic Secretary on the staff of any such Ambassador, High Commissioner, Commissioner, Minister, Counsellor, Chargé d'Affaires, or Head of Mission.

Compare: 1908 No 56 s 48A

1433 See EV5.01. Section 24(e) of the Bill of Rights and s 66(1) of the Summary Proceedings Act provide the right to a jury trial in any criminal proceeding where the penalty upon conviction could exceed three months' imprisonment.

1434 *R v Goodyear-Smith* 26/7/93, Anderson J, HC Auckland T332/92, 5.

EV190.01   Interpretation

Section 190 is a definitional provision setting out the meanings of various terms used in Subpart 3 of Part 4 of the Act — which deals with New Zealand High Court procedures for the taking of evidence to be used in overseas criminal proceedings.

According to the 2006 *Departmental Report for the Justice and Electoral Committee* prepared by the New Zealand Ministry of Justice:[1435]

> "[Sections 190-198 of the Act] substantially repeat sections 48-48F [of the] Evidence Act 1908 relating to evidence for use in overseas proceedings.

> "The major substantive change is that with the inclusion of Subpart 2 [of Part 4 of the Act ('Evidence for use in civil proceedings overseas and evidence for use in civil proceedings in High Court')] these provisions now relate only to criminal proceedings. Previously they applied to both civil and criminal proceedings. The drafting style in the [Act] is also different from that in the Evidence Act 1908."

191   Relationship with subpart 1

This subpart does not affect the application or operation of subpart 1.

EV191.01   Relationship between Subparts 1 and 3 of Part 4

See EV183.01 (which deals with the relationship between Subparts 1 and 2 of Part 4 of the Act pursuant to s 183).

192   Examination of witness at request of overseas court

(1)   If any criminal proceedings (not being criminal proceedings of a political character) are pending before any overseas court of competent jurisdiction, and that court wishes to obtain the evidence of any witness in New Zealand for the purposes of those proceedings, the High Court or a Judge of that court may order the examination of the witness on oath, by interrogatories, or otherwise, before any person named in the order.

(2)   An order under subsection (1) may be made on the application of the parties to the proceeding before the overseas court or on the application of the Solicitor-General.

(3)   Despite subsection (2),—

    (a)   an application for an order under subsection (1) must be made in accordance with any requirements prescribed in regulations made under section 200:

    (b)   the right of the Solicitor-General to make an application of that kind is subject to any restrictions set out in regulations made under section 200.

1435   *Departmental Report* (EV/MOJ/3), 5.

(4)   An order made under subsection (1) may be enforced in the same manner as if it were an order made by the High Court or the Judge in proceedings pending in the High Court or before the Judge.

Compare: 1908 No 56 s 48A

EV192.01   Examination of witness for overseas criminal proceeding

While dealing only with foreign criminal proceedings (foreign civil proceedings now being dealt with under ss 184-187 of the Act), s 192 replaces s 48A of the Evidence Act 1908. When a criminal case is pending in an "overseas court" (defined in s 190[1436]), s 192(1) gives the High Court the power to order the examination of a witness in New Zealand for the purpose of providing evidence in that foreign proceeding.

(1)   High Court Registrar

See EV193.01 for discussion of the power of a High Court Registrar to make an order under s 192(1).

EV192.02   Applying for order under s 192(1)

Section 192(2) states that a request under s 192(1) can be made "on the application of the parties to the proceeding before the overseas court or on application of the [New Zealand] Solicitor-General". However, pursuant to s 192(3), applications under s 192(1) can only take place in accordance with any regulations promulgated under s 200 — which provides for the making of rules and regulations to carry out the provisions of Part 4 of the Act (including s 192). To date, no such rules or regulations have been enacted under s 200.[1437]

(1)   Evidence in support of application under s 192(1)

See EV194.01 for a discussion of the giving of evidence in support of an application under s 192(1).

EV192.03   Form of examination

Section 192(1) permits the High Court to order the examination of a witness in New Zealand "on oath, by interrogatories, or otherwise, by any person named in the order". For a case dealing with the making and carrying out of such orders under s 48 of the Evidence Act 1908, see the discussion of *Re Nattrass* at EV185.04.[1438]

(1)   Solicitor of the High Court

See EV197.01 for a discussion of the authority of a solicitor of the High Court to take the affidavit or declaration of witness examined in New Zealand pursuant to an order made under s 192.

1436   See EV190.01.
1437   See EV200.01.
1438   *Re Nattrass* (1997) 10 PRNZ 335 (HC).

EV192.04   Criminal proceedings "of a political character"

Section 192(1) does not permit a witness examination order to be made in New Zealand if the pending criminal proceeding in the overseas court is "of a political character". The language is copied from s 48A(1) of the Evidence Act 1908 and repeats: (a) grounds for the New Zealand Attorney-General to refuse assistance to a foreign country under s 27(1)(a) or (b) of the Mutual Assistance in Criminal Matters Act 1992;[1439] and (b) grounds for a New Zealand court to refuse extradition of an alleged foreign offender from New Zealand under s 7(a) or (b) of the Extradition Act 1999.

Like s 27 of the Mutual Assistance in Criminal Matters Act and s 7 of the Extradition Act, s 192(1) makes no attempt to define when an overseas criminal proceeding deals with an offence "of a political character". Nor has the phrase ever been the subject of a decided New Zealand case. However, in *Dutton v O'Shane*, a judgment dealing with the "political offence" restriction on surrender pursuant to s 7(a) of the Extradition Act 1988 (Aust), the Federal Court of Australia observed:[1440]

> "The words 'political offence' in the Act have been defined by reference to a formula (that is, an offence 'of a political character') that itself has 'so far defied precise definition': *Cheng v Governor of Pentonville Prison* [1973] AC 931 at 942; [1973] 2 All ER 204 at 206. It is well accepted … that there are two analytically distinct kinds of political offence, the one being 'the pure political offence', the other, 'the relative political offence': see Aughterson, [*Extradition — Australian Law and Procedure*, 1995], pp 90ff; Stanbrook and Stanbrook, [*Extradition Law and Practice*, 2nd ed, 2000], p 69; 31A Am Jur 2d 'Extradition' §44.

> "Illustrative of pure political offences are offences such as treason, espionage, sabotage, subversion and sedition. Such are offences 'directed solely against the political order': Shearer, Extradition in International Law, 1971, p 151. Their purpose has been described, variously, as to protect the political institutions of the state (Aughterson, p 91), the state itself (34A Am Jur 2d §44) or the sovereign or public order (Bassiouni, *International Extradition*, 3rd ed, p 512). Relative political offences, in contrast, are common crimes which acquire their political character from the political purpose sought to be achieved by an offender in committing them: see *Ex parte Cheng* at 945; *Minister for Immigration and Multicultural Affairs v Singh* (2002) 209 CLR 533; 186 ALR 393 at [44] …"

EV192.05   Enforcement of High Court order

With respect to its enforcement, s 192(4) gives an order "made under" under s 192(1) the same status "as if it were" a High Court order made in proceedings pending before that court. See, however, EV195.01 for a discussion of the rules related

---

1439   See EV192.06.
1440   *Dutton v O'Shane* (2003) 200 ALR 710 (FCA), paras 185-186.

---

to the non-compellability of witnesses in New Zealand otherwise subject to an examination order under s 192(1).

EV192.06   Mutual Assistance in Criminal Matters Act 1992

Sections 190-198 provide a method by which the New Zealand High Court can act on a request from a foreign court to examine a witness in New Zealand in order to provide evidence for a foreign criminal proceeding. However, those sections do not provide for requests from the New Zealand High Court for the overseas examination of a witness for the purpose of a New Zealand criminal proceeding.

The High Court has no inherent jurisdiction to issue Letters of Request to a foreign court for aid in criminal cases. [1441] However, Part 2 of the Mutual Assistance in Criminal Matters Act 1992 remains in effect. That Act provides for evidence obtained overseas to be admitted in a New Zealand criminal trial. It also provides for bringing witnesses from overseas to give evidence in a New Zealand criminal case and, supplementing ss 190-198 of the Evidence Act 2006, for New Zealand to assist foreign jurisdictions in obtaining evidence from New Zealand for use in a foreign criminal proceeding. [1442]

(1)   Relationship between Evidence Act and Mutual Assistance in Criminal Matters Act

Section 36 of the Mutual Assistance in Criminal Matters Act 1992 states that "[n]othing in this Act limits or effects the Evidence Act 2006". The language appears aimed at allowing both ss 192-96 of the Evidence Act 2006 and the provisions of Part 3 of the Mutual Assistance in Criminal Matters Act (ss 24-62: "Requests to New Zealand") to operate for the benefit of foreign jurisdictions seeking various types of assistance in New Zealand relating to criminal matters overseas.

193   Powers may be exercised by Registrar

(1)   A Judge may authorise a Registrar of the High Court to exercise the powers of the High Court or the Judge under section 192, either—

    (a)   generally; or

    (b)   in respect of a particular case or class of case.

(2)   An authorisation under subsection (1) may be revoked at any time by any Judge.

(3)   If, in the opinion of the Registrar, any matter that he or she has jurisdiction to deal with under an authorisation under subsection (1) is of special difficulty, the Registrar may refer the matter to a Judge who may—

    (a)   dispose of it; or

    (b)   refer it back to the Registrar with any directions that he or she considers appropriate.

1441   See *Samleung International Trading Co Ltd v Collector of Customs* [1994] 3 NZLR 285 (HC).

1442   See Part 3 of the Mutual Assistance in Criminal Matters Act 1992 (ss 24-62: "Requests to New Zealand").

(4)　　Nothing in this section prevents the exercise by the High Court or any Judge of any powers conferred on a Registrar under this section.

Compare: 1908 No 56 s 48B

EV193.01　　Judge can authorise Registrar to exercise powers under s 192

Section 193 repeats s 48B of the Evidence Act 1908. It allows a "Judge" — defined in s 190 as a "Judge of the High Court of New Zealand" — to authorise a "Registrar of the High Court" to exercise the "powers of the High Court or Judge under s 192" either: (a) "generally" (s 193(1)(a)); or (b) "in respect of a particular case or class of case" (s 193(1)(b)).

There is no comparable provision in Subpart 2 of Part 4 of the Act (ss 182-89), which deals with the taking of evidence in New Zealand for use in civil proceedings overseas and vice versa.

EV193.02　　Scope of Registrar's powers

Powers granted under s 193(1) would allow a High Court Registrar to formulate orders for the examination of witnesses in New Zealand pursuant to proper requests made to the High Court under s 192 and for use in pending criminal proceedings overseas. The grant of authority may be revoked by a High Court Judge at any time (s 193(2)) and does not limit the concurrent exercise of jurisdiction under s 192 by any High Court Judge (s 193(4)).

EV193.03　　Exercise of judicial discretion

Section 193(1) gives no guidance as to when it will be appropriate for a High Court Judge to authorise a High Court Registrar to handle applications for the examination of witnesses pursuant to s 192. However, despite the grant of any authority under s 193(1), the registrar may refer the matter back to the High Court Judge if the registrar feels that providing for the requested witness examination poses "special difficulty" (s 193(3)).

What may amount to a "special difficulty" is left undefined by s 193. By way of example, questions might arise regarding the prerogative of a witness to refuse to give evidence under s 192 that the witness "could not be compelled to give in criminal proceedings in New Zealand" (s 195(1)).[1443] By contrast with a non-contentious witness examination that could be handled by a High Court Registrar, such matters would need to be resolved by a legally trained High Court Judge. Nonetheless, a High Court Judge faced with a referral from a High Court Registrar under s 193(3) may dispose of the matter himself or herself (s 193(3)(a)), or send the matter of the witness examination back to the High Court Registrar with "any directions that [the Judge] considers appropriate" (s 193(3)(b)).

1443　　See EV195.01.

194   Evidence in support of application

(1)   Evidence that any criminal proceedings are pending in an overseas court and that the court wishes to obtain the evidence of the witness to whom the application relates for the purposes of those proceedings, may be given by—

(a)   Letter of Request; or

(b)   another document issued by that court; or

(c)   the certificate of an overseas representative given under subsection (3); or

(d)   any other process that the High Court or a Judge may accept.

(2)   Any Letter of Request or other document purporting to be sealed with the seal of any overseas court or signed by a Judge or other judicial officer or by a Registrar or other officer of the court must for the purpose of this section and section 192 be received in evidence without proof of—

(a)   the seal of the court; or

(b)   the signature of the Judge or other person; or

(c)   the judicial or official character of the Judge or other person.

(3)   A certificate purporting to be signed by an overseas representative to the effect that any matter in relation to which an application is made under section 192 is a criminal proceeding pending in a court having jurisdiction in the proceeding in the country of which he or she is a representative and that the court having that jurisdiction wishes to obtain the testimony of the witness to whom the application relates, is sufficient evidence of the matters set out in the certificate.

(4)   A certificate given under subsection (3) must be received in evidence without proof of—

(a)   the signature of the person who signed the certificate; and

(b)   the official character of that person.

Compare: 1908 No 56 s 48C

EV194.01   Evidence in support of s 192 application

Section 192 permits the High Court to order the examination of a witness in New Zealand at the request of an "overseas court" (defined in s 190) and in order to obtain evidence for pending criminal proceedings in that court. Section 194 sets out requirements for evidence in support of such applications. Although limited to active criminal proceedings abroad, the provision substantially restates s 48C of the Evidence Act 1908.

EV194.02   Requirement to accept evidence

As noted immediately above, the conditions for receiving evidence under s 194 are pegged to the authority of the High Court to order the examination of witnesses in New Zealand pursuant to a foreign court's request under s 192. Accordingly, s 194(1) requires the application under s 192 first to allege "[e]vidence that … criminal proceedings are pending in an overseas court and that the court wishes to obtain the evidence of the witness to whom the application relates for the purposes of those proceedings". Section 194(1)(a)-(d) then go on to specify the manner in which such material can be presented.[1444] Pursuant to ss 194(2) and (3) — and assuming various formalities are complied with — certain written statements from an "overseas court" or "overseas representative" (defined in s 190) are self-authenticating and must be received in evidence as proof of the matters required to be demonstrated under s 194(1).

The irrefutable presumptions set out in s 194(2) and (3) parallel the one found in s 198(2) of the Act (which, with respect to prosecutions in New Zealand for false affidavits or declarations taken by solicitors of the High Court in response to a s 192 request from an overseas court, creates a conclusive presumption that criminal proceedings were pending in the court and that a certificate was provided to the solicitor in accordance with s 194(3)).[1445] Their inclusion in s 194 is designed to avoid challenges to High Court orders under s 192 based on the sufficiency of proof regarding: (a) the existence of a pending overseas criminal proceeding; and/or (b) the desire of an overseas court to obtain evidence from a witness in New Zealand for the purposes of those proceedings. However, what if cogent evidence actually exists to rebut one or both of the propositions rendered legally irrefutable by s 194? In such circumstances, a witness required to attend for examination might still be able to argue that any High Court order was not "made under" s 192(1) — a prerequisite to enforcement of the order in New Zealand pursuant to s 192(4).[1446]

195 Protection of witnesses

(1) A person may not be compelled by an order under section 192 to give evidence which the person could not be compelled to give in criminal proceedings in New Zealand.

(2) A person may not be compelled by an order under section 192 to give any evidence if the giving of that evidence would infringe the jurisdiction of New Zealand or would otherwise be prejudicial to the security or sovereignty of New Zealand or would be likely to be prejudicial to the trading, commercial, or economic interests of New Zealand; and a certificate signed by the Attorney-General to the effect that it would be or, as the case requires, is likely to be so prejudicial for that person to do so is conclusive evidence of that fact.

(3) In this section **giving evidence** includes—

(a)   answering any question:

1444   For an example of a "Letter or Request" (see s 194(1)(a) and (2)) issued by the Supreme Court of Hong Kong to the New Zealand High Court pursuant to s 48A of the Evidence Act 1908 (now incorporated as s 192 of the Evidence Act 2006) and seeking to take the evidence of witnesses in New Zealand for pending criminal proceedings in the Supreme Court, see *Re Nattrass* (1997) 10 PRNZ 335 (HC).

1445   See EV198.05.

1446   See EV192.05.

(b)　　producing any document.

Compare: 1908 No 56 s 48D

EV195.01　　Privileges of witnesses

In the relevant part, s 195 repeats and extends ss 48D and 48H of the Evidence Act 1908. In certain situations, it permits a witness in New Zealand to resist giving evidence he or she would otherwise be compelled to provide pursuant to a High Court order under s 192. Section 186 of the Act creates comparable (but not identical) exemptions where evidence is sought from witnesses in New Zealand for foreign civil proceedings.[1447]

EV195.02　　Scope of s 195

Section 195(1) and (2) set out two separate circumstances[1448] under which a witness otherwise obliged to give evidence for use in an overseas criminal proceeding cannot be compelled to do so pursuant to s 192. Section 195(3) defines "giving evidence" in the same manner as s 186(5).[1449]

EV195.03　　Exemption under New Zealand law

Questions of non-compellability under s 195(1) will be settled by reference to other provisions of the Evidence Act. Successful claims are likely to be rare since, as a general matter, s 71 of the Act makes most persons eligible and compellable witnesses in New Zealand civil and criminal proceedings.[1450] However, where relevant, s 195(1) will encompass non-compellability based on the grounds discussed at EV186.04.

EV195.04　　Prejudice to New Zealand national interests

The bases of non-compellability incorporated in s 195(1) are buttressed by the broader grounds of New Zealand national interests contained in s 195(2). The provision parallels the narrower basis of non-compellability contained in s 186(4) of the Act. See the discussion of ss 186(4) and 195(2) at EV186.05(1).

EV195.05　　Witnesses are eligible to testify voluntarily

Like s 71 of the Act, s 195 does not forbid witnesses in New Zealand from giving, if they so choose, the kinds of evidence that would be shielded from disclosure under s 195(1) or (2). See the discussion of this issue under s 186 at EV186.06.

196　　Witnesses' expenses

Every witness required to attend for examination by an order made under section 192 is entitled to a sum for his or her allowances and travelling expenses and loss of time in accordance with the scale prescribed for the time being by regulations made under the Summary Proceedings Act 1957.

Compare: 1908 No 56 s 48E

1447　　See EV186.01.
1448　　See EV195.03-04.
1449　　See EV186.02.
1450　　See EV71.01.

EV196.01   Expenses of witnesses

With respect to evidence taken in New Zealand for use in overseas criminal proceedings, s 196 provides for the reimbursement of a witness's time, labour, disbursements, travel and associated expenses when required to attend for examination pursuant to a High Court order issued under s 192 of the Act. The scale of reimbursement will be provided by the Witnesses and Interpreters Fees Regulations 1974 and its subsequent amendments, these being the "regulations made under the Summary Proceedings Act 1957" (s 196).

An example of the manner in which a High Court Judge may provide for such reimbursement can be found in *Perry v Molteno*[1451] — a civil case dealing with a witness's time and expenses under the equivalent provision in s 48E of the Evidence Act 1908.

197   Solicitor may take affidavit or declaration

(1)   It is lawful for any solicitor of the High Court to take the affidavit or declaration of any person in relation to any criminal proceedings that are certified in accordance with this section to be pending in any overseas court.

(2)   An affidavit or declaration referred to in subsection (1) must be intituled "In the matter of section 197 of the Evidence Act 2006", and a declaration referred to in subsection (1) may be expressed to be made under the provisions of this section.

(3)   No affidavit or declaration referred to in subsection (1) may be taken unless the solicitor taking it has received a written certificate—

(a)   from the overseas court that the affidavit or declaration is required for the purpose of criminal proceedings pending in the court; or

(b)   from an overseas representative of the country in which the overseas court exercises jurisdiction that he or she believes the affidavit or declaration to be required for the purpose of criminal proceedings pending in the overseas court.

(4)   A certificate for the purposes of subsection (3)(a) may be given by any Judge or judicial officer of the overseas court, or by any Registrar or other officer of that court.

(5)   If a certificate is given under subsection (3)(b), the jurat or attestation of the affidavit or declaration must state the name and official designation of the overseas representative on whose certificate the affidavit or declaration has been taken.

(6)   In this section—

affidavit means any affidavit or affirmation made before a solicitor of the High Court

---

1451   *Perry v Molteno* (1999) 13 PRNZ 546 (HC).

declaration means any written statement declared by the maker of the statement to be true in the presence of a solicitor of the High Court.

Compare: 1908 No 56 s 48F(1)-(6)

EV197.01   Solicitor may take affidavit or declaration under s 192

Section 197 supplements the High Court procedures contained in ss 192-96 for the examination of a witness in New Zealand to provide evidence for a pending overseas criminal proceeding. The provision repeats s 48F(1)-(6) of the Evidence Act 1908.

In furtherance of a proper request made from a foreign jurisdiction to the High Court under s 192(1), s 197(1) permits a New Zealand solicitor to take the "affidavit" or "declaration" (defined in s 197(6)) of a witness in New Zealand for use in a pending criminal proceeding overseas.

EV197.02   Requirements for solicitor to take affidavit or declaration

Section 197(3)-(5) sets out the form and substance of certifications required from an "overseas court" or "overseas representative" (defined in s 190) before a New Zealand solicitor can take an affidavit or declaration pursuant to s 197(1).

With respect to pending criminal proceedings in an overseas court, certifications of the type listed in s 197(3)(a) and (b) would also qualify under s 194 as evidence in support of an application from the overseas court to the High Court for the examination of a witness in New Zealand. Pursuant to s 194(2) and (3), and provided certain conditions are fulfilled, such certifying documents comprise self-authenticating proof — which must be accepted in evidence — that: (a) criminal proceedings are pending in the overseas court; and (b) such court wishes to obtain the evidence of a witness in New Zealand for the purposes of those proceedings.[1452]

Section 197(2) sets out the required formalities for the titling of an affidavit or declaration taken by a New Zealand solicitor pursuant to s 197(1).

198   False affidavit or declaration

(1)   Every affidavit or declaration taken under section 197 is deemed to have been made in a judicial proceeding within the meaning of the Crimes Act 1961, and any person who falsely makes an affidavit or declaration of that kind is guilty of perjury or of making a false declaration accordingly.

(2)   In any prosecution in respect of an affidavit or declaration taken under section 197 it must be conclusively presumed that criminal proceedings were actually pending in the overseas court and that a certificate was given in accordance with section 194(3).

Compare: 1908 No 56 s 47F(7), (8)

EV198.01   Offence to make false affidavit or declaration

Section 198 repeats s 48F(7)-(8) of the Evidence Act 1908. It creates separate offences for making a false affidavit or false declaration under s 197 — which establishes a

---

1452   See EV194.02.

procedure for affidavits and declarations to be taken from witnesses in New Zealand by a High Court solicitor and for use in pending overseas criminal proceedings pursuant to s 192.[1453]

EV198.02   Definition of "affidavit" and "declaration"

See s 197(6) for the definitions of "affidavit" and "declaration" as used in s 198.

EV198.03   Applicability of Crimes Act 1961

Section 198(1) mandates that any affidavit or declaration taken pursuant to s 197 be "deemed to have been made in a judicial proceeding within the meaning of the Crimes Act 1961". Accordingly, any person who "falsely makes an affidavit or declaration" under s 197 will have such conduct treated as, respectively: (1) perjury (false affidavit) — carrying a sentence of up to 7 years' imprisonment under s 109 of the Crimes Act 1961; or (2) making a false declaration — carrying a sentence of up to 3 years' imprisonment under s 111 of the Crimes Act 1961.[1454]

The potential 3-year penalty for the latter s 198 offence (making a false *declaration* as prescribed by s 111 of the Crimes Act 1961) parallels that for a false statement made, otherwise than on oath, in violation of s 189 of the Evidence Act — which deals with evidence taken in New Zealand for use in overseas civil proceedings pursuant to s 185(1).[1455] See the discussion of s 189. The greater available penalty for making a false *affidavit* under s 198 (7 years for perjury as prescribed by s 109 of the Crimes Act 1961) undoubtedly reflects the fact that affidavit evidence is given on oath.

EV198.04   Elements of offence: intent to mislead

Like ss 109 and 111 of the Crimes Act 1961, an offence under s 198(1) will likely require that the declarant make a false statement in a s 197 affidavit or declaration knowingly and with the intent to mislead.[1456]

EV198.05   Conclusive presumption

Section 198(2) makes it clear that, in any prosecution related to a false affidavit or declaration made pursuant to s 197, it must be "conclusively [irrefutably] presumed" that: (a) "criminal proceedings were actually pending in the overseas court"; and (b) a certificate was given to the High Court solicitor taking the affidavit or declaration (a requirement of s 197(3)[1457]) "in accordance with s 194(3)" — which states that certain "overseas representatives" listed in s 190 can furnish a certificate to the High Court providing sufficient evidence that criminal proceedings are pending in the overseas court and that the court wishes to obtain the testimony of a witness in New Zealand pursuant to s 192.[1458]

1453   See EV197.01.
1454   For a discussion of s 111 of the Crimes Act 1961, see *Kwong v Department of Labour* 7/11/05, Venning J, HC Auckland CRI-2005-404-209.
1455   See EV189.02.
1456   See *Adams on Criminal Law*, CA108.04-05; CA111.02.
1457   See EV197.02.
1458   See EV194.02.

With respect to a criminal prosecution under s 198(1), the goal of the conclusive, irrefutable presumption of s 198(2) is to avoid any defence based on the argument that procedures for the taking of evidence under s 197 were not properly instituted or invoked. However, where there is evidence suggesting that such defects in procedure did actually exist, an accused might still be able to argue that the allegedly false affidavit or declaration was not "taken under s 197" — a requirement for any prosecution under s 198(1).

Subpart 4—Rules and regulations

(s 199 to s 200)

199   Rules

(1)   In the case of the High Court and the Court of Appeal, rules may be made for the purposes of subpart 1 of this Part under section 51C of the Judicature Act 1908 that make provision for or relate to—

(a)   the issuing of New Zealand subpoenas and the service of those subpoenas:

(b)   the hearing or disposal of applications for orders under any specified provisions in this Part:

(c)   the lodging of documents or things with an Australian court in compliance with a New Zealand subpoena that requires only the production of documents or things by a witness:

(d)   the transmission of documents or things lodged with a New Zealand court in compliance with an Australian subpoena to the Australian court that issued the subpoena:

(e)   the giving of evidence and the making of submissions by video link or telephone conference in connection with proceedings before a New Zealand court or an Australian court:

(f)   the receiving of facsimiles of documents or things:

(g)   the form of New Zealand subpoenas and other documents:

(h)   such other matters as are contemplated by or necessary for giving full effect to subpart 1 of this Part.

(2)   In the case of any other New Zealand court, rules or, as the case may be, regulations may be made under the authority of any enactment that provides for the making of rules or regulations governing the practice and procedure of the court that make provision for or relate to any of the matters referred to in paragraphs (a), (c), and (e) to (h) of subsection (1).

EV199.01   Overview

Subpart 1 of Part 4 of the Act (ss 150-181), referred to in s 199(1), contains the rules governing trans-Tasman litigation assistance.[1459] Those sections in the main re-enact

---

1459   See EVPt4Sub1.01-03.

the Evidence Amendment Act 1994 and s 199 repeats the substance of s 33 of that Act.

200   Rules and regulations

(1)   Without limiting section 199 or the power to make rules of procedure conferred by the Judicature Act 1908, the District Courts Act 1947, and the Family Courts Act 1980,—

(a)   rules may be made under those Acts prescribing anything that is required to be prescribed or necessary for carrying this Part into effect:

(b)   the Governor-General may, by Order in Council, make regulations prescribing anything that is required to be prescribed or necessary for carrying this Part into effect.

(2)   The Governor-General may, by Order in Council, make regulations—

(a)   fixing, and requiring the payment of, fees and expenses for or incurred in taking evidence under this Part:

(b)   prescribing the matters in respect of which fees are payable under this Part and the amounts of those fees:

(c)   regulating the payment of expenses in respect of expenses incurred in complying with New Zealand subpoenas.

Compare: 1980 No 27 s 47

EV200.01   Overview

Section 200 provides for the making of rules and regulations for the carrying out of the special procedures included in Part 4 of the Act. This reflects the discrete nature of this largely procedural part of the Act. The regulation making power for the Act in general is set out in s 201. The regulation making power in s 200 is referred to in ss 184, 188 and 192 of the Act. The only regulations promulgated under s 200 to date are the Evidence Regulations 2007 (SR 2007/204) (see further the discussion at EV201.01).

Part 5
Miscellaneous
(s 201 to s 216)

Regulations

201   Regulations

The Governor-General may, by Order in Council, make regulations—

(a)   prescribing the procedure to be followed, the type of equipment to be used, and the arrangements to be made where a person's evidence is to be video recorded:

(b)   providing for the approval of interviewers, or classes of interviewers, for child complainants, and providing for such approvals to be proved by production of certificates in the prescribed form:

(c)   regulating the way in which evidence of a witness may be given in an alternative way:

(d)   prescribing the form of certificate by which an interviewer is to formally identify a video record:

(e)   regulating the video recording of evidence:

(f)   providing for the consent of persons to be video recorded and specifying who may give consent on behalf of children who are to be video recorded:

(g)   prescribing the uses to which any video records may be put and prohibiting their use for other purposes:

(h)   providing for the safe custody of video records intended to be offered as evidence:

(i)   providing for the preparation of transcripts of video records and for their uses and safe custody:

(j)   regulating the provision of communication assistance to defendants and witnesses:

(k)   providing for requirements, in addition to those set out in section 45(3), for formal procedures that are held to obtain visual identification evidence:

(l)   providing for the determination of the amount of fees and expenses, including minimum and maximum amounts, payable in respect of professional services provided by counsel appointed under section 115:

(m)   regulating the form of warnings or information that can be given by a Judge in relation to evidence given by children under the age of 6 years in a proceeding tried by a jury:

(n)   regulating the translation of documents into English or Maori:

(o)   providing for any other matters contemplated by this Act, necessary for its administration, or necessary for giving it full effect.

Editorial Note: Evidence Amendment Bill (No 2) 2007

Section 201 may be amended by the Evidence Amendment Bill (No 2) 2007 which, if passed, will add paragraph (p):

"(p)   prescribing offence in respect of the contravention of any regulations made under this Act and prescribing fines, not exceeding $2,000, in respect of those offences."

EV201.01   Overview

Section 201 contains the regulation making power. In response to a submission that the wording of s 201(o) was too broad, the Ministry of Justice confirmed that it is a common form of wording and is limited in application to situations where there is "a reference in the primary legislation that intends that regulations be made."[1460] However, the sections in the Act that refer to regulations under s 201 (ss 45, 80, 105, 106, 115, 125, and 135) are all covered by a specific paragraph in s 201. It is unclear then what matters will be caught by s 201(o).

A number of those specific references were added during the Select Committee process (s 201(c), (k), (l), (m), and (n)) after the Ministry of Justice identified that a number of the provisions of the Act referred to a regulation-making power.[1461] Section 201(m) was added as a consequence of the content of the Law Commission's draft Code's recommended directions in the case of young children being removed prior to the introduction of the Bill.[1462]

The only regulations promulgated under s 201 to date are those dealing with the video recording of the evidence of complainants (see the discussion at EV106.03) and the content of warnings in relation to young children.[1463]

Periodic review of operation of Act

202 Periodic review of operation of Act

(1)   The Minister must, as soon as practicable after 1 December 2011 or any later date set by the Minister by notice in the *Gazette*, and on at least 1 occasion during each 5-year period after that date, refer to the Law Commission for consideration the following matters:

    (a)   the operation of the provisions of this Act since the date of the commencement of this section or the last consideration of those provisions by the Law Commission, as the case requires:

    (b)   whether those provisions should be retained or repealed:

    (c)   if they should be retained, whether any amendments to this Act are necessary or desirable.

(2)   The Law Commission must report on those matters to the Minister within 1 year of the date on which the reference occurs.

(3)   The Minister—

    (a)   may not set a date later than 1 December 2011 for the commencement of the initial periodic review of this Act under subsection (1) unless the Minister is satisfied that, because of the limited number of cases concerning the provisions of this Act decided by the superior courts of New Zealand or for any other reason, it is appropriate to defer the date of the initial periodic review; and

    (b)   must not set a date later than 1 December 2014 under subsection (1).

1460   *Departmental Report* (EV/MOJ/4), 1.
1461   *Departmental Report* (EV/MOJ/4), 2-3.
1462   See EV125.04.
1463   Evidence Regulations 2007 (SR 2007/204). See also EV125.04.

EV202.01   Overview

Section 202 reflects the inevitability that problems with the drafting of the Act will be exposed as it is scrutinised and applied by lawyers, judges and commentators. Additionally, the law of evidence has always required flexibility and capacity to adjust in order to keep pace with changes in technology and social attitudes. The process of codification carries an obvious potential to stultify the process of evolution of the law of evidence. The requirement to periodically review the operation of the Act set out in s 202 is the Select Committee's solution to these issues, reflecting their view that "the Law Commission is the most appropriate agency to review the Act."[1464] The rationale for this type of periodic review was further explained in the House:[1465]

> "I commend this [clause of the Bill] to the Committee as a good model for post-legislative review. I am not saying that it should be all legislation, but, certainly, with this kind of legislation we do not want those finicky amendments that sometimes bedevil legislation. It will be good for the body that authored the reports that gave rise to the legislation to look at this legislation after it has been in operation for 5 years, and in a principled way go through the various provisions to see whether the sorts of innovations we have been talking about this afternoon actually work and, if they do not, what changes need to be made. So I simply say that it is a good and workable clause, and it will enable this very important area of the law to be kept up to date, not in a piecemeal or an episodic fashion but in a principled way."

Transitional provisions

EV203.Intro.01   Overview

Many of the transitional provisions, namely ss 203-205 and 208-214, anticipated that these sections would come into force before the particular provisions to which those sections refer (which occurred when ss 203-214 came into force on 18 July 2007). The problem aimed at by these sections was caused by s 5(3), which imposes the general rule that the Act applies to all proceedings, whenever commenced, as soon as the Act comes into force. Accordingly, when the Act came into force on 1 August 2007, matters such as notice requirements (referred to in ss 203-205, 212, and 213) or required applications to the court (ss 208-211) were immediately effective, despite no previous legislative justification for a party meeting these requirements. If the hearing of the proceedings was to take place on 2 August 2007 the difficulties presented by the required notices and applications are obvious. The transitional provisions were designed to cater for these potential difficulties.[1466]

1464   *Select Committee Report on the Evidence Bill*, 14.
1465   Hansard, *Christopher Finlayson: Evidence Amendment Bill: Second Reading*, 21 November 2006 ((2006) 635 NZPD 6652). Other options for review and amendment were outlined by Chris Finlayson MP in his capacity as a consultant to the Law Commission: see the letters contained in the Appendix to NZLS *Submission on the Evidence Bill*.
1466   LC *Evidence Code*, para C441.

203 Notice of hearsay before commencement

The requirements of section 22(2) may be complied with before the commencement of that provision, for the purpose of ensuring that compliance with those requirements occurs in sufficient time before a hearing that may or will take place after the commencement of that provision.

204 Notice before commencement relating to co-defendants' veracity

A notice under section 39(2) may be given, before the commencement of that provision, for the purpose of ensuring that it is given in sufficient time before a hearing that may or will take place after the commencement of that provision.

205 Notice before commencement concerning propensity evidence about co-defendants

A notice under section 42(2) may be given, before the commencement of that provision, for the purpose of ensuring that it is given in sufficient time before a hearing that may or will take place after the commencement of that provision.

206 Identification already carried out

Subpart 6 of Part 2 (identification evidence) does not apply in relation to an identification made before the commencement of that subpart.

EV206.01   Overview

Despite s 206 coming into effect at an earlier date, it does not suffer from the problem described in the discussion at EV203.Intro.01. The former law governing identification evidence will govern the cases described by s 206.[1467]

207 Transitional provisions relating to Law Practitioners Act 1982

(1)   Until the commencement of section 6 of the Lawyers and Conveyancers Act 2006, section 51(1) must be read as if for the definition of lawyer there were substituted the following definition:

"**lawyer** means a barrister or solicitor, as those terms are defined in section 2 of the Law Practitioners Act 1982".

(2)   Until the commencement of section 112 of the Lawyers and Conveyancers Act 2006, section 55(1)(a) must be read as if the reference to section 112 of the Lawyers and Conveyancers Act 2006 were a reference to section 89 of the Law Practitioners Act 1982.

(3)   Until the commencement of section 96 of the Lawyers and Conveyancers Act 2006, section 55(1) must be read as if for paragraph (b) there were substituted the following paragraph:

"(b)   by any solicitors' nominee company operated by a solicitor with the consent of the relevant District Law Society as a nominee in respect of securities and documents of title held for clients."

1467   *Adams on Criminal Law — Evidence*, EC7.

EV207.01   Overview

Section 207 remains an important transitional provision because the Lawyers and Conveyancers Act 2006 is not yet in force.[1468]

208   Transitional provision relating to communication assistance

(1)   A defendant may apply under section 80(2), before the commencement of that provision, for communication assistance after the commencement of that provision in criminal proceedings.

(2)   A witness or a party to civil proceedings may apply under section 80(4), before the commencement of that provision, for communication assistance after the commencement of that provision in civil proceedings.

209   Transitional provision relating to cross-examination by unrepresented parties

A witness, or a party calling a witness, may apply under section 95(2), before the commencement of that provision, for an order under that provision, restricting any cross-examination that is to take place after the commencement of that provision.

210   Transitional provision concerning alternative ways of giving evidence

A party may make an application for directions under section 103(1), before the commencement of that provision, for the purpose of ensuring that the application for directions permitted under that provision in respect of the giving of evidence in chief by a witness and his or her cross-examination after the commencement of that provision in any proceedings, is made as early as practicable before the proceeding is to be heard.

211   Transitional provision concerning giving of evidence by child complainants

The prosecution may make an application for directions under section 107(1) before the commencement of that provision, for the purpose of ensuring that the application required under that section in respect of the giving of evidence in chief by the complainant and his or her cross-examination after the commencement of that provision, is made as early as practicable before the case is to be tried.

212   Transitional provision relating to offering documents in evidence without calling witness

(1)   A party may give notice under section 130(4), before the commencement of that provision, for the purpose of ensuring that the notice is given in sufficient time before a hearing that will or may take place after the commencement of that provision.

(2)   A party may give notice of objection under section 130(5), before the commencement of that provision, for the purpose of ensuring that the notice is given in sufficient time before a hearing that will or may take place after the commencement of that provision.

1468   The Lawyers and Conveyancers Act 2006 is likely to come into force on 1 July 2008: New Zealand Law Society, *Law Talk*, Issue 697, 15 October 2007, 16.

213   Transitional provision relating to translation and transcripts

A party may give notice under section 135(1) or 135(3) of the translation of the document or the offer of a transcript, before the commencement of those provisions, for the purpose of ensuring that the notice is given in sufficient time before a hearing that will or may take place after the commencement of those provisions.

214   General

If, under any of sections 203 to 213, any person is empowered to apply to a Judge under any provision before its commencement for any order or directions, the Judge also has power, before the commencement of the provision, to exercise any of the powers conferred by that provision on a Judge.

Repeal and amendments

215   Repeal

The enactments specified in Schedule 1 are repealed.

EV215.01   Overview

The rationale for the repeal of the enactments listed in Schedule 1 was discussed in the Ministry of Justice's advice to the Select Committee.[1469] However, there is no comment as to why only s 366(1) of the Crimes Act 1961 was repealed rather than the entire provision.[1470]

216   Consequential amendments

The enactments specified in Schedule 2 are amended in the manner set out in that schedule.

EV216.01   Overview

The consequential amendments list some of the Acts affected by the Evidence Act 2006 (however see s 115 of the Care of Children Act 2004) but do not include all of the relevant regulations, some of which still refer to the Evidence Act 1908 (see, for example, the Armed Forces Discipline Rules of Procedure 1983).

Schedule 1
Enactments repealed

s 215

Evidence Act 1908 (1908 No 56)

Crimes Act 1961 (1961 No 43)

Sections 344D, 366(1), and 369.

Juries Act 1981 (1981 No 23)

Section 28.

1469   *Departmental Report* (EV/MOJ/4), 8-9.
1470   See further the discussion of s 366(2) of the Crimes Act 1961 at EV33.01.

Summary Proceedings Act 1957 (1957 No 87)

Sections 3(1)(k), 60, and 178A.

Schedule 2
Amendments to other enactments
(Part 1 to Part 2)

s 216

Part 1
Amendments to other Acts

Acts and Regulations Publication Act 1989 (1989 No 142)

Insert, after section 16:

"Judicial notice and evidence of New Zealand legislation

"16A Judicial notice of Acts of Parliament

"Judicial notice must be taken by all courts and persons acting judicially of all Acts of Parliament.

"16B Judicial notice of regulations

"(1) Judicial notice must be taken by all courts and persons acting judicially of all regulations.

"(2) In subsection (1) and sections 16C and 16D, **regulations**—

"(a) has the same meaning as in section 2; and

"(b) includes any instrument that, under section 14, has been printed and published as if it were a regulation.

"16C Copy of Act of Parliament, Imperial legislation, and regulations printed as prescribed to be evidence

"(1) Every copy of any Act of Parliament or of any Imperial enactment or any Imperial subordinate legislation (as defined in section 2 of the Imperial Laws Application Act 1988) being a copy purporting to be printed or published (whether before or after the commencement of this section) under the authority of the New Zealand Government is, unless the contrary is shown, deemed—

"(a) to be a correct copy of that Act of Parliament, enactment, or legislation; and

"(b) to have been so printed or published.

"(2) Every copy of any Imperial enactment or Imperial subordinate legislation (as so defined), being a copy purporting to be printed (whether before or after the commencement of this section) by the Queen's or King's Printer or under the superintendence or authority of Her Majesty's Stationery Office in the United Kingdom, is, unless the contrary is shown, deemed—

"(a)   to be a correct copy of that enactment or legislation; and

"(b)   to have been so printed.

"(3)   Every copy of any regulations (as defined in section 16B(2)) purporting to be printed, whether before or after the commencement of this section, under the authority of the New Zealand Government is, unless the contrary is shown, deemed—

"(a)   to be a correct copy of those regulations; and

"(b)   to have been so printed or published; and

"(c)   to be evidence that the regulations were notified in the *Gazette* on the date printed on that copy as the date of their notification in the *Gazette*.

"16D   Copy of reprint of Act, Imperial legislation, or regulations to be evidence

"(1)   This section applies to any copy of a reprint of any legislation, where that copy purports to be printed or published (whether before or after the commencement of this section) under the authority of the New Zealand Government.

"(2)   Unless the contrary is shown, every copy of a reprint to which this section applies is to be taken—

"(a)   to be a copy of a reprint that correctly states, as at the date at which it is stated to be reprinted, the law enacted or made by the legislation reprinted and by the amendments (if any) to that legislation; and

"(b)   to have been printed or published under the authority of the New Zealand Government.

"(3)   To avoid any doubt, the presumption contained in subsection (2) applies to a copy of a reprint in which changes authorised by section 17C have been made.

"(4)   The presumption contained in subsection (2) may be rebutted by the production of the official volume in which the relevant legislation or any amendment to that legislation, as the case requires, is contained.

"(5)   Subsection (4) does not limit any other means of rebutting the presumption contained in subsection (2).

"(6)   In this section, unless the context otherwise requires,—

"Imperial enactment and **Imperial subordinate legislation** have the meanings given to them by section 2 of the Imperial Laws Application Act 1988

"legislation means any Act, Imperial enactment, Imperial subordinate legislation, or regulations "**official volume** means any volume containing copies of legislation that are deemed, by section 16C, to be correct copies of that legislation.

"16E   Copies of parliamentary Journals to be evidence

"All copies of the Journals of the Legislative Council or the House of Representatives, purporting to be printed by the Government Printer or published by order of the House of Representatives, must be admitted as evidence of those matters by all courts and persons acting judicially without proof being given that those copies were so printed or published."

Omit from the definition of "reprint" in section 17A "section 29A of the Evidence Act 1908" and substitute "section 16D".

Armed Forces Discipline Act 1971 (1971 No 53)

Section 147(1): omit "Evidence Act 1908" and substitute "Evidence Act 2006".

Commonwealth Countries Act 1977 (1977 No 31)

Repeal section 2(5) and substitute:

"(5)   For the purposes of this section,—

"**court** includes the Supreme Court, the Court of Appeal, the High Court, and any District Court

"**District Court** includes—

"(a)   a Family Court; and

"(b)   a Youth Court

"**person acting judicially** means any person having in New Zealand by law authority to hear, receive, and examine evidence

"**proceeding** means—

"(a)   a proceeding conducted by a court; and

"(b)   any interlocutory or other application to a court connected with a proceeding."

Companies (Bondholders Incorporation) Act 1934-35 (1934-35 No 39)

Section 13(2): omit "Evidence Act 1908" and substitute "Evidence Act 2006".

Copyright Act 1994 (1994 No 143)

Section 215(4): omit "Evidence Act 1908" and substitute "Evidence Act 2006".

Crimes Act 1961 (1961 No 43)

Section 216C(2)(iii): omit "Evidence Act 1908" and substitute "Evidence Act 2006".

Section 369A(1): omit "section 13A(6)(d) of the Evidence Act 1908" and substitute "section 109(1)(d) of the Evidence Act 2006".

Section 379A(1)(e): omit "section 13A(6)(d) of the Evidence Act 1908" and substitute "section 109(1)(d) of the Evidence Act 2006".

Section 379A(1)(f): omit "section 13C of the Evidence Act 1908" and substitute "sections 112 and 113 of the Evidence Act 2006".

Section 379A(1)(g): omit "section 23A of the Evidence Act 1908" and substitute "section 44 of the Evidence Act 2006".

Customs and Excise Act 1996 (1996 No 27)

Section 161(2): omit ", despite section 47B or 47C of the Evidence Act 1908," and substitute ", despite section 75 of the Evidence Act 2006,".

Hawke's Bay Earthquake Act 1931 (1931 No 6)

Section 23(2): omit "Evidence Act 1908" and substitute "Evidence Act 2006".

Human Rights Act 1993 (1993 No 82)

Omit from section 106(4) "Evidence Act 1908" and substitute "Evidence Act 2006".

Immigration Act 1987 (1987 No 74)

Omit from clause 11(2) of Schedule 2 and clause 9(2) of Schedule 3C "Evidence Act 1908" and substitute in each case "Evidence Act 2006".

Judicature Act 1908 (1908 No 89)

Repeal section 51A(2) and substitute:

"(2)   Sections 16B, 16C(3), and 16D of the Acts and Regulations Publication Act 1989 apply accordingly."

Land Transport Act 1998 (1998 No 110)

Section 209(2): omit "(as defined in section 2 of the Evidence Act 1908)".

Add to section 209:

"(4)   For the purposes of this section, a **person acting judicially** means any person having in New Zealand by law authority to hear, receive, and examine evidence."

Lawyers and Conveyancers Act 2006 (2006 No 1)

Section 151(4): omit "Evidence Act 1908" and substitute "Evidence Act 2006".

Section 239(4): omit "Evidence Act 1908" and substitute "Evidence Act 2006".

Local Government Act 2002 (2002 No 84)

Section 35(1): omit "Evidence Act 1908" and substitute "Evidence Act 2006".

Maori Fisheries Act 2004 (2004 No 78)

Section 203(2): omit "section 48G of the Evidence Act 1908" and substitute "section 4 of the Evidence Act 2006".

Maritime Transport Act 1994 (1994 No 104)

Clause 9 of Schedule 2: omit "Evidence Act 1908" and substitute "Evidence Act 2006".

Mortgagors and Lessees Rehabilitation Act 1936 (1936 No 33)

Section 18(2): omit "Evidence Act 1908" and substitute "Evidence Act 2006".

Mutual Assistance in Criminal Matters Act 1992 (1992 No 86)

Repeal section 36 and substitute:

"36 **Evidence Act 2006 not affected**

"Nothing in this Act limits or affects the Evidence Act 2006."

Oaths and Declarations Act 1957 (1957 No 88)

Section 13(1): repeal and substitute:

"(1) A witness under the age of 12 years who is required, under section 77(2) of the Evidence Act 2006, to make a promise to tell the truth, must, before being examined make the promise:

'I promise to speak the truth, the whole truth, and nothing but the truth'.

"(1A) That promise has the same force and effect as if the witness had taken an oath."

Plant Variety Rights Act 1987 (1987 No 5)

Repeal section 29(3) and substitute:

"(3) For the purposes of subsection (2),—

"**Court** includes the Supreme Court, the Court of Appeal, the High Court, and any District Court

"**District Court** includes—

"(a) a Family Court; and

"(b) a Youth Court

"**person acting judicially** means any person having in New Zealand by law authority to hear, receive, and examine evidence."

Reprint of Statutes Act 1931 (1931 No 13)

Section 4: omit "section twenty-nine of the Evidence Act 1908" and substitute "section 16C of the Acts and Regulations Publication Act 1989".

Reserve Bank of New Zealand Act 1989 (1989 No 157)

Section 156A(4)(b): omit "section 47B of the Evidence Act 1908" and substitute "the Evidence Act 2006".

Sale of Liquor Act 1989 (1989 No 63)

Section 109(2): omit "Evidence Act 1908" and substitute "Evidence Act 2006".

Social Workers Registration Act 2003 (2003 No 17)

Clause 6(4) of Schedule 2: omit "Evidence Act 1908" and substitute "Evidence Act 2006".

Status of Children Act 1969 (1969 No 18)

Section 8(1): omit "section 44A of the Evidence Act 1908" in both places and substitute in each case "section 141, or any of sections 145 to 149 of the Evidence Act 2006".

Summary Proceedings Act 1957 (1957 No 87)

Omit from sections 157(1A) and 161A "section 13A(6)(d) of the Evidence Act 1908" and substitute in each case "section 109(1)(d) of the Evidence Act 2006".

Section 168AA(5): omit "section 13C of the Evidence Act 1908" and substitute "section 112 of the Evidence Act 2006".

Section 178A(1): omit "section 13A(2) of the Evidence Act 1908" and substitute "section 108(5) of the Evidence Act 2006".

Section 178A(2): omit "section 13B or section 13C of the Evidence Act 1908" and substitute "sections 110 to 112 of the Evidence Act 2006".

Section 182(1): omit "section 13A(2) of the Evidence Act 1908" and substitute "section 108(2) of the Evidence Act 2006".

Tariff Act 1988 (1988 No 155)

Repeal section 7(1C) and substitute:

"(1C)   For the purposes of this section,—

"**court** includes the Supreme Court, the Court of Appeal, the High Court, and any District Court

"**District Court** includes—

"(a)   a Family Court; and

"(b)   a Youth Court

"**person acting judicially** means any person having in New Zealand by law authority to hear, receive, and examine evidence

"**proceeding** means—

"(a)   a proceeding conducted by a court; and

"(b)   any interlocutory or other application to a court connected with a proceeding."

Taxation Review Authorities Act 1994 (1994 No 165)

Section 17(3): omit "Evidence Act 1908" and substitute "Evidence Act 2006".

Te Ture Whenua Maori Act 1993 (Maori Land Act 1993) (1993 No 4)

Section 69(3): omit "Evidence Act 1908" and substitute "Evidence Act 2006".

Trans-Tasman Mutual Recognition Act 1997 (1997 No 60)

Section 63(4): omit "Evidence Act 1908" and substitute "Evidence Act 2006".

Treaty of Waitangi Act 1975 (1975 No 114)

Clause 6(3) of Schedule 2: omit "Evidence Act 1908" and substitute "Evidence Act 2006".

United Nations Convention on the Law of the Sea Act 1996 (1996 No 69)

Repeal section 3(5) and substitute:

"(5)   For the purposes of subsection (4),—

"**court** includes the Supreme Court, the Court of Appeal, the High Court, and any District Court

"**person acting judicially** means any person having in New Zealand by law authority to hear, receive, and examine evidence

"**proceeding** means—

"(a)   a proceeding conducted by a court; and

"(b)   any interlocutory or other application to a court connected with a proceeding."

Part 2
Regulations amended

Designs Regulations 1954 (SR 1954/224)

Regulation 73(1)(a): omit "prescribed by the Justices of the Peace Act 1927 or by the Evidence Act 1908, as the case may be" and substitute "required by the Oaths and Declarations Act 1957".

Patents Regulations 1954 (SR 1954/211)

Regulation 143(1)(a): omit "prescribed by the Justices of the Peace Act 1927 or by the Evidence Act 1908, as the case may be" and substitute "required by the Oaths and Declarations Act 1957".

Legislative history

3 May 2005	Introduction (Bill 256-1)
10 May 2005	First reading and referral to Justice and Electoral Committee
24 October 2006	Reported from Justice and Electoral Committee (Bill 256-2)
15 November 2006	Second reading
21 November 2006	Committee of the whole House (Bill 256-3)
23 November 2006	Third reading

This Act is administered by the Ministry of Justice.

Chapter 2

Evidence Regulations

Evidence Regulations 2007

SR 2007/204

Contents

At Wellington this 23rd day of July 2007

Pursuant to sections 200 and 201 of the Evidence Act 2006 and, in relation to preliminary hearings, pursuant also to section 212 of the Summary Proceedings Act 1957, His Excellency the Governor-General, acting on the advice and with the consent of the Executive Council, makes the following regulations.

REGULATIONS

1 Title

These regulations are the Evidence Regulations 2007.

2 Commencement

These regulations come into force on 1 August 2007.

3 Interpretation

In these regulations, unless the context otherwise requires,—

Act means the Evidence Act 2006

authorised advisor means—

(a) the Secretary for Justice; or

(b) a person engaged by the Minister of Justice or the Secretary for Justice to give advice about a review application

Commissioner means the Commissioner of Police

interview means an interview with a complainant whose evidence is being video recorded

lawyer's copy, in relation to a video record, has the meaning given to it by regulation 30

master copy, in relation to a video record, has the meaning given to it by regulation 15

responsible department means the department that is, with the authority of the Prime Minister, for the time being responsible for the administration of the Children, Young Persons, and Their Families Act 1989

review application means—

(a) an application for the exercise of the prerogative of mercy; or

(b) an application under section 406 of the Crimes Act 1961

working copy, in relation to a video record, has the meaning given to it by regulation 16.

Part 1
Video record evidence in criminal proceeding

(reg 4 to reg 48)

Subpart 1—Recording video evidence

(reg 4 to reg 18)

4 Application of subpart

This subpart applies to the video recording of a complainant's evidence if it is intended that the video record may be offered later as evidence in a criminal proceeding.

Who may be present at video recording of interview

5   Only certain persons may be present during interview

The following persons are the only persons who may be present at the video recording of an interview:

(a)   the person facilitating the interview (the **interviewer**):

(b)   the complainant:

(c)   any person needed to operate the recording equipment:

(d)   if regulation 6 applies, a person who is present to support the complainant:

(e)   if regulation 7 applies, an interpreter.

Compare: SR 1990/164 r 4(1)

6   Person to support complainant may be present

(1)   A person may be present at an interview to support a complainant if the interviewer considers that—

(a)   it is in the interests of the complainant; and

(b)   the person is an appropriate person to support the complainant.

(2)   A person present at an interview under subclause (1) must not take part in the interview.

Compare: SR 1990/164 r 4(2)

7   Interpreter may be present

An interpreter may be present at an interview if—

(a)   the complainant does not have sufficient proficiency in the English language to understand the interview if conducted in English; or

(b)   the complainant has a communication disability.

Compare: SR 1990/164 r 4(3)

What must be on video record

8   What must be on video record

A video record of an interview must show the following:

(a)   the interviewer stating the date and time at which the interview starts; and

(b)   each person present identifying himself or herself; and

(c)   subject to any contrary direction of a Judge, in the case of a complainant who is of or over the age of 12 years, that person taking an oath or making an affirmation; and

(d)   in the case of a complainant who is under the age of 12 years,—

(i)   the interviewer informing the complainant of the importance of telling the truth and not telling lies; and

(ii)   subject to any contrary direction by a Judge, the complainant making a promise to tell the truth (in any form, provided the overall effect is a promise to tell the truth); and

(e)   any interpreter present taking an oath or making an affirmation; and

(f)   the entire interview; and

(g)   a clearly visible analogue clock, with a second hand, correctly recording the time; and

(h)   the interviewer stating the time at which the interview finishes; and

(i)   if any of regulations 9 to 12 apply, the matters required by those regulations.

Compare: SR 1990/164 r 5(1)(a)–(d), (g), (3)

9   Additional requirement if break taken

A video record of an interview must also show the interviewer stating the following matters if the interviewer decides that a break is to be taken during the recording of the interview:

(a)   the fact that a break is being taken; and

(b)   the estimated duration of the break; and

(c)   the reason for taking it.

Compare: SR 1990/164 r 5(1)(e)

10   Additional requirement if premature conclusion

A video record of an interview must also show the interviewer stating the following matters if the interviewer decides to conclude the interview without asking all the intended questions:

(a)   the fact that the video record is concluding prematurely; and

(b)   the reasons for that.

Compare: SR 1990/164 r 5(1)(f)

11   Additional requirement if person present to support complainant

A person present at an interview to support a complainant must be clearly visible throughout the video recording of the interview.

Compare: SR 1990/164 r 5(4)

12   Additional requirement if interpreter present

An interpreter present at an interview must be clearly visible throughout the video recording of the interview.

Equipment failure

13   Equipment failure

(1)   The following steps are to be taken if any recording equipment (including the video record itself) fails during the video recording of an interview and the failure is not able to be fixed immediately:

(a)   the video record must be removed from the video recording equipment and dealt with under the following regulations in this Part; and

(b)   the interview must be recommenced on another video record as soon as practicable.

(2)   A video record of an interview that is recommenced must—

(a)   show the interviewer stating that this is a new video record of an interview that started on another video record but was interrupted by equipment failure; and

(b)   recommence approximately at the point it was interrupted by the equipment failure.

Compare: SR 1990/164 r 6

Master copy and working copy

14   Copies of video record

(1)   There must be at least 2 video records made of an interview.

(2)   The video records must include—

(a)   a master copy (the "master copy"); and

(b)   a single working copy of the master copy (the "working copy").

Compare: SR 1990/164 r 7(1)

15   Master copy

A master copy is either—

(a)   a single video record of an interview; or

(b)   if 2 or more video records are made of an interview (for example, if 2 or more video records are made simultaneously in a multi-deck machine or linked machines), 1 of those video records.

Compare: SR 1990/164 r 7(2)(a)

16   Working copy

(1)   The working copy is,—

(a)   if regulation 15(a) applies, a copy of the master copy made as soon as practicable after the making of the master copy is complete; or

(b)   if regulation 15(b) applies, 1 of the simultaneously made video records.

(2)   If more than 2 video records of an interview are made simultaneously, the record or records that are not the working copy or the master copy—

(a)   must, subject to paragraph (b), be identified, kept, and dealt with under these regulations as if they were the working copy; but

(b)   may be treated as if they were a copy of a working copy—

(i)   for the purposes of regulations 21(2)(b), 22(2)(b), and 30(1) (which allow a copy of a working copy to be supplied to certain other persons); and

(ii)   if supplied under those regulations, for the purposes of these regulations generally.

Compare: SR 1990/164 r 7(2)(b)

17   How master copy identified and kept

(1)   A master copy must be—

(a)   sealed with a certificate in the form set out in the Schedule; and

(b)   placed in safe custody with the police.

(2)   The police must keep a record of—

(a)   the date on which the master copy was received into safe custody; and

(b)   the particulars of—

(i)   who has dealt with the master copy from that date; and

(ii)   the reasons for dealing with it.

Compare: SR 1990/164 r 8

18   How working copy identified and kept

(1)   A working copy must be—

(a)   identified as a working copy by a copy of the certificate in the form set out in the Schedule; and

(b)   placed in safe custody with the police.

(2)   A record of every person who views, or had custody of, a working copy must be kept with it.

(3)   The record must include—

(a)   the name and occupation of the person who viewed, or had custody of, the working copy; and

(b)   the date on which that person viewed it or, as the case requires, the period during which the person had custody of it.

(4)   Nothing in subclause (1)(b) prevents the police from—

(a)   supplying the working copy under subpart 2; or

(b)   making or supplying a copy of a working copy under subpart 2 or 3.

Compare: SR 1990/164 rr 9, 11(1)

Subpart 2—Restrictions on showing, viewing, copying, and supplying working copy and master copy

(reg 19 to reg 28)

19　Application of subpart

This subpart applies to a video record that has been made of a complainant's evidence under subpart 1.

20　Limited purposes for which police may show working copy

The police may only show a working copy for the following purposes:

(a)　to seek advice from a lawyer or any other person to determine whether—

　(i)　any, and if so what, charges ought to be laid; or

　(ii)　any care or protection proceeding ought to be instituted:

(b)　to allow any of the following persons to know the case against them:

　(i)　a person suspected of having committed an offence to which the video record relates:

　(ii)　a defendant to any charge laid in relation to which the video record may be used in evidence:

　(iii)　an accused against whom an indictment has been filed in relation to which the video record may be used in evidence:

(c)　to allow any lawyer representing any person referred to in paragraph (b) to view it:

(d)　to allow the complainant to view it:

(e)　for the purpose of making a transcript:

(f)　to allow any lawyer representing the complainant or the Crown to view it:

(g)　to enable any Judge to view it in order to—

　(i)　determine whether it is admissible in a proceeding; or

　(ii)　comply with any requirement in an enactment or imposed by a rule of law:

(h)　to enable the Commissioner or any other member of the police to discharge his or her duties under an enactment:

(i)　to assist the police in any further investigations of suspected offences that may have been committed by any person referred to in paragraph (b).

Compare: SR 1990/164 r 10

Request for video record made by responsible department or Family Court Judge

21 Responsible department may request video record of certain complainants

(1) The responsible department may ask the police for a copy of a video record of a child complainant or any other complainant of the kind described in section 185CA(1)(a) of the Summary Proceedings Act 1957 for the following purposes:

  (a) allowing the complainant to view the video record:

  (b) enabling the Director-General of the responsible department, or any social worker employed by the responsible department, to discharge his or her duties under an enactment.

(2) In response to a request made under subclause (1), the police must supply one of the following to the responsible department:

  (a) the working copy; or

  (b) a copy of the working copy.

(3) The responsible department must place the working copy or the copy of the working copy in safe custody.

(4) This regulation does not give any person authority to make a copy of the working copy or a copy of the copy of the working copy supplied to the responsible department under subclause (2).

(5) A working copy supplied to the responsible department under subclause (2)(a) must be returned to the police on request.

Compare: SR 1990/164 r 11A

22 Family Court Judge may request video record of certain complainants

(1) A Family Court Judge may ask the police for a copy of a video record of a child complainant or any other complainant of the kind described in section 185CA (1)(a) of the Summary Proceedings Act 1957 (the **child**) for the Family Court for any of the following purposes:

  (a) allowing parties to a proceeding under the Care of Children Act 2004 or the lawyer for any of those parties to view the video record:

  (b) assisting a person that the Family Court Judge considers qualified to prepare a cultural, medical, psychiatric, or psychological report on the child under section 133 of the Care of Children Act 2004:

  (c) allowing parties to a proceeding under Part 2 of the Children, Young Persons, and Their Families Act 1989 or the lawyer for any of those parties to view the video record:

  (d) assisting a person to prepare a medical, psychiatric, or psychological report on the child under section 178 of the Children, Young Persons, and Their Families Act 1989.

(2)   In response to a request made under subclause (1), the police must supply one of the following to the Family Court:

(a)   the working copy; or

(b)   a copy of the working copy.

(3)   The Family Court must place the working copy or the copy of the working copy in safe custody.

(4)   The Family Court may only show the video record if—

(a)   a Family Court Judge is satisfied that showing it is in the best interests of the child who is the subject of the proceeding under the Care of Children Act 2004 or the care or protection proceeding under the Children, Young Persons, and Their Families Act 1989; and

(b)   a Family Court Judge authorises in writing the viewing of it by the person or persons concerned; and

(c)   the viewing takes place within the Family Court premises; and

(d)   the viewing is supervised by a registrar of the Family Court or by any person nominated by a registrar; and

(e)   the Family Court Judge is satisfied that showing it is not likely to jeopardise any pending criminal proceeding.

(5)   This regulation does not give any person authority to make a copy of the working copy or a copy of the copy of the working copy supplied to a Family Court under subclause (2).

(6)   A working copy supplied to a Family Court under subclause (2)(a) must be returned to the police on request.

(7)   This regulation does not affect whether or not a video record is admissible as evidence in any proceeding.

Compare: SR 1990/164 r 11B

23   Transcript to accompany video record supplied to responsible department or Family Court

(1)   The police must also supply a copy of any existing transcript of a video record if the video record is supplied to—

(a)   the responsible department under regulation 21; or

(b)   a Family Court under regulation 22.

(2)   A copy of a transcript supplied to the responsible department or a Family Court under subclause (1) must be placed in safe custody with the working copy or the copy of the working copy to which it relates.

Compare: SR 1990/164 r 11C(1), (2)

24　Copying or showing transcript limited to certain purposes

(1)　The responsible department may only copy or arrange for the copying of a transcript in its custody under regulation 23 in relation to a purpose specified in paragraph (a) or (b) of regulation 21(1).

(2)　A Family Court may only copy or arrange for the copying of a transcript in its custody under regulation 23 in relation to a purpose specified in any of paragraphs (a) to (d) of regulation 22(1).

(3)　Despite subclauses (1) and (2), the responsible department or a Family Court may copy or arrange for the copying of a transcript in its custody under regulation 23 if—

(a)　satisfied that doing so is in the best interests of the child who is the subject of the proceeding under the Care of Children Act 2004 or the care or protection proceeding under the Children, Young Persons, and Their Families Act 1989; and

(b)　satisfied that doing so is not likely to jeopardise any pending criminal proceeding; and

(c)　a record is kept of every person to whom a copy of the transcript is given.

(4)　No person may make a copy of a transcript supplied under this regulation other than as provided for in this regulation.

(5)　A copy of any transcript supplied to the responsible department or a Family Court under regulation 23 must, if regulation 21(5) or 22(6) applies, be returned to the police on request along with the working copy to which it relates.

(6)　The responsible department or a Family Court may only show a transcript in its custody under regulation 23 to a person if—

(a)　satisfied that doing so is in the best interests of the child who is the subject of the proceeding under the Care of Children Act 2004 or the care or protection proceeding under the Children, Young Persons, and their Families Act 1989; and

(b)　satisfied that doing so is not likely to jeopardise any pending criminal proceeding; and

(c)　a record is kept of every person to whom a copy of the transcript is shown.

Compare: SR 1990/164 r 11C(3)–(7)

Request by authorised advisors

25　Authorised advisor may request copy of video record

(1)　An authorised advisor who requires a copy or copies of a video record of a complainant for the purpose of giving advice about a review application may ask the registrar of the court responsible for the custody of a master copy under regulation 38 to supply a specified number of copies of it.

(2) On receiving a request under subclause (1), the registrar must supply the specified number of copies of the master copy requested.

Compare: SR 1990/164 r 13A

26 Conditions of supply of copy of master copy to authorised advisor

(1) A copy or copies of a master copy supplied to an authorised advisor under regulation 25 may only be viewed by—

(a) the authorised advisor; and

(b) any person the authorised advisor considers can help with the giving of advice about the review application.

(2) An authorised advisor must place every copy of a master copy supplied to that advisor in safe custody.

(3) An authorised advisor may supply the copy or 1 of the copies of the master copy in his or her custody to another person if the authorised advisor considers that person can help with the giving of advice about the review application.

(4) An authorised advisor who supplies a copy of a master copy to another person under subclause (3) must take all reasonable steps to ensure that the person to whom it is supplied—

(a) places it in safe custody; and

(b) prevents any other person from viewing it; and

(c) returns it to the authorised advisor as soon as is reasonably practicable.

(5) This regulation does not give any person authority to make a copy of any copy of the master copy supplied to that person under regulation 25.

(6) Every copy of a master copy supplied to an authorised advisor under regulation 25 must be returned by the authorised advisor to the registrar who supplied it as soon as is reasonably practicable after the authorised advisor finishes giving advice about the review application or any related matter.

Compare: SR 1990/164 r 13B

27 Transcripts to accompany copy of master copy supplied to authorised advisor

(1) A registrar of a court who supplies a copy or copies of a master copy to an authorised advisor under regulation 25 must also supply the authorised advisor with the number of copies of the transcript that the authorised advisor requests.

(2) Subclause (1) only applies if a transcript of the master copy already exists.

(3) Every copy of a transcript supplied to an authorised advisor under subclause (1) must be placed in safe custody with the copy or copies of the master copy to which it relates.

(4) An authorised advisor may only copy or arrange for the copying of a transcript in his or her custody in relation to the purpose specified in regulation 25(1).

(5)   An authorised advisor may only copy or arrange for the copying of a transcript under subclause (4) if—

    (a)   satisfied that doing so is not likely to jeopardise any pending criminal proceeding; and

    (b)   a record is kept of every person to whom a copy of the transcript is given.

(6)   No person may make a copy of a transcript supplied under this regulation except as provided for in this regulation.

(7)   If regulation 26(6) applies, every copy of a transcript supplied under subclause (1) and every copy made under subclause (4) must be returned along with the copy or copies of the master copy.

(8)   An authorised advisor may only show another person a copy of a transcript if—

    (a)   satisfied that doing so is not likely to jeopardise any pending criminal proceeding; and

    (b)   a record is kept of every person to whom a copy of the transcript is shown.

Compare: SR 1990/164 r 13C

Prosecution to give transcript to defence before preliminary hearing

28   Prosecutor to give transcript to defence before preliminary hearing or defended summary hearing

(1)   The prosecutor must ensure a typed transcript of a working copy is given to the defendant or the defendant's lawyer,—

    (a)   if there is to be a preliminary hearing, at least 7 days before the date on which a video record is given in evidence at a preliminary hearing:

    (b)   if the defendant is to be tried summarily, as soon as is reasonably practicable after the defendant has pleaded not guilty.

(2)   The typed transcript is to be prepared by the police.

(3)   The Court may adjourn the hearing to allow further time for the defendant to consider the transcript if satisfied that subclause (1) has not been complied with.

Compare: SR 1990/164 r 13

Subpart 3—Lawyer's copy

(reg 29 to reg 34)

29   Application of subpart

This subpart applies if a copy of a video record of a complainant's evidence to which subpart 2 applies is to be given to a lawyer for a party to a criminal proceeding under section 106(4)(a) of the Act.

30   Lawyer's copy

(1)   If this subpart applies, the police must make a copy of the working copy and supply it to the lawyer (the "lawyer's copy").

(2) A lawyer's copy must be identified as a lawyer's copy by a copy of the certificate in the form set out in the Schedule.

31   Custody of lawyer's copy

(1) A lawyer who has a lawyer's copy supplied to him or her under regulation 30(1) must place it in safe custody.

(2) A lawyer who has a lawyer's copy must return it to the police as soon as practicable after the criminal proceeding to which it relates is finally determined or discontinued.

(3) Nothing in subclause (2) prevents a lawyer from returning a lawyer's copy to the police at any earlier time.

32   Purposes for which lawyer's copy may be used by lawyer

(1) A lawyer may only use a lawyer's copy for the following purposes:

(a) preparing a case for the person he or she is representing in the criminal proceeding to which the video record relates:

(b) showing the video to any expert from which the lawyer wished to seek advice in connection with the criminal proceeding:

(c) giving legal advice to the person he or she is representing in the criminal proceeding to which the video record relates.

(2) A person to whom a lawyer is authorised to show the lawyer's copy under subclause (1) may view the copy only in the presence of the lawyer.

33   Prohibition on copying lawyer's copy

No person may make any copies of a lawyer's copy without the permission of a Judge.

34   Restriction on supply of lawyer's copy

(1) A lawyer who has a lawyer's copy in his or her custody must not give it to any other person without the permission of a Judge.

(2) Nothing in subclause (1) prevents—

(a) the defendant or any expert from viewing a working copy under regulation 20(b) or a lawyer's copy under regulation 32; or

(b) the lawyer from returning the copy under regulation 31.

Subpart 4—Retention and destruction of master copy, copies of master copy, working copy, copies of working copy, and lawyer's copy

(reg 35 to reg 48)

35   Application of subpart

This subpart applies to a video record of a complainant's evidence to which subpart 2 or 3 applies.

36   Meaning of destruction date A and destruction date B

In this subpart,—

(a)   destruction date A means the date that is 10 years after the date on which the criminal proceeding to which a video record relates is finally determined or discontinued; and

(b)   destruction date B is the date that is 7 years after the date on which a master copy is made.

Privacy preserved

37   Privacy to be preserved

Until destruction date A, destruction date B, or the date referred to in regulation 47 (whichever applies) the master copy, working copy, every copy of the master copy and working copy, and every lawyer's copy, must be kept in a way that preserves the privacy of the persons recorded on it.

Compare: SR 1990/164 r 14(8)

Master copy to be used in criminal proceeding

38   Producing and retaining master copy for criminal proceeding

(1)   The following must be produced at a criminal proceeding if a video record is to be offered as alternative evidence:

(a)   the master copy; and

(b)   a typed transcript of the master copy prepared by the police.

(2)   Once given in evidence at a criminal proceeding, the master copy must be retained in the custody of the court until destroyed or erased in accordance with regulation 39.

(3)   Despite subclause (2), a master copy may be removed from court custody for the period necessary to make a copy or copies of it for the purpose of responding to a request under regulation 25 (which relates to a request by an authorised advisor).

Compare: SR 1990/164 r 12

Court retention and destruction obligations

39   Obligations of court to retain and destroy master copy and copy of master copy

(1)   If a master copy is produced in court, the court must retain custody of it until destruction date A.

(2)   On destruction date A, the court must destroy or erase—

(a)   the master copy; and

(b)   all copies of the master copy returned to the registrar under regulation 26(6).

(3)   If a copy of the master copy is returned under regulation 26(6) after destruction date A, the court must promptly destroy or erase it.

Compare: SR 1990/164 r 14(3), (3A), (3B)

Police retention and destruction obligations

40 Obligations of police to retain and destroy master copy

(1) The police must retain custody of a master copy until—

    (a)   it is produced in court; or

    (b)   if no proceeding is brought, destruction date B.

(2) On destruction date B, the police must destroy or erase the master copy.

Compare: SR 1990/164 r 14(2), (3)

41 Obligations of police to retain and destroy working copy and copy of working copy

(1) The police must retain custody of the working copy until destruction date B.

(2) On destruction date B, the police must destroy or erase the working copy.

(3) On destruction date B, the police must destroy or erase any copy of the working copy in their custody.

Compare: SR 1990/164 r 14(4), (6)(a), (7)(a)

42 Obligations of police to retain and destroy lawyer's copy

(1) The police must retain custody of any lawyer's copy returned to them until destruction date B.

(2) On destruction date B, the police must destroy or erase the lawyer's copy.

Responsible department and Family Court retention and destruction obligations

43 Obligations of responsible department to retain and destroy working copy

(1) This regulation applies if the responsible department has custody of a working copy supplied to it in response to a request made under regulation 21.

(2) The responsible department must retain custody of the working copy until destruction date B unless it is sooner asked to return the working copy to the police under regulation 21(5).

(3) If the responsible department retains custody of the working copy on destruction date B, it must destroy or erase it on that date.

Compare: SR 1990/164 r 14(5), (6)(b)

44 Obligation of responsible department to retain and destroy copy of working copy

(1) This regulation applies if the responsible department has custody of a copy of a working copy supplied to it in response to a request under regulation 21.

(2) The responsible department must retain custody of the copy of the working copy until destruction date B.

(3)   On destruction date B, the responsible department must destroy or erase the copy of the working copy.

Compare: SR 1990/164 r 14(5), (7)(b)

45   Obligations of Family Court to retain and destroy working copy

(1)   This regulation applies if a Family Court has custody of a working copy supplied to it in response to a request made by a Family Court Judge under regulation 22.

(2)   The Family Court must retain custody of the working copy until destruction date B unless it is sooner asked to return the working copy to the police under regulation 22(6).

(3)   If the Family Court retains custody of the working copy on destruction date B, it must destroy or erase it on that date.

Compare: SR 1990/164 r 14(5A), (6)(c)

46   Obligations of Family Court to retain and destroy copy of working copy

(1)   This regulation applies if a Family Court has custody of a copy of a working copy supplied to it in response to a request made by a Family Court Judge under regulation 22.

(2)   The Family Court must retain custody of the copy of the working copy until destruction date B.

(3)   On destruction date B, the Family Court must destroy or erase the copy of the working copy.

Compare: SR 1990/164 r 14(5A), (7)(c)

Exception

47   Destruction before destruction date

(1)   Nothing in this Part prevents the destruction of the master copy, any copy of the master copy, the working copy, any copy of the working copy, or any lawyer's copy before the date until which the copy would otherwise be required to be kept under this Part if—

     (a)   no criminal proceeding is brought; or

     (b)   any criminal proceeding brought is discontinued because the video record evidence is considered to be of insufficient probative value.

(2)   If subclause (1) applies, any reference in this subpart to a destruction date must be read as if that reference were a reference to the date on which that master copy, any copy of the master copy, the working copy, any copy of the working copy, or any lawyer's copy was destroyed.

Compare: SR 1990/164 r 14(10), (11)

Transcripts

48 Retention and destruction of transcripts

Any reference in this subpart to a master copy, a copy of a master copy, a working copy, or a copy of a working copy must also apply, with any necessary modifications, to any transcript or copy of a transcript in the custody of any of the following:

(a) any lawyer for a party to a proceeding to which the transcript relates:

(b) the police:

(c) the responsible department:

(d) the Family Court:

(e) an authorised advisor.

Compare: SR 1990/164 r 14(9)

Part 2
Warning or informing jury about very young children's evidence

(reg 49)

49 Warning or informing jury about very young children's evidence

If, in a criminal proceeding tried with a jury in which a witness is a child under the age of 6 years, the Judge is of the opinion that the jury may be assisted by a direction about the evidence of very young children and how the jury should assess that evidence, the Judge may give the jury a direction to the following effect:

(a) even very young children can accurately remember and report things that have happened to them in the past, but because of developmental differences, children may not report their memories in the same manner or to the same extent as an adult would:

(b) this does not mean that a child witness is any more or less reliable than an adult witness:

(c) one difference is that very young children typically say very little without some help to focus on the events in question:

(d) another difference is that, depending on how they are questioned, very young children can be more open to suggestion than other children or adults:

(e) the reliability of the evidence of very young children depends on the way they are questioned, and it is important, when deciding how much weight to give to their evidence, to distinguish between open questions aimed at obtaining answers from children in their own words from leading questions that may put words into their mouths.

Part 3
Revocation and transitional provision

(reg 50 to reg 51)

50   Revocation

The Evidence (Videotaping of Child Complainants) Regulations 1990 (SR 1990/164) are revoked.

51   Transitional provision

A videotape made before the commencement of these regulations in accordance with the Evidence (Videotaping of Child Complainants) Regulations 1990—

(a)   is deemed to have been made in accordance with these regulations, for the purposes of any proceedings to which the Act applies; and

(b)   may be kept, shown, given, returned, or destroyed in accordance with subparts 2 to 4 of Part 1, which apply with any necessary modifications.

Schedule
Form
(Form)

rr 17(1)(a), 18(1)(a), 30(2)

Form
Certificate for video record of interview

Type of copy: [*specify whether master copy, working copy, lawyer's copy, or other*]

Type of electronic record: [*specify whether videotape, DVD, or other*]

Reference number of electronic record:

File number (if applicable):

Date of interview:

Name of person interviewed:

Date of birth of person interviewed:

Name of guardian(s) (if person interviewed is under 18 years or mentally impaired):

Name of interviewer:

Designation/rank of interviewer:

Name and designation of all other persons present:

Reasons for interview: [*type of incident or offence*]

Location of interview:

Time interview commenced:

Time interview concluded:

Duration of interview:

Number of tapes/DVDs used for this interview:

Number of breaks in interview:

Reasons for breaks, eg, to speak to another person, for refreshments, or toilet breaks (if applicable):

Reasons for premature conclusion of interview (if applicable):

Cross-reference(s) to other tape/DVD records of person interviewed:

Other:

I certify that the contents of this certificate are correct.

Dated:

Signed:

(Signature of interviewer or member of police)

Rebecca Kitteridge,
for Clerk of the Executive Council.

Explanatory note

This note is not part of the regulations, but is intended to indicate their general effect.

These regulations are the Evidence Regulations 2007 (the "regulations").

The regulations, which comes into force on 1 August 2007, are made under the Evidence Act 2006 and the Summary Proceedings Act 1957. The regulations revoke the Evidence (Videotaping of Child Complainants) Regulations 1990.

Subpart 1 of Part 1 provides for certain requirements that must be complied with when video recording the evidence of a complainant if it is intended that the video record may be offered later as evidence in a criminal proceeding.

Subpart 2 of Part 1 specifies restrictions on the showing, viewing, copying, and supplying of working copies and master copies of video evidence that has been recorded in accordance with subpart].

Subpart 3 of Part 1 sets out restrictions on the use, copying, and supply of any video record evidence by a lawyer for a party to a proceeding who is in possession of a copy of the video record as a consequence of it being offered in evidence at a criminal proceeding (see section 106(4)(a) of the Evidence Act 2006).

Subpart 4 of Part 1 sets out the obligations relating to the period of retaining and the time for destroying master copies, copies of master copies, working copies, copies of working copies, and lawyers' copies.

Part 2 sets out the form in which a Judge may warn or inform a jury if evidence is given in a criminal proceeding by a child who is under the age of 6 years.

Part 3 revokes the Evidence (Videotaping of Child Complainants) Regulations 1990 and contains a transitional provision allowing existing videotapes to continue to be used in proceedings under the Evidence Act 2006.

PROMULGATION

Issued under the authority of the Acts and Regulations Publication Act 1989.
Date of notification in *Gazette*: 26 July 2007.
These regulations are administered by the Ministry of Justice.

Table of Statutes and Regulations

Abbreviations

s 58(2)	EV58.01(2)	s 63(3)	EV63.02,04,05, 67.05(1)
s 59	EV51, 51.11(2), 53, 53.02, 59.01,03,04,05, 05(1),(2),(3),06,07,08, 09,10,11, 66.01(1), 67, 67.01,04, 69.02(2)	s 64	EV4.13.01, 51, 51.11(3), 53, 53.02,04, 64.01,02, 65, 66, 66.01,04, 67, 67.01,04
s 59(1)(a)	EV59.01,05(2),(3)	s 64(2)	EV64.01
s 59(1)(b)	EV59.04	s 64(2)(a)	EV51.11(3), 64.03,06
s 59(2)	EV59.02,05(3)	s 64(2)(b)	EV64.03,04
s 59(3)	EV59.02,05(3)	s 64(3)	EV64.01,04
s 59(4)	EV59.02,05(3), 65.03(6)	s 65	EV39.04, 52.04, 57.03, 08, 58.05, 59.08, 60.06, 61.03, 65.01, 67.06, 69.07
s 59(5)	EV51.11(2), 59.03,06	s 65(1)	EV58.05, 59.08, 60.06, 61.03, 65.01,03(1)
s 59(6)	EV59.03,05(2)	s 65(2)	EV65.03,03(1),(2),(6), (7),04(1), 66.02(1)
s 60	EV51, 51.06,08,12, 53, 53.04, 60.01,02,04, 04(1),(2),(3),(6),(7), 05(1),(2),06,07,09,10, 61.01,02,03, 62.01, 01(1), 63, 65, 66, 66.01(2),04, 73.03	s 65(3)	EV65.03,03(1),04(1),(3)
		s 65(3)(a)	EV65.04,04(1),(2),(3)
		s 65(3)(b)	EV65.04(3)
		s 65(4)	EV53.05, 65.03,05
		s 65(5)	EV57.12, 65.03
s 60(1)	EV60.02,05,06, 62.01	s 66	EV58.07, 59.10, 60.09, 66.01,01(2),02
s 60(1)(a)	EV60.01,04(1),(2),(4), 61.02, 62.01(1)	s 66(1)	EV58.07, 59.10, 60.09, 66.01,03,04(1),06
s 60(1)(a)(i)	EV60.04(1), 73.03	s 66(1)(a)	EV66.04
s 60(1)(a)(ii)	EV60.04(1), 62.01, 66.01(4)	s 66(1)(b)	EV66.03,04
		s 66(1)(c)	EV66.01(2),(3),(4),06
s 60(1)(a)(iii)	EV60.04(1),(2), 62.01, 66.01(4)	s 66(2)	EV66.01,04,04(1),(2), 05,06
s 60(1)(b)	EV60.01,04(3),(5), 61.01,02, 73.03	s 66(2)(a)	EV66.05
		s 66(2)(b)	EV66.04(1)
s 60(2)	EV51.07, 60.02,03, 04(4),(6)	s 66(3)	EV66.04,04(2),05
		s 66(4)	EV66.01,01(3),04(2),06
s 60(2)(a)	EV60.01,04(1)	s 67	EV57.09(1), 58.06, 59.09, 60.07, 64.05, 67.01, 68.Intro.01, 69.07, 186.04(2)
s 60(2)(b)	EV60.01	
s 60(3)	EV5.01, 60.03,05(1)	
s 60(3)(a)	EV60.03, 61.03	
s 60(3)(b)	EV60.03	
s 60(4)	EV60.05, 61.02	s 67(1)	EV60.07, 67.01,02, 02(1),03,03(1),04, 69.07
s 60(4)(a)	EV60.05(1)	
s 60(4)(b)	EV51.12, 60.05(2), 66.01(2)	s 67(2)	EV60.07, 64.05, 67.04, 04(1),05, 69.07
		s 67(3)	EV63.04, 67.05,05(1)
s 60(4)(c)	EV60.05(3)	s 68	EV68.Intro.01, 68.03, 05, 69.02,03, 70.02, 186.04(3)
s 60(5)	EV60.10	
s 61	EV60.04(5), 61.01,02, 03,04, 186.03	
		s 68(1)	EV68.01,02,05,06
s 61(1)	EV61.02,03	s 68(2)	EV68.06,07
s 61(1)(a)	EV61.02,03	s 68(2)(a)	EV68.06
s 61(1)(b)	EV61.02, 144.02	s 68(2)(b)	EV68.06
s 61(1)(b)(i)	EV61.02	s 68(3)	EV68.08
s 61(1)(b)(ii)	EV61.02	s 68(4)	EV68.09
s 61(2)	EV4.26.01, 61.02,04	s 68(5)	EV68.03,04,07, 69.06
s 61(3)	EV61.02,03	s 69	EV52, 52.01,05,06, 58.08, 59.01,03,06,11, 68.02,03,05, 69.01,02, 02(1),(2),06,07, 70.02, 71.01
s 62	EV61.03, 62.01,01(1), (2),02,03	
s 62(1)	EV4.26.01, 60.08, 61.03, 62.01,01(1),02, 03, 65.03(1)	
		s 69(1)	EV58.08, 69.01,02(2), 04
s 62(2)	EV62.01,01(2),02	s 69(1)(a)	EV52.05
s 63	EV51, 51.06,08, 60, 60.10, 63.01,02,03,05	s 69(1)(b)	EV52.05
		s 69(1)(c)	EV52.05
s 63(1)	EV63.01,04,05	s 69(2)	EV69.02(1),05,06
s 63(1)(a)	EV63.02,03	s 69(2)(a)	EV69.05
s 63(1)(b)	EV63.02,05	
s 63(1)(c)	EV63.02,05	
s 63(1)(d)	EV63.02,03,05	
s 63(2)	EV63.01,04,05	

Table of Cases

Abbreviations

Subject Index

Abbreviations

ER   Evidence Regulations 2007: ch 2   EV   Evidence Act 2006: ch 1

B

C

D

E

F

G

J

L

M

P

U

V

W

Y